'With chapters written by field-leading experts, this collection sheds a great deal of light on the reality of drug dealing today. Rather than succumb to the usual stereotypes, contributors explore a diverse range of drug markets and the various strategies adopted by suppliers as they seek to profit from and remain afloat in the drugs business. On every page there is something new and worthwhile for students and intrigued social scientists to explore.'

Simon Winlow, *Professor, Northumbria University, UK*

'This excellent and much needed book engages with the complexities of "drug dealing" giving space to the diverse ways of dealing drugs. The fascinating insights gained from exploration of the hidden worlds of those who deal drugs are eloquently captured in this edited collection. The impressive array of authors engage with the nuances and intersections involved in the dealing of drugs, while also challenging stereotypes and stigma surrounding the ultimate contemporary folk devil – "the drug dealer".'

Fiona Hutton, *Associate Professor, Victoria University of Wellington, New Zealand*

'Bringing together some of the most prominent voices in the field, Ayres and Ancrum compile a truly interdisciplinary and critical approach to the clandestine world of drug dealing. Addressing myths and realities about drug violence, markets, and policy, they weave in important structural and interpersonal realities that truly make this a holistic and cutting edge must-read!'

Victoria E. Collins, *Professor, School of Justice Studies, Eastern Kentucky University, USA*

'One of the most vilified and misunderstood characters, drug dealers get the treatment they really deserve in this new volume – a nuanced, unvarnished and critical analysis that reveals and informs the reader of the diverse motivations, mundane realities and real harms of drug markets and supply chains. While prohibition continues to fail, alongside two-dimensional political and journalistic treatments, this book takes an unblinking look at those responding to the desires or desperation of drug users. From international mafias to local "lads" and friendly neighbourhood dealers, from the desperate hinterlands of cities to college dorms, gyms, suites and on to the opaque systems of crypto currencies and postal drops, this is a fresh and essential briefing on a perennially thorny set of issues. A truly global collection of detailed and close-up investigations, brings new insights, analytical depth and ideas to a subject that has for too long been crying out for insights anchored in thorough academic enquiry.'

Rowland Atkinson, *Chair in Inclusive Societies, University of Sheffield, UK*

UNDERSTANDING DRUG DEALING AND ILLICIT DRUG MARKETS

This book examines the drug dealer in contemporary society from an interdisciplinary perspective and considers the increasingly blurred demarcation between illegitimate and legitimate drug markets. It explores the motives and drivers of those involved in drug supply and dispels common and stereotypical myths and misconceptions surrounding illegal drug markets and those who operate within them.

The drug dealer has become one of our foremost contemporary 'folk devils'. Those who trade in substances prohibited by law are the subject of an array of inaccurate myths and urban legends. Criminology has tended either to shoehorn drug dealers into neat typologies or portray them as 'victims' of an uncaring, predatory post-modern society. In reality, we know relatively little about the complex and diverse world of drug markets and our concentration inevitably falls on low-end 'retail' dealers who operate in the most visible sectors of the illegal economy. Bringing together an international group of experts, this book considers perspectives from around the world, including UK, USA, South America, Spain, India and Australia.

This book will be of interest to students and researchers across criminology, law, sociology, criminal justice and public health, and will be an essential reading for those taking courses on drugs, drug markets and substance misuse.

Tammy C. Ayres is an associate professor of Criminology at the University of Leicester. She is an interdisciplinary scholar whose research focuses on drugs, consumerism, prisons and terrorism.

Craig Ancrum is a senior lecturer in Criminology at Teesside University. His research teaching is around drugs and drug markets, local crime and consumerism, violence and ethnographic methods.

UNDERSTANDING DRUG DEALING AND ILLICIT DRUG MARKETS

National and International Perspectives

Edited by Tammy C. Ayres and Craig Ancrum

Routledge
Taylor & Francis Group
LONDON AND NEW YORK

Cover image: © Getty Images

First published 2023
by Routledge
4 Park Square, Milton Park, Abingdon, Oxon OX14 4RN

and by Routledge
605 Third Avenue, New York, NY 10158

Routledge is an imprint of the Taylor & Francis Group, an informa business

British Library Cataloguing-in-Publication Data
A catalogue record for this book is available from the British Library

Library of Congress Cataloging-in-Publication Data
Names: Ayres, Tammy, editor. | Ancrum, Craig, editor.
Title: Understanding drug dealing and illicit drug markets : national and international perspectives / edited by Tammy C. Ayres and Craig Ancrum.
Description: Abingdon, Oxon ; New York, NY : Routledge, [2023] |
Includes bibliographical references and index. | Summary: "This book examines the drug dealer in contemporary society from an interdisciplinary perspective and considers the increasingly blurred demarcation between illegitimate and legitimate drug markets. It explores the motives and drivers of those involved in drug supply and dispels common and stereotypical myths and misconceptions surrounding illegal drug markets and those who operate within them. The drug dealer has become one of our foremost contemporary 'folk devils'. Those who trade in substances prohibited by law are the subject of array of inaccurate myths and urban legends. Criminology has tended either to shoehorn drug dealers into neat typologies or portray them as 'victims' of an uncaring, predatory post-modern society. In reality, we know relatively little about the complex and diverse world of drug markets and our concentration inevitably falls on low-end 'retail' dealers who operate in the most visible sectors of the illegal economy. Bringing together an international group of experts, this book considers perspectives from around the world, including UK, USA, South America, Spain, India and Australia This book will be of interest to students and researchers across criminology, law, sociology, criminal justice and public health, and will be essential reading for those taking courses on drugs, drug markets and substance misuse"– Provided by publisher.
Identifiers: LCCN 2022059715 | ISBN 9781138541801 (hardback) |
ISBN 9781138541825 (paperback) | ISBN 9781351010245 (ebook)
Subjects: LCSH: Drug traffic. | Drug dealers.
Classification: LCC HV5801 .U468 2023 | DDC 362.29–dc23/eng/20221216
LC record available at https://lccn.loc.gov/2022059715

ISBN: 978-1-138-54180-1 (hbk)
ISBN: 978-1-138-54182-5 (pbk)
ISBN: 978-1-351-01024-5 (ebk)

DOI: 10.4324/9781351010245

Typeset in Bembo
by Newgen Publishing UK

This book is dedicated to our parents
John and Doreen
&
William and Colleen

CONTENTS

CONTRIBUTORS

Paul Andell is an experienced researcher and practitioner in the field of drugs and more latterly gangs. He is currently a senior lecturer in criminology at the University of Suffolk. Paul has more than 25 years of experience of working in the criminal justice and community safety field. He has worked in the statutory, voluntary and private sectors undertaking criminal justice-related work in practice, policy and research.

Craig Ancrum is a senior lecturer in criminology at Teesside University. His research teaching is around drugs and drug markets, local crime and consumerism, violence and ethnographic methods. He has published on cannabis markets, 'taxing' and the use of biographic methods in teaching and research. He is a co-author of the 2008 book *Criminal Identities and Consumer Culture.*

Georgios A. Antonopoulos is a professor of criminology at Teesside University. His research interests include 'organised crime' and illegal markets. He is the editor-in-chief of *Trends in Organised Crime.*

Tammy C. Ayres is an associate professor of criminology at the University of Leicester. She is an interdisciplinary scholar working in the area of drugs, consumerism, prisons and terrorism, which are reflected in her research as well as her publications. Writing on drug policy, drug use and the intersection of drugs, pleasure and consumer capitalism, she uses critical theory and continental philosophy in an attempt to proffer new ways of theorising drugs in contemporary society.

Angus Bancroft lectures at the University of Edinburgh, examining illicit markets, digital platforms in the illicit drug economy and the uses of digital platforms for harm reduction.

Daniel Briggs is a researcher, writer and interdisciplinary academic who studies social problems. Over the last 20 years, he has undertaken mixed-methods and ethnographic research into various social issues from street drug users to terminally ill-patients; from illegal immigrants to football hooligans; and from gypsies to gangs and deviant youth behaviours. He has published over 100 books, chapters and articles and presented at over 50 conferences worldwide. He has written *Deviance and Risk on Holiday: An Ethnography of British Tourists in Ibiza* (2013, Palgrave MacMillan), *Crack Cocaine Users: High Society and Low Life in South London* (2012, Routledge). He is the editor of *La Criminología Del Hoy y Del Mañana* (2016, Dykinson) and *The English Riots of 2011: A Summer of Discontent* (2012, Waterside Press). He is a co-author of *The Consequences of Mobility: Reflexivity, Social Inequality and the Reproduction of Precariousness in Highly Qualified Migration* (2017, Palgrave MacMillan), *Riots and Political Protest* (2015, Palgrave MacMilan), *Culture and Immigration in Context* (2014, Palgrave MacMilan) and *Assessing the Use and Impact of Anti-Social Behaviour Orders* (2007, Policy Press). His penultimate book, which was based on a two-year photo-ethnographic project, titled *Drugs, Crime and Life in the City Shadows* (2017, Policy Press) won the Distinguished Book Award from the International Division of Criminology at the American Society of Criminology. He has recently concluded *Climate Changed: Refugee Border Stories and the Business of Misery* (2020, Routledge) and *Researching the Covid 19 Pandemic: A Critical Blueprint for the Social Sciences* (Bristol University Press, 2021). *Global Lockdown: A Critical Study* (2021, Palgrave MacMillan)continues his research into the Covid-19 pandemic and next year will be writing up his work on luxury brothels.

Ross Coomber is Professor Emeritus of Criminology and Sociology at the University of Liverpool. Prior to joining the University of Liverpool in 2018, he was professor and director of the Griffith Criminology Institute, Griffith University, in Brisbane and Gold Coast Australia, and before that, he was professor of sociology, and director of the Drug and Alcohol Research Unit at the University of Plymouth. He has more than 30 years of research experience in the drug and alcohol field and has written extensively and broadly in this area – particularly on the nature of, and the machinations of, illicit drug markets.

Jake Coomber-Moore is a research assistant in the Christie Patient Centered Research (CPCR) team at the Christie National Health Service (NHS) foundation Trust in Manchester, England. He has experience working on a variety of commercial and academic studies.

Jennifer Fleetwood is a senior lecturer in criminology in the Department of Sociology at Goldsmiths, University of London. She is the author of *Drug Mules: Women in the International Drug Trade*, which jointly won the British Society of Criminology Book Prize in 2015.

Erik D. Fritsvold serves as the founding faculty member and Academic Director for the Master of Science in Law Enforcement and Public Safety Leadership program at the University of San Diego. Fritsvold earned his BA in sociology from the University of San Diego, and his MA and PhD from the Criminology, Law & Society Department at the University of California at Irvine. His primary expertise is applying core tenets of academic criminology and criminal justice to dynamic, modern-day law enforcement. Fritsvold has been a full-time faculty member at USD in various capacities since 2005. He has authored numerous scholarly articles and book chapters. Fritsvold is also the co-author, with A. Rafik Mohamed, of *Dorm Room Dealers: Drugs and the Privileges of Race and Class.*

Alexandra Hall is an associate professor in criminology at Northumbria University. She is an interdisciplinary criminologist whose research interests extend across the social sciences. She is currently working on research and writing projects focusing on the enhancement drug trade and the criminological dimensions of special economic zones. Her books include *Fake Meds Online* (2016) and *Fake Goods, Real Money* (2018).

Angie Heal has many years' experience of working in public and voluntary sector organisations, including NHS, drug services, police and local authority posts. She completed her PhD in criminology at the School of Law, University of Sheffield. She has authored publications including *Journeys into Drugs and Crime: Life Stories of Jamaican Men Involved in the UK Drugs Trade* (2015, Palgrave) on which her chapter in the volume is based and *Child Sexual Exploitation after Rotherham: Understanding the Consequences and Recommendations for Practice* (Gladman and Heal, 2017, Jessica Kingsley Publishers). She now works with adult social care departments in local authorities around the country and is a volunteer in the local Covid-19 vaccination programme. She previously spent 15 years as a trustee and volunteer with an organisation working with women involved in street prostitution. She is a very amateur potter and a poor golfer but enjoys both, as well as being a serial adopter of greyhounds.

David James is an associate professor in sociology at the University of Suffolk and a course leader. He has undertaken evaluation work that has examined social policy interventions for young people, city centre policing practice and crime reduction interventions. He has a wide interest in social theory and social change, with a recent focus on the implications of a well-considered materiality.

Craig Kelly is a lecturer in criminology at Birmingham City University. He is currently enrolled on a PhD which focuses on experiences of violence within the British homeless milieu. His previous research has focussed upon violence in a range of areas including drug markets, music, video games and serial murder.

Travis Linnemann is an associate professor of sociology at Kansas State University. He is the author of *Meth Wars: Police, Media, Power* (2016, New York University Press [NYUP]) and *The Horror of Police* (2022, University Of Minnesota Press [UMNP]). He is also the current co-editor of *Crime, Media, Culture.*

Dev Maitra is a lecturer in criminology and law at the University of Suffolk. He holds degrees from the University of Cambridge (MPhil, PhD) and University of Bristol (LLB Hons.), and was called to the Bar of England and Wales at Lincoln's Inn. His research interests focus on street gangs, prison gangs, organised crime and prisoner radicalisation.

Corina Medley is an interdisciplinary researcher interested in theory, culture, criminology, sexuality, and animals and the environment. She is currently a lecturer in sociology at Kansas State University.

A. Rafik Mohamed is the dean of the College of Social & Behavioral Sciences and a professor of sociology at California State University, San Bernardino. Mohamed holds a BA in sociology and criminal justice from the George Washington University, and an MA in social ecology and PhD in criminology, law & society from the University of California at Irvine. Mohamed's research has focused on domestic drug policy, sports sociology and issues of racial identity and inequality in the United States. He is the co-author, with Erik D. Fritsvold, of *Dorm Room Dealers: Drugs and the Privileges of Race and Class.* His most recent book is titled *Black Men on the Blacktop: Basketball and the Politics of Race.*

James Morgan is a senior lecturer of psychology at London Metropolitan University. James has been researching drug issues since beginning his doctoral studies in 2010 and focuses on the lifestyle of heroin users while taking a special interest in the intersection of using and dealing amongst this population. In addition to continuing research with heroin users James co-hosts and curates the Street Drugs Discussions series of symposia and webinars.

Leah Moyle is a senior lecturer in criminology and sociology at Royal Holloway, University of London. Leah's research interests focus principally on illicit drug supply, and she has published widely in this area, with recent work spanning the policing of street-level drug markets, the sentencing and punishment of low-level 'drug dealers' and the use of social media in recreational drug markets. From 2016 to 2018 Leah worked as a Research Fellow at the world leading criminological research institute at Griffith University (Australia). Leah's work is internationally recognised and has featured on *BBC News, the Independent,* and *the Guardian.* Her findings have informed policy reports by the Global Commission on Drug Policy, the UK Government, the Advisory Council for Misuse of Drugs (ACMD) and Europol.

Kyle J.D. Mulrooney is a senior lecturer in criminology at the University of New England where he occupies a number of leadership roles including the co-director of the Centre for Rural Criminology. He also serves as the Vice President of the International Society for the Study of Rural Crime and on the Executive Board of the Human Enhancement Drug Network. Kyle's primary field of research is the sociology of punishment in which he has examined issues ranging from the nexus between penal populism and political culture to the areas of (enhancement) drug policy and rural crime. Kyle holds a PhD in cultural and global criminology from the University of Kent and Universität Hamburg, an MA in the sociology of law from the International Institute for the Sociology of Law and a BA (honours) in criminology and justice from the University of Ontario Institute of Technology.

Rob Ralphs is a professor in criminology and social policy, deputy director of the Research Centre for Applied Social Science (RCASS) and co-convenor of the interdisciplinary Substance Use and Associated Behaviours (SUAB) Research Centre at Manchester Metropolitan University. He has over 20 years of research experience dating back to 1997 that spans substance use and drug markets. Rob's interest in drug markets emerged from the three-year Economic and Social Research Council (ESRC)-funded 'Youth Gangs in an English City: Social Exclusion, Drugs and Violence' study for which he was the lead researcher. More recently, he has conducted research exploring new psychoactive substance (NPS) drug markets in prison and homeless populations. He is the principal investigator on a programme of annual research that is focused on emerging drug trends and changing drug markets in Greater Manchester (GM TRENDS).

Mike Salinas is a senior lecturer in criminology at Manchester Metropolitan University. He earned his doctorate from the University of Manchester. His research work includes ethnographies of various illegal drug markets and various stages of the supply chain. He writes on 'traditional' illegal drug supply chains, offending careers over the life course, as well as use and policy surrounding image and performance enhancing drugs. In 2015 he was awarded 'Best PhD' in Organized Crime by the International Association for the Study of Organized Crime (IASOC, Washington D.C.).

Daniel Silverstone is the director of the School of Justice Studies at Liverpool John Moores University. The school consists of three cognate but distinct disciplines, Criminology, Criminal Justice and Policing studies. Daniel has a long-standing research interest in the activities and organisation of Serious and Organised Crime and is currently working with colleagues evaluating the government response to the threat from 'County Lines'. He also has a research interest in the issue of human trafficking and works on behalf of the courts as an expert witness in this area.

Nigel South is a professor of sociology and director of the Centre for Criminology, University of Essex, UK. He has worked on drugs-related topics since the 1980s, co-authored *Traffickers: Drug Markets and Law Enforcement* and *Eurodrugs*, co-edited *Drug Use and Cultural Contexts*, edited *Drugs: Cultures, Controls and Everyday Life* and is currently working on the development of drug markets on the web. He is a fellow of the Academy of Social Sciences and in 2013 received a Lifetime Achievement Award from the American Society of Criminology, Division on Critical Criminology and Social Justice.

Stuart Taylor is a senior lecturer in criminal justice in the School of Justice Studies at Liverpool John Moores University, UK. His main academic interests centre upon social, cultural and legal construction of drugs, drug use and drug users and how these interact with and influence drug policy. His recent publications focus on media representations of intoxication, the cultural juxtaposition of the stigma applied to different substance uses, and the use of drug checking technologies among ecstasy users.

Honor Townshend is a PhD student and a visiting lecturer in the Criminology Department at the University of Hertfordshire's School of Law. She holds a BA (Hons) in criminology (Birmingham City University) and an MSc in criminology and criminal justice (City, University of London). The focus of her doctoral research is the role of idealised gender identities on the uptake of IPEDs.

James Treadwell is a professor at Staffordshire University. He started his academic career as a lecturer in criminology at the University of Central England, having previously worked for NACRO and the National Offender Management Service. He is a member of the executive board with the British Society of Criminology and was an academic advisor on the Howard League Commission into Ex-Military Personnel in Prison (advising the inquiry chair Sir John Nutting QC). His recent research has considered issues of prison violence and disorder, and violent and organised crime against the backdrop of deindustrialised locales in the Centre and North of England. His research tends to involve qualitative and ethnographic research, prison research and interviewing and often centres on aspects of the drug trade. He has also recently authored *Criminological Ethnography: An Introduction* (2019, Sage)

Tim Turner is an assistant professor of criminology at Coventry University, UK. He volunteers as a senior researcher with The Loop, a non-profit organisation delivering innovative drug checking services to music festivals, clubs and city centres.

Katinka van de Ven is a senior lecturer at the Centre for Rural Criminology, University of New England, and a visiting fellow as part of the Drug Policy Modelling Program (DPMP), Social Policy Research Centre (SPRC), University of New South Wales. Katinka specialises in the use and supply of performance and image-enhancing drugs (PIEDs), which includes projects surrounding steroids and the law, harm minimisation policies, and improving healthcare services for people who use enhancement drugs. Katinka also conducts research in relation to alcohol and other drug (AOD) treatment services systems more broadly, amongst others around funding mechanisms, workforce characteristics and client outcomes. Katinka is the Editor-in-Chief of *Performance Enhancement & Health* and the director of the Human Enhancement Drugs Network (HEDN).

Andrew Wilson recently retired as a senior lecturer in criminology and is now a research fellow at Manchester Metropolitan University. His PhD research at the London School of Economics (LSE) was published as *Northern Soul: Music, Drugs, and Subcultural Identity*. The research drew on his own experience of amphetamine use, burgling chemist shops and supplying of drugs in the 1970s northern scene. After completing his PhD in 1999 he was the lead researcher on a Home Office study assessing the impact of drug markets on neighbourhood regeneration. He later worked for Nacro on the evaluation of drug testing arrestees at police stations. From 2015 to 2018 he served the Welsh Government on the Advisory Panel on Substance Misuse.

FOREWORD

It is always time to update knowledge around legal and illegal drugs, their damaging, healing and radiant effects. This is because all research on the topic is partial, at times being focused on specific populations of users, at other times on specific substances popular amongst users. Moreover, funding and other bureaucratic hurdles, often clumsily dressed as ethical concerns, slow down the process of disseminating findings, so that by the time these are known the reality described has changed.

This is a very welcome collection of papers that address what seems a comprehensive range of issues surrounding drugs. Prohibition, racism and sexism feature in persuasive and nuanced contributions, as does the relationship between the drug business and the global economy. Advanced countries, which are major producers of legal drugs, stigmatise and penalise developing ones, deemed monopolisers of the production of prohibited substances. But are we sure that the former are not engaged in a competitive battle to produce all sorts of drugs? Total legalisation, after all, is invoked by business as well as users, although the latter would opt for protected and safe markets rather than the drug supermarket model advocated by pharmaceutical companies.

The stereotypical association of some substances with precise ethnicities is well documented, and this book adds original material to what I would describe as a subtle supplementary aspect of competition. Harsh punishment of those involved in the marketing of 'radically evil' drugs, for example, aims to nudge distributors towards other occupations, namely, badly paid and precarious jobs in the hidden and illicit economies. Of concern is the loss of the labour drug dealers could provide, rather than the damage they might cause to users. Nor is it easy to demonstrate that legitimate precarity is preferable, materially and ethically, to an equally precarious position in the illegal drug market. In this sense, prohibitionists seem to be upset by those who imitate them by pursuing an entrepreneurial, if illegitimate, career. This reminds me of the similar envious distress felt by official entrepreneurs when members of organised crime argue that, unlike the former, they are stigmatised because they manage to extract profits even from lice.

The book covers not only prohibited drug use, but also the consumption of addictive medications, performance enhancement drugs, dietary supplements, vitamins and beauty augmentation, all part and parcel of diverse widespread lifestyles. The concept of 'drug apartheid' is well explicated with arguments that resound old, glorious conflict theories, whereby privilege entails the right to name 'things and others' while averting being named by others. The drug offer today is differentiated and *ad personam*, with legitimate and illegitimate providers adopting a just-in-time model: legal and illegal mixtures, innovative cocktails and individually designed blends lead the market. Abundance and diversity, in turn, determine the involvement of a variety of operators unseen in previous periods. In one of the last research project I conducted, the majority of heroin distributors serving a prison sentence had a degree in marketing, not a criminal apprenticeship.

Underlying prohibitionism is the tendency to impute to drug use all the unpleasant features of contemporary societies. Users and distributors are said to lack the *socius*, namely, the capacity to engage constructively in the public sphere. However, this is denied the very moment in which punitive institutional measures are imposed on them. Here is the paradox: in penalising users and dealers, one removes them from the social arena because they are incapable of engaging in the Platonic pleasure of public dialogue. Therefore, the *socius* is taken away from them because they do not have it.

This book also addresses the role of banks and other financial institutions in the global drug business. Surely, those involved in processing profits from drugs cannot claim social sensitivity, unless they implicitly support any form of wealth generation because the trickle-down principles will benefit all. One wonders why the same argument is not mobilised when addressing cocaine producers and traffickers. The reality is that in the drugs economy costs and benefits are not equitably distributed, as those who are unsuccessful in the legitimate world find it difficult to make it in the illegitimate world too.

The present book inspires many questions, provides responses to some and, rightly, encourages plural answers to others. One key stimulation that readers will probably find pertains to the debate around the legalisation of all drugs. Why is this debate stalled or avoided? Is it because legalisation would yield fewer monetary benefits? Or because it would erase the distinction between benefactors and enemies of the public? In fact, governments need the friend/enemy opposition, as identifiable enmity is indispensable for their action and for their very survival. Perhaps, drug legalisation would leave many social service providers bereft of clients and many criminological researchers idle. The latter would have to shift their object of study from merchants of death to cholesterol dealers, focussing on the dangerous effects of items such as American chickens and English sausages.

Vincenzo Ruggiero, *Professor of Sociology at Middlesex University, London*

INTRODUCTION

> I knew there was never anyone to blame when people get into drugs. They're always responsible for their own behavior, and it's not the dealer, it's not the friend, it's not the bad influence, it's not the childhood.
>
> *Anthony Kiedis*

> A priest and a drug dealer both sell products that offer everlasting joy … although the drug dealers product is cheaper with fewer strings attached.
>
> *Chris Haslam*

The making, supply and use of drugs change continuously. Keeping on top of new developments and trends can be challenging. Research may become quickly outdated and can skew our knowledge by focusing on particular populations or drugs. This means that uncovering the realities and consequences of new drugs, shifting drug markets, their manufacturing, trafficking and supply is often partial and tends to lag rapid new developments and innovations. In recent years these have included the use of psychoactive substances, particularly synthetic cannabinoids (Spice), the opioid crisis in America and the increasing use of social media and the Internet to supply an array of substances, some of which remain prohibited. Prohibition remains contested not least because a key consequence is that the drugs world becomes a more enclosed, secretive and sometimes dangerous domain that clogs up the criminal justice system, raises the bar of health costs and makes these spaces more inaccessible to researchers as traffickers know the risks arising from disclosing too much information about their business. This is particularly true of the successful drug dealers and those that occupy the higher echelons of the drug trafficking business, which is often linked to significant transnational trade that may be legitimate or to organised crime and terrorism, which are not.

DOI: 10.4324/9781351010245-1

The chapters of this book therefore seek to address these complexities, many of which are similarly bound by the limitations of trying to do socially relevant and important research in this field. Although there is already a range of texts straddling different disciplines on drug supply, there are few books that focus exclusively on this topic and those that do are increasingly dated (see Coomber, 2006; Ruggiero and South, 1995) as drug markets shift and change. This book arrives at a time of continuing concern about the impact of prohibition, calls for the reformation of the current (outdated) drug laws,[1] the emergence of new synthetic psychoactive drugs and a widespread appetite for the kind of knowledge that might help to see progress on these issues. This book responds to these concerns by offering nuanced insights from cutting-edge researchers working on modern drug markets and with drug dealers to examine the way that these have altered and developed internationally.

The contributions collected here elucidate on the realities of drug supply at both a local and global level, offering interdisciplinary perspectives with contributions from international scholars, from professors, early career academics, professionals and PhD students. This book examines the modern-day drug dealer and contemporary drug markets. While this book cannot claim to offer a comprehensive and total understanding of the complexities of drug markets, it does provide a cutting-edge perspective that gets inside the reality of drug supply and its subsequent issues to capture and illustrate the finer nuances of these often clandestine markets and how they are inextricably tied to the global political economy, which is largely disavowed and omitted from the official discourse. Consequently, this new and exciting collection is not only relevant to academics and students alike, but also to those working in this area, from the police and the National Crime Agency to international organisations like the United Nations Office on Drugs and Crime and the European Monitoring Centre for Drugs and Drug Addiction (EMCDDA). This chapter introduces the ensuing contributions that comprise this edited collection by contextualising the modern-day drug dealers in contemporary society. It does this by looking at the myths surrounding drug traffickers compared to the reality and how all of this is tied to the wider political economy, inequality and culture. The overarching aim of this edited collection therefore is to provide an up-to-date insight into modern-day drug markets and the contemporary drug dealer.

Death dealers and pushers

Those who trade in drugs have historically been demonised constituting one of history's most prominent and pervasive scapegoats (Berridge, 1999, 2013; Szasz, 2003). As Linnemann and Medley highlight in Chapter 20, drug dealers have haunted the American imagination, which is also true in the UK as well as around the globe. Historically drug dealers have been blamed for many of society's ills. Whether it was the Chinese in London in the early nineteenth century peddling opium or the more recent Yardie gun wielding crack dealers, the supply of illicit drugs has always been associated with 'otherness', particularly foreignness, race and ethnicity, alongside danger and death. In fact, drug dealers/suppliers have often been referred to as 'death dealers' or 'merchants of death' as they are held responsible for the demise of drug users as well as the destruction and corruption of society (e.g. drug trafficking causes crime/violence, corruption and death). Therefore, they not only warrant condemnation but also vilification and social control through punishment.

Drug dealers often receive some of the harshest punishments and longest prison sentences available, not only in the UK but also around the world, despite it being a largely victimless crime (or at least a crime where the victim consents to any harm that occurs as a result of the drugs being sold and used). This is problematised further since the evidence base underpinning prohibition, the criminalisation of drugs and their supply is largely missing, or at least, not premised on scientific evidence. Despite this, however, drug dealing/trafficking is still punishable by death in 35 countries (e.g. Saudi Arabia, China, Iran, Vietnam and Singapore) (see HRI, 2021). It is in this context that drug dealers are often portrayed as a personification of evil – preying on the young and the vulnerable, forcing drugs onto innocent by-standers in order to get them hooked – tropes that continue today and are often reinforced by drug policy and legislation.

Drug policy and legislation have indoctrinated many of the myths spiralling around drug dealers. Yet there is a need to be able to calibrate the extent of these harms and differentiate myth from reality, particularly in this multi-mediated landscape. In fact, it is the mediated stereotypical representation that dominates the view of the drug dealer/trafficker, as the hyper-reality surrounding drug supply has become more real than reality itself (Baudrillard, 1994). This has distorted society's perception of the contemporary drug dealer and thus the research and knowledge base in this area, while the impact of prohibition – and its subsequent legislation – is ignored. The violent trade in drugs made lucrative by prohibition has generated its own harms. For example, the so-called county lines supply of drugs[2] has been linked to the exploitation of vulnerable people and increased levels of violence. However, this may also be attributable to its illicit nature and the draconian punishments facing anyone willingly involved in drug dealing, rather than being a true representation of these complex issues. Instead, stereotypes and mythology – like the idea that women do not choose to sell drugs, see Chapter 7 in this volume – have been indoctrinated as fact despite many of these occurrences being shown to be 'urban legends' that inappropriately influence policy and practice (see Coomber, 2006).

One prolific example of an urban legend relates to the widely held perception that drug dealers prey on young children and stand at the school gates pushing their drugs on to them, just to get them hooked, which is for the most part a myth. For many reasons children are not good, profitable customers with large disposable incomes and yet this myth is legitimised in legislation and is widely regarded as fact. For example, the Drugs Act 2005 and more recently the Sentencing Guidelines for Drug Offences (2012) requires a court to consider aggravating factors such as drug dealing near a school when sentencing a dealer, which merely results in those selling drugs in built-up (often poverty stricken) inner-city areas being more likely to be in the vicinity of a school and thus more likely to receive a longer prison sentence. Similar myths can be found globally (see Chapter 3 in this volume on how the moral panic about 'Yardies' impacted law enforcement initiatives and changed immigration policy). However, the reality is starkly different.

As illustrated in the ensuing chapters, the reality surrounding the manufacture and supply of drugs illustrates that drug dealers are not evil and amoral people, but instead they are just like the rest of us. Rather than having some malevolent innate property to corrupt, drug dealers are not inherently evil and yet, like the drugs themselves; drugs and their suppliers are often blamed for many societal ills. Instead, drugs are just commodities to be bought, sold and consumed (see Ruggiero and South, 1995). Like with drugs, knowledge around drug supply is largely influenced by the research in this area – as highlighted by Coomber in the first chapter and Ayres and Taylor in Chapter 19 later on in the book – and although, research has debunked many of the more pervasive and stereotypical myths surrounding drug dealers, these have not been widely disseminated outside of academia to become part of the official everyday discourse.

Instead, official discourse often incorporates and perpetuates these myths. While drugs are not really pushed but pulled (by demand), research has also shown that drug dealers often follow a moral code not to deal with children, and may sometimes mete out consequences (e.g. violence and cut supply) to those that do (see Broadhurst, 2005). Who we see as the drug dealer is also rather narrow, because as Coomber highlights in Chapter 1, researchers often focus on that which is most visible and assumed from previous research. In this context, affluent and well-educated people are rarely seen as drug dealers (or drug users, particularly problematic users) (see Chapter 8), nor are doctors or big pharmaceutical companies despite the role they both play – and have played – in the supply and subsequent use of drugs (licit and illicit) throughout history. Consequently, the stereotypical drug dealer invokes one of the highest levels of public concern (often alongside that of sex offenders/paedophiles), despite the fact that the dominant perception of drug dealers/traffickers has been created in a 'infinite hall of mirrors' (Ferrell, 1999: 397).

In contemporary society, the line between reality and fiction has become blurred. The media no longer merely reports on the news. Instead, it defines it, including who we see as the drug dealer/trafficker – the evil other – which structures the reality surrounding drug supply. The messages reverberating through the mainstream media reflect the dominant ideologies of the capitalist system while also functioning as an ideological system that 'comes to act as the cultural wallpaper in our lives' (Taylor, 2010: 97). It is in this wider context – the wider political economy and the consumer responsibility agenda – that drug dealing must be viewed as it not only strengthens and ignores the harms arising from legitimate laissez-faire practices by businesses, doctors and pharmaceutical companies, but also simultaneously reinforces the need for a system of drug prohibition and its draconian sentences, which are saved for the evil drug dealer. In fact, in some instances drug dealers get longer sentences than murderers, rapists and paedophiles, illustrating their standing in contemporary society. This is because the media – alongside political discourse – have constructed the drug dealer/trafficker within various guises of otherness, premised on race/ethnicity, gender, criminality, risk, corruption and evilness: themes that have been replicated throughout history, which have led to 'knee jerk' reactions and punitive responses that often lack a legitimate evidence base (see Ayres and Jewkes, 2012; Murji, 1998; Silverman, 2012). It also distinguishes us from them and our idealized and entrepreneurial selves – the normal from the deviant – which not only helps to engender conformity, but also permits those in power to pass legislation and policy restricting the intolerable behaviour of society's evil undesirables – in this instance, the drug trafficker. The ideological message construed by the media is representative of the government's stance on illicit drugs, their manufacturer and supply, alongside the state's aspirations for a drug-free society full of drug-free individuals. It is in this world where 'the street scripts the screen and the screen scripts the street' that drug supply must be viewed (Ferrell, Hayward and Young, 2008: 114).

The subsequent 'loops and spirals' (Ferrell et al. 2008: 119) mean that stereotypical tropes dominate, while others outside the dominant typecast are disavowed. This is partly attributable to the dominant portrayal of drug dealers, which focuses on the powerless rather than the powerful as those in power label difficult, dangerous, minority ethnic groups as outsiders – a threat – in their exertion of state power, which also led to the War on Drugs. As Wacquant (2009: 69) outlines, the:

> "War on drugs"— [is] an ill-named policy since it refers in reality to a guerilla campaign of penal harassment of low-level street dealers and poor consumers, aimed primarily at young men in the collapsing inner city for whom the retail trade of narcotics has provided the most accessible and reliable source of gainful employment in the wake of the twofold retrenchment of the labor market and the welfare state.

Instead, those in power, alongside the media – with its reductionist discourse – have created the spectacle of the drug dealer, which as Debord (1967: 11) highlights 'serves as a total justification of the conditions and goals of the existing system'. Thus, the dominant portrayal of the drug dealer has tended to feed into law enforcement initiatives as part of the 'Prison-Industrial-Complex', which is increasingly used to address problems that are essentially social, political or economic in nature but which have provided lucrative returns for private providers who have acted in concert with the state. The dominant tropes surrounding drug supply subsequently focus on the usual suspects, which include criminals, organised crime groups and terrorists, while ignoring the unusual suspects like doctors, big pharma and states. Tropes that adopt and perpetuate racialised/ethnic stereotypes (e.g. Turkish heroin dealers, Black Jamaican Yardies dealing crack, white working-class males that are violent), which is legitimised and personified in the UK by policy campaigns,[3] while other groups – women in particular – are omitted and invisibilised (see Chapter 7) alongside wealthy white (college) kids (see Chapter 8), professional people, doctors and legitimate businesses (see Chapters 19 and 20).

Consequently, the reality of drug supply/dealing and the agents that operate within drug markets are quite different from the dominant status quo and the mainstream imaginary. For example, we see in Chapter 3 how Jamaican men migrated to the UK looking for a better way of life where they could achieve their dreams, but due to the furore around violent 'Jamaican Yardies' at the time – which subsequently impacted immigration policy – the only means of achieving these aspirations was via the illegitimate economy and the UK drug trade. Therefore, while the first half of the book (Part 1, Chapters 1–14) examines drug dealing among the usual – albeit diverse – suspects, the second half of the book (Part 2, Chapters 15–18) looks at how drug markets are changing and have changed – alongside technology. The last two chapters take a look at the unusual suspects (e.g. big pharma) as well as the limitations of research and knowledge in this area to acknowledge the changing landscape.

The changing landscape

The topic of drugs, their manufacture and supply has changed alongside contemporary society, from which it cannot be separated as under neoliberalism human existence and all subsequent interactions have been brought within the domain of the market. In accordance with the neoliberal[4] ethos, every aspect of life has been commodified, which has resulted in 'social incoherence' and the

> creative destruction, not only of prior institutional frameworks and powers (even challenging traditional forms of state sovereignty) but also of divisions of labour, social relations, welfare provisions, technological mixes, ways of life and thought, reproductive activities, attachments to the land and habits of the heart … [as] deregulation, privatization, and withdrawal of the state from many areas of social provision.
>
> *Harvey, 2007: 3*

It is in this context that drugs must be understood, whether we are talking about their manufacture, supply or use, or drug policy, the war on drugs and its resultant legislation, all are tied to capital and its neoliberal hegemonic ideology (see Ayres, 2019, 2020; Courtwright, 2001; Paley, 2014).

Neoliberalism exacerbates inequalities and prioritises individualism, entrepreneurialism, a free market, deregulation and privatisation, which rather than benefit the masses benefit a tiny percentage of the population as everything is increasingly managed as a business and profit is prioritised over people (Chomsky, 1998). The result is that drug laws and their enforcement – particularly when it comes to the manufacture and supply of drugs – become yet another attack on poverty and the poor as 'class inequalities upon which capital accumulation rests are frequently defined by identities of race, gender, ethnicity, religion and geographical affiliations' (Harvey, 2010: 240–241). Here the media, the prison industrial complex and the criminal justice system are used as a 'cultural engine and fount of social demarcations, public norms and moral emotions', as the 'the state stridently reasserts its responsibility, potency, and efficiency in the narrow register of crime management', which demarcates the deserving from the undeserving, the legitimate suppliers of drugs from the illicit dealers, and the criminal from the law-abiding citizen all of which determine whether these groups/individuals warrant excommunication, punishment and, in some instances, death[5] as they are used to 'enforce hierarchy, and control contentious categories' (Wacquant, 2009: xvi, xviii). Here issues of power, labelling and capital result in the unequal enforcement of drug laws around the world, which disproportionately target (and criminalise) the most vulnerable and the most powerless, while big corporations, states and those in power – despite their involvement in the drug trade, which often causes more harm – are disavowed as 'neoliberalism is a failed utopian rhetoric that masking a successful project for the restoration of ruling-class power' of the economic elites (Harvey, 2007: 203). This dichotomy is very much evidenced in the chapters of this book, which focuses on 'drug dealers proper' rather than those omitted from and legitimised by the official discourse that loops and spirals around drugs and those that manufacture and supply them. Subsequently, if we are ever to understand the root causes and people's involvement in the drug trade (and criminality more widely), then the structural factors arising from the political-economy must be considered (Ayres, 2020; Contreras, 2012; Hall et al., 2008; Treadwell and Ayres, 2014) as illustrated in the subsequent chapters of this edited collection.

The ensuing chapters show that illicit drug dealers sell drugs to stave off poverty, starvation, and social death. Exercising their freedom of enterprise and adorning themselves with the material markers that illustrate ideological success, they strive to survive in the situations they find themselves in, while also heeding the neoliberal call to consume, be entrepreneurial and take advantage of every opportunity available to them in a society where everything is instant and individuals are blamed for their own misfortune including those arising from wider structural issues (e.g. deindustrialisation, privatisation, unemployment and poverty), which are largely disavowed. What is evident from the ensuing chapters is a clear capitalist ethos motivated them to enter the drug market (Ayres, 2020; Contreras, 2012; Hall et al. 2008; Wacquant, 2009; Treadwell and Ayres, 2014). However, the demonisation of illicit drug dealers and their symbolic representation dominates, which has resulted in their punishment, control, vilification and exclusion, as some of the most hateful and evil depictions are reserved for the illicit drug dealer. Illicit drug dealers are largely seen as something we are not – folk devils – when the reality is, they are not very different from the rest of us or the legitimate manufacturers and suppliers of drugs (whoever they may be) as such market distinctions are increasingly becoming blurred.

There is also much debate about what constitutes a drug, particularly since drugs appear to have diversified to include a range of substances that incorporate prescription medications, human enhancement drugs (HEDS), performance- and image-enhancing drugs (PIEDS), dietary supplements, vitamins, alcohol and tobacco, as well as the more traditional illicit drugs (e.g. cannabis, cocaine and heroin). This diversification cannot be divorced from neoliberal subjectivity – the individual as the sovereign of their own entrepreneurial self – and the subsequent changes to the beauty, body and lifestyle ideals that accompany it as everyone is invested in 'project Me' (Bröckling, 2016). It is in this context that the consumer relies on an ever-increasing array of transient commodities to help inform, create and transform the self, and this includes drugs (see Ayres, 2019, 2020; Hall, 2019). 6: 76) highlights, in contemporary society, the 'only constant left to the individual is the necessity of constantly transforming … [them]self to cope with the discontinuities and accelerating turbulence of the market'. In order to achieve this, there is an increasing array of substances that promise to improve our appearance, make us happier, healthier, more muscular, smarter, thinner (Evans-Brown, McVeigh, Perkins and Bellis, 2012) and so on, as appearance, identity and life have become an 'economic function', and in this context, 'disinvestment means death' (Bröckling, 2016: 53) as individuals are blamed for their own misfortune and poor consumption choices (Bauman, 2000) as everyone strives for perfection.

As Bauman (2000) highlights in neoliberal society

> you owe your body thought and care, and if you neglect that duty you should feel guilty and ashamed. Imperfections of your body are your guilt and your shame. But the redemption of sins is in the hands of the sinner, and in his or her hands alone.
>
> *p. 35*

This perspective is exacerbated by the role of the media, particularly social media that engenders the ideal image that everyone desires as 'capitalism needs more than simply justifications; it also needs mechanisms for getting people to get themselves into the right shape to actively participate in it' (Bröckling, 2016: 181). We are constantly reminded that there is room for improvement in all aspects of our life (Featherstone, 1982) as 'self-management is supposed to activate the potential of the whole person, not just [thei]r ability to work' (Bröckling, 2016: 32). As part of 'project Me', the branded entrepreneurial self draws upon the processes, symbols, and market logics of the mainstream image-economy of the culture industries as they preserve, reproduce and reconstruct their own human capital (Hearn, 2008) as everyone strives to make themselves more marketable, desirable and competitive as they are 'trapped in the narcissistic, self-surveillance world of images' (Featherstone, 1982: 22), which has increased mental ill-health, anxiety and body dysmorphia as everyone is striving for the unrealistic and imaginary good life that can only be achieved via consumption. Instead, everyone is busy consuming themselves into being (Bauman, 2000), through an increasingly diverse array of products, services, lifestyles, experiences and substances.

As the substances being used have diversified, so too have the actors that supply them and their respective skill set. The skills necessary for more traditional forms of drug dealing are very different from those that are needed to set up an online drug market, particularly on the darknet. In fact, this diversity in supply and in those now participating in drug dealing also means that the levels of violence vary despite the stereotypical perception that all drug markets are inherently violent. The reality is, however, that the violence present in drug markets and supply chains is often attributable to other wider socio-political and economic factors (e.g. failed states, weak and corrupt governments) as research shows that unless drug dealers already have a penchant for violence (see Ancrum and Treadwell, 2016; Ayres and Treadwell, 2012; Contreras, 2012; Treadwell and Ayres, 2014), they are often reluctant to become involved in violence (see Broadhurst, 2005; Coomber, 2006). Instead, like most legitimate businesses, the majority of drug dealers would rather implement marketing strategies like starting a price war, discounts on multiple buys – Buy One Get One Free (BOGOF) – and/or providing tasters to their customers, than become involved in violence (Broadhurst, 2005; Coomber, 2006). For example, cocaine is often sold in half grams for forty pounds in the UK, but many dealers have a 'three for a hundred' policy or offer similar bulk deals like two white (crack) and one brown (heroin) for twenty-five pounds.

Ironically, prohibition and law enforcement have been shown to actually incite as well as exacerbate levels of violence in drug markets (see Rolles et al., 2016). However, as the chapters of this book show, violence is not used by everyone involved in the drug trade. Some violent individuals are instead attracted to drug dealing or use their violent persona to rob or 'tax' drug dealers in a society where their skill set is no longer valid and it becomes their only means to earn a living, providing them with an alternative form of work (Ayres and Treadwell, 2012; Bourgois, 1995; Collison, 1996; Contreras, 2012; Preble and Casey, 1969; Treadwell and Ayres, 2014; Treadwell et al., 2018). For many, drug dealing is a job that provides meaning/purpose and economic survival, not only to the disenfranchised and dispossessed, but also to increasingly diverse sections of the populace, which constitute some of the more unusual suspects. Against a backdrop of deindustrialisation, macro-economic policies, precarious employment, competition and the decline in more traditional forms of work that offered job security, career advancement and a living wage, the drug trade has for many provided an alternative and more viable form of work than the more precarious and transient alternatives available to them in the legitimate economy (Ancrum and Treadwell, 2016; Contreras, 2012; Hall et al., 2008; Treadwell and Ayres,

2014), where they might be lucky to earn a minimum wage and instead face becoming one of the working poor.

From the early work of Preble and Casey (1969) to the chapters of this book (alongside others), drug dealing can be seen – for increasingly diverse sections of the populace – as an alternative form of work, and for many, more desirable than other 'work/employment' options available to them (e.g. unemployment, welfare/benefits, earning minimum wage and being one of the working poor). A successful drug dealer may have a more fulfilling and rewarding life than if they had opted for some of the realistic and legal alternatives available to them. While drug dealing used to be seen as employment for disenfranchised and dispossessed individuals/groups, like most things related to drug dealing, this is also an inaccurate representation. As outlined in the ensuing chapters, entrepreneurs from all walks of life are attracted to drug dealing/trafficking often due to the money to be made, although this was not the only motivating factor (see Chapter 8). Other motivating factors also involved the procurement of drugs and the supply of drugs among friendship groups, which was more engrained in the socio-cultural fabric of regular drug use and has been termed social supply and/or part of the moral economy rather than drug dealing proper (see Chapters 2 and 6 as well as Moyle and Coomber, 2015; Wakeman, 2016). For those that did deal drugs to make money – whether drug supply was their only source of income or a means of supplementing their wages – many dealt drugs so that they might afford the finer things in life as they all partook in conspicuous consumption (e.g., see, Chapters 4, 8 and 11). Thus, the individual actors involved in drug dealing – like any legitimate business – sold drugs to earn a living and to survive financially as their sale provided them with 'economic freedom' (see Chapter 11).

Many drug dealers saw themselves as entrepreneurs, heeding the neoliberal call to be competitive and enterprising individuals striving for success and economic security, while also being responsible for their own fate. In contemporary neoliberalism, we are all expected to exploit unexploited opportunities and become burgeoning 'entrepreneurs', which 'produces a model for people to understand what they are and what they ought to be' – a form of subjectification – as 'acting entrepreneurially is the very condition of participation in social life' (Bröckling, 2016: iii). As Hobbs (2013: 158) points out, there is an 'entrepreneurial symbiosis associated with a wide range of skills, acumen and logistics common to both criminal and legitimate enterprise', including drug dealing. In fact, the contemporary drug market and its transactions stress flexibility, autonomy and independence, reflecting similar trends in the legitimate market and its global gig economy (see Chapter 11) as people increasingly occupy precarious employment with zero-hour contracts and/or cannot find employment at all, particularly employment that provides enough to live on and pay the bills (see Chapter 16). Therefore, drug dealers – on both a local and a global level – exploit the opportunities they have for illicit gains, using skill sets that are often no longer valued in the legitimate economy in order to 'stand out and fit in' as people seek individual recognition and distinction (Hall et al., 2008: 203), while believing that 'human wellbeing can best be advanced by liberating individual entrepreneurial freedoms and skills' (Harvey, 2007: 2). Therefore, drugs – their production, supply and use – must be understood in the political-economy of neoliberal consumer capitalism, which promotes the entrepreneurial values of competitiveness, self-interest, individual empowerment and decentralisation creating self-interested actors that embody the neoliberal ideal of market-orientated entrepreneurship (Ayres, 2019, 2020). However, rather than being seen as a rational and valid response to their wider socio-economic circumstances (see Chapter 3), drug dealers are individually pathologised and demonised as evil and amoral people that get people addicted to drugs and deal in death. The fact is that drugs are not only a crucial part of the irregular economy – which creates counter-economies not only locally (see Hammersley, 2008) but also globally – they are also part of the legitimate economy as boundaries between the two are becoming increasingly blurred (see Chapters 17–20).

Drug supply: who are the criminals?

Consequently, the blurring between licit and illicit pervades the global trade in drugs/substances, which includes HED/PIEDS (see Chapter 17), the supply of illicit medicines (see Chapter 18), dietary supplements (Ayres, 2020) and pharmaceuticals (see Chapter 20). Despite being legal/quasi-legal, these substances are also potentially, if not equally as or even more, harmful than illicit drugs. In fact, evidence suggests that despite being legal – and thus one would expect regulated and safe – legitimate products often contain banned (e.g. natural dietary supplements,[6] human enhancement drugs) and harmful ingredients that can negatively affect people's health and well-being (Evans-Brown et al., 2012; Singer and Baer, 2009; Tucker et al., 2018). However, the harms arising from non-drugs – including their manufacture and supply – are largely ignored and commodified. Instead, the focus and blame is placed on illicit drugs and those who manufacture and supply them as outlined in Chapter 19. While consumers expect the contents of illicit drugs to be subject to inconsistencies – due to the market being unregulated and illicit – they do not expect inconsistencies in the legal drugs they buy from reputable companies, let alone think that these substances might actually harm them (see Singer and Baer, 2009). Nobody really sees big pharma and the doctors they pay to prescribe their drugs or the alcohol industry and its marketing campaigns as being akin to drug dealing and drug dealers. Suppliers of substances they might be, but dealers of drugs they are not, at least not in contemporary society, but is this a constraint imposed by the research in this area?

As with most areas of criminology, drug scholars have predominately focused on the use and supply of drugs by the powerless, while ignoring the powerful. While there has been some work on the pharmaceutical industry as a form of state-corporate crime and the harms arising from their practices (e.g. Braithwaite,

1984; Griffin and Miller, 2011; Singer and Baer, 2009), it is not a common and integral component of the drug dealing literature and discourse, which largely focuses on the unprivileged drugs, their users and suppliers (see Taylor et al., 2016). It is not just the drugs/substances themselves that blur the boundaries between legitimate and illegitimate, as diverse sections of the populace are drawn to the trade in drugs. This is because the drug trade exists in a power vacuum, so theoretically it is open to anyone. No qualifications or experience is needed, meaning that drug dealing is an equal opportunities employer. In fact, in some countries the illicit drug trade far exceeds the size of the legitimate economy, while the penetration of illicit drug profits into the legitimate economy is so extensive that it is impossible to tell where the boundaries lie, let alone how one would begin to disentangle them. This is further exacerbated by the legitimate people and businesses who are also involved in the illicit drug trade – lawyers, accountants, bankers, governments and states, to name just a few. For example, HSBC Bank in 2012 was fined for laundering USD$881 million drug cartel money but never indicted; however, they instead agreed to be monitored by a court-appointed watchdog and allowed to pay a USD$1.92 billion settlement. Such cases illustrate how the legal actors (e.g. doctors) and businesses (e.g. big pharma) involved in the illicit drug trade avoid criminalisation and are instead – as with most corporate criminality – regulated and fined. This blurring between licit and illicit is further exacerbated since many legal pharmaceutical drugs are illicitly traded and consumed (see Chapter 2) alongside illicitly manufactured and sometimes fake pharmaceutical products (see Chapter 18). However, the drug dealing/trafficking literature and research largely remains narrowly focused on criminal/deviant individuals and/or on certain types of (unprivileged) drugs in what has been described elsewhere as the 'Drug Apartheid' (see Taylor et al., 2016).

The Drug Apartheid

The Drug Apartheid is an arbitrary division of substances 'that has privileged the use of certain substances and outlawed the use of other substances, a corrupt system that has much to do with who uses the drugs and little to do with the risks posed by the drugs' (Taylor et al. 2016: 459). Thus, the supply of legal drugs and their market prosper within neoliberalism, while the illicit drug trade is framed as corrupting society causing many of its ills, while the substances themselves are deemed so harmful that they warrant criminalisation and punishment, despite the fact that there is much crossover (pharmacologically) between privileged/legal and unprivileged/illegal substances and their markets. Instead, prohibition disproportionately targets already marginalised groups, like the poor and ethnic minorities, which is largely disavowed and ignored in the official discourse. This also explains why drug prohibition has been described as the new Jim Crow Laws[7] (see Cohen, 2006), ignoring the unusual suspects – white affluent college kids as Mohamed and Fritsvold outline in their chapter on 'Dorm Room

Dealers' – as well as ignoring scientific evidence.[8] As they highlight, 'drug laws have more often mirrored social privileges and social prejudices than they have served as an objective and proportional assessment of public harm', illustrating that attention focuses on the unprivileged, illicit drugs and their users/suppliers – a minority – while disavowing the harms arising from privileged legal drugs that are used (and supplied) by the majority. Thus, this edited collection examines drug dealers in the twenty-first century, and although it has been nearly thirty years since *Eurodrugs* (1995) was published, many of the themes present are still evident today.

Eurodrugs (1995: 3) always resonated with us as one of its primary orientations was to see illicit drugs as commodities, commodities that 'shape and are shaped by demand, supply, exchange and consumption', which is something we have both focused on over the course of our careers (Ancrum, 2011; Ayres, 2019, 2020; Hall et al., 2008). The other orientating perspective that has always influenced our writing is to see drug dealing as a form of work that harks back to another influential academic text by Preble and Casey (1969): *Taking Care of Business*. Often the typology of actors involved in drug dealing, such as those identified by Preble and Casey (1969), appears broadly comparable to the actors identified in more recent studies as well as in the subsequent chapters of this book (see Chapters 5 and 6). Although the ensuing chapters capture the reality of drug dealing in contemporary society and the changes that have occurred – including the growth of the Internet and the dark net; cryptocurrency; the sale of new drugs/substances – it also looks at the similarities inherent in all drug markets past and present, legitimate and illegitimate, to offer a more nuanced and critical overview of drug dealing and supply.

As the chapters of this book show, the reality of drug dealing is often very different from the myth. The drug market is decentralised, highly fragmented and diverse. In fact, it is a constantly mutating network of diverse actors and organisations that are transient and reactive so as to avoid detection, enforcement and prosecution. These characteristics also mean that our understanding of drug markets is incomplete and limited due to their highly secretive and criminal nature. What we do know for definite about drug dealing and trafficking – particularly in the higher echelons and in some of the more unstable and violent countries – is that it is an under-researched area, which is unlikely to change as research-intensive universities are increasingly neoliberalised, meaning that academic autonomy is managed, criticality is discouraged and risk management is prioritised, particularly when it comes to research, and risky drug-related research at that, which now seems to fall under the new PREVENT duty on handling/researching sensitive, extreme or radical material. Also, when we say under-researched, we mean very little is actually known about the successful drug dealers, the ones that do not appear in any official (criminal justice) statistics or who partake in any research for fear of the consequences of disclosing too much, as drug-related research – particularly that which focuses on the manufacture and supply of drugs – is highly sensitive, risky (see Chapter 10), narrow (see Chapter 19) and for most drug dealers, not worth participating in. Whether we will ever obtain an accurate picture of the drug trade is questionable, particularly while it remains an illicit activity. For example, how many successful drug dealers would risk a long prison sentence, particularly those with legitimate businesses and supposedly law-abiding lives, just to participate in a piece of academic research? Consequently, the true nature of drug supply remains hidden, and unfortunately, looks set to stay that way.

What we do know, however, is that drug markets are dynamic and differentiated depending on cultural context, country (stability, wealth), and the social and economic circumstances of the people involved – factors that also influence the level of risk and violence, as well as the complexity of buyer/seller interactions. Drug networks vary from disorganised crime to organised crime; some are about mutual acquaintances rather than anonymous exchanges, while others are about friendship groups and the moral economy, as well as those that are all about profit and conspicuous consumption – all of which are captured in this edited collection.

The chapters of the book

The collection then looks at the way drug markets, and drug dealing, have altered and developed in contemporary society, not only in the UK, but also around the world, to elucidate the realities of drug markets on both a local and an international level. While this book cannot claim to offer a comprehensive and total understanding of the complexities of drug markets, it does provide a much-needed re-examination of the modern global drugs trade. It illustrates the diversity and heterogeneity of drug markets – or as Coomber (2010) describes it, as highly differentiated – as evidenced across the chapters of this book and has evolved over time as outlined in the first chapter, which is followed by Wilson and Ralphs' chapter. Wilson and Ralphs' chapter continues on from Coomber's chapter by looking at the supply of amphetamines in the 1960s Northern Soul scene to show not only how policy (e.g. that controlled drugs [Classes A and B] needed to be stored in a secure cabinet, safe or room) led to a plethora of unintended consequences for users and suppliers (see Wilson 2008) but also how drug supply was less about profit and more about the scene. This is followed by Angie Heal's chapter on Jamaican men in the UK who came looking for a better life, but ended up selling drugs due to economic marginalisation, lack of legitimate employment opportunities and visa restrictions related to immigration policy, which further serves to debunk the stereotypical image of the drug dealer. A theme continued in Ayres and Treadwell's chapter looking at the usual suspects – drug dealers proper – by focusing on criminal entrepreneurs – some of whom had a reputation and penchant for violence – to show that drug dealing must be seen against the backdrop of an economic austerity and a political economy of neoliberal consumer capitalism that prioritises and promotes individualism, entrepreneurialism, pervasive consumerism and compulsive (conspicuous) acquisition. To the men in this chapter, like many others, drug-dealing was a viable employment option that allowed them to draw upon their violent (hard-man) image to ensure the survival of their (sometimes illicit) entrepreneurial businesses, since many were no longer valued or could find work in the legitimate economy.

Morgan's chapter highlights the varied motivations for selling drugs, with some participants maintaining a middle market position in the drug trade while being a dependent user of heroin, thus debunking the stereotypical image of the junkie. This chapter also illustrates how the user-dealers attributed this to their personal characteristics that set them apart from the crowd (e.g. self-discipline, astuteness and intelligence) and made them distinct from other heroin users. The next chapter by Leah Moyle looks at social supply and discusses how young drug users drift in (and out) of supply, and occupy varying roles and distribution behaviours, which illustrate there has been a relative normalisation of drug supply in contemporary society, although in legal terms, these individuals are still conceived of as 'dealers'. This is followed by Fleetwood's review chapter on women's role in the drug trade, which provides a comprehensive overview of the literature on an under-researched and often invisibilised group, despite growing evidence that 'women are ubiquitous to the drug trade' on a global scale. In fact, scholarship can no longer continue to describe the drug market as if women were not there, and this includes other actors involved in it like businessmen and white, affluent college kids, which is the focus of the next chapter by Mohamed and Fritsvold. Their chapter on *Dorm Room Dealers* illustrates how the drug dealing of the well-off is largely overlooked, particularly by law enforcement agencies, illustrating how the stereotype surrounding drug dealers influences policing and thus prosecution decisions that nearly always exclude the 'boys and girls next-door'. Instead, this group remain 'comfortably shielded from criminal justice scrutiny by race and class-based privileges' which is 'woven into the fabric of US society.' The chapter on *Dorm Room Dealers* leads nicely into the next chapter on *Steroid Vacations*, where IPED users from countries where the non-medical supply of steroids is prohibited purposely visit countries such as Thailand to access cheap, and although still controlled, easily available IPED so as to combine holidays with intensive training and body sculpting. Providing another insight into a group of drug dealers often omitted from the popular narrative, this chapter shows a trend that mixes self-regard, competitive individualism, fear of missing out and a form of drug tourism with some parallels with the motivations and behaviours of cosmetic surgery tourists.

Tourism and hedonism are trends continued in Turner's chapter on drug supply in Ibiza, which using Bryman's (2004) influential *Disneyization* framework shows that for many seasonal workers, engaging in drug dealing can be partially explained by widespread ambivalence (and complicity) of door security and the police in Ibiza, as sellers saw it as an easy way to make money. Here Turner argues that the differential normalisation of drugs in Ibiza – a form of Disneyized hybrid consumption – together with a deep level of performative labour, combines to make drug use and dealing seem completely *natural* within this context. The money-making theme is extended in the chapter by Mike Salinas, which shows how doubling up on their income by selling drugs can provide an essential financial crutch for people, which he has framed under three distinct financial motives: its use for non-essential spending (pocket money); its use as a financial safety-net during economically precarious times; and its use as investment capital in legitimate occupational endeavours (such as business or study). Making money was also evident in Andell and colleague's chapter looking at county-lines – a phenomenon currently dominating the headlines around drug distribution – which goes back to looking at drug supply as an organised, competitive, albeit illegal business that is often associated with gangs.

Gang involvement in the drugs trade is also a feature of Kelly and Treadwell's chapter, which looks at the finer nuances associated with drug supply and gang involvement in an attempt to unpick the complexities and to provide an alternative characterisation of the role, place and function of drug economies and cultures in urban estates marked by cultural anelpis[9] (Hornsby and Hall, 1995). Briggs' chapter follows on from this by examining the distribution of drugs by Spanish gypsies who were subject to aggressive social policies which criminalized their businesses and led to the historical-generational transfer of drug dealing businesses within the gypsy networks. This is the final chapter in the first half of the book that covers the more traditional and recognized forms of drug supply, before the second half of the book goes on to look at more contemporary forms of drug dealing, which have largely been facilitated by technological advancement and the diversification of substances.

The second half of the book kicks off with a chapter by Angus Bancroft looking at the impact digital technology has had on drug supply to produce hybrid distribution strategies that combine online and offline strategies. Kelly's chapter on cryptomarkets continues this theme as it examines how technology has converged with global organised crime to change the nature of British drug markets at a 'grass roots level', which now also includes a range of increasingly diverse substances that is the focus of the subsequent chapters. The next two chapters go on to discuss the supply of PIEDS both for profit and non-profit (social supply) from Van de Ven, Mulrooney and Townshend, which is followed by Hall and Antonopoulos' chapter on the trade in illicit pharmaceuticals. This chapter offers a prescient example of late-modern shifts in the way drugs are bought and sold, challenging many of the common assumptions currently held about drugs and drug dealing, which is elaborated in the chapter by Ayres and Taylor.

Ayres and Taylor propose that there is a need to reconceptualise our understanding of drugs, drug dealing and drug markets in order to contest the Drug Apartheid, by showing that the supply of legal drugs by large corporations is as, if not more harmful than the supply of illicit drugs by the evil and amoral drug dealers, and yet it is largely omitted from the drug dealing literature. When discussing drug supply and trafficking, large companies and multi-national corporations are largely omitted from the discussion – as evidenced by their absence within the content of this book, barring Medley and Linnemann's chapter, which focuses on the opioid crisis in America and the role of big pharma in what they describe as 'palliative capitalism'. The final chapters of this book seek to revisit what is meant by drug dealing in an attempt to move the field forward and capture the changes that drug cultures and markets have undergone in recent years. Changes and developments that demand a reappraisal of drug dealing and supply; something this edited collection seeks to do.

Some final thoughts

This book therefore provides a much-needed re-examination of the global drugs trade. Drug markets and those that operate within them – both locally and globally – can be linked to the deteriorating economic, cultural and political conditions characteristic of contemporary society and the material and cultural markers that illustrate ideological success. However, this is largely omitted from the official discourse, policy and practice. Instead, the hyper-reality surrounding drugs – their manufacture, supply and use – dominates, and has actually become more real than reality itself, as the loops and spirals circulating around this topic, in true neoliberal ethos, blame the evil and amoral drug dealer who is individually responsible for an array of societal ills as well as their own poor choices, particularly if they fit the stereotype of the traditional drug dealer. It is in this context that states, legitimate business, doctors and pharmaceutical companies are ignored despite their role in the manufacture, supply and final use of some of these substances not only now, but throughout history. Alternatively, we see the scapegoating of drug dealers, and some unprivileged, illicit drugs, and their users in what has been termed the Drug Apartheid (see Taylor et al., 2016), while the harmful capitalist dynamic remains hidden. While drug traffickers and their drugs are often blamed for many of society's ills, these ills are actually a consequence of the ramping up of neoliberal consumer capitalism and the disintegration of the underlying order, rather than its cause (Ayres, 2019, 2020; Žižek, 1989; Hall et al., 2008).

Therefore, the chapters of this edited collection emphasise the importance of understanding and addressing the underlying and deep-seated social and economic inequalities that characterise not only drug supply, but also crime more generally, which are an integral part of capitalism. A system that thrives on exploitation, competition and inequality and has resulted in diminished opportunities and increasing insecurity for the majority of its citizens. While this is nothing new and resonates with research conducted many years ago by Preble and Casey (1969), what this edited collection seeks to do is proffer a need to reconceptualise drugs – their manufacture and supply – and the harms arising not only from prohibition, which has been excellently outlined elsewhere (see Rolles et al. 2016), but also the harms arising from a capitalist ideology and its global political economy. Like other areas, surely it is time to refocus the lens of drug manufacture and supply to include the powerful and the more unusual suspects.

Notes

1 A hundred years since the Dangerous Drug Act 1920 and fifty years since the Misuse of Drugs Act 1971 was introduced has seen demands for drug law reform gathering momentum (see Commons Health and Social Care Committee, 2019; Scottish Drug Deaths Task Force, 2021).
2 According to the National Crime Agency, 'County Lines is where illegal drugs are transported from one area to another, often across police and local authority boundaries (although not exclusively), usually by children or vulnerable people who are coerced into it by gangs. The 'County Line' is the mobile phone line used to take the orders of drugs. Importing areas (areas where the drugs are taken to) are reporting increased levels of violence and weapons-related crimes as a result of this trend' (see www.nationalcrimeagency.gov.uk/what-we-do/crime-threats/drug-trafficking/county-lines).
3 A good example of this type of campaign is the 'Too Much Bling, Give Us a Ring' campaign run by the Police where the image of a young black male driving around in a BMW, dripping with gold and carrying a gun was used on its accompanying posters to encourage members of the public to ring the police to let them know if someone in their community was living beyond their means in order to help the police recover criminals assets.
4 Harvey (2007: 2) describes neoliberalism as 'a theory of political economic practices that proposes that human well-being can best be advanced by liberating individual entrepreneurial freedoms and skills within an institutional framework characterized by strong private property rights, free markets, and free trade'.
5 Some countries still implement the death penalty for a range of crimes that include drug trafficking (see HRI, 2021).
6 Natural dietary supplements have been shown to contain banned and harmful ingredients (about 25%) and also contain more than one unapproved pharmaceutical ingredient, which can cause harm (see Tucker et al., 2018).
7 The Jim Crow Laws referred to legislation – both state and local laws – that enforced racial segregation in the USA.
8 A good example of this is the sacking of Professor Nutt as chair of the Advisory Council on the Misuse of Drugs (ACMD) for saying that some illicit drugs – cannabis, ecstasy and LSD – were less harmful than legal drugs like tobacco and alcohol (see Nutt et al., 2010).
9 Anelpis 'pertains to groups of people in states of extreme pragmatic stress: who have suffered a series of crises which have resulted in the complete dislocation of the productive base, and therefore the practical purpose, of their own existence as social subjects' (Hornsby and Hall, 1995: 7).

References

Ancrum, C. (2011) 'Knowing the dance': The advantages and downfalls of a 'criminal biography' in teaching criminology in higher education, *Enhancing Learning in the Social Sciences*, 3 (3): 1–21.

Ancrum, C. and Treadwell, J. (2016) Beyond ghosts, gangs and good sorts: Commercial cannabis cultivation and illicit enterprise in England's disadvantaged inner cities. *Crime, Media, Culture*, 13 (1): 69–84.

Ayres, T.C. (2019) Substance Use in the Night-Time Economy: Deviant Leisure? In T. Raymen and O. Smith (Eds.), *Deviant Leisure: A Criminological Perspectives on Leisure and Harm* (pp. 135–160). Basingstoke: Palgrave MacMillan.

Ayres, T.C. (2020) Substances: The luxurious, the sublime and the harmful. In S. Hall, T. Kuldova and M. Horsley (Eds.), *Crime, Harm and Consumerism* (pp. 108–122). London: Routledge.

Ayres, T.C. and Jewkes, Y. (2012) The Haunting Spectacle of Crystal Meth: A Media Created Mythology. *Crime Media Culture*, 8 (3): 315–332.

Ayres, T.C. and Treadwell, J. (2012) Bars, Drugs and Football Thugs: Cocaine Use amongst English Football Firms. *Criminology and Criminal Justice*, 12 (1): 83–100.

Baudrillard, J. (1994) *Simulacra and Simulation*, Translated by Sheil Faria Glaser. US: University Michigan Press.

Bauman, Z (2000) *Liquid Life*. Cambridge: Polity.

Berridge, V. (1999) *Opium and the People: Opiate Use and Drug Control Policy in Nineteenth Century England*. London: Free Association Books.

Berridge, V. (2013) *Demons: Our Changing Attitudes to Alcohol, Tobacco, and Drugs*. Oxford: Oxford University Press.

Bourgois, P. (1995) *In Search of Respect. Selling Crack in El Barrio*. New York and Cambridge: Cambridge University Press.

Braithwaite, J. (1984) *Corporate Crime in the Pharmaceutical Industry*. London: Routledge and Kegan Paul.

Broadhurst, K., Duffin, K., Owen, K. and Gill, M. (2005) *Research into the Views and Perceptions of Drug Dealers*, Leicester: PRCI Ltd.

Bröckling, U. (2006) *The Entrepreneurial Self*. London: Sage.

Bryman, A. (2004) *The Disneyization of Society*. London: Sage.

Chomsky, N. (1998) *Profit over People*. London: Seven Stories Press.

Cohen, M.M. (2006) Jim Crow's Drug War. *Southern Cultures*, 12: 55–79.

Collison, M. (1996) In Search of the High Life: Drugs, Crime, Masculinities and Consumption. *British Journal of Criminology*, 36 (3): 428–444.

Commons Health and Social Care Committee (2019) *Drugs Policy*. London: CHSCC.

Contreras, R. (2012) *The Stickup Kids: Race, Drugs, Violence and the American Dream*. California: University of California Press.

Coomber, R. (2006) *Pusher Myths: Re-Situating the Drug Dealer*. London: Free Association Books.

Coomber, R. (2010) Reconceptualising drug markets and drug dealers — the need for change. *Drugs and Alcohol Today*, 10 (1): 10–13.

Courtwright, D. (2001) *Forces of Habit: Drugs and the Making of the Modern World*. Cambridge: Mass.

Debord, G. (1967) *The Society of Spectacle*. New York: Zone Books.

Evans-Brown, M, McVeigh J, Perkins C. and Bellis, M.A. (2012) *Human Enhancement Drugs: The emerging challenges to public health*. Liverpool: Northwest Public Health Observatory.

Featherstone, M. (1982) The body in consumer culture. *Theory, Culture and Society*, 1(2): 18–33.

Ferrell, J. (1999) Cultural criminology. *Annual Review of Sociology*, 25: 395–418.

Ferrell, J., Hayward, K. and Young, J. (2008) *Cultural Criminology: An Invitation*. London: Sage.

Griffin, O. and Miller, B.L. (2011) OxyContin and a regulation deficiency of the pharmaceutical industry: Rethinking state-corporate crime. *Critical Criminology*, 19: 213–226.

Hall, A. (2019) Lifestyle drugs and late capitalism: A topography of harm. In O. Smith and T. Raymen (Eds.), *Deviant Leisure and Social Harm* (pp. 161–186). London: Policy Press.

Hall, S., Winlow, S. and Ancrum, C. (2008) *Criminal Identities and Consumer Culture: Crime, Exclusion and the New Culture of Narcissism*. Cullompton: Willan.

Hammersley, R. (2008) *Drugs and Crime: Theories and Practices*, Cambridge: Polity Press.

Harm Reduction International (HRI) (2021) *Death Penalty for Drug Offences: Global Overview 2020*. London: HRI.

Harvey, D. (2007) *A Brief History of Neoliberalism*. Oxford: Oxford University Press.

Harvey, D. (2010) *The Enigma of Capital: And the Crises of Capitalism*. Oxford: Oxford University Press.

Hearn, A. (2008). Meat, mask, burden: Probing the contours of the branded self. *Journal of Consumer Culture*, 8: 197–217.

Hobbs, D. (2013). *Lush Life: Constructing Organized Crime in the UK*. Oxford: Oxford University Press.

Hornsby, R. and Hall, S. (1995) Anelpis: A preliminary expedition into a world without hope or potential. *Parallax: A Journal of Metadiscursive Theory and Cultural Practices*, 1(1): 81–92.

Moyle, L. and Coomber, R. (2015) Earning a score: An exploration of the nature and roles of heroin and crack cocaine user-dealers. *British Journal of Criminology*, 50 (3): 534–555.

Murji, K. (1998) The agony and the ecstasy: Drugs, media and morality. In R. Coomber (Ed.), *The Control of Drugs and Drug Users: Reason or Reaction?* (pp. 69–85). Amsterdam: Harwood Academic Publishers.

Nutt, D., King, L.A. and Phillips, L.D. (2010) Drug harms in the UK: A multicriteria decision analysis. *Lancet* 376(9752): 1558–1565.

Paley, D. (2014) *Drug War Capitalism*. Edinburgh: AK Press.

Preble, E. and Casey, J. (1969) Taking care of business. *International Journal of Addiction*, 4 (1): 1–24.

Rolles. S., Murkin, G., Powell, M., Kushlik, D., Saunter, N. and Slater, J. (2016*) The Alternative World Drug Report* (2nd Edition). Bristol: TDPF.

Ruggiero, V. and South, N. (1995) *Eurodrugs: Drug Use, Markets and Trafficking in Europe*. London: UCL Press.

Scottish Drug Deaths Task Force (2021) *Drug Law Reform*. Scotland: SCCTF.

Sentencing Guidelines for Drug Offences (2012) *Drug Offences: Definitive Guidelines*. London: Sentencing Council.

Silverman, J. (2012) *Crime, Policy and the Media: The Shaping of Criminal Justice*. London: Routledge.

Singer, M. and Baer, H. (2009) *Killer Commodities: Public Health and the Corporate Production of Harm*. Lanham: AltaMira Press.

Szasz, T.S. (2003) *Ceremonial Chemistry: The Ritual Persecution of Drugs, Addicts and Pushers* (Revised Edition). New York: Syracuse Press.

Taylor, P. (2010) *Žižek and the Media*. Cambridge: Polity.

Taylor, S., Buchanan, J. and Ayres, T.C. (2016) Prohibition, privilege and the drug apartheid: The failure of drug policy reform to address the underlying fallacies of drug prohibition. *Criminology and Criminal Justice* 16(4): 452–469.

Treadwell, J., Ancrum, C. and Kelly, C. (2018) Taxing times: Inter-criminal victimization and drug robbery amongst the English professional criminal milieu. *Deviant Behavior*, 41(1): 57–69.

Treadwell, J. and Ayres, T.C. (2014) Talking prada and powder: Cocaine use and supply among the football hooligan firm. In J. Treadwell and M. Hopkins (Eds.), *Football Hooliganism, Crime and Crowd Control: Contemporary Themes in Relation to Research and Theory* (pp. 49–70). Basingstoke: Palgrave Macmillan.

Tucker, J., Fischer, T., Upjohn, L., Mazzera, D. and Kumar, M. (2018) Unapproved pharmaceutical ingredients included in dietary supplements associated with US Food and Drug Administration warnings. *JAMA Net Open*, 1(7): e185765.

Wacquant, L. (2009) *Punishing the Poor: The Neoliberal Government of Social Insecurity*. London: Duke University Press.

Wakeman, S. (2016) The moral economy of heroin in austerity Britain. *Critical Criminology*, 24: 363–377.

Wilson, A. (2008) Mixing the medicine: The unintended consequence of amphetamine control on the northern soul scene, *Internet Journal of Criminology*, 1–22.

Žižek, S. (1989) *The Sublime Object of Ideology*. London: Verso Books.

1

THE CHANGING SHAPE OF ILLICIT DRUG MARKETS

Differentiation and its consequences for understanding and researching illicit drug markets

Ross Coomber

Introduction

The nature and shape of illicit drug markets have been, and are continuing to, change and vary. Change is occurring, on the one hand, due to the development of technology, such as anonymised cryptomarkets on the dark web and the use of encrypted smartphone app technology affecting, and mediating, exchange spaces between the physical and online but, on the other hand, also because of developments in the culture(s), practice(s) and environmental contexts surrounding the supply of drugs in offline spaces. Coalescing with these material changes, there have been recent shifts in the *conceptual understanding* of traditional drug markets and those that populate them. In part, this shift in understanding is to do with an overcoming of the ways that illicit drug markets have been historically (mis)understood and consequent developments in the critical lens through which drug markets are increasingly viewed. This latter shift has seen some moves towards more nuanced ways of policing and prosecuting those that would otherwise be seen, one dimensionally, as simply drug dealers. Arguably, it has been the adoption of unreasonably narrow methodological and stereotyped lenses through which drug markets have been historically viewed, both by the criminal justice system and, importantly, by many drug field researchers, that has led to the largely one-dimensional perspective that still effectively predominates and the unhelpful interventions levied on many of those prosecuted for supply offences when they might have been seen, and dealt with, differently. In addition to a growing acknowledgement that 'social suppliers' and other minimally commercial suppliers do not necessarily constitute 'drug dealers proper', for example, there is also an increasing recognition, in countries such as the UK, that certain drug supply contexts such as County Lines (see below) often involve varying types of exploited and vulnerable persons and that traditional attributions of culpability

DOI: 10.4324/9781351010245-2

are now problematised. This has led to a new context of intervention discourse and practice where, although many agencies, including the police, are cognisant of these vulnerabilities, they are struggling to respond appropriately or effectively to the needs of those involved. For policing this means a changed context whereby the policing of vulnerability, especially where those involved are at one and the same time both criminal and exploited/vulnerable and victim/perpetrator, is challenging the very nature of enforcement itself. Given these changes, it is not an exaggeration to suggest that policing in general (vulnerabilities confront them in many areas) but particularly with regard to drug supply, will, over time, be fundamentally transformed by each aspect of this 'new' milieu.

The traditional supply landscape(s)

All commercial landscapes change over time, but some aspects persist in essence and evolve. Drug market landscapes in the UK and many other 'Western' nations, over the last half century at least, had mainly involved variations on what was a relatively consistent and basic extant practice (Coomber and Moyle 2018). In the UK for example, the main landscape for drugs such as heroin and cocaine related to greater or lesser levels of hierarchical predominance at the level of importation and/or wholesale management (in other words, a mix of levels and types of 'organised crime' activity down to a variety of 'independent' operator sourcing which themselves would vary over time and in each space – each city/town) (Dorn et al. 1992; Lewis 1994; Pearson and Hobbs 2001; Paoli 2002; Lupton et al. 2002). For UK-based wholesalers or serious dealers outside the main hubs of, for example, London, Liverpool, Manchester, Birmingham and Glasgow, access meant either travelling to, and sourcing from, the hub and taking it back to use or sell, or having a delivery arrangement whereby drugs were sent from the source hub to the wholesaler(s) in the larger towns/cities not themselves a source (Coomber and Moyle 2018). At the retail, 'street', sale and buy level, a combination of indigenous/local runners and sellers would supply either independently or for others. For recreational drugs, this 'surface level' supply was intersected by less commercially oriented (social) supply by friends to friends and acquaintances whereby many of those sourcing recreational drugs could do so without really engaging with the 'drug market proper' (Coomber and Turnbull 2007; Murphy et al. 1990). Such 'surfing above' the market without having to really engage with it is also commonly found, for example, with the supply of image- and performance-enhancing substances (IPED) at the local level (Coomber et al. 2015; van de Ven and Mulrooney 2017; Turnock 2021). In other parts of Europe and the world, most specifically in the so-called developed nations, variations on the above broad landscape would have been in place, with some spaces eliciting greater levels of gang or other organised crime control, more/fewer 'open' or so-called 'open-air' markets (May and Hough 2004) and meaningful variance in the levels of conflict, intimidation and violence present (Coomber 2015; Coomber and Maher 2006; Reuter 2009). So, lest we forget (and we will return to this later), even *within* each of these basic forms, important degrees of, and types of, differentiation of personnel, culture and practice has manifested meaningfully across time, place and space (Coomber 2015, 2010; Spicer et al. 2020) and as such any broad understanding of 'drug markets' needs to be accommodating of any evolving intra-dynamics and difference. Hence, whilst drug markets have always been more complex and nuanced than generally perceived or depicted, they have nonetheless, mostly tended to operate within the broad structural parameters outlined above. In the last twenty years however, there have been both some incremental and relatively seismic changes that have significantly, and irreversibly, altered the drug supply and sourcing landscape in the UK and internationally.

New developing and evolving drug supply forms: from pagers to cryptomarkets – the technological revolution

Low mobile tech to cryptomarkets (and back again[1]...)

From a relatively slow, low-tech, start, vis-à-vis pagers (an early small mobile wireless telecommunications device that receives/sends and displays alpha-numeric or voice messages) in the 1990s (Curtis and Wendel 2000; Curtis et al. 2002), through to the now ubiquitous smartphone and highly specialised online darknet cryptomarkets from the mid-late 2010s, technology has, and continues to, impact on the drug supply milieu exponentially (see the chapters by Bancroft and Kelly in this volume). Early adopted technology through the use of pagers made supply more mobile and responsive than ever before (Curtis et al. 2002; Natarajan et al. 1995) and even facilitated (at least in many contexts) a shift from relatively 'open' and fixed or static 'open air' markets (e.g. a known 'corner' on certain streets in certain parts of a town – the so called 'hot-spots' vulnerable to law enforcement due to their visibility) to exchange 'meets' that could be easily controlled by pre-arranging locations and times, both of which could vary, through this new mobile technology. This then accelerated with the relative ubiquity of mobile phones (where disposable 'burner' phones[2] could also aid anonymity and then smartphones with encrypted, and thus safer[3], messaging platforms. These improvements also facilitated 'anytime' communication. Such 'always on', accessible suppliers, which could either deliver a sale or arrange quick meets, effectively *enhanced* extant modes of drug supply. In this sense, early technology was not essentially transformative in the way that online sales – particularly those exchanges undertaken through darknet cryptomarkets such as Silk Road (initially) and other popular platforms to emerge – have been since (Barratt 2012; Martin 2014; Moyle et al 2018).

Drug cryptomarkets located on the so-called darknet or dark web and hidden from surface web view have been transformative and landscape changing because they employ technology that protects both buyers and sellers from law enforcement and provides a platform to enhance the exchange process and reduces risks related to fraud and 'rip-offs' (Aldridge 2019; Martin 2018) as well as changing the market shape overall. They have also attracted buyers and sellers averse to the relative risks (real or imagined) of offline markets (Martin et al. 2020; Barrett et al. 2016) hoping for and expecting a different kind of drug selling/buying experience. Darknet cryptomarkets can only be safely accessed through browsers – such as the Tor (The Onion Router) browser – that anonymise users' locations and, when used with VPN software, encrypt all activity (such as searches and exchange-related communications). Safely accessing and using drug marketplaces via Tor and other similar browsers however, at the current time, requires a meaningful level of computing capability and know-how that can be intimidating to the average surface level platform user (Aldridge and Askew 2017) and helps to explain why more risky options such as app-mediated supply or even surface web-mediated supply (see below) are preferred by many (Moyle et al. 2019 Child et al. 2022). The trading structures of darknet drug marketplaces however (i.e. anonymised browsing, confidential exchanges, seller and buyer ratings and escrow payments where – similar to, e.g., eBay – payments are (with) held by a third party until both parties are happy with the exchange) mean that most normative risk associated with drug purchasing/supply is significantly reduced in relation to law enforcement intervention, possible violence/intimidation, as well as product quality. Although the interception of posted purchases by enforcement agencies is potentially meaningful (Aldridge and Askew 2017), in practice, operations to effectively trace and follow darknet purchases such that it could reduce supply are mired in attendant difficulties. For example, the use of sniffer dogs (that are few in number and tire quickly) or scanning technology at postal sorting centres (again, few in number) requires both these in situ infrastructure and personnel resource to operate and then respond to 'findings' (locate and retrieve the package, open it, process the package, re-start the process) and as such are effectively prohibitive in high-volume, fast-paced settings such as postal sorting spaces. Add in the attendant ethical and civil liberties concerns (the scanning of all private mail), the inability of enforcement to follow up on all but a few of the seizures to each address we can see that the approach is of high cost in terms of resources, subject to various inefficiencies that confound routine/continuous intervention, involve disruption of the postal service, and are thus, unsurprisingly rare and likely to remain so for the foreseeable future (Personal Communications, Australian Federal Police 2018; Queensland Police Service 2017). Because such 'end of line' tactics targeting buyers appear to be rarely used, other than for occasional symbolic acts (Coomber et al. 2017) or for random monitoring, in comparative terms, darknet trading probably provides the lowest level of exchange risk(s), to both buyer and seller, particularly with regard to the criminal justice system than almost any other form of illicit drug market exchange (Moyle et al. 2019).

It remains unclear as to the extent to which darknet drug cryptomarkets, which are currently estimated to account for only around 1% of the global drug trade (UNODC 2020), will become more accessible, grow exponentially and thus fundamentally transform the nature of drug supply and access but, given the general trend for user facing complexity around technology to become 'friendlier' and easier, some significant growth going forward seems inevitable. Indeed, at the time of writing – during the COVID-19 pandemic where access to traditional markets has been more challenging – cryptomarket sales are reputed to have grown significantly across a number of specific darknet drug market platforms (ECMDDA 2020).

As stated earlier, drug markets shift and change but this is not always towards a more sensible, 'rational' or even logical approach. Intrinsic to much traditional offline drug supply is the building up of trust and relationships between supplier and purchaser due to the benefits this is seen to incur – loyalty of custom, safety from enforcement due to the 'known' quantity of buyer/seller to each other, trust perceptions that the product will be more reliable than from an unknown source, and so on. The over-riding benefit of supply/purchase via the darknet is security and yet, recent evidence suggests that some vendors and some buyers are seeking to gain market advantage by initially establishing cryptomarket relations on seller platforms and then offering, more expedient, exchanges by moving away from the darknet platform to direct exchange via encrypted messaging (Childs et al. 2020a . This mutation of supply activity merges (at least to begin with) the security benefits of cryptomarkets with the 'premium' protective aspects of familiar 'offline'[4] exchange. In practice, however, the vendor makes themselves more vulnerable to covert enforcement operation officers pretending to be buyers and buyers make themselves vulnerable to both being 'ripped-off' (no escrow, no ratings or scoring) and to enforcement targeting buyers. Despite this shift to a riskier exchange strategy, such deviations from the safer platforms provided by cryptomarkets appear to be attractive to at least a particular type of buyer/seller who will both see such a move as potentially beneficial from a financial sense (Childs et al. 2020a and who may also not, despite the enhanced safeguards, necessarily have experienced trouble-free cryptomarket exchange activity prior to the switch (Dupont and Lusthaus 2022). Other shifts involving the fragmentation of darknet drug supply include moves to smaller 'hidden service platforms' provided by individual vendor arrangements or through using decentralised crypto market platforms such as Black Dog (UNDOC 2020).

Clearly, cryptomarkets – even for those vendors and buyers with direct experience of it – do not provide a wholly satisfactory approach for all. Such dissatisfaction, and some consequent resistance to the initially formed cryptomarket structures, has led to some to seek (perceived) advantage elsewhere and for the market to broaden and diversify. Childs et al. (2020b) have suggested that the continual making and re-making of such online exchange processes, that then in turn provide another set of structural situations to work within or adapt to, can be likened to 'assemblages of online exchange' that allow for an interpretation and understanding of change and diversification as it occurs in this milieu as they do elsewhere. Although, for those willing to negotiate the current technological challenges of buying from cryptomarkets, the advantages are clear, there is one important demand that cryptomarkets, so far, are unable to accommodate, the immediacy of need, on the part of the buyer, that sometimes accompanies drug transactions. It is in this aspect that social media app mediated supply excels.

Social media app mediated supply

Buying and selling through the medium of smartphone hosted social media apps such as Whatsapp, Wikr, Telegram and so on, that utilise full encryption technology, has become a standard method for many to access illicit, especially recreational, drugs since around 2016 (Moyle et al. 2019; Demant et al. 2019). Buyers/sellers can become regulars on this platform, but many utilise it as a facilitator of anytime/anywhere access to drugs as buyers can respond to, for example, Whatsapp adverts of sellers local to their immediate location. This approach to buying and selling situates both buyer and seller somewhere between the relative safety of drug cryptomarkets and the more overtly exposed risks of open 'street' supply where both are at greater risk from either undercover enforcement (e.g. undercover policing/entrapment), fraud (e.g. fake or poor-quality drugs) or robbery from the other party (Moyle et al. 2019). Although many buyers/sellers are reassured by the encrypted capability of smartphone messaging, and are 'seduced' by the immediacy of a possible exchange wherever they are, the real risks come from buyers and sellers having to meet to exchange goods and thus to the possible insecurities that accompany in person exchange with unknown, un-vouched for, persons.

Surface web mediated supply–grey market supply and facilitation platforms

In technological terms, situated somewhere between social media and encrypted smartphone app supply, is supply via the 'surface web'. This is the platform level of Google and all normative, 'open' and easily visible internet sites that host everyday commercial (e.g. online shopping, advertising, financial and associated activities) social (e.g. Facebook; blogging; personal web pages) governmental (online information, payment and other services) and so on. Obviously, this is the online 'space' level most familiar to, and most accessible to, most users of the internet. It is in this space that we find what has been termed 'grey' drug market transactions. This is where the substances involved are either not illegal to produce and/or distribute in all jurisdictions but can be bought from countries where they are, or where the substances are not, often disingenuously, apparently being sold as psychoactive substances. Perhaps unsurprisingly, the type of substance supply found on the surface web, because of the high levels of visibility and opportunities for law enforcement to track and trace the website's owners, tend to be where there is some 'greyness' to the legality of the transactions offered. Sales of various steroids and other image- and performance-enhancing drugs (IPED) that are not covered by international conventions and which are legal in some locations, most usually where they are produced and sold from, are one example. Indeed, it has been speculated that for IPEDs, online supply may now be the primary route of initial sourcing/exchange (van de Ven, K., and Koenraadt 2017) and importation–as opposed to 'supply' *per se* as it is likely that the way that social supply is embedded within IPED supply (cf. Coomber and Salinas 2020; Turnock 2021 Coomber 2015; van de Ven et al and Mulrooney 2017 and van de Ven et al.'s chapter in this volume), particularly in gyms, will mean that this will predominate in terms of *numbers* of actual exchanges carried out. Other common substances will be medicines such as benzodiazepines (both diverted and 'fake') and many other common pharmaceuticals which can be accessed easily and cheaply from these online 'pharmacies' that range from the fully legal to the unlicensed and fake (Hall and Antonopoulos 2016, and Hall and Antonopoulos' chapter in this volume).

The emergence, from around 2009, of various so-called synthetically produced legal highs or novel (or new) psychoactive substances (NPS) as they were subsequently labelled, but sold as, for example, 'plant food' or 'bath salts' online also provided 'grey market' opportunities for surface web platform supply in this area – albeit pretending, quite openly but disingenuously, to be something other than what they really were (Measham et al. 2010; Ayres and Bond 2012). However, once NPS were banned internationally by countries around the world, online surface platform presence claiming to sell completely legal substances covered by the sanctions diminished significantly as demand has waned (EMCDDA 2017) and the legal context has made such presence riskier[5]. Darknet availability of NPS continues (Scourfield et al. 2019) but surface web presence – whilst still apparent – is riskier for buyers and sellers and likely includes many fake sites where supply does not result similar to those fake 'pharmacies' found by Hall and Antonopoulos (2016).

One current area of growth and diversification for surface web level platforms, particularly related to recreational substances such as cannabis, is that of *mediated supply* where those that supply, and those that want to buy, can connect via a dedicated platform such as *LeafedOut* (Childs et al. 2022). LeafedOut, initially designed to facilitate cannabis exchange, does not, itself, provide a central service through which exchanges can be made (e.g. in the way that Amazon does or even cryptomarket platforms) but, instead, it provides a peer-to-peer (P2P) mediation or 'hook-up' service. As a geolocation-based programme it provides an immediate visual map (see Figure 1.1) of registered buyers and sellers in any one postcode area, region, or city. Buyers, for example, can click on a seller and immediately see what services they offer, how to contact them, and how they have been rated by other buyers to date. Despite the fact that such an approach to purchase/supply is riskier than many other forms of supply, because, like app-mediated supply, it leaves sellers wide open to enforcement operations and buyers to entrapment (Childs et al. 2022) it does so by broadcasting their whereabouts and their online identifier. Nonetheless, despite these risks, we will likely see a

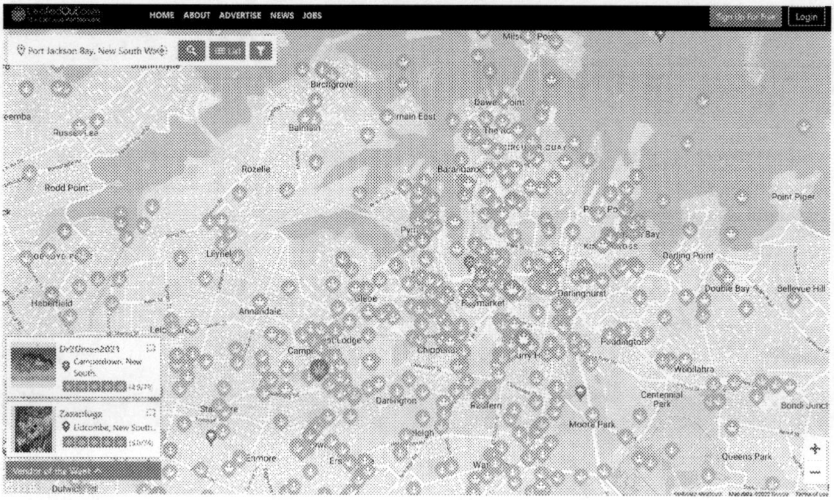

FIGURE 1.1 A LeafedOut page grab of Sydney Harbour on February 3, 2021. Green cannabis leaf icons indicate a signed-up vendor, blue a consumer.

proliferation and diversification of mediating platforms of this kind as well as motivations for use (see Bancroft's chapter in this volume for a more in-depth insight).

Social supply, minimally commercial supply, exploitation and vulnerability

In addition to shifts in the technological terrain, a range of observations, commentaries and researches over the last twenty years have also pointed to the extant and burgeoning forms of materially ('offline') situated supply that have become prominent; the positioning of new ways of seeing old supply structures; a recognition of new forms of criminal exploitation in the supply context, and, relatedly, a new awareness of supply context vulnerabilities that present new challenges for policing and the criminal justice system.

In 2000 the Police Foundation (Runciman) Report *Drugs and the Law* noted the disjunct between the aims of the UK's 1971 Misuse of Drugs Act to deal with serious forms of drug dealing and those 'user-dealers' (mostly addicted, injecting heroin users, selling to other already addicted users to get enough money to ensure their own supply) that were, somewhat erroneously and contradictorily, most affected by arrest and prosecution. Until this point – by and large – those arrested and convicted of drug supply were all seen, somewhat simply, as 'drug dealers' and of contributing fairly equal levels of harm and culpability to societies' drug-related ills. In 2003 an adjunct conversation was also burgeoning around the 'social supply' of recreational street drugs where concern was being expressed around the criminal justice system understanding acts of drug sharing, brokering or perhaps 'supply' for little or no profit at all as equal in measure by otherwise law abiding citizens (often schoolchildren) to 'drug dealing proper' and prosecuting young people and adults as though this was the case (Hough et al. 2003). Later research (Coomber and Moyle 2015, and see Moyle's chapter in this volume), building on the momentum of both these positions, suggested the 'minimally commercial supply' of addicted user-dealers would be better dealt with through a public health rather than a criminal justice lens and process and that, correspondingly, the huge growth of non-predatory, nominally profitable, social supply in a context of relative drug normalisation (South 1998; Coomber et al. 2016) should be considered to sit outside of the remit of the Misuse of Drugs Act (Coomber and Turnbull 2007; Moyle et al. 2013; see also Morgan's chapter in this volume). Whilst social suppliers of recreational drugs would not, normatively, be understood as constituting a particularly exploited or vulnerable group, drug-dependent dealers, selling for minimal commercial gain and, primarily, with a purpose to reproduce their own supply *can* be seen as vulnerable[6] (Moyle et al. 2013) and as deserving of a public health intervention rather than a criminalising one and prison as a mode of 'treatment'. User-dealers of drugs such as heroin and crack cocaine however, once the predominate mainstay of the local street level supply of drugs of dependence, have themselves, in recent years, in much of England and the UK, seen the selling landscape transformed before their very eyes.

County Lines drug (heroin/crack – mostly) supply

Slowly building since around 2009, the adoption of a new transactional approach to the sale of heroin and crack cocaine beyond the major city hubs has also seen changes to the way vulnerabilities play out in the drug market context. With new intensive modes of exploitation introduced into the exchange milieu and new 'players' entering and then, often, dominating the heroin/crack selling spaces across the country (Coomber and Moyle 2018; Harding 2020; McLean et al. 2019, and Andell et al.'s chapter in this volume). The outcome form of this transition in the heroin and crack cocaine market has been dubbed 'County Lines' in the UK, an approach that has been attributed with strong typifying characteristics (see below) but can be, and has, manifested differently in different spaces – to mitigate risks and accommodate cultural and demographic difference – and will likely evolve further because the approach has inbuilt capability to be flexible in its application.

Whilst traditional heroin and crack cocaine supply in the UK relied either on key wholesale suppliers from, for example, London, Liverpool, Glasgow, Manchester and Birmingham, connecting with, and sending drugs to, wholesale level receivers in smaller towns and cities (e.g. down the 'M6 corridor') where they would then be sold at street level by local heroin/crack user-dealers, many of whom (likely most) would only make enough money or drugs to satisfy their own drug use needs. Prior to County Lines incursion, most of those involved in such street sales at the local level, in line with the relatively ageing heroin/crack using population would have been over thirty years of age. The growth of the County Lines approach to heroin/crack supply has turned much of this on its head (Coomber and Moyle 2018).

County Lines supply takes the following basic form (see also Andell et al.'s chapter in this volume for further in-depth insight): a range of wholesalers based in major city 'hubs' (some are organised crime groups, some 'gangs', some independents) with access to importer/wholesale levels of heroin and crack, have expanded their direct selling retail activity from geographically close to home to, tentacle like, many other smaller locations in parts of the country. Early County Lines sellers would 'commute' by train or car to towns and areas within an hour or so from the hub and either return at the end of day or establish short and longer stay accommodation (for themselves and others from the same 'gang' or associated group) at the site from which to run their operations (Coomber and Moyle 2012; Coomber 2015). The new incomers had a reputation for intimidation and violence and often either displaced local sellers, subsumed them or co-existed with them (with varying levels of tension and conflict). The incomers soon built a reputation for being available 24–7, which existing local sellers were not, and in many cases to be more reliable (these incomers tend not to be users) than local, dependent, sellers. In addition, over time they gained a reputation to hold better-quality drugs than local sellers but at the same price. Each tentacle from the hub operates on a dedicated phone 'line' with contacts established (often purchased) at the satellite town/area and with the hub able to control those selling for them in the satellite through specific lines. This model has grown quickly with over 2000 branded 'lines' reported to be present in 2019 (NCA 2020) and to be established, to varying degrees (from saturation, co-existence and toe-dipping), in every police force area in the UK. On its own – a geographical expansion of direct selling activity – this operational approach is *not* a seismic shift in the workings of a national drug market. It is meaningful but not substantially so. However, the particular *form* that this methodology has adopted and evolved in the UK means that it has other significant structural aspects that have led higher levels of, and qualitatively different types of, exploitation of young and vulnerable people than what was previously the case. It is important however to distinguish County Lines methodology from the common tropes relating to children so common in public discourses of drug use, addiction and supply.

There is a historical tendency for media and other reporting on drug use and drug markets to sensationalise and greatly exaggerate, largely through insinuation from individual cases or unsubstantiated anecdote, both the involvement of young children in the delivery or supply of drugs such as heroin or how they become entwined in the world of addiction by unscrupulous dealers predating upon them (Flacks 2019; Coomber 2006). The use of fear rooted in exaggerated risks to children as a lever for symbolic policy and issue diversion is thus well established in relation to drugs, drug users and drug supply (Coomber 2006; 2011; 2013; Flacks 2019; Berridge 1998). Most famously, one journalist was even awarded a Pulitzer Prize for Journalism for fictitiously exploiting such an angle in relation to an eight year old heroin addicted child (cf. Sager 2016) where the real lesson is not that journalists sensationalise (or sometimes deceive) but that the story was considered both plausible and likely by those that read it because it fitted the tropes about drug dealers and their morality. At the time of writing, the latest (2021) media contribution to this trope was provided by SHOWTIME's high-profile crime drama Your Honour (2021) where, relating despondently to an area of town to be avoided, it is simply stated that is where there are 'ten year olds selling shit' and is proffered in such a way as to suggest a sad but acknowledged norm.

However, although, as indicated, most drug market anecdotes and stereotypes involving young people, especially those under 12, remain essentially mythical (Coomber 2006), the current County Lines distribution methodology predominantly involves a new approach in which unprecedented numbers of vulnerable young people (predominately aged 14–17, and male) are variably, either 'groomed', enticed, inspired, or, through forms of debt bondage or other pressures, are forced to become involved in the distribution and sale of heroin and crack cocaine. In a context of relative precarity and neoliberal insecurity (see Andell et al.'s chapter as well as Treadwell and Kelly's chapter in this volume) along with the belonging, identification and esteem opportunities provided by 'gang' or other forms of meaningful connectivity/'membership' (Andell and Pitts 2018; McLean et al 2019), however loose, the conditions for the systematic recruitment of young vulnerable people to engage in risky, illegal remunerative activity such as drug supply have grown. The real numbers of young people involved in County Lines supply are difficult to determine but the UK's National Crime Agency (NCA) reported in 2019 that after a single week of coordinated enforcement activity across the UK the previous year that this had 'resulted in over 600 arrests. [and that] Approximately 400 vulnerable adults and 600 children were offered safeguarding advice and support'. Given that there are up to 2,000 'lines' and that police disruption of drug markets is rarely that meaningful this would perhaps suggest that these figures would be a nominal/small number of those involved nationally.

The fact that significant numbers of these individuals will, by dint of age and the contexts from which they were recruited, be deemed by many as vulnerable and exploited is not in question (or at least few questions that is the case). The issue of ongoing concern, however, is how young, vulnerable, exploited people should be managed by the criminal justice system such that they are supported effectively (Moyle 20219 Windle et al. 2020; Coomber and Moyle 2018) and, what the broader ramifications for the policing of vulnerability, and exploited people are more generally (cf. Wroe 2021; McLean et al. 2019). Although the emergence of the County Lines supply methodology presents quantitatively, and qualitatively, new levels and forms of systematic exploitation of young people (as, e.g., commuting couriers and in situ 'runners' and 'sitters' (Moyle and Coomber 2015 McLean et al. 2019; Harding 2020 and thus suppliers) within the heroin and crack supply milieu, there is a further aspect to County Lines exploitation that is also significant in its adoption, manifestation and prevalence – that of 'cuckooing'.

Cuckooing – a particular form of criminal exploitation

Te so-called 'cuckooing' has developed as a component part of the County Lines approach to drug supply. Cuckooing occurs when vulnerable people, such as those with learning or mental health difficulties, disabilities, or with drug use problems, are 'persuaded' to, or forcibly made to, for example, either leave their housing completely, or decamp to a single room whilst out of town drug sellers take over their 'nest' like a cuckoo (Coomber and Moyle 2012, 2018; Spicer et al. 2020). Out of town sellers then establish a short to medium term base in these homes, exploiting, and perhaps intimidating, those cuckooed to varying degrees (Coomber and Pyle 2015; Spicer et al. 2020; Harding 2020). Hitherto, only a nominal footnote in previous criminological literature, cuckooing is now established as one of *the* methods County Lines suppliers use to establish a foothold in a new satellite location and there is some evidence that cuckooing as an exploitative criminal methodology has expanded to broader crime groups and practices and may spread internationally (Spicer et al. 2020; Personal Communications, Belgium Police, 2018; EMCDDA 2021).

County Lines – not necessarily as big as deal as it is made out to be?

Whilst the County Lines methodology in the UK does currently use vulnerable and exploited young (and other) people in strategic ways, as outlined above, it is important to realise that this is not a necessary or required aspect of the model. The same model *could* be operationalised using adults typical of the model(s) preceding County Lines and/or by relying more directly on local user-dealers run by hub wholesalers – in the satellite towns and cities as has already started to happen in some spaces (Harding 2020). Likewise cuckooing. Cuckooing may currently be a convenient model for those managing County Lines, but it is also not an essential aspect. Cuckooing could easily morph into a far less exploitative model (as is the case in some circumstances anyway – see Spicer et al. 2020) where premises are occupied for reasonable amounts of time and with respectful relations and/or where local user-dealers are utilised to sell for the hub but doing so locally and providing some short-term accommodation if/when needed. Alternatively, short-let arrangements enabling local hub accommodation but also flexibility could, with a little thought, be introduced, as could a variety of workable alternatives. The importance of County Lines as a supply methodology would, in the absence of excessive levels of exploitation of vulnerable people, diminish in terms of its distributive significance and merely become a minor shift in managing distribution from what preceded it. Given this rationale, even if County Lines-type methodology does evolve to a greater degree than at present across Europe and other spaces, its fundamental significance will ultimately depend on the extent to which the exploitation of the young and vulnerable is utilised[7].

Each of the above examples (from cryptomarkets to minimally commercial forms of supply to County Lines) provides insight into how drug markets have transformed, and/or are transforming, in the UK specifically but also internationally, and, in the case of darknet drug cryptomarkets, across, time, space and (virtual) place.

'Knowing' drug markets: methodological limitations, trope, stereotype and researching the 'visible'

Earlier parts of this chapter point to some transitional realities of drug markets and drug supply. Some of these supply modes and facets of them are wholly new, for example: cryptomarkets; social media app-mediated supply; cuckooing. Some, however, such as minimally commercial supply, social suppliers, the vulnerable but criminal, have been present in one form or another for some time but were effectively invisible to the criminal justice system and most of those researching drug markets (as is evidenced by a general lack of reference to them in most drug market research and publications). As such there was a strong tendency in academic research to default to researching what was 'visible' (i.e. what was assumed or 'known' from prior research) and to continue to oversimplify and overhomogenise what, and 'who', a drug dealer *is* and what a drug market looks like, how *the* drug market functions and what can be assumed about what is standard and predictable within them.

The use of various administrative data to understand crime and criminality can have some serious limitations – not least in how it can lead to obtuse constructed classifications of both (Young 2004; Matthews 2009). Why, how and what administrative data is collected can mean that classifications of types of crime and criminality are predetermined (by administrators in many cases and/or by historical data collection practices but also by adherence to cultural scripts on how the world is configured) and unreflexively accepted by data analysts. By definition, administrative data is exclusive of classifications that sit outside those (pre)selected for collection. It commonly has a myriad of weaknesses in terms of data limitations (e.g. for UK police forces there is frequently a lack of compatibility and comparability even between individual forces on how to record, classify and analyse crime types). It can also suffer analytically if the analysis and consequent reporting is weakly contextualised due to a focus on the (assumed) strength or utility of the data (and type of data) collected and thus of scientific method over and above 'the lived reality of crime' and criminality (Matthews 2009).

Intuitively, most qualitatively minded researchers would (sometimes perhaps too smugly) assume that the flexibility of qualitative research approaches that are designed to garner unexpected data, to provide depth of understanding and nuance would trump administrative and other forms of constrained positivist research when it comes to understanding essence and complexity – unfortunately however, this is too often not the case. All tools, including research tools, are only as effective as the capabilities, and/or focus, of those that wield them and when it comes to adopting qualitative methods of various kinds to research drug markets and those that populate them the primary issue has not necessarily been the data per se (which is of course affected) but, again, the classificatory preconceptions that inform the focus and design of the project(s) to begin with. At its most basic, and most unhelpful level, this can involve (and I would argue, too often has done) a relatively uncritical acceptance of the big picture, 'visible' understanding of the broad milieu to be researched. In short, qualitative researchers researching drug markets, whether those using depth ethnography, or other, less immersive approaches, have overall tended to focus on, and more readily 'see' and report on, the sexier (in research terms), the 'visible' and, therefore ironically, the 'surface' aspects of drug supply and exchange. This can result in the predominate, day-to-day, relative *absence* of something like violence and intimidation being ignored for the less common but occasional occurrence in whatever form it takes.

Drug market research and the need for a critical lens that neither privileges the 'sexy' or the assumed nor seeks to aggregate too simply

That drug markets have significant difference within and between them and thus that meaningful differentiation manifests is, arguably, now well established (cf. Coomber 2006; 2010; 2015), there is however a need for more discussion on *how* illicit drug markets should be both researched and reported on.

Differentiation of structure apart, drug markets have also, mostly, not manifested as they have been commonly depicted in terms of their broader essences (Coomber 2004, 2006, 2010; Beckett et al. 2006; Blum et al. 1972; Chaiken and Chaiken 1994). The widely portrayed and generally assumed presence of routine excesses of violence and intimidation in academic work (e.g. see Singer et al. 2001; Marsh 2021 Werb et al. 2010; Schneider 2013; Gerell et al. 2021 to name just an indicative few) in practice varies hugely across time, space and place and that is itself within a general context whereby most drug markets in 'Western' societies are in fact, most of the time, relatively *peaceful* (Reuter 2009; Coomber 2015; Coomber and Maher 2006). Similarly, the extent of predatory behaviour that, through acts of enticement ('freebies') or direct pharmacological compulsion through the 'spiking' of recreational drugs with drugs like heroin, has little (e.g. 'freebies' handed out to 'hook' non-users) to no (e.g. 'spiking' to hook) evidential basis (Coomber 2003, 2006). Numerous other assumed heinous acts, such as dangerous adulteration (i.e. the *routine* use of poisons to dilute street drugs such as heroin or cocaine for greater profit, either on purpose or through a heinous disregard of care for the substitute 'cut'), are similarly unevidenced[8] (Coomber 2006, „c1997ab; Broséus et al. 2016; Cole et al. 2010, 2011). Each and all such practices can vary widely across, time, space and place, if they take place at all, and rely, in part, on the personnel engaged in the supply act (e.g. young otherwise non-deviant 'social suppliers', middle class suppliers, brokers or go-betweens; women sellers and so on rather than the evil – non-white and male – dealer of trope) as to the degree they are likely to manifest (Coomber 2004, 2010, 2008). Regardless, much attention is nonetheless paid to these widely assumed essences of stereotype and trope in media reporting; politicians' statements, and law enforcement-derived discourse and statement, and as such, we might argue, the public imagination. Indeed, even drug dealers themselves often believe these acts to be true, routine and typical of 'other' drug dealers even when their own first-hand practice and knowledge contradict it (Coomber 1997, 2006) as we shall see below. However, whilst it will not surprise many that the media, politicians, law enforcement and fearful members of the public work readily with generalisations, stereotype and tropes, we do not necessarily expect such a positionality to be assumed, exacerbated and/or reinforced by academic research but unfortunately, in the study of drug markets this has occurred far too often. In part this is due to a lack of broader awareness of the literature and the research lens adopted, but it is also in part the result of methodological weakness.

This narrowness of focus and (relatively) uncritical 'chasing' or choosing of the visible, assumed and accepted is not new to the illicit drug-related research arena per se, but research on drug markets lags somewhat behind where we are with researching drug *use*. The historical tendency to overly aggregate and generalise both user populations (deviant/problematic) and risks pertaining to 'drugs' (e.g. Anslinger regarding Drug Enforcement Administration propaganda that set a tone from the 1930s in the US but also various international treaties, UN declarations and national drug laws depicted and classified many drugs as having similar high riskiness/dangers) is well documented (e.g. Boyd 2009; Coomber and South 2004; Labate and Cavnar 2014; Labate et al. 2016; Klein 2014; Musto 1987; Inciardi 1986) and has gradually been amended over time such that we are now slowly seeing significant shifts in policy and levels of regulation around some substances/types of use and users partially on this basis (Collins 2018). To understand meaningful nuance in drug use, the need was, and is for, a *research framework* or pre-design lens that looks for and has an expectation of difference rather than there being an almost Foucauldian like (Foucault 1972) 'will to aggregate' to classify, to 'round up' and thus produce more acceptable levels of perceived generalisability in the data. Because there is now greater understanding and broader acceptance that drugs (and their effects) differ, that use contexts differ and thus that users and their motivations will differ, a research milieu has been produced that is more sensitive to nuance than was once the case.

Arguably, by adopting a lens of differentiation whereby there is an expectation of, and desire to reveal, meaningful difference (rather than seeking to aggregate understanding across milieu and behaviours) more research designs might avoid the less critical stance of focussing on the supposedly visible and commonly assumed. Specifically, adopting such a lens and critical stance, we might hope, would result in fewer projects exploring (or just describing) how and why violence occurs in drug markets and more will focus on why and under what conditions it might be (and commonly is) generally absent, managed or avoided (see Ayres and Treadwell's chapter and Treadwell and Kelly's chapter in this volume). One pertinent example might be Coomber and Maher's (2006) research in Sydney's Cabramatta where the lived experience of street located heroin sellers strongly countered a widely accepted and assumed 'reality' of prevalent and heightened violence that was simply believed to be 'there' and was supposedly visible to media, politicians and enforcement and accepted by other drug field researchers at the time. Clearly, much research and reporting will continue to be carried out on those aspects that have attracted so much attention to date. Whilst this will reinforce some aspects of the directly visible as essence, if the aspect in question is suitably situated vis-à-vis the confounding literature and appropriately justified in its focus, then the impact of this will be lessened (e.g. see Ayres and Treadwell's chapter in this volume in relation to drug market violence).

Adopting a critical lens that also expects (or is sensitive to) differentiation is one aspect that will help change how drug markets are researched. Another is an improved awareness from drug market researchers of the broader literature prior to honing in on a research topic. It is not uncommon for new researchers to the field to be PhD students and whilst they may have sufficient critical awareness of the drug market literature before they choose their topic area, often this will not be the case. Where this is not the case, the chances of opting for one of the perceived sexier aspects of drug markets are likely heightened and thus the unhelpful circle of simply researching the visible is perpetuated. It is also the case that many supervisors (unless sufficiently expert in drug markets) will not have the kind of broad critical awareness of how drug markets differ from trope and stereotype and as such the student may not be encouraged to widen their choice or adopt a lens that will help them avoid a focus on the visible and assumed.

Analysing and reporting research on drug markets

Whilst the research design framework and adopted lens are, as related above, undoubtedly important for how particular aspects of any drug markets continue to be classified in particular, overly homogenised, ways, how drug markets are referred to, and reported on, in outputs related to the research is also of great importance. Many years of peer reviewing illicit drug market research articles and books by drug field researchers (I am more forgiving of media, police, lay and 'official' reporting that has, in general, lower standards of reporting and weaker understanding) has shown me that it is common for respective authors to simply refer to 'the drug market' or 'drugs' in their background review, findings or discussion when they actually mean a very specific segment or intersection of the drug market and particular (not 'all') drugs. The unspoken insinuation is that there is a level of commonality across *the* drug market that allows the mixing of a broad 'drug market' literature on different substances and organisational contexts to allow broad points to be drawn upon and referred to unproblematically as though the differences bore no significance in their relational relevance. Clearly, the heroin and/or crack cocaine market is not, in general, the same as the cannabis, or other parts of the recreational drugs market and those that populate it by way of buyers/users and suppliers/sellers can also differ significantly. Heady overlaps may, of course, be present (but often are not) but there will be meaningful differences even *within* these market/drug types in different spaces/places and moments in time. Reasserting the unhelpful 'drug market', unprefaced with, e.g., 'heroin', or 'cannabis' or 'recreational' or failing to provide a geographical pointer to the research being referenced (UK, US and other markets can differ enormously and uncritically mixing geographically located research is not unproblematic), as a simply knowable broad phenomenon and thus as a phenomenon with understood essences is unhelpful and merely perpetuates this primary stereotype (that all drug markets are similar) and the next level stereotypes that sit beneath it (inherently violent, predatory, dealers as essentially evil individuals and so on). By providing clarity on the specific phenomena being considered and providing clear signalling with regard to the type of market being referred to and where and how it is situated, we can move away from overly abstract and homogenised concepts.

Another commonly observed weakness in both analysis and reporting, predominately in (various) qualitative research, is the almost automatic attribution of veracity given to 'key person' respondents by researchers. Too often there is no, or insufficient, reflexive (and thus sufficiently critical) situating of key respondents' statements, beliefs, stories and reflections as to how and why the collected data reports what it does. And yet, we know that drug sellers commonly hold many of the same beliefs about specific drug risks, *the* drug market and drug supply practices as the general public, certainly for drugs or practices outside their direct experience and often even when it is. An acute illustration of this in relation to drug dealers and dangerous adulteration is found in Coomber (1997) where the interviewed retail/'street' drug dealers confirmed that their own practice, *consistent with the forensic evidence* also collected (but in contrast to commonly believed practice), was to *not* 'cut' or 'step-on' the heroin they sold and certainly not with dangerous substances. They cited good reasons for why this made no sense for them to do it (e.g. 'why would I want to hurt anyone'; 'I want to be known to sell good gear'; 'I don't need to, I just skim off the top'; 'the comeback'; 'why would I want to kill my customers?'), consistent with stereotype however, nearly all nonetheless believed that most 'other' dealers did cut heroin, routinely, with dangerous cutting agents. Aware that some might wish to hide their own guilt in this regard, interviewees were also asked if they had first-hand knowledge (e.g. had witnessed) dangerous cutting by other drug dealers. None took the opportunity to substantiate their belief that others cut heroin dangerously – despite believing it to be the case – by citing first-hand knowledge (they could also have transposed their own guilt onto a mythical other at this point if they wanted if it was something they did really do). As such, this suggested that the idea of dangerous cutting was so engrained into both lay and 'professional' consciousness that even drug dealers, that do not do it nor have experience of it being done, believe it to be common. This demonstrates that even those closest to a phenomenon ('key' of all key persons – the people that actually 'do' the job) actually may have little idea about what happens beyond their own personal experience and construct a world view of 'what goes on' that is at odds with the reality (reality in this sense being both the forensic evidence and their lived experience). Believing that drug markets are routinely inflected by such purposively violent practice imagines a different type of drug market (and drug dealer) if the opposite is in fact the norm. This indicates quite clearly that researchers wherever possible need to triangulate evidence/data and be aware that 'key person' interviews/beliefs or ethnographic accounts cannot (and should not) be accepted uncritically – regardless of their closeness to the issue in hand.

It is firmly the illicit drug market researcher's responsibility to situate how and to what extent their respondents' (and their own) views on the respective areas under consideration are considered to be *reliably* informed (rather than just believed) have been derived from first-hand 'knowledge' or interpretation of first-hand experience rather than them 'just knowing' it to be true. An insufficiently critical situating of, and reporting of, key respondent data obviously runs the risk of simply providing belief or interpretation of common tropes as 'fact' and providing it with credibility simply through the assumed 'closeness' (and thus attributed default credibility) of the 'key' respondent status.

The lens of differentiation is a surface level methodological framing approach which simply suggests, for a research milieu that is too often unhelpfully bent towards simplifying and homogenising observed phenomena (or accepting existing simple, homogenised understandings), that it would be helpful to assume that detecting meaningful difference is of value. Recent illicit drug market research that has been progressive and is potentially transformational has shown the benefits of not seeing all drug dealers as similar and/or acting similarly and not seeing all markets as having the same fundamental characteristics. It is an observational framing approach that evokes complexity, encourages emergent knowledge and makes a plea to see what is hidden, changing and evolving rather than paying lip service to what is already assumed.

Conclusion

This chapter aimed to provide some insight into both how, and in what ways, drug market structures and processes have been changing internationally and specifically/locally but perhaps most indicatively in the UK since the turn of the century. A complementary aim was to also provide a broad based, up-to-date, conceptual and empirically situated context for the subsequent chapters in this book. It was suggested that a key conceptual (re)positioning has been to consider the way that drug markets are highly *differentiated* phenomena and how a failure to appreciate this historically has led to cumbersome and an overly simple understanding of what drug markets are, who populates them, how they operate and how they might be managed in prohibitionist criminal justice systems. It has been argued that this historical failure is in part a result of an over-reliance of stereotypes and tropes about 'who' the drug dealer is (evil, predatory, profit-maximising, violent) and the supposed inherent nature of the drug market and how it operates (through intimidation/violence, hierarchical and top-down and controlled by organised crime groups of varying levels). This has rendered a variety of differentiation either partly or wholly invisible and this has too often been (often unintentionally, but often naively) reinforced by academic research on illicit drug markets that has focussed almost exclusively, and uncritically, on the visible and/or the preferred ('sexier', more interesting) aspects pertaining to fear, violence and heinous behaviours (some real, others not) of some suppliers/markets. Research focus on the visible has also been, unhelpfully, complemented by a tendency for positivist approaches to be over-reliant on enforcement and other administrative data that, again, records the visible (e.g. homicides, violent attacks, hospital admissions and police reports) and rarely differentiates between categories of, say, homicide 'involvement' or is able to capture the *absence* of market behaviours (such as violence) either geographically or across the intersectional milieus, or when they are muted and/or rare. Qualitative research (across the spectrum but including depth ethnographies) also has to accept some blame in this respect by also focussing on the sexier rather than mundane aspects. Because of these limitations in understanding there has been a historical failure to separate out, even within Western criminal justice systems largely bent on proportionate punishment, to police, 'manage' and punish, the most culpable from those we should view differently and to (extensively) criminalise, for example, friend 'dealers', dependent (and often traumatised) user-dealers and 'vulnerable'/exploited young people rather than support and assist them. That such populations need a criminal justice approach and response that equates to their positioning within drug exchange/markets and not punitive ones that all too easily default to 'crackdowns' and a fetishism of arrest numbers is slowly being recognised in a world that is increasingly being forced to acknowledge that the policing of vulnerabilities or of relatively minor criminality (as in the case of brokering or social supply) needs to be approached with an understanding of those aspects and with informed and sensible guidance on how to do so.

Notes

1 As will be outlined further below, some online practices are being partially abandoned in favour of more traditional technological approaches.

2 Burner phones are still used to aid anonymity in many drug exchange contexts.

3 'Safe' is a relative term when it comes to drug markets. Each method and mode of exchange will be on a spectrum of riskiness for seller and buyer. Some are less subject

to enforcement intervention than others, but even encrypted platforms, such as EncroChat, a platform purposively used by numerous criminal groups, were infiltrated by an international policing effort and led to the arrest of 746 individuals in the UK alone (BBC July 2 2020).

4 'Offline' in this sense, away from the cryptomarket. Such moves to private exchange arrangements will almost certainly all be still online via encrypted messaging and online monetary exchange.

5 There remains some surface web presence but where this is the case it is now clear that those selling and those receiving are aware that the product may not be legal in the receiver's country.

6 The extent to which an individual can be vulnerable and/or exploited and thus a victim rather than simply a criminal in these circumstances can be contested – not least by those being labelled as vulnerable and exploited (cf. Windle et al. 2020; McLean et al. 2019) and individuals will likely, in reality, situate on a intersectional spectrum. However, for the purposes of delineation of the wholly unprotected, vulnerable and exploited which at least some of those that become County Lines engaged individuals we need to recognise that vulnerability to exploitation and harms can accrue more vigorously in this new structural context to some more than others and how they are then viewed needs a sympathetic/empathetic, informed and appropriate response.

7 Obverse in some ways to cuckooing but often involving the exploitation of vulnerable (often young) trafficked people is that of cannabis 'farms'. Cannabis farms – whereby the use of specific houses or premises is transformed such that its purpose is to mass cultivate cannabis, in situ, for commercial gain commonly use 'sitters' to guard and tend the plants. Whilst cannabis farms have not significantly transformed supply processes in many other regards, as with County Lines, the variable use of young trafficked people from countries such as Vietnam who would classify directly under the Modern Slavery Act, is an important differentiator from that which preceded its emergence (Bokhari 2008; Ramiz et al. 2020).

8 Purposive and routine adulteration/cutting with various substances for the purpose of dilution and/or enhancement (e.g. caffeine, paracetamol, lactose and various others) is common but this is not the same as hap-hazard, uncaring or purposive adulteration with toxic substances. The presence of fentanyl in heroin in some countries has a complex aetiology but the aim is not to produce a more dangerous product.

References

Aldridge, J. (2019) 'Does online anonymity boost illegal market trading?', *Media, Culture & Society*, 41(4): 578–583.

Aldridge J. and Askew, R. (2017) 'Delivery dilemmas: How drug cryptomarket users identify and seek to reduce their risk of detection by law enforcement', *International Journal of Drug Policy*, 41: 101–109. doi: 10.1016/j.drugpo.2016.10.010

Andell, P., James, D. and Maitra, D. (in press) 'County lines and the transformation of middle drug markets within a local organised crime context'. In T. Ayres and Ancrum (eds.), *Understanding Drug Dealing and Illicit Drug Markets in the 21st Century: National and International Perspectives*. London, UK: Routledge.

Andell, P. and Pitts, J. (2018) 'The end of the line? The impact of County Lines drug distribution on youth crime in a target destination', *Youth & Policy*, January.

Ayres, T. C. and Bond, J. W. (2012) 'A chemical analysis examining the pharmacology of novel psychoactive substances freely available over the internet and their impact on public (ill)health. Legal highs or illegal highs?', *British Medical Journal Open*, 2012(2): e000977.

Ayres, T. C. and Treadwell, J. (in press) 'Entrepreneurs: Just taking care of business, the drug business'. In T. Ayres and Ancrum (eds.), *Understanding Drug Dealing and Illicit Drug Markets in the 21st Century: National and International Perspectives*. London, UK: Routledge.

Bancroft, A. (in press) 'The dark net, bitcoins and the role of the internet in drug supply'. In T. Ayres and Ancrum (eds.), *Understanding Drug Dealing and Illicit Drug Markets in the 21st Century: National and International Perspectives*. London, UK: Routledge.

Barratt, M. (2012) 'Silk Road: eBay for Drugs', *Addiction*, 107(3): 683.

Barratt, M. J., Ferris, J. A. and Winstock, A. R. (2016) 'Safer scoring? Cryptomarkets, social supply and drug market violence', *International Journal of Drug Policy*, 35: 24–31.

BBC (2020) 'Hundreds arrested as crime chat network cracked'. July 2. www.bbc.com/news/uk-53263310

Beckett, K., Nyrop, K. and Pfingst, L. (2006) 'Race, drugs, and policing: understanding disparities in drug delivery arrests', *Criminology*, 44(1): 105–137.

Berridge V. 1998. *Opium and the People*. London: Free Association Books.

Blum, R. H. and Associates (1972) *The Dream Sellers*. London: Jossey-Bass Inc.

Bokhari, F. (2008) 'Falling through the gaps: safeguarding children trafficked into the UK', *Children & Society*, 22(3): 201–211.

Boyd, S. C. (2009) *Hooked: Drug War Films in Britain, Canada, and the United States*. Toronto: University of Toronto Press.

Broséus, J., Gentile, N., and Esseiva, P. (2016) 'The cutting of cocaine and heroin: a critical review', *Forensic Science International*, 262: 73–83.

Chaiken, J. J. and Chaiken, M. R. (1994) 'Drugs and predatory crime', in Coomber, R. (ed.), *Drugs and Drug Use in Society: A Critical Reader*. Dartford: Greenwich University Press.

Childs, A., Bull, M. and Coomber, R. (2022) 'Beyond the dark web: navigating the risks of illicit drug supply of cannabis over the surface web', *Drugs: Education, Prevention and Policy* (Special Issue), 29(4): 403–414. doi: 10.1080/09687637.2021.1916439

Childs, A., Coomber, R., and Bull, M. (2020a) 'Do online illicit drug market exchanges afford rationality?', *Contemporary Drug Problems*, 47(4): 302–319.

Childs, A., Coomber, R., Bull, M. and Barratt, J. M. (2020b) 'Evolving and diversifying selling practices on drug cryptomarkets: an exploration of off-platform "direct-dealing"', *Journal of Drug Issues*, 50(2): 173–190.

Cole, C., Jones, C., McVeigh, J., Kicman, A., Syed, Q. and Bellis, M. (2010) *CUT: A Guide to Adulterants, Bulking Agents and Other Contaminants Found in Illicit Drugs*, Liverpool: Liverpool John Moores University.

Cole, C., Jones, L., McVeigh, J., Kicman, A., Syed, Q. and Bellis, M. (2011), 'Adulterants in illicit drugs: A review of empirical evidence', *Drug Test Analysis*, 3: 89–96.

Collins, J. (2001) 'Why are so many countries now saying cannabis is OK?',' *BBC News*, December 11. [Accessed 03/05/21]. www.bbc.co.uk/news/world-46374191

Coomber, R. (1997a) 'Adulteration of drugs: The discovery of a myth', *Contemporary Drug Problems*, 24(2): 239–271.

Coomber, R. (1997b) 'The adulteration of drugs: What dealers do, what dealers think', *Addiction Research*, 5(4): 297–306.

Coomber, R. (1997c) 'How often does the adulteration/dilution of heroin actually occur: An analysis of 228 'street' samples across the UK (1995-1996) and discussion of monitoring policy', *International Journal of Drug Policy*, 8(4): 178–186.

Coomber, R. (2003) 'There's no such thing as a free lunch: how 'freebies' and 'credit' operate as part of rational drug market activity not as a device for 'pushing' drugs onto the innocent and uninitiated', *Journal of Drug Issues*, 33(4): 939–962.

Coomber, R. (2004) 'Drug use and drug market intersections'. Editorial in *Addiction Research & Theory*, 12(6): 1–5.

Coomber, R. (2007) 'Drug trafficking, drug dealing and drug markets: a need for new research and new concepts'. Editorial/Introduction to the Special Issue in *Journal of Drug Issues*, 37(4): 749–754.

Coomber, R. (2010) 'Reconceptualising drug markets and drug dealers–the need for change', *Drugs and Alcohol Today*, 10(1): 10–13.

Coomber, R. (2011) 'Social fear, drug related beliefs and drug policy'. In Geoffrey Hunt, Maitena Milhet and Henri Bergeron (eds.), *Drugs and Culture: Knowledge, Consumption and Policy*, pp. 15–31. Farnham: Ashgate.

Coomber, R. (2014) 'How social fear of drugs in the non-sporting world creates a framework for policy in the sporting world'. Special Issue: Anti-Doping Rational Policy or Moral Panic?', *International Journal of Sport Policy and Politics*, 6(2): 171–193.

Coomber, R. (2015) 'A tale of two cities: understanding differences in levels of heroin/crack market related violence–a two city comparison', *Criminal Justice Review*, 40(1): 7–31.

Coomber, R. and Maher, L. (2006) 'Street-level drug market activity in Sydney's primary heroin markets: organisation, adulteration practices, pricing, marketing and violence', *Journal of Drug Issues*, 36(3): 719–754.

Coomber, R. and Moyle, L. (2012) *A Rapid Appraisal of the Illicit Drug Market in Southend-on-Sea, Essex*. Full Report. Plymouth University, Drug and Alcohol Research Unit (August).

Coomber, R. and Moyle, L. (2014) 'Beyond drug dealing: developing and extending the concept of 'social supply' of illicit drugs to 'minimally commercial supply', *Drugs Education, Policy and Prevention*, 21(2): 157–164.

Coomber, R. and Moyle, L. (2018) 'The changing shape of street-level heroin and crack supply in England: commuting, holidaying and cuckooing drug dealers across 'County Lines', British Journal of Criminology, 58(6): 1323–1342.

Coomber, R., Moyle, L., Belackova, V., Hakkarainen, P., Hathaway, A., Laidler, K.J., Lenton, S., Murphy, S., Scott, J., Stefunkova, M., Van de Ven, K., Vlaemynck, M., and Werse, B. (2018) 'The burgeoning recognition and accommodation of the social supply of drugs in international criminal justice systems: an eleven-nation comparative overview', *International Journal of Drug Policy*, 58: 93–103.

Coomber, R., Moyle, L., and Knox-Mahoney, M. (2017) 'Symbolic policing: situating targeted police operations/'crackdowns' on street-level drug markets', *Policing and Society* [early online].

Coomber, R., Moyle, L. and South, N. (2016) 'The normalisation of drug supply?: the social supply of drugs as the 'other side' of the history of normalisation of use', *Drugs: Education, Prevention and Policy*, 23(3): 255–263.

Coomber, R. and Pyle, E. (2015) *A Rapid Appraisal of the Illicit Drug Market in the Unitary Authority of Torbay, Devon*. Full Report. Plymouth University, Drug and Alcohol Research Unit. April.

Coomber, R., Pavlidis, A., Hanley Santos, G., Wilde, M. Schmidt, W., and Redshaw, C. (2014) 'The supply of steroids and other performance and image enhancing drugs (PIEDs) in one English city: fakes, counterfeits, supplier trust, common beliefs and access', *Performance Enhancement & Health*, 3(3): 135–144.

Coomber, R., and Salinas, M. (2020) 'The supply of Image and Performance Enhancing Drugs (IPED) to local non-elite users in England Resilient traditional and newly emergent methods. In K. van de Ven, K. Mulrooney and J. McVeigh (eds.), *Human Enhancement Drugs*, pp. 230–246. Oxford: Routledge.

Coomber, R. and South, N. (2004) 'Drugs, cultures and controls in comparative perspective'. In Ross Coomber and Nigel South (eds.), *Drug Use and Cultural Context 'Beyond the West': Tradition, Change and Post-Colonialism,* UK: Free Association Books, pp. 13–26.

Coomber, R. and South, N. (2014) Fear and loathing in drugs policy: risk, rights and approaches to drug policy and practice. In Beatriz Caiuby Labate and Clancy Cavnar (eds.), *Prohibition, Religious Freedom, and Human Rights: Regulating Traditional Drug Use.* Springer Berlin Heidelberg.

Coomber, R. and Sutton, C. (2006) 'How quick to heroin dependence', *Drug and Alcohol Review*, 25(5): 463–471.

Coomber, R. and Turnbull, P. (2007) 'Arenas of drug transaction: adolescent cannabis transactions in England–"social supply"', *Journal of Drug Issues*, 37(4): 845–866.

Curtis, R. and Wendel, T. (2000) 'Toward the development of a typology of illegal drug markets'. In Natarajan, M. and Hough, M. (eds.), *Illegal Drug Markets: From Research to Policy. Crime Prevention Studies*, Vol. 11. New York: Criminal Justice Press.

Curtis, R., Wendel, T. and Spunt, B. (2002) *We Deliver: The Gentrification of Drug Markets on Manhattan's Lower East Side*, Final Report. U.S. Department of Justice, Rockville, MD.

Demant, J., Anderdal Bakken, S., Oksanen, A. and Gunnlaugsson, H. (2019) 'Drug dealing on Facebook, Snapchat and Instagram: a qualitative analysis of novel drug markets in the Nordic countries', *Drug and Alcohol Review*, 38 (4): 377–385.

Dorn, N., Murji, K. and South, N. (1992). *Traffickers: Drug Markets and Law Enforcement.* London: Routledge.

Dupont, B., and Lusthaus, J. (2022). 'Countering distrust in illicit online networks: The dispute resolution strategies of cybercriminals'. *Social Science Computer Review*, 40(4): 892–913. https://doi.org/10.1177/0894439321994623

Edelman, M. (1988) *Constructing the Political Spectacle.* Chicago, IL: University of Chicago Press.

EMCDDA/European Monitoring Centre for Drug Dependency and Addiction (2020) *COVID-19 and Drugs: Drug Supply via Darknet Markets*, EMCDDA: Lisbon, 22pp. www.emcdda.europa.eu/system/files/publications/13042/EMCDDA-report_COVID19-darknet-final.pdf

EMCDDA/European Monitoring Centre for Drug Dependency and Addiction (2020) *New Psychoactive Substances: Global Markets, Glocal Threats and the COVID-19 Pandemic*—an update from the EU Early Warning System, December. EMCDDA: Lisbon. www.emcdda.europa.eu/publications/rapid-communication/new-psychoactive-substances-global-markets-glocal-threats-and-covid-19-pandemic_en

EMCDDA/European Monitoring Centre for Drug Dependency and Addiction (2017) *Synthetic cannabinoids in Europe.* EMCDDA: Lisbon, 9pp. www.emcdda.europa.eu/system/files/publications/2753/POD_Synthetic%20cannabinoids_0.pdf

Flacks, S. (2019) 'Making drug harms: punishments for drugs offenders who pose risks to children', *European Journal of Criminology*, 16(6): 652–670.

Foucault, M. (1972) *The Archaeology of Knowledge.* London: Tavistock.

Fratila, I. and Berdychevsky, L. (2020) 'Understanding drugs as leisure through the (de) differentiation lens and the dialectic of Logos–and Eros-modernity', *Leisure Studies*, [Published online: 08 Nov 2020].

Gerell, M., Sturup, J., Magnusson, M., Nilvall, K., Khoshnood, A., and Rostami, A. (2021) 'Open drug markets, vulnerable neighbourhoods and gun violence in two Swedish cities', *Journal of Policing, Intelligence and Counter Terrorism* (early online March 2021).

Hall, A. and Antonopoulos, G. (in press) 'Illicit pharmaceutical supply: moving beyond common assumptions about drugs and drug dealing'. In T. Ayres and Ancrum (eds.), *Understanding Drug Dealing and Illicit Drug Markets in the 21st Century: National and International Perspectives*. London, UK: Routledge.

Hall, A. and Antonopoulos, G. (2016) *Fake Meds Online: The Internet and the Transnational Market in Illicit Pharmaceuticals*. London: Palgrave Macmillan.

Harding, S. (2020) *County Lines: Exploitation and Drug Dealing Amongst Urban Street Gangs*. Bristol: Bristol University Press.

Hough, M., Warburton, H., Few, B., May, T., Man, L. and Turnbull, P.J. (2003) *A Growing Market: The Domestic Cultivation of Cannabis*. York: Joseph Rowntree Foundation.

Inciardi, J. A. (1986) *The War on Drugs: Heroin, Cocaine, Crime and Public Policy*, Palo Alto: Mayfield Publishing Company.

Klein, A. (2014) 'Framing the chew: narratives of development, drugs and danger with regard to Khat (Catha edulis)'. In Beatriz Caiuby Labate and Clancy Cavnar (eds.), *Prohibition, Religious Freedom, and Human Rights: Regulating Traditional Drug Use*. Switzerland: Springer.

Labate, B.C., Cavnar, C., and Rodrigues, T. (2016) 'Drugs and politics in the Americas: a laboratory for analysis'. In Beatriz Caiuby Labate, Clancy Cavnar and Thiago Rodrigues (eds.), *Drug Policies and the Politics of Drugs in the Americas*. Switzerland: Springer.

Labate, B.C. and Cavnar, C. (2014) 'Controversies on the regulation of traditional drug use'. In Beatriz Caiuby Labate and Clancy Cavnar (eds.), *Prohibition, Religious Freedom, and Human Rights: Regulating Traditional Drug Use*. Switzerland: Springer.

Lewis, R. (1994) 'Flexible hierarchies and dynamic disorder–the trading and distribution of illicit heroin in Britain and Europe, 1970–90'. In John Strang and Michael Gossop (eds.), *Heroin Addiction and Drug Policy: The British System*. Oxford: Oxford University Press.

Lupton, R., Wilson, A., May, T., Warburton, H., and Turnbull, P. J. (2002) *A Rock and a Hard Place: Drug Markets in Deprived Neighbourhoods*. Home Office Research Study 240. London: Home Office.

Marsh, B. (2021) *The Logic of Violence: An Ethnography of Dublin's Illegal Drug Trade*. Routledge.

Martin, J. (2014) *Drugs on the Dark Net: How Cryptomarkets Are Transforming the Global Trade in Illicit Drugs*. UK: Palgrave Macmillan.

Martin, J. (2018) 'Cryptomarkets, systemic violence and the "gentrification hypothesis" ', *Addiction*, 113: 797–798.

Martin, J., Munksgaard, R., Coomber, R., Dermant, J., and Barrett, M. J. (2020) 'Selling drugs on darkweb cryptomarkets: differentiated pathways, risks and rewards', *The British Journal of Criminology*, 60 (3): 559–578.

Matthews, R. (2009) 'Beyond 'so what?' criminology: Rediscovering realism', *Theoretical Criminology*, 13(3): 341–362.

May, T. and Hough, M. (2004) 'Drug markets and distribution systems', *Addiction Research & Theory*, 12:6, 549–563. DOI: 10.1080/16066350412331323119

McLean, R. A., Robinson, G., and Densley, J. A. (2019) *County Lines: Criminal Networks and Evolving Drug Markets in Britain*. Cham: Springer.

Measham, F., Moore, K., Newcombe, R. and Zoë (née Smith), Z. (2010) 'Tweaking, bombing, dabbing and stockpiling: the emergence of mephedrone and the perversity of prohibition', *Drugs and Alcohol Today*, 10(1), pp. 14–21.

Moffat, P. (2021) *Your Honour.* TV series, https://www.imdb.com/title/tt7440726/

Morgan, J. (in press) 'Heroin users who deal: getting high on their own supply'. In T. Ayres and Ancrum (eds.), *Understanding Drug Dealing and Illicit Drug Markets in the 21st Century: National and International Perspectives.* London, UK: Routledge.

Moyle, L. (in press) 'Just sorting my mates'?: the identities, roles and motivations of social suppliers'. In T. Ayres and Ancrum (eds.), *Understanding Drug Dealing and Illicit Drug Markets in the 21st Century: National and International Perspectives.* London, UK: Routledge.

Moyle, L. (2019). 'Situating vulnerability and exploitation in street-level drug markets: Cuckooing, commuting, and the "county lines" drug supply model', *Journal of Drug Issues*, 49(4): 739–755.

Moyle, L., Childs, A., Coomber, R., and Barratt, M. (2019) '#Drugsforsale: an exploration of the use of social media and encrypted messaging apps to supply and access drugs', *International Journal of Drug Policy*, 63: 101–110.

Moyle, L. and Coomber, R. (2017)'Bourdieu on supply: utilizing the "theory of practice" to understand complexity and culpability in heroin and crack cocaine user-dealing', *European Journal of Criminology*, 14(3): 309–328.

Moyle, L. and Coomber, R. (2015) 'Earning a score: an exploration of the nature and roles of heroin and crack cocaine "user-dealers"', *British Journal of Criminology*, 55, 534–555.

Moyle, L., Coomber, R., and Lowther, J. (2013) 'Crushing a walnut with a sledge hammer? Analysing the penal response to the social supply of illicit drugs', *Social & Legal Studies*, 22(4): 446–466.

Murphy,S., Waldorf, D., and Reinarman, C. (1990) 'Drifting into dealing: Becoming a cocaine selle', *Qualitative Sociology*, 13: 321–343.

Musto, D. F. (1987) *The American Disease: Origins of Narcotic Control*, Oxford: Oxford University Press.

Natarajan, M., Clarke, R.V., and Johnson, B.D. (1995) 'Telephones as facilitators of drug dealing', *European Journal on Criminal Policy and Research*, 3(3): 137–153.

National Crime Agency. (2020). National Strategic Assessment of Serious and Organised Crime.

Paoli, L. (2002) 'Flexible hierarchies and dynamic disorder: the drug distribution system in Frankfurt and Milan', *Drugs: Education, Prevention and Policy*, 9(2): 143–151.

Pearson, G., Hobbs, R., Jones, S., Tierney, J. and Ward, J. (2001) *Middle Market Drug Distribution.* Home Office Research Study 227. London: Home Office.

Personal Communication (2018) Team Leader, Forensic Drug Intelligence Specialist Operations, Australian Federal Police, Sydney.

Personal Communication (2017) Inspector, Drug Investigation Unit, Queensland Police Service.

Police Foundation (2000) *Drugs and the Law: Report of the Independent Inquiry into the Misuse of Rugs Act 1971.* London: The Police Foundation. 148 pp.

Ramiz, A., Rock, P., and Strang, H. (2020) 'Detecting modern slavery on cannabis farms: the challenges of evidence', *Cambridge Journal of Evidence-Based Policing*, 4: 202–217.

Reuter, P. (2009) 'Systemic violence in drug markets', *Crime, Law and Social Change*, 52: 275–284.

Sager, M. (2016) The fabulist who changed journalism, *Columbia Journalism Review*, June 1. < https://www.cjr.org/the_feature/the_fabulist_who_changed_journalism.php >

Salinas Edwards, M. (2014) *Men at Work: An Ethnography of Drug Markets and Youth Transitions in Times of Austerity*, PhD Thesis, University of Manchester.

Singer, M., Simmons, J., Duke, M., and Broomhall, L. (2001) 'The challenges of street research on drug use, violence, and AIDS risk', *Addiction Research & Theory*, 9(4): 365–402.

Schneider, S. (2013) 'Violence, organized crime, and illicit drug markets: a Canadian case study', *Sociologia*, 71: 125–143.

Scourfield, A., Flick, C., Ross, J., Wood, D.M., Thurtle, N., Stellmach, D. and Dargan, P.I. (2019) 'Synthetic cannabinoid availability on darknet drug markets—changes during 2016–2017', *Toxicology Communications*, 3:1, 7–15. DOI: 10.1080/24734306.2018.1563739

South, N. (1998) *Drugs: Cultures, Controls and Everyday Life*. London: Sage.

Spicer, J., Moyle, L., and Coomber, R. (2020) 'The variable and evolving nature of "cuckooing" as a form of criminal exploitation in street level drug markets', *Trends in Organized Crime*, 23: 301–323.

Syvertsen, J.L., Ohaga, S., Agot, K., Dimova, M., Guise, A., Rhodes, T., and Wagner, K.D. (2016) 'An ethnographic exploration of drug markets in Kisumu, Kenya', *International Journal of Drug Policy*, 30: 82–90.

Treadwell, J. and Kelly, C. (in press) 'Violence, grime, gangs and drugs on the south side of Birmingham'. In T. Ayres and Ancrum (eds.), *Understanding Drug Dealing and Illicit Drug Markets in the 21st Century: National and International Perspectives*. Oxford, UK: Routledge.

Turnock, L. A. (2021) 'Polydrug use and drug market intersections within powerlifting cultures in remote South-West England', *Performance Enhancement & Health*, 8(2): 100186.

Torres, C.E., D'Alessio, S.J., and Stolzenberg, L. (2020) 'Market dynamics and systemic violence: a longitudinal examination of market penetration, entry deterrence, and excess capacity in the illicit drug market', *Journal of Drug Issues* 51(1): 143–158. https://doi.org/10.1177/0022042620963074.

United Nations Office on Drugs and Crime (UNODC) (2020) *In Focus: Trafficking over the Darknet–World Drug Report 2020*. Vienna: UNODC.

van de Ven, K., Mulrooney, K.J.D., and Townshend, H. (in press) 'Image and performance enhancing drug (IPED) suppliers and their motives: following the evidence'. In T. Ayres and Ancrum (eds.), *Understanding Drug Dealing and Illicit Drug Markets in the 21st Century: National and International Perspectives*. London, UK: Routledge.

van de Ven, K. and Mulrooney, K. (2017) 'Social suppliers: exploring the cultural contours of the performance and image enhancing drug (PIED) market among bodybuilders in the Netherlands and Belgium', *International Journal of Drug Policy*, 40: 6–15.

van de Ven, K., and Koenraadt, R. (2017) 'Exploring the relationship between online buyers and sellers of image and performance enhancing drugs (IPEDs): quality issues, trust and self-regulation', *International Journal of Drug Policy*, 50: 48–55.

Werb, D., Rowell, G., Guyatt, G. Kerr, T., Montaner, J. and Evan Wood (2010) *Effect of Drug Law Enforcement on Drug-Related Violence: Evidence from a Scientific Review*. International Centre for Science in Drug Policy.

Windle, J., Moyle, L., and Coomber, R. (2020) '"Vulnerable" kids going country: children and young people's involvement in County Lines drug dealing', *Youth Justice*, 20(1–2): 64–78.

Wroe, E.L. (2021) 'Young people and "county lines": a contextual and social account', *Journal of Children's Services*, 16(1): 39–55.

Young, J. (2004) 'Voodoo criminology and the numbers game'. In J. Ferrell, K. Hayward, W. Morrison and M. Presdee (eds.), *Cultural Criminology Unleashed*, 13–28. London: The Glasshouse Press.

PART 1

The usual suspects

Traditional forms of drug dealing

2

DRUG DEALING WITH AMPHETAMINES

From over the counter to subcultural thefts, three phases of supply

Andrew Wilson and Rob Ralphs

> They [the teenagers] are looking for, and getting, stimulation not intoxication. They want greater awareness, not escape. And the confidence and articulacy that the drugs of the amphetamine group give them is quite different from the drunken rowdiness of previous generations on a night out.
>
> *Sharpley 1964: 18*

The above quote, taken from the *London Evening Standard* journalists that expose of amphetamine use by teenagers in Soho is not framed in the usual language of moral panics. Yet the series of reports published by the *Evening Standard* in February 1964 prompted the government to rush through legislation to criminalise the possession of amphetamines, making the criminalisation of central nervous system (CNS) stimulants (amphetamines hereafter) in the Drugs (Prevention of Misuse) Act enacted in July 1964. The publicity marked a turning point on amphetamines that we will be using in this chapter to illustrate the way context influences the culture of drug supply. The importance of situational effects on drugs markets draws on Blum (1972: 91) study of drug dealing in Britain and America, which revealed disparities that implied 'national cultural differences do effect drug use and dealing careers'. Despite the shortcomings of Blum's sample of British users and dealers predominantly drawn from the London hippie drug scene, his point about cultural influences retains its value. Drug use and dealing is never a static. The market is dynamic, made up of many aspects, that can change (whether in nature or just in emphasis) in response to fashion, technology, policing and laws. The use and supply of amphetamines offers a good illustration of those influences in the rise, response and fall of a drug. We divide the chapter into three distinct periods of amphetamine use and supply: the golden age of amphetamines from 1945 to 1964 when they were legal to possess; 1964

DOI: 10.4324/9781351010245-4

to 1973 which was marked by the heavy-handed policing of young people using amphetamines to attend mods and northern soul all-night dances; and, finally, post-1973 when the battle to control the supply by restricting the availability of pharmaceutically produced amphetamines was lost as illicitly manufactured amphetamine dominated the market.

Amphetamines: a post-war tonic

Amphetamine was discovered in 1887 but it was only after Gordon Alles in his search for a more effective decongestant than ethedrine that its stimulant properties were recognised (Heal et al. 2013: 479). Alles found that when inhaled or taken orally the drug 'dramatically reduced fatigue, increased alertness, and caused a sense of confident euphoria' (Hanson 2004: 93). By 1940 amphetamine had become a 'miracle drug' to be ranked alongside insulin and penicillin (Rasmussen 2006 1). After the Second World War, Bett (1946) found that amphetamines were prescribed for 39 separate conditions. These included the 'first specific medicine for mood disorder' (Rasmussen 2009: 3) as well as 'obesity, alcoholism, bed-wetting, depression, schizophrenia, head injuries, seasickness, and persistent hiccups' (Hanson, Rau et al. 2004: 93). After the war amphetamines may have been 'aggressively promoted' as a treatment for obesity through appetite suppression (Chesher 1991: 299) but this underplays the widespread enthusiasm for a miracle drug that was prescribed 'readily and light-heartedly' (Kiloh and Brandon 1962). After a decade of growth enthusiasm for amphetamines meant some 5,600,000 prescriptions were issued in 1959 for stimulants (Brain 1961: 89), with most of them being prescribed to women in the 36–45 years age group (Kiloh and Brandon 1962: 43). When Laurie (1971) extrapolated the ratio of dependent users of amphetamines from Kiloh and Bradon's (1962) Newcastle prescription rate, he estimated that 23,000 people in receipt of a prescription may be dependent. There were warnings about the risk of dependency to amphetamines and the chance that heavy use may cause problems like psychosis (Friedenberg 1940; Monroe and Drell 1947; Bethell 1957; Connell 1957; Connell 1958; Beamish and Kiloh 1960). Most of these problems occurred behind closed doors so as Laurie (1971) pointed out, that there was public complacency about the necessity of amphetamines in thousands of homes. The 'public horror', Laurie (1971: 84) goes on to say, was reserved for the teenage users. Yet as Connell (1964: 24) pointed out, 'adult habitation' was the most problematic because it involved high levels of constant use which was more likely to require psychiatric treatment. The habituated user was more likely to be in receipt of a prescription for amphetamines, but they were also the more likely to use deception to gain more supplies, by claiming to have lost or destroyed their prescription, or to commit crime by forging a prescription (Connell 1964: 24). He was less concerned about the 'teenage weekend consumer' whose pep pill use could be explained by the 'cultural factors' related to attending Soho-type clubs to be 'with it' (Connell 1964: 24). Linken (1963), a doctor who researched drug use across London, offered insights into the cultural factors at play. He estimated that about 30 out of 150 people attending an all-night coffee bar would have smoked hemp/cannabis or taken a pep pill that evening. He was impressed by the easy attitude towards drugs and the openness with which the young people talked about their drug use. He went on to say, 'one fact that stood out: among young people drug-taking is not considered a vice or a potential criminal activity.' The use of the nickname sweets, or sweeties, for some amphetamines shows just how far removed they were from narcotics in the minds of the young people.

The mixture of complacency on the part of doctors along 'with the demands from their patients for the drugs' (Connell 1964: 21) contributed to increasing the availability of amphetamines and in doing so making them appear an accepted and routine pick-me-up. Consequently, there was no moral line to cross in the initiation to amphetamine use; no legal barrier loaded with stigma. It was just a pep pill from a friend, workmate or hairdresser. Whatever the technical merits of the concept of normalisation there is perhaps no surer sign of a drug's acceptability than a girl's mother taking her child some pills to cheer her up while in a remand home (Scott and Willcox 1965). This lack of legal and moral obstacle to the use of pep pills also played a part in the trade of amphetamines that were legal to possess but not to sell on the open market. So, when it came to buying pills that were likely obtained by deception or stolen, the legal status of the amphetamines gave them a status similar to goods procured through a workplace fiddle.

Grey Two markets for pep pills

There is no way of knowing the precise number of tablets and capsules were prescribed because the amount in each prescription could vary greatly, though a survey of prescribed amphetamines in Newcastle in 1960 found an average of 77 per prescription (Laurie 1971: 84). Whatever the medical justification for prescribing stimulants, these two elements, staying alert and being cheerful, underpinned the development of the term 'pep-pills' and the relatively benign image of the drug. It is important to emphasise that the legal process to possess the status of amphetamines was an essential feature of the grey market for pep pills. Just as the colloquial name 'pep pills' shows how amphetamines avoided the negative connotations loaded on terms like 'narcotic' or 'drug' (Seddon 2016) prior to 1964, the same applies when using terms like 'drug market' and 'drug dealing' to describe transactions carried out in this period. When amphetamine use by young people appeared in the media before criminalisation, the dealers were described as drug pedlars but the activity had more in common with the moral ambiguity of the war time Spiv. By grey market we do not imply the conventional economic meaning where legally produced products sold outside the manufacturer dealer network (Mackenzie and Yates 2017: 71). The amphetamines sold in bulk prior to criminalisation in 1964 were ones that had been legally manufactured under conditions of lax security for low-value goods. The cost of the pills to manufacturers was miniscule with 5,000 costing around £1 at wholesale price (estimated from MIMS 1978). It was within this context, the moral ambiguous status of pep pills and the acceptance of workplace theft, that 'the customs of the fiddling subculture are delicately balanced between legitimate and criminal activity' (Ditton 1977: 193). Amphetamines may have been legal to possess under the drugs legislation but in some cases the possessor was charged with receiving stolen property. This placed the substances in the category similar to the products sold by 'spivs'. The spiv was an individual regarded as 'young, working class, and always on the make' (Hornsey 2010: 20) at a time of post-war shortages and rationing, such as nylons and rationing coupons. Even outside London the spiv became a common description for working class entrepreneurs who 'had their finger on everything going… half of it was legal and the other half wasn't' (Joyce 2008: 249). Spivs formed bridging capital between different parts of the market, to obtain pep pills by buying prescriptions or ones stolen from the workplace and selling them directly to customers or to coffee bars where they were sold 'under the counter' (Wilson 2008).

There was little academic research on amphetamines after criminalisation, so it is not surprising that the substance was largely ignored before 1964. The fragmented picture of amphetamine use and supply in this period is pieced together from a combination of press reports of prescription fraud, journalist looking into concerns about young people using pep pills, and the accounts of patients after seeking medical attention. The few academic studies that were carried out are useful but only provide a parochial snapshot. One often cited study of amphetamine prescribing in Newcastle did not find any evidence of 'organised illicit sales' (Kiloh and Brandon 1962: 41). Instead Kiloh and Brandon found small-scale exchanges of 50 tablets for 14 shillings from a known seller or a fellow factory worker selling them for 3d (about 2 pence in today's money) each. While identifying sellers in Newcastle may have required local knowledge, there is evidence to show that the knowledge of where to buy pills in London had spread outside the capital. An article in *The Lancet* discussing the mental illness suffered by three patients after consuming phenmetrazine (Preludin) revealed that they had all obtained them 'in the same London coffee bars and clubs where Preludin was used frequently as a pep pill' (Evans 1959: 155). A letter to the editor of *The British Medical Journal* shows how the reputation of the grey market extended beyond London. It gave an account of a 17-year-old who had been taking drinamyl and Dexedrine regularly for 12–18 months who travelled from Sheffield to a 'fairly notorious public house' in London 'to obtain a new supply of drinamyl tablets' (Bachrich 1964: 834). Anne Sharpley's (1964) account of a 'teenage pusher' who had recently bought 25,000 purple hearts suggests that he had paid £25 for them (less than half the 3d per pill). Sharpley contacted Smith, Kline, and French (SK&F), the Welwyn Garden-based manufacturer of the Drinamyl tablets, to point out that they were targets for pilfering. The company assured her that their security was effective but those of other manufacturers and warehouses may be the problem. SK&F did not make public the production and sales figures for Drinamyl, so there is no way of knowing whether their factory was as secure as they claimed.

Prior to Sharpley's (1964) series of articles in the *London Evening Standard* little attention was given to amphetamines, though a criminal case in 1961 propelled them to national headlines as a drug misused by teenagers. Victor John Terry was convicted of shooting a security guard during an armed robbery which focused attention of the coffee bar 'juke box jive' culture that the 20-year-old Terry inhabited (Johnson and Saker 1961). In the same issue of the *Daily Mirror* another article speculated on the way supplies of pep pills and cannabis were reaching the south coast (James and Tullett 1961). The police told the journalists that the cannabis and pep pills originated from two sources: smuggled by foreign ships and fishing boats; and pedlars (dealers) from London at weekends, and that pep pills were obtained with forged prescriptions. An 18-year-old interviewed for the article claimed 'they come in on boats at Shoreham Harbour… we get reefers ad pep pills, cheap cigarettes and whisky that way' (James and Tullett 1961: 5). A 17-year-old girl added, 'whatever they do we'll get the stuff… Most of us get our drugs from Ireland. But there are always lads coming from Brighton or London who bring the stuff with them'. Another 18-year-old said, 'Purple Heart is kid's stuff. I go for reefers for a real kick' (James and Tullett 1961: 5). The interviews in the article help to illuminate some of the points made above: the link between the coffee bar juke box culture of the 1950s with pep pills; the fragmented nature of the market; and the place of pep pills within a grey market for smuggled goods. The report went on to say that the police had carried out dozens of raids on south coast clubs and coffee bars without being able to capture the dealers. Adding that the use of pep pills in London, especially Chelsea and Hammersmith, is so common among teenagers that the Home Office is considering a nationwide hunt for the pedlars.

The focus of the police on pedlars is a sign of their misunderstanding pep pill use as an illicit supply side problem. A report in the *Evening Standard* from 1 October 1962 on drug menace that risked 'infecting teenagers' (cited in Mills 2013: 131) is a good example of failure to see the elephant in the room. In the period from 1945 to 1964 the pharmaceutical companies aggressively marketed amphetamines in pursuit of profit. As Inglis (1965: 150) points out, if the drug companies had promoted heroin in the same way as they did pep pills and tranquilisers, 'the same as they employed selling cosmetics…there would have been a public outcry'. In the USA annual spending on advertising in 1957 was over three times the combined $200 million spending of all the medical schools in America. In Britain the major spending went on sales representatives who used gifts and other promotional gimmicks to have direct influence over prescribing decisions of doctors. It was not until after criminalisation in 1964 that the medical profession began to seriously question the over-prescription of amphetamines and other CNS stimulants.

Prior to that, amphetamine was seen as a wonder drug prescribed for 39 conditions (Bett 1946) that was routinely passed around between family and friends as a pick-me-up. Up to 150 amphetamine tablets could be purchased over the counter at a chemist shop. The first stage in the development of an illicit market began in 1950 after amphetamine sales were placed under schedule 4 of the poisons rule which restricted sales to 'a fit and proper person' with each sale signed off in a register. This was monitored by regulators who made test purchases to check on compliance with the rules. In 1952 a pharmacy in Leamington Spa was fined £45 for selling Dexedrine tablets to someone without a prescription who was not 'fit and proper' without recording the sale (Leamington Spa Courier 1952). Pharmacists complained about the 'fit and proper' stipulation because they often had to deal with 'disgruntled customers' after refusing to sell them amphetamines (Pleasants 1954: 185) so the pharmacists supported the move to limit availability to prescription only in the 1954 Pharmacy and Poisons Act. There may have been an absence of evidence that tighter regulation was a response to the abuse of amphetamines (Bean 1974: 86) but the move exposed a strain between demand and supply. It was a soft form of regulation that did not criminalise possession, and left stimulants such as Benzedrine inhalers freely available. As Connell pointed out, the increased sales of inhalers which contained the equivalent of around 110 5-mg amphetamine sulphate tablets was a gap in the law that exposed the demand for these stimulants (Connell 1957: 582). The new restriction quickly gave rise to the practice of prescription forgery (Pharmaceutical Journal 1954: 282). Three years later an editorial draws attention to the increased problem of amphetamines being obtained with forged prescriptions, notably at 'various London West End pharmacies during the last twelve months' (Pharmaceutical Journal 1957: 217). At the time prescriptions could be written on scraps of paper so forgery was relatively a simple way to obtain amphetamines. The various illicit methods of obtaining amphetamines expose the points where amphetamines crossed the boundary from being a substance that avoided moral censure and was legal to possess into the crime of obtaining by criminal means or receiving stolen property. Under these conditions the notion of grey market captures the unclear status of the amphetamines, their widespread use and acceptance, and the fragmented nature of the way pep pills were obtained and sold. The research studies of amphetamine use in this period found the introduction to stimulants came from a friend, workmate, and in one study more frequently than anticipated, the hairdresser. The initial encounter tended to be followed up with a request to their doctor for a prescription (Brandon and Smith 1962; Kiloh and Brandon 1962). In places where demand was not met by a friendship network, the spiv like dealers, the roguish working class entrepreneurs, stepped in to ensure that those who could obtain a supply, whether from a prescription or workplace theft, could profit from the demand.

The theft of 4,500 'energy pills' from a Sheffield hospital dispensary offers good insight into the lax security around the substance and offers some indication of the way pep pills could enter the grey market. The Dexedrine tablets were stored in two large glass bottles. It was not until the second bottle was stolen that the dispensary noticed that the other had been missing for a week (Birmingham

Daily Post 1962: 1). The low cost value of the pills can be gleaned from a hospital in Cambridge where 2,000 tablets were stolen, leading the group secretary to comment that they were only worth about £1 to the hospital. The street value of the 4,500 tablets would have been in the range of £100–150, but there is a dearth of information on the balance between pills that were consumed, given away to friends and sold. Our lack of knowledge about the grey market in this period makes it impossible to estimate the proportion of stimulants consumed without prescription that originated from individuals selling their prescription, thefts or forgeries. Nor does the market in this period appear to have a form of supply that is exclusive enough to hold sway over the market and exploit the limited demand. It was, as our earlier description of the many small-scale suppliers indicated, misleading to focus attention on the pedlars from London when the market was so fragmented. Another problem for the authorities is that amphetamines were legal to possess so action against those selling the drug had to be taken by the Pharmaceutical Society for 'illegally selling Schedule 4 poisons contained in Drinamyl and Dexedrine tablets' (Birmingham Daily Post 1962). The 17-year-old from Rubery living in St Ives bought 100 tablets from a Beatnik in a Soho café for £1 4s before selling 50 of them to a youth in St Ives. He also said he bought some from a Teddy Boy in St Ives on the beach for two shillings. This was the only case of prosecution for supply we found in a British Library newspaper search, with variations of keywords such as amphetamines and pep pills. There is little doubt that Soho, with its long history of providing illicit leisure to the neighbouring theatres of London wealth, offered many opportunities for young people to buy amphetamines.

Drugs (Prevention of Misuse) Act 1964: policing drug users

Despite the relatively benign status of amphetamines as prescribed medicines the use of pep pills by young people made it the first drug in Britain to 'draw political reaction' (British Medical Association 2013: 90). This can be missed when looking to heroin as the reason for British drugs policy changes (Coomber, Moyle et al. 2016: 13). Certainly more academic attention was given to cannabis, perhaps in part because of Becker's (1963) highly influential book and the mythology of lysergic acid diethylamide (LSD) being on middle class/student life in the 1960s (Neville 1970; Young 1971). The rapid criminalisation of amphetamines and the associated crime after 1964 made it ripe for analysis. Wilson (2008) identified four key influences that led to the criminalisation of amphetamines in 1964: the professional constituents of the World Health Organization, politicians who took on the issue, the media and the self-proclaimed moralist Lee Harris. The latter was instrumental in motivating the Labour MP Ben Parkin to take an interest in the issue. He had worked closely with the *London Standard* journalist Anne Sharpley in a campaign for greater tenancy protections from rogue landlords. Parkin contacted her about the claims that young teenagers high on amphetamines were wandering around

Soho on Sunday morning after spending the night in seedy clubs. The element missing from Wilson's (2008) account is that earlier media reports about delinquency related to pep pills and drug use were likely to have created fertile ground for Harris's intervention. It is worth noting that this move to control pep pills began over a month before the mods and rockers moral panic (Cohen 1972). In fact, at the end of February the Home Secretary announced he would introduce legislation (Craig and Tullitt 1964: 1). That is not to suggest the drama of the seaside resort clashes did not have a negative influence on teenage use of amphetamines. Headlines like 'Drug check on "wild ones"' (Mirror Reporter 1964: 1) and editorial comment on the young people as 'victims of a dangerous racket' that called for 'the pedlars of pep-pills for "kicks"' to be 'driven out of business' sharpened the resolve of the Home Secretary Henry Brooke to act to stop this 'growing evil' (Staff Reporter 1964: 1)

It is difficult to establish the precise effects of the new legislation on both the illicit supply and consumption of amphetamines. But within a month of the July enactment of the 1964 regulations the Coventry Pharmacy Committee was warning its members to guard pep pills after three burglaries in one month where they were the only item stolen (Coventry Evening Post 1964) . Supplies may have been squeezed by tighter regulations at places of manufacture which may not have eliminated thefts, but it did draw a line under casual fiddles. Not simply because of the more stringent auditing and security but also because the criminalisation created a sharper moral boundary. The changed status did not slow down the prescription of amphetamines, though it did mark the start of a debate within the medical profession about the usefulness of amphetamines. In 1967 the BMA Science Committee set up a working group to assess the usefulness of amphetamines. They concluded that the compounds were of little therapeutic value (USA Congress 1972: 92). This conclusion was arrived at after local investigation in Ipswich, which was followed up with a ban on prescribing and stocking amphetamines in 1969. It was effective in reducing the use of amphetamines and 'two months after the ban there was no sign of abuse in the Ipswich area whatsoever' (USA Congress 1972: 92).

It was around this time, the 1967 summer of love, where the mods fragmented along class lines with the hippies and students forming one strand, and the more working class element moving into a style that would go on to shape skinheads, scooter clubs and the soul scene (Cohen 1972; Hebdige 1979; Cohen 1997; Wilson 2007). Essentially this marked a divided drug culture with the all-night dances becoming a touchstone for some members of all three working class styles. Although it was the soul scene that kept alive the amphetamine fuelled all-night dancing, by the end of 1967 cannabis, LSD and hippies had become a central concern for authorities while users of pep pills faded into the background. This is not to argue that they were no longer a policing interest, it is more to point out that the other two strands came to define drug use as the media cast hippies as the new folk devils (Young 1971; Cohen 1997). After 1968 police raids on all-night clubs outside London received little attention in the national media, instead the focus moved to raids on hippie and student users of cannabis and LSD. The effect of this was to shape drug use in the public eye as one related to hippies, students, and the use of heroin by 'junkies' at a time when there was strong belief that the use of soft drugs like cannabis inevitably led to the use of harder drugs like heroin (Connell 1968; Noble 1970; Bean 1971; Young 1971). The point is made here because the stereotypical view of the drug user had considerable influence on shaping the amphetamine ethos that formed in the wake of criminalisation (Wilson 2007).

Before taking a closer look at supply, we need say more about policing in this period to emphasise the part it played in changing cultural setting of drug use and dealing. The one important effect of criminalisation was the licence it provided for proactive policing of young people to deter them from drug use. Although it is important to appreciate that the move against drug use by young people was one element of an attempt to regulate the conduct of teenagers that began in the 1950s (Jackson 2008; Jackson 2015). Drugs provided evidence of youthful waywardness that turned the attention of the authorities on the 'coffee clubs' where they were being traded and consumed. Police drug raids on clubs took place from the early 1950s but it was stepped up after criminalisation with a special squad of 50 London police assigned to raiding clubs and coffee bars at the end of 1964 (Special Correspondent 1964: 8). We do not have figures for the number of raids in 1964–1965 but in 1966 there were 100 raids on clubs and coffee bars (Anon Reporter 1967: 1). While the report implied these were London raids, the practice was carried out across the nation. That includes a raid on the Dungeon Club in Nottingham that deployed 114 police officers to search over 600 young people. The raid received national attention after parents from as far away as London had to attend the police station to pick up the 60 young people under the age of 17 (Plaice 1967: 14). One month later, 100 police officers raided the London mod club Tiles where they stripped young people to their underwear in the search for drugs, and then held 182 (including 120 females) found to be under the age of 17 at the police station until their parents could collect them (Coolican 1967: 2). The media added a level of sensationalism to reports about the raids, focusing on the ages of those arrested, their gender and their presence at 'Teenage drug clubs' (Read 1966: 19). This all added pressure to regulate the clubs. In May 1967 the Licensing Act was amended to grant the police absolute right of entry.

Supplying amphetamines after the Act to Prevent Misuse

> As a general proposition, the secret society emerges everywhere as correlate of despotism and of police control. It acts as protection alike of defence and of offence against the violent pressures of central powers. This is true, not alone in political relations, but in the same way within the church, the school, and the family.
>
> *Simmel 1906: 472*

The first point to make is that the police raids, the strip searches, the prosecutions for possession and the closure of clubs eventually created a cohesive subculture among the relatively small number of young people attending the soul clubs in the north of England (Wilson 2019). The second point is the rather obvious one that the new law removed any grey areas from the use and supply of amphetamines. The law made amphetamine using teenage club goers as criminal as those supplying the drug. The observation that supply was put in the hands of criminals is axiomatic; but the statement needs qualifying. It would be hard to argue that the pre-criminalisation market for pep pills was completely crime free on the supply side and some of the suppliers will have continued. One of those is Ahmet Bekir who worked as a waiter and bouncer in London from the late 1950s. In 1964 he was twice charged with violence-related offences but accumulated enough money to open a 'teenage beat club' called Gigi's (his nickname) in Stoke Newington. In August 1965 he appeared in court charged with possession of 'Indian Hemp' (cannabis) and 'purple heart', amphetamine tablets. He later used his Turkish Cypriot connections to import heroin to the UK, illustrating the way entrepreneurs who could exploit the unregulated club scene of the 1960s were able to build capital and exploit new trends, which he did. According to Peter Walsh (2018), Bekir became one of the main suppliers of heroin to the UK in the 1970s.

The production of illicitly manufactured amphetamines is one activity that can be clearly linked to external criminal exploitation. Amphetamines for the oral mod culture needed to be produced in tablet form while this was less of an issue in the hippie/student market. Leech (1973: 35) observed that the two strands in London became closer in 1967 with the availability of injectable methylamphetamine. In the spring of 1968, in a ten-week period, most of the 80 people who appeared in court on Methedrine charges had injected the substance (Bean 1971: 81). There is little evidence to suggest the same happened outside London where prescription seepage and thefts from factories and chemist shops maintained supplies. We did not encounter evidence that counterfeit pills were seized by the police, but it is possible that the pills may have passed for bona fide ones. John Pearson's book on the Kray twins offers the best illustration of criminal movement into the market. In the summer of 1967 'they began a racket peddling purple hearts from an address in Soho; they had an old acquaintance who was manufacturing them by the million in an Essex farmhouse' (Pearson 1985: 248). While illicitly manufactured amphetamines were present in this period, within the oral mod drug using culture they were considered a poor substitute for the 'good gear' as the legally manufactured pharmaceuticals were called.

Seepage from prescribed medications, falsification of a need more such medication and prescription forgery (Lascelles and Sturrock 1967) were some of the methods used to obtain supplies. But curtailing grey market of workplace fiddles created a pressure on supply that was met by a range of criminal responses: thefts from warehouses, lorries transporting drugs, burglary of chemist shops (Pharmaceutical Society 1965) and importation from countries where stimulants were legally available. Reports and studies suggest a link between amphetamine use and prior delinquency (Linken 1963; Scott and Willcox 1965; Noble 1970; Bean 1971), so it is perhaps not surprising that the loss of plentiful supplies would provide motivation for some delinquent mods to turn to burglary of chemist shops. This raises a conceptual problem, not least because it is not what is implied by the statement that criminalisation puts supply in the hands of criminals. That suggests the criminals are separate in some way from those buying and consuming the drugs. The statement also implies supplying as a form of 'work' that can be reduced to profit-seeking activity (Ruggiero and South 1995: 4). In reality the theft of amphetamines from chemist shops could be described as a form of internal exploitation. Wilson (1999) used the notion of internal exploitation to explain the effects of commercialisation on a subculture. The argument is that any grouping that forms around social activity creates a need for organisation, whether booking a room, finding an empty space and entertainment such as music. This creates a need which is met by insiders who have a mix of specialist knowledge and an interest in the same values espoused by the group.

Chemist shop burglary: a job for an insider

The burglary of a chemist shop could be committed by individuals with three different objectives: a criminal stealing goods of value, which may include the drugs; an opioid user who would break open the locked (usually) wooden box where they were stored; and the amphetamine user in search of the different brands stored in alphabetical order on the shelves of the pharmacy. Each of those three types is likely to include crossover, so the opioid user may also take amphetamines to use or sell, and likewise with the amphetamine user that may also take opioids to use or sell, and each of those may also steal goods of value like cameras. While such an assumption is logical, the pattern burglary for just pep pills that had been observed in Coventry (Coventry Evening Post 1964) was repeated just over two years later in the Pharmaceutical Journal:

> The offences carry identical characteristics. No excessive damage is caused and the stock remains intact except a small range of specified drugs. The offender can recognise these tablets and capsules at sight and departs immediately with as many as he can carry.
>
> *Pharmaceutical Society 1967: 428*

In April 1966 the *Birmingham Post* reported that in the previous year, 34 of the city pharmacies had been raided for drugs. A similar pattern was reported for Manchester a year later, with 16 of Salford's 47 pharmacies being burgled (Pharmaceutical Society 1967). The high level of prescribing in this period meant the chemist shops carried high levels of stock. So, a burglar would expect a haul of a few thousand pills, but sometimes it involved large amounts like the 50,000 stolen in 1967 from a pharmacy in King's Norton (Pharmaceutical Society 1967: 159). It is possible that the theft of amphetamines was carried out by criminals not involved in attending the all-night clubs, but the folklore tales passed on by members of the soul scene suggest that a good number of these burglaries were carried out by 'insiders' (members of the scene). Dave Owen (2018) is a good example of an insider from this era. He burgled his first chemist shop in 1967. When asked why he felt the need to burgle when pills were readily available, he replied, 'when I first went to the Mojo (an all night club in Sheffield) purple hearts were 3d each', though you could pay by the handful, 'about 1967 they went up to a shilling each'. He was working as a window cleaner in Grantham when he burgled his first chemist shop in Grimsby. He stopped window cleaning and lived off the money he made breaking into chemist shops and signing on the dole. There is little doubt that Dave Owen became criminal, but interviewing him amidst his considerable record collection, talking about attending a soul weekender, should leave no doubt about his insider credibility.

The association of soul clubs with drugs, together with the frequent chemist shop burglaries by members of the scene, ensured that the soul clubs in the north were policed as heavily as the rest of England was for cannabis. In 1971 a raid on Wakefield's Metro Club resulted in two coachloads of young people being transported to the local police station. A couple of weeks later, a newspaper report on a police raid at a nearby club, Hernies in Leeds, provides good insight into the drug culture and the way in which such issues were reported. The *Leeds Evening Post* reporter talked to members of what the reporter called the 'soul sect' (the term northern soul did not gain common currency until 1973).

> One boy said: 'it is becoming more and more difficult to get drugs. Most of it comes from chemists which are broken into. Pushers are usually people who find out where the 'scene' will be and bring the drugs along. But the (drug) squads seem to be finding out where we are going each weekend, and they never seem to leave us alone.'

It went on to quote members of the scene talking about pushers 'who make big money from peddling drugs and the people who raid shops to get them'. It also noted that 'The kids were half expecting a raid. Clubs in Manchester and the Midlands had been closed after police visits, and now most of the devotees were now well accustomed to being searched'. The reporter could have added that an article in the same paper disclosing the whereabouts of the new venue for the drug using teenagers had raised fears of a raid. One of the boys cleared by the police commented that it was not much of a raid as raids go. 'He explained that because of the threat of the raid many had taken drugs before going on the premises and were not carrying anything' (EP Reporter 1971). We asked a member of the scene who worked at the club, Pete Dillon (2018), what the response was to the newspaper report. He said 'we all thought joke'. In fact, he said, 'the raid was expected because Flash told a reporter that with the Metro closing everyone would be going to Hernies'. When they did come it took the police a long time to gain entry because the club had a secure door with an inspection slot. He dismissed the suggestion that gear was 'pushed' on members of the scene by outsiders, calling it a fiction. He confirmed that pills at that time were supplied by members of the scene. I also asked whether that was the kind of language that would have been used by any of the lads giving an interview. He did not think it would, it was one of the reasons they all thought the article to be a joke.

Whatever the inaccuracies in detail the report still managed to convey some of the tensions around amphetamine use, including the growing constraints on supplies and the adaptations users needed to make when faced with pro-active policing (language, secrecy, stashing and heavier dose). The description of the way that strangers were treated with suspicion, that they may be either members of the drug squad or their informants, reflected the increased insularity and secrecy of the scene. Those factors go some way to explaining why the interviewees wanted to move drugs to arm's length from themselves: who would admit to a reporter that their friend was the one burgling a chemist shop and selling the amphetamines to fellow members of the scene? They 'insisted that they did not use hard drugs' and defended use of the drugs on instrumental grounds, 'we do not harm anyone except ourselves… To keep dancing all night we need the drugs… Pot and pep pills should be legalised. This would cut out the pushers' (Evening Post 1971). We pressed Pete Dillon on whether he would have thought of people selling pills at the club as drug pushers. It was only by asking the question that he could see that the term was totally inappropriate. At a time when the soul scene was relatively small, it was common sense that the individuals selling the pills were friends or, at worst, associates. He could not recall the names of 'the lads from Barnsley' who had burgled a chemist shop the week before the raid.

In the early 1970s there were two other significant sources of supply. One came about after two members of the soul scene persuaded a worker at the Kerfoot's pharmaceutical factory in Ashton-under-Lyne to regularly throw a bag of 10,000 pills over the factory fence. The exchange was carried out in Ashton library at £40 per 1,000 pills which were sold on for a £20 profit. The claim that 'millions' of pills were obtained this way may be an exaggeration, but enough exchanges occurred to have accumulated a substantial number of pills. This kind of theft from the workplace was more like the bakery fiddles Ditton (1979) described, which was regarded as more a kind of 'spiv' activity than outright criminal. This may have been 'something more' than social supply (see Moyle's chapter on social supply in this volume) but it was a form internal exploitation that delivered more reward through the accumulated subcultural than it did financial benefits and was far removed from the stereotypical notion of the drug pusher (see Coomber 2006).

The second source of supply was the same type of enterprise as the Krays became involved with in the late 1960s: illicitly manufactured pills. In the early 1970s substantial amounts of blue and yellow (replicating Drinamyl and

Dexedrine) tablets were available, selling at 7–9 pills per one pound. The bulk seller was based in Cambridgeshire. He was reputed to have bought the pills directly from the illicit manufacturer in Welwyn Garden City, then sold them to middle level dealers, including the two living in Selby who sold some of the pills at the Central Soul Club in Leeds, and took orders for them that would end in an exchange at the Birch service area on the M62 en route to the all nighter in Bolton. All of those involved in the supply network, including the seller in Cambridgeshire, were members of the soul scene. The pills were consistently good quality and with some discounts for bulk buying. In 1973 the distribution network was busted and the two sellers from Selby were given long-term prison sentences. The manufacturers of the pills were clearly engaged in a form of external exploitation but the bulk buy stages could still be regarded as a form of internal exploitation was more than social supply but significantly less than the image of the pusher that influenced their harsh sentences. They are both still involved in the soul scene, one of them as DJ. At least two people in Wilson's (2007) study began burgling chemist shops after the supply of illicit pills ended. The bust also encouraged some members of the scene to buy illicitly manufactured amphetamine (often crystals) from dealers selling in the Skyrack pub in the student area of Leeds.

Chemist burglars: heroes or villains?

> I suppose the comical thing that would happen is somewhere along the line, some of the bad lads must've reconnoitred all the different ways into Wigan and looked at the chemist shops that didn't look like they had the greatest security… And whichever way they came in you could almost bet your life that a chemist would be broken into and done… I used to hear about people getting busted. It used to be a contributory factor into why those places always got closed down.
>
> *Former DJ Ian Dewhirst (1998)*

The quote perpetuates a myth made real by the occasional burglary on route to an all-night dance, whether local or over a hundred-mile journey. The recollection of chemist burglary as a comical enterprise is revealing. In the interview Dewhirst named three known chemist burglars and their home town reflecting a good level of subcultural knowledge even though he denied personal use of amphetamines. He was also aware of the harmful effects, including arrests and clubs being closed down. But it is the nostalgic tone and acceptance that offers good indication of the way the use, supply and theft of amphetamines became contextually normalised (Coomber, Moyle et al. 2016), to the extent that non-drug using members of the northern soul scene accommodated the method of obtaining the pills they consumed at the weekend. It would be unthinkable to apply any of the attributes of the mythical pusher (Coomber 2004) to dealing within this context. Demand for 'good gear' always exceeded supply, so there was never good reason to introduce someone to amphetamines to boost sales. Not selling to someone could be interpreted as a snub (Coomber, Moyle et al. 2016: 260), which risked damaging the reciprocal arrangements that existed with the peer group clusters (Oetting and Beauvais 1987; Wilson 1999; Parker 2000). As well as the moral barrier to adulterating drugs sold to friends, the stolen pharmaceuticals had attested purity that was impossible, in the case of pills, and difficult for capsules, to tamper with.

While there is an obvious problem with applying the term 'social supply' to those selling the proceeds of a chemist burglary, there were similar features. It may have been more than simple possession and nothing like 'something less' than drug dealing (Coomber, Moyle et al. 2016: 256), but for most of the nine chemist shop burglars in Wilson's (2007) study the criminal act was motivated by personal supply and not profit. However, the nine burglars varied from the one-timer to a pair of prolific burglars who broke into over one hundred shops. It would be hard for the prolific burglars to evade the dealing for money label, but even they talked about the importance of personal supplies, being in control, having the ability to give gear to their friends. Aside from the criminal act of burglary, the motives have much in common with those expressed by the marijuana dealers in Goode's (1970) study. After the common sense benefits of making money and free drugs, he lists the mystique of dealing, and the respect gained from playing a more dangerous game than the users. Goode (1970: 257–258) suggests some dealers enjoy the 'cloak and dagger intrigue, at least at first' and has specialist knowledge 'from which the nondealer is to some degree excluded'. All of the repeat burglars in Wilson's (1999, 2007) study had a prior history of delinquency with time spent in youth offender institutions, so being valued within a 'subcommunity' where they could gain status from their willingness to break the law to acquire subcultural capital (Thornton 1996) made chemist shop burglary an attractive proposition. One more similarity with marijuana dealing was that there were no tangible signs of long-term profit from the burglaries. In part that may be explained by the easy come nature of the drugs – they were free so, like the hippies in Langer's (1977: 384) study, selling might 'not been entirely co-ordinated or systematized'.

Commercialisation and control: effects on demand and supply of amphetamines

The third phase of amphetamine supply covered in this chapter describes the cultural impact of the commercialisation of northern soul after 1973 which created a demand for amphetamines that far outstripped the shrinking amounts obtained through chemist shop burglary. Laycock's (1984: 6) assertion that target hardening significantly reduced chemist shop burglary was flawed because it did not give enough weight to the effects of destocking amphetamines. More significantly, because the Home Office had a narrow interest in reducing burglary, they paid no attention to the displacement effects of target hardening. Discussions about chemist shop security began in 1969 after the sharp rise in burglaries. The industry rejected the high cost of installing alarms to protect low-value goods in favour of a lower cost option of a secure cabinet, safe, or room to store the controlled drugs (both Classes A and B). This measure entered the statute book in 1973 (Carr 1973) though a shortage of cabinets caused a short compliance delay. The unintended consequences of this change have been documented elsewhere (Wilson 2008) so here we will give an outline of the effects.

Prior the change the chemist burglar needed a good knowledge of the various brands of CNS stimulants to pick them out among the array of medicines on the shelves of the pharmacy. Afterwards they simply needed to locate the white cabinet which contained all of them in one place. Most cabinets could be opened within ten minutes with a couple of screwdrivers and a crow bar. Once opened the burglar could sweep the entire contents into a bag to be sorted in a safe place. Initially some burglars flushed the opiates or disposed of them safely by posting them through the letterbox of a chemist shop (Wilson 2008). When it became known that opioids were being 'wasted', either a contact within the northern scene or a connection to the home town opiate users offered to buy the next batch. This is not to suggest that opiate use and selling did not occur within the soul scene prior to this change. Dave Owen (2018) said he began mixing opiates with amphetamines in the late 1960s when he moved to Sheffield. In that period weekend amphetamine users were more likely to use barbiturates as a means of gaining a good night sleep to be ready for work on Monday, but the use of opiates for this reason became more common among those with access to opioids from 1974. Dave also sold opioids to local users, which included the musician Joe Cocker when he was homeless living in a pink Jaguar. While Dave Owen's actions reflect a calculated choice to take opiates, the new storage regulations made it a necessity. Furthermore, it did so precisely at a time when commercialisation was diluting the amphetamine ethos of the scene by making the use of amphetamine powder the new norm. The old pill-based ethos stemmed from detailed knowledge about each brand of CNS stimulant – strength, dosage, duration, what not to mix with – as well as tacit rules about not using during the week and not injecting. The golden rule was to not use opiates. Within a matter of months chemist burglars who could argue were only serving the needs of their friends and associates became one of the main sources of opiates in the north of England.

A court case involving 33 people where drugs and money were exchanged along the M62, a road the judge called 'thieves highway' (Johnson 1975: 6), illustrates the trade well. The headline "How the soul-scene pushers were trapped" presents the stereotypical image of the predatory drug dealer, this time set within a 'ring spanning the northern counties'. Brian Taylor (2019) was one of the chemist burglars caught up in what today would be defined as 'organised crime' crossing 'county lines'. His contact with the rest stemmed from selling his drugs to a former member of the scene, Alf Hockedy. It was the one and only link to the other 33. Another one of the loosely connected group gave a similar account, adding that the police failed to arrest the two main people based in Stockport. His contact with the group stemmed from the opposite relationship Brian (who sold opiates) had with the grouping; he was buying amphetamines from the 'hippie' types who were burgling chemist shops. In the shadow of the 'organised' exaggeration the case shone light on the drugs trade within this period. Most of the opiate traffic travelled westwards along the M62 from Yorkshire, though it later went to the north east and Scotland.

This 1970s version of 'county lines' dealing could sometimes make the occupation of the opiate users home a necessity. This tended to happen when two elements were in short supply: money and trust. A lack of funds to buy the full consignment meant sitting around until enough sales had been made to cover the costs. This kind of deal involved a lot of risk to the burglar. Notifying opiate users that supplies were available raised the possibility someone would sell the information to the police (common practice in the early 1970s). The user/dealer gained two advantages: the first was to make enough money to support their personal drug use; the other was having the pick of the consignment. The usually meant first to the Diconal, a strong opioid analgesic that was often more sought after than morphine and heroin. The pharmacology of the pill, a mix of dipipanone and cyclizine (which inhibited histamine release, reducing the nausea and vomiting associated with opiates) does not capture the almost mystic qualities users ascribed to the drug. Everything in the drugs cabinet had value – including the suppositories that could be boiled up to release the morphine from the wax like casing. There was also a demand for barbiturates among the opiate users, so they were sometimes included as a 'free' item in the deal. However, some of the opiate users considered intravenous use of barbiturates to be the definition of a junkie. The strong anti-opiate ethos among the soul scene burglars could raise moral dilemmas when it came to requests to buy from friends on the soul scene. In one case after being refused a request to buy some he said to the seller 'if I don't get it from you I'll get it somewhere else, somewhere with no guarantee over its purity'. He had a point because the opioids being sold were pharmaceutically pure, though that did not prevent the challenge to morality from overdose deaths. It is worth noting that prior to the changes in storage regulations, Wilson (2008) only found one recorded death related to amphetamine use, which the coroner said was related to a pre-existing condition. After the storage changes, together with the dilution of the amphetamine ethos, fatalities became a relatively common feature (Wilson 2007, 2008). Crucially, the interaction between two drug user cultures together with the effects of commercialisation (higher demand from increased numbers and dilution of the amphetamine ethos) created not just a pathway to the use of amphetamine powder, but also to the spread of an injection culture within the scene. This aspect came to have a significant impact on the lives of those infected with hepatitis C.

Concluding observations

Taking a historical approach to the supply and use of amphetamines within the dance culture that emerged in the late 1950s gives an insight into the way extraneous changes had a profound effect on the way drug use and supply was framed and continues to be framed. The promotion of amphetamines as miracle drugs that could treat anxieties, excess weight and fatigue helped to give it a socially acceptable reputation. That status may have been tarnished a little by criminalisation, but its main effect was on the cultural context of those using amphetamines at the weekend to attend the all night dance clubs. We take issue with the claim that the changed legal status put supply in the hands of criminals for two reasons. Even though the burglary of chemist shops was a criminal act it was not in the hands of individuals external to the scene driven by the profit motive. The second reason is that the statement distracts attention from the wider criminalising effects of prohibition. The raids, strip searches, arrests, holding young people at police stations for parents to pick up may have lacked the 'violent pressures of central powers' Simmel (1906: 472) described, but it did promote a defensive reaction against the wholesale criminalisation of previously legal cultural practice. This policing of leisure may lack the deep-seated racism that Alice Goffman (2014) encountered but her description of the way the war on drugs promoted a defensive community reaction has many similarities. It not only produced a situation where chemist burglars were celebrated, it also propagated a culture where individuals with no prior history of delinquency were prepared to carry or hide drugs, drive burglars to a chemist shop, harbour fugitives, allow a burglar to use their home to count their proceeds, and give a false alibi to the police to help someone avoid arrest.

The changed dangerous drugs storage regulations inadvertently created a link between two different drug use cultures that changed the nature of chemist shop burglary. The theft of opioids by members of the soul scene and their sale to members of an opiate user culture (even where it involved former members of the soul scene) changed the nature of the enterprise. However, the exchange was not all one way with some payments being made in amphetamine powder. Crucially, along with the money and powder came an introduction into an injecting culture that was previously scorned by members of the soul scene. It was not unknown, but the pill culture ethos was upheld by the relatively small and close knit scene. Commercialisation and the dilution of that culture exasperated the effects of the wider acceptance of intravenous drug use. These exchanges should not be interpreted in a way that supports the notion of the pusher. Many of the opiate users in this period eked out their supplies and when dependent turned to other substances such as barbiturates to ease withdrawal symptoms. The chemist burglars seldom sold to individual users unless cajoled by a friend or associate. It would be reasonable to say that the tighter regulations failed because it was a cheap option.

The attempt to reduce recreational use of CNS stimulants and the illicit use of opioids by stemming pharmaceutical sources in the early 1970s was ineffectual. The policy made sense at the time because illicit supplies of both were limited, and the pharmaceutical products had a good reputation. The move to change the habits of doctors by encouraging them to restrict their prescription of amphetamines did help to reduce the problem of adult habituation as the Ipswich example illustrated. It is something of an oddity that the advertising and promotion given to amphetamines by the pharmaceutical companies was not subjected to more criticism at a time when young people using the miracle drug were talked about as being infected by the pushers and pedlars. This chapter should leave no doubt that the image was wrong, even if the harsh sentences under prohibition encourage users to draw on the mythical image to distance themselves from responsibility for their own actions (Young 1971: 188).

References

Anon Reporter (1967). "Police raid London Club: 192 held." *Aberdeen Press and Journal*. Aberdeen.

Bachrich, P. R. (1964). "New drugs of addiction." *British Medical Journal* 1(5386): 834–835.

Beamish, P. and L. G. Kiloh (1960). "Psychoses due to amphetamine consumption." *Journal of Mental Science* **106**(442): 337–343.

Bean, P. (1971). "Social aspects of drug abuse: A study of London drug offenders." *The Journal of Criminal Law, Criminology, and Police Science* **62**(1): 80–86.

Bean, P. (1974). *The Social Control of Drugs*. Oxford, Martin Robertson.

Becker, H. (1963). *Outsiders: Studies in the Sociology of Deviance*. London, Free Press.

Bethell, M. F. (1957). "Toxic psychosis caused by 'preludin'." *The British Medical Journal* **1**(5009): 30–31.

Bett, W. (1946). "Benzedrine sulphate in clinical medicine." *Postgraduate Medical Journal* **22**(250): 205.

Birmingham Daily Post (1962). "4,500 'Pep' Pills Stolen." *Birmingham Daily Post*. Birmingham: 1.

Blum, R. H. (1972). *The Dream Sellers: Perspectives on Drug Dealers*. London, Jossey-Bass.

Brain, W. R. (1961). *Drug Addiction: Report of the Interdepartmental Committee on Drug Addiction*. London, HM Stationery Office.

Brandon, S. and D. Smith (1962). "Amphetamines in general practice." *The Journal of the College of General Practitioners* **5**(4): 603.

British Medical Association (2013). *Drugs of Dependence: The Role of Medical Professionals*, January 2013. London, British Medical Association.

Carr, R. (1973). *The Misuse of Drugs (Safe Custody) Regulations 1973. 798*. H. Office. London, HMSO.

Chesher, G. B. (1991). "Hazardous amphetamine use: The need to consider dosage." *Drug and Alcohol Review* **10**(4): 299–303.

Cohen, P. (1997). *Rethinking the Youth Question: Education, Labour and Cultural Studies*. London, Macmillan.

Cohen, S. (1972). *Folk Devils and Moral Panics: The Creation of the Mods and Rockers*, MacGibbon and Kee.

Connell, P. (1958). *Amphetamine Psychosis*. Oxford, Oxford University Press.

Connell, P. (1964). "Amphetamine misuse: The present position with regard to misuse of amphetamine and amphetamine barbiturate mixtures." *British Journal of Addiction to Alcohol & Other Drugs* **60**(1): 9–27.

Connell, P. (1968). "Amphetamine dependence." *Proceedings of the Royal Society of Medicine* **61**(2): 178–181.

Connell, P. H. (1957). "Amphetamine psychosis." *British Medical Journal* **1**(5018): 582–582.

Coolican, D. (1967). "Drug raid girls told to strip." *Daily Mirror.* London.

Coomber, R. (2004). "Drug use and drug market intersections." *Addiction Research & Theory* **12**(6): 501–505.

Coomber, R. (2006). *Pusher Myths: Re-situating the Drug Dealer.* Free Association Books. ISBN: 1853439487.

Coomber, R., et al. (2016). "The normalisation of drug supply: The social supply of drugs as the 'other side' of the history of normalisation." *Drugs: Education, Prevention and Policy* **23**(3): 255–263.

Coomber, R., et al. (2016). *Friendly Business: International Views on Social Supply, Self-supply and Small-scale Drug Dealing.* B. Werse and C. Bernard (eds.). New York, Springer: 13–28.

Coventry Evening Post (1964). Chemists told: guard pep pills. Coventry.

Craig, W. and T. Tullitt (1964). "Brooke acts on purple hearts." *Daily Mirror.* London: 1.

Dewhirst, I. (1998). *Ian Dewhirst, Northern Soul DJ. B.* Brewster. London, Red Bull Music Academy.

Dillon, P. (2018). *Recollections of Drug Dealing on the Soul Scene.* A. Wilson.

Ditton, J. R. (1977). *Part-time Crime: An Ethnography of Fiddling and Pilferage.* London, Macmillan.

EP Reporter (1971). "Sect call for legal 'pot': A night with the soul devotees in Leeds." *Leeds Evening Post.* Leeds: 5.

Evans, J. (1959). "Psychosis and addiction to phenmetrazine (Preludin)." *The Lancet* **274**(7095): 152–155.

Friedenberg, S. (1940). "Addiction to amphetamine sulphate." *Journal of the American Medical Association* **114**(11): 956–956.

Goffman, A. (2014). *On the Run: Fugitive life in an American City.* Chicago, University of Chicago Press.

Goode, E. (1970). *The Marijuana Smokers.* New York, Basic Books.

Hanson, G. R., et al. (2004). "The methamphetamine experience: A NIDA partnership." *Neuropharmacology* **47**: 92–100.

Heal, D.J., Smith, S.L., Gosden, J. and Nutt, D.J. (2013). "Amphetamine, past and present--a pharmacological and clinical perspective." *Journal of Psychopharmacology* 27(6): 479–496. doi: 10.1177/0269881113482532. Epub 2013 Mar 28. PMID: 23539642; PMCID: PMC3666194.

Hebdige, D. (1979). *Subculture: The Meaning of Style.* London, New Accents.

Hornsey, R.Q.D. (2010). *The Spiv and the Architect: Unruly Life in Postwar London.* London: University of Minnesota Press.

Inglis, B. (1965). *Drugs, Doctors and Disease.* London: Mayflower.

Jackson, L. (2015). *Policing Youth: Britain, 1945–70.* Manchester, Manchester University Press.

Jackson, L. A. (2008). "'The coffee club menace'." *Cultural and Social History* **5**(3): 289–308.

James, P. and T. Tullett (1961). "The pep kids sneer at CID." *Daily Mirror.* London.

Johnson, H. and H. Saker (1961). "Terry the drug thug." *Daily Mirror.* London.

Johnson, P. (1975). "How the soul-scene pushers were trapped." *Yorkshire Post.* Leeds.

Joyce, S. (2008). "The black economy in the Soar Valley, 1945–1971." *Transactions of the Leicestershire Archaeological and Historical Society* **82**: 245–254.

Kiloh, L. and S. Brandon (1962). "Habituation and addiction to amphetamines." *British Medical Journal* **2**(5296): 40.

Langer, J. (1977). "Drug entrepreneurs and dealing culture." *Social Problems* 24(3): 377–386.

Lascelles, B. D. and G. R. Sturrock (1967). "Forged prescriptions." *The British Medical Journal* **1**(5538): 494–494.

Laurie, P. (1971). *Drugs: Medical, Psychological and Social Facts.* Harmondsworth, Penguin Books.

Laycock, G. (1984). *Reducing Burglary: A Study of Chemists' Shops.* London, Home Office London.

Leamington Spa Courier (1952). "Slimming tablets sold without prescription." *Leamington Spa Courier.* Leamington Spa.

Leech, K. (1973). *Youthquake: The Growth of a Counter-Culture through Two Decades.* London, Sheldon Press.

Linken, A. (1963). "The young drug-takers." *Sunday Times.* London**:** 1.

Mackenzie, S. and D. Yates (2017). "What is grey about the 'grey market' in Antiquities?" *The Architecture of Illegal Markets: Towards an Economic Sociology of Illegality in the Economy.* J. Beckert and M. Dewey (eds.). Oxford, Oxford University Press.

Mills, J. H. (2013). *Cannabis Nation: Control and Consumption in Britain, 1928–2008.* Oxford, Oxford University Press.

MIMS (1978). *Monthly Index of Medical Specialities.* London, Haymarket. **20**.

Mirror Reporter (1964). "Drug check on the 'wild ones'." *Daily Mirror.* London: 1.

Monroe, R. R. and H. J. Drell (1947). "Oral use of stimulants obtained from inhalers." *Journal of the American Medical Association* **135**(14): 909–915.

Neville, R. (1970). *Playpower.* London, Jonathan Cape.

Noble, P. J. (1970). "Drug-taking in delinquent boys." *The British Medical Journal* **1**(5688): 102–105.

Oetting, E. R. and F. Beauvais (1987). "Peer cluster theory, socialization characteristics, and adolescent drug use: A path analysis." *Journal of Counseling Psychology* **34**(2): 205.

Owen, D. (2018). *Personal Recollections of Drug Use 1964 to 2018.* A. Wilson. Unpublished.

Parker, H. (2000). "How young Britons obtain their drugs: Drugs transactions at the point of consumption." *Crime Prevention Studies* **11**: 59–82.

Pearson, J. (1985). *The Profession of Violence: The Rise and Fall of the Kray Twins*, originally published 1972. London, Panther Books.

Pharmaceutical Journal (1954). "Comment." *Pharmaceutical Journal.* London, Royal Pharmaceutical Society. **119**: 282.

Pharmaceutical Journal (1957). "Editorial." *Pharmaceutical Journal* **124**: 217–218.

Pharmaceutical Society (1965). "Theft of Drugs." *Pharmaceutical Journal* **198**(165): 428.

Pharmaceutical Society (1967). "Chemist shop burglaries." *Pharmaceutical Journal* (198): 428.

Plaice, E. (1967). "Drugs: CID hold sixty children." *Daily Mirror.* London.

Pleasants, R. E. (1954). "Letters." *Pharmaceutical Journal* **119**.

Rasmussen, N. (2006). Review: LIVES OF A BLOCKBUSTER DRUG. Reviewed Work: Interferon: The Science and Selling of a Miracle Drug by Toine Pieters. Minerva, Vol. 44, No. 2, pp. 229–234.

Rasmussen, N. (2009). *On Speed: From Benzedrine to Adderall.* New York, NYU Press.

Read, T. (1966). "Teenage drug clubs–by a headmaster." *Daily Mirror.* London.

Ruggiero, V. and N. South (1995). *Eurodrugs: Drug Use, Markets, and Trafficking in Europe.* London, Routledge.

Scott, P. D. and D. R. C. Willcox (1965). "Delinquency and the amphetamines." *British Journal of Psychiatry* **111**(478): 865–875.

Seddon, T. (2016). "Inventing drugs: A genealogy of a regulatory concept." *Journal of Law and Society* **43**(3): 393–415.

Sharpley, A. (1964). "Purple heart trip in Soho." *Evening Standard.* London.

Simmel, G. (1906). "The sociology of secrecy and of secret societies." *American Journal of Sociology* **11**(4): 441–498.

Special Correspondent (1964). "Surprise raids reduce Soho's youth problem." *Coventry Evening Telegraph*. Coventry: 8.

Staff Reporter (1964). "Action to stop purple heart evil: Mr Brooke had tour with police." *Birmingham Daily Post.* Birmingham: 1.

Taylor, B. (2019). *Burgling Chemist Shops and Selling Drugs.* A. Wilson.

Thornton, S. (1996). *Club Cultures: Music, Media, and Subcultural Capital.* London, Wesleyan University Press.

USA Congress (1972). *Amphetamine Legislation. Hearings Before the Subcommittee to Investigate Juvenile Delinquency.* S. C. o. t. Judiciary. Washington, Congress.

Walsh, P. (2018). *Drug War: The Secret History.* Lancashire: Milo Books Ltd.

Wilson, A. (1999). "Urban songlines: Subculture and identity on the 1970s Northern Soul Scene." Unpublished PhD Thesis. London, LSE.

Wilson, A. (2007). *Northern Soul: Music, Drugs and Subcultural Identity.* Cullompton, Willan.

Wilson, A. (2008). "Mixing the medicine: The unintended consequence of amphetamine control on the Northern soul scene." *The Internet Journal of Criminology.* Available at SSRN: https://ssrn.com/abstract=1339332

Wilson, A. (2019). "Searching for the subcultural heart of northern soul: From pillheads to shredded wheat." *Northern Soul.* S. Raine, T. Wall and N. Watchman-Smith (eds.). Sheffield, Equinox Publishing.

Young, J. (1971). *The Drugtakers: The Social Meaning of Drug Use.* London, Paladin.

3

LIFE STORIES OF JAMAICAN MEN INVOLVED IN THE UK DRUGS TRADE

Angie Heal

> … many of the stereotypes attached to those that deal in illicit street drugs are difficult to sustain for the vast majority of those who would be classified as drug dealers, whilst some such stereotypes are simply untrue. Although an attribution of evilness suggests the problem lies in individual pathology–they do the things they do because they are bad people (or in some versions the drugs turned them bad)–this attribution of evilness itself needs to be understood within a broader historical and contemporary context.
>
> *Coomber, 2006:2*

Introduction

Since the 1940s, many people have journeyed from Jamaica to the United Kingdom (UK) to seek new opportunities for themselves and their families; they hoped to obtain employment, income and a lifestyle that they could not achieve at home. Immigration 'push' factors (Thomas, 1973) like unemployment, low wages and poor housing, for example, meant they needed to go abroad to attain these goals. The UK was a natural destination for many because of the close ties between the two countries; Jamaica was a British colony until 1962, therefore its language, institutions and national administration systems came from the same roots. For some Jamaican men however, their journeys ended in a life of drugs supply, and ultimately prison.

The respondents in this research were involved in the UK drugs trade at a time when 'Yardie' dealers were seen as the latest 'folk devils', to which there was a 'moral panic' (Cohen, 1972).

DOI: 10.4324/9781351010245-5

> Societies appear to be subject, every now and then, to periods of moral panic. A condition, episode, person or group of persons emerges to become defined as a threat to societal values and interests.
>
> *Cohen, 1972, p. 28*

In regular speech, a 'yardie' is someone who is Jamaica-born living abroad or a recent arrival from Jamaica ('yard' means home in Patois). In written text, it generally refers to Jamaicans involved in drugs supply or other organised crime (Heal, 2015). The 'Yardie' legacy of violence, drugs and fast living has been significant and influential. They have been portrayed in film (e.g. Elba, 2018), books (including Headley 1992; Blake, 2004), games (Grand Theft Auto) and much music. Jamaican drug suppliers in London were some of the first to be involved in establishing out-of-town operations, in Aberdeen, for example (The Guardian, June 2003). What is now known as county lines operations (Home Office, 2017) is nothing new. Whilst the moral panic about 'Yardies' is largely over, the impact was so significant that it resulted in long-term law enforcement initiatives such as Trident[1] and changes in immigration policy.[2]

This chapter explores respondents' life stories – their trajectories and when, how and why they became criminalised – whilst contextualising their experiences within relevant literature. It is based on research completed for doctoral research and published in *Journeys into Drugs and Crime: Jamaican Men involved in the UK Drugs Trade* (Heal, 2015).

Jamaica context

Cocaine first arrived in Jamaica in about 1980 (Gunst, 1995; Sives, 2010). Cannabis had previously been the drug of choice, but Jamaica's geographical position between the producers and the coca-growing fields of South America to the end users in the United States and Europe was a key factor in the arrival of cocaine. Cocaine powder is made by stripping the active ingredient cocaine hydrochloride from the leaves of the coca bush and converted to liquid, then to a thick paste. The paste is then 'purified' and dried to form cocaine powder. Crack cocaine is the result of cooking cocaine powder with sodium bicarbonate or ammonia which, when smoked, gives a far more intense high than snorting powder. Cocaine powder is a relatively easy product to transport, first overland and then by boat.

Once the crack trade had been established in Jamaica, it enabled wealthy, violent and politically associated gangs to create new opportunities and markets. For some, this included moving abroad, and establishing themselves in the United States, Canada and England (Gunst, 1995). An excess of money, an increase in flight routes and few visa restrictions enabled easy travel between countries at that time. The global links for Jamaicans operating in the cannabis and cocaine trade had been established; they had developed a 'transnational criminal profile' (Sives, 2010: 133).

The present-day social, political, economic and cultural position of Jamaica is inextricably bound with the slave trade, when Britain was the main trader and financial beneficiary of the exploitation and abuse of hundreds of thousands of African slaves (Anti-Slavery International, undated). Pryce (1979, p. 67) notes: '... the contemporary misery and deprivations of the Jamaican masses derive from and are rooted in the history of colonialism and imperialism'. To this day 'narcotics trafficking, corruption, and related crime undermine the rule of law, democratic governance, economic growth, and the quality of life for all Jamaicans' (Home Office, 2018). High unemployment exacerbates the crime rate, including gang violence fuelled by the drug trade; it has one of the highest murder rates in the world (United Nations Office on Drugs and Crime, undated). As Gordon says,

> Caribbean people have death in their roots, in the fabric of their culture and in their connection to the spirit world. We've become so used to abandonment, losing people early and seeing death on a regular basis, that it's become a transitory part of life, rather than being the end.
>
> *Brinkhurst-Cuff, 2018, p. 204*

These factors all have a negative impact on economic growth, which is inevitably felt more deeply in the most socially and economically deprived areas of the country (Harriott, 2000).

Whilst the cocaine/crack cocaine trafficking routes between Caribbean and the UK are not now as important as they had been when the respondents in this research were active, at the time Jamaica was a key player (Bowling, 2010). In 2010 the International Narcotics Control Board estimated 40% of European cocaine came via the Caribbean, although by 2013 the importance of the region had declined significantly due to combined intensive action, including immigration policy changes, naval operations and law enforcement activities.

UK context

Until the early 1980s, most drugs markets in the UK were closed and drug sales were conducted away from the public eye (Edmunds et al., 1996). But the 1980s and 1990s witnessed an increase in the demand for heroin and an escalation in the number and geographical spread of local markets (Brain et al., 1998). It was, however, the result of an increase in crack cocaine supply in the 1990s that heroin and crack street selling in open markets became commonplace in many communities (Edmunds et al., 1996).

At the time, the arrival of crack cocaine was portrayed as the latest American trend for Britain to inherit. Exaggerated claims of cocaine's addictive nature ('one hit and you're hooked') were reported in the press (DrugWise, 1989). Britain was waiting for the 'explosion in crack cocaine use' as had happened in the US (Shapiro, 1993: 12), but a different pattern emerged which was a more gradual rise in the use and supply of crack. Until then, crack and heroin had mostly been used by two different sets of users – one seeking a high, the other something more tranquil. Another customer then emerged, one who liked to experience heroin and crack cocaine together, known as 'speedballing' (Home Affairs Committee, 2010). This has had a fundamental effect on UK drug markets, and the communities which have to host them. The physical, psychological and financial impacts of entrenched drug use and supply for the drug users themselves, their families and friends and their local communities remain, for many, overwhelming. They include petty and serious crime, antisocial behaviour, violence, intimidation, mental and physical ill health, the safety and well-being of children, family stress and breakdown, poverty, imprisonment, and poor quality and unstable accommodation and homelessness. At that time, the country was looking for 'others' to blame.

Hall and colleagues (2013) note the social construction of an association between mugging and black people, 'evidenced' by the police and the judiciary and reported by the press for the public – notions which were based on American experiences. A similar construction subsequently took place in relation to crack cocaine use and supply. UK drug specialists expressed concern at the time about how quickly associations were made between crack cocaine and black users and suppliers, despite the majority of users being white (Shapiro, 1993; Bean, 1993; Pearson et al., 1993). Pearson et al. noted that in one area of London – Lewisham – around 95% of those arrested were black (ibid). The response to the increase in crack cocaine availability was a repetition of the mugging 'crisis', ignoring the role that everyone not black played in its supply and casting all who were in the role of the evil dealer (Coomber, 2006).

The respondents

To find out about some of the men behind those media headlines and about whom there was no previous research, the study utilised life history and life course theoretical frameworks to aid understanding of the journeys each man had taken – from growing up in Jamaica to being imprisoned for drug-related offences in the UK. The research criteria were that respondents were male, had been born in Jamaica and were involved in the UK drugs trade. Jamaican women were excluded as other studies found the reasons for their involvement were usually different (including Fleetwood, 2011; Hibiscus Initiatives).

The fieldwork encountered significant challenges in interviewing willing and eligible respondents. Whilst it had been anticipated it would not be easy to access a group with a reputation of having ambivalent relationships with authorities, it was harder than expected. As well as there being a limited number of men willing to participate who did not get deported or moved prisons before interview, there were also significant difficulties in negotiating different prison and national administration systems. The final sample group was therefore small; it constituted eight men, aged 23 to 67 years old. At their initial interview, seven were serving prison sentences, ranging from 15 months to 9 years; one was on parole. Some respondents participated in more than one interview, bringing the total number to 20. Below is a profile of each man, as at first interview, with a given pseudonym; their identities have been protected.

Christopher (23 years old) had been in the UK for 5 years and in prison for 18 months. He was serving a 5-year sentence for supplying heroin and crack cocaine as a street-level retailer. He grew up in Kingston; his father left home when he was six, leaving his mother to bring him up with his two sisters and running the family business. Christopher initially came to London to study but found living in the capital too expensive, so he moved north to stay with a family member. He overstayed his visa so therefore became an illegal immigrant, but by then he had two children. He worked as a labourer, but when the business closed, he was offered a 'job' by a friend of his employer selling drugs which he felt he had little option but to take. He sold drugs from a house for six months before he was arrested. He said he had never been in trouble with the police before, either in Jamaica or in the UK.

Steadman (35 years old) was serving a 5-year sentence for grievous bodily harm (GBH); he was also serving a further one year from a previous sentence (conspiracy to supply Class A drugs) for which he was on licence at the time of the GBH offence. He grew up in poverty in Kingston; his father left when he was five, but he had a good relationship with his mother, stepfather and sister. He said that he had no previous history of involvement in drugs and no criminal record in Jamaica and that he had always worked. As for many though, he got caught up in gang violence in Jamaica; he had injuries as a result of a shooting that also killed his girlfriend. He became a significant figure in the drugs trade in the UK, including a retail seller of cannabis, heroin and crack, wholesale seller of crack cocaine, a crack cocaine cook and cocaine importer. He also admitted his involvement in firearms offences, violence and people smuggling.

Dwight (aged 48) came to England when he was 10. He had been brought up by male relatives in rural Jamaica, when his mother and stepfather emigrated to the UK. He was serving a 15-month sentence for cultivating cannabis, for which he also had numerous other convictions. Dwight had been involved in crime since his early teens and had spent much of his life in prison. He had many previous convictions including violence, drugs and sexual offences, including rape. In addition to being a grower of cannabis he was also a street-level retailer.

Devon (aged 35) had grown up in a large family in Kingston. He said he had always worked in the business and retail sectors in Jamaica. He had no previous criminal record, but he also got caught up in gang violence in Kingston. He was serving a 9-year sentence for intent to supply cocaine, which was reduced to 7 years on appeal. He had first come to the UK legally with his brother as their lives were under threat, but were both subsequently deported due to his brother's involvement in a shooting. Devon left Kingston a second time following another attempt on his life, using a false passport. His brother was subsequently murdered. He felt he had no option but to commit the offence of drugs supply as he had to repay the cost of the passport. He lived with a cousin in the north of England until he was arrested. He did painting, decorating and DIY work to earn money to live. Whilst in prison he unsuccessfully applied for asylum on humanitarian grounds, as he believed his life was in danger if he returned to Jamaica.

Velmore (aged 67) was on licence after serving half of his 4-year sentence for cocaine importation. He thought he was bringing cannabis into the country for personal use, as he had done in the past, but was duped into bringing cocaine instead. He grew up in rural Jamaica in extreme poverty with his parents – the youngest of nine children. Velmore came to England in the early 1950s to seek work, aged 20; he was part of the Windrush generation (Phillips and Phillips, 1998). He had a number of different labouring jobs over a 20-year period before retiring due to ill health.

Patrick (aged 27) was serving a 6-year sentence for supplying heroin and crack cocaine. He said he had not previously been involved in criminality, either in the UK or in Jamaica. He grew up in Kingston; his father left the family when he was a teenager. As a result, his family lost their home and had significant financial problems. He later reunited with his father and worked with him in construction. He came to the UK aged 21, to join his English girlfriend. He lived with her and their child, but he was unable to get employment, legal or otherwise, and was introduced to selling drugs by friends.

Claude (aged 57) was serving a 7-year sentence for intent to supply crack cocaine. He had come to the UK in 1967 aged 17 to join his parents, who had emigrated some years earlier. He had been brought up by his grandmother in rural Jamaica, in relative financial comfort. He said he had a good employment record in the UK, working in factories before running his own small businesses but said he became greedy when persuaded by others to sell crack cocaine.

Marlon (aged 35) had been in the UK for 10 years. He was serving a 7-year sentence for blackmail, firearms offences and kidnap; a drug dealer who worked for him had failed to repay a debt. He said he had grown up 'in the ghetto' in Kingston; he did not know his father. Marlon was the only respondent who admitted prior involvement in supplying drugs before coming to England and immediately on arrival. He said he was part of a gang importing cocaine from the Caribbean via cruise ships. Despite being an illegal immigrant from the point of arrival, he said he was trained in health care in the UK, presumably on false documents.

These men, therefore, constituted the research sample. This work is indebted to them, to which they enthusiastically gave their time and their life stories.

As will be demonstrated the respondents had different roles in the drugs markets, some having more than one. May et al.'s (2007) and Matrix's (2007) definitions are used to analyse their involvement but are not always a good fit; it can be difficult to accurately categorise dealers due to their complex circumstances.

Getting involved in selling drugs

As with any activity, legal or otherwise, there is a process of initial engagement. May et al. (2000) and Matrix (2007) both noted the influence of friends and sometimes family in becoming involved in selling drugs; due to the illegal nature of the 'work', people must already be known or be recommended by a trusted other. Sandberg and Pedersen (2009) analysed the trajectories of dealers, many of who were African and Middle Eastern immigrants, to the River street market in Oslo. They noted that economic and social motives were usually the reason why their subjects became involved in drugs supply, but that the River also offered a scene of friendship and membership of a hidden society with the added attraction of excitement and easy money.

Some of the respondents in this research admitted that they were motivated solely by making money. Claude said he was tempted by a suggestion that he could make more money by selling crack cocaine than working in his business.

> I was selling crack cocaine and I get catch… I get into selling it through friends of friends of friends. … Life was sweet and then I make a mistake.

Another dealer/seller (May et al., 2007), Patrick, had been living in England for six months before becoming involved in drug dealing. He said he got to know a couple of other Jamaican men already involved in drug supply:

> Most of them used to go there [a house] to get their hair plaited were drug dealers. There were a few black English lads went there as well. I get talking to JJ and another guy. … I see JJ one day. I say just give me something to sell. But he say you can't do it like that, the police will jump on you straight away. So I start to roll with them. I used to hang out and observe what they do.

Steadman decided to become a dealer/seller, having been told about selling drugs by someone he met whilst on remand in prison for attempted murder soon after he arrived in the UK. Although he had a very 'successful' career – with over £1m confiscated via a Proceeds of Crime Act order, he said he had not intended to get involved in crime when he came to England. He was resolute that if he had been legally able to work, he would have easily found employment and would not have sold drugs in order to survive (see also Paoli, 2000).

> I was an innocent guy until I come to this country. Weed, ganga was all I saw in Jamaica. … When I start to sell drugs…my friend give me a hundred pounds. I go and buy half ounce weed and some bags. And I go and wrap up that half ounce weed and I go and start to sell that. When I start to sell that weed I was brave–right outside the Crown Court. That's where I sell my weed from. The reason why…. 'cos the police are not going to expect you to sell it from the Crown Court.
>
> *(Steadman)*

Marlon, the only man involved in the drugs trade prior to arriving in the UK was also a dealer/seller. Although he did not say how he first became involved, he said he was charged with importation offences via cruise ships in the Caribbean. He did work in the UK, however, so his decision to migrate to the UK may not have necessarily been about selling drugs and making money.

> My first night in England I stopped with friends in London. I went to this house and there was a Luger[3] on the table and a kilo of crack they were cutting up into £20 stones. I stayed there for my first few days; I didn't leave the house to start.

Devon had a very short and reluctant position in the drugs market.

> When I was in Jamaica and needed to get out quickly, a man came to offer me a passport. But I didn't have no money. He played the Good Samaritan. But I had to transport drugs for him. He put them in a clothes bag, in a shoe box. I never knew who would meet me when I got there. I did it twice in between [southern UK city] and [northern UK city]. Police said they got information. I was grassed up. I was never really in the drugs scene.

Whilst he fits the definition of a transporter/runner, someone who 'transports drugs between locations and actors' (Matrix, 2007: 12), he saw himself very much as a victim of tragic circumstances; a law-abiding man by nature who did not want to get involved in the drugs trade.

Velmore was a user/dealer (May et al., 2007) who imported cannabis, albeit at a very low level. He admitted that he had occasionally imported cannabis from Jamaica to the UK over a period of 20 years, when he returned home. He said it was for personal use for him and his friends, and he usually brought it through Customs in his hand luggage. He was a not-for-profit sole operator, which neither Matrix's nor May et al.'s classifications include.

> This last time now, I get set up. It was 10 oz of weed I was looking after bringing. … This guy ask me if I need any help. When I take my thing back, I just put it in my hand luggage. He say 'no, put it in your shoes'. So he take my shoes and it's two days before he come back with the shoes. It was all right and he gave me a bottle of rum and a packet of cigarettes, to give to his friend Bob in England. I say 'who is Bob, cos a lot of my friends in England they have a pet name'. 'Bob know me', he said. Anyway when I reach at Custom, they take me and they search me. They take the shoes and they come back and say 'it's cocaine '. I say Can I see it?' and they say 'No' and I say 'Cos it's supposed to be ganga'.
>
> *(Velmore)*

Whilst Dwight did not say about how he started selling cannabis, he said 'smoking'; it was a fundamental part of his Rastafarian belief. His flat where he was growing it was raided by the police; he was serving a sentence for cultivation.

This is a specialist role (Matrix, 2007). He had numerous cannabis-related offences, including intent to supply.

Christopher said his initial involvement in drug supply, as a dealer/seller, was solely to support his family. He became a user/dealer, however, as unlimited access to crack cocaine was too tempting (see Morgan's chapter in this volume on user-dealers also). He had not sold drugs previously. Within six months he was arrested for supplying crack cocaine and heroin, twice unwittingly selling to undercover police officers. Christopher was very much of the opinion that his boss had known of his difficult situation and took advantage.

An emerging typology

In addition to analysing the Jamaican respondents' roles in the markets, this research noted a new typology based on the reasons for their involvement. As the number of respondents was low, in some sub-categories there is only one respondent. It would be appropriate, therefore, to describe this typology as 'emerging' rather than definitive. Analysis of interview data suggested the emergence of four types of drug dealer: willing, reluctant, coerced and duped.

A willing drug dealer is someone who knows what he/she was doing, is an eager participant and willingly enters into the role. This was the largest category, involving five of the eight respondents (Marlon, Steadman, Patrick, Dwight and Claude). A reluctant drug dealer is someone who does not want to get involved in selling drugs but did not make much attempt to avoid doing so and therefore was complicit in the activity (Christopher). A coerced drug dealer is someone who is threatened with violence into supplying drugs and therefore feels they have no option but to acquiesce (Devon). Finally, the duped drug dealer is someone who is set up to carry drugs for another. They may either be completely unaware that they are carrying drugs or think they are carrying drugs of a lower classification (Velmore).

The reluctant, coerced and duped categories debunk the 'contemporary depictions of the drug dealer … of particularly evil, amoral individuals' (Coomber, 2006, p. 1). Even Steadman and Patrick, categorised as willing dealers, said they had no legitimate redress to money and felt they had no other options than to sell drugs.

Learning the trade

Whatever their involvement, all of the respondents had to learn their trade. Becker (1963) outlines the role of the experienced cannabis user in initiating the novice in how to get the most effective smoking experience, whilst minimising the possibility of side effects. Data analysis revealed a similar process for trainee drug dealers. Apart from Marlon, none of the respondents had prior involvement in drug supply before living in the UK; the majority said they had not even seen Class A drugs and some had even heard of them before. For those with such inexperience, a process of initiation was necessary in order to become proficient.

Patrick described how he served his apprenticeship:

> They used to make me wrap out, with a black scale and a razor. I used to take out the 'cheese' [crack] and wrap it into point 4, ½ teenths[4], teenths, and eighth. So cutting it and wrapping it was my job. I used to take the cling film, tear off a strip, wrap the rock in it and then use a lighter to heat it so that it would seal it up. JJ say some people bring it in their mouths so that the police couldn't get it, but you have to be able to talk with it in your mouth so the police don't suspect it if they stop and talk to you. So they make me practice with peanuts in my mouth! But then someone say don't put it in your mouth 'cos saliva has DNA and if they get hold of it they can test it for your DNA.

He was clearly being instructed not only in the practicalities of how to cut, weigh and wrap street deals of crack cocaine, but also about arrest and conviction risk reduction strategies. He described the open market in which he was selling as well as how to convert cocaine powder to crack cocaine.

> I used to sell it on the line up in …. There would be about 6 of us. We would take it in turns on the line. I would buy ½ oz and pay it back when I'd sold it. I just make up a name and tell it to them (buyers)… So I just start there, giving out my number to lots of people. Then my phone start to ring, ring, ring. All the time it was ringing. I arrange where to meet them …. CID, they were driving past every day. We had to run then….
>
> JJ got this link from outside, from [northern city]. We were getting ½ ki [kilogramme] or a ki of cocaine from there. They wanted a man to distribute it. That was me. The guy would bring the drugs. They had a value of £25,000. He would say give me 20 grand, and so 5 grand would be my own. He would just bring it in a shopping bag. I got into cooking it up. The cocaine come in like a coconut oil bottle. You pour it into a tray with the bicarb and put it in a tray like you put in the oven. To every ounce of coke you put ½ oz bicarb and you get nearly 3 oz of crack. Just put it in the microwave, use defrost, not too much heat. Then you get it out and whip it with a whisk and put it in again. Then you can get it out, cool it and then turn the tray upside down and bang it to get the crack out. It only take 5 or 6 minutes to cook.

Christopher was also a 'retailer' (Matrix, 2007), to whom someone had to show him the ropes:

> Sometimes there were two of us selling drugs from the house. D showed me what to do to start with.

Once he had learnt how to sell, like any other job, there were required routines to which he had to adhere:

> Bigman's mobile was ringing all the time. He left me with 20 deals at a time to sell. Users would ring Bigman and he would tell them where to go to meet me. Then he'd then tell me where to go to meet them.... I was selling about 10 Bs [heroin] and 10 Ws [crack] at a time. I did this about 7 or 8 times a day. When I got down to my last 5, I'd have to ring Bigman who would bring me more.

Once dealers have learnt the ropes and have gained experience, like other jobs they can instruct others, as this quote from Steadman demonstrates:

> Once you have the money to buy the crack you can go and get it like that and start to sell it. You just have to know how to do your cutting. Or if you get the powder, you got to know how to cook it. You got to know how to cook it 'cos it you don't you could lose everything. That's a part of me, 'cos I used to teach people. Somebody teach me and then I teach other people.

He was a 'wholesaler' at international, national or regional levels, as well as a 'mixer' (Matrix, 2007).

The above quotes from the respondents suggest, therefore, that the majority became criminalised in the UK as a direct result of learning from others already embroiled in drugs supply.

Progressing a career in drugs sales

Whilst there is research related to drug using careers (e.g. Parker et al., 1998; Brain et al., 1998), there is little evidence about drug dealing careers; May et al. (2005: 18) state: 'little is known about the "careers" of those who sell drugs at a local level'. Some of the respondents in this research talked about their increasing levels of involvement.

Steadman described how he purposefully moved from selling cannabis to 'hard drugs'.

> So I moved from the weed now. I met a friend, and he said we could start a business selling more drugs and he was the one who bring me to the hard drugs. I buy half ounce of hard drugs and give him to wrap up and watch him wrap it up and then start to sell the crack. So I start to sell half ounce of crack, I cut it and sell from there. I got a guy, he start to lay me on by giving me an ounce and I pay him back his money. So what I used to do is he charge me £1,000 an ounce. I used to cut it, sell it, and give him his £1,000. The profits left were for myself. So I start to build up myself until I used to buy ounces from him instead of half, so I end up taking bigger amounts until I end up being one of the big guys. I got loads of people work for me. Not runners, but sometimes if I'm out of town, if I go and

> cool at a woman house, somebody used to take my phone and work it. Or I'd phone somebody to drop off that stuff for me.

Here Steadman demonstrates how he moved from retailer to wholesaler, whilst also being a mixer/preparer (Matrix, 2007). He was also the boss, in charge of operations and paying wages. He also operated across international borders, noting his career progression and an increase in profits:

> Now, because I get so big at it I start to get it from outta town because I'm buying big. Half ki, 9 bar [9 ounces], or a ki, sometimes I might fly abroad and it come from abroad cos it cheap. You go to Holland and you pay a little bit of money and three grand and you get set up. A couple of thousand pound and you can come out of it with seven grand easy.
>
> *Steadman*

Marlon also described the different roles that he had. In the Caribbean, he was an international wholesaler; in the UK he was involved in retail sales. His quote above described his first night in the country spent at a friend's house cutting up crack for retail sales. He said he also ran a crack house, in charge of the closed market operation and employing 'staff'.

Steadman was clearly still involved in the sale of drugs whilst in prison, as he admitted to being caught with £1,000 of heroin. For this offence he served four weeks on the segregation wing and was then immediately moved to another prison.

Level of involvement in the UK drugs trade

Apart from Christopher and Devon, the other respondents had been involved at some level over significant periods of time – ranging from 15 months to 30 years. Their level of engagement and positions in drugs markets did vary though; they were not constant.

The UN Convention against Transnational Organized Crime defines organised crime as committed by a structured group of three or more persons, existing for a period of time and acting together with the aim of committing one or more serious crimes, which would warrant prison sentences of at least four years (United Nations Office of Drugs and Crime, 2004). Murji (2007, p. 786), however, has a simpler definition:

> Crime and drugs, however chaotic they may at times seem, have to be organized in the most basic sense that two or more parties have to connect to engage in some form of transaction. Anything beyond this simple dyad … requires a further degree of coordination and organisation.

Patrick agreed:

> Jamaicans aren't organised criminals. You just know people. It's who you know. Jamaicans don't own airplanes and boats and stuff.

Most respondents in this research were reticent to discuss the others with whom they worked, which makes analysis of whether they could be categorised as organised criminals difficult. Some would undoubtedly be assessed by law enforcement agencies as serious and organised criminals, as the level of their involvement ensured they were targets for county-wide, regional and sometimes national and international level criminal investigations. This is evidenced by their convictions and length of sentences. Yet data analysis suggests that their criminal networks were much more fluid and that they may not have been regularly reliant on at least another two operators to conduct business; the number of participants varied according to the job in hand.

Making money

May et al. (2005) averaged the weekly wage of the dealers in their research to be £7,500 (between £900 and £20,000); for runners it was £450 (£140–4,000; ibid). Not all the respondents in this research, however, gained financially. Velmore, importing cannabis in his hand luggage for personal use, made no money. Devon, who had to transport drugs in return for a false passport, did not receive any actual cash. However, other respondents were, at times, making money from selling drugs.

> He paid me about £100 a day, but sometimes I'd manage to keep about another £300–400. I was also smoking about £60, or about a gram of crack a day. In all I was selling about £4,000 crack and heroin a day for Bigman.
>
> *Christopher*

> I'd been dealing for about 15 months. I made about £100,000 in that time.
>
> *Patrick*

> I was selling over £1,000 of crack a day there. (Marlon)
>
> Sometimes I used to make £1,000 in half an hour, selling crack cocaine ...... Drugs is an up and down thing. In one week I could made £5,000–£10,000 or £200-£400 if I'm not working hard.
>
> *Steadman*

> I was selling about 2oz of crack a day; about £15,000 a week.
>
> *Claude*

Some respondents also used other methods to make money, using innovative if sometimes risky strategies over straightforward supply.

> One time in London, we rob these African guys of three kilos of crack. One was a big black African guy in slippers. We'd planned to do it, but when they arrive I was really worried as he was so big and the gun I had had little bullets. They weren't gonna do him any damage. The big man said it was a nice sunny day to do business. We had stuffed a case with paper to make it look like money. We got away with it.
>
> *Marlon*

> The phone keep ringing 'til the battery dead. Later, I rent my phone to a friend. I was just collecting off the phone. I get £1,000 every 3 or 4 days for renting the phone.
>
> *Patrick*

Patrick's phone, containing customers' contacts, was clearly a valuable commodity. Neither of these approaches fit within any of the Matrix's (2007) or May et al.'s (2007) definitions.

Because of the profits the authorities believed they had made, Claude and Steadman both had Confiscation Orders (Proceeds of Crime Act, 2002). This forces them to repay the amount they were calculated to have benefitted from the supply of drugs. Steadman stated that he had over £1m taken from him, including houses, cars and cash. The police also track money sent abroad:

> It was over £100,000 .... They want me to make them a deal. But I ain't got the any money to make them a deal .... I had money in Jamaica but they found it.
>
> *Claude*

Whilst clearly some respondents making money, not everyone involved complies with the myths of drug dealers earning vast sums of money (Coomber, 2006, p. 157).

Involvement in other crimes

There was a mixed picture in relation to respondents' convictions for other offences. Christopher, Patrick and Devon each had one conviction for drugs supply, for which they were serving a sentence. Velmore and Claude had previous convictions for cannabis: possession with intent to supply and importation. There was no evidence at interview that any of these men had been involved in any other crimes. The other three respondents had quite different histories.

> I got charged with murder. But I got off. I was just in the wrong place at the wrong time.
>
> *Marlon*

> I'd already done nine months on remand for attempt murder. Then it was changed to Section 18 [wounding] and then the judge directed the jury to find me not guilty....
>
> *Dwight*

Following a fight in a bar, Steadman was remanded for a year for attempted murder before the case was dismissed. He was later convicted of grievous bodily harm, for which he received a five and a half year sentence.

Marlon described how he was convicted of blackmail, firearms and kidnap offences:

> I had been selling a kilo of crack to this guy to sell. But he owed me money, he was smoking too much of it himself and not selling enough. So I call him up and tell him I have ½ a ki for him to come and pick up. When he arrived, I held a gun to his head, made him strip his clothes off and held him hostage, demanding money. When the guy got out, he called the police and I was prosecuted.

In addition to drugs offences, Dwight had convictions for burglary, shop lifting, robbery, indecent assault and assault of police officers. He said in the interview that he had also previously served a 7-year sentence for rape and after the fieldwork period was convicted for two historical rapes.

Steadman also admitted to organising people smuggling:

> If you have a family abroad and you say 'I have a sister, mother, brother', if I can see a way to help you I will do it. 'Cos I know it is hard, 'cos of my background and where I come from, I know it is hard sometime in certain countries. I will help them. And I used to do a lot of that. When they come over I used to get documents so they could get jobs. I would put them up too. I had an empty house, where if I kick off with my woman that's where I used to go to sleep. So I used to put them up there. Loads of my friends who come from Jamaica I used to put them up in my own house, until them foot can touch the ground and they on their own way. Or they find a woman or something.

Again, there is a mixed picture in relation to respondents' involvement in violence and other crimes, with the majority of them debunking the myth of the violent drug dealer (Coomber, 2006).

Respondents' outcomes

The National Probation Service (NPS) provided follow-up data about the participants at the end of their sentence, from the Case Recording and Management System. Internet searches were also conducted to see if additional information could be gleaned regarding their post-interview trajectories.

Christopher said in the interview that he wanted to return to Jamaica and work again in the family business. He accepted deportation via the Early Release Scheme (HM Prison Service, 2005). Steadman was also deported at the end of his prison sentence, which he fought against but lost but then returned to England illegally. He was arrested the following year, held in a detention centre and again deported.

Dwight was convicted of the two historical rapes two years after he was released from prison and sentenced to 15 years. Velmore was interviewed whilst he was already out on parole. He was supervised on licence by NPS for one year and then granted permission by the Home Office to return to Jamaica permanently, having lived in England for 40 years.

Devon lost his application for asylum on humanitarian grounds. He was sent to a deportation centre at the end of his sentence, from where he was deported. Patrick was also deported at the end of his sentence. Claude was granted parole during the fieldwork period; he was not charged with any further offences; he also returned to Jamaica to live. Marlon was deported to Jamaica at the end of his sentence. He then moved to America, where he was subsequently found guilty of immigration offences and sentenced to 18 months in prison. Anecdotal information suggests that Claude and Velmore have subsequently died.

For those who were deported or returned home voluntarily, what awaited them in Jamaica is unclear. Some of the respondents had only been away for a few years and may have found it easier to re-integrate back into Jamaican life, with their families and friends. Others had been in the UK for many years and might have found it harder to settle back into a country where places and people had changed since they left – with friends and family members having moved away, died or been killed. The majority of respondents had children in the UK who they had to leave behind, some of whom were quite young. Unless the children could afford to visit them in Jamaica, future contact would only be via phone. Steadman and Devon realistically faced possible further attempts on their lives. Feuds have long memories; just because they have been out of sight from their enemies for years does not mean that they would be safe when they returned to Jamaica.

Conclusion

This chapter outlines how a small number of Jamaican men operated in the UK drugs trade. Whilst this research does not necessarily debunk all the myths of drug dealers, it demonstrates they do not all fit the stereotypes of being violent, greedy and amoral (Coomber, 2006); it is a much more mixed picture. The research gives the men's lives context and provides the opportunity for them to narrate their own stories. It aids understanding of their life stories, from growing up in Jamaica to serving prison sentences in the UK for drugs supply and related offences. It outlines how their lives in the UK were significantly affected by economic, social and immigration policy – a landscape which often changed during the time they lived in the UK and continues to do so. Whilst interviews conducted for this research significantly predated the Windrush scandal (Guardian, 2018), immigration policy clearly impacted their lives and post-release outcomes.

For the majority, the length of time and the level of drugs supply at which they had been operating were significant, yet the number of offences for which they had been convicted was relatively few. This suggests that, overall, the odds on their ability to evade law enforcement were in their favour – for some time at least – and that for those with no other recourse to money the rewards outweighed the risks of arrest. Most of the respondents had suffered some degree of social and/or economic marginalisation, in Jamaica, the UK or both countries. For those with legitimate employment opportunities – Claude, Dwight and Velmore – it may be that as a result, they felt they had little to lose and at the time the risk may have seemed worth it. Christopher, Patrick and Steadman believed that no legitimate options were available to them. They argued that it was employment-related visa restrictions that forced them into selling drugs. Whilst some may purport that the respondents could have made other choices, it could also be said that their situation was a result of constructed criminalisation through the implementation of immigration policy. With Marlon the picture was less clear, and Devon's experience did not fit either scenario.

All of the respondents said they came to the UK looking for an improved way of life – whatever that meant to them – and had planned to work or study in order to achieve their goals. The data therefore suggests the majority of them did not migrate with the express intent of getting involved in the UK drugs trade, which challenges their media image. Whatever their initial goals, all potential prospects ended with their involvement in the drugs trade and their subsequent imprisonment.

Notes

1 Trident – formerly known as Operation Trident, a long running Metropolitan Police operation targeting drug-related gun crime within the black community (BBC Online News, May 2013).
2 Legislative changes in 2003 to immigration policy to curb entry to those suspected of being a threat to the UK (House of Commons, 2003).
3 A Luger is a pistol.
4 A teenth is a drug using term for a sixteenth of an ounce.

References

Anti-Slavery International. Recovered Histories www.recoveredhistories.org/index.php [Accessed 27 October 2018].

BBC Online News 13 May 2013 The Met's Trident unit loses its gun murders brief, www.bbc.co.uk/news/uk-england-london-21773275 [Accessed 14 December 2018].

Bean, P. (1993) Cocaine and crack; the promotion of an epidemic. In Bean, P. (ed.), *Cocaine and Crack: Use and Supply*, MacMillan: Basingstoke, pp. 59–75.

Becker, H. (1963) *Outsiders: Studies in the Sociology of Deviance*, Free Press: New York.

Blake, D. (2004) *The Shower Posse: The Most Notorious Jamaican Crime Organization*, Diamond Publishing: Brentford.

Bowling, B. (2010) *Policing the Caribbean*, Oxford University Press: Oxford.

Brain, K., Parker, H., and Bottomley, T. (1998) *Evolving Crack Cocaine Careers: New Users and Quitters and Long Term Combination Drug Users in NW England*, University of Manchester: Manchester.

Cohen, S. (1972) *Folk Devils and Moral Panics*, MacGibbon and Kee: London.

Coomber, R. (2006) *Pusher Myths: Re-Situating the Drug Dealer*, Free Association Books: London.

Drugwise. (1989) *Crack Myths and Realities in the UK*. www.drugwise.org.uk/wp-content/uploads/Crack-myths-and-realities.pdf [Accessed 14 December 2018].

Elba, I. (2018) *Yardie* StudioCanal.

Edmunds, M., Hough, M., and Urquia, E. (1996) *Tackling Local Drugs Markets*, Police Research Group Crime Detection and Prevention Series: London.

Fleetwood, J. (2011) Five kilos: Penalties and practice in the international cocaine trade. *British Journal of Criminology* 51, 375–393.

Gordon, N. (2018) Nine night in Brinkhurst-Cuff (Ed). *Mother County: Real Stories of the Windrush Children*, Headline Publishing Group: Croydon, pp. 203–216.

Grand Theft Auto Gaming. Yardies, www.gtagaming.com/gta-united-gang-pack-f3033.html [Accessed 14 December 2018].

Gunst, L. (1995) *Born Fi' Dead: A Journey through the Yardie Underworld*, Canongate Books: London.

Hall, S., Critcher, C., Jefferson, T., Clarke, J., and Roberts, B. (2013) *Policing the Crisis: Mugging, the State and Law and Order*. MacMillan: Basingstoke.

Harriott, A. (2000) *Understanding the Jamaican Crime Problem: Peace Building and Community Action*. Kingston, Department of Government, University of West Indies.

Headley, V. (1994) Yardie. X Press: London.

Heal, A. (2015) *Journeys into Drugs and Crime: Jamaican Men involved in the UK Drugs Trade* Palgrave: Basingstoke.

Hibiscus Initiatives. http://hibiscusinitiatives.org.uk/index.php/project/advocacy-prison/ [Accessed 14 December 2018].

HM Prison Service. (2005) Prison Order 6000: Parole Release and Recall. www.justice.gov.uk/downloads/offenders/psipso/pso/pso-6000.pdf [Accessed 14 December 2018].

Home Affairs Committee. (2010) The cocaine trade. House of Commons: London https://publications.parliament.uk/pa/cm200910/cmselect/cmhaff/74/7402.htm [Accessed 14 December 2018].

Home Office. (2017) Criminal exploitation of children and vulnerable adults: County lines. www.gov.uk/government/publications/criminal-exploitation-of-children-and-vulnerable-adults-county-lines [Accessed 27 October 2018].

Home Office. (2018) Country policy and information note–Jamaica: Background information, including actors of protection, and internal relocation https://assets.publishing.service.gov.uk/government/uploads/system/uploads/attachment_data/file/685577/Jamaica_-_Background_-_CPIN_-_v2.0__March_2018_.pdf [Accessed 27 October 2018].

House of Commons. (2003) Statement of changes in immigration rules. www.official-documents.gov.uk/document/hc0203/hc01/0180/0180.pdf [Accessed 14 December 2018].

Matrix Knowledge Group. (2007) *The Illicit Drug Trade in the United Kingdom*, Home Office Online Report 20/07. http://webarchive.nationalarchives.gov.uk/20110218135832/http://rds.homeoffice.gov.uk/rds/pdfs07/rdsolr2007.pdf [Accessed 14 December 2018].

May, T., Harocopos, A., Turnbull, P., and Hough, M. (2000) *Serving Up: Impact of Low Level Police Enforcement on Drug Markets*, Home Office Police Research Series Paper 133. London.

May, T., Duffy, M., Few, B., and Hough, M. (2005) *Understanding Drug Selling in Communities*, Joseph Rowntree Foundation. www.academia.edu/32141098/Understanding_Drug_Selling_in_Local_Communities [Accessed 14 December 2018].

Murji, K. (2007) Hierarchies, markets and networks: Ethnicity/race and drug distribution. *Journal of Drug Issues* 37, 4, 781–804.

Paoli, L. (2000) Pilot project to describe and analyse local drug markets–First phase final report: Illegal drug markets in Frankfurt and Milan. EMCDDA: Lisbon.

Pearson, G., Mirza, H., and Phillips, S. (1993) Cocaine in context: Findings from a South London inner-city drug survey. In Bean, P. (ed.) *Cocaine and Crack: Use and Supply*, MacMillan: Basingstoke, 99–129.

Phillips, M., and Phillips, T. (1998) *Windrush: The Irresistible Rise of Multi-Racial Britain*. Harper Collins: London.

Proceeds of Crime Act 2002 www.legislation.gov.uk/ukpga/2002/29/contents [Accessed 14 December 2018].

Pryce, K. (1979) *Endless Pressure: The Study of West-Indian Lifestyles in Britain*. Penguin: Harmonsworth.

Sandberg, S., and Pedersen, W. (2009) *Street Capital: Black Cannabis Dealers in a White Welfare State*. Policy Press: Bristol.

Shapiro, H. (1993) Where does all the snow go?–the prevalence and pattern of cocaine and crack use in Britain. In Bean, P. (ed.), *Cocaine and Crack: Supply and Use*, MacMillan: Basingstoke, 11–28.

Sives, A. (2010) *Elections, Violence and the Democratic Process in Jamaica 1944–2007*, Ian Randle Publishers: Kingston.

The Guardian (14 June 2003) *Euan's story: Caught in the Yardies' web of crack and violence–in Aberdeen*. www.theguardian.com/uk/2003/jun/14/ukcrime.drugsandalcohol [Accessed 27 October 2018].

The Guardian. (December 2018) *The Windrush Scandal*, www.theguardian.com/uk-news/windrush-scandal [Accessed 14 December 2018].

Thomas, B. (1973) *Migration and Economic Growth: A Study of Great Britain and the Atlantic Economy*. Cambridge University Press: London.

United Nations Office on Drugs and Crime. (2004) *United Nations Convention against Transnational Organised Crime and the Protocols Thereto*, www.unodc.org/documents/treaties/UNTOC/Publications/TOC%20Convention/TOCebook-e.pdf [Accessed 14 December 2018].

United Nations Office on Drugs and Crime. (n.d.) *Intentional Homicide Victims* https://dataunodc.un.org/crime/intentional-homicide-victims [Accessed 28 October 2018].

4

ENTREPRENEURS

Just taking care of business, the drug business

Tammy C. Ayres and James Treadwell

Introduction

This chapter revisits our earlier work on drug supply among criminal entrepreneurs by catching up with some old respondents, as well as introducing some new, and drawing on empirical field data we have gathered with men who have entered the illicit drugs trade, often due to receding legitimate opportunities or to supplement their no longer acceptable incomes (Ayres and Treadwell, 2012; Treadwell and Ayres, 2014; Salinis' chapter in this volume). In keeping with much of the research in this area (see Coomber, 2006), the authors acknowledge that drug markets are for the most part not violent. However, this chapter provides a slightly different perspective, focusing more closely on those familiar with violence linked to drug supply. In recent years the dominant criminological cannon on drugs has considered and focused on the footprint of quite normalized 'social supply', as it has become known (see Moyle's chapter in this volume). However, such framing risks overlooking the more negative, violent and harmful practices, which while no means dominant are an important facet of illicit enterprise generally (Hobbs, 2013).

At a time when criminology seeks to connect criminal commerce and organised crime with drugs and drug markets almost exclusively within a framework that recognizes exploitation, vulnerability and what is now commonly known as 'county lines' (see Coomber and Moyles, 2018; see Andell's chapter in this volume), or through problematic narratives of gangs (see Treadwell and Kelly's chapter in this volume), this chapter serves to provide a rebalancing act by considering an alternative. Principles such as market dominance, outsourcing, risk management and various other logics of business and enterprise have long been associated with some illicit drug markets and are common in discussion on the transnational trade. Yet at a more everyday national level, criminal violence,

DOI: 10.4324/9781351010245-6

both as a regulatory logic and an organizing principle, is needed. Threat, intimidation, exploitation, manipulation and coercion are hardly just the stuff of criminal enterprise; violence has long been an established practice both within and outside criminal networks. This is despite the fact that comparatively little academic research exists about the nature and role of violence and enforcement in criminal markets (Rahman et al., 2020). In fact, there is a shortage of academic literature that seeks to apply theories of violence to illicit drug markets, and what there is, is largely descriptive or journalistic in style, providing sensationalist and often highly personal accounts of ferociously violent drug markets (e.g. Farrell, 2020; Grillo, 2017; Woods and Rafaeli, 2019).

The data presented here focuses on men with well-cultivated reputations for violence, who have carved out a niche for themselves, alongside other criminal enterprises, but which largely centre around middle market drug supply. This chapter draws on data taken from both the 'usual and unusual suspects' and comes from research undertaken by both authors with individuals who have been involved in criminal violence and drug supply, whose involvements and biographies in most cases involve time spent in both community and carceral settings. Here the data is used to argue that illicit drug dealing must be seen against the backdrop of an economic austerity and a political economy of neoliberal consumer capitalism that prioritises and promotes individualism, entrepreneurialism, pervasive consumerism and compulsive (conspicuous) acquisition. It is within this context that drug supply must be considered. As wealth is now concentrated in the hands of a few, there is a growing inequality gap, which has widened as austerity measures negatively impact the most vulnerable (Ellis, 2019) and illicit drugs have become the mainstay of organised crime at every level of the strata.

In fact, drug markets provide an opportunity – *par excellence* – to get ahead and become involved in rapacious consumption and create an intimidating reputation for themselves as successful men of action. However, in using ethnographic material, we also seek to challenge some of the highly mediated representations of drug markets and present a more realistic picture of what is a complex world where participants' lives (like the lives of users) are full of episodic highs and lows. Violence in illegal drug markets, when understood from the perspectives of those who have participated in it, is often quite different from the tabloid simplicity. The potential profits to be made from trafficking, distributing and dealing drugs – entirely a construct of illegality – means the drug trade is steeped in a toxic mix of quite routine violence in the background even to more convivial forms of dealing (Marsh, 2020).

Illicit markets, violence and criminal entrepreneurs

An array of criminological works attests to the fundamental skill set that is often possessed by men involved in criminality where violence is more commonplace (see Hobbs, 2013; Rahman et al., 2020; Winlow, 2001). Like many of these men,

Marty is a fighter, and largely always has been. He grew up part of an extensive family on a tough estate, and that brought its own troubles with other figures. His life is a complex web of connections and contacts, but it is a world removed from the myth of drug dealing that is largely given by the media:

> there is a lot of bullshit, and that bullshit starts to change peoples minds, you see these lads today, they want to look like a dealer, dress like they are straight out of fucking Compton because they have watched some shit gangster film and talk about the endz and being on road when they have never lived. Its fucking myth, you know who looks like that. Pricks who get caught, dickeads that get shot and stabbed. I say it is like this right, you look at the media has a lot to do with it. It is like prostitutes. You look at the media, what do they say a hooker looks like? They are street walking in a fucking Basque and suspenders and high fucking heels in November. The real girls on the street it's a puffer jacket and jeans and trainers... What does a drug dealer look like, it's always a street gangster, gold teeth, Gucci and a BM. A runner, that will be a young lad, baseball cap push bike. Its bollocks. The reason I say this, there might be some element of reality to some of it, but it is more complex than the picture that is often painted.

As Marty is keen to suggest, mediatised representations and dominant modes of thinking may capture some element or caricature of cultures, but often they are simple and underdeveloped, moreover Marty can play off just such stereotypes as he shifts decent amounts of cocaine, cannabis and anabolic steroids.

> Drop the stash in the Gym Bag, I have one that I use just for it, filled with skipping ropes, sweaty boxing gloves, a tub of protein powder, the gear goes in there... I drive around in a pair of tracksuit bottoms, [names brands] t shirt, jeans or shorts, people would see me and I am what an average guy. I do not get pulled by the old bill, I do not look like a fucking drug dealer do I?.... but this is the thing, too understand the scene you need to get it more, get what it is about, it is not what people think it is, and that is the same for violence. It is not violent all the time. It is not all guns and fucking scarface, but at the end of the day, yes there is violence there, it's a fucking reality.

Marty looks very different to the media made representation of the drug dealer he critiques. He suggests that this is but one reason that he has managed reasonably successfully to avoid much criminal detection and sanctions directly related to his involvement in illicit activity, including drug supply (although he has spent several considerable periods in prison on remand for serious offences) and manages to live a secure life of meeting various financial obligations without too much of a problem. What is common for him and the others who feature in this chapter is that their starts in life have largely involved post-industrial council estates in urban areas in large cities, comprehensive schools to drug supply, sometimes alongside legitimate business opportunities and other forms of (often casual) work, sometimes not, but always in lives where violence is common and regular. Here dealing can provide income, status, reputation, entertainment, stigma, shame and release, but where rates of violence tend to run far higher (Ellis, 2019).

Increasingly it is in this context that drug supply, and the violence around it, must be seen against the backdrop of an economic austerity and receding legitimate opportunities for increasingly precariously positioned populations (Ellis, 2019; Hall et al., 2008), but particularly among those already marginalised communities that are disconnected from social institutions and the legitimate economy due to the decline in manufacturing in the UK[1] (see Hall, 2012; Hall et al., 2008; Hobbs, 2013). It is in this context that entrepreneurship, which dominates all markets (legal and illegal), must be seen alongside the values of competitiveness, self-interest, individual empowerment and the decentralisation that it promotes to create self-interested actors that embody the neoliberal ideal of market-orientated logic of supply and demand, winner and loser (Hall, 2012; Hall et al., 2008; Hobbs, 2013). The role of criminal entrepreneurs in the drug markets, however, is nothing new, but increasingly there is a blurring between legitimate and illegitimate entrepreneurialism as individuals are held accountable for themselves in all matters of life (health, well-being, economic success), which includes 'the individual as self-provider and entrepreneur of their own labour' (Bröckling, 2007: xi).

It is this type of labour that merits some attention. Marty is indicative of the sort of self-reliant man embroiled in much illegal enterprise and mid-level, criminal drug distribution (Pearson and Hobbs, 2003). He has a long-standing reputation for being very capable and 'handy' when it comes to violence, both legitimate and less legitimate forms. This has not only involved boxing, kick-boxing and mixed martial arts, security and door work, but more than his fair share of street violence. Marty has cultivated both an ability and a reputation for just that since his school years and regards this as a core aspect of being involved in proto-criminal settings and the criminal milieu:

> you get it, but a lot don't, there is a presence … ultimately it is actions and words, and sometimes words are not enough. When it comes on top, you have to be able to fucking act, you have to be able to handle yourself.
>
> *Marty*

This is largely due to the illicit and criminal nature of drug markets, which 'by definition, cannot be regulated by contracts and courts' (Reuter, 2009 as cited in Rahman et al., 2020). Instead, transactions are enforced (typically) by 'systemic violence'[2] (Goldstein, 1985). Media portrayals tend to depict such violent enforcers as burly wide necked men, tattooed and muscle bound, physically intimidating and unthinking, often acting on behalf of ruthless criminal networks located in a hinterland of backroom bars, usually very much hidden from the general public. Sat atop the pile are ruthless suited criminal businessmen. While there may be elements of truth in such representations, Marty, like many around him, suggests that comprehensive schooling, tough estates, a desire for money and a keen eye for enterprise are, for the most part, the stuff of the contemporary drug trade, which is more diverse than many recognise. Yet Marty notes that violence, while far from common, is a not infrequent part of the scene, it is merely that it involves a smaller cast of individuals than is often recognised, is under-reported and involves much more threat and coercion than routine violence. It is a complex world where avoidance of violence is also important. For example, Marty's friends and contacts are serious criminals and violent men who sit atop the drug trade, but who also work with a number who are far from that. At the top tier of serious drug dealer groups there will almost always be violent men, but not all the men in this top tier will do violence. Men who have been involved in both legitimate and illegitimate forms of violence, from security work and debt collecting for local businessmen, to football violence. A remarkably consistent pattern of biographical influences features (Marsh, 2020; Rahman et al., 2020). Yet as Marty notes, violence is in many ways bad for business. Rather there is a common theme here that is significant, violence has an economic rational and a regulatory function.

In the contemporary drug marketplace, the supply of substances crosses the licit (e.g. pharmaceuticals, cosmeceuticals, dietary supplements and human enhancement drugs) and illicit economy (e.g. drugs, fake medications and synthetic psychoactive substances), and this is increasingly becoming blurred (Ayres, 2020; Hall and Antonopoulos, 2016). The majority of criminal entrepreneurs in this chapter had turned their hand to supplying illicit substances like cocaine, alongside cannabis, crack and heroin, to not only satisfy demand,[3] but also as a response to the changing economy where their principal skill set was no longer valued, could not ensure enough financial success to survive, and where they either adapted or perished (Ancrum and Treadwell, 2016; Ayres and Treadwell, 2012; Hall et al., 2008; Hobbs, 2013; Treadwell and Ayres, 2014). As Craig Ancrum highlights, 'the cocaine trade provides both a means of income and status in a disenfranchised post-industrial area which all too often fails to offer a viable alternative' (cited in Daly and Hall, 2018: 3). Thus, drug supply fulfilled a number of functions in these criminal entrepreneurs' lives; it provided viable employment for some and thus a dignified, and much easier, in fact for some, the only way of financing their lifestyles; for others it supplemented a legitimate income or business (see also Salinas' chapter in this volume); while others flitted in and out of criminality depending on their needs, wants and desires (Treadwell and Ayres, 2014). What was common across all of our respondents was that they all did it to buy '*the nice things in life*', to bankroll a luxurious and desirable lifestyle, afford exotic holidays, fancy cars and designer clothes – the 'ornamental trinkets that bestow existential significance and social distinction' on people in contemporary society (Hall et al., 2008:77), which often revolves around money and overt demonstrations of wealth.

Money, money, money! the root of much violence

We introduced Carl and Rick in detail elsewhere (see Ayres and Treadwell, 2012). They operate as a group separate from Marty (although we acknowledge in the odd and small world of middle market drug dealing, there may possibly be overlap or contact between their respective groups that we are unaware of). Carl was, at that time, an up and coming drug dealer, a man with a considerable reputation for violence who became involved in the retail supply of drugs to consumers as part of his main way of generating an income. His routeway and reputation was through a football firm, a subculture where violence is largely not driven by a profit imperative. Yet cocaine and alcohol use in such a context can also become an integral component of the men involved in mainstream leisure pursuits, as well as within the night-time economy more generally (see Ayres and Treadwell, 2012). Carl now sports a wider array of tattoos and a broader frame and has recently been involved in violence linked to drugs mainly in the context of prison. He is no longer at liberty. Rick remains his friend but is now a less close associate but continues to be involved in scaled back drug supply with a somewhat reconstituted network. Rick now goes to football less and has settled down but remains involved periodically in criminal activity and drug brokerage and distribution:

> I had to settle down a bit and keep quiet. When it came on top for the lads I knew, like with Carl inside, well you have to be careful. I work and I am legit, well mostly. Most of my cash now comes from mainstream graft, but I keep doing a bit. The thing is now, the lads that like gear, it's not like it was where it was. You have new lads involved now and it is on top a lot, Somalis, Asians, and Albanians. That is all they are about, and unlike Carl, like most of us have legit businesses and that and we do not want to be making like 6 quid a fucking week in prison.
>
> *Rick*

Others in their once drug dealing network are now making legitimate incomes (or attempting to) in a range of enterprises. Indeed, it ought to be noted that having spent several years involved in ethnographic research with criminals and active offenders in various settings, the perpetual drift into and out of crime is for the most part the emotional and existential precarity now confronting many young people as they attempt to negotiate the complex life worlds of late modernity. That drift into and out of crime, in Britain at least, is perhaps seedier and less romanticised than some accounts acknowledge[4] (e.g. Ferrell, 2018). As Ellis and colleagues (2017) have noted, the contours of organised crime can be choppy and turbulent, a maelstrom of arrest and imprisonment, or violent victimisation, and trauma and injury that can arrive unexpectedly. Not all such troubled waters are short-lived or fast arising, some come in the form of addictions or relationship breakdowns. Those with a one-time criminal reputation and status can fall from grace quickly, a historical reputation for violence does not necessarily act as a safeguard in terms of others exploiting or taking liberties.

Mac is one such man. In the 1990s 'Mac' was a bouncer and hard man used as muscle for hire on doors, in debt collecting and on cannabis runs where substantial amounts were imported in cars with false tanks from the Netherlands. Now he is a shadow of his former self, he associates with an 'old and more relaxed crowd'. He laments the changing scene in a bar where he is now regularly mocked by a generation of younger men, he would probably at one time have beaten savagely for the slights and remarks he now routinely feels he has to tolerate:

> Back in the 1990s as you know, I knew the door scene well, knew lads and that, I was involved in some naughty things, some proper bad things. Back then you had some of the influx of the gangster stuff in places like Manchester, but a lot of those lads were mugs. They had chips on their shoulders and no respect, but the last thing they wanted was for it to come on top with an older generation, because seriously, most of them, without a tool, they could not fight their way out of a paper bag. Nowadays though that is everywhere. They get what they think is respect for being a little twat who will shoot someone, and a lot of them today do not give a fuck about 25 or 30 year bird. It is not respect like it was, it is fear, stupidity and bravado. People rise high quick and then someone else, some nobody will come along and put them down quickly. That was never what it used to be like for most lads [the drugs scene] it was about the money, being able to have a fight and handle yourself was like the standard expectation. Now they will drop on one bloke all tooled up six or seven handed to fight over a fifty quid deal, it is fucking mad.
>
> *Mac*

For Mac, a changing and more violent drug scene is a given. For Mac another given is that there are two things that are the root of all violence:

> Ask me then most violence is about one of two things, it is either women or money, at root, it is about possession.
>
> *Mac*

In recent research that we have undertaken in both prisons and the community, we have routinely heard such laments. We have also heard much about the changing nature and character of violence around the supply of drugs involving, for example, the emergent narrative of county lines. Yet Mac's very involvement in the door security of raves in the 1990s and the security around drug deals suggests that such a narrative might be a little one dimensional. There is very little broader discussion of the place of violence in drug marketplaces and during much of the 1990s while the academic literature tended to be framed around social supply and presenting a market of non-commercial supply of drugs to friends and acquaintances for little or no profit, the dominant now cultural representation is of Essex boys with shotguns in Landrovers. In fact, there were plenty of shootings, stabbings and violent beatings in Macs day. As an unregulated market with large profits, violence is, and always has been very much one part of the picture, even if it is not well documented in academic accounts framed by students who saw normality in the friendly supply of drugs involving mates. While not everyone involved in the drugs trade makes money or makes the huge profits we are led to believe that come from supplying drugs (see Coomber, 2006, 2010), the entrepreneurs in this chapter have all organised their trade as much along the lines of a legitimate businesses as possible and were primarily involved in the drug dealing business to make a profit (or claimed to be).

Although some of our respondents would rather avoid violence (or say that they would), all were drawn to the drug trade with extensive exposure to violence, and it was those who had acted as perpetrators that were often the most extreme and involved actors due to their involvement in 'enhanced cultures of violence anyway' (Coomber, 2010, p.12). Some like Carl and Ryan were ex-football hooligans. Some sold drugs to supplement their income and avoided violence unless it was necessary, whereas for men like Danny and Marty, violent reputations were at the centre of their involvement in local drug markets. As Ryan, who is connected to well-known crime families, suggests:

> Not every drug dealer is a hard man, but in every drug dealing firm, every group, you are going to have some, and they are going to be somewhere near the top of the tree. They might not be [understood as] leading role, they might not be the importers or the one calling all the shots, but at the same time, they are not going to be a dickhead or someone you can take for a dickhead. Let's be honest, it is not always a nice business and people push at the boundaries and sometimes have to be put in their place. That is human nature.
>
> *Ryan*

Ryan's functional view and networked perception of understanding violence recognise its communicative function, but of course, any reputational dimension in many ways has an expressive physical connotation, as Marty suggests:

> Occasionally you can let something slide, but If you give someone stuff on tic and they don't pay, you haven't got much option but to humiliate them and put them in their place, With what people are like, they will take the piss, and if you didn't it would be like a green light to others, and this is business. Business is business. How bad, well that depends, a grand I might give them a slap and have their car. But if someone is taking a serious liberty, if we won't be doing business again and the gloves are off they will get badly hurt, very badly hurt, humiliated too.
>
> *Marty*

Therefore, although in some instances drug dealers avoid violence, there are a group of criminal entrepreneurs with a penchant for violence that are attracted to the drug market, mostly because of the amount of money and profit they can make selling drugs by using their skills and reputation for violence. Their involvement then is exacerbated either by the lack of legitimate opportunities available to them – some did not have the skills necessary to earn decent money in the legitimate economy, which left them with little choice but to deal drugs – or by the lure of the profits from dealing (often that come alongside legitimate work, as there is a strong connection between illegitimate activity and legitimate business to clean the cash). Moreover, in this respect the world of community drug dealing is not too dissimilar to that of the drug dealing that occurs inside of prisons, where the drug trade is rife.

To illustrate that point, Jason, a stocky and well-built young man with prominent tattoos and a serious stare who has been heavily involved in serious crime from his teens and frequently incarcerated for most of his adult life for drug and violent offences makes the point that in many respects, the custodial realm and prison is little different:

> In here, no different to out there, people bitch and compete, what man has got the best trainers, the best gear. No man wants to be taken for a dickhead. You are forced to decide in a way, its predator and prey, dog eat dog. There are more drugs in jails than outside, and just as much money to be made. Dickheads get in debt, someone is going to collect that, inside and out, it's the same, a dog don't pay, you send in the wolves bruv.
>
> *Jason*

For Jason that involvement means frequent moves around the system and through the Incentive and Earned Privileges scheme (IEP) prison discipline system, connection to OCGs and frequent charges for serious violence, as well as the distribution of drugs from outside of prison custody inside on a scale that was about significant profit. This for him suggested the difference between '*those who can get their hands really dirty*' and those who have to keen up appearances and keep themselves seemingly straight or manage that 'law abiding' appearance. Ryan, talking about his friend Carl (who is now incarcerated), makes a similar point when describing his friend's temporary situation:

> He isn't bothered by it [prison] to be honest or wasn't when last I went to see him. He was sound, in a Boss T Shirt and Nice Trainers, having a laugh. He said he was in for about 3 days before he was dealing in subbies and pills and that, and now him and a few of the lads are all over the vapes and the mamba. He doesn't want for nothing and knows half the lads in there. He is sound. The only thing now is he will be less willing to get caught filling some cunt in. Long term, he will probably learn from it truth be told.
>
> *Ryan*

In contrast, Lee, who is a reasonably successful independent businessman, who is also involved in distribution of class A drugs stressed for him, violence was not something he wanted to do (or be perceived to be actively physically involved in himself), because he simply had too much to lose to spend time in jail for that sort of offending. Moreover, he is not a violent man and never has been. However, he recognised the function of being connected to those who can do, as the following illustrates:

> one of the biggest load of bollocks is drug dealing is that it is all massive money, or that it is a replacement for a job. Is it fuck. No way, fuck off, I do both. I make good money, but life is expensive, if you want to have the best, it [dealing] is what you do. I run a decent business, and I make money on the side, but like, you never know when hard times are going to come. I grew up sat in the back of a police car while me mom nicked for shoplifting, I hid from bailiffs and debt collectors behind the sofa, had no gas and electric in our flat as kids. I am not having my kids grow up wanting for nothing. But I cannot fucking go and collect and I am not going to fucking do it [violence] myself, look at me, but I know people and that, you have to. I am useful as I can pay wages, put stuff through the books. I am good with money, good in business side. I am not a hardman, but I know lads who are. I have good lads with me who are.
>
> *Lee*

For one such lad, Danny – who is a renowned local character drawn from a family known to the authorities – the drug scene is almost the opposite of that described by Lee. He describes his involvement not in terms of dealing or distribution, but as a lad involved infrequently in his mate's business. Yet even here, when pressed it is the economic factors and not the bounds of friendship that are most significant. Danny [like Marty] will spend hours at a local gym with well-known hard men, training weights, hitting punch bags, comparing notes on protein intake and training regimes. He is well built and more than capable of violence, as well as infrequent and unregulated work in the security business. Yet while Danny might occasionally suggest he is merely someone interested in helping his mates out, there is clearly an economic imperative to many of the acts he initially presents as altruistic:

> I help my mates out, sure, I will go a long way for my mates because loyalty matters a lot to me. I can graft, but I am not earning a big wedge from it, look at jobs I have, I have no great qualifications, a CSCS card. I can earn a few quid on sites or doing security, but its low pay and it's a fucking bother with some twat in your ear. I lose near as much as I gain to be honest. Yet I can be down the gym, quick chat, two or three hours later have a word with someone about some money that is owed and I have earned a grand or more in notes in my pocket helping my mates out, so It's a no brainer basically.
>
> *Danny*

As Danny suggests, not all such disputes that he mediates will be about illegality, a car deal gone wrong, a dispute between private citizens, a landlord not payed rent, but he often cannot tell, and is not interested what the story is or the truth in it, if a mate needs help and there is money to be made, Danny has a willingness to act. If the former condition was to be met without the later though, that help might not be so forthcoming:

> Basically, we get asked to go collect and told, you will get this much, then I say fair enough, I am in, and that is it really. You get a story often, but that might be a load of bollocks, who knows. "He hasn't payed me for this unit he rented off me", What the fuck do I know if that is true? What the fuck do I give? End of the day its money isn't it. Money is money.
>
> *Danny*

The position in society of the people involved in this research ranged from ex-industrial workers and football hooligans to ex-armed robbers to those that for the most part operated successfully in legitimate businesses (from Cafes to building services, Plumbing and double glazing, supplement stores to newsagents, mechanics and car trading to property rental to gardening services, antiques dealing, eBay trading and more still besides), or were employed albeit often in low-paid low-skilled jobs like driving, security, building, scaffolding, and/or personal training which they often used as a front for their drug dealing. When they did implement violence, it was to collect debts incurred from offering bail, credit or gear on tic. In fact, some dealers refused to offer credit merely to avoid having to implement violence to collect debts as they could not be seen to be a 'pushover' otherwise '*everyone will just start taking the piss, and before you know it, everyone owes you money*'. Others implemented violence to see off more ruthless competition, to tax other dealers or to enhance personal reputations (Treadwell, Ancrum and Kelly, 2018). But violence was often just a part of these men's lives. Some were undoubtedly violent in their personal relationships. They could deal with their children with anger and violence. Violence was a likely result if someone cut them up driving. Violence could also come for entirely unrelated reasons that were then speculatively linked to the drug trade. As Ryan suggests:

> people look and if it's a drug dealer who has been violent, they automatically think, it must be drugs. It might not be. Look at Carl, he would glass some cunt because he did not like the way they looked. Then if the police look at it, if it gets reported, they will probably put it down to drugs. Its complex. You are more likely to hurt someone if they diss you, if they take you for a cunt, it can be anything. Drugs might be part, debts and that, but who knows? There are all sorts of things the police don't know, and sometimes lads themselves will keep the myth going. It was over a drug debt might be better than, "I didn't really have a reason, I am just a cunt when I have a few drinks", or "I heard he got a blowjob off my ex-girl". Let's be

> honest, sometimes the real reason for violence, only the one who did it can know, and what they tell you might not be fucking true.
>
> *Ryan*

Unfortunately, the illicit nature of the drug market – a result of prohibition – means systemic violence does exist and tends to dominate the literature on drug markets that has been indoctrinated in drug policy (see Goldstein, 1985 cited in Home Office, 2016: 30). It must also be noted that a large amount of violence that is present in drug markets is attributable to prohibition and their illegal status, with research showing how prohibition exacerbates and increases levels of violence not only at a local level, but also across the globe (Rolles et al., 2016; Werb et al., 2010). Although violence is a regulatory strategy in any illicit market, 'illegality alone is insufficient on its own to generate high levels of violence' (see Reuter, 2009, p. 275), which often depend on the wider socio-economic context. It also depended on an individual's proclivity for violence, which seems to (for the most part) lessen as they got older and the more socially integrated and acceptable lives they begin to lead, particularly if they have a family with children, a mortgage to pay or simply acquire more to lose. Indeed Marty, still quite a young man recognised this:

> look I am earning, but I have plans too, my own little gym and a tattoo studio, maybe. I will keep a little bit of a hand in, but it is like fighting, you have limited time. I want to have a nice life all settled and that. Prison is shit and if you are doing this as business then you must see it that way. When I was a kid and did not give a fuck. I have been stabbed up in rows over [mo]peds and as a kid on the estate, we had lads killed over a bit of fucking weed [cannabis].... I am careful, this is about the money and the life you want to have you do what you have to, but you want to wake up tomorrow free and happy, definitely.
>
> *Marty*

As Coomber (2010, p. 11) highlights, 'sellers in the drug market are highly differentiated' and clearly not all those involved are violent. The place of violence in the drug scene, even for men who had been quite frequently violent, is complex, and rather than perpetuating again and again the same myths, it is worth noting that the role, function and place of violence are often too little considered.

Business as usual: to be violent or not, that is the question?

Consequently, it is clear to see that drug dealing operates on a continuum. Some actors are criminal drug dealers and that was their only source of income, while others used it to supplement their income and had a legitimate business that operated as a front for their illicit activity (see also Salinas' chapter in this volume).

In years of qualitative work in prisons and communities we have met many respondents, even the most chaotic, who regard themselves as entrepreneurs taking individual responsibility and responding to changes in the market – which is heavily influenced by consumer habits. No matter what position they occupied they all responded to glocal trends in the drug market. They continuously revisited, evolved and re-invented themselves and their businesses. From Kinder eggs full of spice being conveyed into prison to meet the new demand for synthetic cannabinoids, and often due to the threat from violent men, dealers who would flog M-cat while legal and those who learned how to make synthetic spice once it had been criminalised, as demand remained. In a society where individual responsibility is emphasised and has been 'recast as an entrepreneur of the self who becomes responsible for their own fate' (Goodwin and Griffin, 2017, p. 21) mean they only have themselves to blame if they do not seize every opportunity, make the right – life and consumer – choices in a society where you increasingly adapt or die (Hall et al., 2008). Of course, some will adapt to face less risk, some will do so because of coercive pressure, and the motives for individuals will vary significantly, what will not alter is the economic imperatives that often and usually underscore such adaptions.

In line with the neoliberal entrepreneur the drug dealers we have known and spoken to over years of fieldwork on an array of projects have frequently capitalised on every opportunity, every gap in the market and, investing in themselves (e.g. physically, health wise, economically, conspicuously), this group acknowledged that 'when life becomes an economic function, disinvestment means death' (Bröckling, 2007, p. 53). This was very much the case with committed dealers who looked for opportunities in what is largely a cash economy. A girlfriend's nail bar or beauty parlour would be an opportunity to clean money through the books, as well as an opportunity to gain more social status. The foreign holidays to Mexico and the Caribbean could then be explained with business success, as could the new cars and detached houses. But such trappings would also bring jealousy and declining trust. A frequent issue when using ethnographic research is long-term contacts would simply break off contact and become uncommunicative, or more guarded. Some fair badly from their involvement and disappear, some into prison, others move areas. Some simply decide the game is over (e.g. it's a young man game) and desist, or certainly, desist from talking about their activities. Often there were more willing participants all too ready to step into the front-end tasks of distribution, taking the lead role in the retail end for what was not always a substantial income. Just as their entrepreneurial spirit was often channelled into legitimate ventures, they also understood good business. In their drug dealing they offered promotions on the drugs they sold (BOGOFF, 3 for 2) and used marketing strategies you would find in any legitimate business (e.g. free tasters/samples, text messages when new merchandise was received, free delivery) that included credit to their customers. Credit in this area can be important, however, in drug worlds not everyone pays debts. Therefore, the slip into a heady mix of drugs, power and money meant some dealers ruined their own, once successful businesses, and that included both legitimate and illegitimate business.

> It is easy to fuck it all up, I have seen it happen all too often, look at ★★★★★★★ [names a well-known local dealer recently jailed after packages destined for his business address were seized by border force] he claimed turned to dealing to prop up firm when it was failing, its bollocks, he just got greedy… fucking smuggling big shipments through a fucking Airport. He had a nice cash business, could clean money, but all it says to me is he got to greedy and someone grassed him up. But when you are out every night, round too many people, talking to much, you are a fucking liability to yourself, but the other thing is people did not fear him man, what was he, he was no fucking Scarface, could not have had a row ever. He always had a fall coming because who was frightened by him?
>
> *Ryan*

The ability of this group to adapt and move with the markets depended on their capital and this is frequently tied to their capacity for and/or reputation for violence, latent threat, or lack thereof. Talking of two associates who had at one point run a small drug dealing enterprise and car valeting business on the outskirts of the city, but had left the trade, Ryan noted:

> I will tell you honestly what happened to them mate, they were doing business but mainly for them, car valeting and that was legit, it is a front for dealing a lot, but for them, to be honest, it was more than just a way to account for the money, they were making cash, decent money too with the cars. But what happened to them mate, the fucking Albanians, that is what happened. They got told, you can sell to us or you can both disappear, and this was not a light threat. You know these lads who had the business, they could have a row, but the people we are talking about, who came in and took over, let's just say that counted for fuck all. If you get offered a few grand or a bullet, which do you take?

The competitive and ruthless undertaking implemented by some drug dealers can not only be seen in the operation of county lines (e.g. exploiting vulnerable populations and children) (see Coomber and Moyles, 2018 and Andell and colleague's chapter in this volume), but also the example provided above. Extreme violence, or the threat of extreme violence, implemented as part of the business plan/strategy can either be about reputation maintenance, competition (enhancing it or eliminating it), debt collection or much more everyday things such as perceived slights, insults and disrespect. As the marketplace has been democratised, some violent individuals have found a profitable outlet for their now redundant skill set (Treadwell and Ayres, 2012; Treadwell et al., 2018). These violent individuals are attracted to the drugs trade because they perceive it to be a place where their skill set is still of use, and because it accords with a sense of self. It allowed them to use violence or just the threat of it, to make money. Violence was or had been a normal part of their everyday lives and how they resolved conflict regardless of their drug business, so it was easy work. The attention on county lines and violence, and the conflict between dealer groups was regarded as overexaggerated by many of our more entrepreneurial dealers but was also useful in that it kept the light away from them. So too, the confusing opaque reasons behind violence when it did play out, was for them, also important to recognise though a less frequent theme in the criminological literature, as Danny suggests in such a world the true motives for violence can be difficult to disentangle:

> I've been part of situations where it's[violence] been over drugs, but you are dealing with a legitimate straight goer [businesspeople] who owes money, and you cannot always just go steaming in with threats and that, and not violence anyway, well, not straight away. If you are dealing with seemingly normal 9 to 5 people, who would happily call the police, you want to be more careful, so, you're better off reasoning with them and having a conversation, and I do that too, but it's still lads like me rolling up to collect, so that tells you something I suppose. But when you're dealing with those that are involved in drugs, they often only respect one way of doing things, or need to know where it will go if they try and take the piss, but most importantly, most of all it is nearly always about how you're able to get that money back.
>
> *Danny*

As was suggested on numerous occasions, vital aspects of being able to keep your head above water in criminal worlds were trusted contacts and self-resilience. '*It's not what you know, it's who you know*'. However, contacts can matter little when an individual is alone or incapable of standing up for themselves. Stevie put it that many people could pretend and play a role, but the real world was such that there would be a situation where you were likely to be put to the test and words and image alone was not enough. If that happened, as Marty was keen to assert, '*you can talk like Mike Tyson, but at the end of the day, you get lots of lads that bulk up and come the big man, but then "put to the test, they have fuck all in the chamber*', a point on which he elaborates:

> lad I know, he was remanded in HMP, he does not look all that, so the fucking wide neck cunt who thinks he is tries to sound him out.... When he goes onto another wing, some big cunt, supposed big man and his mates tried to bring it on with him, well, you know where it goes down when he goes for a shower, big man decides he is having trainers off him. They try to do him there... well this is the think, he does not give a fuck, and the big main lad gets it first, but you know he roles, he has fucking brick hands

> and this big lad gets done pretty fast, a 20 inch neck doesn't mean you can really roll. His mates though seeing what he does, do they all pile in? do they fuck? Notice how these lads are brave in groups…But… that is what I always say. No man will ever always be backed up. There will always be a time with everyone when you are alone'.
>
> *Marty*

Stevie suggests that it is a combination of this violent reputation, and violent contacts that often leads to long-term success in criminal business ventures:

> 'If I have never heard of you or you ain't got nothing about you in terms of you being able to look after yourself or being associated to a certain group or name, then I'm just going to tell you to fuck off. However, if I know that you're affiliated or have done something serious in the past then people are more like respectful, then it's a whole different thing. The thing about crime is, there is not too much trust, and basically a lot of people will act like dickheads unless they fear the fucking consequences'
>
> *Stevie*

While this might seem to be articulating the significance of a sort of social capital, many of our participants were keen to make it very clear that a past violent reputation alone was not necessarily enough to maintain a stable market position in the drug trade. Established reputation and the respect for it in the criminal world of today could be relatively short. Reputation was quickly lost and won.

> I am a hard bastard yes, in a fight not many are going to have a go, so what are they going to do, come four or five handed or come tooled up, I am realistic about that, I am at risk in what I do, any lad is. A couple of my lads, they are not daft lads, two of them work together, but they have been done, robbed of gear, it can happen. That is why your reputation only takes you so far, and only with people who think in that way, there are always dickheads and people looking to take advantage. It is worth remembering that.
>
> *Marty*

Although all were aware of the risks – that they did their best to mitigate and manage – it was seen as a hazard of the job, and worth it if it meant they could afford the '*finer things in life*'.

Conspicuous consumption and the importance of having it all

Men like Marty, Danny and Marty mentioned here train their bodies to be functional when it comes to violence, they pride themselves on knowledge and physical fitness, as well as a fundamental willingness to go to extreme lengths and to have that capability to be able to maintain their place in the market. In criminal dealings with money involved, nobody wants to be a pushover, even those not directly associated with violence. Unlike Wakeman's (2016) moral economy around heroin dealers, the more instrumental and entrepreneurial dealers we have encountered have often been keen to make as much profit as possible while seeking to avoid detection or sanction. In their world, 'the market was not a realm of peaceful pursuit of mutual interests by exchange, but rather an intricate and perpetual series of windows of individual opportunity opening and closing again' (Bröckling, 2007, p. 60). If they did not take full advantage of them, they risked economic and cultural insignificance, and would only have themselves to blame.

The democratisation of the drug market, alongside the democratisation of criminal opportunity more generally, has also meant more people from very diverse backgrounds have moved into the supply of drugs taking advantage of the profits/money to be made, which has partly been fuelled by the growth of the internet (see Bancroft's chapter and Kelly's chapter in this volume). In today's 24-hour marketplace even drug dealers are working around the clock and adapting their supply methods to capitalise on trade opportunities. For most commercial drug dealers, it is about making a profit and making as much money as possible, compared to user-dealers, who although might want to make money, settle for being able to fund their often very expensive drug habit via drug supply bringing into question the true levels of altruism evident in social supply chains. However, the differing motivations for selling also translated into different expectations and tolerances for violence. For all of the actors in this chapter, drug supply provided a more attractive alternative than other (employment) options, which for some was other forms of criminality while for others it was engaging in the legitimate economy where their skill set was no longer appreciated, where there were bosses, regular working hours, rules and barely enough money at the end of the week to survive (Treadwell and Ayres, 2012). However, even worse, would have been living in poverty and disappearing into social, cultural and symbolic insignificance, which now supersedes the more traditional threats that once concerned this group (e.g. loss of reputation) (Hall et al., 2008).

Consequently, drug dealing for this group of criminal entrepreneurs not only facilitated the purchase of luxury items, but it fuelled the luxurious lifestyle they all desired. It was seen as a solution to their problems by offering upward mobility, success, status, reputation, economic stability and respect (see also Hall et al., 2008; Ayres and Treadwell, 2012; Treadwell and Ayres, 2012). It allowed this group of dealers and their associates to climb the social ladder, bringing them status distinction and economic wealth (Daly and Hall, 2018; Hall et al., 2008; Treadwell and Ayres, 2014). These criminal entrepreneurs were also buying into the 'celebrity lifestyle' where they acted and occupied a celebrity-like status (Daly and Hall, 2018) as they literally bought the time of their lives (Žižek, 2014) so they could 'have the best of things' (Treadwell and Ayres, 2014). This was not an exceptional view, especially when those involved were younger or at the start of their involvement in dealing. In our research, and in both prison and the community we have met criminal entrepreneurs who have owned businesses, top end sportscars, wardrobes full of designer clothes, been on holidays in the most exclusive resorts in the world and bought expensive luxury homes, things that given their limited backgrounds would never have likely been in reach. Of course, not all enjoyed such wealth, and when a criminal is successful that lifestyle is often connected with legitimate business interests. Not all manage a collection of Omegas, Rolex and Breitling watches, and instead many find themselves in periodic poverty, fear and precarity (Marsh, 2020). Yet the appeal to young men is palpable and the opportunity to be one of the successes is an immense draw:

> If I am honest, I like the fact that if I need too, I could fly out the country in what a few hours, I know lads all over the world, lads in South America, Spain, Dubai. Look at ★★★★★ [names a well know local criminal who has fled overseas], he is still living the high life, having a laugh. He has sun, nice clothes, nice cars, there are plenty of places you can go. I like it here, basically I can walk into stores in town, drop a few grand on Moncler and Gucci, go to the club with the lads, all throw a grand or two in, get best tickets for the boxing, a box at the football. If I go anything, I go executive, high class.
>
> *Lee*

> Honestly, if you look at me, I am careful with it, with what I do because being a really flash cunt has its drawbacks, I do not need that in my life now, I want to be sound, I want to have enough money yes, but I have to be careful.
>
> *Stevie*

Drug dealing allowed them to live the life and afford the lifestyles and experiences that we are all told we want and need, and which in consumer society depict success and elicit envy (Hall et al., 2008).

Conclusion

Much academic work that considers those who operate in criminal enterprises for monetary gain emphasises the rationality of perpetrators as well as their ability to maximise their operations subject to constraints. Yet as Bakkali (2019) argues that economic capital 'on road' can be entrenched in the form of cultural capital (an individual's embodied, linguistic, objectified and institutionalised state) and social capital (the networks that individuals are connected to) (see Bourdieu, 1986). Likewise, a person's social and cultural capital can be institutionalised in the form of economic capital. Good ethnographers of organised crime and male violence have long suggested such interconnectedness, although they may not draw directly on Bourdiesian sociology when stating that (see Ellis, 2016; Winlow, 2001). Drug dealing is complex, and there are a range of motives and factors that underpin it, just as there are a number of forms that it can take illustrating its increasingly differentiated nature.

While the drug dealer has historically been portrayed as challenging and problematic, subverting capitalism and corrupting the norms and values of mainstream economic and enterprise model (Agar, 1973) and while both users and dealers come from diverse backgrounds and interact symbiotically with 'respectable' society (Adler and Adler, 1995), it is also true that such a line risks overlooking the common harms encountered in such worlds that are not so common in mainstream society (Marsh, 2020). Additionally, those who climb to the top of the trade are often deeply conformist (violent adherents) to the sorts of ideas about enterprise and self-reliance, and personal responsibility that feature prominently in broader political discourses. What is more is that our contacts themselves are all too alert to the utility and value, to them, of rather problematic and narrow (stereotypical) framings of drug dealing that often depict contemporary forms of drug supply, such as a current concern with the county lines phenomenon, or street gangs, as useful distractions and diversions which disproportionately highlight distracting and narrow (stereotypical) tropes surrounding drug dealers. Thus, it is integral to understand and examine the context in which drug market violence occurs (Goldstein, 1987; Coomber, 2015). Entrepreneurs are cashing in on this market to provide meaningful work and status (see also Preble and Casey, 1969) and the financial resources to buy the luxury items society tell us we not only want but need (Hall et al., 2008; Treadwell and Ayres, 2014). Throughout history the corporations and entrepreneurs, sometimes criminal, have implemented the same ruthless undertaking in the supply of luxurious (licit and illicit) substances for profit, as they all partake in special liberty (see Hall, 2012) driven by the market economy, which prioritises the exigencies of capitalism (see Ayres, 2020). Yet they also stimulate the local (and global) economy and create degrees of order, structure and security in doing so. As Hammersley states (2008:77), 'drugs and crime can bring cash into social networks and neighbourhoods that have few other economic resources . . . pull the drug dealing from some areas and there would be almost no economy'.

To many of the men we have interviewed, this tension was all too apparent, hence drug-dealing was a viable employment option that allowed them to draw on their violent (hard-man) image, which was often accompanied by their own subjective schema. This not only put them in a perfect position to ensure the survival of their illicit entrepreneurial business, but to survive in such an unregulated and occasionally ruthless and untrusting world, one in which they would occasionally have to fight for survival, to get the money paid as well as for distinction.

Notes

1 Similar trends can also be seen in the USA.
2 Systemic violence commonly refers to violence intrinsic to illicit drugs and traditionally refers to the violence and aggression associated with illicit drug 'interactions within the system of drug distribution and use' that includes turf disputes, debt collection and retaliation/disputes (Goldstein, 1985, p.497).
3 Despite a steady decline in the use of most drugs over the last 20 years, cocaine has bucked this trend, and is one of the few substances that has gradually increased, being used by increasingly diverse sections of the population.
4 It must be noted that some of our longer term participants drifted in and out of crime and drug dealing, as well as violence, and their willingness to be violent and implement violence.

References

Adler, P.A. and Adler, P. (1995) Dynamics of inclusion and exclusion in preadolescent cliques. *Social Psychology Quarterly*, 58(3): 145–162.

Agar, M. (1973) *Ripping and Running: A Formal Ethnography of Urban Heroin Addicts.* London: Academic Press.

Ancrum, C. and Treadwell, J. (2016) Beyond ghosts, gangs and good sorts: Commercial cannabis cultivation and illicit enterprise in England's disadvantaged inner cities. *Crime, Media, Culture*, 13(1): 69–84.

Ayres, T.C. (2020). Substances: The luxurious, the sublime and the harmful. In S. Hall, T. Kuldova and M. Horsley (eds.), *Crime, Harm and Consumerism* (pp. 108–122). London: Routledge.

Ayres, T.C. and Treadwell, J. (2012) Bars, drugs and football thugs: Cocaine use amongst English football firms. *Criminology and Criminal Justice*, 12(1): 83–100.

Bakkali, Y. (2019) Dying to live: Youth violence and the munpain. *Sociological Review*, 67: 6.

Bourdieu, P. (1986) The forms of capital. In J. Richardson (ed.), *Handbook of Theory and Research for the Sociology of Education* (pp. 241–258). Westport: Greenwood.

Bröckling, U. (2007) *The Entrepreneurial Self.* London: Sage.

Coomber, R. (2006) *Pusher Myths: Re-situating the Drug Dealer.* London: Free Association Books.

Coomber, R. (2010) Reconceptualising drug markets and drug dealers–A need for change. *Drugs and Alcohol Today*, 10(1): 10–13.

Coomber, R. (2015) A tale of two cities: Understanding differences in levels of heroin and crack. *Criminal Justice Review*, 40(1): 7–31.

Coomber, R. and Moyles, L. (2018) The changing shape of stree-level heroin and crack supply in England. *British Journal of Criminology*, 58(6): 1323–1342.

Daly, M. and Hall, A. (2018) Cocaine is the hidden mixer in Newcastle's economy. *Vice*, 20th March.

Ellis, A (2016) *Men, Masculinities and Violence: An Ethnographic Study.* Abingdon: Routledge.

Ellis, A. (2019) A de-civilizing reversal or system normal? Rising lethal violence in post-recession austerity United Kingdom. *The British Journal of Criminology*, 59(4): 862–878.

Ellis, A., Winlow, S. and Hall, A. (2017) Throughout my life I've had people walk all over me: Trauma in the lives of violent men. *The Sociological Review*, 65(4): 699–713.

Farrell, J. (2020) *County Lines.* London: John Blake.

Ferrell, J. (2018) *Drift.* California: University of California Press.

Goldstein, P.J. (1985) The drugs/violence nexus: A tripartite conceptual framework. *Journal of Drug Issues*, 39: 143–174.

Goldstein, P.J. (1987) The impact of drug-related violence. *Public Health Reports*, 102(6): 625–627.

Goodwin, I. and Griffin, C. (2017) Neoliberalism, alcohol and identity: A symptomatic reading of young people's drinking cultures in a digital world. In A. Lyons, T. McCreanor, I. Goodwin and H. Barnes (eds.), *Youth Drinking Cultures in a Digital World: Alcohol, Social Media and Cultures of Intoxication* (pp. 15–30). Abingdon: Routledge.

Grillo, I. (2017) *El Narco*. New York: Bloomsbury Press.

Hall, A. and Antonopoulos, G. (2016). *Fake Meds Online: The Internet and the Transnational Market in Illicit Pharmaceuticals*. Basingstoke: Palgrave Macmillan.

Hall, S. (2012) *Theorizing Crime and Deviance*. London: Sage.

Hall, S., Winlow, S. and Ancrum, C. (2008) *Criminal Identities and Consumer Culture: Crime, Exclusion and the New Culture of Narcissism*. Cullompton: Willan.

Hammersley (2008) *Drugs and Crime: Theories and Practices*. Cambridge: Polity Press.

Hobbs, D. (2013) *Lush Life*. Oxford: Oxford University Press.

Home Office (2016) *Modern Crime Prevention Strategy*. London: Home Office.

Marsh, B. (2020) *The Logic of Violence: An Ethnography of Dublin's Illegal Drug Trade*. Abingdon: Routledge.

Pearson, G. and Hobbs, D. (2003), King PIN? A case study of a middle market drug broker. *The Howard Journal of Criminal Justice*, 42: 335–347.

Preble, E. and Casey, J. (1969) Taking care of business. *International Journal of Addiction*, 4 (1): 1–24.

Rahman, M:, McLean, R., Deuchar, R. (2020) Who are the enforcers? The motives and methods of muscle for hire in West Scotland and the West Midlands. *Trends Organized Crime*. https://doi.org/10.1007/s12117-020-09382-y

Reuter, P. (2009) Systemic violence in drug markets. *Crime, Law and Social Change*, 52(3): 275–284.

Rolles, S., Murkin, G., Powell, M., Kushlik, D., Saunter, N. and Slater, J. (2016*) The Alternative World Drug Report* (2nd Edition). Bristol: TDPF.

Treadwell, J., Ancrum, C. and Kelly, C. (2018) Taxing Times: Inter-criminal victimisation and drug robbery amongst the English professional criminal milieu. *Deviant Behavior*, 1–13.

Treadwell, J. and Ayres, T.C. (2014) Talking Prada and Powder: Cocaine Use and Supply among the Football Hooligan Firm. In J. Treadwell and M. Hopkins (eds.) *Football Hooliganism, Crime and Crowd Control: Contemporary Themes in Relation to Research and Theory*. Basingstoke: Palgrave Macmillan, pp. 49–70.

Wakeman, S. (2016) The moral economy of heroin in Austerity Britan. *Critical Criminology*, 24: 363–377.

Werb, D., Rowell G., Guyatt, G., Kerr, T. Montaner, J., and Wood, E. (2010) *Effect of Drug Law Enforcement on Drug Related Violence: Evidence from a Scientific Review*. Vancouver: International Centre for Science in Drug Policy.

Winlow, S (2001) *Badfellas: Crime Traditions and New Masculinities*. Oxford: Berg.

Woods, N. and Rafaeli, P. (2019) *Drug Wars: A Terrifying inside Story of Britain's Drug Trade*. London: Ebury Press.

Žižek, S. (2014). The Impasses of Consumerism. In teNeus (Ed.) *Prix Pictet 05: Consumption*. London: teNeus.

5

HEROIN USERS WHO DEAL

Getting high on their own supply

James Morgan and Daniel Silverstone

The motivation for drug dealing has been characterised as a rational route to financial gain, as a pursuit for people who want to live out an excessive extravagant consumer lifestyle and as a way for addicts to fund their drug use (Desroches 2007; Matrix 2007; Bullock, Clarke & Tilley 2010; Briggs 2013; Hobbs 2013; Taylor & Potter 2013; Shammas Sandberg & Pedersen 2014; Tzvetkova et al. 2014). This chapter aims to shed light on the under-researched area of drug dealing amongst heroin users. Although the existence of drug dealing amongst occasional heroin users has been recorded (Zinberg 1984; Warburton et al. 2005; Shewan & Delgarno 2005, this chapter looks at the dealing activities of people who use heroin every day. Much could be said as to whether these participants were in control of their heroin use. The interviews for this study were biographical and retrospective, with diverse narratives both between participants and across their heroin using careers. All participants, however, described at least some lengthy periods of being dependent heroin users.

User-dealers can be defined as 'users first and dealers second who primarily supply to support their own drug use' (Coomber 2006, p. 141). Similarly, Akhtar and South tell us that user-dealers work to 'regulate one's own [drug] habit' (2000, p. 160). Pearson (2007, p. 77) agrees suggesting the main motive is to 'maintain his or her own drug habit'. In accordance with these authors, this study is concerned with those who supply drugs primarily to support their own consumption; however, additionally, it examines the activities of users who are able to generate financial profit through drug supply.

Much of the user-dealer literature concerns social supply, where friends supply drugs to one another (Coomber & Turnbull 2007). Sandberg (2012, p. 1138), studying culture in Norway's cannabis economy has described social suppliers, who 'sell small quantities to friends; they do not usually regard themselves as dealers, but as "helpers", and they do not make much money'. Although

DOI: 10.4324/9781351010245-7

theorisation of the term has been more recent, the idea of, especially, cannabis users selling in small quantities to their friends is not a newly discovered phenomenon, with Young (1971) discussing this in his seminal study. In *The Drug Takers* (Young 1971) cannabis supply was said to involve young bohemian travellers who would supply their friends following trips to Morocco or India. More recently, social supply has also been discussed in the context of dance drugs (Measham 2004) and prescription stimulants (Murphy et al. 2018) showing social supply is nothing new (see Moyle's chapter in this volume).

Another way to differentiate different sorts of drug dealing has been to look at the 'level' at which trades in drugs occur. Although different typologies have been proposed by different authors[1], at the lowest level, a term used in multiple studies and which is relatively uncontested is 'retail'. These are dealers who sell to users at the street level (Matrix 2007, p. 17). Above this, for our study is the 'middle market'. Pearson and Hobbs (2001) have acknowledged a lack of clarity in understanding what the 'middle market' is but consider the most useful definition to be the drug dealing activity which connects importation and production of drugs with retail. Above this, Desroches (2007) reviewed literature relating to 'higher level drug traffickers. While accepting that the terms 'higher level' and 'upper level' are contested, Desroches (2007, p. 828) defines 'higher level traffickers as importers, growers, manufacturers or wholesalers who market large quantities of illicit drugs to other dealers'. Coomber and Turnbull (2007) in seeing that we do not possess an adequate language for differentiating between different sorts of drug supply. Although the authors accept the boundaries are fuzzy, being able to categorise drug dealing as retail level, middle market or higher level is of use for this chapter.

A common practice?

Research has also focused on user dealing amongst heroin and crack users, with some of these studies suggesting that the practice is not rare. Out of an impressive sample of 275 intravenous drug users, Debeck et al. (2007) found that 41% had supplied drugs. Some other smaller and primarily qualitative studies also reported the proportion of their samples who had at some points in their heroin using careers sold drugs. Waldorf (1973) found that one in three of his participants used dealing as their primary method of funding, while a further 48% sometimes did. Overall, this added up to 81% of his respondents having at some points used drug dealing to fund their heroin use. Rosenbaum (1981) studied *Women on heroin* and found that 61% of her participants had sold drugs as heroin users. Parker et al. (1988), however, found that only 13% of their sample self-reported supplying drugs. The variation in figures reported is striking. Firstly, only the study from Debeck et al. (2007) sought to estimate the prevalence of user-dealing at the population level, the others simply aimed to tell us about their samples of non-randomly chosen participants. However, this might also reflect how 'dealing' is defined, operationalised and understood by participants. As will be seen in the paragraphs below, there are a great many roles to be played in the drugs economy which a heroin user can make use of. Some of these activities could be understood as dealing by some heroin users and not by others.

Small et al. (2013) and Moyle and Coomber (2015) specifically sought to understand the roles played by user-dealers of heroin and crack cocaine within the street drugs scenes that they studied. Although they did not formalise or validate these typologies, the following roles for user-dealers were identified: middling; freelancing; and corporate. Middling is where someone buys drugs on behalf of someone less well connected than themselves and acquires a cut of the drugs purchased for their own consumption (Moyle & Coomber 2015; Small et al. 2013). This might take the shape of buying for someone else and taking a cut, or else a group of users pooling their money and the best-connected buying on their behalf. Freelancing was described by Small et al. (2013) as buying enough drugs so that they can reserve a small amount for personal use while selling the remainder. Corporate sales were defined by Small et al. (2013) as working for an established dealing network as an employee. In a study of heroin use and dealing within a British Asian community Akhtar and South (2000) found evidence of this practice in the form of heroin users working as delivery drivers for higher level dealers.

Recently, there has been much discussion on the 'county lines' phenomenon, where dealers from big cities expand their dealing operations into smaller towns and mobile phone 'lines' are used to communicate drug orders (Windle & Briggs 2015; Coomber & Moyle 2018; NCA 2019; Moyle 2019; see Andell and colleague's chapter in this volume also). If user-dealers are involved in this sort of trade, it would be described as 'corporate' dealing. In a recent study, Coomber and Moyle (2018) suggested that in many provincial areas of the UK the presence of out-of-town dealers dominating the local heroin market means that corporate user-dealing is now the norm. One common arrangement is for the out-of-town dealers to take over a user's house and use it as a base for operations, with this practice referred to as 'cuckooing' (Spicer et al. 2019). However, in areas which are a significant distance from the drug supply centres such as London, Glasgow, Liverpool, Birmingham and Manchester, user dealers are more likely to work on a freelance basis, as out-of-town dealers are less likely to make the journey (Coomber & Moyle 2018).

'The best hustle for a narcotics addict is selling drugs, especially heroin' (Waldorf 1973, p. 50)

Further qualitative studies discussed user-dealing amongst heroin users even though this was not the principal focus. Preble and Casey (1969) introduced the idea of the 'juggler', equitable to the 'freelancer' described above. Waldorf (1973) and Hanson et al. (1985) also referred to this sort of dealing in their studies of heroin use in big cities on America's east coast. Hanson et al. (1985) went on to describe further roles which could be played. 'Touts' and 'Steerers' would be given either drugs or money to direct users to a dealer. The role of the 'copman' involved buying on behalf of someone who did not wish to buy for themselves, of course taking a cut themselves. 'Pooling' involved groups of users combining their resources to buy in bulk. In the typology presented by Small et al. (2013), both roles would be subsumed under 'middling'. Johnson et al. (1985) also noted that some users received heroin for managing 'shooting galleries' where other heroin users could come to inject, for renting out their needles and syringes or for using their skills to inject others. Further roles outlined by Johnson et al. (1985) included testing batches of heroin on behalf of non-using dealers, holding onto and guarding drugs for dealers and acting as lookout. Finally, the 'house connect' sells drugs out of a residential property on behalf of a bigger dealer. More recently, Gamero and Briggs (2017) found in the wastelands around Madrid that the most desperate addicts would act as doormen at drug dealing locations as well as doing odd jobs such as sweeping the floors. In this case, payment was always received in drug form. All of these studies have looked to user-dealers who fit the definition used above, in that their dealing is a means of subsisting as heroin users.

But what does research say about the way that heroin user-dealers understand their own behaviour? Akhtar and South (2000), Moyle and Coomber (2015) and Small et al. (2013) all suggested that small-scale dealing was preferable to alternatives such as shoplifting and burglary. Low-level dealing was seen as more morally virtuous than thieving. It was also seen as more convenient since instead of having to exchange stolen goods for money and then buy drugs, they always had a supply with them. Crucially, people involved in supply did not have to worry about suffering withdrawal. Women interviewed by Moyle and Coomber (2015) and Small et al. (2013) also found selling drugs to be less onerous and unpleasant than selling sex.

But are the self-understandings of heroin users who deal exclusively related to managing dependence to the drug? Some studies of heroin users which have happened upon dealing amongst users have painted a more complex picture. Faupel (1991) recounted the narratives of heroin users who acted as 'freelancers' (Small et al. 2013; Moyle & Coomber 2015) or 'jugglers' (Preble & Casey 1969; Hanson et al. 1985; Waldorf 1973) but also describes the excesses that might occur when a heroin user achieves success in their dealing. In his typology, Faupel (1991) described 'stable addicts' who had a good supply of heroin (especially if they were dealing) but also a regular and stable lifestyle. Some of those who dealt (as well as some bank robbers and other lucrative earners) lived out a party lifestyle and became, according to Faupel's (1991) typology, 'freewheeling junkies. Here heroin was used to excess alongside other activities such as drinking and womanizing.

Some studies have found heroin users who dealt in order to make money. Taylor (1993), in her ethnography, encountered women who dealt heroin in order to manage their heroin dependency but also some women who sold heroin so they could 'get stoned' on heroin rather than using the bare minimum to avoid withdrawal symptoms. In an illustration of female users making financial profit, Taylor (1993) also refers to 'Judy' who boasted that she was 'dripping in jewelry... two rings on each finger and chains around my neck. Leather jackets, hundreds of clothes' (Taylor 1993, p. 70). Another participant described how when she was dealing, she never ran out of money and was able to fully provide for her child. Lalander (2003) unpicked some complex narratives from some of his heroin using informants. Although some sold heroin at a wholesale level and reported cash profits, they also held scorn for anyone who was not a user and profited from selling heroin. Nonetheless, whether this was an aim of their dealing or simply an accident of their success in the field, these heroin-using dealers did more than just get by.

'Never get high on your own supply'

As made famous in the film *Scarface* (de Palma 1983), higher-level drug traffickers seek to avoid using the drugs that they sell. But according to empirical research, how far up the drug dealing hierarchy can heroin users be found? Waldorf (1973) identified four types of heroin seller. 'Pushers' and 'dealers' sell retail or small wholesale units on the street and, according to Waldorf (1973), would almost always be users. Above this were ounce and kilo dealers, and above them importers. The 'dealers' interviewed by Waldorf (1973) reported that the people they bought from were never users. Waldorf (1973) also saw that those arrested with large amounts of high-purity heroin were rarely users. It might be instructive that Akhtar and South (2000) introduced the case study of someone who while a heroin user worked as a delivery driver. After desisting from heroin use following a prison sentence he restarted dealing and grew to the point where he had user-dealer drivers working for him.

Although the issue is rarely described in detail, studies of middle market and upper level drug dealing tend to suggest that people in these positions eschew daily heroin use. One of Desroches' (2007) key findings was that the main motive of 'higher level traffickers' was almost exclusively high-level profit. Indeed, in his own seminal study of imprisoned higher level drug traffickers, Desroches (2005) found a great many businessmen who diversified to illegal drugs when their legitimate businesses were flagging. Even amongst many of those who did not move to drug dealing from a business background, there was often a strong ethos that they were primarily businessmen, rather than gangsters. Getting high on their own supply would be sacrilege for this group.

Literature has also posited a different set of motives for medium and high-level drug dealers. Desroches (2005) described a second class of wholesale dealers who were more criminal and less business like. For these middle market and higher level players, it was important to be the 'man about town', to be able to buy people expensive drinks in expensive venues and be seen to have succeeded. Hobbs (2013) sought to understand the social construction of organised crime and in the course of his study also spoke to people involved in middle-market drug dealing. Included in his book is a cannabis wholesaler who did the work very much in order to make ends meet. However, others sought the *'Lush life'* of luxuries and conspicuous consumption (see Ayres and Treadwell's chapter and Salinas' chapter in this volume). Hall et al. (2008) looked at consumer culture as an explainer for many sorts of criminal activity. They too spoke to middle market drug dealers as well as aspirants. Motivations here were theorized as wishing to carve out a niche as a respectable person and to be seen as apart from the crowd. Material ends, always valued for symbolic value more than their practical utilities, were expensive electrical goods, fashion items and recreational use of powder cocaine. Heroin use was only briefly mentioned in this book, name-checked by a respondent as 'the dirty brown stuff'. Due to the scruffy appearances and lack of self-determination evident in users, heroin use was anathema to those researched. There was also a belief that heroin users were not to be trusted and could be prone to informing on others under police interrogation.

As previously alluded to, having plentiful supplies of drugs and/or money can create problems for heroin users. Faupel (1991) was cited above showing how 'stable users' can morph into 'freewheeling junkies' when in the business of supplying heroin. According to the narratives of his participants, mishaps inevitably occurred during the latter phase, leading to lost trust from whomever they were buying their stock. In the end 'freewheeling junkies' would be on the streets and destitute having blown their riches. Taylor (1993) shared anecdotes from her study which show that for the same reasons there was a perception that whatever goes up then comes down. Hanson et al. (1985) did not describe the same dramatic rises and falls but indicated that profits made would almost always be consumed through the needle. Small et al. (2013) showed how this could present physical dangers to those who bought their stock on credit or worked directly for bigger dealers. As well as indebted user-dealers suffering violence from their suppliers they might also be excluded from doing future business with them or forced to work off the debt with added interest. Some participants in their study suggested that it was safer to play the role of 'middling' so this could be avoided.

Responding to challenges

The respondents in Lalander's (2003) ethnography regularly discussed being under threat from the police and related their continued freedom to having their wits about them. They saw themselves as natural quick thinkers and valued being mentored into their dealing roles by more experienced heads. Some users who also dealt in Lalander's (2003) study lauded talents which they believed allowed them entry into the field of heroin dealing:

> [H]e 'behaves himself' which means that he managed to live up to the norms that are expected of him by the gatekeepers of the underworld.

> Ultimately it is about being as sufficiently calm/cool that the calm can be used to counteract various types of risk.
>
> *Lalander 2003, p. 77*

Moyle and Coomber (2017) theorised the characteristics needed for heroin users to also deal. Invoking Bourdieu's (1990; Bourdieu 1977) theory of practice they viewed the street drugs scene as a 'field' in which certain competencies were desirable, in order to have a 'feel for the game'. These competencies are seen as 'capital', which someone accumulates due to their 'habitus', which roughly refers to their demeanour, manner and comportment of the body and includes their class background. In the main Moyle and Coomber (2017) found that the habitus of long-term heroin and crack users meant that dealing felt natural and became normalized for them. Their histories as drug users, as people from criminal neighbourhoods, as people who grew up in care and as people who have been homeless, meant that they were well enough connected to buy drugs for others and also competent in how it should be done. The same habitus also prevented legitimate income.

Available literature largely focuses on user-dealers who work low-status roles in retail drug dealing simply earning enough heroin to get by. In this analysis, dealing represents an easy and comparatively ethical way to persist in daily heroin use. However, there are some accounts of heroin users who have taken up roles which could fall under 'middle market' (Pearson & Hobbs 2001) or 'higher level' (Desroches 2007) drug dealing. Although accounts are often thin on detail and from texts not primarily aimed at understanding dealing amongst users, some themes can be identified. Sometimes this activity supports hedonistic patterns of partying and drug use somewhat departed from stereotypical images of the dependent heroin addict. There were also some accounts of heroin users who enjoyed luxuries or used dealing to support domestic expenses. These narratives sit awkwardly alongside research which posits that middle market and higher level drug dealers are fearful and scornful of dependent heroin use. Literature reviewed also pointed to inherent difficulties experienced by heroin users who also sell drugs. In addition, the literature pointed to talents which users who deal believe help to overcome these difficulties (e.g. Lalander2003; Moyle & Coomber 2017). The narratives of participants recruited for this study are used to build on this picture, adding to what is known about roles played, motives and ends reported as well as difficulties and talents discussed by heroin users who sell drugs.

Research methodology

The interviews used for this chapter came from two sources. Twenty-three of these were derived from Morgan's (2017) doctoral study into persistent heroin use. This study comprised of 51 semi-structured interviews. Morgan and Bennett (under review) have used the findings from this study to present a typology of heroin using lifestyles. It was an unexpected finding that a number of participants sold drugs as well as using heroin every day. Most of the sampling for this study took place at a street drugs project where the researcher volunteered in the needle exchange. If service users requested injecting equipment and related paraphernalia which suggested heroin use, then they would be asked if they would like to participate in return for a £10 shopping voucher. Those who agreed had a mobile phone number taken and were phoned the day before the planned interview. Many were hard to contact later revealing their mobile phones ended up in pawn shops on a biweekly basis. As well as the study attracting users who had more settled lifestyles and were more interested in the shopping voucher, recruitment was also biased towards people who did not pawn their phones and also those who could give contact details for their partner. This led to a sample who were older and had less chaotic lifestyles. To seek out younger and more chaotic respondents, some extra recruitment was conducted at two hostels where eleven participants were sought, including an extra five who sold drugs while using heroin.

Whilst planning for this chapter further participants were sought. For this stage of the research, several drugs projects were contacted, although only one could facilitate interviews. A contact of the researcher who is a drugs worker was very quickly able to speak to their manager and facilitate use of a room at the project, and crucially, access to service users. For this stage of the research £20 shopping vouchers were offered and eight users who deal interviewed. The first round of interviews was conducted between 2011 and 2012, the second round in 2018. Interviews were conducted across two cities in South Wales. Both series of data gathering comprised of tape-recorded semi-structured interviews. While interviews conducted in the first round discussed all aspects of lifestyle from when the participant was first using heroin every day up until the present, the second round of interviews focused specifically on user-dealing activity. In both rounds of interviews there was variation between those which were more interviewer led and others where the participants very much took the lead and told their own story. Interviews were transcribed verbatim and then thematically coded using NVIVO 11 software.

All thirty-one participants were men. In the first phase of data gathering where heroin users were sought, nine of the sample of 51 were women, and none of the women talked about selling drugs. During the second phase of the research where heroin users who had sold drugs were specifically sought, only eight were recruited and all were men. Studies already cited by Rosenbaum (1981), Hanson et al. (1985), Taylor (1993), Moyle and Coomber (2015) and Small et al. (2013) have shown that heroin using women have been involved in dealing. Future research should aim to add to this literature. Of the 31 men who partook in this study 30 are white, with one British Asian man also participating. A more ethnically heterogeneous sample would also be of benefit.

The analysis focused on narratives of the participants. Using the methods of narrative analysis described by Presser (2009) and Fleetwood (2014), the veracity of claims made is open to challenge, whereas their narratives are key to understanding how the participants understand themselves and how they wish to present themselves. The findings section starts with discussion of the roles played by the user-dealers interviewed. Although this picture will be compared to the findings of similar qualitative studies there is no way to verify whether the accounts given in the semi-structured interviews reflect reality. However, these stories will tell us about culture amongst the user-dealers interviewed. If a story is fantasy, then we will have learnt about the aspirations of the participant. If we hear about motives we will at least understand more about what is important to the participants. Overall, we will find out about how the respondents used storytelling to communicate their identities to the researcher. When hearing about challenges we will learn about users and dealers understanding of the difficulties in their lifestyles. Narrative criminology is a forerunner and close relation of symbolic interactionism, so using the Thomas' theorem (Thomas & Thomas 1928, pp. 572), 'if men define situations as real, they are real in their consequences'. Therefore, the thoughts of participants as projected in their narratives will be relevant to their actions.

Making ends meet, partying and profit

As reported by Moyle and Coomber (2015) and Small et al. (2013), participants told stories of working as retailers of heroin and earning just enough money or heroin to pay for their own habits. This fits with definitions of 'user-dealers' cited above (e.g. Coomber 2006). This included a small number of 'freelancers' who would buy amounts such as a 'teenth' (nominally 1.7 grams, or a six*teenth* of an ounce), perhaps for £60 and break it into ten £10 bags and then administer the profits. As 'Jack' said, *'You just keep up your own habit sorted'*. Another freelancer ('Bernie') covered his habit and also generated some extra cash for essentials such as cigarettes:

> I used to, years ago but just to cover my own habit, nothing major, I used to sell half of it, keep my own habit going, it was £20 a day then, to spend on fags and things, happy days.

There were a larger number of 'middlers' who would buy on behalf of others and take a cut for themselves. 'Tom' played this role and would buy heroin on behalf of a small group of associates who would provide the money. He claimed to have better contacts than most others in his local scene and also had a nice flat where his friends could consume the drugs he supplied. Throughout his heroin using career he claimed that his job seekers allowance covered food, bills and furnishings for his flat, his heroin use was paid for by others due to his position as a middle-man. Some participants talked about buying heroin for others due to their 'interlocking paydays', as 'Ben' explains:

> When I didn't have [heroin], the boys would turn up on their pay-days. It used to all interlock basically. I'd get paid on this day, one of the other boys

> would get paid a couple of days later, another boy and couple of days later. We'd all be helping each other out.

Earlier in his heroin using career 'Ben' started working as a 'runner' for his uncle, delivering small amounts of heroin and being paid a 'teenth' a day. Under the taxonomy described by Small et al. (2013) this form of user-dealing is 'corporate' as he is working for someone else. Despite a 'teenth' a day heroin habit being higher than reported by many participants, 'Ben' did not report having surplus funds while working for his uncle. Other participants have described 'corporate' roles where their house has been used as a premise for the sale of drugs.

In both of the South Wales locations where fieldwork took place, respondents' described 'London blacks' and 'scousers', who originated in Liverpool, setting up heroin and crack dealing operations in the local areas. Although the encroachment of these groups into the local scene, at the cost of local actors, was described as a notable recent change by participants, echoing the analysis of Coomber and Moyle (2019), their presence crops up in narratives dating back to the turn of the millennium (see Hales & Hobbs 2010). The rise in their activity corresponds with law enforcement data which documents a sharp rise in so called 'county lines' activity within Wales (Thomas & Jackson 2018). None of the participants discussed working for 'scousers', a few had worked for drug dealers from London. In the London cases, dealers set up shop in their flats. As well as hosting the operations these heroin users might also act as runners delivering the product, but for fairly meagre pay:

> I would have a couple of stones. I would have a couple of shots a day. I would go out there and if anyone wanted [heroin or crack] I'd run back to the house, grab it, and then run it down to them.
>
> *Gerard*

Another narrative present in participant's accounts was that of dealing in drugs other than heroin at the point they became heroin users. 'Seymour' was selling amphetamines, which as well as heroin he also felt dependent upon. Together with his legal income this meant that he and his partner could make ends meet:

> That paid for my gear and my speed, plus my rent, my girlfriend was working, she was working full time, I was working full time.

Participants' narratives also featured accounts of drug dealing above the retail level and in many cases activities which allowed for financial profit and heavy patterns of drug use, beyond simply managing heroin dependency. 'Colin' and 'Tony' both managed crack houses, where customers would visit the property to buy heroin and crack cocaine, sometimes also consuming their drugs on site. They were both working directly for bigger dealers, so this is 'corporate' dealing. 'Tony' as well as other participants suggested that such commercial 'crack house' operations are largely a thing of the past, saying that Police action made them no longer viable. 'Tony' and 'Colin's narratives are, respectively, set in the early 1990s and the beginning of the millennium. In more recent narratives, drugs were delivered to customers rather than sold on site.

'Colin' was allowed to consume one £10 deal for ever five that he sold. Both 'Colin' and 'Tony' talked of chaotic lifestyles dominated by partying:

> We use to have a shift pattern... but it never used to work... one of us used to man the phone... one of use would sleep, and then you'd fit your partying in, but it never use to really work like that, it was always just partying constantly twenty-four seven.
>
> *Tony*

The party lifestyles described by these crack house managers may be seen as qualitatively different from those of heroin using dealers who only sold enough to avoid withdrawal symptoms. However, some participants claimed to have found even greater levels of success through their dealing.

'A bit of luxury' (Harry)

Participants also discussed corporate rolls which Pearson and Hobbs (2001) would consider as middle market. 'Derek' was convicted for his part of an armed robbery as a teenager. His older accomplices valued him as he *'knew how to use a bat'*. He also claimed to have had a stocky and muscular build, which is perhaps why on his release from prison he began working for a group of heroin dealers providing the security when they bought in bulk. This was in the mid-1980s and he claims he was paid £500 for each trip. 'Alex' was paid both to be a driver and for additional tasks. He collected heroin in bulk from a big city and returned it to the small provincial area where he also weighed and bagged the heroin. Participants in these roles emphasized their connections to more organised criminals. 'Alex' suggested that his affiliation with known crime groups in the city where he bought their heroin protected them from predators who might have wished to barge in on their business or rob them. 'Tony' went further suggesting his employers were able to divert police action away from their operation. Despite 'Alex' describing his lifestyle during this period as 'shit' there was some lingering pride that he was part of a substantial and feared organization. 'Tony' also looks back on this period in his life with some shame but was proud of the alleged bullet wound he showed off to me.

Narratives also featured stories of freelancers who worked in middle market rolls. 'Mo' was a significant wholesaler of cannabis resin at the point he became a heroin user, he was earning six figure sums per annum and in his own words was *'absolutely smashing it'*. However, stories of profit from freelance drug dealing more often involved lucrative sales of heroin and crack. 'Ben', as we heard above, began in a corporate roll but moved on to be a freelancer after his uncle offered that he take over the business. As well as paying for his own heroin use he also generated surplus funds: *'I had a raging habit that I could control and I was making money as well'.* 'Harry' claimed he was earning £1,000 a day. He says he spent around half and saved half. A lot of his outgoings were on drug use, while he also enjoyed: *'a bit of luxury, couple of cars, y'know, go shopping every day, buy clothes every day'.* Although participant's explanations of where the money went focused on heavy consumption of heroin and crack as well as material goods such as cars, narratives also alluded to some more wholesome ends. 'Paul' said that a lot of his money was spent on family: *'I put my daughter through uni and I paid my other daughter's mortgage and things and I just spend on them really'*, while 'Gerard' suggested that four-figure profits accrued from selling opioid substitutes in prison were used to furnish his home upon release. Respondents of this study did not want to suggest that they had sought a celebrity lifestyle. Instead they talked about wanting the things that everyone else had.

The more I was making, the more I was smoking (Harry)

Especially in the narratives of more commercially successful dealers were challenges inherent to supplying drugs while being a heroin user. Some participants reported some highly excessive patterns of drugs use, albeit that the veracity of such claims cannot be verified in a study such as this. 'Jonny' reported that if he was buying heroin in £10 bags he would have spent around £320 per day, with daily crack, cannabis and benzodiazepine use on top. 'Harry' suggested that his lifestyle amounted to little more than *'smoking all day'*, claiming both his heroin and crack use were more or less constant during waking hours. But, how did they fare keeping the business alive despite such heavy drug use?

As previously mentioned, 'Mo's' highly successful cannabis wholesaling enterprise failed to survive his drug use:

> I did it [supplying cannabis], I'd say for about a year, if that, if that, six months, basically it just went out the window… well basically when I was smoking the gear[2], I'd just switch into a different zone, I just didn't want nothing to do with all that crap, didn't have time to go driving around here dropping off here, dropping off there, so it just stopped like that.

'Paul' suggested some level of 'chaos' was inevitable when both selling and using:

> They always get chaotic do you know what I mean… If someone says that they don't… They are lying… Just losing things, losing ounces and stuff.

Another common difficulty was how to desist from heroin use, while being engaged in supply. 'Calum' specifically suggested he was unable to avoid getting high on his own supply:

> The longest I lasted was two or three days. That never, ever fucking worked out... the whole fucking Scarface thing and all of that, and I tried and tried. I would have loved to do that.

Another complaint was that drug use prevented enjoyment of the spoils generated by selling drugs. 'Calum' claimed to have made substantial profits and enjoyed travelling. However, having a heroin dependency created practical problems:

> [W]e never went anywhere for more than a week because of how much gear that you would have to take. And this was the other thing, these were the considerations that we had, you know, that even though we had money and freedom, we were still shackled. So were never completely free.

I certainly was a lot more organised than a few of them (Tony)

Some of the issues described by participants relate to the challenges faced by drug dealing in general, such as the need to have a reputation which prevents people from robbing them or reneging on debts. In addition, many respondents saw themselves as particularly security conscious, being that bit cleverer and more careful than other people in avoiding robbery or arrest. However, others focused on how they were able to manage the inherent difficulties of being user and dealer. Despite the chaos, 'Tony' and 'Colin' (both crack house managers) claimed to keep things ticking over thanks to them being more reliable and self-disciplined than others who attempted to play these roles. 'Colin' was placed in charge of a crack house because the previous manager had been using more than he could sell, 'Colin' was perceived as being relatively trustworthy. 'Tony' also considered himself as distinguished from his colleagues:

> Oh, we were always careless, always, you know, we'd always think we were being more organised than we were, I certainly was a lot more organised than a few of them.

Some lower level 'freelancers' also believed that their levels of self-control set them apart. 'Ross' was a freelancer and worked in partnership with someone who we will call 'Jack' who did not participate in this study. I asked 'Ross' if he had ever messed up his dealing operations and got into debt: *'I didn't. 'Jack' did on the crack, and I had to shoplift again and back to square one'*. The idea of control went further in some narratives. 'Jonny' spoke at length about his difficult experiences growing up, not least feeling controlled by his stepfather as well as coping with bone diseases. Themes of control crop up regularly in his stories, how heroin allowed him to control his pain, how keeping one step ahead of the police gave him feelings of self-determination. He *'was a stickler for hygiene'*, demanding that friends and hangers-on would not inject heroin on his premises. Indeed 'Jonny' was not the only heroin-using dealer interviewed who preferred to smoke rather than inject heroin. Although their high earnings and reserves of consumable heroin made the efficiency savings of injection less vital, there is also a suggestion that these men were apt to set themselves rules which they would keep to and exercise some levels of self-control.

It is the need for control and self-determination, which created the most tangled knot of difficulties for the participants of this study. 'Calum', as we have heard, wished he could desist from heroin so that he could live out a jet-setting drug dealer's fantasy lifestyle, unencumbered by dependence to a drug he would rather not smuggle across international borders. 'Jonny' often discussed quitting drug dealing with a close confidant:

> Wanna get out of here, she'd say, well why don't you do it? I'd go like that, I'd say well, tell me where I'm gonna get all this from, and I'd pull out my pocket, maybe two grand from one pocket, and a big bag of mixed, drugs in the other pocket, and I'd be like, where am I going to get this from, at my age, and a car, and everything else I've got, and without helping my mum pay the mortgage and without doing this and other things were going on as well, erm, how else could I possibly do this?

There were variations in how far participants felt they could control their drug use in the face of incessant opportunities to consume at a high level, but none described managing to fully desist while still selling drugs. Although they subscribed to the maxim 'never get high on your own supply', participants did not report being able to sell heroin without also using the drug.

Conclusion

Coomber (2006, p. 141) suggested that 'user-dealers' are 'users first and dealers second who primarily supply to support their own drug use'. This may well be a useful definition, especially in his research which seeks to delineate social suppliers from drug dealers. However, narratives dissected for this chapter suggest that some heroin users who sell drugs do not necessarily fit this image. Firstly, a number of participants' narratives suggested that they maintained middle market drug dealing whilst dependent users of heroin. This was not expected. The dichotomy between social suppliers supporting their own drug consumption and commercial dealers who make large profits and do not consume drugs does not seem to reflect the diversity of lifestyles amongst heroin users who deal. Moyle and Coomber (2015) focused on the narratives of those who felt they needed to use a certain amount of heroin every day due to their dependencies. However, narratives from this study featuring excessive drug use and party lifestyles point at least to some variation to how far the dealing activities of heroin users are only conducted to make ends meet. A second key finding was that some heroin users described selling drugs for a profit which might be spent on modest and typically conformist expenses such as having highlights in one's hair, 'nice clothes' and camping trips. Additionally, participants spoke about spending more significant sums of money on providing for family members' housing or higher education. In addition to these surprisingly benevolent outgoings, there were also references to conspicuous consumption and foreign holidays. This is not to moralize, but to suggest that some new terminology might be needed for those who do not fit with the image of user-dealers portrayed by Coomber (2006), Moyle and Coomber (2015, 2017), Small et al. (2013) and Akhtar and South (2000).

The methods of data gathering used for this study (and also for Moyle & Coomber 2015, 2017 and Small et al. 2013) were retrospective interviews. Especially since the researcher in this case was an outsider rather than native to the heroin and crack scene investigated, some could question the findings of this study. Indeed, the factuality of the accounts given could not be firmly verified. Although it is a strength of retrospective interviewing that it enables access to older criminals whose drug use and criminal exploits have reduced in scale over time (Maruna 2001), it is a weakness compared to ethnographic research that participants are not observed in the act. However, participants of this study might not have agreed to be interviewed and the middle- to high-level drug dealers would not have consented to an ethnographic approach either (save for exceptional circumstances, such as the study by Sadler 1985), during the heydays of their drug supply for fear of law enforcement. Likewise, one could speculate that not all participants had indeed retired from drug dealing (as they all claimed to).

Narrative theory was used as the main approach for analysing the data for this study. One strength of this is that the sequencing of events by storytellers is put under the spotlight. The mythology of a rise of fall in fortunes was in evidence. Participants discussed utilising personal characteristics including aspects of their masculinities such as violence and aggression in order to carve out a niche. Other personal characteristics were lauded as setting them apart from the crowd, such as self-discipline, astuteness and intelligence. There were stories of serendipitously taking advantage of good fortune as well as rags to riches tails of triumph. There were also tails of how drug use and drug dealing could be emancipatory in enabling individuals to live hedonistic lives as well as possessing status symbols and living comfortably. Participants' narratives also tended to reveal a humility to the idea that despite some hubris in their younger years, they now see that drug use and dealing are awkward bedfellows. Whereas Hall et al. (2008) included a quotation from a successful criminal that heroin addicts were anathema due to their dirty appearance and slavery to a drug, many participants in this study tried to be free and respectable while also being heroin users.

Notes

1 For example, the largest and most recent interview study with convicted drug dealers in the UK splits the market into Retail, Local, National, and International (Matrix, 2007, p. 17).

2 For the participants of this study 'gear' tends to mean heroin.

References

Akhtar, S. & South, N. (2000) Hidden from Heroin's History: Heroin Use and Dealing within an English Asian Community–A Case Study. *Crime Prevention Studies*, 11: pp. 153–178.

Bourdieu, P. (1977) *An Outline of a Theory of Practice*. Cambridge: Cambridge University Press.

Bourdieu, P. (1990) *The Logic of Practice*. Cambridge: Polity Press.

Briggs, D. (2013) *Deviance and Risk on Holiday: An Ethnography of British Tourists in Ibiza*. Basingstoke: Palgrave Macmillan.

Briggs, D. & Monge Gamero, R. (2017) *Dead-end Lives: Drugs and Violence in the City Shadows*. London: Policy Press.

Bullock, K., Clarke, R.V. & Tilley, N. (2010) *The Situational Prevention of Organised Crime*. London: Routledge.

Coomber, R. (2006) *Pusher Myths: Re-situating the Drug Dealer*. London: Free Association Books.

Coomber, R. & Moyle, L. (2018) The Changing Shape of Street-Level Heroin and Crack Supply in England–Commuting, Holidaying and Cuckooing Drug Dealers Across 'County Lines'. *British Journal of Criminology*, 38(6): pp. 1232–1342.

Coomber, R. & Turnbull, P. (2007) 'Arenas of Drug Transaction: Adolescent Cannabis Transactions in England-Social Supply'. *Journal of Drug Issues*, 37(4): pp. 845–865.

de Palma, B. (1983) *Scarface*. Universal Pictures.

DeBeck, K., Shannon, K., Wood, E., Li, K., Montaner, J. & Kerr, T. (2007) Income–generating activities of people who inject drugs. *Drug and Alcohol Dependence*, 91(1): 50–56.

Desroches, F. (2005) *The Crime That Pays: Drug Trafficking and Organised Crime in Canada*. Toronto: Canadian Scholars.

Desroches, F. (2007) Research on Upper Level Drug Trafficking: A Review. *Journal of Drug Issues*, 37(4): pp. 827–844.

Faupel, C.E. (1991) *Shooting Dope: Career Patterns of Hard-Core Heroin Users*. Gainesville: University Press of Florida.

Fleetwood, J. (2014) *Drug Mules: Women in the Cocaine Trade*. Basingstoke: Palgrave MacMillan.

Hales, G. & Hobbs, D. (2010) Drug Markets in the Community: A London Borough Case Study. *Trends in Organised Crime*, 13(1): pp. 13–30.

Hall, S., Winslow, S., & Ancrum, C. (2008) *Criminal Identities and Consumer Culture: Crime, Exclusion and the New Culture of Narcissm*. Cullompton: Willan.

Hanson, B., Beschner, G., Walters, J.M., & Bovelle, E. (1985) *Life with Heroin*. Lexington, MA: Lexington Books.

Hobbs, D. (2013) *Lush Life: Constructing Organised Crime in the UK*. Oxford: Oxford University Press.

Johnson, B.D., Goldstein, P., Preble, E., Schmeidler, J., Lipton, D.S., Spunt, B. and Miller, T. (1985). *Taking Care of Business: The Economics of Crime by Heroin Abusers*. Lexington, MA: Lexington Books.

Lalander, P. (2003) *'Hooked on Heroin'*. London: Berg.

Maruna, S. (2001) *Making Good: How Ex-Convicts Reform and Rebuild Their Lives*. 1st edition. Albany, NY: American Psychological Association.

Matrix Knowledge Group (2007) *The Illicit Drug Trade in the United Kingdom*. Home Office Online Report.

Measham, F.C. (2004) Play Space: Historical and Socio-Cultural Reflections on Drugs, Licensed Leisure Locations, Commericialisation and Control. *International Journal of Drug Policy*, 5–6(11): pp. 337–345.

Morgan, J.C. (2017) *Long Term Heroin Careers: Narratives of Persistence.* Unpublished doctoral thesis.

Moyle, L. (2019) Situating Vulnerability and Exploitation in Street-Level Drug Markets: Cuckooing, Commuting, and the "County Lines" Drug Supply Model. *Journal of Drug Issues*, 49(4) 739–755.

Moyle, L. & Coomber, R. (2015) Earning a score: An exploration of the nature and roles of heroin and crack cocaine 'user-dealers'. *British Journal of Criminology*, 55(3): pp. 534–555.

Moyle, L., & Coomber, R. (2017) Bourdieu on Supply: Utilizing the 'Theory of Practice' to Understand Complexity and Culpability in Heroin and Crack Cocaine User-Dealing. *European Journal of Criminology*, 14(3): pp. 269–289.

Murphy, F., Murphy, S., Sales, P., & Lau, N. (2018) Examining Social Supply among Nonmedical Prescription Stimulant Users on the San Francisco Bay Area. *International Journal of Drug Policy*, 54: pp. 68–76.

NCA (2019) County Lines Drug Vulnerability and Harm 2018, National Crime Agency.

Parker, H., Bakx, K., and Newcombe, R. (1988) *Living with Heroin: The Impact of a Drugs Epidemic in an English Community.* Milton Keynes: Open University Press.

Pearson, G. (2007) Drug Markets and Dealing: From 'Street Dealer' to 'Mr Big'. In M. Simpson, T. Shildrick & R. MacDonald (Eds.), *Drugs in Britain: Supply, Consumption and Control* (pp. x–y). Basingstoke: Palgrave.

Pearson, G. & Hobbs, D. (2001) *Middle Market Drug Distribution.* Home Office Research Study 227. London: Home Office.

Preble, E. & Casey, J. J. (1969) Taking Care of Business, the Heroin User's Life on the Street. *Substance Use & Misuse*, 4(1): pp. 1–24.

Presser, L. (2009) The Narratives of Offenders. *Theoretical Criminology*, 13(2): pp. 177–200.

Rosenbaum, M. (1981) *Women on Heroin.* New Brunswick, NJ: Rutgers University Press.

Sadler, P.A. (1985) *Wheeling and Dealing.* Columbia University Press.

Sandberg, S. (2012) The Importance of Culture for Cannabis Markets: Towards an Economic Sociology of Illicit Drugs Markets. *British Journal of Criminology*, 52: pp. 1133–1151.

Shammas, V., Sandberg, S. & Pedersen, W. (2014) Trajectories to Mid-and Higher Level Drug Crimes: Penal Misrepresentations of Drug Dealers in Norway. *British Journal of Criminology*, 54, 592–612.

Shewan, D. & Delgarno, P. (2005) Evidence for Controlled Heroin Use? Low levels of Negative Health and Social Outcomes among Non-Treatment Heroin Users in Glasgow (Scotland). *British Journal of Health Psychology*, 10: pp. 33–48.

Small, W., Maher, L., Lawlor, J., Wood, E., Shannon, K. & Kerr, T. (2013) Injection Drug Users' Involvement in Drug Dealing in the Downtown Eastside of Vancouver: Social Organization and Systemic Violence. *International Journal of Drug Policy*, 24: pp. 479–487.

Spicer, J., Moyle, L., & Coomber, R. (2019) The Variable and Evolving Nature of 'Cuckooing' as a Form of Criminal Exploitation in Street Level Drug Markets. *Transnational Organised Crime.* Available at: https://doi.org/10.1007/s12117-019-09368-5

Taylor, A. (1993) *Women Drug Users: An Ethnography of a Female Injecting Community.* Wooton-under-Edge: Clarendon Press.

Taylor, M. & Potter, G. (2013) From "Social Supply" to "Real Dealing": Drift, Friendship, and Trust in Drug-Dealing Careers. *Journal of Drug Issues*, 43(4): pp. 392–406.

Thomas R. & Jackson, C. (2018) County lines: Why drug phenomenon has hit Wales so hard, BBC News, 16 May 2018. Available at: www.bbc.co.uk/news/uk-wales-44127068

Thomas, W.I., & Thomas, D. S. (1928) *The Child in America: Behavior Problems and Programs*. New York, NY: Knopf.

Tzvetkova, M., Pardal, M., Rena, A., Liquori, A., Libianchi, S., Disley, E., et al. (2014) *Drug Dealers' Careers, Behaviours and Strategies–In Their Own Words. A Study of Imprisoned Drug Dealers in Italy, Slovenia and Germany. Addiction and Lifestyles in Contemporary Europe: Reframing Addictions Project (ALICE RAP).* Report to European Commission.

Waldorf, D. (1973) *Careers in Dope*. Englewood Cliffs, NJ: Prentice Hall.

Warburton, H., Turnbull, P. & Hough, M. (2005) *Occasional and Controlled Heroin Use: Not a Problem?* York: Joseph Rowntree Foundation.

Windle, J. & Briggs, D. (2015) 'It's Like Working Away for two weeks', The Harms Associated with Young Drug Dealers Commuting from a Saturated London Drug Market. *Crime Prevention and Community Safety*, 17(2), pp. 105–119.

Young, J. (1971) *The Drugtakers: The Social Meaning of Drug Use*. London: MacGibbon and Kee.

Zinberg, N.E. (1984) *Drug, Set, and Setting: The Basis for Controlled Intoxicant Use*. Newhaven, CN: Yale University Press.

6

JUST 'SORTING' THEIR MATES?

The identities, roles and motivations of social suppliers

Leah Moyle

Background

The image of the drug dealer in which profit-driven wholesalers or drug addicted 'junkie' retail distributors (Pearson and Hobbs, 2001 are presented as predatory, unscrupulous and immoral (Coomber, 2006; Speaker, 2002) has been suggested to be culturally omnipresent (Berridge, 1999; Kohn, 1992; Musto, 1999). However, over time, various research on drug markets (e.g. Blum, 1972; Dorn, Murji, & South, 1992; Parker, Aldridge, & Measham, 1998) has demonstrated that not all drug dealers are the same (Coomber & Moyle, 2013). Indeed, many of the stereotypes attached to those that deal in illicit street drugs have been difficult to sustain for the vast majority of those that would be 'classified' as drug dealers (Coomber, 2006). The young adults participating in this research are one example of a group that tend not to fit these stereotypes of the 'drug dealer', which have become enshrined in the laws around supply and the 1971 Misuse of Drugs Act (see Police Foundation, 2000). Instead, they are indicative of a growing population who are able to source an ever increasing range of substances through a variety of emerging and evolving technologies such as darknet markets (Martin, 2014), and social media apps (Moyle et al., 2019) and who are found to be more likely to access drugs from friends or known individuals than commercial sellers (see Barratt et al., 2016). At the same time and accompanying the normalization of drug use (Parker et al., 1998; Aldridge et al. 2011; South, 1999), there also exists a relative normalisation of drug supply in society (Parker, 2000). This, as the chapter will go on to document, is constituted by drug users commonly engaged in low-level acts or sharing, reciprocal exchange, along with demonstrating an openness to undertake more involved forms of social supply – distributing larger quantities of drugs, including Class A substances, to acquaintances as well as friends (Coomber et al., 2015).

DOI: 10.4324/9781351010245-8

This chapter aims to present an in-depth analysis of these varying roles and distribution behaviours undertaken by drug users, stretching from acts that may not even be understood as normatively constituting supply, to those that may, on paper, seem to represent something more commercial. It draws upon interviews with young adults who describe the ways in which they drift into this activity, and the motivations that lead them to continue to buy from or supply drugs to friends or acquaintances over time. Social supply has tended to be conceptualized as 'not-for-profit' supply or 'friendly business' (Werse & Bernard, 2016. This chapter will begin by exploring existing literature that has contributed to framing this distinctive supply act. In doing so it also identifies gaps and some areas of blurring (Potter, 2009), along with how this can present challenges for working with these kinds of offences in a legal context (Coomber et al., 2018).

Many of those participating in this research could not be categorised as operating with a complete 'absence of any financial gain' or on a purely 'non-commercial basis' – categorisations which, for example, have been utilized in attempt to differentiate social supply type offences in England and Wales (e.g. Sentencing Council 2012: 8). While these types of approaches are progressive for recognizing different levels of culpability and harm evident in supply and legally challenging the trope that all drug dealers are the same (Coomber, 2006), as this chapter will go on to detail, there is still more work to be done to appropriately identify the scope and nuances of social supply as it takes place in the real world if we are able to impart more proportionate legal responses towards this group (Coomber et al., 2018).

Conceptualising social supply: social supply as 'not-for-profit'

Although definition of social supply has largely tended to be a slippery business characterized by an absence of an accepted definition criterion (Taylor & Potter, 2013), nonetheless, there are two central elements that are often associated with the term: social supply as 'non-profit', and as 'non-stranger' supply (Potter, 2009). To begin with, the idea of social supply as owning an inherent non-commercial character appears to have been widely supported in the literature base (e.g. Hough et al., 2003; Coomber & Turnbull, 2007). Early studies identified either the latent symbolism of distributing and/or introducing friends to mind-altering substances (Goode 1969; Blum et al., 1972), or the social significance of the related mutual assurance of low or non-profit trading of drugs (Dorn et al., 1992). In a contemporary context, the reciprocal nature of social supply, where exchange-based supply functions to support peer group drug supply, together with the altruism loaded within sentiments of 'helping friends out', has similarly been emphasised as meaningful (Belackova & Vaccoro, 2013; Aldridge at al. 2011; Parker et al., 1998).

At a practical level, literature elsewhere (e.g. Hough et al., 2003; Duffy et al., 2008; Aldridge et al., 2011; Lenton et al., 2016) has also depicted the regularity and high incidence of drug users sharing, swapping and 'chipping in' (combining funds to buy a quantity of drugs as a group). This has been identified as an important means of negotiating drug prohibition through providing access to those without contacts to drug supply networks (Jacques & Allen, 2014; Measham et al., 2001), as well as offering users the prospect to share drug costs and protect themselves from the threat of the police and prosecution (Potter 2009; Parker et al., 1998). Purchasing from a friend or as part of a group could often therefore ensure greater security since buyers felt there was less possibility of being supplied low-quality or fake drugs, thereby increasing the perceived levels of safety (Measham et al., 2001; Murphy et al., 2005; Jacinto et al., 2008).

Yet, while research tracing motivations for accessing drugs through social suppliers have prioritized the relational and non-commercial nature of social supply, a closer more critical examination of the data suggests that these transactions are often more nuanced. Research literature indicates that some forms of profit or reward commonly feature in most transactions. Suppliers are routinely given free drugs or a monetary contribution for their troubles and risk (Parker, 2000; Coomber & Turnbull, 2007), or effectively earn their drugs for free through retail 'markup' (see Goode, 1969; Dorn et al., 1992; Murphy et al.,1990; Jacques & Wright, 2015; Velackova & Zabransky, 2016). The routine inclusion of gain and financial profit through taxing, bulk purchase and markup has elicited a call for social supply to be understood as part of a broader concept of 'minimally commercial supply' (see Coomber & Moyle, 2013; Coomber et al., 2018) where the routine inclusion of gain is conceded as intrinsic to almost all non-commercial drug deals or exchanges. It is argued that extending the parameters of the concept would more accurately describe the nature of low-level drug transactions (including 'problem drugs' such as heroin and crack cocaine), whilst also acknowledging the seemingly artificial boundary between involved drug use and low-level sharing and supply behaviours (Chatwin and Potter, 2014; Coomber et al., 2018).

Social supply as 'friendly business'

Another central theme linked with social supply is the notion of friendship. Empirical studies have invariably reported meaningfully high proportions of study populations having received illegal drugs from friends (see, e.g.,, Duffy et al., 2008; Murphy et al., 2005; Nicholas 2008; Belackova & Vacarro, 2013). While the notion of friendship is commonly utilised and even seems to signify the key characteristic of this practice (e.g. Police Foundation, 2000), there has also been broad consensus within the academy that these social drug networks also incorporate 'acquaintances' (Hough et al., 2003; Murphy et al., 2005; Potter, 2009). The difficulty with the association of acquaintanceship to social supply relates to the intricacies surrounding the point at which a stranger stops being a stranger, and becomes an acquaintance (see Morgan, 2009). Indeed, as Potter (2009) has noted, the scope of social supply as found in the literature also appears to include 'known individuals', who are not quite friends but who ostensibly tend not to be strangers. Accordingly, Potter (2009, p. 69) consequently argues that supply to 'non-strangers' may be a helpful way of defining such networks. This is reasoned as appropriate since friendship is itself a subjective conception and therefore it is problematic–particularly at policy level – to base the definition of social supply solely on this idea. In illustrating the premise behind this notion, it is also instructive to reflect on the empirical observations of Belakova and Vaccaro (2013), who explicate the nuances inherent in relationships between social networks while also noting the importance of 'friendly business' in both facilitating distribution and protecting users against the risks of illicit cannabis markets. Such themes (see also Measham et al., 2001 and Parker, 2000) serve to reflect the increasingly blurred distinction between 'dealer' and 'friend' (Parker, 2000; Potter, 2009; Taylor & Potter, 2013) and the complex minutiae of constructing an accurate definition of social supply as it occurs in a real-world context.

The voices of those included in this research expose these aforementioned blurred boundaries or the often 'fuzzy' overlap between consumption and supply evident within the so-called social supply networks (Coomber et al., 2015). As such, this chapter seeks to unpack such nuance, providing in-depth qualitative data examining the meanings, motivations, benefits and lived experience of involvement in the social supply of recreational drugs.

Methodology

The original data presented here formed the basis of a PhD study on non-commercially motivated forms of drug supply (specifically social supply and 'addicted' user-dealing). This explorative qualitative project employed interviews and case studies garnered from 60 social suppliers comprised of a 'student sample' (a group of 30 second and third-year undergraduates from a range of subject groups including but not limited to sociology, business studies and geology) and the *principal research population* – referred to as 'the Somerset sample' – which these research findings are largely based upon. In recruiting both groups, the inclusion criteria were set to incorporate anyone over the age of 18 who had distributed illicit drugs to friends or acquaintances 'for little or no profit' in the last year, thereby capturing a sample with a range of experiences and involvement in social supply. While some had dipped in and out of the practice and others described more sustained participation in supply, the principal 'Somerset sample' could be described as fairly 'drug involved' (see demographics) and had been since first attending university. Conducted in 2013, this research generated thematic data exploring the types of roles that social suppliers played, as well as data pertaining to routes into supply, motivations and relationships between suppliers and users. Access to these respondents was achieved through the researchers' pre-existing relationships with individuals known – on some level – to have some involvement in social supply activity. The principal gatekeeper was contacted, and through snowball or 'respondent-driven sampling' – where respondents offer referrals to those who possess similar characteristics that are of interest to the researcher (Biernacki & Waldorf, 1981) – he was able to contact and recruit friends and acquaintances through direct communications and via social media.

Ethical approval was obtained from the University Ethics Board and normative anonymising and confidentiality measures were employed to protect respondents from harm and identification. As is common with this type of research (see Ritter et al., 2003), respondents were offered a £15 reciprocity payment for their contribution to the research to acknowledge their time and effort. After the transcription process, the data was uploaded into a computer-assisted qualitative data analysis software program (NVivo 9), where codes were generated and resulting themes and typologies were created. Below these themes are explored, beginning with an outline of demographic trends, broad typologies, and motivations and rationales for involvement in social supply activity.

Findings

Social supply demographics

Of the principal research sample, 86% were male. The age of the respondents ranged from 23 to 32 years, with the average age being 27. All respondents were employed at the time of interview, with a range of roles including media executives, teachers, chefs, construction managers, journalists and architects. Social suppliers were most likely to have had their first drug use experience at the age of 15, with ages ranging from 11 to 17 years. Of the sample 87% had used drugs in the last one month and 83% had provided access to drugs (social supplied) in the last six months. At the time of the research, respondents reported 'regular' use of cocaine (28%), 3,4-Methylenedioxymethamphetamine (MDMA) (23%), cannabis (17%), ecstasy (15%), ketamine (11%), Valium (2%), mushrooms (2%) and mephedrone (2%). Use of lesser known hallucinogenic substances, such as 2C-B (4-bromo-2,5–dimethoxyphenethylamine) and 2C-I (2,5-dimethoxy-4-iodophenethylamine), were also cited. With regard to the amount of drugs social suppliers themselves used, cocaine users most commonly stated using 1 g (range 0.2 g–2 g), MDMA users 0.5 g, ketamine consumers 1 g and cannabis users a 'teenth' (1.75 g) *per occasion* (modal quantity). In terms of cost, this group indicated spending anything between £10 and £200 a month on drugs, and the average expenditure was reported by social suppliers as being around £70.

Introducing the 'social suppliers': typologies

What follows will outline the research findings, beginning with an analysis of the differing social supply roles taken on by the respondents and moving on to a description of the core motivations offered for continued involvement in social supply. The following typologies represent the most prevalent styles in which individuals would become involved in social supply. It should be noted that these roles were not definitively adopted by individuals; instead, they represent differing modes of supply that social suppliers drifted in and out of in a fluid fashion, according to the wider context or situation (see Coomber et al., 2015; Murphy et al., 1990). Social suppliers may therefore act principally as 'designated buyers' who periodically engage in 'party buying', or equally, they may describe themselves as 'stash dealers' who graduate to an 'entrepreneur role' – these choices are mediated over time by factors ranging from their levels of social capital (Bourdieu, 1990), their ability to fund a drugs buy or the frequency of their drug use.

The 'designated buyer'

The 'designated buyer' represents the most common form of social supplier identified within this data set. As suggested by the title, the typology refers to an individual who will buy a quantity of substance on behalf of the group. Once purchased, the substance will be split between those other group members who have 'chipped in' to finance the deal, either before or after the transaction takes place. A typical example of this practice is presented below.

> If it's a night out at 'Motion' or something, then what would probably happen is that you'd, like all four of you from the office are going out so it's like '*what do you fancy doing...a few grams of cocaine or something*?'. We've all got a couple of numbers that we can ring up, we can drive somewhere...if one number doesn't work, I can ring my guy and he'll meet me at the pub. I'll get the money, go in there and then maybe go and meet at the terrace, or meet at the pub...sometimes you can meet at a venue... it's always a good idea to meet up first because it's not fair for one person to take the full risk of carrying everyone else's drugs in.
>
> *Tom, 27, Somerset Sample*

Consistent with academic research elsewhere (Police Foundation, 2000; Duffy et al., 2008; Potter, 2009), data reinforced the notion that a 'designated buyer' acts on behalf of the group, and is simply the actor who happens to 'pick up' the product. This data is therefore supportive of the point made by the Police Foundation Report (2000) – that each member of the group shares a 'common objective' or intention in the pursuit of and personal consumption of these substances and does little more than pass on a drug from one person to another (Coomber, 2006). The supply activity undertaken by the 'designated buyer' can be likened to that of the 'broker' (see Duffy et al., 2008), a role characterised by assisting others to access a drug without profit. While many designated buyers procured no tangible *financial* benefit for their work, for those that did, the data revealed that the size of the group, the perceived quality of friendship and associated risk of carrying a substance provided the basis to decide whether financial gain should be taken as recompense.

'The party buyer'

The 'party buyer' typology describes a supplier who purchases larger (sometimes bulk) amounts of drugs for a specific occasion or event, most notably for club nights or festivals. The 'party buyer' is characterised by his or her distribution of a relatively sizable quantity of drugs for a large group of people – beyond their personal friendship group and what might be assessed as reasonable for personal possession. When distributing for a festival, this would often require the party buyer to purchase sufficient quantities of drugs to cover members of the group (and sometimes their contacts) for two or three days. Interestingly, entrée into this typology was not established through the individual's frequency, or experience of drug supply. Instead, it was predicated on the party buyer's access to adequate quantity of drugs at the particular time that coincides with the 'party'.

> If I'd been to a drug dealer it would be for a lot of people, it would be for…I mean I've bought for ten people before so that would be over £100, so that would be over 100 pills it might be even 200 pills or something… it sounds stupid to say it out loud. I mean, that's a serious amount of drugs! But yeah if you're going to a festival or something and you've got 10-15 people, that's not even that much and then they've got girlfriends or friends that want some, so yeah…it sounds stupid to say it out loud! But yeah, I've done that before…
>
> *Andy, 29, Somerset Sample*

In the context of this data, this indicates that party buyers were often individuals who had some experience of acting as a 'designated buyer' but had not drifted into an 'entrepreneur' role (see below) or drug dealing proper. But for many of the party buyers, the only tangible differences between party buying and acting as a 'designated buyer' lie in the amount of drug purchased and the individual from whom the drugs were purchased. The act itself was often 'neutralised' (Sykes & Matza, 1957) through 'mental gymnastics' (Mohamed & Fritzvold, 2010), with the social supplier deconstructing both the quantities purchased in relation to the amount of members of the group they were providing for, as well as the amount of days for which the substances were required. The party buyer is therefore an individual involved in irregular and exceptional supply events; examples from both research populations suggest that these events may only occur perhaps once or twice a year.

'The entrepreneur'

'Entrepreneurs' are individuals, who, when the opportunity arises, buy a 'weight' (most popularly cited as an ounce or more) of a particular substance, in order to distribute substances for *profit* (see Ayres and Treadwell's chapter and Salinas' chapter in this volume). For the eight 'entrepreneurs' found in this research, their involvement in this more serious level of supply was not something that was actively sought out, nor something they necessarily aimed to be involved with again. Jacob explains:

> It was an opportunity that kind of came out of the blue and I kind of just saw it as a one off chance to make a bit of money...I wouldn't ever have wanted to carry it on afterwards but it was just kind of an opportunity that sort of came around and I sort of thought...why not? So, it was a real one off situation, it was a fair amount and I was able to make some money... so yeah...
>
> *Jacob, 29, Somerset Sample*

Although the relatively large quantities distributed may ordinarily be indicative of a potential customer base made up of strangers, the 'entrepreneur' primarily distributed to those described as friends and acquaintances, demonstrating the blurring of boundaries in low-level drug supply and complexities surrounding definition (Coomber et al., 2015). Despite the socially orientated aspect of distribution, this act could, nonetheless, be understood as fitting more within the parameters of commercially motivated supply, due to the respondents' *primary aim* for supply acting as a means of obtaining financial capital. Many of the respondents who were involved in this distribution style had substantial experience of previously acting as a 'designated buyer' or a 'party buyer'. Blum et al. (1972) suggest that getting 'acquainted with dealers' can be taken as being essential for later dealing. Transition into higher level opportunistic selling was likely propelled by a propensity to have taken on a number of social supply roles, the development of consequent contacts at retail level and the construction of a customer base. Jack describes his journey into an entrepreneurial role:

> Yeah, [entrepreneurial supply took] probably a couple of years, probably because there were the links and I suppose a bit of business sense so it was like, might as well ... and then I suppose I had a friend that could get a big amount and previously, I wouldn't have known that ... you gradually mix with more and more people maybe, and you know it's just one of those things ... and then you probably will eventually hear of opportunities like that and they become available. So you think "*I might as well go and do this*" so instead of £40 for one [gram] you pay £400 for 28 [grams of MDMA] so that means think I've only got to sell 10 and then...it's free (laughs). So yeah, but then you are aware that you're taking a bit of a risk...(laughs).
>
> *Jack, 26, Somerset sample*

Being active in supply for a number of years also provided necessary 'street capital' (Sandberg, 2008) – an internalised 'sense' of effective supply methodologies which minimize 'hassle' and promote profit – for successful dealing. Much like the rational cost–benefit' decisions taken by young drug takers described by Parker et al. (1998), 'entrepreneurs' reported analysing the potential rewards available (including free drugs, social status and capital) against the ease of distributing these substances (e.g. how many potential customers who would want to buy, how much effort would be required to distribute substances), and the prospective risk of being found in possession of these substances. Notably, the 'entrepreneurs' found in this research were far more likely to be individuals who perceived themselves as being in financial difficulty. For the student sample – who had historic expertise in low-level social supply – boosted social capital and the interconnectivity of the university population (see Jacques & Wright, 2015) very often presented straightforward, lucrative supply opportunities that offered respondents an attractive means to supplement their income or drug use (see Moyle & Coomber, 2018 for a full discussion and Mohamed and Fritsvold's chapter in this volume).

Social supply motivations and rationales

Economies of scale – incentivised discounts and buying 'more for less'

Overall, the motivation that featured most widely in the narratives of social suppliers was based upon the idea that buying a larger quantity of drugs – either to share within a group or to sell on – was the *cheapest* way of purchasing drugs. Many of the respondents stressed what they saw as 'basic' economic principles, 'economies of scale', stating that purchasing more always worked out as cost effective, and in this sense, it was the most 'obvious' and logical option. For the majority of the social suppliers, particularly those who supplied cannabis, the benefit of buying larger quantities was both understood and operationalised at an early stage of the social supply career, rather than a practice that was learnt through engaging in further transactions:

> Immediately, when we started doing it, we realised that there was a clear benefit in that if we were going to all do it then it's just a simple hang on a minute, we're doing this, so why don't we get more? It was a rational choice because you're thinking, hang on a minute I'm only going to buy more of this in a day or two, so why don't we just buy more of this now and get it cheaper, that just seemed like a logical thing to do.
>
> *Colin, 29, Somerset sample*

Social suppliers as well as buyers described the desire from potential customers, particularly cannabis users, to obtain a 'good deal' themselves. This suggests that the need to obtain value for money and maximise 'economies of scales' in order to buy 'more for less' is prevalent at *both* ends of the supply transaction:

> If people are asking if you've got it, they will also ask if you can do more than the minimal amount, do you know what I mean? Because they want

> to get the benefit, so if they ask if you've got any then you say 'yeah', and then the next question is 'how much have you got'? Not normally 'can I have an eighth?'. So, if you've got a lot I'll have a half ounce or I'll have an ounce, because then they'll give it to their mates and do the same as you. So, everyone wants to get and make that different breaking point, where you go 'why would I want to spend…why would I want just one transaction when I know my mate wants it as well?'. I'll get enough for him and then…
>
> *Joe, 27, Somerset sample*

As the above quote indicates, an entrepreneurial spirit (see Salinas, 2018) and pragmatism was therefore often so inextricably linked and tied into drug use that low-level social supply was felt to be part and parcel of any regular drug user's practices (Coomber et al., 2015).

'If I've got the hassle, I'll get the benefit': hassle tax

Contrary to scholarship that has postured low-level social drug supply as an activity tied up with the 'pursuit of coolness' (Jacques & Wright, 2015), while there appeared to be some perceived status associated with being known as a source of supply by a small number of respondents, the vast majority of psychoactive drug suppliers described the social supply of 'party drugs' as an experience characterised by inconvenience, risk and hard work:

> I hate it – I wouldn't say there was any status – I mean, obviously if I was a *drug dealer* then I'd probably feel that there was some status with that, but I think because it's always like '*oh Mike can you get me some*', then it's just more of a ball ache, especially if there's a big night on and you've got ten or fifteen people who want one pill each. It's trying to sort that out…it's just like, '*I just want to have a good time*', I don't want to be chasing people for a tenner…I think I'm more of a drug mule than anything (laughs)… but then if I was adding a bit on for myself then it would probably make a lot of difference…
>
> *Mike, 24, Somerset sample*

Supporting wider research, social suppliers of cannabis generally found the supply transaction to be a less taxing experience since it normally included some kind of social aspect, such as smoking or 'chilling' with the supplier as part of the supply transaction (see Coomber & Turnbull, 2007; Dorn et al., 1990; Belackova & Zabranky, 2016). However, at a broader level, particularly when distributing 'party drugs' social suppliers felt that an important rationale for taking small remuneration related to acquiring some recompense or 'reward' for their efforts. Supporting the findings of Werse and Müller (2016: 98), an openness to receiving some form of monetary gain was specifically related to higher risk supply practices, particularly when being in possession of Class A drugs. Above all, however, this gesture acknowledged the *effort* a social supplier would take on for the benefit of the receivers of the drug, and this benefit was widely referred to by respondents as a 'hassle tax'. In practical terms the 'hassle tax' was most commonly explicated as equating to the 'few quid', or the amount it would take social suppliers to round costs up to the nearest £5 or £10 note. Social suppliers suggested that taking a 'hassle tax' from a supply transaction is firmly embedded within supply culture, both approved and expected by receivers of drugs. As Joe describes:

> I think so…I think it's just an unwritten rule really, it's not really something that's ever asked, so say if a friend's got a gram of MDMA or something, I'd ask how much and they'd be like '£40' and I'd be like, 'fine'. Even if it was good friends, I probably wouldn't quiz them that hard on it…
>
> *Joe, 27, Somerset sample*

The 'hassle tax', in most cases, was rarely cogitated when respondents were questioned regarding the amount of gain, they acquired from the drugs transaction. Instead, it represented a relatively small amount of financial capital that was described as so culturally fixed within social supply transactions, that it was rarely either considered or conceived as gain by those who received it.

Drugs 'for free'

In addition to taking small financial recompense for occupying a supply role, supporting previous academic studies (see Coomber, 2010; Lenton & Davidson, 1999; Nicholas, 2008), respondents recalled being strongly motivated to engage in social supply activity as a simple means of acquiring 'free drugs'. For social suppliers that were habitual, or even regular recreational users, buying a larger quantity of drugs in order to sell on to friends provided a relatively straightforward solution for subsidising their use. This motivation was particularly prevalent with cannabis users who were smoking on a daily or weekly basis (see below). With an acute awareness of how the costs of smoking cannabis on a regular basis could mount up, getting drugs for free through 'sorting' mates out enabled users – particularly when they were studying (see Moyle & Coomber, 2018) – to continue using without a sense of guilt regarding the accumulated costs. For the respondents who used 'club drugs' like MDMA and cocaine, getting free drugs was perceived as a reward for undertaking the risk and hassle of sourcing and collecting Class A drugs for friends. This practice was also viewed as a way of financing a particular night or nights out rather than general substance use:

> (It was) something I drifted into to be honest, if someone asks you to help them out, you help them out, don't you? I kind of didn't realise early on that if you're getting some pills for a pound and selling them for a pound

> fifty – which people are more than happy to pay–then you can get your stuff for free. That becomes quite apparent quite quickly, that's probably why I was more than happy to do it as time went on…it was just enough to have free nights because obviously nobody's got too much money when they're in their second and third year (at university).
>
> *Josh, 21, Somerset sample*

The method used in order to obtain 'free drugs' varied between social suppliers according to their level of access, the drugs they were planning to distribute and the buyer. Typically, respondents described purchasing a larger quantity of drugs than needed – this immediately reduced the cost of each deal. The social supplier could then choose how good a 'count' they will sell on to the receiver of the drug – i.e. whether they would sell them the correct quantity of drugs, or whether they might 'skim' off the top of the weight (e.g. selling an eighth which is supposed to weigh 3.5 g as 3.2 or 3.0 g). Leo explains how this worked with club drugs:

> At the moment, say if we were going out…say if we were sorting out a night out and some people wanted coke then it would be three people who wanted a gram each split between three people and then get a half a gram split between you all for free…so if you bought an eighth–so there's three and a half grams in an eighth–so everyone would get a gram and then you'd have half a gram for free.
>
> *Leo, 27, Somerset sample*

Many different ways of getting 'free' cannabis were described; for social suppliers acting at a very low level, who brokered relatively small amounts such as 'eighths' and 'teenths', the amount of free drugs obtained could be relatively minimal – equating to a 'a joint' or 'a couple of smokes'. However, for those who were smoking more regularly and were struggling to subsidise this use, namely students, it was not unusual for respondents to describe selling quantities ranging from half an ounce up to 4.5 ounces. Social suppliers selling half an ounce of cannabis reported selling three out of four eighths in order to get an eighth of an ounce (equating to £20) for free, while a student who obtained an ounce described selling six eighths in order to gain a quarter (two 'eighths' or 7 g) for their own consumption.

'Doing your bit' for the group

Apart from acting as a means to subsidise their own use or enable the social supplier to get their drugs 'for free', the idea of supply being undertaken as a means of fulfilling obligation to the group proved to be a popular discursive thread. Much like work tracing supply trends in the 1970s (e.g. Blum et al., 1972), this supply motivation was found to encompass classical notions of reciprocity and exchange. For example, if a member of a social group had initiated 'sourcing plans' – particularly for an event in which all members of the group were attending – they would then be expected to provide for the rest of their network. Planning access to drugs for events was found to be routine and therefore acquiring drugs on an individual basis, or just for themselves, did not appear to represent a viable option for social suppliers:

> Yeah for sure, you know I wouldn't go hunting for pills unless I knew something big was on, if there was a night coming up or...you wouldn't ever go on a night like that on your own, you're always going to go with people and they're always going to be very likeminded so you'd already know other peoples' wants and requirements so you'd cater for them because... you're their friend...it's like you wouldn't go to the off license and just get a load of beer for yourself.
>
> *Adrian, 29, Somerset sample*

As the narrative indicates, entrenched cultural practices and codes guide etiquette relating to the sourcing of drugs and are understood by those who experience them as 'distribution norms' (Dorn et al., 1992). Following wider structures of reciprocity (Gouldner, 1960; Mauss, 1990), there is a clear expectation for group members to all take their turn and provide for the group. Thematically, this data is consistent with the work of Dorn and South (1990) and their conceptualisation of 'mutual societies' (see also Dorn et al., 1992). 'Mutual societies' are described as friendship networks of user-dealers, who support each other and sell or exchange drugs amongst themselves in a reciprocal fashion (Dorn & South, 1990, p. 177). At the heart of this conceptualisation is the notion that everyone will do their bit, or as Dorn et al. (1992, p. 10) suggest, 'where every user is a supplier and everyone is expected to help out' in order to keep the group supplied. While reciprocity is 'the name of the game' (Auld 1981 as cited in Dorn et al., 1992, p.182), within the context of this research, rationales for social supply motivation were also reliant on the values and ethos associated with what it means to be a friend. In this respect, rather than representing a purely functional act characterised by individuals simply volunteering to 'take on supply', supporting the findings of Jacques and Wright (2015), respondents additionally exhibited clear signs of altruism and a desire to *want* to help good friends acquire drugs:

> No it feels fine, it doesn't feel risky, it's just like...I don't want to say it but I'm going to say it anyway, you kind of feel like the 'big dog' because you're sorting all your mates out, you like the feeling of helping your mates.
>
> *Craig, 28, Somerset sample*

> I first started doing it because...it's a hassle for everyone else to get it and you don't want to always be the person that always receives things and that doesn't go out and buy it, so you know, it was more of a (pauses)...doing my bit I suppose.
>
> *Ben, 27, Somerset sample*

Notions of membership, subculture, responsibility and obligation are particularly relevant here and they interlink and express themselves in complex ways. As Andy explains:

> If you're going to a festival particularly, it's common for, if someone knows someone, to get orders for other people, it's just polite (Laughs)...to offer it up. Just like I would if I knew somebody and I was going to see someone... there's an expectation, definitely. It's like, I was just talking to Tim and we're going to Secret Garden Party next week and I said 'well if you're going to get something then'...(laughs). So yeah, it's an expectation really that you'd do that for your mates...
>
> *Andy, 29, Somerset sample*

As Andy's quote suggests, in some circumstances, expectation therefore carried so much weight that certain members of these social groups would not only take advantage of emerging chances, but would also actively *seek out* opportunities for group supply.

Discussion

Despite social supply encompassing a key area of importance both in the UK and internationally with a number of jurisdictions acknowledging this as a distinct form of distribution (see Coomber et al., 2018), there remains a misunderstanding of the reality of social supply as it occurs in the real world. This chapter provides in-depth, qualitative findings, which highlight some of the subjectivities, shared meanings and cultures of social supply. While conventional understandings of drug dealing are associated with rational calculated action and with economic profit as the end goal (Jacques et al., 2014; Coomber, 2006), research here suggests that social supply is *firmly embedded in the socio-cultural fabric of regular recreational drug use* (see Coomber et al., 2015). Mirroring extant literature, social supply is described by respondents as being enacted as a way of managing the difficulties associated with gaining access to a prohibited substance (see Murphy et al., 1990; Taylor & Potter, 2013). For social suppliers (apart from the 'entrepreneur' typology), financial profit was fundamentally considered as a subsidiary issue, and supply was primarily entered into with the aim to keep a group of drug users supplied at a lower cost and with the intention to help out friends and to get better 'deals'.

Findings suggested that gaining a financial bonus may be a consideration for some social suppliers, however, significantly, financial profit was not cogitated as a *primary rationale* for engaging in supply. Further, though the Police Foundation (2000) noted that 'social supply' may involve 'some element of gain', this research has found the acquisition of 'gain' such as markup 'hassle tax' as routine and implicit to *all* transactions. Interestingly, data not only suggests that gain is a central aspect of social supply transactions, it also indicates that the vast majority of this gain could be classified in courts as 'financial' (Moyle et al., 2013).

Traditionally, social supply has been conceived as a mode of distribution limited to friends (RSA, 2007; Police Foundation, 2000) and acquaintances. In contrast, according to the narratives gathered in this study, although social suppliers will almost certainly have a core group of close friends that they will routinely distribute to, supporting existing research (e.g. Belackova & Vaccaro, 2013; Potter, 2009), data shows they may also supply to other acquaintances or 'known faces', who have been directed to the supplier by other contacts. This research therefore presents further evidence of complexity with regard to supply relationships, with social suppliers often describing 'becoming friends' with drug receivers (through the supply relationship) and regularly demonstrating an inability to recall which came first, drug supply or friendship. Consistent with Potter (2009), this results in a 'grey area' in the conceptualisation of social supply indicating that relying on the relationship between the supplier and the receiver of the drugs as a core component of the definition is problematic, particularly in a legal context (Potter, 2009; Lenton et al., 2016).

Social supply also encompasses the distribution of quantities of drugs that exceed some normative thresholds for possession (e.g. Sentencing Council, 2012). The relative normalisation of social supply engenders not only an inclination to engage in less involved designated buying acts, but in addition, it can lead otherwise non-criminal populations to buy large quantities of drugs for friends for specific events or 'parties' without any commercial intent. Yet larger purchased quantities do not necessarily equate to a higher level of culpability. As much as a dealer (proper) found with a small amount of drugs but evidence of involvement in a larger scale of operation corresponds to a low level of culpability (see Moyle et al., 2013; Harris, 2011), a social supplier found with an amount considered beyond personal possession may not always signal a more serious level of supply.

Conclusion

In England and Wales the Sentencing Council (2012) has acknowledged important heterogeneity in supply and competing levels of culpability (demonstrated through role) and harm (indicative of the quantity of substance supplied) (see Moyle et al., 2013; Coomber et al., 2018) – and internationally has demonstrated a relatively progressive legal response to this type of the supply offence acknowledging heterogeneity in supply forms. The way social supply is defined and delineated is still, however, not wholly commensurate with the behaviours outlined by the social suppliers in this research, and is instead built upon rigid and undeveloped understandings of how social suppliers commonly operate in the real world. Though there appears to be evidence of blurring and diversity, there are some commonalities that have emerged through numerous studies (e.g. New Zealand Law Commission, 2011; Potter, 2009; Moyle, 2013) and that could more accurately encapsulate this activity along with emergent data, as the entrepreneur typology showed us, of the point at which social supply moves towards dealing proper.

Drawing upon this evidence in order to conclude, research-based characteristics for the categorisation of social supply might, for example, comprise:

> the individual using the drugs that were being supplied; the transaction as not primarily motivated by the aim to gain financial profit; the social supplier distributing drugs to friends, acquaintances or 'known individuals' (non-strangers), and the transaction being characterized by some element of gain such as 'free drugs' or a small sum as means of recompense for the social suppliers' effort.
>
> *Moyle, 2013*

The incorporation of evidence-based sentencing matrix could thus make a meaningful difference to the outcomes for an established yet growing population of individuals who drift into distribution through drug use (Murphy et al., 1990), but in legal terms are still conceived as 'dealers'.

References

Aldridge, J., Measham, F., Parker, H., & Williams, L. (2011) *Illegal leisure revisited: changing patterns of alcohol and drug use in adolescents and young adults*. London: Psychology Press.

Auld, J. (1981) *Marijuana use and social control*. London: Academic Press.

Barratt, M. J., Ferris, J. A., & Winstock, A. R. (2016) Safer scoring? Cryptomarkets, social supply and drug market violence. *International Journal of Drug Policy*, 35, 24–31.

Belackova, V., & Vaccaro, C. A. (2013) "A Friend with Weed Is a Friend Indeed": Understanding the relationship between friendship identity and market relations among marijuana users. *Journal of Drug Issues*, 43(3), 289–313. https://doi.org/10.1177/0022042613475589

Belackova, V. & Zabransky, T. (2016) "Friendly" marijuana markets in the Czech Republic and in the U. S.–drug policy outcomes and risks, in C Bernard and B Werse (eds.), *'Friendly Business. International Views on social supply, self-supply and small-scale drug dealing'*. Frankfurt: Springer VS.

Berridge, V. (1999). *Opium and the People*. London: Free Association Books.

Biernacki, P., & Waldorf, D. (1981) Snowball sampling: Problems and techniques of chain referral sampling. *Sociological Methods & Research*, 10(2), 141–163.

Blum, RH and Associates (1972) *The dream sellers*. San Francisco: Jossey-Bass Inc.

Bourdieu, P. (1990) *The logic of practice*. Cambridge: Polity Press.

Chatwin, C., & Potter, G. (2014). Blurred boundaries: The artificial distinction between "use" and "supply" in the U.K. Cannabis market. *Contemporary Drug Problems*, 41(4), 536–550. https://doi.org/10.1177/0091450914567120

Coomber, R. (2006). *Pusher Myths Re-situating the Drug Dealer.* Free Assn Books.

Coomber, R. (2010) 'Reconceptualising drug markets and drug dealers—the need for change'. *Drugs and Alcohol Today*, 10 (1), 10–13.

Coomber, R., & Moyle, L. (2013) Beyond drug dealing: Developing and extending the social supply of drugs to 'minimally commercial supply'. *Drugs: Education, Prevention & Policy*, 21, 157–164.

Coomber, R., Moyle, L., & South, N. (2015) The normalisation of drug supply: The social supply of drugs as the "other side" of the history of normalisation. *Drugs: Education, Prevention and Policy*, 23, 1–9.

Coomber, R., Moyle, L., Belackova, V., Decorte, T., Hakkarainen, P., Hathaway, A., … & Stefunkova, M. (2018) The burgeoning recognition and accommodation of the social supply of drugs in international criminal justice systems: An eleven-nation comparative overview. *International Journal of Drug Policy*, 58, 93–103.

Coomber, R. & Turnbull, P. (2007) Arenas of drug transactions: Adolescent cannabis transactions in England–social supply. *Journal of Drug Issues*, 37(4), 845–865.

Dorn, N., Murji, K., & South, N. (1992) *Traffickers: Drug markets and law enforcement*: Psychology Press.

Dorn, N., & South, N. (1990) Drug markets and law enforcement. *British Journal of Criminology*, 30(2), 171–188.

Duffy, M., Schafer, N., Coomber, R., O'Connell, L., & Turnbull, P. (2008) *Cannabis supply and young people: "It's a social thing"*. York, England: Joseph Rowntree Foundation.

Goode, E. (1969) *Marijuana*. New York: Atherton Press.

Gouldner, A. W. (1960) The norm of reciprocity: A preliminary statement. *American Sociological Review*, 25, 161–178.

Harris, G. (2011) *Conviction by Numbers, Threshold Quantities for Drug Policy.* London: International Drug Policy Consortium.

Hough, M., Warburton, H., Few, B., May, T., Man, L., Witton, J., et al. (2003) *A growing market: The domestic cultivation of cannabis.* York: Joseph Rowntree Foundation.

Jacinto, C., Duterte, M., Sales, P. & Murphy, S. (2008) 'I'm Not a Real Dealer: The Identity Process of Ecstasy Sellers'. *Journal of Drug Issues*, 38(2), 419–444.

Jacques, S., Allen, A., & Wright, R. (2014) Drug dealers' rational choices on which customers to rip-off. *International Journal of Drug Policy*, 25(2), 251–256.

Jacques, S. &Wright, R. (2015*) Code of the Suburb. Inside the World of Young Middle Class Drug Dealers.* Chicago: University of Chicago Press.

Lenton, S. & Davidson, P. (1999) Raves, drugs, dealing and driving: Qualitative data from a West Australian sample. *Drug and Alcohol Review*, 18(2), 153–161.

Lenton, S. Grigg, J., Scott, J., & Barratt, M. (2016) 'The social supply of cannabis in Australia: Definitional challenges and regulatory possibilities', in C. Bernard and B. Werse '*Friendly Business. International Views on social supply, self supply and small-scale drug dealing*. Frankfurt: Springer VS.

Martin, J. (2014) *Drugs on the dark net: How cryptomarkets are transforming the global trade in illicit drugs*. Springer.

Mauss, M. (1990) *The gift: The form and reason for exchange in archaic societies*, trans. WD Halls. New York and London: WW Norton.

Measham, F., Aldridge, J. & Parker, H. (2001) *Dancing on drugs: risk, health and hedonism in the British club scene*. London: Free Association Books.

Mohamed, A.R. & Fritzvold, E.D. (2010) *Dorm room dealers: drugs and the privileges of race and class*. Boulder, CO: Lynne Rienner Publishers.

Morgan, D. (2009) *Acquaintances: The space between intimates and strangers*. Milton Keynes: Open University Press.

Moyle, L. (2013) An exploration of how the social supply and user-dealer supply of illicit drugs differs to conventional notions of drug dealing and consideration of the consequences of this for sentencing policy (PhD thesis, University of Plymouth, UK).

Moyle, L., Childs, A., Coomber, R., & Barratt, M. J. (2019) #Drugsforsale: An exploration of the use of social media and encrypted messaging apps to supply and access drugs. *International Journal of Drug Policy*, 63, 101–110.

Murphy, S., Sales, P., Duterte, M., & Jacinto, C. (2005) *A Qualitative Study of Ecstasy Sellers in the San Francisco Bay Area*, Final Report to the National Institute of Justice Grant # 2002-IJ-CX–0018 [online]. Available from: www.ncjrs.gov/pdffiles1/nij/grants/209267.pdf.

Murphy, S., Waldorf, D., & Reinarman, C. (1990): Drifting into dealing. Becoming a cocaine seller. *Qualitative Sociology*, 13(4), 321–343.

Musto, D. F. (1999) *The American Disease: Origins of Narcotic Control*. Oxford University Press.

New Zealand Law Commission (2011) *Controlling and regulating drugs: A review of the Misuse of Drugs Act 1975*. Wellington, New Zealand: Law Commission.

Nicholas, R. (2008) *The impacts of social networks and not-for-profit illicit drug dealing on illicit drug markets in Australia*. Tasmania: National Drug Law Research Fund.

Parker, H. (2000): How young Britons obtain their drugs: Drugs transactions at the point of consumption. *Crime Prevention Studies*, 11, 59–82.

Parker, H., Aldridge, J., & Measham, F. (1998*) Illegal leisure: The normalization of adolescent recreational drug use*. Adolescence and society series. London: Routledge.

Pearson, G. & Hobbs, D. (2001) Middle market drug distribution. *Home Office Research Study* 227. London: Home Office.

Potter, G. (2009) Exploring retail-level drug distribution: Social supply, 'real' dealers and the user/dealer interface. In Z. Demetrovics, J. Fountain, & K. Kraus (Eds.), *Old & new policies, theories, research methods and drug users across Europe* (pp. 50–74, ESSD Series). Lengerich: Pabst Science Publishers.

Ritter, A. J., Fry, C. L., & Swan, A. (2003) The ethics of reimbursing injecting drug users for public health research interviews: what price are we prepared to pay? *The International Journal of Drug Policy*, 14(1), 1–3.

Royal Society for the Encouragement of Arts, Manufactures and Commerce (RSA) (2007) *Drugs–the facts: The report of the RSA Commission on illegal drugs, communities and public policy*. London: RSA.

Salinas, M. (2018) The unusual suspects: An educated, legitimately employed drug dealing network. *International Criminal Justice Review*, 28(3), 226–242.

Sandberg S. (2008) Street capital: Ethnicity and violence on the streets of Oslo. *Theoretical Criminology*, 12(2), 153–171.

Sentencing Council (2012): *Drug offences definitive guidelines*. London: Sentencing Council.

South, N. (1999) Debating drugs and everyday life: normalisation, prohibition and 'otherness'. In: South, N. (Ed.), *Drugs: Cultures, controls and everyday life*. London: Sage.

Speaker, S.L. (2002) Creating a monster: Newspapers, magazines, and America's drug problem. Molecular Interventions, 2(4), 201–204. doi: 10.1124/mi.2.4.201MI. https://triggered.edina.clockss.org/ServeContent?url=http://molinterv.aspetjournals.org%2Fcontent%2F2%2F4%2F201.full

Sykes, G., & Matza, D. (1957) Techniques of neutralization: A theory of delinquency. *American Sociological Review*, 22, 664–670.

Taylor, M., & Potter, G. R. (2013) From "social supply" to "real dealing": Drift, friendship, and trust in drug dealing careers. *Journal of Drug Issues*, 43(4), 392–406.

The Police Foundation (2000) *Drugs and the law: Report of the Independent Inquiry into the Misuse of Drugs Act 1971*. London: The Police Foundation.

Werse, B., & Bernard, C. (2016) Introduction. In: C. Bernard and B. Werse (Eds.), '*Friendly business. International views on social supply, self-supply and small-scale drug dealing*. Frankfurt: Springer VS.

Werse, B., & Müller, D. (2016) Drifting in and out of dealing–Results on career dynamics from the TDID project. In: C. Bernard and B. Werse (Eds.), *Friendly business. International views on social supply, self-supply and small-scale drug dealing*. Frankfurt: Springer VS.

7

WOMEN'S ROLE IN ILLEGAL DRUG PRODUCTION, SELLING AND TRAFFICKING

Jennifer Fleetwood

According to the United Nations Commission on Narcotic Drugs (UNCND 2011, 1), women represent around 20% of those involved in drug seizures worldwide. Women may be a minority in the drug business (with some exceptions), but their involvement is not merely minor or inconsequential. Women are, inevitably, present wherever drugs are grown, cooked, transported, brokered or sold. But, as this chapter shows, women's experiences and roles in the illegal drug trade[1] are extremely varied, reflecting the diverse experiences of women internationally.

Quantitative data – like the above statistic from the United Nations – are recorded by law enforcement agencies. As such, they reflect policing and drug policy as least as much as women's actual involvement in the drug trade (Fleetwood and Haas 2011). Data comprehensively demonstrate the sheer scale of women's incarceration for drug offenders internationally, especially foreign women and women of colour (Boyd and Faith 1999; Bush-Baskette 2004; Giacomello 2013b; Green et al. 1994; Green (ed.) 1996; Iakobishvili 2012; Jeffries and Chuenurah 2016; Joseph 2006; Reynolds 2008; Sudbury 2002; Mauer et al. 1999). Recent research documents rising numbers of women receiving the death penalty for drug offences (Cornell Centre on the Death Penalty Worldwide 2018; Fleetwood and Seal 2017; Harry and Girelli 2019).

Recorded crime data can offer scant insight into the realities of women's involvement or circumstances of their criminalisation. Venezuelan criminologist Rosa del Olmo, one of the first scholars to examine women's role in the drug trade (1986), found that many women were arrested simply for being at home when the police came despite having little knowledge or involvement in the business. Thus, to understand women's role in the drug trade, we need to draw on qualitative data.

DOI: 10.4324/9781351010245-9

There exist several reviews of women's role in drug dealing and drug trafficking (Buxton 2020; Anderson and Kavanaugh 2017; Fleetwood 2015; Maher and Hudson 2007). These reviews tend to focus on Europe and the USA, focussing on women's role in street-level crack cocaine or heroin markets in large cities in developed countries like New York or St Louis, or on women arrested trafficking drugs *into* European or American cities. This chapter seeks to extend our focus beyond the global north. The UK and the USA are nations in which drugs are mostly *consumed* rather than produced, representing only part of the drug trade. This chapter seeks to include women who grow, manufacture, coo, transport or distribute drugs, as well as those who traffic or sell to customers. Increasingly criminology is aware of its bias towards studying the developed global north (Aas 2012) and the geopolitical dynamics underpinning criminology as a discipline (Agozino 2003).

Undertaking a global review is admittedly ambitious given the vast array of illicit drugs,[2] modes of drug production, transport and selling worldwide. To complicate this task further, academic journals tend to be dominated by research from the global north (Aas 2012). A further problem is that good research on women in the drug trade often fails to include women, or to consider gender in their analysis. The following review draws on research that gives sufficient analytical space to consider the position and role of women in the drug trade, and ideally employs gender as an analytical concept rather than a descriptive category. Readers are invited to take this chapter as a starting point, rather than the final word.

This chapter is organised as follows. Firstly, it gives an overview of the main questions and debates in research on women in the drug trade: what do women do in the drug trade, and why are they involved? Is women's involvement in the drug trade changing? Has women's 'emancipation' in the legal world resulted in changes in the drug trade? Next, I present research on women's involvement in cultivation, international transporting/trafficking and street-level drug selling. Although women are ubiquitous to the contexts in which drugs are cultivated, brokered, transported and sold, their role varies considerably, reflecting diverse gender orders, and meanings given to gender across the world (Connell 2014). Throughout, I demonstrate that women's labour is fundamental to all aspects of the global drug trade, following Anderson (2005). I also demonstrate that women's involvement in the drug trade is globally heterogeneous. I conclude by suggesting some possible future research on women's involvement in emerging drug markets.

The 'emancipation' thesis

Fierce debate has raged (although mainly in the USA) about whether women's involvement in the drug trade has increased, whether as a result of the changing status of women in society, or changes in the drug market (for reviews, see Maher and Hudson 2007; Anderson and Kavenaugh 2017). Fagan (1994) famously argued that the advent of rapidly expanding crack cocaine markets created 'new opportunities' for women in contrast to stable, highly gender-stratified heroin markets. He also noted the rise of female-headed households, and the importance of the informal economy for women living in the inner city, concluding:

> the expansion of drug markets in the cocaine economy has provided new ways for women to escape their limited roles, statuses and incomes in previous eras. It also provides an outlet for women to achieve conventional goals for family through illegal work.
>
> *1994, 210*

Drawing on his now famous fieldwork in New York's East Harlem in the early 1990s, Bourgois likewise claimed that 'greater female involvement in crack reflects in a rather straightforward manner the growing emancipation of women throughout all aspects of inner-city life, culture and economy' (1989, 643), although he also acknowledged that women were often victimised as a result of their participation in the drug trade. Similarly, drawing on ethnographic research in Ciudad Juarez/El Paso on the US/Mexico border, Howard Campbell argued that women's participation in cross-border cocaine trafficking 'can be linked to the interacting effects of greater social freedoms for women and economic marginalisation' (2008, 259). Campbell interviewed women who were employed directly by organisations ('cartels'), or smaller local networks. Women already occupying privileged social positions were better able to profit from trafficking, earning money and a degree of independence and personal freedom. Nonetheless, most women were mules: a role characterised by lack of control and few prospects for 'moving up' the career ladder (2008).

The notion that women's participation in the drug trade results from or offers emancipation for women has been roundly critiqued (inter alia Denton 2001; Maher 1997; Fleetwood 2014a). Whist some women may exercise agency and occupy positions of relative power and control, it is not clear how this relates to wider social processes of emancipation, if at all. As Maher, who researched women in Brooklyn drug markets, succinctly observes: 'activity is confused with equality, and presence is read as participation' (1997, 18). Even those women who hold positions of power and who garner capital in the drug trade are unlikely to be able to translate it into legal opportunities. Even when women act autonomously, the capital they earn supports others including family and children, as well as partners who use drugs (Anderson 2005). For example, Dick Hobbs describes Yvonne, a grandmother who cares for and provides for her children and grandchildren through selling cannabis in London (2013). For Hobbs, Yvonne's involvement in the drug trade is exemplary of cultural change, especially a shift from 'traditional' masculine criminal associations to loose networks (1995; 2013). While criminal subcultures may have altered to enable Yvonne's participation in dealing cannabis, dealing ultimately enables her to fulfil her traditional role by as providing for their family, not only in terms of household caretaking but also financial stability (Hobbs 2013).

The United Nations found that although the number of recorded drug crimes is rising, women's involvement 'has not increased disproportionately in comparison with that of men' (UNCND: 1), suggesting little change in women's overall participation in the drug trade worldwide, although there are serious issues with this data (Haas and Fleetwood 2011). A historical view demonstrates that women have long been involved, sometimes in agential roles. Between the 1920s and the 1970s *La Nacha* (Ignacia Jasso Gonzalez) dominated the heroin and morphine trade in Ciudad Juarez, Mexico (Campbell 2010; Carey 2014). Although her husband also sold drugs, her career long outlasted his (ibid.). *La Nacha* began selling in 1920s Ciudad Juarez, which was then a tolerance zone in which alcohol and sex were sold to both US citizens and locals. Academics disagree as to whether her business was merely local (Campbell 2010), or extended into the USA (Carey 2014). Nonetheless, the USA set up sting operations in the effort to arrest and extradite her (Carey 2014, 130). Although *La Nacha* is perhaps one of the best well-known (perhaps because of her interest to US law enforcement) she is one 'exceptional' woman of many described in Carey's historical account of women traffickers in the USA/South America. Griselda Blanco Restrepo (Medellin/Miami) and Lola 'La Chata' (Mexico City) also had long careers, not to mention their modern equivalents, such as Sandra Avila Beltran the so-called *Reina del Pacifica* (Carey and Cisneros Guzmán 2011). Seeking to recuperate the histories of women in the drug trade in the twentieth century, Carey argues that: 'The great male narrative, whether of the capo or the cop, is only a small part of the story' (Carey 2014, 197). While it is impossible to disagree, historical research sheds little light on the realities of women whose careers may have been shorter, less notable or less successful.

Rather than asking whether women's position is changing, this chapter takes up Dietzer et al.'s intriguing proposition that: 'the contextual circumstances of drug economies affect women's ability to enter specific markets and the positions they enjoy within them' (2019, 271). As such, the following sections examine how diverse global contexts shape women's involvement and the roles they play in the drug trade.

Drug cultivation, processing and manufacture

Women's role and experiences in drug production are under-researched in comparison to street-level drug markets.[3] Nonetheless, available research shows that women undertake a variety of roles in the cultivation of plant-based drugs such as coca (the organic base for cocaine), cannabis and opium (poppies), reflecting women's integral role in subsistence farming in the global south.

Women constitute up to half of the workforce involved in harvesting opium poppies in Turkey, India, Laos and Burma (Mansfield 2002, 10). In Afghanistan, women are involved in cultivating, harvesting and processing, despite traditions that would normally confine them to the home (known as Purdah) (Mansfield 2002). Amongst the Hmong people in Lao, women are responsible for most farming and household tasks, including opium farming, although they do not keep or control earnings (Oparaocha 1998). In Cambodia, Chin found that the majority of low-level opium buyers in the Bangkang marketplace were women (2009). The job involved a lot of waiting around in order to buy small quantities of opium (which has a legal status here) from farmers in town for the regular markets, then brokering on larger quantities. This job was framed as women's work: it was a relatively low-level, although a moderate amount of money could be made. Some women reported having a boss, but others worked independently (Chin 2009).

In Colombia, coca leaf cultivation is a family business offering little more than a subsistence income (Carrillo Gonzalez 2014; Gómez Fernández 2017; Bautista Revelo et al. 2018). Against the backdrop of rural poverty and lack of economic opportunities – especially for women – as well as violence and displacement, farming coca offers a meagre means of survival. Women are involved in transferring seeds, planting and harvesting leaves but can be found undertaking all jobs, including as 'chemist' processing leaves into paste (Carrillo Gonzalez 2014; Gómez Fernández 2017). Nonetheless, women's participation is not on equal term: women are underpaid compared to men and the work environment may be hostile to them (Gómez Fernández 2017). Coca cultivation may offer a means of survival, but it also increases women's vulnerability to violence connected to the drug trade. Nonetheless, for some women, coca cultivation has provided women with an opportunity to increase their power within the household (Bautista Revelo et al. 2018).

Women are involved in the domestic cultivation of cannabis in Africa where it is often planted alongside food crops, as coca is in Latin America (Afsahi 2011, 2015; Diarisso and Goredama 2014; Hübschle 2014). In Senegal women are often in charge and farming cannabis can earn a good income (Diarisso and Goredama 2014). In Morocco, cannabis has been cultivated for centuries in the Rif region and continues to be tolerated. Since the 1970s, its production became much more widespread due to European demand (Afsahi 2011). Here, women represent a 'considerable proportion' of the 800,000 rural inhabitants that are involved in the production of cannabis (Afsahi 2011). In the Rif, cannabis cultivation and processing involve the whole family but the work is gender-stratified: men manage the land and family finance while women play an 'invisible but fundamental' role (2011, 51). Women may be consigned to household tasks such as cooking food for the workers, but elsewhere they may weed and harvest. According to Afsahi, some women, 'through their high level of involvement in the cultivation of cannabis, have gained recognition in certain villages. This is mainly demonstrated by the fact that they receive income, gain access to places that until then had only been reserved for men, make their own decisions and obtain luxury items such as jewellery' (2011, 49, see also Afsahi 2015).

Women comprise 40% of Vietnamese cannabis cultivation suspects in the Netherlands, where the sale of small amounts of cannabis has been decriminalised, but production remains illegal (Schoenemakers et al. 2012, 2013). By comparison, women comprise between 10 and 30% of those involved in cannabis cultivation in the UK (Potter 2010 138). Vietnamese women apparently play a significant role in cannabis production as 'trusted representatives' and partners in crime. They set up cannabis plantations; undertake gardening and odd jobs, as well as transporting and guarding cannabis and cash (Schoenemakers et al. 2013, 329). Far from being victims of human trafficking, most are first generation migrants with legitimate legal status. The average age of women arrested for cannabis cultivation is 40 and those women were typically on low income or on benefits and became involved through debts, especially gambling (Schoenemakers et al. 2012). Interestingly, gambling debts were the main pathway for Vietnamese women's involvement in the drug trade in Australia where they may tend cannabis farms (Le and Gilding 2016). Le and Guilding (2016) describe gambling as an important leisure activity for Vietnamese women, and cultural practices of shared banking and lending that enabled women to fall into debt. Although some described themselves as forced, some continued to be involved long after their debt had been paid.

August's ethnographic fieldwork of cannabis production in northern California reveals quite a different picture. She reports 'while women occupy many of the same roles as men, their experiences are markedly different from those of their male counterparts' (2013, 93). Men dominated cannabis production, and while some women were entrepreneurs, they often relied on men to sell their cannabis for them. Women mainly undertook a variety of 'behind-the-scenes' jobs, including cleaning equipment and grow rooms, tending to plants and baking 'edibles'. Women were especially employed as 'trimmers' – a tedious, time-consuming job clipping harvested cannabis plants for sale. This was an especially feminised form of labour. Owners preferred to employ women, considering them less likely to steal or reveal the location of the farm to others. Often required to live on-site in remote rural locations, trimmers are vulnerable to sexual harassment and exploitation. August's review of job adverts reveals outright sexism and expectations that trimmers be sexually available, including extra pay for working partially nude (2013). Bouchard et al. found that labouring in cannabis production was relatively common for youth in rural Quebec (2009), estimating that adolescent girls comprised almost half of youth labourers. Anderson and Kavanaugh argue that 'the upward mobility and success of women in the emerging legal cannabis industry in the USA is a notable departure from their subordinate positioning in past illegal cannabis networks', citing that women represent 36% of all executives in the burgeoning legal cannabis trade in the USA, far surpassing the national average (2017, 346). Nonetheless, these opportunities seem to have been afforded primarily to middle-class, white women – quite a distinct cohort from those involved in cultivation and harvesting.

Changes in drug policy in the USA have afforded women greater participation in methamphetamine production. Tighter regulation of precursor chemicals caused a shift towards 'shake and bake' methods (Deitzer et al. 2019). This low-tech process combines pseudoephedrine (a decongestant) with reactants in a plastic bottle that is shaken and 'burped' to release gasses from the chemical reaction. Large labs have been replaced by a decentralised, less hierarchical, less-gender segregated trade (ibid.). Deitzer et al. found that although some women worked alongside men in traditional caretaking or supporting roles, others cooked and used methamphetamine in friendship groups, offering relative freedom and autonomy (Deitzer et al. 2019). Likewise, Miller and Carbone-Lopez's research in rural Missouri found that 'production and consumption went hand in hand' (2015, 700). Although the role of 'cook' had once been high status, the shift to 'shake and bake' opened up new, admittedly low-status roles for women. Fewer women reported exchanging sex for drugs and seemingly lower levels of sexual violence as a direct function of changes in the methamphetamine market. Whilst making meth could offer women greater autonomy over their drug use, it did not shift conservative gendered expectations about women's role as carers and partners (Miller and Carbone-Lopez 2015). These changes have mainly affected white women in the rural American south (Sexton et al. 2006, see also Boeri 2013).

Overall, women undertake a wide variety of tasks in the cultivation and manufacture of illegal drugs. Gender is always significant but plays out differently, reflecting international diversity in gender norms and roles. To a considerable extent, women's role in drug production reflects and is shaped by women's social position and gendered norms although sometimes drug market changes may offer women opportunities but these tend to be low-status roles.

Women in the street-level drug trade

Women's participation in the street-level trade in drug in cocaine, crack and heroin is the most well-researched aspect of the drug trade. Two key works have shaped the research agenda. Lisa Maher's ethnographic research on women in a Brooklyn street-level crack cocaine market in the 1990s found that: 'Drug economies take complex and multiple forms, but cultural practices within them remain embedded in broader relations and structures of gender, race and class' (1997, 193). She demonstrates the importance of seeing *both* structural disadvantage *and* women's agency and choice in negotiating their drug use and activities in the drug trade. Although women were generally consigned to marginalised positions by dint of their gender (sexist attitudes positioned them as less capable), 'race' also structured vulnerabilities and opportunities. For example, white women were considered easy objects of exploitation and were more likely to draw attention from police, but were able to earn more from sex work than Black or Latina women. Even in positions of compound vulnerabilities, women could carve out spaces for agency, including robbing 'dates', or short-dealing men they had agreed to 'cop' (buy drugs) for.

Secondly, Tammy Anderson challenges assumptions that women's involvement in the street-level drug trade is only of a minor of peripheral nature, arguing that research had 'neglected vital "behind-the-scenes" activities where women play important roles in facilitating drug deals or making the market thrive' (2005, 376). Such activities include providing housing, where drugs may be stored, 'cut' and packaged for sale, and money may be a stored; and purchasing drug, including for male partners (ibid.). This aspect of the drug trade continues to be under-researched. The following reviews research on the street-level drug trade, drawing on research from beyond the USA where possible.

Gendered motivations

Research mostly ascribes women's involvement in drug selling (like other aspects of the drug trade) to an economic imperative tied to women's social position as carers for men, children and parents. A common theme is the rise in female-headed households and the feminisation of poverty, although these experiences are far from uniform. Researchers increasingly appreciate that selling drugs may also be a purposeful choice for women, albeit in constrained circumstances.

In Costa Rica, where more than 80% of women in prison are convicted of drug offences, Campos found that selling cocaine, crack cocaine and cannabis was a way for women on the breadline to provide for their families, drawing attention to the large percentage of female-headed households (40%), financial precarity and gender norms that responsibilise women for the care of their loved ones (2011). In Chile, Ortiz and Barriga reported that selling cannabis, cocaine base and cocaine was, on the one hand, a response to poverty and maternal caring roles, and, on the other hand, a way for women to establish some autonomy from their male partners (2015). For women in Burma, low-level opium brokering was a means to financially support themselves and families (Chin 2009). Writing about the Wa area of Burman, Chin describes a woman in her forties who was married with three children who had sold heroin previously but was currently selling methamphetamine tablets: 'I saw other people selling and they made a lot of money. My whole family relied on me for support and I did not have enough money to conduct other businesses, so I decided to sell speed pills' (2009, 132). She asked a local 'boss' to give her pills to sell on credit and set up a business selling from her home. Grundetjern's research on women selling 'hard' drugs in Norway notes that the presence of a strong welfare state ensured housing and necessities but drug selling was typically necessary to fund drug use (2015).

Drug selling can offer women stability, routine and control over their lives (Morgan and Joe 1996; Denton 2001), as well as a sense of self-efficacy and control (Grundetjern and Miller 2019). For some, selling drugs may simply be seen as the 'least bad' way to fund a drug habit. Moyle and Coomber's (2015, 546) study of user-sellers in England found that: 'for the women interviewed… drug supply also offered an opportunity to temporarily avoid or reduce their involvement in sex work, and thereby moderate their exposure to the risk of violence and abuse' (see Moyle's chapter and Morgan's chapter in this volume).

In the recreational drug scene, women – like their male contemporaries – are generally less motivated by poverty and more by entrepreneurial opportunism. Jenni Ward's ethnography of the rave scene in London reveals that many of those involved were students or working (2010). Women here were not motivated by caring responsibilities and instead seemed to drift into dealing through relationships and their own recreational drug use. Social supply generally involves webs of reciprocity and friendship, and the distinction between drug sharing and selling is rather blurry. Coomber and Turnbull found that 70% of the young people they interviewed (of whom a quarter were young women) 'chipped in' to buy cannabis with friends, and a similar portion reported sharing with friends (2007, 856). Women who access drugs via prescription, or who share with friends, don't tend to fit the notion of a drug 'market'. Murphy et al. (2018) describe social supply amongst 'off-prescription' stimulant drug users (i.e. drugs such as Adderall), of whom a third were women. Prescription drugs were often exchanged for favours or gifts as well as other drugs (see Mohamed and Fritsvold's chapter in this volume). Many respondents were motivated by a positive belief in the medication rather than by profit. In summary, the street-level drug trade encompasses a wide array of activities, not all of which involve making money. Whilst economic need may drive some women's involvement it is not the only motivation.

Gendered styles

Women deal drugs differently than men, reflecting the fact that women who sell have to negotiate the apparent threat of violence and additional stigma faced by women who use or sell drugs. Dunlap et al.'s ethnography of Rachel, a 'successful' crack dealer (1994) in New York City was ground-breaking in its examination of how women sell drugs. At the time, Rachel, who was around 40 years old, sold to a small number of customers from her apartment but never on the street (Dunlap et al. 1994). Rachel distinguished herself from fellow dealers, capitalising on her gender to create a niche market, hosting customers in her house offering a relatively safe environment as part of the 'deal' (ibid). Rachel prepared meals for customers and made sure that they did not spend all their salary. She was known for 'high quality' crack and was selective about her customer base. Publicly, Rachel was invested in a conventional identity, and sought to run her business quietly to avoid attention from police, neighbours or other dealers.

Subsequent research finds that women's dealing styles continue to reflect conventional notions of femininity. Heidi Grundetjern described women enacting 'emphasized femininity' as a resource for dealing, with limited success (2015).

Likewise, Maher described women 'copping' drugs for middle-class men who drove to the neighbourhood to buy drugs. Buyers trusted them not to be violent or rob their customers, as *women*, although they usually 'skimmed' purchases before passing to the customer (1998). A slightly different presentation can be described as 'service-mindedness' (Grundetjern and Sandberg 2012). Like Rachel, women dealers may develop niche markets offering reliable, good service and high-quality drugs (see also Morgan and Joe 1996; Denton 2001). I interviewed one woman who sold crack cocaine to just five customers at the weekend in an English town (Fleetwood 2014b). Although she did not offer any special customer care, she sold promptly enabling her to choose professional, employed customers. As 'good' dealers, women justified seldom offering credit; dealing with debts was often considered to be far more trouble than it was worth (Fleetwood 2014b).

Women dealers may also care for their 'employees' and fellow dealers as a way of securing respect in the business. Kate sold cannabis to fellow cocaine dealers, and hosted summertime parties (Fleetwood, 2014b). Denton describes women dealers caring for their drug-selling employees, as a 'soft' form of managerial power that enabled them to develop trust via extended social networks (2001). Social networks could also enable women to draw on the violent capital of partner and family (Hutton 2005; Denton 2001; Hobbs 2013) although some women can create their own reputations for violence (Denton and O'Malley 1999; Jacobs and Miller 1998; Grundetjern and Sandberg 2012; Grundetjern 2015; Maher 1997). However, violence was just one aspect of the importance of kin networks for women sellers. Denton and O'Malley's research on successful women in the Melbourne drug market found that family networks provided trustworthy labour (1999). While some women relied on actual family, others set up quasi-familial relationships based on trust and mutuality. For example, two women set up a house together and shared childcare enabling one to deal drugs.

Women may also seek to perform gender to avoid arrest, described by Jacobs and Miller as 'contextual assimilation' (1998). They describe women dressing and acting conventionally to avoid suspicion. These activities reflect the inner-city context, and women's activities there (see also Morgan and Joe 1996; Ludwick, Murphy and Sales 2015). Women in England were likewise invested in maintaining a respectable front, and typically avoided dealing from home and switching off their 'dealing phone' in the company of family (Fleetwood 2014b). But, contextual assimilation may be as much about avoiding stigma as avoiding arrest.

Many of the strategies employed by women dealers in their diverse contexts draw on traditional notions of women's role. These homologous practices reflect a drug trade that is almost uniformly male-dominated, and where violence may be employed to resolve conflicts and debts. Interestingly there may be some settings in which gender performances were not required. For example, Deitzer et al.'s (2019) research on women manufacturing methamphetamine found small, non-hierarchical groups with little hierarchy. In Norway, gender was relatively unimportant in drug dealing styles, and women performed relatively gender-neutral roles as small business manager (Grundetjern 2015, 272). Ward dedicated a chapter of her book to examine women's role in recreational drug dealing which she describes as a 'semi-open' market; although drugs were mainly distributed through friends, raves offered a pluralistic, friendly setting where gender seems to have mattered less than in 'street' markets (2010).

Gendered hierarchies/institutional sexism

Women's role in the street-level drug trade is (with some exceptions) confined to peripheral activities due to a combination of mutually reinforcing system of institutional sexism and on-street gendered hierarchies. Steffensmeier refers to this as 'institutional sexism', arguing that men prefer to work with other men and that women are seen as lacking qualities such as toughness and violent potential, to successfully manage employees or customers (1983). Lisa Maher found that women in a Brooklyn drug markets were generally excluded from dealing by men, who thought they lacked 'muscle' or 'heart' (1997). Women instead could be found 'copping' (buying) drugs for others and selling paraphernalia (Maher 1997). In Mexico City, Zamudio found women mainly involved in packaging drugs or taking care of administration in small-scale drug selling (2013). In the UK, researchers describe a new form of drug selling called 'county lines', where drug dealers from large cities send out individuals to sell from small, rural towns 'renting' private households as temporary bases for selling drugs, typically in return for drugs (Moyle and Coomber 2017). Some women described renting their house as 'mutually beneficial', but for others it was highly exploitative (Moyle 2019). For some, it was simply the least bad way to support their drug habits. Whilst women do have 'power' as householders that can be a resource for involvement in the drug business (Anderson 2005), the returns are small and 'renting' one's place risks arrest, exploitation and violence. Yet women respond to institutional sexism in a variety of ways. Some argue that being female makes one less suspicious, offering an advantage (Dunlap et al. 1994; Fleetwood 2014b; Jacobs and Miller 1998). Nonetheless, this gendered advantage is also structured by 'race' with white women retaining the advantage of apparently appearing 'less suspect'.

Women's entry into drug dealing is not always met with resistance. In some contexts, women may be recruited for particular roles. Curtis and Wendel describe how, in New York City, pager and then mobile phones changed drug dealing (2007). Women were employed in customer-facing roles to take phone calls and dispatch male 'runners' to deliver drugs. Women found it relatively easy to set up in business in 'Easton', a small city in England (Fleetwood 2014b). Many were 'fronted' (given drugs on credit which they sold to repay the seller) by friends, boyfriends or dealers and worked on a freelance basis after that, able to stop and start business whenever they wanted. Whilst some sold in a 'closed' market (i.e. only to people that they knew) usually in social settings, the advent of mobile phones reduced the significance of their gender. Selling via a phone was seen as relatively safe, especially since women did not deal from home as a rule to avoid being robbed (Fleetwood 2014b). Even in this apparently less-sexist market, none progressed 'upward' in the careers. Most drifted out of dealing after deciding to stop or limit their drug use, or moving into legitimate careers or education. Similarly, 'Robin', one of Ward's club drug-dealers, left behind her dealing career to start a new job (2010). Although academics might ask whether a glass ceiling exists, this is the wrong question. Having made some money (and usually spent it), had 'free' drugs and a good time (mostly), they got out before they got arrested (mostly). In this respect, these women could be said to have had very successful drug selling careers.

Women in the international drug trade: drug mules

Contemporary research on women's involvement in international drug trafficking emerged from the 1990s onwards, largely in response to media reports about women from Jamaica, South America and Nigeria arrested in the UK and the USA, as so-called 'drug mules'. Whilst acknowledging that likening humans to animals is problematic, alternative terms – such as 'courier' – are no less loaded, suggesting that the work parallels legal work (which it does not) (see Fleetwood 2014a, 7). Researchers commonly understand drug mules to be people who carry drugs for others across international borders, whether for financial reward, pressure or threat (Fleetwood 2014a; EMCCDA 2012).

As Cunneen succinctly observes, '...much of the work on globalization and criminology is still distinctively Eurocentric. Human trafficking, the war on terror, illegal immigrants and the transnational flow of peoples are still approached largely as a "problem" for Western states' (Cunneen 2011, 251). With some important exceptions, 'drug mule' research is Eurocentric – that is, 'drug mules' appear as foreign others, especially women, washed up in European prisons. But, with the rare exception of Vietnam where the vast majority of arrested drug couriers *are* women (Luong 2015), they typically represent only about 20–30% of those arrested crossing international borders with drugs. This means that at least 70% of those carrying drugs across borders are men (Fleetwood 2014a, 6). But, with some exceptions (Green 1996, 1998; Harper et al. 2002; Fleetwood 2014a), research on mules draws on all-female samples, reproducing gendered discourses about the drug trade in which men are willing criminals and women are involuntary victims (Fleetwood 2014a).

Since much research on drug mules is on women who come from poor countries in the global south, poverty dominates explanations for their involvement. Drawing on interviews with women serving long sentences for drug importation on Rikers' Island, NYC, Tracy Huling stated: 'it is *obvious* that the poor and unfortunate women of Jamaica have become yet another cheap and expendable labour in the deal' (1996, 57, my emphasis). Desperate poverty is part of the picture, but Olmo rightly emphasises that women are especially hard hit by financial crisis:

> economic hardship, which affects women more severely than it does men in times of crisis and unemployment, pushes them towards illegal activities which provide greater employment.
>
> *1986, 167, see also Sudbury 2005a*

The feminisation of poverty is the main explanation for women's involvement in drug trafficking as drug mules, according to research in the Caribbean (Bailey 2013), Mexico (Giacomello 2013a), the UK (Sudbury 2005a; Dorado 2005) and Cambodia (Jeffries and Chuneurah 2019).

The notion that women are forced to traffic drugs, especially by swallowing them, has become received wisdom. Researchers report women being 'groomed' (Dorado 2005), or 'tricked, trapped and compelled' (Sudbury 2005a, 181, see also Huling 1995, 1996; Bailey 2013). Whilst women might be especially vulnerable to exploitation due to the feminisation of poverty, this does not rule out trafficking being a choice for women. Andreina Torres' (2008) life histories of three women imprisoned for drug trafficking in Quito, Ecuador highlight women's agency as partners, wives and girlfriends. She proposes that love should be taken seriously as a purposive motivation for women's involvement in drug trafficking, even in the context of gendered inequalities. Following Torres' approach, I examined how culturally significant notions such as love and caring figured in women's motivations (2014a). Women's involvement in the drug trade was typically both an outcome of social structural inequality *and* women's self-narratives about themselves as caring mothers, daughters and partners (Fleetwood 2014a).

Research has mainly focussed on *why* women become involved in drug trafficking rather than what they do once they *are* involved. Harper et al.'s analysis of arrested drug traffickers in the UK found that, counter-intuitively, women were carrying drugs of a higher class[4] and a greater quantity than men (2002). Drawing on interviews with women and men who had been employed as drug mules and with recruiters and managers, I found that gender mattered much less than might have been expected (Fleetwood 2014a). In fact, drug mules – regardless of their gender – have little to no control over their work (ibid). Both men and women were misled about what they were carrying and because packages arrived tightly sealed, they were often carrying vastly larger amounts than they had agreed. Contextualising women's experiences in the drug trade shows that the role of mule is characterised by a lack of control, and vulnerability to exploitation. In this sense, exploitation was not a gendered phenomenon.

Women in the international drug trade: beyond drug mules

Women have been involved in international drug trafficking for at least a hundred years (Carey 2014). They undertake a variety of roles in the international drug trade. They may recruit others as drug mules, mind them, train them how to swallow capsules of cocaine, dress them in underwear containing concealed cocaine or heroin, or act as 'minders (Fleetwood 2014a, see also Hübschle 2014). Women also work in a variety of 'invisible' roles: as secretaries in legitimate companies where money as laundered, receiving international shipments of legal goods (and cocaine), employed to play the role of secretary for a trafficker transporting cocaine in a false-bottomed briefcase, as well as minding money and drugs (Fleetwood 2014a).

Women are sometimes present in the upper echelons of drug trafficking organisations. Patti Adler's ethnographic research on a community of cocaine traffickers in California in the late 1970s remains unequalled (1993). As 'old ladies', women sometimes took over business when their partners got arrested. Taking over from partners when they are killed or arrested is an important route for women into the upper echelons of criminal organisations (Allum 2007; Arsovska and Allum 2014; Arsovska and Begum 2014; Fiandaca 2007). Yet, drugs are not only trafficked by hierarchical criminal organisations but also in loose familial arrangements as in Curaçao. Here, as girlfriends and wives of trafficking-involved men, women undertook a variety of supporting activities including stashing drugs and weapons, but were rarely involved in organisational roles (Van San 2011).

Echoing the wider popularity of 'narco-culture' in Mexico (Mondaca Cota 2015), there exist an array of biographical accounts of women in the Mexican cocaine trade (García 2011; Gómez 2012; Valdéz Cárdenas 2009). These accounts offer fabulous tales of beautiful, daring women making their way as *sicarios* (assassins), drug traffickers and 'Queen pins'. Nonetheless, these biographies are journalistic in style, offering little analysis of how gender works (Bórquez 2015). Howard Campbell's research into women in the drug trade on the US/Mexico border offers a soberer account, depicting an array of women involved in the drug trade as mules, brokers and in some instances as organisers too (Campbell 2008. Rarely, his fieldwork does not rely on a sample drawn from prison, and captures women as a heterogeneous group who may both benefit from, and be disadvantaged by their involvement in the drug trade.

Conclusion

It is customary to conclude reviews such as this by stating that the subject is under-researched. Hopefully this chapter persuades the reader that, in fact, a great deal has been written on women in the drug trade. The question of whether women are involved in the drug trade is no longer up for debate: they clearly are. The global drug trade is undoubtedly a man's world, dominated by, and mainly controlled by, men: they own the land that cannabis is cultivated on and the cocaine smuggled into JFK, Heathrow and Schiphol. Women comprise the minority, and are often relegated to lower-status, low-reward roles but they nonetheless play a fundamental role in the production, transport and sale of drugs. Echoing Anderson's call to note the vital but invisible role of women in the street-level drug trade (2005), this chapter draws attention to sheer scale and variety of women's invisible labour on a global scale: they labour in the fields cultivating coca, cannabis and opium, transport drugs across borders and sometimes recruit others to do so too.

In rare instances, involvement in the drug trade does seem to open up new opportunities for women – we might recall women in the Rif afforded economic and social power as (legal) cannabis farmers, or the fact that women may dominate opium brokering in rural Burma. We might recall that dealing drugs can, perhaps counter-intuitively, offer women stability and routine (Morgan and Joe 1996; Denton 2001). Yet, it is notable that these opportunities for women within drug markets have little to do with women's supposed emancipation. Indeed, the question of 'emancipation' and drug trade participation starts to look somewhat absurd in global context: opportunities for women in the drug trade bear no correlation to those contexts in which women have achieved greater economic, political and cultural power. It is hard to conclude that emancipation is either the cause or consequence of women's involvement in the drug trade. And, as this chapter hopefully persuades, women are ubiquitous to the drug trade: scholarship can no longer continue to describe the drug market as if they were not there.

Future research

Drug markets are dynamic, and future research can fruitfully examine women's involvement in emerging drug markets drawing on an excellent array of theory (see especially Anderson 2005; Campbell and Herzberg 2017). As the legal cannabis trade in the USA expands and the trade in Canada develops, research might explore change and continuity in cannabis production cultures (Anderson and Kavanaugh 2017). We might consider whether legal production will offer women protection from exploitation. But since Uruguay fully legalised both the sale and production of cannabis in 2013, what might we learn by turning our gaze south? What might research from Uruguay tell us about the relationship between gender and changes in the drug trade?

Another important frontier in drug research is online drug markets. Whilst some research exists, so far little has focussed on women or questions of gender (Fleetwood, Aldridge and Chatwin, 2020). Might anonymous online markets offer new possibilities for women to become involved in illegal drug sales? Might online settings disrupt gendered hierarchies or will they simply be reproduced online? Qualitative research tends to focus on a particular geographic locale, but ethnography is well placed to follow things as they travel internationally. Anthropologist Nancy Scheper-Hughes' (2004) ethnography of the global organ trade is exemplary here. She visited the places where organs are bought and sold, using observations and interviews to build a picture of the geopolitics of organ donation on a global level. And, in taking a global view, we might start to develop more comparative work to better understand the intertwinements between social and technological changes, women, gender and drug markets.

Notes

1 I use 'trade' rather than 'market' here. For a more detailed critique of the language of the market for sidelining notions of gender, see Fleetwood (2014: 23–25).
2 I have not employed strict criteria as to which 'drugs' are included. This chapter mainly discusses illegal drugs, but also includes discussion of legalised drugs such as cannabis. This reflects that the same substance may be considered legal or illegal in the same country (depending on context and use), and the extremely wide range of drug legislation internationally.
3 One likely cause is the dominance of social science in nations characterised by drug use rather than production.
4 For international readers, sentencing of drugs reflects quantity and drug class. Class A (the highest class) includes drugs like heroin and cocaine; Class B includes drug such as cannabis and ketamine, and Class C includes anabolic steroids and benzodiazepines.

References

Aas, K.F., 2012. 'The earth is one but the world is not': Criminological theory and its geopolitical divisions. *Theoretical Criminology, 16*(1), pp. 5–20.

Adler, P.A. 1993. *Wheeling and Dealing: An Ethnography of an Upper-Level Drug Dealing and Smuggling Community,* 2nd ed., New York: Columbia University Press.

Afsahi, K. 2011. Cannabis cultivation practices in the Moroccan Rif. In *World Wide Weed, Global Trends in Cannabis Cultivation and Its Control* (pp. 39–54). Surrey, England/Burlington/USA: Ashgate Publishing Limited/Company.

Afsahi, K., 2015. No cannabis cultivation without women. The case of Rif in Morocco. *Deviance et Societe, 39*(1), pp. 73–97.

Agozino, B. 2003. *Counter-Colonial Criminology: A Critique of Imperialist Reason.* London: Pluto Press.

Allum, F. 2007. Doing it for themselves or standing in for their men? Women in the Neapolitan Cammorra (1950–2003). In G Fiandaca (Ed.), *Women and the Mafia: Female Roles in Organized Crime Structures.* New York, London: Springer.

Anderson, T.L. and Kavanaugh, P.R., 2017. Women's evolving roles in drug trafficking in the United States: New conceptualizations needed for 21st-century markets. *Contemporary Drug Problems, 44*(4), pp. 339–355.

Anderson, T.L., 2005. Dimensions of women's power in the illicit drug economy. *Theoretical Criminology, 9*(4), pp. 371–400.

Arsovska, J. and Allum, F., 2014. Introduction: Women and transnational organized crime. *Trends in Organized Crime, 17*(1–2), pp. 1–15.

Arsovska, J. and Begum, P., 2014. From West Africa to the Balkans: Exploring women's roles in transnational organized crime. *Trends in Organized Crime, 17*(1–2), pp. 89–109.

August, K., 2013. Women in the marijuana industry. *Humboldt Journal of Social Relations, 35*(1).

Bailey, C., 2013. Exploring female motivations for drug smuggling on the island of Barbados: Evidence from Her Majesty's prison, Barbados. *Feminist Criminology, 8*(2), pp. 117–141.

Bautista Revelo, A.J., Capacho Niño, B., Cruz Olivera, L.P., Martínez Osorio, M., Periera Arana, I., and Ramirez Bolivar, L., 2018. Voices from the coca fields: Executive summary, Bogotá: Dejusticia. https://cdn.dejusticia.org/wp-content/uploads/2018/07/Voces-desde-el-cocal-executive-summary.pdf

Boeri, M., 2013. *Women on Ice: Methamphetamine Use among Suburban Women*. Rutgers University Press.

Bórquez, K.H., 2015. Las jefas del narco. El ascenso de las mujeres al crimen organizado de Arturo Santamaría (coord.)(2012). *Critical Reviews on Latin American Research-CROLAR*, *4*(1), pp. 28–30.

Bouchard, M., Alain, M. and Nguyen, H., 2009. Convenient labour: The prevalence and nature of youth involvement in the cannabis cultivation industry. *International Journal of Drug Policy*, *20*(6), pp. 467–474.

Bourgois, P., 1989. In search of Horatio Alger: Culture and ideology in the crack economy. *Contemporary Drug Problems*, *16*, pp. 619–649.

Boyd, S. and Faith, K., 1999. Women, illegal drugs and prison: Views from Canada. *International Journal of Drug Policy*, *10*(3), pp. 195–207.

Bush-Baskette, S., 2004. The war on drugs as a war against black women. In M. Chesney-Lind & L. Pasko (Eds.), *Girls, Women, and Crime: Selected Readings* (p. 257). London: Sage.

Buxton, J., 2020. Women as actors in the drug economy. In *The Impact of Global Drug Policy on Women: Shifting the Needle*. Emerald Publishing Limited.

Campbell, H., 2010. *Drug War Zone: Frontline Dispatches from the Streets of El Paso and Juárez*. Austin: University of Texas Press.

Campbell, H., 2008. Female drug smugglers on the US-Mexico border: Gender, crime, and empowerment. *Anthropological Quarterly*, *81*(1), pp. 233–267.

Campbell, N.D. and Herzberg, D., 2017. Gender and critical drug studies: An introduction and an invitation. *Contemporary Drug Problems*, *44*(4), pp. 251–264.

Campos, C.P., 2011. Delito y sobrevivencia: las mujeres que ingresan a la cárcel El Buen Pastor en Costa Rica por tráfico de drogas. *Anuario de estudios centroamericanos*, pp. 245–269.

Carey, E. and Cisneros Guzmán, J.C., 2011. The daughters of La Nacha: Profiles of women traffickers. *NACLA Report on the Americas*, *44*(3), pp. 23–25.

Carey, E., 2014. *Women Drug Traffickers: Mules, Bosses, and Organized Crime*. UNM Press.

Carrillo González, L., 2014. Consecuencias sociales del cultivo de la coca en comunidades afrocolombianas del Caquetá: análisis de la relación entre la economía ilícita, las prácticas campesinas tradicionales y su papel en la seguridad alimentaria. *Revista El Agora USB*, *14*(1), pp. 203–221. http://nbn-resolving.de/urn:nbn:de:0168-ssoar-422715

Chin, K.-L., 2009. *The Golden Triangle: Inside South-East Asia's Drug Trade*. Cornell University Press.

Connell, R., 2007. *Southern Theory: Social Science and the Global Dynamics of Knowledge*. Polity.

Connell, R., 2014. *Gender: In World Perspective*, 3rd ed. Wiley.

Cornell Centre on the Death Penalty Worldwide., 2018. Judged for more than her crime: A global overview of women facing the death penalty. The Alice Project, Cornell Centre on the Death Penalty Worldwide.

Cunneen, C., 2011. Postcolonial perspectives for criminology. In Bosworth, M. and Hoyle, C. (Eds.), *What Is Criminology?* Oxford: Oxford University Press.

Curtis, R. and Wendel, T., 2007. "You're always training the dog": Strategic interventions to reconfigure drug markets. *Journal of Drug Issues*, *37*(4), pp. 867–891.

Deitzer, J.R., Leban, L. and Copes, H., 2019. "The times have changed, the dope has changed": Women's cooking roles and gender performances in shake methamphetamine markets. *Criminology, 57*(2), pp. 268–288.

Denton, B. and O'Malley, P., 1999. Gender, trust and business: Women drug dealers in the illicit economy. *British Journal of Criminology, 39*(4), pp. 513–530.

Denton, B., 2001. *Dealing: Women in the Drug Economy.* UNSW Press.

Diarisso, B. and Goredema, C. 2014. Illicit drug trading in Dakar: Dimensions and intersections with governance, ISS paper. *Institute for Security Studies Papers* 2014, no. 260.

Dorado, M.-C. (2005). Desventajas del castigo penal 'exclusivo' a las colombianas, mensajeras de drogas en Europa. In M. T. Martín Palomo, M. J. Miranda López and C. Vega Solís (Eds), Delitos y Fronteras:Mujeres extranjeras en prisión. Madrid: Editorial Complutense.

Dunlap, E., Johnson, B.D. and Manwar, A., 1994. A successful female crack dealer: Case study of a deviant career. *Deviant Behavior, 15*(1), pp. 1–25.

European Monitoring Centre for Drugs and Drug Addiction (EMCDDA), 2012. Definition of 'Drug Mules' for Use in a European Context.

Fagan, J., 1994. Women and drugs revisited: Female participation in the cocaine economy. *Journal of Drug Issues, 24*(2), 179–225.

Fiandaca, G., 2007. Introduction. In G. Fiandaca (Ed.), *Women and the Mafia: Female Roles in Organized Crime Structures.* New York, London: Springer.

Fleetwood, J., 2014a. *Drug Mules: Women in the International Cocaine Trade.* Basingstoke: Palgrave MacMillan.

Fleetwood, J. and Seal, L., 2017. Women, drugs and the death penalty: Framing Sandiford. *The Howard Journal of Crime and Justice, 56*(3), pp. 358–381.

Fleetwood, J., 2014b. Keeping out of trouble: Female crack cocaine dealers in England. *European Journal of Criminology, 11*(1), pp. 91–109.

Fleetwood, J., 2015. Mafias, markets, mules: Gender stereotypes in discourses about drug trafficking. *Sociology Compass, 9*(11), pp. 962–976.

Fleetwood, J., Aldridge, J. and Chatwin, C., 2020. Gendering research on online illegal drug markets. *Addiction Research & Theory, 28*(6), pp. 457–466.

Fleetwood, J. and Haas, N.U., 2011. Gendering the agenda: Women drug mules in resolution 52/1 of the Commission of Narcotic Drugs at the United Nations. *Drugs and Alcohol Today, 11*(4), pp. 194–203.

García, J.S., 2011. *La reina del Pacífico: es la hora de contar.* Mexico: Grijalbo.

Giacomello, C., 2013a. *Género, drogas y prisión. Experiencias de mujeres privadas de su libertad en México.* Ciudad de México: Tirant lo Blanch.

Giacomello, C., 2013b. *Women, Drug Offenses and Penitentiary Systems in Latin America.* London: International Drug Policy Consortium (IDPC).

Gómez Fernández, R., 2017. Coca *Cultivation in Colombia from a Gender Perspective,* Commentary, 12th April 2017. Washington, Washington Office on Latin America. www.wola.org/analysis/coca-cultivation-colombia-gender-perspective/

Gómez, Arturo Santamaria. 2012. *Las jefas del narco: El ascenso de las mujeres en el crimen organizado.* Grijalbo.

Green, P. (Ed.)., 1996. *Drug Couriers: A New Perspective.* London: Quartet.

Green, P. 1998. Drugs, Trafficking and Criminal Policy: The Scapegoat Strategy. Winchester: Waterside Press. [Google Scholar]

Green, P., Mills, C. and Read, T., 1994. The characteristics and sentencing of illegal drug importers. *British Journal of Criminology, 34*(4), 479–486.

Grundetjern, H. and Miller, J., 2019. 'It's not just the drugs that are difficult to quit': Women's drug dealing as a source of empowerment and its implications for crime persistence. *The British Journal of Criminology*, *59*(2), pp. 416–434.

Grundetjern, H. and Sandberg, S., 2012. Dealing with a gendered economy: Female drug dealers and street capital. *European Journal of Criminology*, *9*(6), pp. 621–635.

Grundetjern, H., 2015. Women's gender performances and cultural heterogeneity in the illegal drug economy. *Criminology*, *53*(2), pp. 253–279.

Grundetjern, H., 2018. Negotiating motherhood: Variations of maternal identities among women in the illegal drug economy. *Gender & Society*, *32*(3): 395–416.

Harper, R.L., Harper, G.C. and Stockdale, J.E., 2002. The role and sentencing of women in drug trafficking crime. *Legal and Criminological Psychology*, 7(1), pp. 101–114.

Harry, L. and Girelli, G., 2019. *The death penalty for drug offences: The impact on women*. Briefing Paper. Harm Reduction International and Centre for Criminology, University of Oxford.

Hobbs, D., 1995. *Bad Business: Professional Crime in Modern Britain*. Clarendon: Oxford University Press.

Hobbs, D., 2013. *Lush Life: Constructing Organized Crime in the UK*. Clarendon: Oxford University Press.

Hübschle, A., 2014. Of bogus hunters, queenpins and mules: the varied roles of women in transnational organized crime in Southern Africa. *Trends in Organized Crime*, *17*(1–2), pp. 31–51.

Huling, T., 1995. Women drug couriers: Sentencing reform needed for prisoners of war. *Criminal Justice*, *9*, pp. 15–19.

Huling, T., 1996. Prisoners of war: Drug couriers in the United States. In P. Green (Ed.), *Drug Couriers: A New Perspective*. London: Quartet.

Hutton, F., 2006. Risky Pleasures? Club Cultures and Feminine Identities. Aldershot and Burlington, VT: Ashgate.

Iakobishvili, E., 2012. *Cause for Alarm: The Incarceration of Women for Drug Offences in Europe, Central Asia and the Need for Legislative and Sentencing Reform*. London.

Jacobs, B.A. and Miller, J., 1998. Crack dealing, gender, and arrest avoidance. *Social Problems*, *45*(4), pp. 550–569.

Jeffries, S. and Chuenurah, C., 2016. Gender and imprisonment in Thailand: Exploring the trends and understanding the drivers. *International Journal of Law, Crime and Justice*, *45*, pp. 75–102.

Jeffries, S. and Chuenurah, C., 2019. Vulnerabilities, victimisation, romance and indulgence: Thai women's pathways to prison in Cambodia for international cross border drug trafficking. *International Journal of Law, Crime and Justice*, *56*, pp. 39–52.

Joseph, J., 2006. Drug offenses, gender, ethnicity, and nationality: Women in prison in England and Wales. *The Prison Journal*, *86*(1), pp. 140–157.

Le, R. and Gilding, M., 2016. Gambling and drugs: The role of gambling among Vietnamese women incarcerated for drug crimes in Australia. *Australian & New Zealand Journal of Criminology*, *49*(1), pp. 134–151.

Ludwick, M.D., Murphy, S. and Sales, P., 2015. Savvy sellers: Dealing drugs, doing gender, and doing difference. *Substance Use & Misuse*, *50*(6), pp. 708–720.

Luong, Hai Thanh., 2015. Transnational drugs trafficking from West Africa to Southeast Asia: A case study of Vietnam. *Journal of Law and Criminal Justice*, *3*(2), pp. 37–54.

Maher, L., & Daly, K. 1996. Women in the street-level drug economy: Continuity or change?. *Criminology*, *34*(4), pp. 465–492.

Maher, L. and Hudson, S.L., 2007. Women in the drug economy: A metasynthesis of the qualitative literature. *Journal of Drug Issues*, *37*(4), pp. 805–826.

Maher, L., 1997. *Sexed Work: Gender, Race and Resistance in a Brooklyn Drug Market*. Clarendon: Oxford University Press.

Mansfield, D., 2002. the economic superiority of illicit drug production: Myth and reality. Opium poppy cultivation in Afghanistan. In *International Conference on Drug Control and Cooperation, Feldafing (January 7–12)*.

Mauer, M., Potler, C. and Wolf, R., 1999. *Gender and Justice: Women, Drugs, and Sentencing Policy*. Washington, DC: Sentencing Project.

Miller, J. and Carbone-Lopez, K., 2015. Beyond 'doing gender': Incorporating race, class, place, and life transitions into feminist drug research. *Substance Use & Misuse, 50*(6), pp. 693–707.

Mondaca Cota, A., 2015. El discurso del cuerpo femenino en la narcocultura. *XXVII Encuentro de la Asociación Mexicana de Investigadores de la Comunicación*, pp. 4–5.

Morgan, P. and Joe, K.A., 1996. Citizens and outlaws: The private lives and public lifestyles of women in the illicit drug economy. *Journal of Drug Issues, 26*(1), pp. 125–142.

Moyle, L., 2019. Situating vulnerability and exploitation in street-level drug markets: Cuckooing, commuting, and the "county lines" drug supply model. *Journal of Drug Issues, 49*(4), pp. 739–755.

Moyle, L. and Coomber, R., 2015. Earning a score: An exploration of the nature and roles of heroin and crack cocaine 'user-dealers'. *The British Journal of Criminology, 55*(3), pp. 534–555, https://doi.org/10.1093/bjc/azu087

Murphy, F., Murphy, S., Sales, P. and Lau, N., 2018. Examining social supply among nonmedical prescription stimulant users in the San Francisco Bay Area. *International Journal of Drug Policy, 54*, pp. 68–76.

Olmo, R. Del., 1986. Female criminality and drug trafficking in Latin America: Preliminary findings. In E. Morales (Ed.), *Drugs in Latin America*. Williamsburg, VA.: Dept. of Anthropology, College of William and Mary.

Olmo, R. Del. 1990. The economic-crisis and the criminalization of Latin-American women. *Social Justice-a Journal of Crime Conflict and World Order, 17*(2), pp. 40–53.

Oparaocha, S., 1998. Hmong women, opium cultivation and livestock production in Lao PDR. *Gender, Technology and Development, 2*(3), pp. 375–395.

Ortiz, G.R. and Barriga, O., 2015. Madres narcotraficantes: Las motivaciones de ingreso al narcomundo en mujeres internas en el Centro Penitenciario Femenino de Chillán, Chile. *Revista Punto Género, 5*, pp. 42–58.

Potter, G., 2010. *Weed, Need and Greed: A Study of Domestic Cannabis Cultivation*. London: Free Association Books.

Reynolds, M., 2008. The war on drugs, prison building, and globalization: Catalysts for the global incarceration of women. *NWSA Journal, 20*(2), pp. 72–95.

Scheper-Hughes, N., 2004. Parts unknown: Undercover ethnography of the organ trafficking underworld. *Ethnography, 5*(1), pp. 29–73.

Schoenmakers, Y., Bremmers, B. and Wijk, A., 2012. Vietnamese cannabis cultivation in the Netherlands. *Research Summary*. Beke Reeks. www.beke.nl/doc/2012/Vietnamese_Cannabis_cultivation_Netherlands.pdf

Schoenmakers, Y.M., Bremmers, B. and Kleemans, E.R., 2013. Strategic versus emergent crime groups: The case of Vietnamese cannabis cultivation in the Netherlands. *Global Crime, 14*(4), pp. 321–340.

Sexton, R.L., Carlson, R.G., Leukefeld, C.G. and Booth, B.M., 2006. Patterns of illicit methamphetamine production ("cooking") and associated risks in the rural south: An ethnographic exploration. *Journal of Drug Issues, 36*(4), pp. 853–876.

Smart, C., 1979. The new female criminal: Reality or myth? *British Journal of Criminology*, *19*(1), pp. 50–59.

Steffensmeier, Darrell. 1983. Organization properties and sex-segregation in the underworld: Building a sociological theory of sex differences in crime. *Social Forces*, *61*, pp. 63–101.

Sudbury (Oparah), J., 2002. Celling black bodies: Black women in the global prison industrial complex. *Feminist Review*, *70*, pp. 57–74.

Sudbury (Oparah), J., 2005a. " Mules", "Yardies" and other folk devils: Mapping cross border imprisonment in Britain. In J. Sudbury (Ed.), *Global Lockdown: Race, Gender, and the Prison-Industrial Complex*. New York, London: Routledge.

Sudbury (Oparah), J. (Ed.), 2005b. *Global Lockdown: Race, Gender, and the Prison-Industrial Complex*. New York, London: Routledge.

Torres, A., 2008. *Drogas, Cárcel y Género en Ecuador: la Experiencia de Mujeres Mulas*. Quito, Ecuador: FLACSO/Abya Yala.

United Nations Commission on Narcotic Drugs (UNCND)., 2011. *Promoting international cooperation in addressing the involvement of women and girls in drug trafficking, especially as couriers Report of the Executive Director Summary, E/CN.7/2011/7*. Vienna: United Nations.

Valdéz Cárdenas, J., 2009. Miss narco. Belleza, poder y violencia. *Historias reales de mujeres en el narcotráfico mexicano*. Mexico: Aguilar.

Van San, M., 2011. The appeal of 'dangerous' men. On the role of women in organized crime. *Trends in Organized Crime*, *14*(4), pp. 281–297.

Ward, J.R., 2010. *Flashback: Drugs and Dealing in the Golden Age of the London Rave Scene*. Collumpton, England: Willan.

Zamudio Angles, C.A., 2013. Jóvenes en el narcomenudeo: el caso de la Ciudad de México. Urvio, *3*, pp. 111–123.

8

DEALING DOPE IN THE DORMS

College drug dealers and anti-targets in the U.S. war on drugs

A. Rafik Mohamed and Erik D. Fritsvold

On August 3, 2016, U.S. President Barack Obama commuted[1] the sentences of 214 federal prison inmates, the vast majority of whom were serving time for low-level drug offences. The President's action set the record for the most commutations issued in a single day, and in his words "altogether, I've commuted more sentences than the past nine presidents combined, and I am not done yet." Befitting a President whom millennials played a significant part in electing, President Obama turned to social media rather than conventional news outlets to explain his decision.

Spotlighting the story of Sherman Chester, one of the inmates who was about to become free after serving more than 20 years on a life sentence without parole for a nonviolent drug crime, President Obama wrote:

> We know that Sherman's story is all too common in this country–a country that imprisons its citizens at a rate far higher than any other. Too many men and women end up in a criminal justice system that serves up excessive punishments, especially for nonviolent drug offenses. But this is a country that believes in second chances. So we've got to make sure that our criminal justice system works for everyone. We've got to make sure that it keeps our streets safe while also making sure that an entire class of people like Sherman isn't relegated to a life on the margins...These acts of clemency are important steps for families like Sherman's and steer our country in a better direction, but they alone won't fix our criminal justice system.

Because of two prior convictions for drug possession, Mr. Chester was subjected to the federal "three-strikes" mandatory sentencing law[2] and, at the age of 27, condemned to life in prison. At his sentencing hearing, even the trial judge voiced objection to the disproportionality of the sentence he was required to

DOI: 10.4324/9781351010245-10

impose upon Mr. Chester saying, "This man doesn't deserve a life sentence, and there is no way that I can legally keep from giving it to him."

By the end of his presidency, Obama had used the constitutional authority granted the chief executive to extend compassion to nearly 2,000 prisoners. Consistent with Mr. Chester's case, most of those granted executive clemency found themselves caught up in the complicated web of the United States' "War on Drugs." Over just a little more than a 35-year period (1980–2016), the number of people in the United States incarcerated for drug crimes grew from approximately 49,000 to 450,000, an increase of 1,000 percent. While overall tougher sentencing practices caused the prison population to increase sharply as a whole, the war on drugs was the single biggest driver of this increase. Starker than the explosion in the U.S. prison population was the alarming rate at which the drug war was resulting in black (and increasingly Hispanic) Americans sentenced to prison relative to their white drug-using and drug-dealing counterparts. Indeed, more than a decade and a half after America's focus shifted from the war on drugs to the "war on terror," black Americans remained imprisoned for drug charges at a rate six times that of whites.[3] Similarly, while African-Americans only make up about 12 percent of the U.S. population and 12.5 percent of the drug-using population, nearly 30 percent of all people arrested for drug crimes in the U.S. are black. While the overall number of black Americans held behind bars has decreased in recent years and the overall "black-white gap" has narrowed in the past decade, the total number of incarcerated black people in the U.S. remains greater than the number of whites or Hispanics.[4] Furthermore, blacks, who again represent only 12 percent of the U.S. adult population, still account for 33 percent of the sentenced prison population (Gramlich, 2019).

In response to these disparities, acclaimed civil rights lawyer and legal scholar Michelle Alexander (2010: 75) wrote:

> We're told that the reason so many black and brown men find themselves behind bars and ushered into a permanent, second-class status is because they happen to be the bad guys. The uncomfortable truth, however, is that crime rates do not explain the sudden and dramatic mass incarceration of African Americans during the past 30 years...The vast majority of that increase is due to the "War on Drugs."

Alexander's analysis as well as Mr. Chester's case also illustrates the aggregate impact of these policies on the lives of individuals, their families, and communities at large. Like the subsequent and equally metaphorical "war on terror" that replaced the war on drugs at the fore of America's law enforcement consciousness following the September 11, 2001 tragedy, the drug war was also "without a clear enemy." As *Time* magazine's Claire Suddath (2009: 1) summarized, "anything waged against a shapeless, intangible noun can never truly be won." However, in spite of the seemingly effortless shift past the drug war to the campaign against non-white domestic and international terrorists, lower income communities of color across the U.S. remained reeling from the devastating toll the drug war's "get tough" approaches took on these populations. To again quote Michelle Alexander (2010: 76) writing in reflective response, "the drug war has been brutal…But those who live in white communities have little clue to the devastation wrought."

Beyond this public face of America's drug war focusing almost exclusively on poorer urban communities and inner-city minority drug use, the vast majority of American drug users and drug dealers were exempt from the public's conversation. Instead, highlighting what criminologist Elliot Currie (1994) referred to as "two drug problems,"[5] the United States' approach to drugs has consistently presented the drug problem as one concentrated in the inner cities and disproportionately empowered the criminal justice system to "treat" the problem. As drug policy historian, Howard Abadinsky (2005: 22) reasoned, "policy decisions…have frequently been based on perceptions, beliefs, and attitudes with little empirical foundation. They have often reflected popular prejudices against a variety of racial and ethnic groups." Simultaneously, the U.S. approach has underemphasized, managed through treatment, or effectively ignored drug problems involving the majority of the population. As we wrote in our book Dorm Room Dealers (2009: 154), "when policing drug crime, it is well documented that inner-city drug raids are relatively successful, efficient, and politically safe expenditures of police resources" while the "boys and girls next-door" remain "comfortably shielded from criminal justice scrutiny by race and class-based privileges woven into the fabric of US society."

The bulk of this chapter focuses on the drug dealing activities of some of the boys and girls next-door, specifically privileged and predominantly white college drug dealers. Before we get into our particular research on their distribution network, we think it useful to explore the social and political processes that permit this overlooking of the drug crimes of the well-off to exist.

The carnival mirror, "folk devils," and anti-targets

In his classic work theorizing the relationship between privilege and criminal justice, Jeffrey Reiman described the U.S. justice system as "a mirror in which a whole society can see the darker outlines of its face. Our ideas of justice and evil take on visible form in it, and thus we see ourselves in deep relief" (Reiman, 2001: 1). While this crime mirror purports to present the real dangers that threaten us, Reiman analogized the reflection cast as akin to that cast by a "carnival mirror." With respect to drug crimes and drug dealers, because the attention of the U.S. criminal justice system is overwhelmingly focused on only a certain subset of the drug dealing and drug using population–one that is noticeably poorer and blacker than the narco-population as a whole–we are presented a misleading and "sketchy" image or understanding of contemporary drug dealers. In Reiman's words:

> Because the system deals with some evils and not with others, because it treats some minor evils as grave and treats some of the gravest evils as minor, the image it throws back is distorted, like the image in a carnival mirror … Like a carnival mirror, although nothing is reflected that does not exist in the world, the image is more a creation of the mirror than a picture of the world.
>
> *Reiman, 2001: 64*

Extending Reiman's critique beyond the image solely cast by the criminal justice system, South African sociologist Stanley Cohen's (1980) "folk devil" construct illustrates a society's tendency to scapegoat during periods of social crisis and moral panic[6]. According to Cohen, in these socially, politically, or economically challenging times, groups of people already on society's margins are publicly defined as a threat to societal values and interests. Their vilification is shaped and promoted by the mass media, and policy solutions to the problems attributed to them – the newly labeled pariahs – are proffered by "socially accredited experts." Ultimately, the folk devil is cast as the clear villain in a dramatic performance that often has serious and enduring repercussions that reshape legal and social policy for years to come.

As Michael T. Davis (2016: 179) wrote of folk devils, "they become disvalued members of society, stripped of their political, social and moral legitimacy and confined to the margins. In that space, folk devils exist as 'visible reminders of what we should not be' and are instantly recognised as 'unambiguously unfavourable symbols". Ron Dudai added,

> folk devils are individuals who become the subject of intense moral concern by the community, the embodiment of a serious threat to collective social and interests … The successful creation of folk devils 'rests on their stereotypical portrayal as atypical actors against a backdrop that is over-typical' and on establishing the folk devil as 'a sort of alter-ego for virtue'.
>
> *Dudai, 2012, p 36*

Reiman's carnival mirror and Cohen's folk devil well capture the face and fate of America's panic during the war on drugs. Beginning in the early 1980s, disproportionately black and poorer Americans were summarily cast as the folk devil in America's drug war and, for decades to follow, placed under correctional supervision at an alarmingly high rate. At the same time, others who engaged in similar forms of illicit drug activity but who did not fit within the folk devil archetype or otherwise were not reflected in the nation's distorted crime mirror and were allowed to retain their virtue. As we wrote in our book discussing the relative immunity from drug warrior persecution enjoyed by white, relatively affluent college drug dealers:

> It seems reasonable, then, to conclude that those in positions to define particular behaviors as criminal and those who construct the overall agenda of the law enforcement community prefer to continue to cast the US drug problem as one primarily located among groups of people different from them, specifically, the minority poor. Yet, the dealers and activities we discussed throughout this book directly rebut this fiction and speak to the extent to which the US drug problem knows no racial or class boundaries yet continues to be constructed as if it does.
>
> *Mohamed and Fritsvold, 2009: 182*

Fueled by hyperbolic characterizations of a new drug scourge taking over America, U.S. media outlets ran with the grossly distorted idea of the drug problem as specifically tied to amoral and predatory urban black drug users and dealers. However, then and now, America's drug problem was not primarily black, white, or brown, or rich or poor. Instead, America's drug problem looks like America; virtually every facet of the U.S. drug culture spans all races and ethnicities, and every social and economic strata. When it comes to abuse of illegal drugs, the non-medical use of pharmaceuticals, and illicit drug sales, our country's drug users and sellers are generally demographically representative of the larger U.S. population.

However, to President Obama's earlier discussed point, a pullback shot of the drug war reveals literally tens of thousands of U.S. prisoners ensnared by drug laws that do not seem to work for everyone. His comments also highlight what laypeople and policy-makers alike have more recently come to view as an approach to drug policy that has privileged some while placing a disproportionate burden on others. None of this is to suggest that the abuse of drugs and the illicit markets where many of these drugs are made available are not costly and, in some cases, devastating to society. As the Secretary of the U.S. Department of Health and Human Services recently wrote, "the effects of substance abuse are cumulative and costly for our society, placing burdens on workplaces, the health care system, families, states, and communities" (HHS, 2016: 1). However, as law professor Michelle Alexander (2012: 99–100) highlighted in her acclaimed book *The New Jim Crow*, "any notion that drug use among blacks is more severe or dangerous is belied by the data." Among young adults in particular, while black people have always been significantly more likely to be arrested for distributing illegal drugs, white people are actually more likely than blacks to sell them.[7] Returning to Alexander's analysis and in light of this reality, "the notion that most illegal drug use and sales happens in the ghetto is pure fiction. Drug trafficking occurs there, but it occurs everywhere else in America as well".

Dorm room dealers

More than a decade ago, we began researching the relatively unexplored world of college drug dealers. Virtually anyone who has attended a U.S. university would be aware of the pervasive and often extensive illicit drug trafficking networks hidden in plain sight on college campuses across the U.S. However, from the perspective of academicians, law enforcement, and the engineers of the U.S. domestic drug agenda, this type of illegal conduct seemingly did not fall within the scope of the "problem of drugs" and was therefore not a major focus of scholarship, news media, or public policy. In the academy, some previous research on drug trafficking has addressed upper-level dealers and smugglers, and middle-class marijuana users (Cave and Reuter, 1998; Cooper, 1989; Reuter and Haaga, 1989; Adler, 1985). However, the overwhelming majority of research on the U.S. drug dealing networks has targeted street-level drug dealing, focusing on the drug trade in poor, marginalized, and overwhelmingly minority communities.[8] For the most part, qualitative and descriptive information on college drug markets was absent from the drug literature. This is in spite of the fact that college-aged Americans are the peak demographic for illicit drug use and, as we already mentioned, drug use and trafficking is abundant on college campuses. Clearly, as we also noted in earlier published discussions of our research, the absence of scholarly work around college drug markets does not result from an absence of thriving drug markets on private college campuses. Rather, we concluded so little is known about these markets because of their sheltered "ivory tower" environments and the secluded context in which many of the characteristic drug dealing transactions take place. Finally, and perhaps more than anything else, the markets have been largely unexplored because of social biases that presume and project the illegal behaviors of well-to-do and predominantly white college students to be less serious than those carried out by poor people of color.

Our curiosity about the functioning of college drug markets was driven by personal observations during our respective undergraduate years at separate private U.S. universities and questions about whether the world of college drug dealing we observed as students was still intact. We were also interested in how these markets may have changed over time and how their existence was affected by the previously discussed "get tough" approaches to drug law violations associated with the war on drugs. We ultimately came to focus our query on one specific group of *anti-targets*, a network of college drug dealers who operated with relative impunity while making little effort to conceal their illicit activities. In spite of the "zero tolerance" zealotry that drove the U.S. drug war for decades, these boys and girls next door were comfortably shielded from criminal justice scrutiny by race and class-based privileges woven into the fabric of U.S. society, and the drug war made no discernible difference in how they elected to construct their drug distribution networks or carried out their routine dealing activities.

Over a period of approximately six years, we were able to access this drug distribution collaborative. The system was almost entirely comprised of relatively affluent current and former college students, and its members provided an array of illegal drugs to several colleges in Southern California. Going into the research, we expected to find somewhat low-level and benign drug peddling between college students. While examples of this low-grade dealing certainly existed, we also uncovered a much more extensive and serious drug-trafficking network – a collection of approximately 50 college drug dealers loosely sectioned into several primary strains of semi-fluid, informally organized distribution channels servicing one common user base.

From the number of network dealers with whom we spoke and the substantial structural barriers toward accessing the user community without legitimate entrée, it is reasonable to conclude that the members of this network supplied the majority of marijuana consumed at one particular medium-sized university. The network also was responsible for supplying significant amounts of marijuana to students at several other local colleges and universities. Over the course of our observations and interviews with the network's dealers, users, university administrators, and other authorities, we also uncovered relatively robust and distinct markets for cocaine, "party" drugs, and prescription drugs, all servicing the same college populations.

We were intrigued why socioeconomically and racially privileged college students would make the seemingly irrational choice to illegally sell drugs, potentially compromising their future legitimate aspirations. By asking this question directly, taking the time to get to know several of our dealers rather closely, and through general observations of their activities, we discovered several distinct motivations for selling drugs. It is worth noting that many of the motives were different from those associated with stereotypical street drug dealers popularized by mainstream news and entertainment media. Their reasons tended to fall into one or more of six categories including underwriting the costs of personal drug use; funding incidental, social, and entertainment expenses; to practice entrepreneurship; ego gratification and the pursuit of status; for the thrill and excitement of knowingly committing crimes and getting away with it; and to ward off the emasculating effects of privilege. These motives demonstrated the angst, insecurities, greed, and often arrogance of the dealers we observed and interviewed. Furthermore, they were often accompanied by a variety of rationalizations and "techniques of neutralization"[9] (Sykes and Matza, 1957) that served, at least in the minds of many of our dealers, to mitigate what they knew to be illegal activity. For example, nearly all of the college drug dealers we interviewed and observed either defined their drug sales as morally acceptable, downplayed their involvement in what was an unambiguously illicit enterprise, or reacted to questions about their criminality with a sense of indignation or moral superiority over other lawbreakers.

Most of the actors in our network were low- to mid-level dealers, and most of those distributing illicit street drugs dealt mainly in marijuana. However, a handful of our network's dealers singularly played substantial roles in the local drug economy. Over the span of our research, one of our key informants evolved into one of the area's foremost marijuana dealers, distributing anywhere from five to ten pounds of marijuana per week and grossing between $80,000 and $160,000 per month in ill-gotten revenue. This particular dealer was a large-volume wholesaler trafficking marijuana primarily in pound or multi-pound increments and only rarely selling quantities of less than one-quarter pound. Accordingly, his profit margins were less than if he were to stretch out the product by selling in smaller increments. This rate of return is common for dealers who "flip weight," electing to move larger quantities of drugs for smaller profit margins in exchange for reduced hassle and lower visibility. Nonetheless, at his peak, this particular dealer took in total weekly profits ranging from $2,500 to $5,000.

Given they were already from privileged backgrounds and therefore not dependent upon drug proceeds to secure their basic needs, our networks dealers tended to spend their takings from illegal drug sales on relatively frivolous things. The larger dealers routinely spent substantial sums partying, supporting the drug use of friends and other hangers-on, and on high-tech media equipment, high-end accessories for their cars, and other whimsical expenditures (see also Ayres and Treadwell's chapter and Salinas' chapter in this volume). For example, Brice, one of our network's key dealers, used some of his profits to fund a three-month excursion to Asia. Similarly, Weasel, another wholesale supplier to mid-level dealers in the network, missed a scheduled interview with us choosing instead to take an impromptu European vacation. At the height of his dealing, LaCoste, one of our network's most interesting characters, was selling approximately one pound of marijuana per week to his fellow students. When asked what he bought with his estimated profits of $1,200 per week, he replied, "whatever I want. I used to go on shopping sprees first semester a whole bunch, like, whatever I want. I just buy shit. I spend lots of money." It is worth noting LaCoste's father was a very successful accounting executive who paid all of LaCoste's college expenses, purchased for him a top of the line SUV, and provided him with a generous allowance. A handful of dealers also channeled some of their proceeds into legitimate business ventures. Like LaCoste, since most of the dealers in our network came from well-off families, these material excesses and available venture capital almost never drew them any unwanted attention from law enforcement or university officials in the way that their street dealing counterparts might. That is not to say that these officials were oblivious to the drug dealing activities of many of our network's members. But, the foundational wealth of these student-dealers offered the authorities, particularly those on campus, a convenient apology for turning a blind eye to their criminality.

The pill mill

As our research took us deeper into the college marijuana and cocaine drug dealing subculture, we inadvertently happened upon a robust parallel market centered on legally manufactured but illicitly used and distributed prescription drugs. This actually caught us a bit by surprise. We knew that the nonmedical use of pharmaceuticals was common among college students, particularly with drugs like Adderall designed to help cognition in people with attention deficit hyperactivity disorder (ADHD). We were already aware that college students have significantly higher rates of nonmedical use of ADHD drugs than their peers who have not matriculated at a university. It is common knowledge among college students that these drugs may help them stay alert and focus while studying for exams. Beyond that more pragmatic usage, we knew the party-going college student set routinely turns to the nonmedical use of ADHD drugs for extended energy during social activities and to otherwise a higher state of stimulation.

However, we were not aware of how vast the market that existed around the distribution of ADHD drugs and other pharmaceuticals among college students was. After gathering a basic sense of its scope, we then initially assumed that this prescription drug trafficking market would function in an analogous way to the marijuana and cocaine markets we had already uncovered. In particular, we speculated that the bulk of the drugs originated on the black market and a few key primary dealers would control the supply. We also figured the motivation for sales would chiefly revolve around material gain and ego-gratification. Finally, we thought the rationales used to neutralize both the use and distribution of illegal pharmaceuticals would be somewhat consistent with those we found among our street user and dealer populations and risk management strategies would be minimal. Only this final assumption about weak risk minimization strategies proved similar to the characteristics of the primary market centered on marijuana and cocaine. For both of our college dealer populations – those who traded in either conventional street drugs or prescription drugs – meaningful efforts to avoid detection by law enforcement or university officials were all but absent. Instead, the most effective risk minimization tool at their disposal proved to be their social and economic statuses.

Beyond that, we found most of the pharmaceuticals sold in this market actually were obtained from lawful sources – generally from doctors with liberal prescribing practices or from student-patients who opted not to keep their appropriately prescribed drugs for personal use. Our network's pharmaceutical dealers were notably different from their dorm room drug dealing counterparts in several significant ways. While making money was certainly not the exclusive driving force behind most of our network's street-drug dealers' entrée into drug trafficking, the desire not to "pay retail" for personal drug use, the yearning for "extra beer money," and other material influences were still significant motivating factors for our cocaine and marijuana dealers (see also Morgan's chapter and Moyle's chapter in this volume). In contrast, the profit motive was an almost nonexistent motivating force in our prescription-drug dealers' choice to sell drugs. Actually, most of the dealers we spoke with were unaware how much money they made on prescription drug sales because they were generally just selling off their surplus pharmaceuticals or trading them for another prescription drug for personal misuse. For those who did incorporate a small markup, they still tended not to be aware of their net profits and only saw the inflated price as a means to occasionally "off a couple of parking tickets" and pay other small expenses.

By our best estimate, our network's prescription drug dealers averaged only between $50 and $100 per month in illegal drug proceeds, a paltry sum relative to even their most modest peers trafficking in marijuana. While occasionally, a dealer would return from nearby Mexico's grey market[10] with a "big score" and turn a reasonable profit, only one of the twenty or so pharmaceutical traders in our network earned any significant money on a consistent basis. This particular dealer earned about $1,000 in profits each time he sold his doctor-prescribed monthly supply of Adderall for its maximum campus "street value" of $5 per pill. While this represented a significant profit margin over the $1 per pill retail pharmacy cost of the drug, his proceeds were still meager in relation to our higher-end street-drug dealers.

Law-abiding lawbreakers

While not entirely surprising given the well-documented tendency of the criminal justice system to closely monitor the illegal activities of the poor while simultaneously turning a blind eye to similar activities carried out by the non-poor, we were still taken aback by the lack of attention paid to our network's dealers by university police and administrators, and local law enforcement. As Cecilia, one of the handful of female dealers we encountered, explained, "well obviously no one was very careful. Hardly anyone talked with code. There wasn't a whole lot of emphasis placed on being careful in any way whatsoever." This brazenness, incompetence, and general dearth of street smarts tended to characterize the dealers' daily practices. Risk minimization strategies were near absent with both our marijuana/cocaine and pharmaceutical dealers. Drugs and drug paraphernalia were routinely on full display in living areas, in plain view of passersby. High levels of customer traffic were common. Some of our network's dealers reported being high or openly smoking marijuana while transporting distribution-level quantities of marijuana up and down California highways or while making local drug deliveries to customers. Given their family's affluence and their place at an expensive private university, these dealers stood to lose a great deal if caught selling drugs, a seemingly irrational choice. However, members of the network managed their extensive drug-dealing activities virtually immune to law enforcement scrutiny. We theorize that our dealers' racial, ethnic, and socioeconomic backgrounds afforded them this luxury, allowing them and their clientele to exist freely as anti-targets in the US drug war.

Indeed, among the most significant findings from our examination of college drug dealers was that, despite their obvious criminality, our dealers were rooted in a culture that cast people like them as inherently virtuous while simultaneously ignoring or downplaying their transgressions. This constant reaffirmation of status coupled with dealers' applications of techniques of neutralization allowed these anti-targets to maintain a legitimate self-identity in spite of their routine and often conspicuous criminality. Again, in Cecilia's words, "I got the impression in college that you were protected by being in college to some extent…that obviously the authorities should be spending their time busting people that are not working toward a potentially better future."

This tendency to diminish the significance of their drug dealing while holding to a different standard less privileged stereotypical street drug dealers and the accompanying positive self-appraisal existed in significant part precisely because theirs were not the images reflected in the crime mirror. In many cases, this self-perception was considerably out of step with the scope of their illicit activity, particularly when contrasted with the reaction their poorer and darker street drug-dealing counterparts garnered from dominant social and legal institutions. But, to the point, society had not branded our network's marijuana, cocaine, or pharmaceutical dealers (and people like them) the "folk devil" and they therefore avoided the associated negative consequences.

Dealers within this population also frequently minimized the perception of their own criminality by subscribing to pervasive society-wide assumptions about crime and caricatures of stereotypical criminals. For example, white Americans in particular significantly overestimate the proportion of crime committed by black and Latino Americans (The Sentencing Project, 2014). Furthermore, in spite of the comprehensive data we already mentioned demonstrating relatively equal involvement in illegal drug activity across U.S. racial and ethnic groups, Americans typically associate drug crime with members of minority groups.[11] A necessary correlate of this stereotyping of minority involvement in drug crime, of course, is the reciprocal downplaying of their own group's involvement in criminal activity. If society's crime mirror consistently reflected drug dealer and other criminal images that were wholly different from them, it makes sense that our network's dealers would reasonably perceive their own demographic as largely non-deviant or at least less criminal than their urban counterparts. After all, they were not likely to see people like themselves doing a perp walk[12] on the evening news, as the objects of police scrutiny for drug and other crimes in entertainment media, or otherwise reflected back in society's crime mirror. Consistent with Cohen's description of the media's role in creating folk devils, research conducted by The Sentencing Project (2014: 2) found "many media outlets reinforce the public's racial misconceptions about crime by presenting African Americans and Latinos differently than whites–both quantitatively and qualitatively. Television news programs and newspapers over-represent racial minorities as crime suspects and whites as crime victims."

Ann, another of our network's few female street drug dealers, captured this awareness of her own symbolic capital and some of the ways these biases likely contributed to the largely non-deviant self-perception that characterized most of the dealers with whom we came into contact. In her words, "I mean if someone really wanted to bust us they could, all they would have to do was get someone to sit on our house to get some evidence against us to be able to go in there. No one cares that much. I think a lot of it has to do with the people we are, we don't live in the ghetto."

Where do we go from here?

Both the data on the disparate mass incarceration of black Americans and our research on the relative immunity offered college drug dealers illustrate the point that the hyperbolic declaration of "war" exacerbated a system of drug policies and drug law enforcement that was already not working for everyone. The war on drugs was neither effective in reducing the supply or demand of illegal drugs in the United States. In fact, if this were truly a war, it would be reasonable to conclude the drugs won while minority communities disproportionately suffered huge losses. As Jon Schuppe (2016: 5) wrote of the drug war's toll, "the era of mass incarceration has profoundly damaged American society, particularly for minorities, the poor and residents of inner cities. Millions are now unable to hold steady jobs, maintain housing, keep their families together or vote". And, as Fordham law professor John Pfaff (2015: 178) added, "States spend several billion dollars a year incarcerating drug offenders, and the personal, familial, and social costs to inmates and their families are greater still; it is unlikely that these costs are justified by whatever benefit drug enforcement produces".

Decades of scholarship have well documented the fact that, from their very beginnings in the late 19th century, U.S. drug laws have more often mirrored social privileges and social prejudices than they have served as an objective and proportional assessment of public harm. As the reaction, or lack thereof, to our network of college dealers underscores, American attitudes toward drug use continue to be shaped by whom the users appear to be and by popular (and often exaggerated) narratives around a drug's particular dangers. Toward this point, the United States is in the midst of what is regularly referred to as "the opioid crisis." The impact of American opioid addiction is undeniable; in just the past 20 years, more than 400,000 people in the U.S. have died from opioid overdoses caused by the misuse of prescription and illicit opioids (see Linnemann and Medley's chapter in this volume).[13] As researchers examining the rise in opioid mortality in the U.S. concluded, "the current opioid epidemic in the United States is unprecedented compared to previous drug crises, in terms of the number of people affected and the rate of increase in overdose deaths" (Alexander et al., 2018: 713).

In what we would argue is an appropriate response to this crisis, for the first time in decades American politicians from both major parties began publicly reassessing the war on drugs. As *Vice Magazine*'s Bill Keller (2016: 3) wrote, "by the beginning of 2014, criminal justice reform was turning mainstream." Accordingly, the collective conversation spearheaded by our "socially accredited experts" in public office and in the press has moved dramatically from the "get tough" rhetoric of the war on drugs toward using the language of "disease."[14] This shift in semantics has subsequently invited the consideration of more rehabilitative and therapeutic approaches to addiction, at least insofar as opioids are concerned.[15] As Republican U.S. Senator Rob Portman (Shesgreen, 2016: 1) said of a 2016 bill that sought to strengthen opioid abuse prevention and treatment rather than increase criminalization, "this is a historic moment, the first time in decades that Congress has passed comprehensive addiction legislation...this is also the first time that we've treated addiction like the disease that it is."

But one cannot help ask the question, what changed? Why, after nearly 40 years of rabidly endorsing "get tough" strategies, are these drug warriors – along with those in the news and entertainment media whose depictions of America's drug problems – presenting such a different image of drug abuse and addiction? Data outlining the failures of mass incarceration to stem drug abuse and eliminate drug sales have been abundant and conclusive since at least the mid-1990s. The fiscal unsustainability of the wholesale incarceration of millions of Americans has also been evident for decades, as has the destabilizing impact of these practices on urban minority communities. So, again, what has changed?

One of the most obvious variations between the current opioid crisis and the 1980s crack epidemic that served as a springboard to the war on drugs can be distilled down to basic demographics. While crack disproportionately affected impoverished black communities in the U.S., opioid addiction and deaths have asymmetrically affected white communities. To be clear, mortality due to opioids has significantly increased among black, white, and Hispanic Americans. However, as Monica Alexander et al. (2018: 713) found in their analysis of long-term trends in opioid-related mortality,

> the nature of the epidemic has changed substantially over the past 35 years, shifting from relatively low heroin mortality, to a prescription drug problem in the white population, and more recently to a heroin/fentanyl epidemic affecting both the black and the white populations.

The acceleration of white mortality from opioid misuse can be directly traced to an increase in the number of opioid pain medications; drugs too willingly prescribed by doctors, and abundantly manufactured and aggressively promoted by the pharmaceutical industry.[16] Unlike the revolting racial minority crackheads and amoral black corner boys who were conveniently vilified as folk devils in the drug war, in the current opioid crisis both the predominant user and dealer populations are white. Like the students at the heart of our research on college drug dealers, privileged socioeconomic status, whiteness, and folkloric notions of who is truly an "American" seem to be serving as protective factors from the wrath of U.S. drug policy. Their superficial sameness with those in positions to influence the drug control agenda has resulted in more compassionate approaches to illegal misuse and sales of drugs. Unfortunately, for the hundreds of thousands of black Americans who have been irrevocably entangled in the full force of the drug war, this change has come too late.

Notes

1 Unlike pardons, which offer full legal forgiveness for their crimes, commutations shorten prison sentences while typically leaving intact other conditions like court supervision after an inmate is released. According to P.S. Ruckman, Jr., a professor of political science who tracks executive pardons and commutations on his website www.PardonPower.com, President Obama's 214 commutations marked the most any president ever granted in a single day. The previous high-water mark for presidential pardons was 151, set by Franklin Roosevelt in 1935 for immigration-related offenses.

2 Signed into law by President Bill Clinton, the U.S. "three strikes" provision of the Violent Crime Control and Law Enforcement Act of 1994 required mandatory life imprisonment without the possibility of parole for federal offenders with three or more convictions in federal or state courts for serious violent felonies or drug trafficking crimes.

3 In 2017, the rate of incarceration for African Americans was 1,549 black prisoners for every 100,000 black adults. In comparison, the imprisonment rate for whites and Hispanics was 272 and 823 per 100,000, respectively. See www.pewresearch.org/fact-tank/2019/04/30/shrinking-gap-between-number-of-blacks-and-whites-in-prison/

4 At the end of 2017, federal and state prisons in the United States held approximately 476,000 inmates who were black, as compared with 436,500 white inmates and 336,500 inmates who were Hispanic. This does not include inmates incarcerated in municipal jails. More information available from: www.pewresearch.org/fact-tank/2019/04/30/shrinking-gap-between-number-of-blacks-and-whites-in-prison/

5 In his 1994 book, *Reckoning: Drugs, the Cities, and the American Future*, sociologist Elliott Currie identified two significant yet different American "drug problems." The first–a drug problem associated with more affluent drug users–Currie characterized as largely manageable presumably because of their socioeconomic status and the fact that their drug abuse is generally outside of the scope of the "war on drugs." The second, Currie describes as "the drug problem of the have nots," and is an "endemic" problem whose persistence reflects deep-seated social and economic issues that "run along the fault lines of our society" (1994: 4).

6 Described by Nachman Ben-Yehuda (2009, pp. 1–2), moral panic "broadly refers to the creation of a situation in which exaggerated fear is manufactured about topics that are seen (or claimed) to have a moral component. Moral panics have to create, focus on and sustain powerfully persuasive images of folk devils that can serve as the heart of moral fears."

7 Source: Ingraham, Christopher. *The Washington Post*, September 30, 2014. "White People are More Likely to Deal Drugs, but Black People are More Likely to Get Arrested for it." In 1980 and 1989, two separate longitudinal studies showed whites were about 45% more likely than blacks to sell drugs. Ingraham's analysis of data from the 2012 National Survey on Drug Use and Health shows that 6.6% of white adolescents and young adults (aged 12 to 25) sold drugs, compared to just 5.0 percent of blacks (a 32 percent difference).

8 I do not mean to suggest that there is not excellent and illuminating research in this realm. A few examples of solid ethnographic work along these lines include *The Cocaine Kids* by Terry Williams, *In Search of Respect* by Philippe Bourgois, *Cop in the Hood* by Peter Moskos, and *Dealing Crack* by Bruce A. Jacobs.

9 In their classic work titled "Techniques of Neutralization," Sykes and Matza argue that individuals learning techniques that allow them to avoid moral culpability for their crimes can explain a good bit of criminal and delinquent behavior. They write, "much delinquency is based on what is essentially an unrecognized extension of defenses to crimes, in the form of justifications for deviance that are seen as valid by the delinquent but not by the legal system or society at large" (1957: 666). Among these techniques are denial of responsibility; denial of injury; denial of victim; condemnation of the condemners; and the appeal to higher loyalties.

10 Some of the network's pharmaceutical dealers would occasionally travel to neighboring towns in Mexico and fraudulently obtain prescription drugs from minimally regulated Mexican pharmacies.

11 Kappeler and Potter, The Mythology of Crime and Criminal Justice; Burston, Jones, and Roberson-Sanders, "Drug Use and African Americans."

12 "Perp walk" is short for "perpetrator walk" and refers to the practice of police walking a handcuffed accused offender in front of a crowd or the media. In its modern version, the perp walk emerged as a result of advancements in camera technology that allowed the photography of moving objects. Perp walks are often used in higher-profile cases, and they have been criticized for undermining the constitutionally guaranteed presumption of innocence for the accused.

13 More information on opioid related deaths through 2017 may be found at www.cdc.gov/drugoverdose/epidemic/index.html

14 See "The Disease Killing White Americans Goes Way Deeper than Opioids," *Washington Post*, March 24, 2017.

15 Messaging from President Trump's administration has been mixed on the issue of drugs abuse and addiction. Generally, over the first three years of the administration, the Trump White House has signified a sharp shift away from the Obama administration's rejection of harsh anti-drug and "get tough" policies. Notwithstanding the very notable exclusion of how his office has chosen to frame the rising number of white Americans addicted to opioids, the Trump administration has largely departed from the previous administration's emphasis on treatment over punishment. Instead, Trump has trained more of his administration's attention on casting illegal opioid use as a problem of border security, rather than one related to access to treatment and health care.

16 According to reporting in *The Washington Post*, America's largest drug companies flooded the United States' licit marketplace with 76 billion oxycodone and hydrocodone pain pills from 2006 through 2012. Just 6 U.S. companies were responsible for distributing 75 percent of these opioids. See "76 Billion Opioid Pills: Newly Released federal data unmasks the epidemic," (July 16, 2019). Available from www.washingtonpost.com/investigations/76-billion-opioid-pills-newly-released-federal-data-unmasks-the-epidemic/2019/07/16/5f29fd62-a73e-11e9-86dd-d7f0e60391e9_story.html

References

Abadinsky, H. 2005. *Drug Use and Abuse: A Comprehensive Introduction.* Boston: Cengage Learning.

Adler, Patricia. 1985. *Wheeling and Dealing: An Ethnography of an Upper-level Drug Dealing and Smuggling Community.* New York: Columbia University Press.

Alexander, Michelle. 2010. "The War on Drugs and the New Jim Crow," *Race, Poverty & the Environment*, Vol. 17, No. 1, 75–77.

Alexander, Monica J., Mathew V. Klang, and Magali Barbieri. 2018. "Trends in Black and White Opioid Mortality in the United States, 1979–2015," *Epidemiology* (September 2018), Vol. 29, No. 5, 707–715.

Beh-Yehuda, Nachman. 2009. "Moral Panics—36 Years On," *The British Journal of Criminology*, Vol. 49, No. 1, 1–2.

Burston, B. W., D. Jones, and P. Roberson-Sanders. 1995. "Drug Use and African Americans", *Journal of Alcohol and Drug Education*, Vol. 40, 19–39.

Cave, Jonathan A. K., and Peter Reuter. 1998. *The Interdictor's Lot: A Dynamic Model of the Market for Drug Smuggling Services*. Santa Monica, CA: Rand.

Cohen, Stanley. 1980. *Folk Devils and Moral Panics: The Creation of the Mods and Rockers*. (First published 1972, reprinted 1980 with new introduction), London: MacGibbon and Kee. 1980 edition published by Martin Robertson & Company Ltd.

Cooper, Mary H. 1989. "The Business of Drugs", *Congressional Quarterly*. Washington, DC: HV5801. C586 Overflow.

Currie, Elliott. 1994. *Reckoning: Drugs, the Cities, and the American Future*. New York: Hill & Wang.

Davis, Michael T. 2016. "The Vilification of Thomas Paine: Constructing a Folk Devil in the 1790s", in Gordon Pentland and Michael Davis (eds.), *Liberty, Property and Popular Politics: England and Scotland, 1688–1815. Essays in Honour of H. T. Dickinson*. Edinburgh: Edinburgh University Press.

Dudai, Ron. 2012. "Informers and the Transition in Northern Ireland", *The British Journal of Criminology*, Vol. 52, No. 1 (January 2012), 32–54.

Gramlich, John. 2019. "The Gap between the Number of Blacks and Whites in Prison is Shrinking", Pew Research Center. Available at: www.pewresearch.org/fact-tank/2019/04/30/shrinking-gap-between-number-of-blacks-and-whites-in-prison/

HHS, 2016. "Facing Addiction in America: The Surgeon General's Report on Alcohol, Drugs, and Health", *U.S. Department of Health & Human Services*. Available at: www.ncbi.nlm.nih.gov/books/NBK424857/pdf/Bookshelf_NBK424857.pdf

Kappeler, V., and G. Potter. 2005. *The Mythology of Crime and Criminal Justice* (4th ed.). Long Grove, IL: Waveland.

Keller, Bill. 2016. "How Criminal Justice Reform Died," *Vice* (September 28, 2016). Available at: www.vice.com/en_us/article/yvewn7/how-criminal-justice-reform-died-bill-keller

Mohamed, A. Rafik and Erik D. Fritsvold. 2009. *Dorm Room Dealers: Drugs and the Privileges of Race and Class*. Boulder, CO: Lynne Rienner Publishers.

Pfaff, John. 2015. "The War on Drugs and Prison Growth: Limited Importance, and Limited Legislative Options," *FLASH: The Fordham Law Archive of Scholarship and History*, Vol. 52, 173–220.

Reiman, Jeffrey. 2001. *The Rich Get Richer and the Poor Get Prison*. Needham Heights, MA: Allyn & Bacon.

Reuter, P. and J. Haaga. 1989. *The Organization of High-Level Drug Markets: An Exploratory Study*. Santa Monica, CA: Rand.

Schuppe, Jon. 2016. "30 Years after Basketball Star Len Bias' Death, Its Drug War Impact Endures," *NBC News* (June 19, 2016). Available at: https://www.nbcnews.com/news/us-news/30-years-after-basketball-star-len-bias-death-its-drug-n593731

Shesgreen, Deirdre. 2016. "Congress Approves Anti-addiction Bill as Funding Fight Continues," *USA Today* (July 13, 2016). Available at: www.usatoday.com/story/news/politics/2016/07/13/congress-approves-anti-addiction-bill-funding-fight-continues/87040856/

Suddath, Claire. 2009. "Brief History: The War on Drugs," *Time* (March 25, 2009). Available at: http://content.time.com/time/world/article/0,8599,1887488,00.html

Sykes, Gresham and David Matza. 1957. "Techniques of Neutralization: A Theory of Delinquency," *American Sociological Review*, Vol. 22, No. 6 (Dec 1957), 664–670.

The Sentencing Project. 2014. "Race and Punishment: Racial Perceptions of Crime and Support for Punitive Policies." Available at: www.sentencingproject.org/wp-content/uploads/2015/11/Race-and-Punishment.pdf

9

'STEROID HOLIDAYS' AS DRUG TOURISM AND DEVIANT LEISURE

Jake Coomber-Moore, Nigel South, Ross Coomber and Leah Moyle

Introduction

Increasing use of steroids and other image- and performance-enhancing drugs (IPED) over the past decade or so has been reported in specialist, lifestyle and also in 'general' news stories (e.g. Strudwick, 2013; *Men's Health*, 2016; Morris, 2018; Walker, 2015; Gallagher, 2017; see also van de Ven and colleague's chapter in this volume). Statistics and studies in Australia, UK and elsewhere indicate a rise from a relatively low prevalence in the mid-2000s (Dunn, 2010) to significant reported use (including intravenously) and related illegal production and trafficking between 2009 and 2015 (Goldsworthy and McGillivray, 2015; Antonopoulos and Hall, 2016; van de Ven and Mulrooney, 2016; Jacka et al., 2017). Zahnow et al. (2017: 69) suggest that although the prevalence of 'anabolic androgenic steroid' use 'in the general population appears to be relatively low, the perception that use is increasing, particularly among young, recreational gym goers and non-athletes, is ubiquitous'. Morris (2018) states that around one million individuals in the UK are using steroids to 'improve' their bodies and Griffiths et al. (2017) have identified similar trends and issues in Australia.

Steroids – or IPED – are at the heart of an expanding culture and market that does not necessarily conform to the expectations raised by many media portrayals which have focused on professional sports and elite athletes. For example, Goldsworthy and McGillivray (2015) suggest that these are in fact the smallest sub-groups of users and the 2015 Australian Crime Commission Report (2015: 49), *Organised Crime in Australia,* attributed 'One of the key drivers of the market' not to elite athlete role models but to lifestyle trends within a more normal and ordinary 'strong youth culture, particularly prevalent among young males, that is focused on a muscular and athletic physical appearance'. In Britain, similarly, according to Walker (2015), experts have

DOI: 10.4324/9781351010245-11

warned of 'an epidemic of anabolic steroid use among image-obsessed young men' with the country facing 'a health time bomb from a problem which is significantly under-represented in official statistics.' The Australia-located Butterfly Foundation, an organisation providing support for body image disorders, has noted in this regard that 'Australia and the UK are writing the same story on steroid abuse' (2018).

As the acceptance and use of IPED increases, along with the normative supply structures commonly described at the local level (cf. Coomber and Salinas, 2019; Fincoeur, van de Ven and Mulrooney, 2014), other distinctive supply and consumption practices have emerged that might be understood as fitting broadly within the conceptual boundaries of 'drug tourism' and the more modern pursuit of 'cosmetic surgery tourism'. One such activity of note is that of the so-called 'steroid holidays', where IPED users from countries where the non-medical supply of steroids is prohibited, purposely visit countries such as Thailand to access cheap, and although still controlled, easily available, IPED so as to combine holidays with intensive training.

Health concerns related to the growth of steroid holidays emphasise the dangers of using IPED in a supply context where easy access, reduced prices and the propensity for intensive use may all elevate already attendant risks to a new level (e.g. ABC News, 2013). This mix of leisure and pleasure with a pursuit of substance involved training in an alien context perhaps highlights the extant irony previously related to IPED use such that, as noted by Zahnow et al. (2017, p. 70) 'while health and fitness pursuits are often cited as the main reasons' for steroid use, various 'adverse health effects' may in fact result, some being 'acute in nature', subsiding with cessation, while others become 'chronic health conditions' as a result of long-term use (e.g. Hepatitis C as a result of injecting, Hope et al., 2017). One report (McLoughlin, 2017) on steroid-related hospital admissions in South Australia noted a 'three-fold increase in recent years' and linked this to adverse reactions to 'black market products packaged as anabolic-androgenic steroids'.

This research does two things: firstly, it provides insight into the activity of steroid holidays as a practice and secondly it draws attention to the context and meaning of this phenomenon by offering some preliminary insights into the experience of, and attitudes towards, non-normative use and access through steroid holidays and exploring these as a specific example of deviant leisure (Smith and Raymen, 2016/2018; Raymen and Smith, 2019). Steroid use and the building of what is seen as a desirable physique (with a belief that this will be accompanied by a similarly desirable personality and lifestyle) will all combine goals that are widely aspired to, with a deviant means of achieving these that may (as stated – ironically) not be beneficial but harmful to an individual's health. Applying the deviant leisure perspective here is useful because, as Smith and Raymen (2018: 65) explain, this offers a 'conceptual foundation' for the examination of forms of

> social deviance in which 'harm' and 'deviance' can *always* be looked at in the same analytical frame. By reframing 'deviant' forms of leisure not as a contravention of norms and values but as a transgression of ...[an] ethical 'duty to the other', we can discuss the harms of commodified leisure as 'deviance' while acknowledging their conformity to social norms and values.

In the context of the relatively mainstream gym culture of the Gold Coast region (located south of Brisbane, east Australia), steroid holidays were seen as a viable and socially normalised way of accessing IPED. Thailand presented, with its climate, training facilities and a reputation for hedonistic nightlife, an environment that could easily accommodate the values, lifestyle and practices associated with the training and bodybuilding subculture of the Australian Gold Coast. At the same time, such tourism raises questions about drug control, drug access, drug safety, commodification of leisure, competition regarding body image, and the relationship of all this to social, and individual self-harms.

Steroid use is at an interesting intersection of approved and disapproved leisure, being accepted and embedded in sports training even if it breaks rules. It is therefore seen as 'edgy' (in multiple senses) and related to other forms of deviance in sport – cheating, stimulant use, etc. – (Mulrooney and van de Ven, 2015). It can therefore usefully be positioned alongside other phenomena and behaviours described by Smith and Raymen (2016: 6) as 'deviant leisure'. Thus, 'Cultural lifestyle sports or forms of "serious leisure" (Stebbins, 2007) such as skateboarding, parkour, and urban exploration (Atkinson, 2009; Garrett, 2013) occupy a curious position at the nexus between deviance and leisure which is riddled with contradictions'. Importantly, breaking rules or laws in order to meet social expectations of high performance and comply with a socio-economically encouraged spirit of competition means that 'in many ways such activities can be conceptualized not as 'deviant' but entirely conformist; embodying the risk-taking entrepreneurial ethos of late capitalism, and part of the drive to discover one's true self and construct a persona of 'cool individualism' (Smith and Raymen 2016: 68).

Background: IPED use, supply, culture and context on the Gold Coast

According to the Australian Crime Commission (2015: 49), the IPED market in Australia has experienced rapid growth in recent years, and now consists of 'users from an increasingly diverse demographic who are using an ever-widening range of substances.' Alongside a traditional repertoire of anabolic steroid use, it is suggested that 'peptides and human growth hormone have gained in popularity among IPED users, and are being used in combination with, and in addition to, anabolic steroids'.

The Gold Coast is a city that has been built on tourism as a holiday destination for people from all over Australia and overseas (West and Bayne, 2002) and it is the epicentre of Queensland IPED use. Being a city with a beach culture means there are 'bodies on show everywhere you look', and Bleeker (2014: 24) emphasises the importance of this visibility and the cultivation of the 'body beautiful' with regard to injecting IPED prevalence in this region. These themes are often observed in media articles with Willacy (2015), for example, reporting for *ABC News* that, 'society's obsession with body image and [communication via] social media is helping to drive a surge in steroid use, particularly in Queensland's south east corner' (the Gold Coast). A local newspaper commentary reinforces these themes stating that the mainstream popularity of gyms on the Gold Coast means that 'Gyms are a must-be-seen-in place' where 'even celebrities such as Dwayne (The Rock) Johnson stop by for workouts' (Gold Coast Bulletin, 2015).

Gym culture as a mainstream culture

To understand the Gold Coast as a particular context for IPED use and a location from which steroid holidays are undertaken and accepted as an aspect of some training regimes, it is important to recognise the extent to which gym culture has become a core feature of mainstream life. In other locations of mainstream leisure, such as bar and club culture, moderate recreational drug use has become sufficiently prevalent and/or embedded to be described as 'normalised' (Coomber et al., 2015), signalling degrees of tolerance or acceptance. In this respect some 'boundaries between convention and criminality' may be blurred (Coomber et al., 2015: 8; van de Ven et al., 2018). Like recreational drug use, IPED use also needs to be located within a context of broader (relatively) normalised drug use.

Normative IPED supply

IPED access and supply has traditionally been through the older 'hardcore' 'serious' gyms, where an individual would become inducted into the weightlifting subculture before initiating use and gym owners would be the likely suppliers (Coomber et al., 2014; Coomber and Salinas 2019). However, with gyms having become mainstream across Australia and especially on the Gold Coast (in terms of the number of gyms, their 24-hour availability and their redesign to appeal to general fitness populations) and with the growth of fitness-related forms of 'social supply' (where users with access facilitate access to friends/acquaintances) also expanding (Coomber et al., 2014), activities that were once confined to hard-core bodybuilders have now widened to encompass 'normal' populations (van de Ven and Mulrooney, 2016). The pursuit of muscle tone, strength and model body composition is no longer limited to the realm of professional body building. Noyce (2018) for example, asks 'who uses steroids in Australia and why are they using them?', considering the experiences of three young, male steroid users, who accessed drugs via online black markets, and gathered information from online forums. Their stories support a common narrative that many users suffer a body image disorder or dysmorphia, and despite apparent risks of side effects, would continue to take illegal substances as a form of self-medication. For others, the 'fitness craze' (Gold Coast Bulletin, 2016) has seen gym memberships offer ordinary people the opportunity to train, make physical transformations 'and become part of the family' (ibid.). In this respect, the Gold Coast presents a unique context in which fitness and body image are intertwined in lifestyle and culture, and as a result, there is a degree of expectation and acceptance of the availability and use of IPED in gyms, constituting a move toward what South (1999: 4) has described as drug use as a 'fact of everyday life'. As Mulrooney and van de Ven (2015: 5) relate:

> in bodybuilding subcultures both the use and supply of IPED is often 'normalized' (Monaghan, 2001) [and, although]...the consumption, possession and trafficking of IPED may be considered unethical, morally wrong and even illegal by society at large, these activities are a normal feature of 'the everyday life' (South, 1999) of many bodybuilders [and].... a wide variety of IPED are often easily accessible through these subcultural groups... [where]... consumption and sale often intertwine.

Because of IPED users' entanglement with everyday cultural pressures surrounding muscle gains, strength and body image, it may not be unreasonable to suggest that within locations of comparatively high and increasing IPED use, such as the Gold Coast, a relative normalisation of IPED use is not only conceivable but also expected. The Australian Gold Coast then not only provides a milieu in which the use of IPED becomes more accepted within day-to-day life and where social supply is routine in this context (Coomber et al., 2014; van de Ven and Mulrooney, 2016) but, as suggested by media reporting, this may lead to a willingness and enthusiasm to seek out new, less traditional forms of access in other arenas of supply, such as the steroid holiday.

Drugs tourism and steroid holidays

Reports on steroid holidays first began to appear in news articles in Australia from around 2012 (Duff, 2012; ABC News, 2013; Skeene, 2014; EFE, 2016) covering the journey of a number of amateur Australian bodybuilders to Thailand whose intent was to purchase cheap, easily accessible steroids and other performance enhancing supplementation. The interest of the media seems to have waned since 2016 although holidaying to procure drugs has not (EFE, 2016; Fink et al., 2018).

This form of drugs tourism is growing in destinations such as Pattaya, Phuket and Bangkok (Thailand), and reported as emergent in other destinations such as Mumbai, Warsaw and Kiev where supply contexts are less restricted than in Australia. While *steroid* 'tourism' may be relatively new, the idea of 'drugs tourism' is not, by itself, new at all and is defined by Valdez and Sifaneck (1997: 880) as 'the phenomenon by which persons become attracted to a particular location because of the accessibility of licit or illicit drugs and related services'. Drug tourism can be traced at least to the 'hippy and hash' travellers of the 1960s (Dorn et al., 1992: 6), through the embrace of the exotic and the search for the authentic in forms of tourism that have sought drug-induced religious experiences (de Rios, 1994; Coomber and South, 2004; Winkelman, 2005), to the heterogeneity of drugs tourism experiences today, where the use of various substances may involve the simple pursuit of hedonism, a more challenging search for meaning, or engagement with different cultures (Uriely and Behlhassen, 2005). Some of this is simply adding pleasure to everyday life; some of it is about changing the everyday to enhance experiences and pursue an 'edge' (Lyng, 1990; Cohen and Taylor, 1992).

While some drugs tourism might be traditionally associated with the pursuit of transcendental experience or inner change, 'cosmetic surgery tourism' has been defined as travel to access procedures to enhance external physical appearance. Cosmetic surgery tourism is a rapidly growing phenomenon, and its emergence comes as part of the broader trend in health, medical or wellness tourism (Reisman, 2010). The ease of travel in a globalised world, along with a rise of health awareness (Carrera and Bridges, 2006) and the normalisation of body enhancement have provided a context in which cosmetic surgery tourism is flourishing. The numbers of people travelling to undergo elective medical procedures has been increasing for some years (Connell, 2006), reflecting a combination of availability of cheap air flights, favourable exchange rates for some, and cheaper costs for procedures. The further driver in cosmetic surgery tourism is the actual *tourism* element (Bell et al., 2011). This often takes the form of holiday packages that can offer surgery plus recuperation in a picturesque resort location or retreat, while also offering more familiar tourist experiences for recovering patients and accompanying travellers. These aspects of cosmetic surgery tourism can be understood as purposeful image enhancement coupled with added indulgence value. These expressions of individualism and narcissism reflect buy-in to 'conformity to social norms and values' but in a context in which these have been 'manipulated by the ideological dominance of consumer capitalism that opens up a space for harm to result from the individualistic pursuit of leisure' (Smith and Raymen, 2016: 65).

Steroid holidays

Steroid holidays may be understood as bearing some of the characteristics of drug tourism and cosmetic surgery tourism, providing a means of accessing IPED that involves travelling to another country, appearing to be doing so for the purposes of a holiday but with the dual (or primary) objective of acquiring pharmaceutical grade IPED to consume in situ or possibly smuggle back home (in countries where personal possession is still permitted). The original empirical research findings reported here add to the limited amount of information available in various international media sources and represent the first, as far as we are aware, published academic contribution to the area.

In Australia, the laws regarding use and distribution of steroids are comparatively strict (van de Ven et al., 2018). Though steroids were previously classified as prescription drugs under the *Poisons and Therapeutic Goods Act 1966*, in early 2014 the government amended certain laws applying to steroids, reclassifying them as narcotics under the *Drug Misuse and Trafficking Act 1985.* Penalties for related offences vary between Australian states and depend upon whether possession is for personal use, or if there is intent to supply. The harshest penalties range from fines (up to $100,000) to imprisonment (up to twenty-five years) for possession of a Schedule 4 [poison] drug (Hughes et al., 2015). In Queensland, steroids were 'unhelpfully' (van de Ven and Zahnow, 2017) reclassified as a schedule-one drug in 2014, placing them in the same category as heroin, cocaine and methamphetamine. Increased penalties do not seem to have curtailed use, suggesting that this is not a very effective strategy (ibid).

The appeal of a steroid holiday stems from what may be a genuine – or a wishful – belief (reflected in media reports and conversations among users of online forums; see, e.g., Anabolic Steroids Forum: http://forums.steroid.com/), that steroids are legally available without prescription in Thailand and hence a visit will offer the opportunity to purchase safe, high-quality IPED, at a price far cheaper than in countries with comparatively effective prohibitions and a stricter policing of such drugs. For example, one ABC News interviewee claimed that steroids accessed in Thailand cost as little as one sixteenth of the equivalent available on the illicit drug market in Australia (ABC News, 2013) while a report on the availability of IPED in Dubai (Webster, 2016) also emphasised reduced cost as a significant motivation for visitors: 'Performance-enhancing drugs are widely and cheaply available in Dubai despite being banned, leading the emirate to attract "drug tourists", former Olympic athletes living in the UAE say' …[with] 'anabolic steroids, human growth hormones and testosterone' easily available at half the price they would cost elsewhere in countries such as Australia, Europe or the USA.

For Australians, alongside the 'pull' of reduced cost, there is also a 'push' in the sense that taking a steroid holiday will provide the opportunity to source and use IPED away from the jurisdiction and constraints of Australian drug law. However, although Thai pharmacies have a reputation for supplying steroids over the counter and despite an apparent ease of availability, purchasing steroids without a prescription in Thailand is in fact a criminal offence (Windle, 2016). The abundant availability of anabolic steroids leads to a common misconception that they have been legalised in Thailand (Zoera, 2014) whereas under food and drug laws, possession and sale can lead to serious fines and harsh jail sentences, while offences charged under the Narcotics Act can carry a maximum penalty of death (Zoera, 2014; Thongmuang, 2013).

Much like perceptions elsewhere regarding the legality of new psychoactive substances or 'legal highs' (Measham et al., 2010), the assumption that IPED are legal, reassures or misleads purchasers in a further assumption that the drugs are more likely to be genuine, regulated and of good quality. Research has however consistently shown that the IPED circulating in the black market are often fake or of poor quality (Coomber et al., 2014). In support of this, Pellegrini et al. (2012) have argued that the rapidly expanding international IPED black market, which includes Thailand as one major point of steroid origin, commonly provides inauthentic IPED with a compromised composition. The use of substandard IPED can be very dangerous, and as individuals look to maximise physical results within the time constraints of their stay, this could lead to short-term excessive consumption in the same way that certain spatial conditions can promote 'rushed' injecting practices leading to drug-related hazard and injury in heroin using populations (Parkin and Coomber, 2011). Constrained or rigid periods for consumption may therefore serve to compromise harm reduction activities such as 'break periods' (Rowe et al., 2017).

Perceptions of, and the doing of, steroid holidays by Gold Coast IPED users

The following sections report on the views and experiences of 22 IPED users recruited from a Needle and Syringe Programme (NSP) on the Australian Gold Coast who participated in semi-structured face-to-face interviews during 2015–2016. Participants were asked what they knew of steroid holidays, if they had personally experienced them, whether they considered them to be a viable means of access, and if they knew of others who had acquired IPED this way. The NSP facilitated the research by advertising the project and helping to recruit respondents. Selection criteria included current or former IPED users (who must have used within the last 3 years) that were over 18. The sample consisted of 21 males and 1 female, broadly consistent with the gender ratios of NSP service users, and were aged between 20 and 45 years (average of 29 years). The longest period of use was 18 years, and four participants had been using for 6 months or under; the average length of use was 4 years.

Normative IPED supply for 18 of those engaged in the study and reflective of other studies on IPED supply elsewhere (Coomber et al. 2015; Coomber and Salinas 2019) was through three now 'traditional' primary sources: 'street' or 'gym'-based supply from a dealer or gym owner/worker (n=5); social supply (n=9) perceived as a growing trend resulting from the relative normalisation of broader drug use (Coomber, Moyle and South, 2015); and the purchasing of IPED online (n=4) where there was seen to be a quick and easy access to IPED and other drugs (Kraska et al., 2010; Antonopoulos and Hall, 2016). Three had also accessed their IPED from private doctors. Only one respondent had actually been on a steroid holiday with a further five personally knowing others, such as 'lifting partners' or gym acquaintances, that had been on steroid holidays. Three had also supplied IPED to gym acquaintances (social supply) for little or no profit as well as received IPED in this fashion.

It is common for IPED users to believe that their sources and supply are legitimate (not fakes) as was the case for this sample. Such belief is however, commonly mistaken (Coomber et al., 2014) regardless of how authentic the appearance of the drugs supplied.

Ease of access

As related above a steroid holiday entails travel to Thailand (or similar such locations) to engage in intensive training with the aid of what is assumed to be legal, cheap yet pharmaceutical grade IPED obtained in local pharmacies in situ. Those interviewed highlighted the ease with which steroids could be obtained in Thai pharmacies or related retailers:

> I was in Thailand with my girlfriend and I walked into a supplement store. I said "do you have steroids", straight out, and they opened this cabinet, and they had everything!...And they had everything, and it was right there, and the guy selling it was huge, and definitely had to be legit because they had a lot of repeat business.
>
> *27-year old, male steroid user–curious holiday maker not a steroid tourist*

That there may be an element of self-deception or wishful thinking about the legal status of IPED in Thailand is illustrated by one interviewee (26 years; steroid user – 3 years of use) who described his experience of purchasing steroids in the following way:

> Go over to Thailand. Walk into a chemist. Ask for what you want, and they will give it to you. That's it. All steroids are legal in Thailand. They're only illegal if you're bringing them back... Yeah, you can just buy them over the counter... *well if you can just buy it over the counter, I'm guessing it's legal.* (emphasis added)

A similar blurring of the legal status of these drugs was expressed by another visitor who explained to a news reporter (see EFE, 2016) that:

> According to the law, a prescription is required in order to purchase these products, but the pharmacies do not strictly follow the rules. Sometimes the prescription can even be issued on the spot by paying a few dollars to the doctor.

Thailand has a high profile in the bodybuilding community as a country where pharmaceutical quality IPED are available at a fraction of the regular price. Those interviewed echoed this belief, suggesting that in Thailand IPED were cheaper and easier to acquire. Although it was commonly reported that price was likely an important incentive for taking steroid holidays, one of the more experienced IPED use interviewees was sceptical about the actual overall savings benefits once travel and time were also considered:

> I think it's ridiculous. I'll tell you why. I've researched this a lot. By the time you get on a plane and go over there, how long can you stay over there as a normal person? Time off work alone is costing you 800 bucks [dollars]. So you go for a month right, you've lost 3200 [dollars], and then you've got to live there and come back. And you've only been on that shit for a month, which isn't going to make a difference in anyone's book really, and what I'm saying is... what are you gaining from going there? You're getting your gear a bit cheaper, that's it. You can use a bit more but look what it's costing you.
>
> *42-year old male steroid user and professional bodybuilder – 18 years of use*

A training or party holiday?

The same participant who had voiced scepticism about cost savings also argued that steroid holidays were an attempt by misinformed users to make quick muscular gains that could not be realistically retained:

> Well you know some of the steroids last 24 hours. Some last two weeks. It depends on the ester, or what you use. You use testosterone and stuff like that, it'll be out of your body in 2/3 weeks, and they are some of the longer lasting ones. Stanozol is 24 hours. So, what I'm saying is that it's a totally uneducated way to go. I've always been inclined to use smaller amounts over a longer period of time. It's not about whacking as much as you can in, it's not going to work mate.

By contrast, however, another interviewee reported that he knew of two professional bodybuilders who would train in Thailand for 12 weeks prior to competition, though he noted that this was likely to be exceptional as they approached their training programme more seriously than most. The same participant contrasted this with cases of other individuals going to Thailand for just two weeks with the intention of 'stacking' in a shorter time period, or using a variety of IPED, with the aim of maximising short-term growth (Kimergard, 2014):

> To me that's stupid, and goes back to people being uneducated about it, and I've heard stories about one specific person who went over and put on 12 kilos of so-called muscle in two weeks, and within 4 weeks it was gone. I do know of people who have gone to do that.
>
> *27-year old, male steroid user – 2 years of use*

This method was not only suggested by some to be ineffective but was also seen as problematic in that it could lead to IPED users taking higher doses on holiday with the hope that the dose would continue to filter through the body on return from the holiday. A number of media reports present a similar story (Duff, 2012; ABC News, 2013; Skene, 2014). This uninformed use may suggest some individuals are new to bodybuilding and rather than spend time training and learning, instead they are looking for the 'quick fix' that will speed up the enhancement process in search of the elusive body they desire and that they see as culturally valued as well as doing so in a context they perceived to be less risky with regard to supply and criminal justice sanctions.

Most suggested that the 'holiday' inflection of 'steroid holidays' was often taken too literally and prioritised over serious training. The general belief was that many individuals taking such a holiday would use IPED in combination with other (illicit) 'party drugs' and excessive alcohol consumption. It has been suggested that holidays offer a social arena which can provide a playground and 'permission' for risky behaviour and excessive consumption (Briggs et al., 2011, see also Turner's chapter in this volume). This seemed to be the case for one interviewee who described his time in Thailand as a 'party holiday' involving the use of various drugs and alcohol (including steroids). Interviewees also reflected on friends' steroid holidays, with one respondent (33-year-old male, steroid user) referring to one friend, who he described as a 'party guy', using 'steroids to look good', and 'party drugs to feel good'. Thailand seemed to present an accelerated and intensified version of Gold Coast gym culture where 'steroid tourists' could be surrounded by similar signs and signifiers of this scene. One interviewee commented:

> They have tons of gyms, they charge like 10 bucks, which is a lot of money there, and there's a lot of huge guys there. You might walk through Surfers Paradise [in Gold Coast, Australia] and think there's a lot of big guys, but walk through the streets of Thailand, Pattaya or wherever... everyone's huge!.
>
> *27-year-old, male steroid user – 2 years of use*

These themes were echoed by another young steroid user who seemed to hint that much like tattoos, recreational drug use was tied up in some aspects of Gold Coast steroids subculture:

> Oh yeah, he parties all the time. Yeah definitely. He does it here anyway, yeah, they all do it. Cocaine. They do everything, steroids and cocaine. They all do it...They do it to feel good, they take it to look good, and they spend their money on women. They think that's the pinnacle of life, looking good, feeling good, and a little line... plus tattoos, and melanotan too. That's a good drug.
>
> *24-year-old, male steroid user – 1 year of use*

This sample is by no means representative of the steroid holiday population but does flag the issue of poly-drug use that has also been raised in media reports. An association between steroid use and partying, alcohol, and violence has also been noted previously in the academic literature (cf. Lopez, 2013; Altheide, 2002; Clark and Henderson, 2003; Pope and Katz, 1994). One interviewee (42-year-old, male, long-term steroid user) suggested that 'Most of the people that use steroids use party drugs. It's all about image', while others also said they believed many IPED users, particularly younger ones, were pursuing a particular image that IPED use offered and that the hedonism, image, plus party combination promised by steroid holidays was seductive to some for this reason. Most of those interviewed provided insight that suggests and supports the argument that there has been a turn towards the use of leisure and consumer markets to seek freedom and identity, and in this sense that people have 'appended their existential security and self-esteem to the 'velocity of fashion' (Appadurai, 1986) within a precarious 'life cycle' of commodities, fads and leisure trends and the spirals and loops of cultural meaning' (Smith and Raymen, 2016: 76).

Steroid holidays, training regimes and health

Drug users stigmatise the behaviours of other users they see as being engaged in 'less responsible' use of the same drugs (Simmonds and Coomber, 2009) and this was also evident among some of those we spoke to. Some 'serious' IPED users interviewed expressed negative views about other IPED users who were pursuing their 'ideal' steroid holiday as an opportunity to mix hedonistic indulgence and relaxation alongside the acquisition and consumption of cheap, quality IPED and some training. For the purists, involvement in holiday hedonism and wider drug taking signalled a lack of dedication or seriousness towards training:

> Yeah, well your body can only take so much, it's bound to happen [risking your health from mixing substances], I've seen a lot of friends that do go over to Thailand and Bali and all that, and mess themselves up for two weeks straight or something like that. It takes a long time to recover, and it's not good for you. I don't do any other drugs… I used to smoke a lot of weed, but not anymore.
>
> *22-year-old, male steroid user – 3 years of use*

and

> When I take steroids, I'm all about the healthy lifestyle mate, not about smoking, drinking, having a snort of this. I'm training you know. It's all about health and fitness. What is the point?.
>
> *48-year-old, male ex-steroid user – 5 years of use*

Attaching negative labels to those deemed 'less serious' can also perform a function of providing justification for their own approach to personal use, that is, unlike others, they are not 'mis-using' or 'abusing' but are behaving responsibly (Simmonds and Coomber, 2009). All respondents were nonetheless clear that they perceived IPED use to be a means of acquiring the kind of positive social capital (Shilling, 2005) required to achieve a desired status within certain social spheres they frequented within Gold Coast culture.

Along with concerns around the incompatibility of recreational drug use and serious training regimes, a number of respondents raised concerns about the safety of the IPED available in Thailand. Several commentators (Kimergard et al., 2014; Coomber et al., 2015; Antonopoulos and Hall, 2016) have suggested there are difficulties in identifying legitimate IPED due to illicit suppliers successfully copying the packaging of authentic pharmaceutical products. If individuals try to take advantage of ease of access and use a large amount of IPED in a short space of time they could be risking their health even if using legitimately produced drugs, with the risk multiplying in cases of use of counterfeit drugs (Kimergard, 2014). One IPED user reflected on stories he had heard from friends who had purchased 'bladders' (500 ml packs of IPED) while holidaying:

> Respondent: They basically said, you can get big fucking bladders, like big plastic bags for drips and stuff like that, for not much, 100 dollars you know… and getting back here and that can't be that hard.
>
> Interviewer: How do you view that as a means of access? Would you say it's a safe way of going about it?
>
> Respondent: Well it depends if it's the product, if it's the real thing. There's a lot of fake um, stuff that goes around in that market. And you wouldn't really know what you were taking, especially if it wasn't in a sealed… thing.
>
> *48-year old, male ex-steroid user – 5 years of use*

Another interviewee commented, 'It's a third world country, to me you've sort of got to question the quality of everything' (22-year-old, male steroid user – 3 years of use). This, however, was not a common anxiety as the majority emphasised the legitimacy and availability of 'pharmaceutical grade' IPED that they believed could be easily obtained in Thai chemists. Such beliefs however are common within the IPED-using community and there is little evidence (and no proof to those purchasing) to suggest that these IPED are any less problematic than those accessed by others elsewhere where packaging and substance appear totally authentic but the product is commonly either incorrect, sub-standard/less than optimal dosage or simply fake (Coomber et al. 2014).

Discussion

As forms of tourism related to drug use and cosmetic surgery see further growth and become a viable option for those wishing to experience inner or aesthetic transformation, steroid holidays might be understood as embodying a *hybrid* form of these activities. Bell et al. (2011: 143) suggest that (surgery) tourists select their destinations at least in part as particular places where they 'expect...certain prices and levels of service'. These themes were interwoven in many of the narratives of Gold Coast IPED users, who conceived Thailand as representing a location in which a range of cheap IPED could be accessed with ease. Significantly, there is a degree of contradiction and self-deceit involved in what individuals say they 'know' or 'believe' regarding the legality of availability and use of steroids in Thailand. This is evident when they also indicate awareness – and some fear – of the strict nature of Thai laws in general and in relation to drugs in particular, as well as the unpredictability of how police might respond to any case which could be interpreted as 'possession' or 'trafficking'.

Rojek (1997) uses the terms 'indexing' and 'dragging' to refer to the ways individuals can collect particular images of tourist destinations and combine these elements to visualise a particular destination. Thailand was said to be imagined as a place where IPED users could combine their pursuit of 'stacking' with hedonism: recreational drug taking, excess alcohol and partying. The overall impression was that steroid holidays were, for the majority, an opportunity to combine a party lifestyle, with the physique that has become synonymous with such a culture. Those who went on steroid holidays tended to be either the party-loving Gold Coast steroid user identified by many throughout the broader interviews, or those going away to engage in serious training camp preparation before a competition, as they believed they would be able to use pharmaceutical-grade steroids and benefit from good training facilities. If there is a stereotype of the steroid holidayer, it appears to be grounded in some segment of reality: the main expressions of interest in this particular activity seem to be from young, male, tanned, tattooed and sociable 'party-people'. For the latter group, unlike the cosmetic surgery tourists who often choose to fly elsewhere seeking relative anonymity to undergo secret procedures, perhaps with minimal engagement with local people and culture (Bookman and Bookman, 2007), steroid holidays instead offered the opportunity to engage in an overt masculine display of what Baudrillard (1998: 129) observes is the most desired object in consumer culture, 'more precious and more dazzling than any other... the BODY.'

Uriely and Belhassen (2005 243) suggest that drug tourism destinations can be understood as 'cultural centres' for subcultures that emerge around particular drugs, providing the example of users of cannabis who 'share certain goals, values, practices and lifestyles that constitute a distinctive subculture within and across national cultures'. Identity construction and meaning are made through 'memorable holiday experiences' (Briggs et al., 2011) and are strongly shaped by the social context, particularly those characterised by aggressive marketing of alcohol, drugs and sex (Sellars, 1998). In many ways, Thailand seemed to offer the perfect context for steroid tourists, offering the climate and environment to display the body, an abundance of gyms, a Muay Thai training culture, and many opportunities for hedonism. It is suggested that body builders who use anabolic steroids often undertake particular performances of health which very often privilege 'self-willed corporeal transformations, experienced as both pleasurable and demanding' (Keane, 2009: 172). Steroid holidays may then be understood as providing one of the more pleasurable aspects of body building/training, offering IPED users an opportunity for an important sub-cultural identity-building experience, along with the deviant leisure prospect of 'acting out' some of the more risky characteristics associated with gym and body building culture.

Most participants warned of the health implications of steroid holidays and stressed the risk of poly-drug use and excess alcohol consumption in Thailand leading to health problems, while also furthering negative stereotypes of aggressive, partying steroid users. Though it was reasoned that it is possible to take the holiday and also achieve muscular gains, most interviewees – making reference to cycle lengths – were sceptical about what could be achieved, and doubtful about the progress that could be made, while on holiday and retained on return. In this respect, the promise of a 'quick fix' tended not to materialise and those who sought this out were considered 'uneducated' and naïve. It has been suggested that while drug tourists are in many cases concerned with legal, social, and medical aspects of risk and take precautions to reduce them, they nonetheless perceive drug use as less perilous in the context of tourism than in the routine of everyday life (Uriely and Balhassen, 2005). These themes are relevant to the circumstances and characteristics of the steroid holiday which presents a unique context in which routine personal rules and limits are relaxed and unanticipated risks and harms may be experienced.

Conclusion

Steroid use as deviant leisure, integrated into holidaying in places with a reputation for the availability of hedonistic experiences, can be seen to reflect a trend that mixes self-regard, competitive individualism and fear of missing out on the fun that others must be having. Social and collective morality are subverted by individualism and moral relativism, 'privileging consumer tastes and desires as a form of 'freedom' and liberal self-expression', meaning that 'capacity for harm is embedded within culturally acceptable, value-normative behaviours, bound inextricably to what Žižek (2002) terms the 'cultural injunction to enjoy' (Smith and Raymen, 2016: 67). Hall (2019) would place all this within the 'new economy of the self' which includes

> a booming market in various lifestyle drugs, otherwise referred to as image and performance enhancing drugs (IPED) or human enhancement drugs …, consumed through personal choice rather than illness, and often used for non-health matters or matters lying at the margins of health and well-being … [and] available to boost sexual performance, speed up weight loss and muscle growth, slow down ageing, and increase physical and mental capacity.

The 'steroid holiday' where IPED users travel abroad to countries such as Thailand to access and use cheaply sourced 'legitimate' IPED while on 'holiday' has not been subject to previous academic study. Within the range of options for obtaining IPED, steroid holidays surfaced as a surprisingly popular choice for a means of supply previously only reported sporadically in the media. Though significant as a form of IPED access, the steroid holiday can also be understood as an important (subcultural) identity-building experience. Steroid holidays might be usefully understood as an emergent form of drug tourism with some parallels with the motivations and behaviours of cosmetic surgery tourists. IPED use is beginning to appear in different repertoires of drug lifestyles and has the potential to gain wider acceptance, making further inroads into mainstream culture, or attract greater condemnation as a threat to health and sports-related values. As van de Ven, Dunn and Mulrooney (2018) note, a growing trend towards criminalisation of suppliers and users can be seen in a number of countries and the possibility is that this will do less to reduce harm and more to create the conditions for a 'self-fulfilling prophecy as it incentivises more criminal actors to enter the market', in turn leading to forms of supply with stronger connections to other criminal activities and crime groups. As in many other areas of drug policy and debate, reactions to IPED use and supply need to carefully consider how to control a growing form of deviant leisure.

References

ABC News (2013) Bodybuilder gives insight into Thailand steroid holidays, doctors warn of health risks. Available at: www.abc.net.au/news/2013-05-30/bodybuilder-gives-insight-into-thailand-steroid-holidays/4723980 [Accessed:17/08/2014).

Altheide, D. L. (2002) *Creating Fear: News and the Construction of Crisis.* New York: Aldine de Gruyter.

Antonopoulos, G. and Hall, A. (2016) '"Gain with no pain": Anabolic-androgenic steroids trafficking in the UK', *European Journal of Criminology*, 1–18.

Appadurai, A. (1986) *The Social Life of Things: Commodities in Cultural Perspective.* Cambridge: University Press. http://dx.doi.org/10.1017/cbo9780511819582

Atkinson, M. (2009) 'Parkour, anarcho-environmentalism, and poesis', *Journal of Sport and Social Issues*, 33: 169–194.

Australian Crime Commission (2015) *Organised Crime in Australia.* Canberra: Australian Crime Commission.

Baudrillard, J. (1998) *The Consumer Society: Myths and Structures.* London: Sage.

Bell, D., Holliday, R., Jones, M., Probyn, E., and Taylor, J. S. (2011) 'Bikinis and bandages: An itinerary for cosmetic surgery tourism', *Tourist Studies*, 11(2): 139–155.

Bleeker, A. (2014) 'The mirror effect: The rising use of performance and image enhancing drugs', *Of Substance: The National Magazine on Alcohol, Tobacco and Other Drugs*, Online, November. 12(3): 22–25. http://search.informit.com.au/documentSummary;dn=779166142273095;res=IELHEA. ISSN: 1449–0021.

Briggs, D., Tutenges, S., Armitage, R., and Panchev, D. (2011) 'Sexy substances and the substance of sex: Findings from an ethnographic study in Ibiza, Spain', *Drugs and Alcohol Today*, 11(4): 173–188.

Bookman, M., and Bookman, K. (2007) *Medical Tourism in Developing Countries*. London: Palgrave.

Clark, A. S., & Henderson, L. P. (2003). Behavioral and physiological responses to anabolic-androgenic steroids. *Neuroscience and Biobehavioral Reviews*, *27*(5): 413–436. https://doi.org/10.1016/S0149-7634(03)00064-2

Cohen, S., and Taylor, L. (1992) *Escape Attempts: The Theory and Practice of Resistance to Everyday Life* (2nd ed.). London: Routledge.

Coomber, R., and South, N. (eds.) (2004) *Drug Use in Cultural Contexts 'Beyond the West': Tradition, Change and Post-Colonialism*. London: Free Association Books.

Coomber, R., Pavlidis, A., Santos, G. H., Wilde, M., Schmidt, W., and Redshaw, C. (2014) 'The supply of steroids and other performance and image enhancing drugs (IPEDs) in one English city: Fakes, counterfeits, supplier trust, common beliefs and access', *Performance Enhancement & Health*, 3(3): 135–144.

Coomber, R., Moyle, L., and South, N. (2015) 'The normalisation of drug supply: The social supply of drugs as the "other side" of the history of normalisation', *Drugs: Education, Prevention and Policy*. DOI: 10.3109/09687637.2015.1110565

Coomber, R., and Salinas, M. (2019) 'The supply of image and performance enhancing drugs (IPED) to local non-elite users in England: Resilient traditional and newly emergent methods', in K. van de Ven, K. Mulrooney, & J. McVeigh (Eds.), *Human Enhancement Drugs*. Routledge Studies in Crime and Society. Routledge.

Connell, J. (2006) 'Medical tourism: Sea, sun, sand and... surgery', *Tourism Management*, 27(6): 1093–1100.

de Rios, M. (1994) 'Drug tourism in the Amazon: Why westerners are desperate to find the vanishing primitive', *Omni*, January. 6.

Dorn, N., Murji, K., and South, N. (1992) *Traffickers: Drug Markets and Law Enforcement*. London: Routledge.

Dunn, M. (2010) 'The non-medical use of steroids in Australia: Results from a general population survey', *Australian and New Zealand Journal of Public Health*, 34: 531–532.

Duff, E. (2012) 'Steroid holiday', *Sydney Morning Herald*. www.smh.com.au/national/health/steroid-holiday-20120526-1zblt.html

EFE (2016) 'Bodybuilders swarm to Pattaya to bulk up as steroid tourism booms', 11th February. Agencia EFE. www.efe.com/efe/english/life/bodybuilders-swarm-to-pattaya-bulk-up-as-steroid-tourism-booms/50000263-2837208

Fincoeur, B., van de Ven, K., and Mulrooney, K.J.D. (2014). The symbiotic evolution of anti-doping and supply chains of doping substances: How criminal networks may benefit from anti-doping policy. *Trends in Organized Crime*. Available at SSRN: https://ssrn.com/abstract=2581555

Fink, J., Schoenfeld, B., Hackney, A., Matsumoto, M., Maekawa, T., Nakazato, K., and Horie, S. (2019) 'Anabolic-androgenic steroids: Procurement and administration practices of doping athletes', *The Physician and Sports Medicine*, 47(1): 10–14.

Gallagher, S. (2017) 'Steroid use increases four-fold in one year, as more young men take muscle-enhancing drugs', *HuffPost UK*, Lifestyle section: www.huffingtonpost.co.uk/entry/steroid-use-increased-four-fold-in-one-year-as-more-young-men-take-muscle-enhancing-drugs_uk_597b05c4e4b02a4ebb74b8cb [Accessed 20/05/2017].

Garrett, B. (2013) *Explore Everything: Place-Hacking the City*. London: Verso.

Gold Coast Bulletin (2015) 'Police seize steroids and arrest a min in a bikie raid at Tugun'. www.goldcoastbulletin.com.au/news/crime-court/police-seize-steroids-and-arrest-a-man-in-a-bikie-raid-at-tugun/news-story/c531b530f88e0f48633a412685454a0f

Gold Coast Bulletin (2016) 'We asked and you voted here are the top 10 gyms on the gold coast as voted by you'. www.goldcoastbulletin.com.au/lifestyle/best-of-gold-coast/we-asked-and-you-voted-here-are-the-top-10-gyms-on-the-gold-coast-as-voted-by-you/news-story/0cddc637a5a6c7b4dafd0692967ac453

Goldsworthy, T., and McGillivray, L. (2015) 'Steroid seizures and arrests soar to record highs in Australia', *The Conversation*, May 20. http://theconversation.com/steroid-seizures-and-arrests-soar-to-record-highs-in-australia-41955

Griffiths, S., Murray, S. B., Dunn, M., and Blashill, A. J. (2017). 'Anabolic steroid use among sexual minority males living in Australia and New Zealand: Associations with demographics, body dissatisfaction, eating disorder psychopathology, and quality of life', *Drug and Alcohol Dependence*, 181: 170–176.

Hall, A. (2019) 'Lifestyle drugs and late capitalism: A topography of harm', in T. Raymen & O. Smith (eds.), *Deviant Leisure: Criminological Perspectives on Leisure and Harm*. London: Palgrave Macmillan.

Hope, V., McVeigh, J., Smith, J., Glass, R., Njoroge, J., Tanner, C., Parry, J., Ncube, F., and Desai, M. (2017) 'Low levels of hepatitis C diagnosis and testing uptake among people who inject image and performance enhancing drugs in England and Wales, 2012–15', *Drug and Alcohol Dependence*, 179: 83–86.

Hughes, C., Cowdery, N., and Ritter, A. (2015) 'Deemed supply in Australian drug trafficking laws: A justifiable legal provision?' *Current Issues in Criminal Justice*, 27: 1.

Jacka, B., Peacock, A., Degenhardt, L., Bruno, R., Clare, P., Kemp, R., Dev, E., and Larance, B. (2017) 'Trends in IPEDs use among male clients of needle–syringe programs in Queensland, Australia; 2007–2015', *International Journal of Drug Policy*, 46: 74–78.

Keane, H. (2009) 'Sport health and steroids', in A. Broom & P. Tovey (Eds.), *Men's Health* (pp. 163–181). Wiley: Sussex.

Kimergård, A., McVeigh, J., Knutsson, S., Breindahl, T., and Stensballe, A. (2014) 'Online marketing of synthetic peptide hormones: Poor manufacturing, user safety, and challenges to public health', *Drug Testing and Analysis*, 6(4): 396–398

Kraska, P., Bussard, C., and Brent, J. (2010) 'Trafficking in bodily perfection: Examining the late-modern steroid marketplace and its criminalisation', *Justice Quarterly*, 27(2): 159–185.

Lopez, B. (2013) 'Creating fear: The social construction of human growth hormone as a dangerous doping drug', *International Review for the Sociology of Sport*, 48: 220.

Lyng, S. (1990) 'Edgework: A social psychological analysis of voluntary risk taking', *American Journal of Sociology*, 95(4): 851–886.

McLoughlin, C. (2017) 'Black market steroids driving rise in hospital admissions in SA', *ABC News*, 26th August. www.abc.net.au/news/2017-08-26/black-market-steroids-driving-rise-in-hospitalisations/8844358

Measham, F., Moore, K., Newcombe, R., and Welch, Z. (2010) 'Tweaking, bombing, dabbing and stockpiling: The emergence of mephedrone and the perversity of prohibition', *Drugs and Alcohol Today*, 10(1), 14–21.

Men's Health (2016) 'Britain's steroid epidemic', *Men's Health*, July 14th. www.menshealth.co.uk/building-muscle/big-read-britains-steroid-epidemic. [Accessed 20/07/2017]

Monaghan, L. (2001) *Bodybuilding, Drugs and Risk*. Abingdon: Routledge.

Morris, S. (2018) 'Up to a million Britons use steroids for looks not sport', *The Guardian*. www.theguardian.com/society/2018/jan/21/

Mulrooney, K., and van de Ven, K. (2015) '"Muscle Profiling": Anti-doping policy and deviant leisure'. Deviant Leisure Research Group [commentary]. January. Available at SSRN http://dx.doi.org/10.2139/ssrn.2581573

Noyce, J. (2018) Inside Australia's underground steroid community: Available at: www.sbs.com.au/news/inside-australia-s-underground-steroid-community

Parkin, S., and Coomber, R. (2011) 'Public injecting drug use and the social production of harmful practice in high-rise tower blocks (London, UK): A Lefebvrian analysis', *Health and Place*, 17(3): 717–726.

Pellegrini, M., Concetta Rotolo, M.,Giovannadrea, R. D., Pacifici, R., and Pichini, S. (2012) A simple toxicological analysis of anabolic steroid preparations from the black market. *Annales de toxicologie analytique*,; 24(2): 67–72 Société Française de Toxicologie Analytique 2012.

Pope, H., and Katz, D. (1994) 'Psychiatric and medical effects of anabolic-androgenic steroid use–A controlled study of 160 athletes', *Arch Gen Psychiatry*, 51(5): 375–382.

Raymen, T., and Smith, O. (2019) 'Deviant leisure: A critical criminological perspective for the twenty-first century', *Critical Criminology*, 27: 115–130. 10.1007/s10612-019-09435-x.

Reisman, D. (2010) *Health Tourism: Social Welfare through International Trade*. Cheltenham: Edward Elgar.

Rojek, C. (1997) 'Indexing, dragging and the social construction of tourism sights', in C. Rojek and J. Urry (eds.), *Touring Cultures: Transformations of Travel and Theory* (pp. 23–51). London: Routledge.

Rowe, R., Berger, I., and Copeland, J. (2017) '"No pain, no gainz"? Performance and image-enhancing drugs, health effects and information seeking', *Drugs: Education, Prevention and Policy*, 24(5): 400–408.

Sellars, A. (1998) 'The influence of dance music on the UK youth tourism market', *Tourism Management*, 19: 611–615.

Shilling, C. (2005). *The Body in Culture, Technology and Society*. London: Sage.

Simmonds, L., and Coomber, R. (2009) 'Injecting drug users: A stigmatised and stigmatising population', *International Journal of Drug Policy*, 20: 121–130.

Skeene, K. (2014) 'Thailand hotspot for young Aussies to home "steroid" holidays', *Gold Coast Bulletin*. March 8th. www.goldcoastbulletin.com.au/news/gold-coast/thailand-hotspot-for-young-aussies-totake-steroid-holidays/story-fnj94idh-1226848524500

Smith, O., and Raymen, T. (2018; online first 2016) 'Deviant leisure: A criminological perspective', *Theoretical Criminology*, 22(2): 63–82.

South, N. (1999) 'Debating drugs and everyday life: normalisation, prohibition and "otherness"', in N. South (ed.), *Drugs: Cultures, Controls and Everyday Life*. London: Sage.

Stebbins, R. (2007) *Serious Leisure: A Perspective for Our Time*. New Brunswick: NJ-Transaction.

Strudwick, D. (2013) 'The Aussie blokes hooked on steroids', News.com.au. www.news.com.au/lifestyle/fitness/the-aussie-blokes-hooked-on-steroids/news-story/0213271d0350d1c256ae828037b5a09c

Thongmuang, P. (2013) 'Drug combinations with steroid dispensing in drugstores: A study in the Center Area of Bangkok, Thailand', *International Journal of Medical, Health, Biomedical, Bioengineering and Pharmaceutical Engineering*, 7, 7.

Uriely, N., and Belhassen, I. (2005) 'Drugs and tourists' experiences', *Journal of Travel Research*, 43(3): 238–246.

Valdez, A., and Sifaneck, S. J. (1997) Drug tourists and drug policy on the U.S.-Mexican border: An ethnographic investigation of the acquisition of prescription drugs. *Journal of Drug Issues*, 27(4): 879–897. https://doi.org/10.1177/002204269702700413

van de Ven, K., and Mulrooney, K. (2016), 'Social suppliers: Exploring the cultural contours of the performance and image enhancing drug (IPED) market among bodybuilders in the Netherlands and Belgium', *International Journal of Drug Policy*, 40: 6–15.

van de Ven, K., and Zahnow, R. (2017) 'Australia should stop beefing up its steroid laws–that won't help users', *The Conversation*, 16th May. http://theconversation.com/australia-should-stop-beefing-up-its-steroid-laws-that-wont-help-users-77343 [Accessed: 25/08/2017]

van de Ven, K., Dunn, M., and Mulrooney, K. (2018) 'Performance and image enhancing drug (IPED) producers and suppliers: A retrospective content analysis of IPED-provider cases in Australia from 2010–2016', *Trends in Organised Crime*. https://doi.org/10.1007/s12117-018-9348-5

Walker, P (2015) 'Spiralling anabolic steroid use leaves UK facing health timebomb, experts warn', *The Guardian*, 19th June. www.theguardian.com/society/2015/jun/19/anabolic-steroid-use-leaves-britain-facing-health-timebomb [Accessed 20/07/2017]

Webster, N. (2016) 'Cheap and easy access to doping "attracting drug tourists" to Dubai', *The National*, July 24th. www.thenational.ae/uae/cheap-and-easy-access-to-doping-attracting-drug-tourists-to-dubai-1.156972 [Accessed 20/06/2017]

West, G., and Bayne, B. (2002) *The Economic Impacts of Tourism on the Gold Coast*, Gold Coast Tourism Visioning Project 3.1 (part la). ISBN 1 86335 492 1.

Willacy, M. (2015) 'Bikie drug rings trafficking illegal steroids bought online from overseas, Queensland Police say', *ABC News*. www.abc.net.au/news/2015-03-09/bikies-queensland-trafficking-steroids-from-overseas-police-say/6290938

Windle J. (2016) Security trumps drug control: How securitization explains drug policy paradoxes in Thailand and Vietnam, *Drugs: Education, Prevention and Policy*, DOI: 10.3109/09687637.2016.1140720

Zahnow, R., McVeigh, J., Ferris, J., and Winstock, A. (2017) 'Adverse effects, health service engagement, and service satisfaction among anabolic androgenic steroid users', *Contemporary Drug Problems*, 44(1): 69–83.

Zorea, A. H. (2014) Steroids- Health and Medical Issues Today- Greenwood. Available at: https://books.google.co.uk/books?id=ajaaBAAAQBAJ&pg=PA77&lpg=PA77&dq=thailand +food+and+drug+steroids&source=bl&ots=IYJldiEjLR&sig=ADSPjC46ucI_sTKTegDxoQ NnK7g&hl=en&sa=X&ved=0ahUKEwjpysXZ5PjQAhUniFQKHaY9A4gQ6AEINDAF#v=o nepage&q=thailand%20food%20and%20drug%20steroids&f=false. [Accessed: 23/11/2016].

10

'EASY MONEY, ZERO RISK'

The role of British seasonal workers in the Ibiza drug market

Tim Turner

Introduction

The Balearic island of Ibiza has a long-standing, indelible reputation as the epicentre of electronic dance music (EDM), a carnivalesque haven themed around narratives of sex, drugs, alcohol and round-the-clock partying. Survey research has documented how regular patterns of drug use can be dramatically transformed on the island (Bellis et al. 2009), while a few scholars have added ethnographic depth to statistical data by exploring the psychosocial and cultural worlds of those involved (see Briggs 2013; Bhardwa 2013; Tutenges 2013). This chapter draws on ethnographic research, conducted over three summers, with British tourists and seasonal workers in Ibiza. The study focuses on the sociocultural processes and situated meaning of both drug use and drug dealing from the perspective of those acting within the chaotic party zones of the island. The aim of the chapter is two-fold. Firstly, it provides insight into the methodological processes and challenges of ethnographic research with drug users and drug dealers in nightlife resorts and similar spaces. Secondly, key findings around drug dealing are outlined, with Bryman's (2004) influential *Disneyization* framework employed to theorise seasonal workers' immersion in Ibiza's drug scene as a form of deep *performative labour* within a context of normalised drug use. It is argued that for many seasonal workers, engagement in drug dealing can be partially explained by widespread ambivalence (and complicity) of door security and police in Ibiza, as they engage in a *performance of control* that enables aspects of the drug market to flourish.

Methodology

The aim of this research was to develop an empathic understanding of the psychosocial and cultural meaning of illicit drugs in Ibiza from the perspective of

DOI: 10.4324/9781351010245-12

those involved. This is important, as research in this field often overlooks both the *meaning* and *social context* of drug use and drug dealing (Hunt, Moloney and Evans 2010, 18). The research was framed by cultural criminology, a theoretical, methodological and interventionist approach to the study of crime (Hayward 2008, 119). The study contributes to a limited evidence base that foregrounds the lived experience of the often-silenced voice of the 'other' (Ferrell and Van de Vorde 2012) by employing a methodology rooted in constructivist grounded theory, an inductive method used to build theory about social issues from the ground up (Charmaz 2006). This rejects the notion of objective reality and recognises the interpretivist role of the researcher. Ethnographic fieldwork was conducted in Ibiza over three consecutive summers, with an aim of capturing moments of chaos, confusion and the 'flashes of fear and transgression' that punctuate the social world (Ferrell, Hayward and Young 2015, 218). The research drew together observations, photographs and semi-structured interviews to gain an in-depth understanding of the situated social meaning of drug use and dealing among a group of British seasonal workers and tourists.

Establishing trust and acceptance in Ibiza

Fieldwork was carried out in a range of tourist locations including airports, beaches, hotels, cafes, restaurants, bars and nightclubs. The gatekeeper (known as 'Brina' – a long-standing friend who owned an events company linked to EDM) proved to be an essential link during fieldwork, gaining us access to super-club guest lists that would otherwise have been off-limits with ticket prices around 80 euros. While Brina's contact list and powers of persuasion were essential in establishing points of access, it was essential to gain a deeper level of trust with participants. As fieldwork progressed, we began to feel increasingly embedded in the scene in San Antonio, particularly as relationships developed with the close-knit group of British workers employed in roles across the night-time economy there. In fact, the longer I spent on the island, the more I felt part of the worker community, separate from tourists. Acceptance by this group seemed to spread organically and gave us an almost instant credibility with some people we met:

> Caught in an afternoon storm, we sit outside a bar under the cover of a canopy. We chat to a group of three male, British bar workers sat drinking at the next table. After an hour of good-humoured conversation, we tell them about the research. They've already heard about us–"ah *you're* the 'researchers' [in finger quote marks, laughing], you need to fucking interview us!"
>
> *Tim Turner, field notes*

This amused reaction to the research was common. People were often incredulous that we had somehow duped the system and were being paid to go on holiday. We played along with this good-natured teasing, a relaxed approach was key to gaining acceptance and trust among participants.

> I meet Ben in a West End bar at 3am. Him and a couple of friends come over and start calling me 'Eyeball Paul' (DJ character in the film *Kevin and Perry Go Large*). I play along with the joke and we chat amiably for the next few hours as they pass a pouch of ketamine between them. We leave there at 6am, swap numbers and they agree to meet later that day for an interview.
>
> *Tim Turner, field notes*

This close proximity to drug use was, of course, inevitable, although I never really felt under any pressure to participate. On some occasions, adapting to the context meant reassuring participants when they felt uneasy about discussing their drug use or their involvement in dealing. British youth in Ibiza and similar European beach resorts have been the source of much media interest in the past, with well-trodden narratives of chaotic, drug and booze-fuelled hedonism. Consequently, many participants started out with a guarded scepticism, and were suspicious of our identities and motives. It was not unusual for people to assume we were working undercover, either as cops or journalists. As the excerpt below shows, gaining trust took time and was subject to rapid shifts:

> After a long night working the bar, Sam sits with me in a café and tells me stories of his time on the island. Then, from nowhere, he pauses mid-sentence, head in hands–"You are *really* a researcher, aren't you? Promise me you're not a journalist". I reassure him and he regains composure, explaining how a tabloid hack duped him last summer, splashing his photo across a British newspaper.
>
> *Tim Turner, field notes*

Immersion represents a deeper level of access, where my role as a researcher moved beyond observation and I became *part of the story*. As Jock Young (2004, 26) asserts, what criminology needs is 'an ethnographic method that can deal with reflexivity, contradiction, tentativeness, change of opinion, posturing and concealment'. The field note below reflects this sentiment and shows how immersion, while fraught with ethical dilemmas, reveals the kind of 'dirty knowledge' that Ferrell 1(997) asserts is necessary to enhance criminological understanding:

> Our guides for the night lead us to a busy bar and shout orders to the waitress. Jugs of some lurid cocktail are dropped on the table. Sean, the same man who had earlier insisted that he had "no interest in drugs", has been dabbing at a pouch of MDMA throughout the night and offers it liberally to anyone in his vicinity. Time accelerates and night descends into blurred

disorientation. Eventually, the group tips out of the bar into the stark daylight of 6am and everyone heads for breakfast.

Tim Turner, field notes

Data collection: participant observation

Fieldwork incorporated three strands of observation. These are delineated here for the purposes of clarity – in the unpredictable reality of fieldwork, observational strategies moved along a dynamic continuum as the rhythm of events unfolded. Firstly, periods of *unobtrusive observation* took place over the 24-hour period. This involved observing a particular setting over a period of a few hours. The locations were often busy and transient, making it easy to observe without attracting any real attention. I used the notes application on a smartphone to record thoughts, feelings and observations, with an aim to capture something of the context and those present. Secondly, *marginal participation* required a level of connection with participants. At times, this involved drinking alcohol in limited amounts to ensure a 'fit' with the context, a key aspect in developing rapport during fieldwork in this area (Thurnell-Read 2011, 39). Thirdly, having gained trust and acceptance, some participants invited me to spend protracted time with them, sometimes throughout the night. This required a deeper level of participation and was ethically challenging at times, as it inevitably meant close proximity to drug taking and drug dealing.

Data collection: semi-structured interviews

The study included 33 semi-structured interviews with individuals and small focus groups. These varied in duration from 30 to 120 minutes. Interviewees (n=56) consisted of 42 tourists (21 males and 21 females), a Spanish police officer and 13 seasonal workers (8 males and 5 females) aged between 18 and 35 years. The workers I met were employed in a range of roles associated with Ibiza's night-time economy – these included bar staff, ticket sellers, dancers, door security and public relations (PR) staff. Interviews were structured around questions that could easily be adapted and changed to fit the natural flow of the conversation. Open questions were used to allow the interviewees to shape their answers. In grounded theory, it is important to approach fieldwork with an open mind and avoid preconceptions, as far as possible (Bryman 2012, 325). As the focus of the interviews was drug use/dealing, the questions were inherently intrusive. Asking such questions, sometimes just a few minutes after meeting someone, is not easy. In this respect, ethnographers need to become adept in reading the dynamics of the situation, knowing when (and when not) to ask these difficult questions. Wherever possible, I arranged to record interviews in a quiet location – no easy task in Ibiza, as music seems to be an ever-present backdrop. An audio-recorder application on a password-protected smartphone was used, with files transferred onto an encrypted laptop. I made notes after each interview, jotting down any thoughts, feelings or ideas relating to the meeting.

Data collection: documentary photography

A total of 580 digital photographs were taken during fieldwork. This was an unobtrusive form of data collection, as taking pictures is hardly unusual in a tourist setting. The photographs added visual depth to the study and helped capture Ibiza's identity and sense of place, two entwined concepts that can generate an understanding of the social world (Spencer 2011).

Ethical issues: consent

In relation to informed consent, Bryman (2012) identifies three principal elements: knowledge and understanding of what is involved; competence to give consent; and voluntary choice. These create significant ethical challenges in relation to fieldwork for drug researchers. For this study, I began by using a simple participant information sheet that outlined the research aims, as well as the limits of anonymity and confidentiality. However, I quickly realised that asking people to sign a consent form felt like an overly formal request in settings that were the antithesis of formal (e.g. a beach!). I found that it acted as a barrier to conversation and switched to asking for verbal consent on the audio-recorded interviews.

Intoxication through alcohol and/or drugs is an obvious issue in ethnographic research of this nature. Interviews and observations took place throughout the 24-hour period, making it inevitable that participants were intoxicated to varying degrees. People in extreme states of intoxication were not interviewed. Observations took place in busy public locations, making it implausible to gain consent from everyone present (Gobo 2008, 140). Observations of this nature were stripped of indicators that might reveal individual identity.

Ethical issues: researcher and participant safety

The safety of the researcher is paramount within social research and represents a central tenet of ethical practice (Botterill and Platenkamp 2012, 75). Fieldwork in party zones and the wider night-time economy is often unpredictable and it's important to stay alert to potential risks. As Ferrell, Hayward and Young (2015, 212) state: 'ethnographic studies generally mix hours of tedium with explosions of surprise and moments of dangerous uncertainty'. An example of the volatile nature of drug research is outlined in the excerpt below, relating to a chance meeting with a female worker who I had interviewed a few days earlier.

> Ella enthusiastically introduces me to Andy, her "fiancé"–a term that strikes me as entirely out-of-place in this context–it seems old-fashioned and this man is wired on pills and wearing luminous yellow gloves. As Ella

> goes to the bar, Andy leans in to me threateningly: "this research thing, if you fuck me over, I will fuck you up. I will FUCK. YOU. UP." He's wide-eyed and jabbing a yellow finger in my chest. I try and reassure him, but he's deeply suspicious. I offer him a drink and suggest we sit outside on the terrace. After ten minutes, we're laughing and joking and he's insistent that I come to his villa for dinner.
>
> *Tim Turner, field notes*

Moments like these punctuated fieldwork, given that interviews centred around illegal behaviour, people were understandably wary of our intentions and identity at times, making it important to carry a university ID badge. On several occasions, this conveyed validity on my role as a researcher in the event of police attention. Cultural criminologists argue that this entanglement 'in the experience of criminality and illegality' (Ferrell and Hamm 1998, 24) is essential to understanding the dynamics of crime at close range. In addition to researcher safety, ethnographers also have a key responsibility to protect participants from harm. The unpredictable and anarchic nature of fieldwork in Ibiza was often a challenging balance between observing and intervening. Take the incident outlined below, situated outside a club in the early hours:

> A young woman is sitting on the floor, clearly very unwell. Her eyes are closed, and her head hangs limply, flopping from side-to-side. Her panic-stricken friend shakes her by the shoulders. I kneel down and her tearful friend tells me they've taken *gold leaf* pills [a brand of ecstasy]. I try and get some water into her, but it just dribbles from her mouth. She needs medical assistance, but the friend argues against this, fearful of reprisal. I make the decision for her and two paramedics arrive within minutes.
>
> *Tim Turner, field notes*

While this kind of intervention oversteps the line of ethnographic observation, it is important to recognise that researchers have a moral obligation to act if someone is perceived to be at an immediate and grave risk of harm. This is an issue that must be given careful consideration before entering the field. In this example, it was my belief that the woman concerned needed urgent medical attention and not acting would make me morally culpable.

Confidentiality and anonymity are essential ethical considerations in drug research (Aldridge, Measham and Williams 2011: 35). Measures to protect participants' identity were taken at the earliest opportunity; participants were given a pseudonym at the time of interview, and irrelevant demographic details were left out. Participants often described how being away from home, in a place where nobody knew them, conferred a sense of anonymity. This seemed to make it much easier for people to discuss sensitive issues and I found participants to be remarkably open about drugs. It was important that participants understood the limits of confidentiality. They were informed that confidentiality could not be maintained if they made disclosures of criminal offences involving serious harm to others, such as violent assaults, for example.

Findings and discussion

The aim of this study was to generate a theoretical understanding of sociocultural, psychological and consumer processes that underpin illicit drug use and drug dealing within 'party zones' – spaces defined by hedonistic pleasure and atypical intoxication, usually stretched over a period of several days. Through constructivist grounded theory, a new theoretical explanatory model was developed around Bryman's (2004) influential framework of *Disneyization* (see Turner 2018). In this chapter, I focus solely on the *performative labour* pillar of this model, with an exploration of drug dealing and drug use among British seasonal workers in San Antonio, Ibiza. This group has received limited academic attention despite occupying a central role in Ibiza's hedonistic night-time economy (Kelly, Hughes and Bellis 2014). This section is structured around three headings. Firstly, I provide an outline of Bryman's (2004) construction of *Disneyized performative labour.* This shows how the theatrical nature of labour, pioneered by Walt Disney, is now a common feature of many other service industry roles. Secondly, I apply Bryman's conceptualisation of performative labour to the party zones of Ibiza, demonstrating how the line between work and pleasure is rapidly blurred as seasonal workers theatrically embody the hedonistic consumer spaces that they are employed within. Consequently, as with their tourist counterparts, the workers I met were, without exception, engaged in high levels of drug use that were out-of-step with their lives back in the UK. Thirdly, I will outline the social processes under which some workers decide to sell drugs, both to their fellow workers and to tourists. Many were financially dependent on income from drug sales, as opportunities within the legal economy were so limited. This was partially sanctioned by what I term, a *performance of control* in Ibiza, with police and door security both ambivalent and complicit to low-level drug use and dealing. Findings therefore indicate that young people working in Ibiza are exposed to significant health risks that come with prolonged, regular use of drugs such as ecstasy and ketamine, *and* multiple risks linked to involvement in the drug trade.

Performative labour as a pillar of Disneyization

Performative labour represents a key pillar of Bryman's (2004) *Disneyization* framework. Theatrical lexicon is embedded within the Disney arena, with employees defined as either front or backstage cast members – their 'ever-present smiles … an indication that they too are having fun and that this is not "real" work [all] conveyed through carefully trained attention to posture, facial expression and behaviour' (Bryman 2004, 101). Performative labour is, of course, no longer confined to Disneyland. Whether you work as an airline cabin crew or as a police officer, your role arguably incorporates some aspect of theatrical performance. In a consumer context, people engaged in performative labour represent an important component of themed space, with an expectation that they will personify the brand of the company or product concerned. This is central to employment within a tourist industry that is subsumed within the experience economy (Pine and Gilmore 1999). The role of summer seasonal workers, whether they are situated in a family holiday camp or within the hedonistic spaces of Ibiza, is essential for creating cherished holiday memories and spectacular experiences. While this performance may be enacted on the surface, tourist workers may also engage on a much deeper emotional level (Bryman 2004; Van Diljk, Smith and Cooper 2011). This is particularly important when it comes to experiential tourism, where workers are expected to embody the sense of adventure and excitement of their arena (Beardsworth and Bryman 2001). In this research, fieldwork showed that for many seasonal workers, the delineation between work and pleasure rapidly disappears as they personify Ibiza's hedonistic spirit in a deep level of performance, putting many of the workers I met in a pivotal role within the island's thriving drug scene.

Disneyized performative labour in Ibiza

The worker participants in this research were employed in performative labour roles across San Antonio's night-time economy. They allowed me to spend significant periods of time with them, both in the daytime and at night. I was present when they used drugs with their friends and when they sold drugs to tourists and to each other. They included bar workers, bouncers, dancers, ticket sellers and PR staff – all roles that require a level of theatrical performance. The role of bar PR, for example, demands a determined display of switched-on zeal in a tireless attempt to pull in passers-by with slashed-price, alcohol deals. The chances of success are hit and miss, to say the least, given the fierce competition for custom in San Antonio's West End. The performative aspect of those working behind the bar was noted throughout fieldwork. The excerpt below, for example, illustrates how the barman transforms the routine act of buying drinks into a memorable consumer experience (Pine and Gilmore 1999, 52):

> The barman, working alone, serves a group of eight raucous women on a hen party. He holds their attention with effortless flirtation and some theatrical cocktail acrobatics. He completes the order in a flourish and then hits them all with a free shot of tequila; he pours one for himself and they chink glasses ostentatiously.
>
> *Tim Turner, field notes*

This excerpt also demonstrates how the line between work and leisure is often blurred for those engaged in performative labour in the night-time economy. The seasonal workers who participated in this study often echoed similar sentiments to tourists with regard to the value of the experience and memories gained from their time on the island, exemplified here.

> When I leave at the end of the season, I'll really miss the atmosphere here. That and the fact that I go out every single night and have a great time. The only commitment I have here is to get drunk and get high.
>
> *Jack, bar worker*

> It's been incredible, but it's exhausting. I work 12 hours a day without a break, for 6 days a week. I go out as much as possible, because it's only for 4 months. I'll look back on this in 10 years with some incredible memories, but it's becoming more and more difficult to function, to work and play.
>
> *Ella, ticket seller*

For some workers, the combination of 12-hour shifts and the intense party scene transformed drug use into a rational means of lasting the pace. In one of the few previous studies carried out, 85.3% of casual workers reported using an illicit drug in Ibiza, with almost half (43.5%) using a drug in Ibiza that they had never used in the UK (Kelly, Hughes and Bellis 2014, 1058). The British workers in this research were deeply involved in drug use, and as with previous findings, this was often more than their tourist counterparts (Hughes and Bellis 2006). As young people arrived in San Antonio looking for work, they were rapidly welcomed into a tight-knit social group, where drugs were culturally embedded and easily available. In comparing his time as both a tourist and a worker, one interviewee stated:

> You make really strong friendships with people. And you know where to get good drugs. I suppose that's the main difference between working here for a summer and just coming for a week–you know how to get hold of the best drugs.
>
> *Jack, bar worker*

This group of young people are therefore exposed to similar drug-related risks as tourists, but over a *much* longer period of time (Kelly, Hughes and Bellis 2014), with a worker's average length of stay 100 days compared to just 7 days for tourists (Hughes, Bellis and Chaudry 2004). The following interview excerpts encapsulate the worker experience:

> The whole place [worker accommodation block] is proper mental. All day, every day. It kicks off about 7am after people pile back there from work or going out and basically doesn't stop all day. Ket and pills everywhere.
>
> *Jack, bar worker*

> How many workers use drugs? All of us! Well, *at least* 90 per cent.
>
> *Nick, bar worker and drug dealer*

> I see it every year. Eighteen-year olds come out here looking for a summer of sun and partying, but they can't handle the pace. They end up leaving after a month with three grand debt and a ketamine habit.
>
> *John, bar worker*

These excerpts show how the line separating workers and tourists is in many ways indistinct. They take the same types of drug, in the same places, but over different timescales. However, for many workers, in a space that can distort risk, there is a point where they decide to start dealing drugs.

The transition to dealing

The performative labour that seasonal workers engage in is almost exclusively low paid and commission-based, with long hours and no employment rights. Poor working conditions and job insecurity is routinely accepted as the norm in this context, as Karen, an experienced PR manager, succinctly stated:

> It's Ibiza. If you didn't like it, you wouldn't be here. You don't come here to be treated nicely at work.

When such volatile, low-paid working conditions are combined with high living costs and a lifestyle built around alcohol and drug use (Kelly, Hughes and Bellis 2014), it can be very difficult for workers to remain in Ibiza for an entire summer. This is especially true when relying on income generated solely within the remarkably unstable and competitive legal economy. Indeed, the Foreign Office recently raised concern that British bar workers in the Balearics were at risk of modern slavery, with evidence of high rents, low wages and passport confiscations (Keeley 2018):

> I've seen PRs work 12 hours through the night and get like 10 euro. The manager will give them 50 cents for every customer they get in the bar, but they don't even see half the punters they get in. It's bullshit.
>
> *Nick, bar worker and drug dealer*

> I don't even know if there's a minimum wage out here. I need to find out. This is my fourth shift and I'm not getting paid for any of it. I'm on a trial.
>
> *Kelly, bar worker*

In one of my first nights in Ibiza, a tourist told me that he needed at least £300 for a good night out; I naively assumed he was exaggerating. On an island where a club ticket is anything up to 100 euros and a small bottle of water inside is more than 12 euros, money runs through your fingers like sand. As a result, with legal opportunities limited, many workers made a choice between going back to the UK or boosting their income through drug dealing. Some I met had abandoned the legal economy altogether and sold drugs as their sole source of income:

> Every other person here is a drug dealer. It starts off every other person is a ticket seller, and then after about three or four weeks, every other person is a drug dealer. It's an easy way to make money. You take ten, fifteen, twenty pills out in your pocket. You make between two and three hundred euros straight up.
>
> *Ella, ticket seller*

> I been working here for two summers, pretty much everyone I've lived with started off working as PRs or bar staff and then just end up dealing pills. They make decent money for a few hours work.
>
> *Jake, tourist*

> I just sell a few pills and a bit of ket to tourists on the side. I have to, you can't live out here on the shitty wages. Easy money, zero risk [shrugs].
>
> *Nick, bar worker and drug dealer*

The pull of the illegal economy in Ibiza is exemplified by Nick, a bar worker and drug dealer who I spent considerable time with over the three summers I was on the island. He was in his early 20s, well-educated and from a middle-class suburb of a UK city. He had worked in Ibiza over several summers and was employed in a busy bar. He had been topping up his income by selling ecstasy on each of the summers he had worked out there. As the field note below illustrates, the process of dealing is often pre-arranged and fast:

> Late afternoon and I meet Nick for a drink before he starts work. Before we find a bar, he says he needs to meet a British tourist to sell some pills. He's carrying 50 *rock-stars* [ecstasy pills], with half stashed in a take-away Coca-Cola cup and half in an empty cigarette packet. Although carrying this quantity could land Nick in a Spanish prison for 4 years, he seems relaxed and in good humour. As we talk, he sees his man, a British lad in his early 20s, and shakes him by the hand. After a brief conversation, Nick passes him the paper cup and then the cigarette packet, and we say goodbye. A few minutes later, sitting in the sun with a couple of beers, Nick takes a sip and tells me he's just made €250.
>
> *Tim Turner, field notes*

Throughout many of my conversations with workers in Ibiza, I was often struck by their blasé attitude to dealing drugs such as ecstasy and ketamine. In their world, drugs were infused into everyday interaction, conveying an entrenched perception that the chances of being caught dealing were negligible.

> No one forced me to sell drugs, but it was an easy option and as long as you're not completely stupid, there's zero chance of getting caught. It's just knocking out pills and no one cares.
>
> *Rob, tourist, discussing his previous summer in Ibiza as a worker*

> Bouncers don't really search you at all. I've walked in with pills in my bag. They'll open the main bit and have a quick glance, that's it. I've taken 50 pills into venues before. Literally had them clenched between my arse cheeks, walk in, sound! I mean us three don't look like drug dealers, do we? Stick 'em in your hair as well. That works.
>
> *Sam, drug dealer*

These excerpts reflect a commonly expressed nonchalance among workers regarding what they perceived to be a relatively risk-free involvement in the Ibiza drug market. I argue that the differential normalisation of drugs in Ibiza – a form of *Disneyized* hybrid consumption – together with a deep level of performative labour, combined to make drug use and dealing seem completely *natural* within the context. This rapidly distorts risk perception in relation to the multiple harms associated with the illegal drug trade. Furthermore, this subjective perception is augmented by the apparent laissez-faire attitude of both police and door security at venues within the night-time economy. In this sense, these controllers are also engaged in a *performance of control*, with fieldwork revealing narratives of police corruption, and door security that is at best ambivalent to drug use, and at worst complicit:

> I never even bother hiding it [from door security]. I just hold it in my hands. The first night we went to [venue]. One of the bouncers caught us doing ket [starts laughing]. He takes the bag off me and just empties it over my head.
>
> *Jed, tourist*

This is further illustrated in the conversation below with two workers, John and Sam. The latter was a well-educated 19-year-old male from a city in England. He was in Ibiza for 12 weeks over the summer and was due to start university in the September. Although he'd arrived on the island looking for a bar job, he'd found it impossible to find work and was relying on drug dealing for his income. He used ketamine several times each week:

> Sam (drug dealer): I've been told not to carry more than 5 pills if you're dealing around the West End. I know someone who got caught with 12 and they got let off. I've never seen door security search anyone. Even in

> the big clubs, they'd just take it off you, chuck you out, and then sell it themselves.
>
> John (bar worker): I know for a fact that door security sell at certain clubs.
>
> Sam (drug dealer): I was in [venue] the other day and I'd got a gram of ket. I couldn't see. I was off my face. This doorman walks up, opens my hand and takes the ket off me. I don't know why, but I just gave him a 20 euro note and he gave me the ket back and let me stay in!

This *performance of control* was illustrated in an interview with a seasonal worker working in various venues as a bouncer:

> Christopher (bouncer): I saw someone dealing in a club I was working in last week. He looked at me and I said, 'mate, don't be a dick, if you're gonna do that, go in the fucking crowd where I can't see you. Don't stand next to the fucking toilet in the middle of everywhere. If I see you doing it again, I'll take all your money and drugs off you.

Despite this ambivalence to the control of low-level drug use, there's little doubt that as young people in Ibiza redefine boundaries of acceptable behaviour, they risk serious legal sanction. Every year, stories emerge of young Brits being sent to prison for amateurish involvement in the Ibiza drug trade, their perception of risk seemingly distorted by the differential normalisation of illegal substances on the island. To take a recent example, in 2018, Jools Riding, 22, was sentenced to almost 7 years by a UK court, after being caught driving 67,000 ecstasy pills into Ibiza by ferry. Riding, who had no previous convictions, had worked in Ibiza on a gap year and accrued debts from ecstasy and cocaine use. In summing up, the prosecution claimed he had been foolishly tempted by the lure of a quick £10,000 (Abel and Milne 2018). And his story is not unusual. British seasonal workers in Ibiza are therefore exposed to significant, multi-level risks as they are targeted by powerful groups keen to exploit their well-established immersion in the local drug scene.

Conclusion

This chapter has outlined the key methodological processes and challenges associated with ethnographic research with drug users and drug dealers in the hedonistic spaces of Ibiza. The study has shown how performative labour, a key pillar of Bryman's (2004) *Disneyization* framework, can help us to understand the sociocultural and consumer processes that underpin the atypical patterns of drug use and drug dealing that are evident in such party zones. For the majority of the seasonal workers who participated in this study, their experience on the island will leave them with the kind of treasured memories and stories that are so highly valued by late-modern 'sensation gatherers' (Bauman 1997, 146). However, fieldwork revealed significant changes in drug-related behaviour among this group, and the potential harm associated with these changes is very real. The poly-drug use that many workers are engaged in, along with high levels of alcohol consumption, is widely acknowledged as dangerous (Hunt et al. 2009, 495). Furthermore, like tourists, many workers describe using drugs for the first time while in Ibiza. This increases risk, as any negative outcomes are compounded by being far away from the support structures of home, as well as the added complications that come with a language barrier and the bewildering lack of familiarity with health and criminal justice systems (Bellis et al. 2009). The chapter also contributes to our understanding of the role of seasonal workers in the Ibiza drug market, and the social processes that lead them there. Drug dealing exposes these young people to multiple risks, including violence associated with organised crime and potentially serious legal sanctions. In combination, these factors make touristic seasonal workers a prime target for innovative harm reduction measures that recognise the temporal, situated risks that run below the neon surface of the island's party scene.

References

Abel, S. and Milne, O. 2018. 'Amateur Ibiza drug dealer caught smuggling a suitcase full of almost £450,000 ecstasy tablets on cross channel ferry', *Mirror* [online] available at www.mirror.co.uk/news/uk-news/amateur-ibiza-drug-dealer-caught-11858540 [19 December 2020].

Aldridge, Judith., Measham, Fiona., and Williams, Lisa. 2011. *Illegal Leisure Revisited: Changing Patterns of Alcohol and Drug Use in Adolescents and Young Adults.* London: Routledge.

Bauman, Zygmunt. 1997. *Post-Modernity and Its Discontents.* Cambridge: Polity Press.

Beardsworth, Alan., and Bryman, Alan. 2001. 'The wild animal in late modernity: The case of the Disneyization of Zoos', *Tourist Studies* 1(1): 83–103.

Bellis, M.A., Hughes, K., Calafat, A., Juan, M., and Schnitzer, S. 2009. 'Relative contributions of holiday location and nationality to changes in recreational drug taking behaviour: A natural experiment in the Balearic Islands', *European Addiction Research* 15(2): 78-86. doi: 10.1159/000189786. Epub 2009 Jan 10. PMID: 19142007.

Bhardwa, Bina. 2013. 'Alone, Asian and female: The unspoken challenges of conducting fieldwork in dance settings', *Dancecult: Journal of Electronic Dance Music Culture* 5: 39–60.

Briggs, Daniel. 2013. *Deviance and Risk on Holiday: An Ethnography of British Tourists in Ibiza.* Basingstoke: Palgrave.

Botterill, David., and Platenkamp, Vincent. 2012. *Key Concepts in Tourism Research.* London: Sage.

Bryman, Alan. 2004. *The Disneyization of Society.* London: Sage.

Bryman, Alan. 2012. *Social Research Methods* (4th ed.). Oxford: Oxford University Press.

Charmaz, Kathy. 2006. *Constructing Grounded Theory: A Practical Guide Through Qualitative Analysis.* London: Sage.

Ferrell, Jeff., and Hamm, Mark. 1998. *Ethnography at the Edge: Crime, Deviance and Field Research.* Boston: Northeastern University Press.

Ferrell, Jeff., and Van de Vorde, Cecile. 2012. 'The decisive moment: Documentary photography and cultural criminology', in *Framing Crime: Cultural Criminology and the Image*, edited by Keith J. Hayward, and Mike Presdee. London: Routledge.

Ferrell, Jeff., Hayward, Keith., and Young, Jock. 2015. *Cultural Criminology: An Invitation* (2nd ed.). London: Sage.

Gobo, Giampietro. 2008. *Doing Ethnography*. London: Sage.

Hayward, Keith. 2008. 'Cultural criminology', in *The Dictionary of Youth Justice*, edited by Barry Goldson. Cullompton: Willan Publishing.

Hughes, Karen., and Bellis, Mark. A. 2006. 'Sexual behaviour among casual workers in an international nightlife resort: A case control study', *BMC Public Health* 6: 39.

Hughes, Karen., Bellis, Mark. A., and Chaudry, Mo. 2004. 'Elevated substance use in casual labour at international nightlife resorts: A case control study', *The International Journal of Drug Policy* 15: 211–213.

Hunt, Geoffrey., Moloney, Molly., and Evans, Kristin. 2010. *Youth Drugs and Nightlife*. London: Routledge.

Hunt, Geoffrey. P., Evans, Kristin., Moloney, Molly., and Bailey, Noelani. 2009. 'Combining different substances in the dance scene: Enhancing pleasure, managing risk and timing effects', *Journal of Drug Issues*, Summer: 495–522.

Keeley, G. 2018. 'Britons become victims of modern slavery in Mallorca', *The Times*, May 25, 2018 [online] www.thetimes.co.uk/article/britons-become-victims-of-modern-slavery-in-majorca-m68mjn5km [19 December 2020].

Kelly, Danielle., Hughes, Karen., and Bellis, Mark. A. 2014. 'Work hard, party harder: Drug use and sexual behaviour in young British casual workers in Ibiza, Spain', *International Journal of Environmental Research and Public Health* 11: 10051–10061.

Pine, Joseph. and Gilmore, James. H. 1999. *The Experience Economy: Work Is Theatre and Every Business a Stage*. Boston, USA: HBS Press.

Robson, Colin. 2002. *Real World Research* (2nd ed.). London: Blackwell.

Spencer, Stephen. 2011. *Visual Research Methods in Social Sciences: Awakening Visions*. London: Routledge.

Thurnell-Read, Thomas. 2011. '"Common sense" research: Senses, emotions and embodiment in researching stag tourism in Eastern Europe', *Methodological Innovations* 6: 39–49.

Tremlett, Giles. and Topping, Alexandra. 2010. "Ibiza police arrest 20 Britons in raid on major drug ring', *The Guardian* [online] 31 August. Available at www.theguardian.com/world/2010/aug/31/ibiza-police-crack-drug-ring [3 June 2016].

Tutenges, Sebastien. 2013. 'Stirring up effervescence: An ethnographic study of youth at a nightlife resort', *Leisure Studies* 32(3): 233–248.

Turner, Tim. 2018. 'Disneyization: A framework for understanding illicit drug use in bounded play spaces', *International Journal of Drug Policy* 58: 37–35.

Van Dijk, Pieter. A., Smith, Liam. D.G., and Cooper, Brian. K. 2011. 'Are you for real? An evaluation of the relationship between emotional labour and visitor outcomes', *Tourism Management* 32(1): 39–45.

Young, Jock. 2004. 'Voodoo criminology and the numbers game', in *Cultural Criminology Unleashed*, edited by Jeff Ferrell, Keith Hayward, Wayne Morrison and Mike Presdee. London: Glasshouse.

11

'DOUBLING UP'

Drug dealing as a profitable side-hustle

Mike Salinas

Introduction

Financially motivated drug dealing has long been framed by scholars in relation to work: with reference to drug markets as an 'employment agency' (Anderson, 1990: 224); the drugs trade as 'an accessible and alternative sphere of enterprise' (Hobbs, 2013: 116); and drug 'gangs' as providers of 'employment opportunities' (Padilla, 1992: 101). Yet aside from a few notable exceptions (e.g. Hobbs, 2013; Adler, 1993; Caulkins and Reuter, 1998) the concept of *drug dealing as work* features largely within the context of geographically concentrated chronic poverty and social marginalisation (e.g. Fagan, 1992; Levitt and Venkatesh, 2000; Duck, 2015). This chapter develops the concept of drug dealing as work and its use a profitable side-hustle via a comprehensive and up-to-date review of the literature, while also extending the concept beyond the confines of chronic poverty to encompass broader, less extreme, forms of social and economic precarity. At a time when occupational insecurities are increasing and many people's prospects of attaining stable work in the legitimate labour economy are diminishing (Cribb and Johnson, 2018; Armstrong, 2017; Allen, 2016),[1] it is important to consider how alternative or additional forms of income within the 'grey' or illicit economies might be drawn upon to compensate (see Heal's chapter in this volume).

Supplying and trading illegal drugs is historically among the most remunerative of 'income-producing criminal occupations' (Fagan and Freeman, 1999: 251; see also MacCoun and Reuter, 1992). The high mark-ups and profits associated with the illegal drug trade stems from traders' risk premiums and the fact that consumer demand for these substances outpaces (illicit) market supply, making these substances relatively scarce commodities (Caulkins and Reuter, 1998; Wilson and Stevens, 2008; Moeller and Sandberg, 2019). Though the underlying

DOI: 10.4324/9781351010245-13

motives to 'deal drugs' are by no means exclusively financial,[2] substantial mark-ups and high degrees of profitability are demonstrable at each stage in the supply chain, especially in the countries of distribution (UNDCP, 1998; Pearson and Hobbs, 2001; Wilson and Stevens, 2008).[3] In short, for those suppliers whose interests are principally economic, it pays (quite literally) to deal drugs.

Yet despite the clear economic incentives of the illegal drug trade, empirical studies have consistently demonstrated that for many commercially orientated drug dealing is merely a part-time role undertaken outside/alongside conventional commitments, such as legitimate paid employment or business (e.g. Fader, 2019; Werse and Muller, 2016; Jacinto, Duterte, Sales and Murphy, 2008; Reuter, MacCoun and Murphy, 1990; Desroches, 2006; Anderson, 1999; Hagedorn, 1994). Fagan and Freeman (1999: 257) referred to such concurrent engagement with legal and illegal forms of income generation as 'doubling-up'. This pattern of behaviour and the paralleled participation in both legal job markets and illegal drug markets (see also Thompson and Uggen, 2012) lies somewhat contrary to popular and poflitical discourse in which drug dealers are positioned as social 'outsiders' (Antonopoulos and Papanicolaou, 2010; Taylor, 2008; Coomber, 2006), who oppose mainstream values (Fader, 2019) and 'threaten the normative bases of (civil) society' (Salinas, 2018: 228). However, as this chapter will demonstrate, the extent to which drug dealers oppose mainstream values and actively position themselves as social outsiders is questionable.

This chapter explores the practice of 'doubling up' via the illicit drug trade (Fagan and Freeman, 1999: 257). It looks at why people who engage in commercially oriented dealing – at times termed 'drug dealers "proper"' (Coomber and Moyle, 2014: 157) – often do so as a means of supplementing, rather than supplanting, legitimate earnings. To explore this phenomenon, the chapter synthesises findings from the empirical literature as well as findings from the author's six-year ethnography, undertaken with 25 drug dealers and traffickers who successfully operated at multiple levels of various supply chains in tandem with legitimate endeavours. The chapter begins by reviewing the empirical literature on commercially orientated drug dealing, assessing the economic returns, the behavioural work patterns and its use (in a range of contexts) as a supplement to legal work. The chapter then explores this practice of doubling up through the author's own in-depth six-year ethnography into the illegal drug trade. In particular, it assesses the practice among those in lower-paid, entry-level work, those experiencing instability as self-employed workers or business owners, and among those studying at university. In a departure from much of the empirical literature, the data shows how doubling up can provide an essential financial crutch to individuals largely removed from contexts of heightened social and economic marginality; which, historically, are the context in which empirical studies of drug markets frequently derive (see Salinas, 2018: 228). In doing so, this chapter demonstrates the importance of understanding changes to 'local life circumstances' (Horney, Osgood and Marshall, 1995) and the increasingly precarious process of transitioning towards stable and gainful employment (Laub and Sampson, 1993). It also illustrates how, during times of economic need – for those situated in networks with opportunities to participate in the illegal drug trade – drug dealing offers a viable yet often temporary 'side hustle'.

This chapter expands upon earlier arguments (Salinas, 2018) by positing that many (if not *most*) people engaged in commercially orientated drug supply are not career criminals committed to a counter-cultural ethos but are instead largely 'conventional' people looking for solutions to financial impediments (see also Askew and Salinas, 2019). The following review of international literature on drug dealing combined with the longitudinal fieldwork findings highlights how drug dealing careers are often time-limited, sporadic and a response to perceived economic constraints arising from inadequate legal opportunities. Both the literature and the fieldwork are analysed in relation to: (i) the work patterns of, and profits from, the illegal drug trade within the context of doubling up; (ii) the motives behind concurrent engagement in the legal and drug market economy, (iii) an assessment of doubling up as a means of supporting university study. Market engagement is framed under three distinct financial motives: its use for non-essential spending ("pocket money"); its use as a financial safety-net during economically precarious times; and its use as investment capital in legitimate occupational endeavours (such as business or study).

Literature: the profits and sales patterns of drug dealing

The primary concern of commercially-orientated drug dealers is to generate an income, rather than supplying drugs as a socially motivated act (see Werse and Müller, 2016) or a means of underwriting one's own drug use (e.g. Moyle and Coomber, 2015). Though truly substantial revenues are obtainable, they are the reserve of an elite few commercial traders operating at the higher levels of the supply chain – the importers, 'mid-level' brokers and wholesalers – whereby a single key operative can net tens of thousands of dollars (or pounds) in profit each month (Reuter and Haaga, 1989; Alder, 1993; Desroches, 2006; Pearson and Hobbs, 2001).[4] Such earnings are unrepresentative of drug dealing at large. As with any kind of illicit economy, "many move little and few move much" (van Duyne and De Miranda, 1999: 245) and most who operate in this economy do so at the lower, less lucrative, retail stages. This section therefore reviews the literature which assesses drug dealing as work at the retail-end of the supply chain, paying particular attention to its financial returns and the work patterns of drug suppliers.

The profitability of commercially orientated retail-level drug dealing

Though numerous studies have touched on drug dealer earnings, very few have systematically attempted to calculate actual take-home revenues – those studies that derive primarily from the United States and from generally within the context of urban deprivation. For instance, in his study of 1,000 cocaine/crack-cocaine sellers in two New York neighbourhoods, Fagan (1992) calculated average monthly drug incomes of around $2,000 and $3,500 – sums that 'exceeded by a wide margin the earnings from legitimate work' (ibid: 120).[5] Among the 186 Washington D.C. drug dealers studied by Reuter, MacCoun and Murphy (1990), equivalent hourly returns of $30 were earned – a sum that substantially out-competed the sample's median legal hourly wages of $7.[6] Similarly, Hagedorn (1994) calculated an income from drug sales of $15 an hour among the Milwaukee gang members he studied; among them, one-third had hourly earnings from drugs on par with the federal minimum wage at $6 or less; roughly a quarter had equivalent hourly earnings of $7 to $12; and one-third equivalent hourly earnings of $13 to $25. Freeman's (1992) analysis of the Boston Youth Survey likewise indicated hourly earnings of $13 to $21 from drug sales, sums that again 'substantially exceeded [legitimate after tax] take-home pay [...] [of] $5.60/hour' (ibid: 230). Most economic analyses of drug selling are over 20 years old and derive from the United States and thus may not be representative of market actors operating presently or in other countries. However, in a departure from the US-dominated data, Moeller's (2012) analysis of two Copenhagen cannabis markets showed that the 'proprietors' (i.e. key market operatives) earned net revenues between €325 and €336 per hour, while 'runners' earned on average between €16 and €23 per hour, and 'look-outs' €13 per hour – sums that exceed the after-tax hourly take-home pay of the city's lower earners, at around €10. Likewise, in England, May, Duffy, Few and Hough (2005) calculated weekly earnings for 68 crack-cocaine and heroin dealers. Many were 'user-dealers' who effectively negated any financial profit through their own use of these drugs (cf. Moyle and Coomber, 2015). Yet, among those who dealt for financial gain, 'profit dealers' earned an average of £7,500 per week, while their 'runners' earned £450 a week. Such earnings exceeded legal alternatives that paid at, or just above, the UK's national minimum wage, that were equivalent to pre-tax earnings of £200–£300 per week.

Generally speaking, though comparatively well paid, the opulent 'Mercedes Benz' lifestyles commonly associated with drug dealing appear to be unrepresentative of drug dealers at large (Reuter et al., 1990: viii; Decker and van Winkle, 1996: 156) with very few dealers reporting the kinds of 'crazy money' people come to expect (Hagedorn, 1994: 202). Nevertheless, the equivalent hourly or weekly returns from drug dealing surpass (in many cases by a wide margin) legitimate alternatives (see Ayres and Treadwell's chapter in this volume).

Sales patterns: 'doubling up' and the fungibility of the drug trade

Though the hourly returns from drug dealing are ostensibly high, actual weekly or monthly take-home returns are often more modest. This is because drug dealing frequently supplements regular incomes and is often undertaken on a part-time or intermittent basis. For instance, the dealers in Reuter, MacCoun and Murphy's (1990) study earned a median $30 an hour from drug sales. However, because drug market activity was confined to just one or two days a week and occurred for only a few hours on each of those days (median of 3 hours per day worked), median net monthly returns from drug sales were just $721 per month. For most (75%) of this sample, drug revenues supplemented median legal incomes of $800 per month, which derived from legitimate employment or legal enterprise. Such patterns of behaviour are an exemplary illustration of doubling up – whereby a few hours of drug sales on intermittent days throughout the month significantly elevated total monthly incomes. However such behaviours are by no means unique to that sample (cf. Hagedorn, 1994; Fagan, 1992) and there is evidence of workers in the legal economy doubling up via the illegal drug economy (Levitt and Venkatesh, 2000; Sales and Murphy, 2007; Jacinto, Duterte, Sales, and Murphy, 2008; Thompson and Uggen, 2012; McKenzie, 2015; Fader, 2019).

Furthermore, participation in the illegal drug trade is rarely sustained; it fluctuates over time, often in response to changing constraints, opportunities or needs. Drug dealing careers are often an 'on-again, off again proposition' (Hagedorn, 1994: 202) with many suppliers 'oscillating' in and out of these markets as economic necessity or indulgence dictate (Adler, 1993). Such intermittent market engagement has been documented widely (e.g. Bourgois, 1995; Johnson, Dunlap and Tourigny, 2000; Windle and Briggs, 2015; Macit, 2018). In addition to the phenomenon of doubling up, this pattern of behaviour exemplifies the 'fluid and dynamic interaction between legal and illegal work' (Fagan and Freeman, 1999: 225).

In the context of severe economic marginality, minimum-wage salaries or irregular employment, doubling up (or 'moonlighting') through illegal drug sales may be viewed as essential (Fader, 2019; VanNostrand and Tewksbury, 1999; Venkatesh, 2006), as one drug dealer in VanNostrand and Tewksbury's (1999: 63) study explained, 'I got a job now. You know, it's decent, but it's not anything for a house payment, car payment, two kids. You know, the money just ain't enough'. In such circumstances drug profits are used to underwrite basic living expenditures – such as rent, food and utility bills, vehicle costs, and at times to support family members in meeting similar financial obligations (Jacobs, 1999; VanNostrand and Tewksbury, 1999; Windle and Briggs, 2015) – while also enabling spending on non-essential yet high-status consumer items such as designer clothes (Anderson, 1999; Jacobs, 1999). Reflecting upon the prevalence of doubling up in their study, MacCoun and Reuter (1992: 489) posit that perhaps a

> useful way of viewing the relationship of drug dealing and legitimate work is to see that the former provides an underground form of "moonlighting"... an opportunity for a few hours of more highly paid work to supplement their primary jobs.

Regardless of whether one 'doubles up' out of indulgence or necessity, an obvious question arises: Why are drug sales so often used to supplement rather than supplant legitimate incomes? As MacCoun and Reuter (1992: 488) put it: 'if drug selling is so profitable, why maintain a legitimate job as well — particularly one with a relatively modest wage?' Indeed, why not simply commit to drug dealing full-time? Various explanations may be advanced. First, drug supply is inherently risky and exposes market traders to severe legal sanctions if caught,[7] as well as systemic market violence (Reuter, 2009). Prolonged market exposure heightens these risks and can, over time, escalate feelings of fear towards feelings of paranoia (e.g. Adler, 1993; Bourgois, 1995; Jacques and Wright, 2015). Limiting one's exposure by dealing at selected times of day, week or month may be an attempt to limit such risks (MacCoun and Reuter, 1992; Fader, 2019). Second, consumer demand is not distributed evenly throughout the course of a day, or even across a week or month, with peak demand often falling in the evenings, at weekends, or on days when welfare or public transfer payments are made (Reuter et al., 1990; Jacobs, 1999; Jacinto, Duterte, Sales and Murphy, 2008; Salinas, 2018). Thus, even if a person wishes to supply drugs all day, market opportunities might simply be absent. Third, despite popularised depictions of the trade as inherently glamorous, the work of a drug dealer is often uninspiring, repetitive and boring (Bourgois, 1995; Jacobs, 1999). There is often 'no adrenaline, no camaraderie, no craft. Just buyers and sellers' (Hobbs, 1995: 28). Therefore, a drug dealer can over time grow 'weary' of the work, its lifestyle and the associated stresses (Søgaard, Haller, Kolind and Hunt, 2019; Jacques and Wright, 2015). There may also be elements of the job that lie uneasily with some sellers, particularly when exploiting a consumer base with serious drug addictions (Fader, 2019; Jacobs, 1999; Waldorf, Reinerman and Murphy, 1992). As one New York crackhouse manager explained: 'I don't like to see people fucked up [...] I don't like this crack dealing' (Bourgois, 1995: 94) and '[Y]ou want the money but you don't really want to do the job. I really hate it, man. Hate it! I hate the environment! I hate the whole shit, man!' (ibid: 97).

In short, the empirical literature demonstrates the wide-spread practice of doubling up from a broad range of studies, though, as noted, such studies have tended to look at drug markets and suppliers in the context of inner-city urban deprivation. In areas disconnected from gainful and meaningful employment opportunities, the illegal drug economy has proven to be one of the few sectors that is in effect always hiring, non-discriminatory and remunerative (Bourgois, 1995; Johnson, Dunlap and Tourigny, 2000; Anderson, 1999) with its use as a supplemental income emerging out of both necessity and desire (Fader, 2019). Yet the risks of drug dealing, the inhibited hours of work and the absence of many substantive returns (aside from financial) likely limits the appeal of this work and confines it to an irregular and time-limited occupation. But in what other ways, and among what other demographics, might perceived economic needs motivate drug market engagement? Extending this work, this chapter reports on the phenomena of doubling up among a sample of drug dealers whose lives are far removed from the context of absolute poverty, which is so often deemed as the catalyst for drug market participation.

The study's methods

The findings presented here originate from an extensive body of data (see also Salinas, 2018; Askew and Salinas, 2019), generated as part of a 6-year ethnography (2006–2012) of 25 males aged in their 20s who, for the purposes of this study, are termed *The Lads*. Participants were located and recruited via the author's social contacts, which were established during adolescence. The use of one's preexisting relations in studying drug offenders is ostensibly one of the few means by which researchers can identify and access clandestine offending networks (e.g. Jacques and Wright, 2015; Hobbs, 2013; Mohamed and Fritsvold, 2010; Winlow, 2001). The study was concerned principally with assessing *The Lads*' seemingly paradoxical commitment to conventional norms/ideals as well as to a deviant and often criminal lifestyle. Thousands of hours were spent in the company of this network, systematically observing participants as they interacted with customers and suppliers (at varying levels of the supply chain), conventional work colleagues, and family members. The author observed many elements of *The Lads*' UK operations (e.g. cash and drug pickups/drop-offs, the selection of stash sites, the processing of drugs, the packaging of consignments and the cultivation of marijuana) and travelled to Ibiza to document and interview those participants involved in cross-border trafficking and supply. Ad hoc semi-structured interviews were undertaken daily, whenever further insight was needed. Field observations and ad hoc interviews were supplemented by more structured interviews, which were audio-recorded and transcribed. These interviews lasted between 30 minutes and 2 hours and were designed to elicit more detailed or reflexive information from participants. Where possible, unobserved events disclosed through interviews and conversations were corroborated via field observations made before or after the event, by speaking to others present or involved (e.g. trade partners or suppliers) or by some other means (e.g. viewing pay-slips, business records or newspaper articles). Interviewees were made aware that they and their responses were anonymised and otherwise kept confidential.[8] Pseudonyms are used throughout (including place names) in order to maintain their anonymity. Ethnographies such as this (see also Adler, 1993; Jacques and Wright, 2015; Mohamed and Fritsvold, 2010) depict burgeoning drug markets far removed from the milieu of social disorganisation, street violence, urban poverty and gangsterdom – and thus diverge from much of the criminological literature. They offer insight into what Mohamed and Fritsvold (2010) have termed 'the silent majority' of drug offender.

Findings

'Doubling up' as the dominant work practice

Of the 25 drug dealers in this study, two were 'social suppliers' who occasionally 'sorted friends' for little or no profit and so are excluded from this analysis (given its economic focus). Among the 23 commercially orientated suppliers, whose primary motive was financial, 21 'doubled up' using drug revenues to supplement (rather than substitute) legal incomes, while only two opted to deal drugs solely during times of joblessness. The occupational contexts in which the 23 commercial sellers operated were as follows:

- 15 dealt drugs while in full-time salaried employment.
- 7 dealt drugs while in full-time education.
- 7 dealt drugs while self-employed or engaged in legal entrepreneurship.
- 5 dealt drugs while unemployed.

(*Note, several (8/23) suppliers feature in one or more occupational categories, as their circumstances changed during the six-year fieldwork period.)

Aside from the five instances in which drugs were dealt in the absence of legal commitments, all other documented instances of drug dealing occurred during periods when the individual was legally working, managing a legal enterprise or studying, meaning that drug revenues overwhelmingly supplemented legitimate incomes in some form or another (e.g. salaried wages, independent business revenues and student loans). Why then did so many of *The Lads* deal drugs commercially, despite having full-time conventional commitments? To answer this, the following section closely examines the work patterns, profits and motives of these 23 commercially orientated drug dealers.

Work patterns and profits

For the purposes of this chapter, the retail stage of the illicit drug economy encompasses the final transaction in a supply chain, that is, sales made to consumers. This was the 'level' at which *The Lads* most commonly participated. The vast majority operated the so-called 'ring and bring' drug delivery services (see also Søgaard, Haller, Kolind and Hunt 2019), which tended to operate between 18:00 and 23:00 hrs Monday to Thursday, and flexible hours on Friday nights and weekends (Salinas, 2018). The hours of operation reflected the sharp increase in consumer demand at those times. It also helped ensure that the 'work' of these dealers did not interfere with their primary legitimate commitments at the time and could be easily integrated into conventional routines (ibid: 233). On average, cannabis retailers [n=9] netted £250–£500 profit per week, while cocaine retailers [n=12] netted between £350 and £1,050 a week. Drug sales at the retail level provided earnings that competed well against the men's legal wages, at times considerably out-competing them. For instance, one of *The Lads*, Pig, averaged a weekly income from taxi driving of around £300 (equitable to £7.50 per hour), yet his supplementary cannabis sales, which required about 10 hours per week, netted him £250–£300 (equitable to £25–£30 per hour). Khalid's net monthly salary while working full-time in an entry-level role in a high street bank was £900 per month (£5.60 net pay per hour), yet his cocaine deliveries netted him weekly profits of £450–£600 (equitable to £56–£75 per hour). Similarly, Marshall took home £1,100 per month through a more senior position in a high street bank (£6.90 net pay per hour), but earned £1,000–£1,200 per week as a cocaine retail and cocaine 'runner', requiring 12 hours (combined) each week (equitable to £83–£100 per hour). Evidently, the limited number of hours devoted to ring-and-bring retail delivery services proved far more profitable on an hourly (and indeed weekly) basis than *The Lads'* legitimate work.

A smaller proportion of *The Lads* opted not to sell direct to consumers (i.e. retail), and instead occupied a slightly higher strata in the market – the so-called 'mid-level' – selling bulk quantities wholesale to retail dealers or other traders. For the purpose of this study, the 'mid-level' included those whose operations included wholesaling, importing or exporting. Mid-level dealers tended to trade one substance at any one time (cocaine [*n*=3], cannabis [*n*=3] and ketamine [*n*=3]); however, one of *The Lads* (Rushton) concurrently brokered wholesale consignments of cocaine, cannabis, ketamine, 3,4-methylenedioxy-methamphetamine - Ecstasy (MDMA) powder and ecstasy. Given the significant variations over time in terms of cost price, mark-ups and volumes sold, it is difficult to provide 'typical' revenues for these drugs. The highest revenues recorded were by the study's premier cocaine wholesaler, Sol. At the peak of his trade he was sourcing weekly consignments of 13.5 ounces at a cost of £5,400 and selling these on in half-ounce and ounce multiples for a net profit of around £3,000 each week (after the staffing costs). By comparison, his most financially prosperous period for legal incomes – which comprised a full-time salaried job, a shift as a nightclub doorman and income from his first business enterprise – netted total weekly incomes of £650. Another mid-level supplier, Bear, redistributed kilos of ketamine (imported from South Asia, from one of *The Lads* who had emigrated there) in one-ounce multiples over two-month selling cycles. Averaged out, his small-scale import/wholesale operation netted over £500 per week. Bear was able to accommodate the 35 (often fewer) transactions around his primary (legal) commitment: a graduate-level profession in the construction industry. Another mid-level dealer, Rushton, the multi-drug dealer, worked in an entry-level role in the financial industries with a take-home pay of just over £1,600 per month. When asked about his illicit revenues, he explained:

> I look at what I earn on a monthly basis, or sometimes a weekly basis, never hourly [...] Three grand (£3,000) is the least I'll earn in a month, but that's because I'm whittling things down and just focusing on the staple lines [of stock]. It's much lower stress level doing it that way. All I have to do is make a few journeys that last a half-hour a few times a month.

As outlined here by Rushton, dealing drugs at the mid-level (i.e. wholesale, import/export) required far fewer transactions than retail-level drug sale (i.e. selling direct to consumers) in order to achieve equitable returns. Mid-level drug dealing within this network proved less time intensive than the retail operations outlined above. The tasks needed to operate successfully at both the retail and mid-levels were straightforward, routinised and easy to accommodate around legal work commitments. As such, work in the observed drug markets was largely confined to those hours outside of the traditional Monday-to-Friday, 9-to-5 working week.

In summary, these findings largely mirror those reviewed earlier in this chapter. These drug dealers were generally working legally at the time of these offending careers and this doubling up of crime and work significantly elevated total weekly/monthly earnings. As in the literature, equivalent hourly earnings from drug dealing significantly outperformed the samples' legal wages or business revenues. This meant that the least well-paid individual, Khalid (the bank employee), was able to increase his net monthly earning from £900 to approximately £2,800–£3,500 through the addition of cocaine retail sales (an increase of 211%–289% in monthly earnings). Likewise, Sol was able to elevate his net monthly earnings of £1,300 to over £14,000 through the addition of mid-level cocaine sales (an increase of almost 1,000%). In short, a few hours of extra 'work' (dealing) during their evenings and weekends elevated *The Lads'* individual net earnings to those of senior working professionals in the UK, akin to those of senior school teachers or medical/general surgeons.

Motivations for 'doubling up'

The combined earnings from drug sales and legal work offered *The Lads* a level of economic freedom to which they aspired but had not previously been afforded. At that time in their lives their legal incomes alone were perceived as inadequate. Gross annual legal earnings for those in full-time salaried employment ranged between £11,500 and £24,000 (not including tax contributions or national insurance deductions). Likewise, the economic lives of the seven business entrepreneurs and self-employed workers were often turbulent and at times unprofitable – with variable periods of underemployment or underperformance. For many, legal earnings during their 20s fell well short of the regional average gross salary for males of a similar age of around £26,000.

> If I wanted to start a future, a family — £900 a month [the wage received while working in a high street bank] — how could I support a kid, a family, mortgage bills? I couldn't do it. I want to treat myself, treat my missus […] [But] that just about covers rent and bills […] What can you do without money? Fuck all.
>
> *Khalid, 24, cocaine retailer (bank clerk)*

> [My salary is] just over £17,000 a year, which works out at about £1,200 a month [take-home pay][…] There's no chance of moving out [of my mums house] just yet […] But my mum's not charging me any keep [rent/bills] and me and Abu are doing our weed thing [cannabis retail sales] […] I'm managing to save loads […] My plan, is to move back to [South City] and get [rent] a place with my missus […] And go do a masters [degree]. So, I'm saving for that. But also want to go away once or twice this summer with [my girlfriend].
>
> *Tee, 22, cannabis dealer (college administrator)*

It is evident from these excerpts that despite their relatively low legal incomes, these men were not 'forced' to engage with the illegal drug economy out of absolute economic necessity or as a means of providing food, shelter or other 'basic living necessities' (VanNostrand and Tewksbury, 1999: 65), which *The Lads'* evidently had. Market entry was driven by a desire to remove the encumbrance of subsistence-level wages and enhance their otherwise limited spending capabilities (cf. Werse and Müller, 2016). It was a response to perceived material and experiential deprivation. Drug dealing helped *The Lads* realise greater financial independence, which provided previously absent opportunities – to move out of the family home, to socialise, to holiday abroad and to shop. For many, this greater financial independence markedly improved their perceived quality of life (Diener, Ng, Harter and Arora, 2010).

> I went back [home] after having money [having served in the armed forces for many years] to a nine-to-five job and paying rent and all the rest of it and was left with something like fifty-quid [£50] a week to spend. So, I thought, "You only get one chance in life and I'm gonna have a good one". […] I fucking seen the fuckin' window [of opportunity] to get into it [wholesaling cocaine] and smashed it! […] "Money can't buy you happiness" is fuckin' bollocks. Money can buy you everything in life […] [Had I not dealt] my average fuckin' days would've been going to work, getting home from work, having me tea, staying in with me missus watching telly. But now I've done fuckin' loads of different things and had the best of everything — travelled the world and all sorts of shit.
>
> *Sol, 28, cocaine wholesaler (logistics manager and business owner)*

A significant proportion of *The Lads'* illicit revenues were spent on non-essential 'luxury' consumables such as designer clothes, cars, motorbikes, holidays and drug consumption. Drug revenues were, in effect, an enhanced form of pocket money. Their motivations for seeking an additional (and, crucially, criminal) income may be perceived as evidence of greed (VanNostrand and Tewksbury, 1999; Desroches, 2006), consumer fetishism (Stratton, 2001) or narcissistic extremism (Hall, Winlow and Ancrum, 2008). Nevertheless, these individuals engaged with this criminal economy in response to the perceived limitations and non-satisfactory wages that they were earning during that period of their lives.

> It's just a comfortable lifestyle [now that I double up via drug sales][...] I don't ever have to really worry about bills or rent, I've got a nice works-van, I go out when I want, take [my girlfriend] out whenever I want [...] If I'm out and about I never have to worry and if I want to spend fifty-quid, I'll spend fifty-quid and not have to worry about it.
>
> *Blaine, 26, cocaine and cannabis dealer ([self-employed tradesman)*

Drug profits did at times provide more essential capital. At various points during fieldwork this secondary income acted as a financial safety-net during times of economic underemployment or underperformance.

> [My wage was] just fuckin' up and down all the time [...] I'd lost a bit of work [for a time] [...] So that [period] I was off [work] for five weeks [...] Then I got sent up [North] for [two months work]. Then I was off work again [...] Whenever I was in a [financial] corner, so to speak, or if there was an opportunity and I wasn't doing anything [...] [and] if I was getting dangerously skint [I'd import a kilo of ketamine].
>
> *Bear, 27, mid-level ketamine trader*
> *(self-employed professional in construction industries)*

> It took the piss [working on my uncle's market stall for that year], you know. I was like "You got to give me something", but that's how it is when you're working for family between Paki's [...] Fair enough, they gave me a job, a room, food, but what about fuel, or insurance [...] what about my phone bill or money to do things with my mates. I couldn't pay for shit [at that time] [...] So I just thought "Right, if you're not gonna pay I'm just gonna go do my own thing on the side"
>
> *Abu, 24, cannabis retailer (market stall trader)*

Doubling up was also used, perhaps paradoxically, to generate revenues for legitimate investment. In the absence of legal and accessible investment capital (e.g. business loans), the drug market provided an ever-accessible and often substantial source of capital which some *Lads* strategically used to pursue legitimate entrepreneurial activities. Drug money was used to establish and develop businesses, including retail shops, drinking establishments, a gym and a food production factory. These business ventures were not established for the purpose of continued money laundering (i.e. 'cleaning' drug money) but rather to provide gainful work adequate to their needs and aspirations. Sol reflected on his past involvement of mid-level cocaine trading:

> [Drug dealing was] purely economic. I wouldn't say I got any real satisfaction [from it] [...] I've literally spent thousands and thousands [of money earned from cocaine] on [this legal business]: doing it up, [...] making it fuckin' mint [...] Where the fuck is a lad like me supposed to get that kind of money? It's cost me 80-grand [£80,000] easy [...] I'm passionate about [the business]. I genuinely like this line of business. It's rewarding, you see your business and work have an impact [...] I'd rather be known as Sol the successful businessman, than Sol the drug dealer who'll break in someone's door with a baseball bat for £500.

Finally, it is worth noting that the underlying economic rationales of the 23 commercially orientated dealers were liable to change over time in response to changing circumstance. This exemplar of Cliff aptly illustrates the shifting occupational terrain that some encountered. It shows how motivations to deal drugs were liable to change. Throughout his five-year dealing 'career', Cliff's underlying motive was consistently financial, yet the economic rationale behind his decisions to double up changed over time. Cliff doubled up as a way to indulge consumer spending habits, as a financial safety net during times of financial instability, and as investment capital in legal enterprise. His case demonstrates the complexities of doubling up and challenges notions of what is meant by 'economic necessity'.

> Cliff initially began retailing cocaine whilst studying full-time towards his bachelor's degree, using the profits from drug sales to supplement his wages from a part-time marketing role. Soon afterwards, he ceased working part-time, unable to justify the requisite investment of hours. He continued to operate his ring-and-bring cocaine delivery service whilst studying towards a master's degree. In the years that followed. Cliff struggled to secure employment in his chosen occupational field and so found interim work as a taxi driver. He continued to deal cocaine, this time using it to supplement his variable (but often low) earnings from taxi driving. Soon into his taxiing 'career' he invested much of his accumulated assets into a legal business venture (and, later, used his drug profits to keep this business afloat).

Doubling up was temporary for most of these men, lasting an average of only a few years. As with Adler and Adler's participants this was partly because 'the novelty gradually faded' (1983: 201). The work was largely monotonous and mundane, requiring little in the way of specific occupational skills (cf. Jacobs, 1999: 34; Bourgois, 1995; Hobbs, 1995). Khalid's comments typified many of *The Lads'* experience of operating a ring-and-bring delivery service: "*If you take the money [element] away, it's a pizza delivery boy job*". Furthermore, as legal earnings increased (at times, quite significantly) or business investments began to pay dividends, the perceived need to supplement this income subsided (cf. Werse and Müller, 2016). Such legal earnings did not need to match the same heights as the revenues from drug sales in order to tip the scales, a finding that has long been evident in the literature (Fagan and Freeman, 1999: 232). As occupational gains increased so too did the stakes of continued drug sales (cf. Laub and Sampson, 2001; Uggen, 2000). Most could no longer justify continuing in this line of illicit work nor risk forfeiting the legitimate gains they had acquired through years of sustained effort and investment. In the final section particular attention is given to doubling up in the context of full-time academic study; a time when many people must forego full-time regular salaries in order to purse (often work-related) qualifications, while incurring debts of around £50,000 (Belfield, Britton, Dearden and van der Erve, 2017).

'Doubling up' in the context of academic study

Student life at university provides a set of social and economic conditions that are potentially conducive to periods of engagement in the illegal drug trade (Moyle and Coomber, 2019). British university students exhibit comparatively high rates of illegal drug use (Bennett and Holloway, 2014; Bennett and Holloway, 2015; Holloway and Bennett, 2018) which provides opportunities for those willing and able to facilitate such consumer demand.[9] Many university students in Britain encounter financial constraints and concerns during their studies (Warrell, 2015; Student Money Survey, 2019) because average living cost for British students is around £800 per month (ibid), yet government-sponsored maintenance loans provide students only £540 per month. This financial shortfall is most commonly remedied through the addition of other funding sources such as part-time work or parental support (Warrell, 2015; Student Money Survey, 2019).[10] Yet these shortfalls in earnings during university presented an economic motive that led those in this study to becoming commercially orientated drug suppliers (cf. Bennett and Holloway, 2019).

Among the 10 *Lads* who had attended university, seven had dealt drugs while studying towards a bachelor's degree. Of these, five had proceeded to deal and study at postgraduate level. Though these dealers sought ultimately to attain a degree qualification that would benefit entry into their chosen occupational field, this was balanced against more immediate desires for financial independence and leisurely activities (cf. Mohamed and Fristvold, 2010). Full-time academic study at university consisted of approximately 12–15 hours of structured classes per week, equating to just 2.5–3 hrs of classes or lectures each day (Monday–Friday), with the onus on self-directed study. Such an abundance of free time provided ample opportunity to socialise, work and supply drugs.

Part-time work was often low-skilled and low paid. Hammer, a business graduate, reflected upon his financial situation as a 'full time' university student. While studying, Hammer had sold both cannabis and cocaine to friends and to associates on his local estate as a means of supplementing his student loan and a part-time salary.

> Thing is, you don't get very far on what I was earning [working part-time in a local pub, while in university]: £100 a week at most, sometimes £60– that's barely enough for the bus fare into town every day and a few ales one night a week [...] I wanna be able to do go out and do things with [my girlfriend] and me pals, I don't wanna have just one night in the week where I have to choose between doing things with me mates or doing things with me missis [...] [Drug dealing enables] a better standard of living [...] Money's not the be-all and end-all in life, people who say that are chatting shit, I should know. You're still able to enjoy yourself without having a load of money, but it [money] defiantly changes how you can live your life, but only up to a point.
>
> *Hammer, 26, cocaine and cannabis retailer (Human Resource manager)*

Some, such as Tee and Nani, chose to forgo any form of paid work during term times, opting instead to rely on the revenues from drug sales. University course mates had introduced Tee to high-potency skunk cannabis wholesalers based in another city who provided weekly consignments which Tee was able to rapidly offload (often via 'pre-orders') among his hometown peer networks. Tee estimated net profits of £200–£300 a week, for roughly three hours 'work'. Though not particularly remarkable, such revenues negated any need to find paid employment during term time.

> I've been working the last two summers [in-between the academic years] at [the local university canteen] doing pot-washing, but no, I haven't worked [during term time] whilst actually being in uni [...] Mum knows I've been selling [cannabis] pretty much since I started [...] She's not exactly happy about it. But she knows it's just for now, until I finish uni and it means I don't have to work [in a part-time job] and so can just concentrate on uni. [...] I don't have to pay any fees, the government pay mine because of what my mum earns isn't much, but I still have all my living costs.
>
> *Tee, 21, cannabis retailer (full-time bachelor's student)*

As with those employed in low-income jobs (see previous sections) drug sales helped to underwrite typical living expenses such as rent and utility bills, as well as extravagant expenditures such as high-end cars, high-tech gadgetry and impromptu holidays. None of *The Lads* financed their undergraduate course fees with profits from drug sales (instead using the government loan scheme); however, two instances were recorded in which drug revenues covered postgraduate course fees in their entirety (approximately £3,000 per year full-time study). Economic constraints did not fully abate upon graduating university. Most continued to deal for a time afterwards. Tee secured relatively low-paid work and continued to deal. Hammer ceased dealing after securing a graduate-level job soon after graduating, however he re-commenced sales after a year, after his employer was forced into making redundancies. Nevertheless, by the time these graduates were in their late-20s all-bar-one had ceased dealing having secured gainful employment adequate to their financial needs and aspirations (cf. Werse and Müller, 2016).

Conclusion

When not being pathologised or presented as inherently 'evil' (Coomber, 2006) drug dealing is often seen as both a symptom of, and response to, extreme conditions of social isolation and economic marginalisation. To be sure, in the absence of accessible and gainful labour markets, localised drug markets have proven to be highly remunerative, non-discriminatory, and always hiring (Bourgois, 1995; Jacobs, 1999; Padilla, 1992). Yet, despite its accessibility and economic allure, very few who engage the market fully commit themselves to this illicit occupation. Instead, as the synthesis of existing research coupled with data from this study has shown, doubling up through legal work and drug markets is in fact commonplace (if not the norm) in many contexts. Indeed, for many, drug dealing appears to be a form of 'moonlighting', a side-hustle, used to top up (albeit significantly) earnings from the legal economy (Reuter, MacCoun, Murphy, 1990; Jacinto, Duterte, Sales, and Murphy, 2008; Fader, 2019). Furthermore, drug dealing is often a time-limited and irregular occupation used selectively in times of financial need (Anderson, 1999; Hagedorn, 1994). Yet as the findings in this chapter have also shown, the supplementing of legal incomes through drug dealing is by no means the preserve of marginalised inner-city residents. As with Reuter, MacCoun and Murphy's (1990) study, the empirical findings presented here show individuals actively participating in the drug trade despite earning above-minimum-wage incomes from legal work (i.e. salaried work, self-employment work, small business enterprise or study). Market engagement was rarely a consequence of absolute economic need. Instead, the economic motives that led the young men in this study towards commercially orientated drug dealing and the doubling up of work and crime could be separated into three distinct categories: (i) the use of drug profits for non-essential spending on 'luxury' goods or experiences (i.e. 'pocket money'), (ii) the use of drug profits as a financial safety net during economically precarious times and (iii) the use of drug profits as investment capital in legitimate occupational endeavours (such as business or study).

A number of conclusions may be drawn. First, participation in legal labour markets or earning just-above-minimum-wages does not by default assuage the desires or perceived needs of individuals. People aspire towards 'living in more complicated ways than simple survival would demand' (Sennett and Cobb, 1972: 53) and thus may be motivated to deal drugs to remove the constrains of subsistence-level wages. In that sense, the underlying financial motives of drug dealers are often linked to relative rather than absolute deprivation; with drug profits often underwriting incidental expenses such as holidays, designer clothing, meals out, or fast cars (items and experiences that denote status, and also imbue the individual with a higher quality of life). Second, as with criminal careers more generally, this form of offending is not static, but dynamic (Laub and Sampson, 1993; Adler and Adler, 1983). Despite being viewed as one of the most 'serious' forms of criminality, those who operate in the drug market are often not full-time serious offenders and their participation is often fleeting. Drug-dealing as a form of work may therefore be best understood as noncommittal, fluid and flexible. Third, 'local life circumstances' and traditional 'turning points' in the life course help to facilitate the onset, escalation and desistance of drug dealing careers. An extended bout of underemployment, a period of underperformance in one's business, the need for additional capital or the desire to start a family can all contribute towards a perceived need for greater income, which can motivate drug market engagement. Conversely, a period of sustained employment, successful performance in one's business or access to alternative (legal) forms of capital can contribute to drug market cessation. Fourth, many drug dealers would prefer to solely work legally, if such work provided incomes relative to their aspirations or perceived needs. Indeed, strong preferences for legal work and explicit aspirations to 'go legit' are even evident among dealers with protracted careers in 'serious' drug markets (e.g. crack-cocaine or heroin) who fundamentally depend upon these illicit revenues to offset serious shortfalls or absences in legal earnings (e.g. Bourgois, 1995; Fader, 2019; Macit, 2018). Legal incomes do not need to equal those of illegal earnings in order to tip the scales in its favour (Fagan and Freeman, 1999) but they do, nevertheless, need to allow for more than mere subsistence level living.

The rites of passage that have traditionally marked the successful transition from adolescence to adulthood (e.g. independent living, parenthood and stable work) are increasingly being delayed. In particular, many young adults find themselves struggling to achieve levels of economic independence enjoyed by the previous generation. Compared to the pre-recession generation, adults in their 20s are experiencing real-term pay declines and are more likely to be in temporary employment (particularly zero-hour contracts) (Cribb and Johnson, 2018; Allen, 2016). During such times of economic uncertainty, it is prudent to consider the means by which individuals look to redress shortfalls in earnings, whether as a consequence of low wages, bouts of unemployment or under-employment. With more British workers now supplementing their primary legal income/job via (legal) 'side hustles' – often motivated out of financial need – it has been said that 'the age of the side hustle is upon us' (Henley Business School, 2018: 2). In many respects, 'doubling up' via the illegal drug economy is akin to working within the emergent 'gig economy'. In both economies, 'independent workers' take on flexible work arrangements within short-term worker–client relationships, earning money per task, assignment or sale. Equally, many who comprise the illicit drug and 'gig' economy workforce use their returns to supplement their primary legal incomes – out of either necessity or choice (see Manyika, Lund, Bughin, Robinson, Mistake and Mahajan, 2016). For many involved in the illegal drug economy, drug dealing is not an occupational calling, nor their *raison d'être*. These people are not 'outsiders', nor are they committed to some counter-cultural ethos. Rather, for those linked to the drug 'scene', drug dealing is often a flexible and relatively well-paid *supplementary* form of work with few barriers to entry and requiring few requisite skills. As regular 9-to-5 salaried employment opportunities diminish, the attractiveness of drug dealing as a 'side hustle' may prove increasingly alluring.

Notes

1 For instance, in the UK, analyses by the Resolution Foundation of the Labour Force Survey, the Anuual Survey of Hours and Earnings and official labour market statistics indicated a 'hollowing out' of weekly pay distribution among males resulting from a reduction in hours worked (Clarke and Bangham, 2018), as well as high levels of 'atypical employment', with 900,000 people working on a zero hour contract, and 800,000 agency workers (Tomlinson, 2018).

2 Rather than looking at profit financial from drug sales a significant proportion of 'dealers' supply drugs to underwrite their own drug using habits (Moyle and Coomber, 2015; Coomber, 2015; May et al. 2005). Others as a means of elevating their standing within their social network via the kudos attributed to being seen as 'gangsta' (Mohammed and Fritsvold, 2010; Jacques and Wright, 2015; Werse and Müller, 2016). And still others do so largely as a form of social reciprocity, helping to 'sort out' friends who are in search of supplies (Coomber and Moyle, 2014).

3 For instance, the UNDCP (1998: 12) report notes that '[m]ore than 90 per cent of the value added (gross profit) of cocaine and heroin is generated at the distribution stage of the illicit drug industry'.

4 Operations at these stages often rely on stratified labour, meaning that many 'runners' – those who undertook the physical drug deliveries for 'profit-dealers') – who work for key operative earn a fraction of the total revenues – e.g. £300–£500 a week (Pearson and Hobbs, 2001).

5 Fifty-two per cent of the sample consumed drugs of a mean monthly value of $400; these costs are not factored into these earnings.

6 Crack-cocaine and cocaine sales were the most frequent sources of revenue among this sample; however, these individuals also sold (in descending order of income share): PCP, cannabis, heroin, methadone, and other drugs.

7 In the UK, for instance, the supply of the cannabis is punishable with up to 14 years in prison and/or an unlimited fine, while the supply of cocaine is punishable by up to life in prison and/or an unlimited fine.

8 For a thorough detailing and discussion of the methods and ethics of this project, see the methods chapter of the doctoral thesis: 'Men at Work: An Ethnography of Drug Dealing and Youth Transitions' (Salinas 2014).

9 Similar patterns of drug use among students have been evidenced in the United States (Mohamed and Fritsvold, 2010; Johnson, O'Malley, Bachman, and Schulenberg, 2016).

10 The Student Money Survey (2019) showed students relying on a wide range of income sources. When asked where they got their money from, the most common

responses were paternal support (73%) and part-time jobs (67%). However students also cited gambling (8%), adult work (4%) and drug trails (2%), perhaps indicating a willingness to assume arguably more risky yet potentially more remunerative work.

References

Adler, P. A. (1993). *Wheeling and dealing: An ethnography of an upper-level drug dealing and smuggling community.* Columbia University Press.

Adler, P. A., and Adler, P. (1983). Shifts and oscillations in deviant careers: The case of upper-level drug dealers and smugglers. *Social Problems*, 31(2), 195–207.

Allen, K. (2016). Top girls navigating austere times: Interrogating youth transitions since the 'crisis'. *Journal of Youth Studies*, 19(6), 805–820.

Anderson E. (1999). *Code of the street. Decency, violence, and the moral life of the inner city.* New York: Norton.

Anderson, E. (1990). *Streetwise: Race, class and change in an urban community.* Chicago: University of Chicago Press.

Antonopoulos, G. A., and Papanicolaou, G. (2010). Asterix and obelix in drugland: An introduction to the special issue on 'drug markets', *Trends in Organized Crime*, 13, 1–12.

Armstrong, S. (2017). *The new poverty.* London: Verso.

Askew, R., and Salinas, M. (2019). Status, stigma and stereotype: How drug takers and drug suppliers avoid negative labeling by virtue of their 'conventional' and 'law-abiding' lives, *Criminology and Criminal Justice*, 19(3), 311–327.

Belfield, C., Britton, J., Dearden, L., and van der Erve, L. (2017). *Higher education funding in England: Past present and options for the future.* Institute for Fiscal Studies Briefing Note.

Bennett, T., and Holloway, K. (2019). How do students source and supply drugs? Characteristics of the university illegal drug trade. *Substance Use and Misuse*, 54(9), 1530–1540.

Bennett, T. H., and Holloway, K. R. (2014). Drug misuse among university students in the UK: Implications for prevention. *Substance Use and Misuse*, 49(4), 448–455.

Bennett, T. H., and Holloway, K. R. (2015). Drug use among college and university students: Findings from a national survey. *Journal of Substance Use*, 20(1), 50–55.

Bourgois, P. (1995). *In search of respect: Selling crack in El Barrio.* Cambridge: Cambridge University Press.

Caulkins, J. P., and Reuter, P. (1998). What price data tell us about drug markets. *Journal of Drug Issues*, 28(3), 593–612.

Clarke, S., and Bangham, G. (2018). *Counting the hours, two decades of changes in earnings and hours worked.* London: Resolution Foundation.

Coomber, R. (2006). *Pusher myths: Re-situating the drug dealer.* London: Free Association Press.

Coomber, R. (2015). A tale of two cities: Understanding differences in levels of heroin/crack market-related violence—A two city comparison. *Criminal Justice Review*, 40(1), 7–31.

Coomber, R., and Moyle, L. (2014). Beyond drug dealing: Developing and extending the concept of 'social supply' of illicit drugs to 'minimally commercial supply'. *Drugs: Education, Prevention and Policy*, 21(2), 157–164.

Cribb, J., and Johnson, P. (2018). 10 years on — have we recovered from the financial crisis. *Institute for Fiscal Studies.* 12 Sept 2018. URL: www.ifs.org.uk/publications/13302

Decker, S. H., and Van Winkle, B. (1996). *Life in the gang: Family, friends, and violence.* Cambridge University Press.

Desroches, F. (2006). *The crime that pays: Drug trafficking and organized crime in Canada.* Toronto, Canada: Canadian Scholars' Press.

Diener, E., Ng, W., Harter, J., and Arora, R. (2010). Wealth and happiness across the world: Material prosperity predicts life evaluation, whereas psychosocial prosperity predicts positive feeling. *Journal of Personality and Social Psychology*, 99(1), 52.

Duck, W. (2015). *No way out: Precarious living in the shadow of poverty and drug dealing.* London: University of Chicago.

Endsleigh (2015). 77% of students now work to fund studies. *Press Release*, 10 August 2015, URL: www.endsleigh.co.uk/press-releases/10-august-2015/

Fader, J. J. (2019). 'The game ain't what it used to be': Drug sellers' perceptions of the modern day underground and legal markets. *Journal of Drug Issues*, 49(1), 57–73.

Fagan, J. (1992). Drug selling and licit income in distressed neighborhoods: The economic lives of street-level drug users and dealers. In Peterson, G., and Harrell, A. (Eds.), *Drugs, crime and social isolation*. Washington, DC: Urban Institute Press.

Fagan, J., and Freeman, R. B. (1999). Crime and work. *Crime and Justice*, 25, 225–290.

Freeman, R. (1992). Crime and the economic status of disadvantaged young men. In Peterson, G.E., and Vroman, W. (Eds.), *Urban labour markets and job opportunities.* Washington, DC: Urban Institute.

Hagedorn, J. M. (1994). *Homeboys, dope fiends, legits, and new jacks. Criminology*, 32(2), 197–219.

Hall, S., Winlow, S., and Ancrum, C. (2008). *Criminal identities and consumer culture: Crime, exclusion and the new culture of narcissism.* Cullompton: Willian Publishing.

Henley Business School (2018). *The side hustle economy. A white paper from Henley Business School.* University of Reading. URL: https://assets.henley.ac.uk/defaultUploads/PDFs/news/Journalists-Regatta-Henley_Business_School_whitepaper_DIGITAL.pdf?mtime=20180703154430and_ga=2.131793419.528961435.1595771595-119668679.1595771595

Hobbs, D. (1995). *Bad business: Professional crime in modern Britain.* Oxford: Oxford University Press.

Hobbs, D. (2013). *Lush life: Constructing organized crime in the UK.* Oxford: Oxford University Press.

Holloway, K., and Bennett, T. (2018). Characteristics and correlates of drug use and misuse among university students in Wales: A survey of seven universities. *Addiction Research and Theory*, 26(1), 11–19.

Horney, J., Osgood, D. W., and Marshall, I. H. (1995). Criminal careers in the short-term: Intra-individual variability in crime and its relation to local life circumstances. *American Sociological Review*, 655–673.

Jacinto, C., Duterte, M., Sales, P., and Murphy, S. (2008). 'I'm not a real dealer': The identity process of ecstasy sellers. *Journal of Drug Issues*, 38(2), 419–444.

Jacobs, B. (1999). *Dealing crack.* Boston, MA: Northeastern University Press.

Jacques, S., and Wright, R. (2015). *Code of the suburb: Inside the world of young middle-class drug dealers.* London: University of Chicago Press.

Johnson, B. D., Dunlap, E., and Sylvie C. Tourigny, S. C. (2000). Crack distribution and abuse in New York. In Natarajan, M., and Hough, M. (Eds.), *Illegal drug markets: From research to prevention policy.* Monsey, NY: Criminal Justice Press, pp. 19–57.

Johnson, L. D., O'Malley, P. M., Bachman, J. G., and Schulenberg, J. E. (2016*). Monitoring the Future: College Students and Adults Ages 19–55.* Ann Arbor: Institute for Social Research: The University of Michigan.

Laub, J. H., and Sampson, R. J. (1993). Turning points in the life course: Why change matters to the study of crime. *Criminology*, 31(3), 301–325.

Laub, J. H., and Sampson, R. J. (2001). Understanding desistance from crime. *Crime and Justice*, 28, 1–69.

Levitt, S. D., and Venkatesh, S. A. (2000). An economic analysis of a drug-selling gang's finances. *The Quarterly Journal of Economics*, 115(3), 755–789.

MacCoun, R., and Reuter, P. (1992). Are the wages of sin $30 an hour? Economic aspects of street-level drug dealing. *Crime and Delinquency*, 38(4), 477–491.

Macit, R. (2018). Becoming a drug dealer in Turkey. *Journal of Drug Issues*, 48(1), 106–117.

Manyika, J., Lund, S., Bughin, J., Robinson, K., Mischke, J., and Mahajan, D. (2016). Independent work: Choice, necessity, and the gig economy. *McKinsey Global Institute*, 2016, 1–16.

May. T., Duff, M., Few, B., and Hough, M. (2005) *Understanding drug selling in communities: Insider or outsider trading?* York: Joesph Rowntree Foundation.

Mckenzie, L. (2015). *Getting by: Estates, class and culture in austerity Britain*. Bristol: The Policy Press.

Moeller, K. (2012). Costs and revenues in street-level cannabis dealing. *Trends in Organized Crime*, 15(1), 31–46.

Moeller, K., and Sandberg, S. (2019). Putting a price on drugs: An economic sociological study of price formation in illegal drug markets. *Criminology*, 57(2), 289–313.

Mohamed, A. R., and Fritsvold, E. D. (2010). *Dorm room dealers: Drugs and the privileges of race and class*. Boulder, CO: Lynne Rienner Publishers.

Moyle, L., and Coomber, R. (2015). Earning a score: An exploration of the nature and roles of heroin and crack cocaine 'user-dealers'. *British Journal of Criminology*, 55(3), 534–555.

Moyle, L., and Coomber, R. (2019). Student transitions into drug supply: Exploring the university as a 'risk environment'. *Journal of Youth Studies*, 22(5), 642–657.

Padilla, F. (1992). *The gang as an American enterprise*. New Brunswick, NJ: Rutgers University Press.

Pearson, G., and Hobbs, D. (2001). *Middle market drug distribution*. Home Office Research Study no. 224. London: Home Office.

Reuter, P. (2009). Systemic violence in drug markets. *Crime, Law and Social Change*, 52(3), 275–284.

Reuter, P., MacCoun, R., and Murphy, P. (1990). *Money from crime: A study of the economics of drug dealing in Washington, D.C.* Santa Monica, CA: RAND.

Sales, P., and Murphy, S. (2007). San Francisco's freelancing ecstasy dealers: Towards a sociological understanding of drug markets. *Journal of Drug Issues*, 37(4), 919–949.

Salinas, M. (2018). The unusual suspects: An educated and legitimately employed drug dealing network. *International Criminal Justice Review*, 28(3): 226–242.

Sennett, R., and Cobb, J. (1972). *The hidden injuries of class*. London: Faber and Faber.

Søgaard, T. F., Kolind, T., Haller, M. B., and Hunt, G. (2019). Ring and bring drug services: Delivery dealing and the social life of a drug phone. *International Journal of Drug Policy*, 69, 8–15.

Stratton, J. (2001). *The desirable body: Cultural fetishism and the erotics of consumption*. Chicago: University of Illinois Press.

Taylor, S. (2008). Outside the outsiders: Media representations of drug use. *Journal of Community and Criminal Justice*, 55, 369–387.

Thompson, M., and Uggen, C. (2012). Dealers, thieves, and the common determinants of drug and nondrug illegal earnings. *Criminology*, 50(4), 1057–1087.

Tomlinson, D. (2018). *The UK's tight labour market and zero hours contract*. Resolution Foundation. URL: www.resolutionfoundation.org/comment/the-uks-tight-labour-market-and-zero-hours-contracts/

Uggen, C. (2000). Work as a turning point in the life course of criminals: A duration model of age, employment, and recidivism. *American Sociological Review*, 16(4), 529–546.

United Nations Drug Control Progtam (UNDCP). (1998). *Economic and social consequences of drug abuse and illicit drug trafficking*. UNDCP Technical Series, Number 6. URL: www.unodc.org/pdf/technical_series_1998-01-01_1.pdf

Van Duyne, P. C., and De Miranda, H. (1999). The emperor's cloths of disclosure: Hot money and suspect disclosures. *Crime, Law and Social Change*, 31(3), 245–271.

VanNostrand, L. M., and Tewksbury, R. (1999). The motives and mechanics of operating an illegal drug enterprise. *Deviant Behavior*, 20(1), 57–83.

Venkatesh, S. A. (2006). *Off the books. The underground economy of the urban poor*. Cambridge, MA: Harvard University Press.

Waldorf, D., Reinarman, C., and Murphy, S. (1992). *Cocaine changes: The experience of using and quitting*. Temple University Press.

Warrell, H. (2015). Students take on more paid employment as living costs rise. *Financial Times*, August 10th, 2015.

Werse, B., and Muller, D. (2016). Drifting in and out of dealing — results on career dynamics from the TDID project. In Werse, B. and Bernard, C. (Eds.), *Friendly business, international views on social supply, self-supply and small scale drug dealing* (pp. 93–120). Springer VS, Wiesbaden.

Wilsons, L., and Stevens, A. (2008). *Understanding drug markets and how to influence them*. London: Becky Foundation Drug Policy Programme.

Windle, J., and Briggs, D. (2015). Going solo: The social organisation of drug dealing within a London street gang. *Journal of Youth Studies*, 18(9), 1170–1185.

Winlow, S. (2001). *Badfellas: Crime, tradition and new masculinities*. Oxford: Berg.

12

COUNTY LINES AND THE TRANSFORMATION OF MIDDLE DRUG MARKETS WITHIN A LOCAL ORGANISED CRIME CONTEXT

Paul Andell, David James and Dev Maitra

Introduction

County lines can be thought of as a hub and spoke distribution model or sometimes simply out of town dealing (Coomber and Moyle 2018; Andell and Pitts 2017). But as a way to recognise more recent human problems of violence and exploitation in drug distribution, the term 'county lines' has high visibility, captures media attention and has high public and criminal justice system recognition (National Crime Agency 2016, 2017, 2018). It works. The concept holds currency in thinking about the harms of the illegal drug distribution trade and the way vulnerable people are part of the process of distribution. This change is potentially a focus towards victims of county lines by grooming and cuckooing and disadvantaged groups such as young people in, or leaving, care. It also captures something about drug distribution in English provinces and the importance of this as an organised competitive illegal business and not a social activity. For these reasons the term 'county lines' can be a useful analytical tool.

In some senses existing understanding of county lines as a middle market is a quite parochial interpretation given the widespread recognition of drug supply as a global business. But as Sergi (2017) has pointed out the term "middle market" is much dependent on the taxonomies of the agencies charged with interventions (Andell 2019). The 'middle market' is an uncertain term and may describe the quantity of illegal drugs being dealt with, which may range from ounces to kilos, or the practices of importation to different geographic and administrative areas. The middle market is below national importation, so it is always sub-national, but above individual supply of consumers. It does however allow us to explore the organisation and links between more wholesale and more retail distribution of illegal drugs. More recently developments in the middle market have

DOI: 10.4324/9781351010245-14

prompted associated concerns regarding significant increases in youth violence (Andell 2019; Black 2020).

On 22nd May 2018, during a debate on the Government's Serious Violence Strategy, David Lammy, MP for Tottenham, raised the issue of cuts to public services and the disproportionate impact this has had on Black communities when he questioned the budget set aside nationally for youth development programmes. He identified the absence of organised crime from public policy debates, and critiqued the Government's Serious Violence Strategy. He argued that any attempt to reduce serious violent crime, and the use of knives in violent gang crime, requires a consideration of local and global organised crime. Criminologists have long identified the merging between global and local criminal activity, with Hobbs (1998) coining the term 'glocal' to denote this convergence of global organised crime and local street gang activity (see also Hobbs 2013). Similarly, Lammy (Hansard 22nd May 2018, Column 794) refers to 'the myriad of organisations that sit well above the youth crime on the ground', drawing attention to the stratified organisation of the criminal marketplace that is often missing from media or policy discourses. This chapter aims to explore how global organised crime is connected to local neighbourhoods in order to fully inform the policy debate, drawing on more contemporary research to update the otherwise often dated work on some of these areas of inquiry.

The local threat of drug markets and gangs is raised in the County Lines, Gangs and Safeguarding report (Andell and Pitts 2017) and the National Crime Agency (NCA 2017) describes the way street gangs, exploiting vulnerable younger adolescents in both the major cities and out of town locations, distribute illegal drugs across wide swathes of the country using vulnerable children and young people. The NCA (2019) describes those involved in these arrangements as 'Urban Street Gangs', 'Organised Crime Groups' or 'Dangerous Dealer Networks'. These terms carry significance regarding the level, appropriateness and cost-effectiveness of responses. Therefore, a more detailed understanding is required if targeted and proportionate interventions are to be effective and earn community support (Lea and Young 1984). Such community-level support is especially necessary in areas which have seen the development of cultures that distrust the police and stigmatise those residents who cooperate with members of law enforcement (Walklate and Evans 1999). In their evaluation of the government's Ending Gang and Youth Violence programme, Disley and Liddle (2016:12) describe how:

> Young people were said to be given targets for selling (drugs) and punished if the targets were not met. Train tickets would be bought in advance by 'the elders', and the fact that young people had valid train tickets for these journeys, which they would not normally be able to afford, provided evidence that their trips were organised.

Additional local empirical studies suggest the involvement of street gangs in the supply of crack and heroin from major cities to smaller cities and towns (Andell and Pitts 2018; Coomber and Moyle 2016; Wendle and Briggs 2015). Questions remain as to the generalisations which can be drawn from these localised empirical studies as well as the dangers of over-reactions through 'gang talk' (Hallsworth and Young 2008:183). Such concerns can be seen as a new iteration of the long-standing criminological focus on the developments of 'moral panics' around certain types of behaviours (Cohen 1972), as well as concerns around the deleterious effects of too readily labelling youth collectives as gangs. This chapter, however, offers a framework of analysis applied to recent observed changes in some drug distribution models in England and explores possible links between gangs, organised crime and the drugs trade.

The findings from the empirical studies above appear to conflict with previous ideas of 'social supply' whereby there is said to be a predominance of unorganised user dealers funding their own habits (Coomber 2004). Recent studies indicate a development of a 'harder-edged' business model designed for minimum risk and higher profits (Andell and Pitts 2018; Andell 2019). Rather than being separate entities, contemporary research shows that street gangs and organised crime groups often operate through a symbiotic relationship, working in an interconnected fashion to better face the demands of contemporary drug markets. This prompts questions regarding the degree of organisation and the divisions of labour involved in new distribution networks in UK crack and heroin markets.

Organised crime and UK drug markets

UK Criminological research has produced a significant body of work which suggests that there are an increasing range of differentiated market arrangements which facilitate the supply of illicit drugs (Aktah and South 2000; Aldridge et al. 2011; Bennett and Holloway 2004; Coomber 2006; Dorn et al. 1992; Dorn and South 1990; Densley et al. 2018, May and Hough 2004 Matrix Knowledge Group 2007; Parker 2001; Parker and Measham 1994; Pitts 2008 Ruggiero 2006; Seddon 2006). Most of these studies agree that there are many misconceptions about drug markets and their participants. It is correctly pointed out that drug markets are not homogeneous, and that the realities of drug markets often differ from the accounts given about them (Coomber 2010). There are also significant differences in drug markets according to country, region and society (see Ayres and Treadwell's chapter in this volume). Moreover, ideas about the use of violence in drug markets, according to Coomber (2015:7), are often overstated, and the realities of violence are:

> contingent on a mix of local supply cultures; supplier rationality; local supply structures as well as supplier characteristics and that each and any

> supply locale is likely, if studied closely, to differ in meaningful respects across time and practice to another.

It is useful to begin with the common assumptions about the differences and organisation of the supply of illegal drugs. These differences are about organisational structure (Hough and May 2004), geographical sphere of operation (Coomber et al 2017), level of market segmentation (Pearson and Hobbs 2001) and the use of technology (Aldridge et al. 2017). This can lead to a convenient functional 'tripartite' model often utilised by enforcement agencies to demarcate international, regional and local market divisions of labour which assist the management of risks and resources. Such models are also present in some of the academic literature on international drug markets, particularly in relation to heroin and amphetamines (Chin 2009). However, Sergi (2017:190) indicates some of the weaknesses in policy responses and conceptualisation when she argues:

Whether a group is local, national or international obviously affects policing responses, because location/geography combined with the level of sophistication of the group will differently affect risk and harm assessments to determine the seriousness of the threat. In the local dimension, organised crime groups and gangs overlap, even more so when their structure or activities remain loose and/or limited to street level. This is mirrored in the fragmentation of the response from the various institutions in law enforcement, and the difficulty to understand the actual threat and the dimensions of organised crime as such. Gangs are locally dealt with, they are usually considered more chaotic, more violent than organised crime groups and subject to power struggles over territories.

The tripartite model allows for the construction of an ideal type (Gerth and Mills 1948) of the organisation and operation of drug markets to compare with empirical knowledge of what is happening at different levels of the market. In this model global importers and exporters belong to organised crime syndicates or cartels that facilitate the sale and passage of drugs from one country to another, the middle market comprises regional wholesale networks that facilitate the retail trade in smaller conurbations, and local markets are largely facilitated by user dealers through 'social supply' networks. While it is likely that this tripartite model is imperfect and cannot correspond to all of the characteristics of any one particular case, it is fair to say that certain elements of the model were once common to most cases but are now subject to change and much of this change is in the middle market within a country or region.

Previous ideas about the lower tiers of drug dealing have suggested a significant enactment of social supply with some diversity of business models. Coomber Moyle and South (2016: 255) argue that a

> …high proportion of user-dealers are found within heroin and crack cocaine markets (Bourgeois, 1995; Coomber, 2015; Johnson et al., 1995), with Jacobs (1999) suggesting that, 'by an overwhelming margin', dealers 'that used' dominate the crack scene. Supporting this, Debeck et al. (2007)

> highlight that 41 percent of their sample had generated money for drugs from dealing, and Small et al. (2013) relate that 'most' of their injecting drug user sample had experience of more than one type of dealing.

A degree of diversity of supply mechanisms is supported by Wilson et al. (2002: 240) in their study of drug dealing in seven English neighbourhoods but they also cast doubt over the viability of freelance dealing in some neighbourhoods when they suggest,

> The high number of runners working for dealers in what appears to be a more or less stable alliance, suggests that it is difficult for freelance (usually user/dealers) to enter the market.

Coomber and Moyles (2016) argue that users often make constrained and strategic choices to engage in dealing to fund their drug habits rather than rely on other forms of crime. This is said to account for the less-than-expected levels of acquisitive crime and violence in more recent crack and heroin markets. However, if constrained, choices become affected by changes in the structure of the social field (Bourdieu 1984) in which drugs are distributed, then it follows that user dealers are exposed to different choices in order to acquire drugs for their own personal use (see also Morgan's chapter and Moyle's chapter in this volume).

Similarly, Maitra (2017: 67) refers to the distinctions that have been apparent within the academic literature when demarcating which groups can be characterized as gangs, and which can also be characterised as organised crime:

> Although there is often an overlap between the activities of street gangs and OCGs [Organised Crime Groups], criminologists acknowledge that there are a set of distinct characteristics which apply to each of these two 'categories'. On the one hand, street gangs–a younger membership base, involvement in general 'low-level' delinquency, spontaneous violence, and street-presence... OCGs, however, are recognised as distinct criminal entities, usually involving older offenders, more systematic and planned offending, a greater focus on pecuniary gain and a level of governance being imposed upon the territories where their members operate.

Pitts (2008:37) suggests less separation between organised crime groups and local street gangs in his 'articulated super gang' model of gang structure. This model suggests the possibility that English street gangs can shade into serious organised crime by providing a semi-structured workforce for the factory floor of the international drugs business (Castells 1997). The model gives a different emphasis from the findings of Decker and Pyrooz (2013:290) who observed that street gangs are unlikely to be involved in high-level organised crime due to their volatility and lack of organisational structure. They suggest,

> ...gangs make unattractive partners for organised criminal groups because of their informal and diffuse organisational structure, public and street-oriented exposure, and expressive and cafeteria-style rather than instrumental and specialised offending patterns. Second, it is inappropriate to conclude, due to their limited organisational structure, that gangs are an association of criminals as opposed to a criminal association.

In order to explore these differences Decker and Pyrooz (2013) suggest that it is useful to explore the structure, processes, cultural orientations and activities of organised crime groups as compared with street gangs. Nevertheless, it is important to remember national differences, apparent between organised crime in different countries. Decker and Pyrooz (2013) primarily focus on organised criminal groups in America, where members of such groups operate on a business model to provide goods and services. Considering these international differences, Sergi (2017) suggests that pressures exist to define English organised crime differently than the widespread definitions of international organised crime groups to avoid the connotations associated with the term 'Mafia'. She argues that,

> Decker and Pyrooz (2013) suggest some overlap in the characteristics of organised crime and gang related crime but point to differences in organisation or the degree in which a group can effectively co-ordinate activities in a structured way. Hagedorn (1993), for example, frames this distinction in terms of the level of organisation in drug markets; i.e. whether gangs were organised drug distributors or gang members were "freelance" drug dealers. Decker and Pyrooz (2013) review mainly US literature on gang organisation and suggest that the debate regarding street gangs as part of organised crime can be divided into two camps...

The two perspectives from this debate include the instrumental-rational (organised) and informal-diffuse (disorganised). These perspectives developed originally out of the debate surrounding the extent to which gangs controlled the increasingly violent street drug markets in the late 1980s and early 1990s in the United States.

While Decker and Pyrooz's (2013) review is mainly of the American literature, such distinctions are by no means confined to the US drug market. Indeed, British criminologists have also formulated differentiations with regard to the varying levels of involvement gangs have with the drug marketplace. For example, Maitra (2017:70) notes:

> One of the principal functions of many gangs is drug-dealing, and different gangs have different levels of involvement within the drug market. In the UK, existing studies have presented a hierarchical model of the drug-market ... ranging from "middle-to-apex market level" to "low-to-mid levels" ... Within Scotland, for example, youth criminal gangs have been identified

as primarily engaging in the latter category of drug-dealing, whilst serious organised crime gangs have been identified as engaging in the former category. Youth street gangs are a further, distinct category: they are looser, less organised entities than either youth criminal gangs or organised crime gangs) and engage predominantly in the social supply of drugs.

In order to analyse the links between English street gangs and organised crime it is useful to explore the context of generative mechanisms in which both street gangs and organised crime arise.

The context of new and emerging crack and heroin markets

Seddon (2006) explains that heroin use in the UK in the 1940s and 1950s was exceptionally rare, before making an upturn in its use in the 1960s, primarily due to over-prescribing. He argues that into the 1970s heroin was not associated with any particular socio-economic group, with links between crime and drugs being limited. The 1980s brought about significant changes with the arrival of cheap 'brown' heroin from Afghanistan via Pakistan which was said to increase the annual numbers of new heroin addicts notified to the Home Office from 1,151 in 1980 to 5,930 in 1985 (Home Office 1990 cited in Seddon, 2006). Seddon further describes the spread of heroin markets across the main cities to the west of the country with new heroin users being reported in Liverpool, Manchester, and Glasgow, where previously heroin use was rare. He argues that the socio-demographic profile of the new heroin users was primarily young unemployed people living in relatively deprived neighbourhoods thus linking heroin use with social disadvantage. Pearson (2001) explains the local backdrop of the 1980s' opiate epidemic as a clustering of social problems which relate to high unemployment, poor housing, high rates of crime, heroin dealing and use.

The UK drug epidemic of the 1980s witnessed a drug–crime connection with users becoming involved in drug dealing, prostitution and acquisitive crime (Parker and Newcombe 1987). Wilson et al (2002) undertook a study of crack and heroin markets in seven neighbourhoods each classified as being among the highest 10% of relatively deprived neighbourhoods in England. In this study they charted a fusion of crack and heroin markets in the mid- to late-1980s – reporting that by 1991/1992 most of the cocaine in the drug market was sold in the form of crack. Since 1994 the growth in both crack users and sellers had risen sharply.

The context of gangs and organised crime in London Liverpool and Manchester

Hobbs (2001) suggests that the fragmentation of both traditional working class neighbourhoods and local labour markets has created arenas that have made it difficult for family-based units to establish the kind of local dominance they enjoyed in the 1950s and 1960s. He argues that these circumstances lend themselves to more flexible networks than the previous neighbourhood family firms such as the Krays and the Richardsons. Hobbs (2013) describes how the 'underworld' of London developed throughout the 20th century so as to become populated by a range of different criminal gangs and networks, rather than solely being the preserve of the 'faces' of the 1950s and 1960s. According to Hobbs (2001), the activities of the local family firm have become 'glocal', that is, local in nature but global in reach. Sergi (2017: 182) develops these themes of transition and change when she describes organisational developments in both gangs and organised crime in Liverpool during the 1980s. She argues,

> The picture of social exclusion, gangs, gun trade and youth crime in Liverpool, therefore, appears mixed up with higher levels crime firms: there is, for example, a link between young people in gangs, firearms and drug trade (Hansard 2007). Liverpool has a reputation of being one of the main hubs of drug trafficking, importation and smuggling in the UK, also thanks to the presence of the most successful drug traffickers and criminal networks, exploiting the port and local gang life (Pearson and Hobbs, 2004) Groups like the Liverpool Mafia, for example, have made the history of the city. The Liverpool Mafia was a drug-dealing alliance emerged after the Toxteth riots in 1981 between white middle-aged bank robbers and young black gangsters.
>
> *Sergi 2017: 182*

Similarly, Pitts (2011:171) also draws on a continuum between international drug supply chains and the local neighbourhood and gangs in analysing Class A drug distribution in Manchester. He argues,

> If we consider class A drugs distribution in Manchester, from the 1980s to the present day, as a social system, constituted by interconnected roles, regulated by inter-related norms and performing a specific set of social functions (Parsons 1937), we are drawn inexorably to the conclusion that a changing cast of around 400 to 500 young people, from a handful of Manchester neighbourhoods, functioned as the economic conduit whereby locally produced dance drugs, heroin from the poppy fields of Afghanistan and Cocaine from the coca farms of South America found their way to 'end-users' on the street corners and in the nightclubs of Manchester for over 20 years.

This relatively recent development, which sees a 'streamlined' model of drug distribution, is indicative of the Hernandez's (2013) 'capitalistic turn' whereby educated competent migrant workers are introduced into the workforce. Pitts's (2011) description of a 'changing cast' of street youth acting as the 'economic conduit' for drug distribution is illustrative of gang practices that place pecuniary advantage ahead of older, orthodox motivations behind gang affiliation, such as kinship and neighbourhood solidarity. Similarly, in Maitra's (2017) study of gangs in Manchester, members of drugs gangs articulated a model of operation similar to that outlined by Pitts (2011), whereby gang members would create distance between themselves and the street dealers to reduce risks. For gang members, the primary, if not sole, motivator behind gang activity was financial gain. However, through 'co-opting' younger, street dealers for the physical act of drug-dealing, gang members could protect themselves from the vicissitudes of the violent, volatile street market place. This rendered the drugs gangs, in some respects, as being closer to the archetypal organised crime group, and these changes to gang activities and practices also caused questions to be raised, in gang members' own minds, as to whether they truly were part of a 'gang'. Maitra (2017:109) quotes one respondent, an importer/middleman, who noted following about his gang's direct relationship with street dealers:

> We'd just get the drugs and then start up by ourselves...go somewhere, like a destination. After importing, we'd set up shop there and sell it on to the street dealers, just Class A's really. I was importing it and I'd make my money off it. And, I suppose, in a way we were a gang, but I think a gang's more when you're doing everything together. Like standing on the street corners. But after making money, we'd go for a drink and then we'd go home to our girlfriends. We wouldn't be out on the streets and stuff like that. For us it was about making money, to buy nice houses, cars, take the kids on holiday. But it gets called a drugs gang.

At the lower tiers of criminal networks, Hobbs (2001) suggests that there is a reserve army of labour to draw on for short term contracts or jobs on behalf of crime groups. Indeed, a parallel can be drawn between the rise of such short term 'contracts' between drug dealers and crime groups, and the rise of precarious employment more generally, again, illustrating the parallels between the legitimate and illegitimate economies. More recently Andell and Pitts (2018) describe an increasingly durable model of gang involvement in the drugs business (see also Treadwell and Kelly's chapter in this volume). This involvement utilises the exploitation of young and vulnerable people in the development of new distribution mechanisms of crack and heroin across the UK. Andell and Pitts (2017) describe a well-organised drug distribution network linking back to second and third generations of London street gangs who exploit a range of vulnerabilities to recruit participants to the lower levels of drug dealing and coerced social supply from cuckooed premises.

English gang involvement in UK markets

There has been increased scrutiny towards the involvement of English gangs within UK drug markets (see, e.g., Densely 2013; Maitra 201 Andell and Pitts 2018). However, in order to situate these gangs within the wider criminal marketplace, one needs to consider the international space within which the production, transportation and consumption of illegal drugs occur. This does not stop at delivering a descriptive account of these transnational drugs networks, but also involves a critical analysis of the role played by state and non-state actors in the drugs economy. This is particularly true for certain drugs, such as heroin (Chin 2009; Paoli et al. 2009), cocaine (Hernandez 2013) and amphetamines (Chin 2009). At a national level in producer countries, there is significant financial gain to be made, often with the implicit or explicit support of agents of the state, including law enforcement and political figures (Hernandez 2013). The financial gains made in these 'upper echelons' of drug trafficking rarely translate down to the 'street' level (Venkatesh 2005). Indeed, it is interesting to note that recent English studies have predominantly focused on these 'street' level dealers. Nevertheless, there is a wider hierarchy that needs to be considered when analysing the involvement of English gangs in UK drugs markets. Maitra (2017:109), for example, presents the following account from a 'gang leader' into how his gang organised its practices in the national crack cocaine and heroin markets:

> My charge is conspiracy to supply Class A's. Heroin. And what about the supply networks? You see, there's people who do it, and they don't do it properly. And there's people who do it, who do it like a business. You get your product. You know there's a market for it. You're marketing. People gonna know you got good stuff. So, you give out your samples, your freebies, so people check it. And they know it's good, yeh? Right. So, everyone's happy. You do your marketing; you got your customers. Wholesale, then you got your retail–your street dealers. So, it works as a proper network. You see people higher up the chain who give it to the kids, they split it up, then to their people, split it up. You got the people who break it down into ounces, then sometimes you have the person who just sells it as 4 ½ ozs, bigger amounts, then they break it down in ounces, break it down to wraps, and then the supplier who gives it to you in keys, gives it to you in kilos, yeh? And the reasons the gangs are formulated is because cos now everyone's trying to rob them. They need protection.

Andell (2019) argues that there is significant evidence to suggest that the practices of some English gangs have evolved into reconstituted drugs distribution networks which now cover large parts of the UK. It is argued that this evolution is not inevitable but contingent on the global features of availability of class A drugs and the local bridging capital of pre-existing criminal networks. Andell (2019:221) asserts,

> Pre-existing crime opportunity structures are an important feature in understanding potential transitions in contemporary UK gangs. An analysis of the opportunities and access to the middle drugs market is crucial

> in explaining the potential evolution of street gangs into the realms of organised crime. Pre-existing criminal structures provide systems of relations which hold between internally related social positions that individuals can occupy and broader organised criminal networks. The position of what Hobbs might term the "family firm" was often located by professionals at the lower tiers of the middle market.

The question remains as to if these reconstituted networks can be classified as organised crime.

Reconstituted middle market networks and local organised crime

At the turn of the century, Pearson and Hobbs (2001:15) described the middle market as a level above retail whereby participants are at arm's length from the retail risks of the street. The more recent organisational transformations of crack and heroin markets undertaken by some former street gangs who have distanced themselves from the streets call into question previous understandings of the middle market and organised crime. The question of whether the middle market can be viewed as 'organised crime' is an issue which Pearson and Hobbs have previously analysed. They suggested that despite differences in ideas about what constitutes organised crime (Hagan 1993; Maltz , 1985; Albanese 1996; Ruggiero 1996), there are significant defining features that constitute organised crime – these include the groups exerting some degree of informal governance over their territories (Varese 2001), the numbers of individuals involved, the time span over which established criminal activities take place and the reach of the criminal network. Indeed, organised crime groups:

> are characterised by a number of specific features: a more systematic approach to their activities, more sophistication in the crime committed, and a greater degree of codification. In particular, their activities are often more serious and endemic in their nature than offences committed by street gangs.
>
> *Maitra 2015:96*

Andell and Pitts' (2018) recent assessment of county lines suggests that some street gangs now operate in the middle market for crack and heroin and shade into what can be described as local organised crime groups. Second- or third-generation street gangs fulfil the criteria of organised crime groups mentioned above by enabling a clear distance between themselves and the retail action by utilising vulnerable children and adults to transport and retail drugs. They have embedded these activities over time whereby individuals may be removed from the network through enforcement but control over drug market activity is maintained by the gang. The NCA (2017) suggests that the majority of the country is covered by county line networks and that these networks are a national threat.

Andell and Pitts (2018) agree that middle level drug markets are flexible and are constantly adapting to changes in enforcement tactics, but they further suggest that hierarchical relations of exploitation and domination also exist in the lower middle market and these power relations are utilised to frequently move relatively small quantities of drugs to a well-established customer base. They found that:

> The drugs coming from the metropolis are usually hidden in luggage or taped to the bodies of the 'Youngers' who transport them from the metropolis on public transport, but they may also be secreted in the bodily orifices of the young people. This latter method, 'plugging', makes the trafficking more secure since the police have neither the equipment nor the powers to detect or detain these 'mules'. As we have noted, the pattern of supply appears to be 'little and often', or 'just in time' to borrow a term from commerce.
>
> *Andell and Pitts 2018:17*

Once drugs are in a reasonable proximity of the end user/buyer, a more flexible model of franchise and entrepreneurship takes place. Drugs are usually delivered to a residence taken over by a local gang (trap house). Gang 'elders' operate and manage the franchise, ensuring that discipline is maintained and the retail end of the drugs business runs smoothly while gang 'youngers' from local or metropolitan gangs are left in the trap house to serve up drugs, keep the tenant under control and collect money from buyers. Evidence from the police and housing professionals suggests that the metropolitan elders may be staying in a separate house or flat maybe belonging to a vulnerable young woman with whom they have deliberately struck up a relationship, while trusted youngers operate and manage the 'cuckooed' flats or trap houses belonging to a local Class A drug addict who is paid in drugs for the use of their homes or subjected to threats or violence to make it available. It is here that the overlap between a new coerced social supply and organised county lines networks is visible.

Andell and Pitts (2018) report co-option of local crime families or the family firm into new arrangements of county line dealing networks from larger cities. Where co-operation has not happened or control is challenged, increases in violence occur, which is sometimes lethal. It would therefore appear that a new middle market is being established, which combines the muscle of street gangs with the connections of the family firm. Arlacchi (1986) describes these practices as building 'protective enclaves' which discourages rivals and competitors. It would appear from Andell and Pitts' (2018) work that gang elders are the middle managers of the crack and heroin business. They organise gang youngers who undertake the local distribution and collect payments. The drugs are packaged for sale and the youngers and other drug users are sent off to deliver the drugs to end users and collect money from them. This new 'business model' for drug-dealing factors in both the practical benefits of exploiting vulnerable young people (e.g. the lower likelihood of very young adolescents and females being stopped-and-searched by the police) as well as forming solidified gang-networks, combining the powers of street gangs and established family firms to better combat the exigent demands of the modern 'underworld'.

In order to understand the described transitions of peer group to gang and then to local organised crime group, it is useful to consider collective subjectivities. Such groupings are not given as finished entities but as emerging social products that are locally and socially constructed in concrete situations of action such as those enacted with county line drug distribution. Vandenbergh (2014) argues that within certain collective subjectivities, symbolic identities can transform and structure individuals into a quasi-group and then into a

n organised group, which in the case of county line drug dealing can represent its members in their absence. These transformations take place as a result of collective actions in an operative chain. Such actions can also be demonstrated in the co-ordination of violence which is associated with county line drug dealing networks (Black 2020).

Changes in supply and the impact on violence

Andell and Pitts' (2017) research suggests that levels of violence in the drugs market depend on both the duration of the relationship between the user and the dealer and whether distribution is controlled by a gang or not (Taniguchi et al. 2011; Venkatesh 2008; Coomber 2015, see also Ayres and Treadwell's chapter in this volume). Referring to gang control of the market, a respondent in Andell and Pitt's (2017:21) study said,

> Now it's not only for financial gain, it's about, you know, the kudos, the respect. They change into a character that they're perceived or expected to be. Yeah. If you're working for a county line you must act like this you must think another way and most certainly look like this (pulls a hard face). There's almost an occupational culture here. Definitely and with that comes the threat of violence.

The use of threats and violence is ever present in markets that lack formal regulation. Pearson and Hobbs (2003) suggest that contracts between drug sellers and customers cannot be enforced through legal recourse and therefore grievances or non-compliance are enforced through slights to reputation, cuts in trading ties (supply ceases), threats or as a last resort violence. Violence is sometimes characterised as an atypical activity, the idea being that violence, albeit a functional tool, is bad for business as it attracts attention of law enforcement agencies (Mohamed and Fritsvold 2010; Taylor and Potter 2013).

However, recent evidence from Carol Black's review (2020:10) suggests

> The rise in the county lines business model seems to be a major factor in increased drug-related violence in the UK, alongside the related factors of the growth in the crack cocaine market and the increasing role of young people in drug supply.

These findings tend to contradict the accepted wisdom that violence is bad for the drugs business and may point to a distribution model in transition. However, violence in new drug dealing arrangements need not be inevitable. If the local community has a high level of 'collective efficacy' with the capacity to band together to mobilise the relevant agencies and individuals, then drug-related violence will be low (Berg and Rengifo 2009).

Andell and Pitts (2018) have analysed the importance of context in their analysis of gangs and county lines. They have observed changes in the economics of drug supply and policy practices that have resulted in the emergence of what can be observed and classified as local organised crime. Andell and Pitts (2017:20) in their research regarding vulnerable young people and gangs in a County town observed recent changes in organisation of the drugs markets. A former drug dealer said,

> What I see now is much more commercial. People coming out constantly 'do you want this do you want that'. Yeah and that's again about that pyramid selling technique you know but the family allegiance is still there…But they (city dealers) steal those gains. The family allegiances are clinging onto it but you've changed from the main dealer with a couple of people, to these unknown faces. …It's much more dangerous. I mean the new round is about the open market drug delivery … the phone comes out … mountain bike delivery or a closed market working from a house which with the old school dealer that would be his home. But when you've got an open market of 10 hoodies on the corner, in a park, who would be replaced by 10 the next day, what is your quality control or your customer service should it all go tits up. So the big risk of going to somewhere like that is going to get robbed … And going to be ripped off.

It is apparent that interactions in some of these new criminal organisations are symbolically regulated by violence and strategically co-ordinated. This impacts the local drug dealing networks that exploit children and vulnerable people in order to meet the most profitable end in the most efficacious way. At this level the alternative economy of drug supply appears to adopt practices which reflect the ruthlessness of exploitation in areas of a legitimate market economy (see Hall and Antonopoulos' chapter, Ayres and Taylor's chapter and Linnemann and Medley's chapter in this volume).

Conclusions

The above analysis contends that local drug markets at the middle and lower ends in the UK (particularly those catering for heroin and crack) are becoming more organised and durable largely due to the greater participation of urban gangs looking to increase their market share through a supply-led increase in demand. It is argued that second- or third-generation street gangs have in some locations expanded and regulated the drugs business by co-opting or eliminating competing distribution mechanisms (Andell and Pitts 2018). It is further suggested that street gang elders operating markets in crack and heroin largely remain free to develop durable business models (Spicer 2018) by maintaining a safer distance from enforcement agencies through the exploitation of vulnerable adults and children in the drugs business. This safer distance is further insulated by the deployment of fewer drug enforcement resources during a time of public sector cuts and economic austerity (Beck 2011). In order to substantiate these claims recent empirical research has been analysed in ways which give priority to potentiality or causal mechanisms over actuality or observed events (Vandenbergh 2014). While earlier gang typologies (see, e.g., Yablonsky 1959) delineate different gang 'types', the increasing fluidity of gang structures, activities and practices is indicative of the fact that contemporary gangs may develop from one 'type' to another. Decker and Pyrooz (2013: 298) suggest that it is possible for gangs to move away from the street and become more organised, and when this happens, they are perhaps better described as durable organised crime groups. They argue,

> It is perhaps more useful to conceptualise gangs along a normal distribution of organisation, with informal-diffuse at one end and instrumental-rational at the other. A point is reached, however, when a gang becomes so organised and institutionalised that it departs from "street gang" criteria and enters into the definitional parameters of an "organised crime group".

At present, policy analysis and recommendations do not appear to be as inclusive as they might be to combat these new arrangements. This is due in part to definitional and methodological problems which feed unhelpful demarcation of professional territory. As highlighted in the introduction to the chapter, David Lammy, MP, reminds us of the need for a more cohesive strategic policy approach. In order to develop such an approach there needs to be a rethinking and exploration of how gangs and organised crime groups interrelate within a multi-layered social field. This may mean a move away from previous classifications which separate agency efforts via 'taxonomic categories' of crime and its attendant jurisdiction and area coverage towards an analysis which understands 'relational and structured groups'. Such a focus would not only promote coordinated drug supply and demand reduction strategies to reduce harms, but also would emphasise actions on the causal mechanisms which sit below these harms.

References

Akhtar, S. and South, N. (2000) "Hidden from heroin's history": Heroin use and dealing within an English Asian community—A case study. In M. Hough and M. Natarajan (eds.), *Illegal Drug Markets: From Research to Prevention Policy . Crime Prevention Studies,* Volume 11. Monsey, NY: Criminal Justice Press.

Albanese, J. S. (1996). *Organized Crime in America.* Wiltshire: Anderson Publishing Company.

Aldridge, J., Measham, F., and Williams, L. (2011) *Illegal Leisure Revisited: Changing Patterns of Alcohol and Drug Use in Adolescents and Young Adults.* London: Routledge.

Aldridge, J., Steven, A. and Barratt, M.J. (2017) *Will Growth in Cryptomarket Drug Buying Increase the Harms of Illicit Drugs?* First published: 02 August 2017. https://doi.org/10.1111/add.13899 (Accessed 30 March 2020).

Andell, P. and Pitts, J. (2017) *Preventing the Violent and Sexual Victimisation of Vulnerable Gang-Involved and Gang-Affected Children and Young People in Ipswich.* Commissioned by Suffolk's Public Health and Community Safety Team. A Report for Suffolk's Public Health and Community Safety Team. ISBN: 978-1-913160-04-3. www.uos.ac.uk/sites/default/files/Research%20Report%20by%20Paul%20Andell%20and%20John%20Pitts.pdf (Accessed 30 March 2020).

Andell, P. and Pitts, J. (2018) The end of the line? The impact of county lines drug distribution on youth crime in a target destination. *Youth and Policy.* www.youthandpolicy.org/articles/the-end-of-the-line/ (Accessed 20 March 2020).

Andell, P. (2019) *Thinking Seriously About Gangs. Towards A Critical Realist Approach.* London Palgrave.

Arlacchi, P. (1986) *Mafia Business: The Mafia Ethic and the Spirit of Capitalism.* London: Verso.

Beck, H. (2011) Drug enforcement in an age of austerity. Key findings from a survey of police forces in England. *UK Drug Policy Commission.* www.ukdpc.org.uk/wp-content/uploads/Evidence%20review%20 %20Drug%20enforcement%20in%20an%20age%20of%20austerity_%20findings%20from%20a%20survey%20of%20police%20in%20England.pdf (Accessed 19 June 2018).

Bennett, T. and Holloway, K. (2004) Gang membership, drugs and crime in the UK. *British Journal of Criminology,* 44(3):305–323.

Black, C. (2020) *Review of drugs: phase one report. The first part of Dame Carol Black's independent review of drugs.* www.gov.uk/government/publications/review-of-drugs-phase-one-report (Accessed 20 March 2020).

Bourdieu, P. (1984) *Distinction: A Social Critique of the Judgement of Taste.* (R. Nice, Trans). Cambridge, MA: Harvard University Press.

Berg, M. T. and Rengifo, A. F. (2009) Rethinking community organization and robbery: Considering illicit market dynamics. *Journal Justice Quarterly,* 26(2): 211–237.

Bourgois, P. (1995) *In Search of Respect: Selling Crack Cocaine in El Barrio.* Cambridge: Cambridge University Press.

Chin, K. (2009) *The Golden Triangle: Inside South-east Asia's Drug Trade.* New York: Cornell University Press.

Cohen, S. (1972 *Folk Devils and Moral Panics: The Creation of the Mods and Rockers, Martin Robertson.* Oxford. 2nd edn first published 1972.

Coomber, R. (2004) Drug use and drug market intersections. *Addiction Research & Theory,* 12: 501–505.

Coomber, R. (2006) *Pusher Myths: Re-Situating the Drug Dealer.* London: Free Association Press.

Coomber, R. (2010) Reconceptualising drug markets and drug dealers—the need for change. *Drugs and Alcohol Today*, 10, 10–13.

Coomber, R. (2015) A tale of two cities: understanding differences in levels of heroin/crack market-related violence—A two city comparison. *Criminal Justice Review*, 40(1): 7–31.

Coomber, R., Moyle, L. and South, N. (2015) The normalisation of drug supply: The social supply of drugs as the "other side" of the history of normalisation. *Drugs: Education, Prevention and Policy*. 23(3): 255–263.

Coomber, R. and Moyle, L. (2018) The changing shape of street-level heroin and crack supply in England: Commuting, holidaying and cuckooing drug dealers across 'county lines'. *The British Journal of Criminology*, 58(6):1323–1342. doi:10.1093/bjc/azx068

Coomber, R., Moyle, L., Belackova, V., Decorte, T., Hakkarainen, P., Hathaway, A., Laidler, K. J., Lenton, S., Murphy, S., Scott, J., Stefunkova, M., van de Ven, K., Vlaemynck, M., and Werse, B. (2018) The burgeoning recognition and accommodation of the social supply of drugs in international criminal justice systems: An eleven-nation comparative overview. *International Journal of Drug Policy*, 58, 93–103, ISSN 0955-3959.

Castells, M. (1997) The power of identity, the information age. *Economy, Society and Culture,* Volume 11. Oxford, Blackwell.

Decker, S.H. and Pyrooz, D. (2013) Gangs: Another form of organized crime? In L. Paoli's (ed.), *The Oxford Handbook of Organized Crime*. New York: Oxford University Press.

Densley, J., McLean, R., Deuchar, R. and Harding, S. (2018). An altered state? Emergent changes to illicit drug markets and distribution networks in Scotland. *International Journal of Drug Policy*, 58, 113–120.

Dorn, N., Murji, K. and South, N. (1992) *Traffickers: Drug Markets and Law Enforcement*. London: Routledge.

Dorn, N. and South, N. (1990) Drug markets and law enforcement. Nicholas Source: *The British Journal of Criminology*, 30(2) (Spring 1990):171–188.

Disley, E. and Liddle, M. (2016) Local perspectives in ending gang and youth violence areas perceptions of the nature of urban street gangs. Research Report 88: 12.

Decker and Pyrooz (2013) Gangs another form of organized crime? In *The Oxford Handbook of Organized Crime* Edited by Letizia Paoli.

DeBeck, K., Shannon, K., Wood, E., Li, K., Montaner, J., and Kerr, T. (2007) Income generating activities of people who inject drugs. *Drug and Alcohol Dependence*, 91(1): 50–56, ISSN 0376-8716.

Dorn, N., Murji, K. and South, N. (1992) *Traffickers: Drug Markets and Law Enforcement*. Abingdon, England: Routledge.

Gerth, H. and Mills, C.W. (1948) *From Max Weber: Essays in Sociology*. London: Routledge and Kegan Paul.

Hagan, J. (1993) The social embeddedness of crime and inequality. *Criminology*, 31(4): 465–491.

Hagedorn, J. (1993) *A World of Gangs, Armed Young Men and Gangsta Culture*. University of Minnesota Press.

Hallsworth, S. and Young, T. (2008) Gang talk and gang talkers: A critique. *Crime Media Culture*, 4:75–195.

Hansard. (2007) Crimes of violence, 457: debated on Wednesday 7 March 2007 https://hansard.parliament.uk/commons/2007-03-07/debates/070307133000008/CrimesOfViolence (Accessed 3.4.2023)

Hansard: Debate on the Serious Violence Strategy, May 30, (2018) David Lammy MP for Tottenham. www.davidlammy.co.uk/single-post/2018/05/30/Debate-on-the-Serious-Violence-Strategy (Accessed 30 July 2018).

Hernandez, A. (2013) *Narcoland: The Mexican Drug Lords and Their Godfathers*. London: Verso Books.

Hobbs, D. (1998) Going down the glocal: The local context of organised crime. *The Howard Journal of Criminal Justice*, 37(4):407–422.

Hobbs, D. (2001) The firm. Organizational logic and criminal culture on a shifting terrain. *The British Journal of Criminology*, 41(4): 549–560.

Hobbs, D. (2013) *Lush Life: Constructing Organized Crime in the UK*. Oxford: Oxford University Press.

Jacobs, B. A. (1999) *Dealing Crack: The Social World of Streetcorner Selling*. Boston, MA: Northeastern University Press.

Johnson, B. D., Golub, A., and Fagan, J. (1995) Careers in crack, drug use, drug distribution, and nondrug criminality. *Crime and Delinquency*, 41: 275–295.

Lea, J. and Young, J. (1984) *What Is to be Done about Law and Order*. Harmondsworth, England: Penguin.

Maltz, M. (1985) Toward defining organized crime. In H.E. Alexander and G. Caiden (eds.), *The Politics and Economics of Organized Crime*. Lexington, MA: D.C. Heath.

Maitra, D.R. (2015 "It's a vicious game": Youth gangs, street violence and organised crime in modern Britain. In S. Harding and M. Palasinski (eds.), *Global Perspectives on Youth Gang Behavior, Violence, and Weapons Use*. Pennsylvania: IGI Global.

Maitra, D.R. (2017) *Gangs, Race and 'the Street' in Prison: An Inductive Analysis*. Doctoral Thesis. Cambridge: University of Cambridge.

Maltz, M. D. (1976) On defining "organized grime": The development of a definition and a typology. *Crime & Delinquency*, 22(3), 338–346. https://doi.org/10.1177/001112877602200306

Matrix Knowledge Group. (2007) *The Illicit Drug Trade in the United Kingdom*. (Home Office Online Report 20/07). London, England: Crown Copyright. Retrieved from https://webarchive.nationalarchives.gov.uk/20110218141356/ http://rds.homeoffice.gov.uk/rds/pdfs07/rdsolr2007.pdf.

May, T. and Hough, M. (2004) Drug markets and distribution systems. *Addiction Research & Theory*, 12(6): 549–563.

Mohamed, A. R. and Fritsvold, E. D. (2010) *Dorm Room Dealers: Drugs and the Privileges of Race and Class*. Boulder, CO: Lynne Reinner Publishers.

National Crime Agency. (2017) *County Lines, Violence, Exploitation & Drug Supply 2017*. London, National Crime Agency (NCA). www.nationalcrimeagency.gov.uk/who-we-are/publications/234-county-lines-violen-ce-exploitation-drug-supply-2017/file (Accessed 30 March 2020).

National Crime Agency. (2019) County lines drug supply, vulnerability and harm 2018. https://nationalcrimeagency.gov.uk/who-we-are/publications/257-county-lines-drug-supply-vulnerability-and-harm-2018/file (Accessed 30 March 2020).

National Crime Agency. (2016) County lines gang violence, exploitation & drug supply 2016. 0346-CAD National Briefing Report. www.nationalcrimeagency.gov.uk/who-we-are/publications/15-county-lines-gang-violence-exploitation-and-drug-supply-2016/file (Accessed 20 March 2020).

Paoli, L., Greenfield, V. A., and Reuter, P. (2009) *The World Heroin Market: Can Supply Be Cut?*. New York: Oxford University Press.

Parker, H. (2001) Unenforceable? How you Britons obtain their drugs. In H. Parker, J. Aldridge and R. Egginton (eds.), *UK Drugs Unlimited: New Research and Policy Lessons on Illicit Drug Use.* Basingstoke: Palgrave.

Parker, H. and Measham, F. (1994) Pick 'n' mix: Changing patterns of illicit drug use amongst 1990s adolescents. *Drugs: Education, Prevention and Policy*, 1(1):5–13.

Parker, H., Bakx, K. and Newcombe, R. (1987) The new heroin users. Prevalence and characteristics in Wirral, Merseyside. *British Journal of Addiction*, 82: 147–158.

Pearson, G. and Hobbs, D. (2001) Middle market drug distribution. *Home Office Research Study* no. 224. London: Home Office.

Parsons, T. (1937). *The Structure of Social Action.* New York: McGrawHill.

Pearson, G. and Hobbs, D. (2003) 'King pin? A case study of a middle market drug broker. *Howard Journal of Criminal Justice*, 42(4), 335–347.

Pearson, G. and Hobbs, D. (2004) "E" is for enterprise: Middle level drug markets in ecstasy and stimulants. *Addiction Research & Theory,* 12(6):565–576.

Pitts, J. (2008) *Reluctant Gangsters: The Changing Face of Youth Crime.* Cullompton, England: Willan.

Pitts, J. (2011) Mercenary territory: Are youth gangs really a problem? In B. Goldson (ed.), *Youth in Crisis? 'Gangs', Territoriality and Violence* (pp. 161–182). Abingdon, England: Routledge.

Ruggiero, V. (2006) *Understanding Political Violence.* London/New York: Open University Press.

Ruggiero, V. (1996) *Organized and Corporate Crime in Europe: Offers That Can't Be Refused*, Aldershot et al. (eds.). Dartmouth.

Seddon, T. (2006) Drugs, crime and social exclusion: Social context and social theory in British drugs–crime research. *The British Journal of Criminology*, 46(4):680–703.

Sergi, A. (2017) *From Mafia to Organised Crime: A Comparative Analysis of Policing Models*, Palgrave Macmillan US.

Small, W., Maher, L., Lawlor, J., Wood, E., Shannon, K., and Kerr, T. (2013) Injection drug users' involvement in drug dealing in the downtown eastside of Vancouver: Social organization and systemic violence. *International Journal of Drug Policy*, 24(5): 479–487. doi: 10.1016/j.drugpo.2013.03.006. Epub 2013 May 8. PMID: 23664788; PMCID: PMC3911907.

Spicer J. (2018) 'That's their brand, their business': How police officers are interpreting county lines. *Policing and Society: An International Journal of Research and Policy.* https://doi.org/10.1080/10439463.2018.1445742 (Accessed 19 June 2018).

Taniguchi, T. A., Ratcliffe, J. H., and Taylor, R. B. (2011) Gang set space, drug markets, and crime around drug corners in Camden. *Journal of Research in Crime and Delinquency*, 48(3): 327–363. https://doi.org/10.1177/0022427810393016

Taylor, M., and Potter, G. R. (2013) From "social supply" to "real dealing": Drift, friendship, and trust in drug-dealing careers. *Journal of Drug Issues*, 43(4), 392–406. https://doi.org/10.1177/0022042612474974

Vandenbergh, F. (2014) What Is Critical About Critical Realism. Essays in Reconstructive Social Theory. Routledge.

Varese, F. (2001) *The Russian Mafia: Private Protection in a New Market Economy.* Oxford: Oxford University Press.

Venkatesh, S. (2008) *Gang Leader for a Day: A Rogue Sociologist Takes to the Streets.* London: Penguin Books.

Walklate, S. and Evans, K. (1999) *Zero Tolerance or Community Tolerance: Managing Crime in High Crime Areas.* Aldershot: Ashgate.

Wilson et al. (2002) Heroin and crack cocaine markets in deprived areas: Seven local case studies. *Supplement to Home Office Research Study 240*, 'A Rock and a Hard Place: Drug Markets in Deprived Neighbourhoods'. www.homeoffice.gov.uk/rds/horspubs1.html).

Windle, J. and Briggs, D. (2015) 'It's like working away for two weeks': The harms associated with young drug dealers commuting from a saturated London drug market. *Crime Prevention and Community Safety*, 17(2):105–119.

Yablonsky, L. (1959) The delinquent gang as a near group. *Social Problems*, 7(2):108–117.

13

VIOLENCE, GRIME, GANGS AND DRUGS ON THE SOUTH SIDE OF BIRMINGHAM

James Treadwell and Craig Kelly

Introduction

This chapter seeks to provide something of an alternative framing of the problems of inner city drug dealing as is commonly understood in criminology, setting to consider context, character and motives of drug dealing particularly in Britain's second city, Birmingham, and amongst young men on and around several of the most deprived estates in the city. In this chapter we suggest that while this has been framed to some extent around the issue of gangs, the reality is that for several years relatively disorganised and chaotic low-level drug dealing has involved an array of young men, some (though by no means all) linked to emerging music scenes. This has led to similar use of the lexicon of gangs, youth, organised crime and 'grime' music, the reality on such estates is high level of quite regular, chaotic and disorganised crime that is linked to both the social structures (including local authority housing policy) that have particularly impacted some of the poorest housing estates to the south of the city. In this piece, based on qualitative and ethnographic engagement on and around those areas (areas where the author and several members of his family were raised, attended schools and resided) and wider cultural criminological analysis of context and place, we seek to provide an alternative characterisation of the role, place and function of drug economies and cultures in urban estates marked by cultural anelpis (Hornsby and Hall 1995)This critical realist representation both challenges some of the logic of criminological work on gangs and organised crime, and particularly emergent notions of county lines, exploited vulnerability (see Andell and colleague's chapter in this volume). Rather, that the instrumental drug dealing and associated crime that tends to run high in some postcodes are much more complex than being gang crime, but rather reflects the messy realities of street-level dealing that is remarkably unprofitable, unfulfilling and unrewarding but forms the first rung of the ladder

DOI: 10.4324/9781351010245-15

in organised criminality that connects local to national and international. It involves substantial risk so much so that it is phenomenally stupid. Its participants run the risk of being robbed, assaulted, caught and jailed (potentially) for many years, and likely risk lifelong marginalisation and exclusion. These settings and places are characterised by incidents of regular and casual violence, some of it linked to petty criminality and drug-dealing.

Welcome to the south side ... of Birmingham

Birmingham is the largest and most populated city in the UK outside of London, with over 1.1 million inhabitants as of 2014, with the wider metropolitan area stretching to a total population of 3.8 million. Today, the city is a major centre for commerce and an important transport hub for the UK. Birmingham is more ethnically diverse than London. According to the UK Census 2011 57.9% of the population in Birmingham were white of which 53.7% of white belonged to Great Britain, 2.1% were Irish white and 2.7% of white relate to various countries. Asians comprised 26.6%, Chinese 1.2% and other Asians 2.9% of Birmingham populace. Blacks made up 8.9% of the population. According to the UK Census 2011, 51% of the population of Birmingham are females and the remaining 49% are males. The ordinary age of residents is 35 years, and hence it has also been described as one of the youngest cities in the UK. However, as of 2019 it was estimated that there are over 100,000 children living in poverty, the equivalent of 37% of all children in the city (after housing costs). This is the second highest rate of child poverty across the UK's core cities.

Birmingham's most affluent areas, such as Edgbaston, Harborne, Moseley, Kings Heath, Bournville and Solihull, are on the south side of the city, and tend to comprise of larger, older properties, where housing prices often average more than £300,000. These areas tend to be where more affluent white population and the most successful minority groups have moved. Disadvantaged communities, and in particular Asian Pakistani and Bangladeshi community, remained in the least desirable neighbourhoods often in close proximity to the city centre; however, the city is split along ethnic and socio-economic lines in a complex way. Poverty is not an issue just for 'black ghettos' in the north of Birmingham that have long been associated with gang crime and were historically the setting for much consideration from academics interested in policing, race and crime. Several predominantly 'white' wards on the south of the city have long been marked by high levels of deprivation and social exclusion. Up until the 1960s Birmingham was one of the fastest growing economies in the UK. During the 1970s and 1980s, however, Birmingham suffered from serious industrial decline. De-industrialisation implied a significant loss of jobs that was not balanced by the creation of new employment prospects in the service sector. Some wards in the inner city were particularly affected by this economic breakdown and became highly deprived areas. This included several estates built on the south side of the city in the period from the late 1960s and early 1970s. These included Druids Heath and its neighbouring The Three Estates near Kings Norton in Birmingham.

The Druids Heath estate was largely constructed during the 1970s as council housing and contains a high number of high-rise tower blocks. Now dubbed Birmingham's 'most neglected council estate' in local media reports, it is largely white, and the estate has become synonymous with social problems, unemployment, crime, drug use and anti-social behaviour. The estate is situated on former farmland on the southern edge of Bells Lane with Druids Lane forming the eastern, southern and western border. When first planned, it was known as Bells Lane Phases 1 and 2 and was part of wider post-war plans for the development of the area to accommodate the growing population of the city.. In walking distance from the Top of the estate where the 50-bus route terminus is located (the most frequent and busiest public transport route in Europe) are the three Kings Norton Estates of Pool Farm, Primrose Hill and Hawksley. Again almost each area traditionally comprised wholly of low-cost local authority accommodation constructed in the 1970s. A concerted programme of modernisation has been undertaken on each of these from 2000, with old buildings demolished, modernisation and renewal, but the areas remain disproportionately poor, and have a far greater indices of almost every social problem. However, these areas have not become synonymous with crime in the way areas such as Handsworth, Soho and Lozells have become. Connected to this is the fact that many of the analysis of Birmingham that is connected to wards and constituencies fails to appreciate the on-the-ground divisions in Birmingham between North and South and the specific dynamics of the city environment as understood by the people within it.

Here we wish to be expressly and unreservedly critical in the first instance of the framing of the Gang problem as the violence problem in Birmingham. Illustrative of this, for example, is a 2017 report by Rev Dr. Carver Anderson, as part of the much officially supported Commission on Gangs and Violence that occurred in recent years. In that report, while Anderson notes the 'absolute devastation that is possible by a small minority of individuals, drawn from different parts of the city and by no means exclusively linked to one geography, community or ethnicity' there is not one mention of any of the locations we describe here or of the communities that occupy them. There are however frequent mentions of primarily black communities of Handsworth, Hockley, Winson Green, Newtown and Lozells. There is specific mention of how 'The present gangs and violence associated challenges should not be seen in isolation of Birmingham's history – The deaths of Charlene Ellis and Latisha Shakespeare, at a New Year's party in Birchfield in 2003' that 'shocked Birmingham awake to gang and gun violence in the city' (Anderson, 2017: 14). Moreover, the abbreviations BYM (black young men), BAME (black, Asian and minority ethnic) and BME (black and minority ethnic) are the first three abbreviations listed in the report. Furthermore, the report suggests that it made the methodological:

> choice to see issues around gangs and violence in Birmingham through 'community led lenses' suggested the use of a 'mixed methods' qualitative approach. This means using a mix of research methods to access, capture and represent the voices, contexts and realities of respondents. These included: reviews of relevant literature and reports; semi-structured interviews with decision makers, service providers and/or key stakeholders working in statutory bodies; focus group discussions with community groups, young people, mothers and with prisoners in HMP Birmingham; consultation seminars and workshops; 'reasoning sessions' with fathers; questionnaires; attendance at commission and SP meetings; outreach interaction in Handsworth, Sparkbrook, Small Heath, Alum Rock, Newtown and Alum Rock; attendance at and review of video footage from 'Faith Matters' seminar.
>
> *Anderson, 2017: 28*

In short, what becomes apparent to anyone knowledgeable about Birmingham is that the problem of 'Gangs' and Youth Violence became reduced largely to a problem of North Birmingham and several disadvantaged and highly ethnically diverse wards. The problem with this is fundamentally that it is framing the youth, violence and crime nexus in racial terms from the outset. However, the problem here is that one need not go too far into the history of organised crime in Birmingham and the Midlands before it becomes very apparent that such a framing is wholly problematic. It is clear that Williams and Clarke are correct to express concern at how 'the "gang" has been appropriated by the state as an ideological device that drives the hyper-criminalisation of black, mixed, Asian, and other minority ethnic (BAME) communities' (Williams and Clarke, 2018), but this has occurred at times with willing participants from black academia framing issues in a rather narrow and naïve manner (Williams, 2015). While 'gang is evoked to explain an array of contemporary "crime" problems, which in turn (re)produces racialised objects to be policed' (Williams and Clarke, 2018: 234), we know that organised crime more generally is the preserve of an array of entrepreneurial men, often those long exposed to the rules of the market and enculturated into specific working class-based habitus (Hobbs, 2013). While some such as Pitts have argued that 'the evidence for the over-representation of Black young people in street gangs … is compelling' (Pitts, 2020), this may simply be an issue of framing, as all a gang is, we contend, is a vehicle for understanding collective endeavour.

Making Anelpis? – drugs, crime and survival dealing on Britain's low-income estates

In 2017 at exactly the same time that Rev Dr Anderson was not considering south Birmingham, Birmingham City Council was considering the fate of one of its large south city estates previously suggested. Druids Heath is in the top 10%

most deprived areas in England. Sixty-five per cent of properties on the estate remain the property of BCC and only 35% were owner occupied. The estate still hosted 15 High Rise Blocks (29% of all homes on the estate) while unemployment is 13% which exceeds Birmingham average of 8%. Residents on Druids Heath with no qualifications total 44% compared to the Birmingham average of 28%. Moreover, as it was developed in the 1960s with design principles of the time, and largely had only really been regenerated in very basic ways (such as road modifications to deter joy riding in the early 1990s). It is perhaps unsurprising given this that this same South Birmingham and its white working-class estates were well known as a proving ground for organised crime. Specifically, its location near to a dual carriageway that quickly took people from the maypole roundabout past the jurisdiction of the West Midlands force and into West Mercia constabulary area made it a prime place for armed robbers.

> The Druids Heath estate for years was the wild west, the pub on it, the Gladiator, we used to joke that there were more firearms in that place than in Tombstone. It was aptly named as well. It was a hard place, a lot of young men who had come up really through the 1970s and 1980s when things were tough for them. It was, well, what we police called a Robbers paradise. It was Birmingham's epicentre for armed Robbery for a long time.
>
> *Former Police Officer*

> There were a lot of crooks on the Druids heath from early on, but also a lot of people that moved there in the 70s felt they had hit the lottery. My old man reminded us, we had an indoor toilet and bath, he grew up with neither and it was only when he got a place on the estate, he got them. That said it was very working class, so there was a certain amount of thieving and kids fighting, but in the early days it was good. Even in the late 80s it was good. But then also things did start to change too. There was the right to buy. People were just getting more ambitious, well some people. I think by the time I was in my teens I was sort of, there is no fucking way I am staying on here for life, and as people started to make money and that, well a lot of folk were moving on.
>
> *Criminal who grew up on estate*

Birmingham's south city white working-class council estates were not really defined by gang loyalties as understood today, but those raised on them in the period of the 1980s and 1990s note much of the continuities and similarities, as Andy who grew up on the state in the 1970s and 1980s explained:

> Now you hear about gangs and its in some ways, well it's a load of shit isn't it. We never had gangs, but we fought kids off pool farm, and then from other areas, other schools. There has always been that thing where young lads will group up with their mates. We never had gangs, but then we had

> football hooliganism. Most of the lads were blue, but if you weren't and you were Villa, that might be a reason for a fight. It's just immature stuff isn't it, so you can say we never had gangs, and in some ways, compared to the kids today we didn't, but then there is a lot that was similar.

While the council estates of South Birmingham had long been the site to a wide range of criminal actors and an array of criminality, including a fair amount of entrepreneurial criminality from robbery and organised theft to commercial burglary and profitable scams, through to lower level and more routine frauds and shoplifting, it remains a criminological truism that what is conventionally understood as crime in the justice system thrives alongside social exclusion, marginalisation, inequality and poverty. Perhaps the most significant was the Right to Buy (RTB), introduced by the Housing Act 1980. It became a flagship policy of the Thatcher government. RTB allowed tenants in publicly owned council housing to buy their rented accommodation at a heavily subsidized price. Overall, RTB was largely responsible for an increase in the share of home ownership amongst householders in the UK from 55% in 1979 to over 70% in the early 2000s, thereby inducing a large-scale change in asset ownership amongst UK households in a relatively short period (Disney and Luo, 2017), but also had the impact of significantly reshaping some estates.

> These places by the 1980s and 1990s, they were hard but a lot of the problems were low level with kids. They would steal badges off cars and car stereo systems around secondary school, move into Cannabis, then twocking, ram raiding and Robbery or drugs, the kids in the school were difficult, to be honest, we constantly had people from the local streets complain about stolen car badges, broken windows, but as they grew up the petty stuff gave way and most grew out of it. They were into crime it was often enterprise; it was about making money. If you grew up on these estates in the 1980s and the 1990s it was all about making the money to get out.
>
> *Local police officer*

Additionally, the volume of crimes recorded by the police increased between the 1980s and the early 1990s, and arguably such shifts were not mere statistical trick. The distinction of deserving and undeserving poor, or society as polarised between a hardworking and law-abiding majority and a feckless and idle criminal minority might be too simple, but crime as a measure of social inequity and poor and not is not mere illusion. While the former has a long history, both in criminology and in social science more generally – for example, between the 'deserving' and the 'undeserving' poor, it is unarguably that conventional crimes tend to play out disproportionately against a backdrop of poor housing, distressed neighbourhoods and disrupted families. Living conditions of this sort are ordinarily defined as social structural consequences of poverty, but so too can cause poverty at the aggregate level by creating an unstable or dangerous environment which is not conducive to economic development. It may also be that those with the financial means will move out of areas with high rates of crime, leaving only those who are economically unable to relocate (Wilson, 2013) and that group includes criminals.

> In the 1980s all the folk I knew made money, lots came from nothing, did right to buy, set up businesses, and then as fast as possible they were out. In one generation you went from parents that had grown up with 8 or 8 siblings in a council house and that had been the family history long back, to lads without a CSE to their name owning a five-bed house in a nice area. You still got some families that had no ambition but to buy a council house and turn it into a palace, but a lot, they could not wait to get out. You also have to remember crime changed as well. Lads that had done blags (armed robberies) if they were smart, they got money into drugs and started making real big money. That is another big social change, from like no drug addicts to a lot of people addicted in the 1980s. If you could stay away from vices, keep hold of money, you get out, you get off the estate.
>
> *Terry, local resident and ex-offender*

The changes in drug crime described above in the 1980s are not just imagined. By the mid-1990s, UK academics developed a theoretical framework in which they argued that the use of some illicit drugs – specifically cannabis, nitrates and amphetamines, and equivocally ecstasy – had become 'normalised'. The proponents of this thesis argued that the recreational use of these drugs had become an unremarkable feature of life for some young people in their pursuit of leisure and pleasure. They also argued that the use of these drugs had become socially and culturally accepted by many members of the non-drug-using population and was increasingly culturally tolerated and acceptable in wider society (Measham et al., 1994; Parker et al., 1995 and 1998). However, numerous sources of evidence agree that the number of heroin users increased markedly through the 1980s and early 1990s and that many also used crack as their drug-using career developed (Briggs, 2013). This 'epidemic' spread from area to area but the national peak probably occurred between 1993 and 2000. Crime peaked between 1993 and 1995 (Morgan, 2014). The 1980s and the drug economy changed much, as did social policy. While not all criminals hailing from South Birmingham's 1970s estates did well because of this (many developed addictions), some more entrepreneurial criminals did, and that success brought them the ability to travel. Not dissimilar to those who benefited from the RTB schemes, many quickly made their way from the setting of their youth to more salubrious settings and homes.

By the 1980s, the estates described here were certainly sites of concern. These estates have a predominantly white, and particularly young population, with almost 29% of the population under the age of 16, and hence it is unsurprising that since the 1990s, they have frequently been blighted by problems of anti-social behaviour, crime and disorder. People on all of these estates were statistically more likely to be unemployed and/or permanently sick or disabled than in the neighbouring area, less likely to be in full-time work (employed or self-employed), and if in employment, more likely to be in a lower skilled occupation. While we do not want to paint a bleak or stigmatising picture, we so too are bounded to recognise that these are not places that the affluent have a stake, something recognised by both those who police them and those who reside on them, and even those who identify themselves as criminals.

> Its generalisations on people, some are just a bit hopeless and you feel sorry for them, some have had some bad luck, and some are genuinely just horrible people, selfish, immoral, feckless, you have like a few bagheads who will just go out and steal and steal. You have plenty of crack heads. You have lots of people doing things off the books, site work, all sorts. Collecting scrap, but there are a lot of people who are just stealing, or doing frauds, but they are not bad, but I would say there is an alternative value system around one lot of people there, there are quite a few that just do not care about anyone or anything.
>
> JT: Would you say there is a common theme with that?
>
> 'Yes, its younger kids, they are totally in the moment, they do not care about if they live or die tomorrow, so they do not care about anyone else or anything, even that is different. Ten years ago you did not get that, now I tell you seriously they would knife your spleen out, but only care if they got your blood on their trainers'.
>
> *West Midlands Police Officer*

> 'Round here, its gangs of youths that rule the streets. Cars stolen, mobility scooters stolen, drug deals all day, fights, they are feral. We are trapped. Living here is like a living Hell. It is awful. The shops are a no-go. I was brought up tough, but this place is something else now. I hate it.
>
> *elderly resident of South Birmingham Estate*

> These streets are our streets, we do what we want, these are our endz, you get me. People look down on man, but these men put in work. Its not all gangs and that, I like grime, but look on this estate man, people not in with the scene (grime crews) just in the roadlife (crime involved) been cheffed [stabbed] up and killed and that round here, it is just the streets are hard on these manors round here. I have my boys, but same time, its all man on his own in the end round here.
>
> *Incarcerated Young Offender from Birmingham in HMYOI Swinfen Hall*

Certainly, it is true that young men on estates, including young black men UK drill and earlier Black music genres, like grime, have been criminalised and policed in ways that question the legitimacy of and reveal the discriminatory nature of policing young black people by the Police as the coercive arm of the British state, but this is an experience far from experienced by black youth alone. Increasingly, as Gilroy argued, the culture of estates is one of a boisterous everyday interaction of different races in parts of city estates and parts of life. Race is not a particular factor, and race has become almost irrelevant for many young and urban Britons. What has not and what is shared is negative perceptions of the state, of an exclusive and uncaring mainstream society, a hypocrisy amongst middle class and mainstream society, yet paradoxically this does not create a solidarity or cohesivity that rejects the dominant mores of neoliberalism, rather it takes on one specific form.

In Britain, while there have been various accounts of the way Drill music scene, for example, has become a site of racialised policing (Fatsis, 2019), such views overlook the more widespread way in which the unique sound of drill music quickly caught the attention of various areas of youth culture, ranging from middle-class teens who spent their Easters Skiing in the Alps to those most marginalised by mainstream society. It is those most marginalised that this chapter will go on to discuss. While for the consumer listening to the latest SBTV release on the slopes of Mont Blanc, the often violent recollections of street culture are undoubtedly nothing more than a perverse thrill, far removed from their lived experience, such lyrics offer a far more personal and perhaps reflective meaning for the consumers who reside in countless deprived and seemingly long forgotten urban estates in Britain.

Those estates are often high-crime places, and a higher proportion of the young men involved in them are likely to be high risk exposed, to return to Anderson's more useful observation on the 'crucial links between the drugs industry, the illegal use of firearms and knives and serious violence' (2017: 14). While it is possible to concur, for example, that 'the volatility of some young people is compounded by their communities' experiences of discrimination and deprivation' (Anderson, 2017:25), trust commonly runs low on class as well as race-based lines, and so true, no race group of young men in Birmingham do not have some members with ties to illicit activity, be it the white, black, Asian and Eastern European community. Low-level involvement in drug dealing cultures where violence is never far from any disadvantaged or impoverished community. These fields are dominated by lower class young men, partly, because as an unregulated shadow market, violence is frequently the regulatory mechanism on which drug markets rely.

Moreover, against a policy vacuum and lack of strategic vision about how to resolve a series of growing divisions, social problems and injustices, low-level involvement for a great many young men becomes not so much a form of resistance or the product of mere strain, but just an everyday reality and a survival mechanism. In 2018, killings by a knife or sharp instrument were the highest recorded and both police-recorded crime and NHS hospital admissions confirmed that there had been consecutive recorded rises in violent offences involving knives or sharp instruments. These offences more frequently involve young men situated at the lowest rungs of society (Ellis, 2019). These estates built as symbols of progress became traps, and while the trap houses frequently mentioned in Grime and Drill are drug dealing places, trap also captures what such places have become. The late 1970s and early 1980s were times of epochal economic change as vital local industries were shattered by increased competition, cheap foreign labour costs, rising domestic inflation and the arrival of a neoliberal government unwilling to support industries that were becoming unprofitable in the globalising economy. But the successful and lucky moved away. The trapped are often the reluctant remaining residents who describe these estates as hellholes caused by criminals, and the criminals who see their estates as underfunded, ignored, stigmatised and overpoliced zones where there is little real escape, but where dreams of the good life and consumer success are encountered in abundance. Dangerous and risky places. They concur with the cultural representation where in recent years, dystopian images of inner urban landscapes populated by gangs of dangerous young men became synonymous with the country's latest 'knife crime crisis' – an association which both revealed and yet, paradoxically, obscure the complexity of violence in contemporary society linked to drug markets. This is all too apparent in notions such as gangs, crime and crime in south Birmingham. Indeed, in recent years much of the explanations for the violence and the drug economies of Birmingham has tied it to gangs, drugs and weapon use (Anderson, 2017). However, here we suggest that a more considered picture might need to be painted (see also Ayres and Treadwell's chapter in this volume).

A brief history of grime, drill and drug criminality in Birmingham

As Lynes et al. (2020) note, hip hop and its various subgenres have long been noted to have a close association with street life and thus gang culture. A brief look over notable recording artists from Birmingham consolidates such propositions. Birmingham has a long history of producing some of grime's most notable stars, such as Devilman. The first trace of gang-affiliated recording artists in Birmingham that rose to a certain level of prominence though is Zimbo, a former member of the Johnson crew. Zimbo has since desisted from gang activity and works to reduce youth involvement in such activities, but while an active member of the Johnson crew he released a series of songs which were extremely popular within the city.

In the years that followed we can see a burgeoning grime scene rapidly develop within the city, though it is frequently pockmarked with instances of criminal activity (usually for crimes around illicit substance distribution or of a violent nature), jail spells and in some instances homicide for some of its most prominent stars. The most notable of such cases is perhaps the untimely death of Joshua Ribiera, known as Depzman.

On 21 September 2014 Kyle Sheehan known as Shamz was killed on Jiggins Lane, Bartley Green. Between 20 and 30 people were involved in an altercation.

During the heated confrontation, fighting broke out and during the melee the 16-year-old rapper was stabbed in the leg. A week later the teenager died due to his injuries. Numerous arrests were made but to date no one has been charged and the death was not treated as gang related.

A year after Sheehan's passing a memorial party was held at TC's club in Selly Oak. In attendance that evening was his close friend Depzman – an up-and-coming grime star who was quickly gaining national attention. During the evening Ribiera came into conflict with Armani Mitchell over a shared loved interest. Following an initial scuffle Armani was ejected from TC's. He returned around quarter of an hour later having changed clothes. Upon his return another confrontation ensued and Ribiera left the club at twenty to eleven. Armani Mitchell followed him out the club and up the road, produced a three inch knife and stabbed him in the heart. Joshua 'Depzman' Ribiera died from his injuries. Armani Mitchel was convicted of the killing and sentenced to a minimum prison term of 18 years.

Prior to his death, Depzman frequently made music with his close friend Jaykae (arguably Birmingham's most successful grime artist). Notably Jaykae, famously stabbed at Sidewinder, has a close relationship with Remtrex. Remtrex was sentenced to 7 years in prison in 2012 for aggravated burglary. While incarcerated he made headlines after amassing over 3 million views on YouTube for short music videos filmed on illicit phones in both HMP Doncaster and HMP Birmingham. These recordings resulted in a recall to prison upon his release. One such recording featured fellow grime artist Big Stygz, who was serving a lengthy sentence for his part in the ambushing of prison van in 2012 which saw John Anslow become the first category A prisoner to escape in 17 years.

Mist, another prominent grime artist from the city, served 14 months in prison for trafficking offences having been involved in a high-speed pursuit on the M6 motorway after police had attempted to stop him for driving without a licence. While no engagement in violence offences or any relating of illicit substances is reported, this relative distance from road life in comparison to his counterparts has evidently not been entirely successful. Notably, Mist was the victim of an armed robbery while in Portugal in 2019 in which jewellery was taken and he received a gunshot wound to the leg. In January 2017, grime artist Safone was arrested for possession of crack, heroin and cannabis. In the following July he was shot in the chest with a shotgun in Qunton, Birmingham. The following may he was again shot in Quinton. Within this incident a bullet entered his buttock and lodged in his thigh. Here we can clearly see the fluid nature of offender and victim found commonly within offending subcultures. In September of 2019 Safone was arrested for possession of a handgun following a police chase through the city centre. A gun was stated to have been thrown from the car during the pursuit with the vehicle later being found torched in Ladywood.

In 2019 the city again hit national news when London-based drill artists Krept and Konan were performing at a 1xtra event. An attempted robbery backstage resulted in Krept receiving a slash wound from a blade on his face. The *Birmingham Mail* was quick to link the Johnson crew to the incident though Zimbo vehemently denied their involvement on social media. This is not the only vague links that can be tied between the older grime artists, the cities' younger drill artists and the established, infamous gangs. The relationship between various artists, some with gang affiliation, is demonstrated once we revisit song collaborations. Safone has previously collaborated with drill artist M10, a member of AR (Armed Response gang).

As should be becoming clear here, there is something of a complex relationship in Birmingham between poverty and social inclusion, gangs, geography, drug-dealing and associated criminality, and the grime music scene. However, the strong associations behind grime, drugs and gangs were re-enforced not only by the traditional framing of a gang, drug, violence nexus with largely black male urban street gangs that existed in North Birmingham, but was then reconnected with a string of around 20 high-profile shootings in 2015 and 2016 that resulted in a major operation being mounted be the West Midlands Regional Organised Crime Unit. In total 18 reported gang members were handed gang injunctions, which prohibited them from entering specific areas and associating with one another alongside access to vehicles and mobile phones. Crucially the injunctions contained prohibition on individuals making music videos that promoted gang violence and the distribution of illicit substances. Included within the injunctions was Reial Phillips, also known as Lynch, who is now serving 20 years for his part in the shootings as well as distribution of class A drugs. Drill artist Lynch appeared in multiple music videos as a prominent member of AR, in which he discussed partaking in shootings against GMG (Get Money Gang). Within the court proceedings it was claimed that AR were an offshoot of the Burger Bar Boys and GMG were an offshoot of the Johnson Crew, noted gangs from North Birmingham's predominantly poor, marginalised and predominantly 'black' areas on the North side of the city.

From this brief overview of the often violent and criminally orientated lifestyles of some of the city's most prominent grime and drill artists we can begin to discern the complex nature of the discussion at hand. Invariably, the involvement of urban street gangs can be found throughout the myriad history offered. It is crucial to note however that some of the most notorious and devastating instances of violence within the subculture, the murders of Depzman and Shamz highlight the complexity of urban violence in contemporary Britain. Invariably, music artists involved in gang activity have offered the media various newsworthy stories which captivate consumers and guarantee clicks. As the song 'Ban Drill' by Krept and Konan declares though, the government's move to ban drill music as it has seen the genre as a causation of violence is short sighted. As the work of Stuart (2020), who conducted an extensive ethnography of drill artists in Chicago, observes, many youths utilise the music as an alternative to gang activity and a path to desistance. Invariably, however, the attention such approach can attract can, on occasion, open such individuals to more risk.

Focussing heavily upon the drill genre, its link to gangs and occasions of violence and criminality in recent years, has created a dystopian image of bleak blocks and run down inner-city urban landscapes populated by dangerous and predatory young men. That image is now the one that is framing some estates on the south side of Birmingham, such as the Fold around Hawksley and Pool Farm, an area that was traditionally overwhelmingly poor and white working class for much of the 1980s and 1990s. Invariably Drill music became synonymous with the country's most recent 'knife crime crisis'. Such associations revealed yet, paradoxically, obscure the complexity of violence in contemporary society which is often linked to drug markets and lower street-level organised crime. In the proceeding section this chapter will demonstrate such complexity using case studies of two murders within the city. From these we can observe that rather than gang-orientated and news grabbing violence scourging the urban centres of the UK, much of the violence is far less organised and regular, with routine violence over trivial issues playing out across estates daily.

Bud, booze, beak, bars and banality – contemporary urban violence reconsidered

By shifting the focus away from the often racialised notion of urban gang studies we begin to discern the more complex, class-orientated issue of violence in the contemporary urban setting and the way that the drug economy forms merely part of the fabric of everyday life. Violence demarked by a sense of hopelessness and invariably tied to the economic deprivation of modern British cities. As Telford and Lloyd (2020) highlight, Stiegler (2019: 19) suggests that today's young people are the 'blank generation'; devoid of a clear biography, job prospects and a future, they are unable to form a coherent self and obtain the goods required to flourish. On impoverished estates it is not simply that involvement in drug markets and its associated violence seem to offer the only feasible route to becoming visible, the hedonism of cannabis (bud) alcohol (booze) cocaine, and throwing out raps that stress ones success and value (spitting bars) are all escape from monotony of convention, and all often an escape, but also a trap. Constructing and articulating that you *matter*, and can access all aspects of the perceived 'good life', becomes the only way to survive and stay still. While grime crews spit their beats about exclusive brands like Stone Island and Gucci, talk up their sexual prowess and pour away bottles of Courvoisier in their online videos, the reality is that many exist in the precarious world of day-to-day survival. That does not stop them from vocally asserting their success against others similarly located in extremely disadvantaged locales.

> Round here, you see nice cars though yeh, people have nice clothes yeh, that's the thing, you get me, we grind. You still get some people who don't, but a lot of us, we do tings, anything to get p [paper, money] you get me. I would say now, there is probably 5 grows by you right now, you get me.

> You get some people, some lazy fat people who won't do nothing, you get me, but we do tings.
>
> *Young offender from south Birmingham*

The young man quoted above hailed from the South Birmingham Estate and was incarcerated for a lengthy spell for involvement in violent crime (although not the one described in the following passage). On 8 October 2015 police responded to reports of gunshots on that same estate. On arriving at the scene officers found 19-year-old Connor Smith with multiple gunshot wounds. By the time paramedics had arrived on the scene, around 11:30 pm, Smith was in cardiac arrest. He was pronounced dead at the scene. On 10 May 2016 two men were charged in relation to Connor Smith's death. Leon Frye, a 28-year-old from Ladywood, Birmingham was convicted of murder. He received a custodial sentence of a minimum 30 years. His associate, Phillip Baillie, was found guilty of manslaughter and received a 20-year sentence. The circumstances around Connor Smith's death exemplify the often-trivial matter in which urban violence often occurs. Frye and Baillie were habitual offenders, each with previous convictions for violence. They were known in the local areas to sell crack, heroin and cannabis, priding themselves on 'running the area'. On the day of Connors' murder the pair used a loaded gun to rob Connor and an unidentified friend of a bag of cannabis. Unlike the taxings connected to the higher echelons of the drug trade which routinely involve firearms (Treadwell et al., 2020), the amount taken by Frye and Baillie was rather trivial, totalling a value of just £50. Connor was then made aware that the pair had also utilised the firearm to intimidate his younger brother.

Enraged at the drugs being relieved and the incident involving his younger sibling, Connor armed himself with a knife. Later that evening Connor and his friend confronted Frye and Baillie in an alleyway. Connor produced the knife and proceeded to stab Frye in the stomach. During the altercation, Fry produced the firearm he had used in the robbery earlier in the day and began shooting. Connor was hit once in his left arm. A second, fatal bullet penetrated his chest. The police were unable to recover the firearm used but ballistic analysis of the bullets recovered evidenced it had previously been used in another shooting.

The murder of Connor Smith, we argue, is atypical of much urban violence which is perpetrated across estates in the UK. Such instances are often underpinned by extreme and sudden acts of violence motivated by notions of disrespect and trivial amounts of money connected to the local drugs trade. Some of these men will have associations that tie them to gangs or crews, but these are often not so clear as the dominant narrative often suggests. These are not simply shown. for example, in Smith's murder, but in the more regular and routine acts of fatal and life-changing violence however happens away from Birmingham's deprived estates and social media. Such instances are usually located within the centre of the metropolis around the bars and clubs of the night-time economy. Such instances are typical of the death of Daniel Baird, in the summer of 2017. Baird, then aged 26, was drinking in Forge Tavern in Digbeth, Birmingham, with his friend Dale Scott and some other friends at an illegal gathering. Security camera footage from the premises shows the group in a dispute with another group of Patrons in the establishment. During the initial heated discussion between the groups Scott is observed striking the pubs punch bag machine. Images from the CCTV show Sashon Brown, a member of the opposing group, standing close to Dale Scott and clutching a knife. Around 4:20 am Baird and Scott left the pub and began to walk home. They were closely followed by Sashon Brown and his friend Carlton Donaldon. As the pair walked down Faizley street and came parallel to the bus stop, Donaldson and Brown struck. Scott received knife injuries in his back but survived. Daniel Baird however died from a single stab wound to the heart measuring less than 3 cm.

The court case that ensued pointed to Carlton Donaldson as the person who stabbed Daniel Baird to death. Alongside the murder charge, Donaldson was found guilty of wounding with intent, attempted wounding, violent disorder and possession of an offensive weapon. He was sentenced to life with a minimum tariff of 23 years before release would be considered. Brown was sentenced to two and a half years in custody for violent disorder and possessing an offensive weapon. Neither of the groups involved in the altercation that culminated in Daniel Baird's death had prior dealings with one another before they entered the bar that evening. The dispute which led to the street stabbings was instigated by a member of Baird's group stumbling onto someone with Donaldson and Brown.

From these examples and considering the murders of Smugz and Depzman we can begin to see the similar and sometimes trivial nature of much urban violence away from the headlines which seek to frame the rise in urban violence as being driven by urban street gangs and drill music. Much of the fatal violence on the streets of Birmingham, and Britain more generally, is driven by much more banal factors, has ties to the lowest rungs of the local drug trade, and matters of respect, jealousy, envy and inebriated perpetrators and victims (on an array of substances from alcohol to cannabis and cocaine) feature prominent. For such dramatic and serious instances of violence to occur of what others would deem rather trivial matters though, it is critical that we begin to understand the driving force and motivating factors for such acts.

It was Horne and Hall (1995) who first began to talk of a criminological value in considering Anelpis, a term literally means no hope, which they averred was relevant to a lower class and overlooked group who are ruled by their emotions and do not fear authority and therefore are not expected to conform. Yet what Anelpis captures was the presence of virtually total cynicism and nihilism, virtually no option, no realistic expectations, no hope and no fear of authority. While we have spoken to young men in the community and in prisons drawn from these estates who believe their bars will lead them to 'blow up like stormzy' and become mega celebrities, the greater reality is one of constant struggle and minimal success. Young criminal men in these anelpic places often held a self-image of success that stands in glaring contradiction with their everyday lives and real prospects. It is just such factors that tend to be experienced across race lines by postcode that unite young white men who are more likely to be the perpetrators, as well as the victims, of violent crime with their black counterparts raised in extremely similar circumstances on estates and places where race actually matters very little.

On such estates race matters little because all too well it is recognised that it is not skin colour or ethnicity that determines your chances of being a victim or a perpetrator, but many other environmental factors – such as disproportionate rates of poverty, unemployment and school exclusions. It is being poor, put in a poor place and having little prospect of escape. Academics ought then to be honest about the fact that youth violent crime is being fuelled by the drug trade, and the palace and function of violence in the wider business of drugs, even if it is not visible in some specific scenes where conviviality and social supply mean that the real harms are very removed. So too the disproportionate impact of poverty impacting on some groups and some communities. While it becomes useful to shortcut these with terms such as 'gang', 'vulnerability', with ever greater calls to be mindful of intersectionality and oppression, the most oppressive force is poverty. Certainly there are complex and interrelated factors at play in people's lives, homes and communities, which can alter the likelihood of someone taking becoming involved in crime as victim or offender, but this also involves deep-rooted and engrained social and economic factors linked to poverty that should make that, and the poverty of place, a significant and universal consideration. Just as the link between drugs, entry-level organised crime and male violence – spread out from the estate firm to involve organised criminal networks that span the globe, with operations the size of large companies, so too the foothold is so frequently the places at the bottom. To highlight this link between poverty, deprivation and crime is not somehow to excuse criminality, just as it is no call to abandon concern with the interconnected nature of social categorisations such as race, class and gender, regarded as creating overlapping and interdependent systems of discrimination or disadvantage where poverty is concerned. So too, the gang talk can obscure commonalities whereas to talk of the bottom and entry-level stages of organised drug crime does not. Refocusing again on the economic drivers and the structural features that give rise to high crime rates, and stripping back the labels and taken for granted descriptors can bring into stark focus the real problem of men, knives and drugs that are frequently found in the urban sprawl of contemporary Britain. The proximate reasons for knife violence involving young people are numerous and varied. Many incidents are triggered by isolated episodes of 'disrespect' that have nothing to do with street gangs or grime scenes, but it is true that in many, drugs and alcohol may form part of the backdrop. Murder is, as Dorling noted some time ago, atop a social pyramid of social harm and its changing numbers and distributions provide one of the key clues as to where harm is most and least distributed. That clue should not lead us to gangs, or grime, or drill, or rap; it is only about ethnicity in so far that poverty is racialised, and the drug market and scenes feature only so far as they are culturally normalised in society. Inequality, curtailed opportunities and hopelessness on inner city estates may not be as exciting as the grime crew, but they are vital if we want to truly understand contemporary serious violence, including that which operates in drug distribution networks.

References

Anderson, C. (2017) *Commission on Gangs and Violence: Uniting To Improve Safety.* Birmingham: Birmingham City Council and West Midlands Police and Crime Commissioner.

Briggs, D. (2013) *Crack Cocaine Users: High Society and Low Life in South London.* Oxford: Routledge.

Disney, R., and Guannan, L. (2017) The right to buy public housing in the United Kingdom: A welfare analysis. *Journal of Housing Economics,* 35, pp. 51–68.

Ellis, A. (2019) A de-civilizing reversal or system normal? Rising lethal violence in post-recession austerity United Kingdom., *The British Journal of Criminology,* 59(4), pp. 862–878.

Fatsis, L. (2019) Policing the beats: The criminalisation of UK drill and grime music by the London Metropolitan Police. *The Sociological Review,* 67(6), pp. 1300–1316.

Horne, R., and Hall, S. (1995) Anelpis: A preliminary expedition into a world without hope or potential. *Parallax,* 1(1), 81–91. DOI: 10.1080/13534649509361995

Hobbs, D. (2013) Lush life: *Constructing Organized Crime in the UK.* Oxford: Oxford University Press.

Lynes, A., Kelly, C., and Kelly, E. (2020) THUG LIFE: Drill music as a periscope into urban violence in the consumer age. *The British Journal of Criminology,* 60(5), pp. 1201–1219.

Measham, F., Newcombe, R. and Parker, H. (1994) The normalization of recreational drug use amongst young people in North-West England. *British Journal of Sociology,* pp. 287–312.

Morgan, N. (2014) *The Heroin Epidemic of the 1980s and 1990s and Its Effect on Crime Trends–Then and Now: Technical Report.* Home Office. URL (accessed 12 January 2021):https://assets.publishing.service.gov.uk/government/uploads/system/uploads/attachment_data/file/332963/horr79tr.pdf

Parker, H.J., Measham, F., and Aldridge, J. (1995) *Drugs Futures: Changing Patterns of Drug Use amongst English Youth.* London: Institute for the Study of Drug Dependence.

Parker, H.J., Aldridge, J., and Measham, F. (1998) *Illegal Leisure: The Normalization of Adolescent Recreational Drug Use.* London: Routledge.

Pitts, J., (2020) Black Young People and Gang Involvement in London. *Youth Justice,* 20(1–2), pp. 146–158.

Stiegler, B. (2019). *The Age of Disruption: Technology and Madness in Computational Capitalism.* Cambridge: Polity Press.

Stuart, F. (2020*) Ballad of the Bullet: Gangs, Drill Music, and the Power of Online Infamy.* New Jersey: Princeton University Press.

Telford, L., and Lloyd, A. (2020) From "Infant Hercules" to "Ghost Town": Industrial collapse and social harm on Teesside. *Critical Criminology,* 28, pp. 595–611.

Treadwell, J., Ancrum, C., and Kelly, C. (2020) Taxing Times: Inter-criminal victimization and drug robbery amongst the English professional criminal milieu. *Deviant Behavior*, 41(1), pp. 57–69.

Williams, P. (2015) Criminalising the other: Challenging the race-gang nexus. *Race & Class*. 56(3), pp. 18–35.

Williams, P., and Clarke, B. (2018) The black criminal other as an object of social control. *Social Sciences*, 7(11), pp. 234–243.

Wilson, J. (2013) *Thinking about Crime*. 3rd edn. New York: Basic Books.

14

THE MORE THINGS CHANGE, THE MORE THEY STAY THE SAME

A structuro-generational perspective of gypsy drug-dealing networks and operations in Madrid, Spain

Daniel Briggs

Introduction

The Spanish drug market has undergone radical changes in recent times with the introduction of heroin in the late 1970s, and from the late 1980s onwards, cocaine (Leal and Sorando, 2016). The evolution of these markets, however, came at a time when rural domestic economies started to evaporate and immigration to the country was welcomed, which essentially resulted in the massive colonisation of Spanish cities, in particular Barcelona and Madrid (Briggs, 2010). The population increase, particularly in these urban areas where manual work had become available until the late 1980s, however, started to coincide with the dismantling of the industrial sectors in the same period, which had massive repercussions for these marginalised groups – rural migrants, immigrants, the urban working class and gypsies (Briggs and Monge Gamero, 2017). Unsurprisingly, the increase in unemployment and inequality resulted in problematic consumption of heroin and cocaine as well as a recruitment opportunity for many into the hierarchies of the country's thriving drug market (Requeña, 2014).

Among those who become central to the distribution of these drugs were the gypsies who, throughout the same period, had also experienced a displacement from urban centres and were subject to aggressive social policies which criminalised their businesses (selling in street markets, collecting scrap metal, etc.). Such was this transformation of their livelihoods that many of the gypsy settlements (known as 'poblados') became open drug-dealing zones. From the mid-1990s onwards in Madrid, hundreds of people each day turned up to take cocaine and heroin in 'fumaderos' (smoking houses) and inject speedballs (heroin and cocaine combined in a syringe) in their cars, in parks and on the streets. Towards the end of the 1990s, however, the local government in Madrid initiated a series of raids and configured social and criminal policies around the total

DOI: 10.4324/9781351010245-16

spatial eradication of these *poblados*, culminating in 2008 with the concentration of drug dealing and problematic use on the outskirts of southern Madrid in a place called Valdemingómez on the Cañada Real Galiana – which is to this day one of the largest ghettos in Europe. Consequently, many of the original gypsy families from these *poblados* simply moved their business to this area.

Today, around 5,000 clients turn up daily to the Valdemingómez where the gypsy clans run the most impenetrable drug-dealing operations in the country. This chapter shows precisely how they do this and charts the historical-generational transfer of drug-dealing businesses within the gypsy networks. It also highlights some of the limp stereotypes around drug dealing and the woeful one-sided depiction of drug dealers in the local media to show that the realities of how people get immersed into these opportunities do not hinge on their own free-will decisions to enter into drug dealing. Rather it is how powerful social and political structures disfavour their economic and social position, leaving them either meagre alternatives for a way of life or high-risk, high-reward illicit avenues such as drug dealing. The data from this work stems from a self-funded photo-ethnographic project which produced 50 open-ended interviews with drug addicts, police, harm reduction workers and gypsies, and direct observations of public drug using sites, fumaderos, rubbish dumps and derelict sites within the Cañada area (for a full account see Briggs and Monge Gamero, 2017). It is available as *Dead End Lives: Drugs and Violence in the City Shadows*.

Europe's largest ghetto: Valdemingómez

Valdemingómez or the sixth of six sectors of the Cañada Real Galiana is a site which stretches 14 km in length and sits only 12 km from the centre of Madrid. The most recent official census estimates that the six sectors house 9,228 people and compose of 2,516 buildings – all illegally constructed (ACCEM and Fundación Secretariado Gypsy, 2010). However, since the publication of these data, the area has continued to expand, largely because the 2008 economic crisis froze thousands of people out of the labour market, many lost their homes in particular, poor families of mostly Arab, gypsy or Romanian origin whom then relocated to the area. There they stay predominantly with other family and friends as a way to survive; some pay no electricity, gas or water bills as these utilities are hijacked from mains sources and are able to take advantage of social security benefits for their children and qualify for further support due to their status as a 'vulnerable ethnic minority'. For this reason, a good estimate would be that the area has between 11,500 and 12,500 people (Figure 14.1).

Valdemingómez is practically a closed community. Though one broken road connects sectors 1 to 5, it is essentially blocked by the A3 – one of the six main roads out of Madrid – thus segregating Valdemingómez. Moreover, there are vast differences in the population demography; sectors 1 and 2, for example, are heavily populated by working-class Spanish families and industrial businesses,

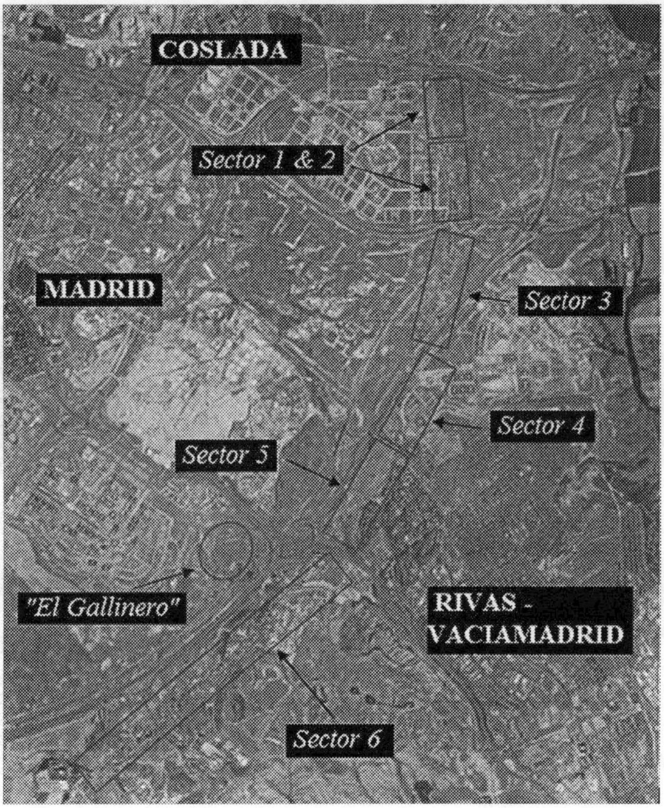

FIGURE 14.1 Ariel view of the six sectors.

respectively. Here, the local government of Coslada has all but incorporated these sectors into their management which is why the houses and buildings in these areas stand decent. There are public services, electricity, water and a good-quality road – even though this area was illegally populated in the 1960s and 1970s by rural migrant workers moving to the city in search of labour opportunities.

Sectors 2 and 3 are divided by a small road between Coslada and Rivas Vaciamadrid (hereafter 'Rivas' – interestingly Vaciamadrid meaning 'empty Madrid') where there are mostly gypsies. Here in sector 3 these people get by on selling used domestic products such as fridges, freezers, washing machines, toilets and baths, while others rob and sell copper and industrial cables. In addition, there are also some cafes and restaurants. However, the largest business without doubt is that which is dedicated to selling scrap metal or 'chatarra'. This sector marks a notable change in the quality of the housing in that it is certainly more improvised. The roads are more difficult to navigate in the absence of asphalt and lining them are large cables which illegally connect the large pylons to the houses and businesses.

Sector 4 comes under their spatial and social management of the Rivas local government but the conditions of the roads and houses are distinctly poor. The area's community are a mix between northern African and Arab families, and gypsies. While there is almost no sign of drug dealing, there are some illegal vehicle workshops and small tool workshops. From here on the electricity, gas and water are also illegally acquired. Small vegetable gardens can be found from time to time and haphazard vehicles passing up and down selling the very same produce to other members of the community.

However, in sector 5, the setting starts to change as well as the perception of the ambiance. In this sector, which lies right next to Rivas town centre, there are similar forms of business taking place among a predominant Arab population – though there are some gypsy families. Perhaps the main differences between this sector and those before them are that a significant number of children in the area attend a nearby school and there is an active community association which seeks to defend the rights of its habitants. This has mostly been set up as a consequence of the increased police raids and demolishing of houses. This is because drugs are sold on a small scale and this has attracted more crime to the area in the form of robbery and car theft.

Around this in Valdemingómez in sector 6 – far more in abundance than in other sectors – are also numerous illegal companies dedicated to construction, transport (bus), furniture and car workshops. The companies know there is no clear political direction in the area and their eviction is just as complex as that of the drug markets. Their most immediate neighbours are the gypsies who construct, occupy and manage the kiosks and fumaderos around them and lead in the organised distribution of drugs. The sector is also similarly diverse. Further up, towards the edge of the sector is an Arab community who have small grocery, general stores and workshops. Additionally, alongside them in the sector live a Romanian community who tend to survive by selling *chatarra* and the purchase and sale of various miscellaneous goods robbed by the sectors' active drug-using population who live and visit the area. This population varies from the 140 machacas who live permanently in the area to the 5,000 clients who come here from all areas around Madrid each day to purchase and/or use drugs.

The drug market in Valdemingómez in the Cañada Real Galiana is a relatively recent development since drug sales evolved around the turn of the 21st century. However, its growth has been on one hand as a consequence of the dismantling of other gypsy drug-dealing settlements or *poblados* in and around Madrid, leading to its consolidation in one drug hypermarket on the outskirts. On the other hand, it has come as a consequence of inept social reintegration policies which have consistently failed and ostracised the gypsies. Perhaps the most significant population growth in Valdemingómez occurred between 2004 and 2006 when a nearby *poblado* called Barranquillas was demolished over a short period of time in an effort to generate support for what was to be another failed Olympic bid essentially transferring what were major parts of Madrid's drug market to Valdemingómez in the Cañada Real Galiana. This transfer was also significant in that it displaced large numbers of people who had come to own properties in sector 6, giving way for the availability of more estates which could be used for the distribution of drugs; in some cases, they were threatened and physically forced from their homes if they did not surrender the space to the gypsy families.

The real boom years for Valdemingómez were then between 2007 and 2008 when it became famous as Spain's drug hypermarket, known nationwide as the place to buy good-quality drugs at cheaper prices than in the local neighbourhood or 'barrio' as we hereafter refer. By then, new young users and dealers had started to visit the area in the absence of political alternatives as law enforcement interventions started to engage in phases of raids and demolitions. Yet Valdemingómez's location was also geographically advantageous for drug distribution as it was well served by main roads and motorways in and around Madrid, in particular the M50 which circumnavigates the capital, as well as the A3 which connects the city centre to the coastal city of Valencia making it easy for new dealing routes to evolve.

Although the 2008 economic crisis massively impacted drug distribution and dealing dynamics around Spain's capital, Valdemingómez still shows little sign of desisting as thousands pour into the sector each day keeping the drug market buoyant. The few families that now run the drug operations in the sector, owning each between 5 and 8 properties in the area to avoid major legal consequences, by keeping only around 200 g of both cocaine and heroin in each sales point while larger quantities are securely located in bunkers. In the main, these families buy drugs in bulk and distribute them to smaller sales points in the area. Indeed, the most popular fumaderos can make between €6,000 and €10,000 each day and for this reason the social hierarchy among the gypsies is determined by the most successful in the drug businesses.

The gypsies are frequently depicted in the media as 'violent criminal gangs'. For example, in one recent news article which reported on the arrest of one of Valdemingómez's most recognised gypsy family clan, they are described as 'heroin and cocaine specialists' and the 'kings of cannabis'.[1] The other typical manifestation of 'criminality' associated with these clans is that led by Spanish TV networks which send presenters alongside police and security teams to make 'controls'[2] (or stop and search) and periodic raids on the drug market.[3] Taken together, these, among other, simplistic explanations confirm to the public that the gypsies are the problem group while deny the real story of the area and how it has come to be Spain's largest drug market.

The historical evolution of the La Cañada Real Galiana

Dating back to the 13th century, the Cañada Real Galiana was a route where goods were transported from the north of the Spanish peninsula to its centre, connecting four autonomous communities (La Rioja, Castilla and León, Comunidad de Madrid and Castilla la Mancha). Known as a 'cattle path', these

Cañadas became increasingly significant during the Middle Ages to transport livestock; their function was to permit farmers and shepherds to move their cattle across the land to take advantage of the best climate for the time of year. Indeed such was their domestic economic significance for agriculture and farming industries that this was reflected by laws set out by the Spanish crown to protect them. As a consequence, there was high competition and rivalry between the shepherds and farmers which caused much conflict, especially when lawful protection from the crown brought significant earnings and profit (ACCEM and Fundación Secretariado Gypsy, 2010).

This continued up until its peak during the 19th century at which point over five million cattle owners were using the Cañadas each spring and autumn to transport livestock. Although the agricultural industry gathered increasing economic importance during the 19th century, by the second part of the 20th century, the Cañadas had practically been abandoned because of advances in technology and transport had led to the construction of rail networks and roads. Consequently, their use dwindled, leaving large sections of the Cañadas across the country disused. Indeed, this included the area where we undertook our research which remained largely deserted until about the 1950s before it started to attract rural migrants who were looking for economical housing near the capital to be able to look for work in Madrid or its expanding outskirts (ACCEM and Fundación Secretariado Gypsy, 2010). This was because the very processes which had given way to a shift in the rural domestic economy essentially uprooted thousands of people in search of work in the city.

These early residents of the Cañada Real Galiana took advantage of free amenities such as water, electricity and gas, and the earliest settlement was populated closest to Coslada (where the present sectors 1 and 2 sit) – a town which too had grown exponentially in the wake of the growth of industry around it. These early residents who were mostly rural Spanish families illegally constructed improvised housing on the Cañada.[4] From the 1950s to the mid-1970s, the population grew, and the sectors extended. New ethnic groups such as Spanish gypsies started to occupy the sectors along with other working-class Spanish families in sector 3 and as sector 4 expanded, Moroccans and Romanians, along with increasing numbers of Spanish families[5] which represented an early form of gentrification in the city, contributed to the formation of new communities, all taking advantage of the financial benefits and the close proximity to the capital (Ministerio de Formento, 2010; ACCEM y Fundación Secretariado Gitano, 2010). Indeed, the spatial juxtaposition coupled with the fertility of the land made it beneficial to have property or land there and these new residents in sectors 3 and 4 also came in the hope that they too would be given land like others had in sectors 1 and 2[6] (Mbomío Rubio, 2012).

This growth gradually continued with the formation of sector 5 and a partial sector 6 or Valdemingómez until the mid-to-late 1990s when Madrid started to instigate large-scale changes to the urban landscape. During this period, similar groups to those who had occupied sector 4 moved in – Moroccans and Romanians along with a scattering of sub-Saharan Africans and sprinkling of Easter Europeans, although gypsies remained the dominant population (Soleares, 2011). However, a series of aggressive social policy efforts initiated by the Operación Barrios en Remodelación or Operation Remodelation of Neighborhoods marked the spatial displacement of the city's main *poblados* where already socially excluded gypsy families engaged in drug sales pushed them to the outskirts.[7] Though the operation was designed to relocate gypsy families, many did not qualify for support or were sidelined from housing opportunities (Lago Ávila, 2014). As noted in other research on the spatial exclusion and attempted forced inclusion of gypsies (see Briggs, 2010), the Plan Nacional de Erradicar del Chabolismo [National Plan to Erradicate Chabolismo] had the reverse effect. From its inception in 1991 up until 1995, major failings resulted in almost no social support for relocated gypsy families and, as a consequence, many simply congregated in other *poblados* in Madrid. The strategy, however, did not anticipate the potential resistance from the gypsy communities and this made each family relocation complicated, expensive and drawn out. For example, it cost the authorities more than €110 million to relocate 499 families from three *poblado* districts (Lago Ávila, 2014). As the years passed, the respective institutions lost motivation to fund the initiative. The more this was neglected, the more these very *poblados* developed crime problems related to drug markets. As these administrational problems and lack of strategic intervention continued, eventually in 1998, the whole operation was disbanded (Lago Ávila, 2014).

All this was taking place as a consequence of massive growth in the city for which the authorities had to balance: mainly because at the end of the 1980s and through to the mid-1990s these spaces which the gypsies occupied were considered to be necessary to the government to allow for the city to grow and expand. However, at the same rate at which the city had expanded, coupled with the authorities' slow progress with relocating the improvised housing known as 'chabolas', only made for the continuing appearance of more *chabolas*. When the Instituto de Realojamiento e Inserción (IRIS) or the Relocation and Insertion Institute was established in 1998 to continue the battle against the improvised housing in which most gypsies used or 'chabolismo', it was never given sufficient direction or funding to make any difference for even in 1999 when a new federation was established to assist with this process and more promises were made by the respective municipal mayors to avoid the creation of ghettos and growth of *chabolas* (Lago Ávila, 2014).

Yet year after year, the *chabolas* were dismantled. From 1999 to 2010, IRIS assisted in the relocation of 1,700 gypsy families and the dismantlement of 60 chabolismo zones (Lago Ávila, 2014). Perhaps regarded as some sort of success, this instead resulted in the increased inhabitation towards the end of the 1990s of the sector most recently formed and least developed of the Cañada Real Galiana at Valdemingómez: and this is one of the main reasons why it became one of the main bastions from where drug sales took place. Hundreds of houses, flats, caravans and warehouses were bought, occupied and, in some cases, forcibly taken by these gypsy families who had been moved from one *poblado* to another in Madrid: their motivation for occupying Valdemingómez mainly involved making it the basis for the new drug-dealing networks. So, the closure of these old *poblados* was significant because they assisted in their spatial mutation in other areas of the city.

As gypsy families installed themselves in Valdemingómez, it took no time to attract the thousands of drug consumers and addicts that had become reliant on other *poblados* for drug purchases. Not only did this then converge the drug market on the outskirts of Madrid but it also concentrated the marginality of the city's most problematic social groups. This then commenced the relocation of thousands of working-class Spanish and immigrants and other unemployed groups with a range of health, drug and practical problems already living in precarious circumstances. This led to the exponential growth of Valdemingómez, making it the main drug market in Madrid. With ideal connections to the M50 (which practically circumnavigates the capital) and the A3 (linking Madrid to the coastal city of Valencia), the new settlement in Valdemingómez could be accessed easily by customers alike from almost any point in the capital. It was also advantageous in that it was in the periphery of Madrid, far from major urban residential settlements and even further from the political focal point of the city centre.

Indeed, Valdemingómez's rapid evolution in the late 1990s was also testament to a historical tolerance by law enforcement agencies as over time national and local governments paid minimal attention to the construction of buildings and properties in the sectors of the Cañadas. There the gypsy clans set up their businesses without any police intervention, at almost no costs, paid no taxes and even were able to hijack electricity and water from public mains sources. The construction of dozens of makeshift buildings dedicated to the sale and consumption of drugs at the turn of the 21st century made its transformation irreversible. Indeed, the period from 2002 to 2010 became known as the 'golden era' of Valdemingómez as it was calculated that there were about 80 different drug sales points operating at the same time. Over this period, there was also a mass exodus from the area with many gypsy and Spanish families leaving the sector because of its social and physical deterioration.

How was it then that the Cañada Real Galiana was occupied given that laws set out in the 1950s – made as a consequence of the Cañadas becoming redundant – protected them from 'threat' and 'deterioration'? It was not until national legislation was made in 1995[8] which declared that the autonomous (local) communities (in this case the local council of Madrid) could protect their 'integrity and conservation' by allowing them for public use such as cycling, horse riding or hiking. By 1998, the local council in Madrid had finally managed to apply this law, essentially making the terrain protected while at the same time prohibited the construction of buildings. Naturally, by the time this law was applied it was too late to deter already-established drug and crime networks which had started to further problematise the application of the law. Deteriorating physical and social conditions and an absence of adequate social support systems had already complicated other formal responses because it involved the collaboration of the regional council of Madrid and local councils of Coslada and Rivas. This was extremely challenging as it took six years for each of the councils to agree to convene to start the process of designing intervention for each of the families in Valdemingómez. During this time it was agreed that the respective government institutions share the cost and responsibility for intervention (ACCEM and Fundación Secretariado Gypsy, 2010) before the initiative grounded to a halt because of 'conflict of interests' between the different administrations (Gómez Ciriano, 2011) and because of disputed urban commercial and economic interest in the land (Soleares, 2011).

Currently, 3,500 people live in Valdemingómez which is only 4 km in length over around 50 hectares. Its position as a sort of no man's land between Madrid, Coslada and Rivas generates numerous problems related to substandard housing or even people living in derelict sites. The scarcity of basic amenities such as water, electricity, public transport and rubbish collection was also prevalent and there was almost no infrastructure, such as asphalt roads, pavements or public space. The absence of basic social services such as schools, health institutions, hospitals, cultural centres or sports facilities made access problematic to basic public services. This was exacerbated by significant levels of drug dealing and drug use and high levels of crime, violence and low-levels of reporting.

In 2007, the police and other law enforcement agencies began a campaign of monitoring and control of Vademingómez with the aim of eradicating the sale of drugs from the sector. The units, comprising the National Police, Local Police and the Civil Guard, attempted a series of coordinated raids and intervention procedures which centred on tackling the gypsy families' grip on the drug market, organised robbery, scrapping of vehicles and general illegal dumping and the robbery of copper. However, there was little attention to the repercussions of a raid and the subsequent demolition of a building, with almost no attention given to the human rights of the people inside or immediate alternative housing solutions. This therefore only increased the risks to those made homeless as well as amplified the dangerous and neglected accumulation of rubbish and dire sanitary conditions. Much of this was continually broadcast by the media and the subsequent attention triggered high levels of social stigma and rejection: many of the other families living in the other sectors have faced discrimination, been blacklisted from possible work opportunities and struggled to register their children in nearby schools precisely because they 'come from the Cañada Real Galiana'. Notwithstanding, the tendency for people living in this area – predominantly gypsies – to have low educational levels, to have difficulty with interpreting and understanding formalised state processes, and a lack of knowledge about their human rights (Soleares, 2011). This has therefore been a deliberate process of subtle social cleansing of the city spaces.

The plot thickens...Madrid, inequality and space

It should be of no surprise that Valdemingómez is situated in one of the poorest areas of suburban Madrid and its immediate surroundings – or the barrios such as Vicalvaro, Villa de Vallecas and Puente de Vallecas – are also similarly deprived. In these areas, indices of youth and general unemployment are high and life expectancy is somewhat lower in comparison to the wealthier centre and northern part of the capital (see Figure 14.2). People living in and around Valdemingómez have a far more precarious existence. Thus, north of these areas in the city centre is where we find high numbers of professionals and fewer unemployed groups, while in the south is where there are higher levels of crime, unemployment and immigration (Clemente, 2015). While it is clear that there have been historical differences between the north and south, and in the periphery, the arrival of the construction boom followed by the labour market vacuum post-2008 only sharpened geospatial inequality (Rivas, 2014; Rojas, 2014). It is fairly safe to say that there exists an invisible dividing line between these two parts of Madrid which determines quite significantly a citizen's socio-economic status and, as a consequence, the urban experience. This is reflected in the high levels of unemployment in the south of the capital (DE, 2016) with many barrios averaging unemployment levels around 30% compared to around 15% in their northern equivalents (Leal and Sorando, 2016).

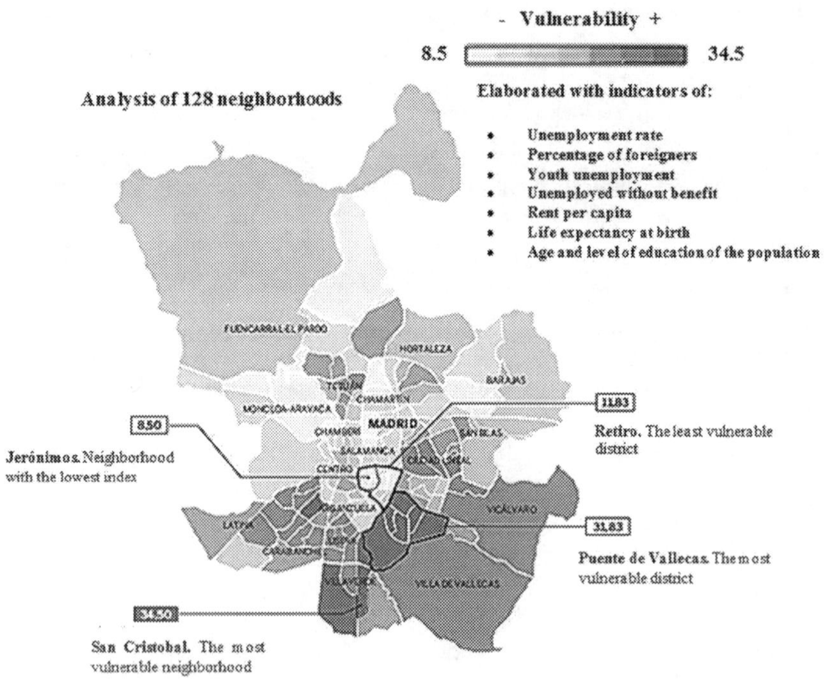

FIGURE 14.2 Indices of geospatial inequality in Madrid.

The metropolitan area therefore reflects serious levels of inequality and this situation of spatial polarisation and social segregation has been aggravated by the economic crisis of 2008, which essentially exacerbated the gap between the two social poles. This is exacerbated further by the sale of 96% of the social housing stock constructed over the last decade by the Madrid government to private companies to make profit. This left only 1,190 properties which essentially blocked access to housing to thousands of people: this despite, in the words of the Mayor, 'not to sell social housing to these types of people [business people]' (Martiarena, 2016). The social strata, it seems, in Madrid are increasingly separated and remote, and this increases the social fracturing of the urban landscape. Madrid is now the European city with the highest levels of social segregation (Tammaru et al., 2015).

This social division and obvious spatial separation is further exacerbated by drastically high levels of corruption which continue to damage the Spanish economy and drain valuable resources from public services. Researchers estimate corruption to cost the Spanish economy €40,000 million each year, and it was estimated that there were still 1,700 open cases as recent as 2013, while only 20 people had been sent to prison (León et al., 2013).[9] Corrupt institutions massively impact a host of different sectors, including public services, the education system, judicial powers, the police and armed forces (Villoria and Jiménez, 2012). The fact that these fraudulent irregularities are endemic to keeping the political elite in power has resulted in a 'politics of austerity' whereby the citizen essentially absorbs the debt generated by the banks and other financial institutions. Therefore, to prop up the economy, citizens pay more for public services, higher taxes, etc., and for this reason people in low-paid work struggle. They cannot access social housing, have benefits cut, cannot access mortgages and their rents increase which puts pressure on maintaining housing payments, utility charges and costs for children, which has led to families being made homeless and having to stay with other family or friends or illegally occupy houses/flats.

In particular, in the poorer areas of Madrid this is felt more than anywhere else. From 1998 to 2008, a consolidated gentrification of the city has taken place, which has separated the city by financial resource and socio-economic status: those with fewer assets have had no choice but to move or stay in the southern areas of the capital where property and standard of living are cheaper (Delgado, 2008; Leal and Sorando, 2016). At the turn of the 21st century, the Madrid government identified four barrios to be those most in need of investment with an aim to reduce inequality between the north and south of the city over a ten-year period. The barrios identified were Tetuán, San Blas, Carabanchel and Vicálvaro (see Comunidad de Madrid, 2009). However, a report published by the Socialist Party in Madrid found that unoccupied properties rose from 49% in 2004 to 56% in 2013 and that in this time of the €1,1170 million available to be invested in those areas, only 61% of the funds had been spent (Belber, 2014).

The creation of these quite separate spaces has been led by strategic private investment and bolstered with other social policies which are associated with maintaining the rank and organisation of those very spaces; that is, once a barrio can peel off symbols of deprivation and destitution – for example, crappy housing, grubby public spaces, problem populations, etc. – it can flourish economically and therefore attract further investment. Naturally, this creates other problems because it merely concentrates the poorer groups in other areas, rendering them more vulnerable. Moreover, this very experience was intensified by the disappearance of public policy for the most unprotected and a political failure to make public institutions respond efficiently to the very process of spatial inequality to which they have generated, essentially multiplying the difficulties people experience in these areas. This is because the social policies have been designed to support the accumulation of capital and economic growth of the city rather than the needs of the collective urban population.

For the people in the economically advantaged areas, this poses little problems as public institutions function better and their sense of individual responsibility is in line with neoliberal expectations of their personal responsibility. However, for families in the poorer areas south of the capital, it is the reverse: pubic services such as education, health and housing struggle under the weight and demand for their assistance while, at the same time, the personal resources to be responsible are somewhat dented by the experience of deprivation and social exclusion. In particular, there exists a massive shortage of affordable social housing in the south of Madrid, so it is perhaps unsurprising to learn that this area of the city reflects the majority of the concentration of illegally occupied housing.

In this context of wealth accumulation, increase of poverty and political abandonment of swathes of the urban populace, Madrid is a clear example of the neoliberal city, characterised by the continual search for competitiveness and new forms of business and profit which sadly shows the power the market has over a society (Requena, 2014). However, the context of my study is exemplified by the spatial and political abandonment of the southern hemisphere of the capital. This only allows for fertile ground for unemployment and crime which is why places like Valdemingomez and Polígono Marconi in Villaverde (also among the most deprived barrios of Madrid) are abundant in organised crime, drugs and prostitution.

The motivation to reverse these trends continues to be piecemeal, and city policymakers and politicians have taken few effective measures to reduce the growth of inequality let alone reduce its concentration in the peripheries of the city. Therefore, the precarious situation of the domestic economy and the deficit in the labour market tend to aggravate this spatial separation. The centre and north of Madrid are areas for business investment given the touristic appeal and represent international opportunities for capital investment, reflecting a cosmopolitan city, global and modern in orientation, even if it has clear problems of homelessness, drug dealing/dependence and socially vulnerable families. There is also certainly no real political interest now in attempting to help – who are portrayed as the main culprits in all this – the gypsies.

The gypsies: a history of working on the margins

Gypsies have often found themselves living outside other people's cultures – as 'people without a history' (Wolf, 1982). Their difference and the racist treatment towards them can be traced back to the advent of the modern period (Bauman, 1998). As countries across Eastern Europe, the ex-Soviet Union and the Third World underwent a process of rapid modernisation, gypsies and other nomadic groups found themselves pushed even further to the edges of European society (Cudworth, 2008). Having moved throughout Europe, escaping discrimination and oppressive policing in Eastern Europe, they encountered similar treatment on arrival in parts of Western Europe (Bangieva, 2007). This historic rejection has meant that gypsies have become highly capable of cultural adaptation in settings where they have had to survive (Gamella, 1999) – interacting in reciprocal contact with hostile host communities in a process of acculturation. They have, as Sway (1984: 83) has noted, 'a flexible and successful way of exploiting the economic margins'. This has, therefore, often promoted unique ways of determining gypsy customs so much so that some suggest many of the behaviours considered unique to their culture have actually been caused by situations related to social exclusion (Quintero et al., 2007).

In Spain, the gypsies have historically suffered varied forms of social persecution, racism and legal discrimination (Poveda and Marcos, 2005) across education, health, employment, housing and the judicial system (Rodríguez et al., 2009). Much of this has been exacerbated by complex urban restructuring processes in city centres over the last 40 years, which has reduced interaction with Spanish communities (Poveda and Marcos, 2005) while confining them to inferior suburban areas with few resources, minimal infrastructure and locking them out of opportunity in city centres (Briggs, 2010). While, there have been increased efforts to integrate gypsies into Spanish life across Spain (Tomás et al., 2004), gypsies remain confined to the margins, drug/criminal networks as well as other informal economies which involve the sale of 'chatarra' (scrap metal), 'cartones' (cardboard boxes) and perhaps 'venta ambulante' (street trading) (Jalon and Rivera, 2000). Increasingly, however, these opportunities have become scanter in the wake of new taxation processes and aggressive social policies prohibiting them which is why from the mid-1980s onwards, with the advent of large-scale drug distribution in Spain, much of their activity has revolved around the trafficking of drugs (Briggs, 2010).

Research has shown that when drugs started to arrive in bulk in Spain, it was the gypsies that started to undercut the competing drug markets by offering high-quality drugs for lower prices (Briggs, 2010). In the main, they dealt in heroin in the barrios of cities like Madrid and, as a consequence, this has come to define the experience of these particular *poblados*. Indeed, from the 1980s, 14 large *poblados* can be identified to have been important in Madrid: they include Pitis, Avenida de Guadalajara, Celsa, Barranquillas and Valdemingómez in the Cañada Real Galiana (Figure 14.3).

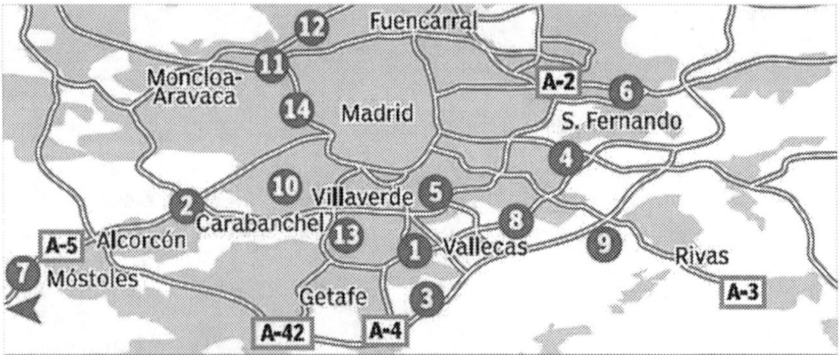

Poblado name	District	Shacks	Poblado name	District	Shacks
1-El Salobral	Villaverde	424	8-Las Barranquillas	Vallecas	120*
2-Mimbreras	La Latina	132	9-Cañada Real	Valdemingómez	2.000
3-Ventorro	Villaverde	?	10-El Aguacate	Carabanchel	30 personas
4-Cañaveral	Vicálvaro	148	11-Puerta de Hierro	Moncloa-Aravaca	16
5-S. Catalina	P. Vallecas	180	12-Las Quinta-Pitis	Fuencarral	12
6-Las Castellanas	S. Fernando	115	13-Plata y Castañar	Villaverde	34*
7-Río Guadarrama	Móstoles	260	14-Valverde	Fuencarral	20

FIGURE 14.3 Spread of the main *poblados* in Madrid.[10]

The sale of drugs occurs in each of these *poblados*, and is often sold from houses, kiosks, fumaderos, improvised buildings, or caravans 24 hours a day. The main drugs available are heroin, cocaine and various types of amphetamines and cannabis. The management of the drug sales is undertaken by gypsy families who operate a strong hierarchy between its affiliates, assigning particular tasks to particular members. Relations between families are generally good and there is cooperation and organisation between them in the trafficking of large amounts of drugs, particularly when it comes to dealing with Colombian cartels (cocaine) and Turkish mafia (heroin). However, when there are disputes between the families or even individuals – which can lead to the involvement of the whole family and the patriarch – it is not uncommon for there to be violence, fights and even deaths. 'La ley gitana' or 'the gypsy law' authorise revenge and the use of violence to resolve conflicts between families or, in some cases, whole *poblados*. It is this same law that permits children to grow up and assume the same cultural attitudes and labour roles as their parents – in this case, working in the drug market from a young age.

For the gypsies, drugs are by far the most profitable commodity and Valdemingómez harbours among the most powerful gypsy families in Spain. We estimate there to be around 13 main families in the area which own between them around 40 drug-selling points: that is either kiosks or fumaderos. The hierarchy is formed of members of the same family, each with between 8 and 20 people, the Matriarch being a woman who has the most important function to manage the organisation while men tend to manage the labour of sales and security. The younger family members access important posts when they arrive at their adolescence, often being instructed and trained by senior family members to inherit the business, hence their position as 'Herederos' or 'Heirs'. In their incorporation, it is common for young boys and girls even much younger than their adolescent ages to also assume some small positions such as look-outs or even to receive clients under the supervision of adults. The 'personas de confianza' or 'trustworthy people' are normally recognised for their working reputation in the trafficking and/or sale of the drugs; most commonly they will buy and sell in bulk or be responsible for drug distribution to and from different places outside Valdemingómez. Even though gypsies often have extensive families, priority for working in the drug market is given to those in closer vicinity and these are called 'Familiares' or 'other family members'. The 'colaboradores' or 'colaborators' are those who exchange stolen goods/information for drugs and/or can also be involved with laundering money in the local area.

Each kiosk and fumadero has various employees. The first of whom are normally located on the outside door are the machacas who let people in, assist with drug deals to clients, look out and clean up. They are located on the outside door to level divots or fill puddles in the road, maintain the fires and warn of police presence. Secondly, within the inside wall of the venue, another machaca will normally open the door after a worded code from another on the outside. This person may direct client's cars if the location has a large parking area. Thereafter, to access the fumadero, the client will need to pass another machaca giving another password to enter in the smoking/dealing area:

> Outside one fumadero, we first get talking to a crowd of four drug users, all of whom practically stand in the fire for warmth. It is quite incredible to look at these people but most seem fairly harmless as they are in a permanent state of intoxication. Daniel smiles at one in particular and when he greets him in the same way in return, he counts four teeth. Beneath his beard and the blackness of his face, he is tanned by orientation, and stands with some toes sticking out of his worn trainers: his clothes ragged and worn, and nails almost as long as his fingers; and as he approaches to shakes Daniel's hand as the dirt from his black palm clasps his.
>
> Minutes later, Diego bangs on the gate of the house at which we stand and the bearded man hurries to him. Diego asks us to be let into the fumadero so the bearded man starts whispering through the gate at the guard on the other side. After a minute or so, the gate slowly opens and the supposed guard is another drug addict, half high and half consciously mumbling as his eyes flicker between closed and ajar. We walk into the courtyard of the fumadero: in front is a house with two fairly robust doors, and to the right a pile of rubbish and rubble, with a makeshift hut for the machacas to sleep in and to the left another hut where some people are permitted to smoke drugs. On the floor, between the dirt and brown puddles,

are literally thousands of castaway drug vials. At weekends Diego says the cars pull in here and come in and stay for the weekend to use drugs. Some, he says, come and spend between €3,000 to €4,000 euros in a weekend. We turn around at the open gate and the machaca stands leaning against it half asleep, high on a dose of heroin and cocaine.

Field notes

The client normally purchases the drugs through a gap which is criss-crossed with iron bars and it is this room which is linked to a high-security room known as a bunker. The access to the bunker is impossible from the fumadero and there is normally a specific entrance for gypsy family members and/or VIP clients. Within the bunker, one person manages the sales with the least amount of drugs as possible and will normally have enough drugs to last 12 hours of sales, so between 150 and 200 g as a means of minimising losses in the event of a police raid. The protection of this interior varies according to the type of construction and importance of the gypsy family. For example, some compose of up to seven armoured doors, reinforced walls and safe boxes. There are also various carbon cookers, drainpipes and corrosive liquids which assist in cutting and preparing the drugs as they do with their elimination. The bunkers never keep large amounts of money, and funds are emptied regularly every 8–12 hours and the cash is transferred to other locations around the capital before being invested in commodities, property and cars. Less common, though it still happens, is that some gypsy families will keep the cash in high denomination notes of €200 and €500 in hidden walls and secret locations in and around the property.

FIGURE 14.4 Inside a fumadero where drugs are mixed and cut and then dealt through the metal door.

Such is the organisation of this that it is estimated that within two minutes of the commencement of a police raid, it is possible to have destroyed all the drugs, money and other incriminating material; two minutes being the estimated time which it takes to batter down the reinforced walls and doors. All these techniques and measures taken by the gypsies have been built up from experience in other *poblados* in Madrid. Notwithstanding, the gypsies will often physically coax potential clients, in particular coming up to passing cars telling them the road has been sealed up ahead and offering "free cocaine hits" while the machaca's role in attracting clients is far more passive largely due to their almost permanent sedentary state.

Wealth is needed to justify the symbolisms of wealth, such as their luxury cars and expensive jewellery. Towards the latter stages of my fieldwork, in the autumn of 2016, some kiosks and fumaderos started to accept things like gold and precious stones as a means of payment for drugs. This is because the gypsies like to exhibit material trinkets as a means of reflecting a superior social status and how they can participate like others as competent consumers. It is also this which determines the key figures in the gypsy families: they are those who are adorned with the most jewels, gold and the like. Key male family members dress in smart suits and hats, perhaps with a gold walking stick while matriarchs will adorn gold, jewellery and often have cosmetic surgery on their bodies. Those further down the family hierarchy normally dress in sports clothes and casual attire. By measure of success and social standing in Valdemingómez, the most important families are those who sell the most amount of drugs, consequently resulting in their ability to display consumer status items, while an inferior family is dependent on those who sell drugs.

These power hierarchies are maintained and reproduced at all levels largely because the gypsy cultural interactions are confined to limited social circles (i.e. only fellow gypsies) and spatially restricted to the area – there is very little contact between the families in Valdemingómez or sector 6 and in sector 5 of the Cañada Real Galiana. This restriction on cultural interactions forces hierarchical relations to revolve around the maintenance of a particular set of symbolic interactions as a means of determining self-respect in a closed space. Taken together, this does not make them socially excluded per se as they demonstrate all the will to want to be socially included as consumers (Nightingale, 2012; Winlow and Hall, 2013; Young, 1999) but they are set in ideological competition with each other. For this to occur, there needs to be a set of norms and codes which place others economically, socially and culturally inferior to them. Those people are the drug users in Valdemingómez and these power relations are reinforced on a daily basis by the adults as well as the young gypsy children:

> As we talk to Roberto, a chorus of half-asleep drug addicts sit and lounge about at the provided dinner tables. The group of Gypsy boys see Margarita (a female machaca) outside one of the fumaderos and start to dare each other to approach her before one decides to steal her coat from her back and tosses it into a nearby fire where another machaca keeps warm. The coat

bursts into flames and Margarita screams and makes one-hand gestures at them. A machaca nearby tries to verbally intervene but can't do anything as these young boys are untouchable–any intervention would mean the quick presence of their parents and would almost certainly end in violence if they had to defend them. As the scene starts to capture the attention of the docile drug addicts in their post-lunch-drug taking, the gypsy kids then steal a blanket from Margarita's back and toss it into the fire. In her fragile state she is helpless and her weak hand gestures only make the children jump up and down in glee. The children then approach her and make faces and insult her as if she was totally alien before she manages to scare them off temporarily, aided in part by the same machaca, who tries to reason with them. As they run off, one falls over in the rubbish and his friends are quick to rescue him thinking perhaps that he has fallen into some used syringes (the area is strewn with used syringes and other paraphernalia). For young boys of no older than 5 years they seem to be aware of these dangers as they strip down the youngest boy, and check for marks. As they dress him again, and in anger, they start to take rocks and throw them in the direction of Margarita.

It is only then that Roberto marches over, waving off the children before shepherding over the bent old woman to the safer territory of the harm reduction bus. It is only then that we realize how startled she is, as she toos and fros from seat to seat, wondering what to do–she seems to feel violated. As she sits, Roberto rubs her back as she puts her bag full of everything she owns and everything she has to sell on the floor. She sits in a pile and puts her dirty black hands on her face and starts to cry. On top of all her suffering, her most basic things to maintain her daily life in this misery are robbed from her for the short-term and aimless entertainment of some gypsy children.

As she gathers her strength back she does some business with other drug addicts who are after clean paraphernalia. Then another female machaca Yolanda, wanders over with four stray-dog pets which follow her as if she is a magical sage. She has come to collect her medication. All we can gather about this woman is she lives alone in the Valdemingómez after having suffered bereavement when her husband died. We have seen her wash cars for the gypsies for only five euros. One dog looks like a bear and has with him several friends of lesser size. All the dogs haphazardly follow their graceful master, Yolanda, this resolute woman in her early fifties with long silver hair and worn face. The dogs' jog around her, in and out of the tables, and in front of cars before circling towards her after she collects her methadone medication.

As they meander off, so do we towards Adrian's chabola on the corner to speak to him. We step up the broken wooden boards, and looking at his collapsing shed, call to him through his wooden structure. He asks us if we are here to cure his dog's leg and it is only then that we see a skinny

> but quite cute dog limp towards us on three legs licking its lips with its little pink tongue. The dog is nervous as Adrian shouts at it to come off the road. As he does, Yolanda passes with the largest of her dogs and suddenly a gypsy driver, much to his amusement, emergency breaks as he almost crashes into the large dog. He drives off laughing to himself while Yolanda yells back and insults at him.
>
> *Field notes*

As we can see in varying intervals of these field notes, at the bottom of the social chain, the gypsies place the drug users; they are a source of entertainment and ridicule, often with extreme consequences:

> As we come to the conclusion of an interview with Nacho, a local policeman who has worked 25 years in Valdemingómez and many of the surrounding poblados, he recalls something quite remarkable as he sits forward sipping his tall beer. He shakes his head as he remembers how devastating the heroin epidemic was in the 1980s. *"In particular, the poor areas south of Madrid were mostly affected, thousands of people lost, a whole generation"* he says. We can't tell if his eyes well with tears or they squint from the fifth cigarette he smokes. We get onto the subject of prostitution and he starts to fiddle around with his phone as if he has got bored with our questioning. Some seconds later, however, he shows us a videoclip recorded by a gypsy in a fumadero where we watch for a few minutes as a woman in her mid-20s dressed in a vest and knickers puts a condom on another drug user, verbally battles off the abuse, jokes and jibs before she starts to suck his dick. As the man exaggerates the pleasure he receives for a few minutes, he turns her around and she drops her knickers. He proceeds to have sex with her quickly and hard much to the cheers of the other people in the fumadero, some of whom are also recording it. A minute or two later, he ejaculates and she walks off swearing at everyone as they jeer at her, while she tries to restore some dignity by pulling up her knickers and dusting herself down. The clip stops and we really don't know what to say as the policeman lights up his sixth cigarette. Most of his colleagues have sent this to each other via Whatsapp.
>
> *Field notes*

The brutality of what it means to live in this open haven for drug dealing and prostitution is evident in these field notes, for as I write these words, it still thrives.

Discussion

For this reason, we can say that drugs will continue to play a part in the day-to-day lives of millions of people – farmers, traffickers, mules, consumers – as long as the global political economy continues to strip away labour markets without replacing decent alternatives for people. Secluded pockets of marginalisation, such as Valdemingómez, where chaotic drug use, drug-dealing and violence are endemic, will continue to thrive because these communities have thus been politically and spatially manufactured to have no interaction with formal economies other than those who offer them some food and clean syringes and those which patrol and arrest them. Furthermore, drugs will also continue to be available, tried, used habitually and problematically so long as cultural attitudes towards our mode of being oscillates around consumerist attitudes mixed with a quest for our own self-gratification and supposed freedom to 'experience' what the world has to offer. So long as consumer culture continues to create in a nagging discontent in people's lives that can be solved by their purchase of an experience/feeling like drugs to temporarily ease the pang, the marketisation of drug use will continue.

While all this indicates some generalised drug-dealing/trafficking myths such as violence, use of minors, organised crime and significant profit, the context is important to consider. This is an area which harbours the city's unwanted social groups and has evolved as a consequence of the closure of other problematic drug markets. Families in this area grow up learning this is the expectation from them – to inherit strategic positions in the drug market. There is no viable alternative for them as racism and exclusionary policies block them from entering mainstream channels such as education and the labour market (see Heal's chapter in this volume). This therefore only perpetuates crime and violence making it inevitable, particularly so when weak social and crime policies are bolstered only with intermittent policing. This area and its conditions then are very specific.

We lack a real clear sense of why people are dealing drugs and this chapter, as well as this collection, aims to remedy this misunderstanding. A common popular misperception about actions attributed to drug dealing is some clear-cut choice, made in the acquisition/absence of knowledge about using a particular substance or engaging in dealing. For example, 'I deal drugs taking a calculated risk knowing that there will be repercussions should I be caught'. I have shown in this chapter that this very philosophy is the thrust of treatment mantras, penal as well as social policy in Spain. Hence, in the wake of the heroin boom of the 1980s and early 1990s, the emphasis was placed on drug education – to make people aware of the risks of certain types of drugs as well as the legal mechanisms which come down on offenders if they are caught.

These depictions are widely found throughout the media as well. Almost all news stories present facts of 'gypsy detentions/arrests' and how 'powerful clans have been raided', coupled with the usual police/political propaganda quotes of how the authorities are working for a safer city. Yet all this does is solidify the public's perception of gypsies and drugs/crime and contributes to blockages in their vertical social mobility. So, one of the main problems of this perspective is that it simply sidelines the role of wider forces which may influence someone from a particular social cohort to deal drugs and thereafter either return to them in the process of continuing to deal drugs.

Here is when we need an appreciation of the political economy in a time when cultural attitudes to consumption are willy-nilly and excessive, and youthful abandonment take precedence and it is this which should explain our attitudes to try substances (Hall et al., 2008; Briggs, 2013). The demarcation from a society, which revolved around notions of community, heritage and established cultural norms made possible by the advent of neoliberalism in the 1970s, has set society in competition with itself and recalibrated subjective identities around the symbolisms provided to us by corporations and marketing experts. From this time onwards our cultural attitudes have started to reflect elements of these structural changes as we place emphasis on 'living for the moment' and 'seizing opportunities' – all of which mirror established neoliberal philosophies that cast aside the future and problems like finding work or establishing a career and family replacing them with the need for personal gratification, risk taking and pleasure-seeking. Yet at the same time we are tasked with being responsible for ourselves and our own health. It is under these cultural circumstances that our research cohort developed consumerist attitudes towards drug dealing and it is where their dilemmas remain as they are caught between extreme, flaunting and opportunistic forms of consumption and safe and healthy consumption. In the end, for these people, this personal quandary is not really resolved as many fluctuate between the two states even if and when they try to take steps towards recovery.

The same transition into the neoliberal period, however, also destabilised the social structure and automatically rendered certain social groups at the bottom of society redundant. Failure to evolve as 'responsible citizens' – regardless of socio-economic status – in a society which ever more gives preference to individual meritocratic initiative coupled with the stark lack of opportunity and economic and educational limitations only serves up viable options in illicit economies, such as drugs, prostitution and crime (see Heal's chapter, Fleetwood's chapter and Ayres and Treadwell's chapter in this volume). While these realities are not certainties for everyone born into these conditions, they are severe impediments to any reasonable alternative especially given the structural and spatial impediments to a better life in and around this area of Madrid.

These problems – far from being locally-born – have global origins. For example, the gypsy dealers described throughout have become the face of the street drug market in Spain but this is largely because of the political scapegoating of the way they have to survive. Criminalising marginal activity like recycling copper, reselling old machines, even applying stricter rules to street market licences, only fosters the need to innovate in the search for other opportunities in other illicit economies. Even then, the gypsies do not simply produce the drugs and are instead part of a global chain of contacts and players in the international drug trade, responding to a market opportunity in a time at which drug consumption has been normalised (see Turner's chapter in this volume). Behind the gypsies, there are political pressures in producer countries which result in the need to cultivate drugs, as there exist thousands of other people who, as a consequence of imbalances in the global political economy, work illegally in the same industry – transporting, dealing, cutting and reselling drugs.

Solutions to these exclusionary predicaments are presented to us as if they hinge on individual decision-making. For example, governments are content to develop policies to support those willing and culturally competent to attain higher levels of education and provide equal access to education and health because social-cultural practices in the field of consumption, education and housing are associated with individual choice: they are realised by private choices which lie outside the realm of government. This is because social institutions now 'filter' out the most deserving, risk free, people in which to invest in: those who will take advantage of what is on offer. However, by comparison, given these emerging spatial dimensions and concentration of deprivation, the resources in hyperghettos like Valdemingómez lack investment for the very same reason – there is almost zero motivation to invest in a dead cause reflected in the slow and drawn-out reluctance to spend dedicated funds on these people who are seen only to squander their own futures. The money 'goes missing' has somehow been 'miscellaneously and mysteriously' spent and this seems to correlate with endemic corruption cases in Spain.

Notes

1 See Hidalgo, C. (2019) 'Cae el historico clan de Los Bruno, una de las familias narcotraficantes más poderosas en Madrid' in *ABC*, cited online on 3rd December 2019 at www.abc.es/espana/madrid/abci-historico-clan-bruno-familias-narcotraficantes-mas-poderosas-madrid-201903191136_video.html
2 See TeleMadrid (2018) 'El drama social de la Cañada Real Galiana' in YouTube cited online on 3rd December 2019 www.youtube.com/watch?v=Uggpr5QAHUI
3 See Sexta (2014) 'Registro en la Cañada Real–Policias en acción' in YouTube cited online on 3rd December 2019 on www.youtube.com/watch?v=iCfwBwEulp8
4 It was not until 1988 that the local government finally agreed to allow for the improvised constructions to be replaced by legal housing and therefore the land was made legal to the owners of the properties – a legal battle led by the resident's association which took 14 years to resolve. Since then, many poor-quality structures have been rebuilt and replaced by stronger, more robust buildings (see Ministerio de Formento, 2010: 12–16).
5 It is suggested that these families were either 'expelled from the city' or 'had significant wealth to be able to build country residences' (see ACCEM and Fundación Secretariado Gypsy, 2010: 45).
6 Spanish families were able to legally acquire the land over a period of time.
7 Interestingly, it is almost impossible to know which part of the Cañada Real Galiana falls under which government entity since the six sectors were demarcated and separated by the Residents Associations in each of the sectors. Over time, this has led to ambiguity in relation to institutional responsibility.
8 See these decrees: La Ley 3/1995, de 23 de marzo De Vías Pecuarias de la Comunidad de Madrid and La Ley 8/1998, de 15 de junio, De Vías Pecuarias de la Comunidad de Madrid.

9 See also cases like Caso Gürtel in which 187 people are implicated, 77 of which are from the Partido Popular (Conservative government) for alleged political corruption (Otero, 2014) and Operación Púnica in which found 100 politicians to have created criminal networks which assisted in the deliberate allocation of €250 million in exchange for illegal commission (Campos, 2015).

10 Statistics taken from data generated and referenced in Briggs and Monge Gamero (2017: 138).

References

ACCEM y Fundación Secretariado Gitano (2010) *Informe diagnóstico sobre la Cañada Real Galiana.* Madrid: Fundación Secretariado Gitano.

Bangieva, B. (2007) 'Italy with special law against Gypsies and travellers', available at: http:// international.ibox.bg/news cited online on 21st February 2019.

Bauman, J. (1998) 'Demons of other peoples fear: The plight of the Gypsies', *Thesis Eleven*, 54, August, 51–62.

Belber, M. (2014) 'Distrito rico, distrito (más) pobre' in El Mundo, 26th April 2014 cited online at www.elmundo.es/madrid/2014/04/26/535bf7c522601d19778b4578.html on 18th January 2019.

Briggs, D. (2010) 'Barriers to reintegration for Los Gitanos (Gypsies) in La Coruña, Spain: Politics, the media and the Spanish community' *International Journal of Migration, Health and Social Care*, 9(1): 17–31.

Briggs, D. (2013) *Deviance and Risk on Holiday: An Ethnography of British Tourists in Ibiza*, London: Palgrave MacMillan.

Briggs, D. and Monge Gamero, R. (2017) *Dead End Lives: Drugs and Violence in the City Shadows.* Bristol: Policy Press.

Clemente, Y. (2015) 'Diferencias entre el norte y el sur de Madrid' in El País cited online at http://elpais.com/elpais/2015/10/14/media/1444838463_647499.html on 29th January 2019.

Comunidad de Madrid (2009) *Planes Especiales de Inversión y Actuación territorial.* Madrid: Comunidad de Madrid.

Cudworth, D. (2008) 'There's a little bit more than just delivering the stuff: Policy, pedagogy, and the education of Gypsy/traveller children', *Critical Social Policy*, 28(3): 361–377.

Departamento de Estadística (DE). (2016) 'Paro registrado' in Ayuntamiento de Madrid cited online at www.madrid.es/portales/munimadrid/es/Inicio/El-Ayuntamiento/Estadistica/Areas-de-informacion-estadistica/Mercado-de-trabajo/Paro-registrado/Paro-registrado?vgnextfmt=default&vgnextoid=a9a2b350526e8310VgnVCM1000000b205a0aRCRD&vgnextchannel=f29e62a006986210VgnVCM2000000c205a0aRCRD on 4th Febuary 2019.

Delgado, B. (2008) Propuestas para un nuevo modelo urbano madrileño en clave de sostenibilidad: del crecimiento a la rehabilitación, *Congreso Nacional del Medio Ambiente.*

Gamella, J. (1999) 'Los gitanos andaluces. Una minoria étnica en una encrucijada histórica', *Revista Demofilo*, 30: 15–30.

Gómez Ciriano, E. (2011) 'Los derechos humanos y la responsibildad de las administraciones en La Cañada Galllinero' in *Trabajo Social Hoy: Revista Editada por el Colegio de Trabajadores Sociales de Madrid*, 62: 7–27.

Hall, S., Winlow, S., and Ancrum, C. (2008) *Criminal Identities and Consumer Culture: Crime, Exclusion and the New Culture of Narcissism.* Cullumpton: Willan.

Jalon, F., and Rivera, A. (2000) *Salud y comunidad gitana. Análisis de propuestas para la actuación*. Madrid: Asociación Secretariado General Gitano.

Lago Ávila, M. (2014) 'Another Madrid: The non-stop growth of shanty towns. Regional rehousing and social integrational policies 1997–2010', *Estudios Geograficos*, LXXV(276): 219–260.

Leal, J., and Sorando, D. (2016) 'Economic crisis, social change and segregation processes in Madrid' in T. Tammaru, M. Szymon Marcizcnak (Eds.), *Socio-Economic Segregation in European Capital Cities: East Meets West* (pp. 214–237). London: Routledge.

León, C., Araña, J., and de León, J. (2013) Estudio de estimación del coste social de la corrupción", realizado por el Instituto Universitario de Turismo y Desarrollo Sostenible (TIDES), Universidad de Las Palmas de Gran Canaria, (2013) Centro de Investigaciones Sociológicas: Estudio nº 3021 del Centro de Investigaciones Sociológicas del mes de abril (2014) y Estudio nº 3114 del Centro de Investigaciones Sociológicas del mes de octubre (2015), disponible en: www.cis.es/cis/opencm/ES/11_barometros/index.jsp

Martiarena, A. 2016. 'Madrid sigue vendiendo vivienda protegida a los "fondos buitre"', La Vanguardia, 12 September, www.lavanguardia.com/local/madrid/20160912/41159445352/madrid-sigue-vendiendo-vivienda-protegida-buitre.html

Mbomío Rubio, L. (2012) *La Cuidad Invisible: Voces en la Cañada Real Galiana*. Unpublished report on a documentary, Antropodocus Productions.

Nightingale, C. (2012) *A Global History of Divided Cities*. Chicago: Chicago University Press.

Poveda D., and Marcos, T. (2005) 'The social organisation of a stone fight: Gitano children's interpretive reproduction of ethnic conflict', *Childhood*, 12(3): 327–349.

Quintero, G., Lilliott, E. and Willging, C. (2007) 'Substance abuse treatment provider views of "culture": implications for behavioural health care in rural settings", *Qualitative Health Research*, 17: 1256–1267.

Requena, P. M. (2014) 'Pobreza y exclusión social en Madrid: viejos temas y nuevas propuestas', *AIBR: Revista de Antropología Iberoamericana*, 9(2): 163–182.

Rivas, P. (2014) 'El mapa de la desigualdad en Madrid' in Diagonal cited online at www.diagonalperiodico.net/global/24735-mapa-la-desigualdad-madrid.html on 14th October 2016.

Rodriguez, A., Leon, A., Garcia, M. and Nunez, J. (2009), 'Attitudes of adolescent Spanish Roma non-injection drug use and risky sex behaviour', *Qualitative Health Research*, 19(5): 605–620.

Rojas, G. J. (2014) *Evolución e impacto del riesgo de la pobreza y la exclusión en la Comunidad de Madrid*. Madrid: EAPN.

Soleares (2011) *Informe Socio-Ambiental sobre la Cañada Real Galiana: Sector 5*, Madrid: Asociación Colectivo Soleares.

Sway, M. (1984) 'Economic adaptability: The case of the gypsies', *Urban Life*, *13*(1): 83–98. https://doi.org/10.1177/0098303984013001005

Tammaru, T., van Ham, M., Marcińczak, S., & Musterd, S. (Eds.). (2015). *Socio-economic Segregation in European Capital Cities: East Meets West* (Vol. 89). Routledge.

Tomás, E., Pérez, J., Tixeira, M., Suarez, J., and Velasco, C. (2004) *Erradicación del chabolismo y integración social de los Gitanos en Avilés*. Avilés: University of Oviedo.

Villoria, M., and Jiménez, F. (2012) 'La corrupción en España (2004–2012): Datos, percepciones y efectos' in *Reis*, 138 abril-junio 2012, pp. 109.134.

Winlow, S. and Hall, S. (2013) *Rethinking Social Exclusion: The End of Social?* London: Sage.
Wolf, E. (1982) *Europe's People Without a history*. London: Allison and Busby.
Young, J. (1999) *The Exclusive Society: Social Exclusion, Crime and Difference in Late Modernity*. London: Sage.

PART 2

New drugs, new technologies and new perspectives

15

THE DARKNET, BITCOINS AND THE ROLE OF THE INTERNET IN DRUG SUPPLY

Angus Bancroft

Drug dealing in a time of illegible capitalism

What is called digital society is really a host and meeting point of a range of technologies, cultures and social practices which reconfigure the opportunities for drug dealers. Mobile apps, internet relay chat programmes, bitcoin and other systems are enabled in specific ways by the underlying technical infrastructure. The political economy of the digital is crucial to understanding the way in which drug dealing and policing of it have developed. Devices are tools and as such are transformational in a socio-technical sense. Mobile phones allow mobility, in theory moving markets away from fixed locations but in practice allowing those locations to be in more than one place. The technology need not be especially advanced. Mobile-mediated drug dealing has brought open-air drug markets indoors (Nicholas, 2008), where after all, everyone prefers to be. This change when dealers can be contacted, text messages and email allows for asynchronous communication.

The political economy of digitally enabled platform capitalism is monopolistic, extractive and illegible (Srnicek, 2016; Zuboff, 2015). It emphasises and values non-material products and labour, and combines informational elements into material production. It generates on a number of myths – that it is flat and data driven, impersonal, automated, networked, transparent and informative, where in reality platform fiefdoms serve the interest of their shareholders, users exist as aggregated data personae, its economy is extractive and sometimes parasitical, it relies on an extensive labour infrastructure, power is concentrated and much is hidden. Power in this economy is both transparent and illegible, meaning that users' actions are visible to the monitoring and mining system, while it resists being analysed for its structural impact and redistribution of wealth and social capital. It is designed to be opaque to and avoidant of established

DOI: 10.4324/9781351010245-18

modes of democratic governance, public oversight and critique (Pasquale, 2015). Enforcement uses some of these tools. It is reconfigured to police the digital street using digital forensics, which leverage these qualities of pattern matching, traceability and associative data to generate narratives of criminal association (Lane, 2018). On the other side, criminal groups can use real-time control systems to manage members' activities (Storrod and Densley, 2017). In terms of research, data collected from multiple sources such as postal intercepts can highlight the existence of rural drug-dealing hotspots and move the criminological lens beyond urban space (Matthews et al., 2019). Technological affordances – technical qualities that permit individual action – generate criminal ecologies, criminalisation processes and crime control modes (Williams et al., 2017; Wortley, 2012). Affordances are significant because they are independent of specific digital platforms.

Internet drug supply and dealing have to be understood as operating within the logics of this techno-political economy in several ways. There is a logic of surveillance. The focus of citizen monitoring is on integration across services and state agencies use different kinds of data – biomedical, facial recognition, financial records and digital fingerprinting – to augment more established kinds of digital surveillance (Valeriano et al., 2018). Researchers, law enforcement, drug dealers and drug users have to work with the opportunities and risks of this kind of digital traceability (Smith et al., 2017). New kinds of investigation and policing are emerging, some of which focus on disruption and denial of service rather than arrest and prosecution (Afilipoaie and Shortis, 2018). Finally, there is a material logic. Rationalised drug supply chains produce commodified entities with a high division of labour, while informationalised markets allow for personalisation and niche products to emerge. Redistribution of labour and accessibility occur along lines of prevailing power and privilege (Urbanik and Haggerty, 2018).

Digitally connected technology has allowed drug dealing to develop in new ways, accelerating an existing move away from open air markets (May and Hough, 2004). Clients do not need to have a high degree of involvement in face-to-face social networks in order to obtain drugs, so there is lower network density in illicit drug-using cultures. Networks of drug distribution can be looser and more agile. New clients and dealers can be drawn into drug use and supply, giving a boost to new forms such as smart drug use (Bakken and Demant, 2019). The geographical place of dealing is also different, but not absent and is still bounded spatially (Demant et al., 2017). Mobile communication technology has meant dealing to users can move indoors, from the street to the sofa (Nicholas, 2008). There is a limited impact of the more specialised dealing modes such as the darknet on the offline, material market as many drug users are impervious to their charms (Spicer, 2019). However, changes in the online can reconfigure other drug markets in three ways: they produce hybrid distribution strategies that combine both online and offline modes (Lusthaus and Varese, 2018), they saturate some markets pushing previous dominant dealer networks to exploit previously marginal opportunities and they open new exploitation vectors (Hall, 2019). On the one hand, highly malicious criminal modes are enabled (Ellis, 2019). On the other hand, digital dealing drives gentrification of norms and interactions in some areas (Martin, 2017).

Routes and modes of digital dealing

There are two main routes of dealing using digital means. One is to employ existing plain sight communication platforms such as email, listservs, Facebook, WeChat and so on (Moyle et al., 2019). The second is to develop dedicated shopfronts and exchange forums on the open web or the darknet (Hall and Antonopoulos, 2015, 2016; Martin, 2014; see Hall and Antonopoulos' chapter in this volume) or channels using Discord, Telegram, Rocketchat and similar apps (King, 2019). These systems offer varying degrees of security, risk and openness, and demand different levels of user expertise and investments of time and resources. Drug users mostly combine online and offline purchase methods depending on the drugs being sought and their availability (Barratt et al., 2016). Many users test out darknet cryptomarkets but desist from use due to the face-to-face market operating just as or more effectively (Barratt et al., 2017). Buyers on social media can use the platform affordances by commenting on dealers' posts advertising drugs or direct messaging them.

Sale methods can be divided into internet-mediated dealing (using apps and so on, essentially mediated in-person purchase) and internet-located dealing (darknet, web purchase) which is ultimately conducted through couriers, postal services and dead drops. When trust is established, darknet dealers sometimes move to off platform direct dealing (Childs et al., 2020). Although internet located dealing is on the rise, most dealing is face to face. Taking drug delivery as a proxy for online dealing, having drugs delivered is most typical of Brazil (47%), Scotland (39%) and England (36%). Hungary and Norway are the fewest with less than 10% (Global Drugs Survey, 2019). Each mode of dealing has varying degrees of scalability. App-based dealing is firmly localised. Cryptomarket dealing has geographical limits but can be more expansive than app dealing. Typically cryptomarket dealers restrict their operations to within a country or region such as the Schengen area, with a risk premium to be paid going beyond that (Cunliffe et al., 2017).

Apps facilitate digitally mediated local markets. The buyer still mostly needs to meet the person to exchange, whereas in cryptomarkets drugs have to be delivered through postal or courier systems. Apps have clear attractions, being immediately available in communication systems that users will be using anyway. They do not have the technical barriers of cryptomarkets nor the problems with using cryptocurrencies – wild swings in value, and the risk the market may collapse with your money when this has happened. They can substitute for absent social supply networks. In the UK apps provide increased range and variety of drugs, but this is a limit for users in other countries where they cannot find what they need on apps. Product promotion is possible. Apps like Snapchat allow dealers to 'spamvertise' products, using a kind of viral marketing to promote their wares. There are no direct ratings but views and likes can function as a proxy. Aside from that, buyers have little comeback from a bad purchase. Users often misattribute security characteristics to apps, assuming some have end-to-end encryption when in fact they do not. As a whole, social supply is still preferred to app-mediated purchase (Bright and Sutherland, 2017).

Dealers locate themselves at different points in the supply chain partly dependent on their commercial acumen and ideology. There are the wholly commercial, profit-driven dealers who see expansion, then there are those who look to reach a stable equilibrium (Masson and Bancroft, 2018). Cryptomarkets are unusual in that they employ both a tailored dealing environment and a means of payment, typically bitcoin. About $76 billion of illegal activity is estimated to be financed using bitcoin, which is 46% of all bitcoin use (Foley et al., 2018). The use of bitcoin as a pseudonymous payment system allows for dealing to take place remotely.

Bitcoin is a decentralised cryptocurrency which is 'produced' and validated by cryptography. Although in theory without central control, in practice the bitcoin network is highly concentrated. Bitcoin is often presented as or blamed for allowing cryptomarket users to buy and sell illicit drugs without monitoring, embedding trust in the technology rather than the face-to-face dealer to user relationship. However, in practice it is not a particularly anonymous technology (Bratspies, 2018). It requires a community of users to sustain (Dodd, 2018). Its attraction is less than its anonymity but that its irreversible payment structure allows users to avoid being ripped off by others and that it fits with the cryptomarket ethic of anonymous decentralisation. In practice it is a risky currency and dealers would be best advised to stick with cash where possible. The technical decision to use bitcoin tends to be driven by its community integration rather than its underlying, shaky, characteristics – for example, it is typically slow, volatile and vulnerable to deanonymisation (Jawaheri et al., 2018) and various system failures (Moore and Christin, 2013). The slow pace at which payments clear makes it tricky to cash out. Law enforcement can successfully target cash-out services and leave dealers with bitcoin that is unusable out with the network. Cryptomarkets have been shut down as the result of coordinated cross-jurisdiction efforts (Afilipoaie and Shortis, 2018; Europol, 2017). Users employ them based partly on ideological preference and a desire for community to share technical know-how and risk management strategies (Ladegaard, 2018).

The labour of dealing is rewritten in this digitally mediated context, changing the time and place of dealing and the qualities of it, who is able to be involved and how, and integrating it into the economy of distributed capitalism. Existing street capital evolved to manage a potentially violent interaction may become obsolete (Sandberg and Pedersen, 2009). Sellers and buyers are more male and whiter than the offline market. Men are more likely than women to pay a dealer for the drugs they consume, and are more likely to purchase online (Vuolo and Matias, 2020). Women tend to have less need to use cryptomarkets and interest in them. Individual dealers who work online are less likely to be gang affiliated, but not wholly disconnected from gang worlds and organised crime (see Kelly's chapter in this volume). These developments bring out combined modes of working which involve licit and illicit activities (Mohamed, 2012). Frequently, the income from either activity is not enough to pay for itself. Spreading work across licit and illicit enterprises ensures a fallback during hard times.

The dealer and user community

Digital dealing consists of instrumental and also political, community and ideological aspects (Ladegaard, 2017; Maddox et al., 2016; Munksgaard and Demant, 2016; Van Hout and Bingham, 2014). Users and dealers are attracted by a combination of instrumental gains such as reliability of income, predictable quality and safety (Barratt et al., 2016). Some characterise their involvement as promoting libertarian or anarchist values and allowing their identities to play out (Bancroft and Scott Reid, 2016). Both dealers and users note benefit to their identity and sense of self, partly because they are validated for their roles and are not subject to stigma. They are also able to benefit from shared information about drug effects and security habits. Interactions between dealers, administrators and users are critical to establishing the markets as viable and ensuring trust as the basis of deals (Dupont et al., 2016). Although the focus is often on the technology, repeated interactions are necessary to apps and the cryptomarkets working as social spaces. In the case of cryptomarkets, interaction is critical to the dealer being able to benefit from the formal market rating mechanisms. With cryptomarkets and app-based dealing, there is a shared language and norms in the market that users have to adapt to and learn, so a period of lurking is typically useful (Afroz et al., 2013).

As with other illicit marketplaces, feedback and sales are concentrated in a small grouping of members (Décary-Hétu and Dupont, 2013). There is a strong centralizing logic to digital dealing in this mode. Concentration of reputation and a client base allows dealers to charge more (Janetos and Tilly, 2017). Instrumentally, dealers change strategy in response to law enforcement action, for example, by maintaining accounts in different cryptomarkets to ensure they can stay in contact with their client base after a market takedown (Broséus et al., 2016). As the cryptomarket ecosystem has matured since the closure of Silk Road in 2013, it has become more finely differentiated. More commercial grade sellers have entered the market, dealing in Xanax, smart drugs and psychoactive substances. One market that specialises in psychedelic drugs benefits from a rich participatory community of users who share both information and drug experiences (Bancroft et al., 2019). The focus on feedback requires a new mode of interaction. In cryptomarkets buyers and dealers are challenged to maintain their reputation through continuous interaction and performance.

More self-enabled online communities are able to assess and choose or reject new drugs. Building up social capital and involvement with others helps reduce drug-related risk but exposes the user to other risks of stigma, exposure, retribution, etc. The user community is a complex social sphere, with material realities (the behaviour of the drugs as biochemical entities, the adaption of the users' body, cue reactivity, etc.) and structured positions and vulnerabilities (age, sex, class, ethnicity, documented migrant status and resources). In the case of synthetic cannabinoids exemplified by Spice it went from an intriguing innovation to an unpredictable and dangerous drug as more user experiences were reported. The digital market's initial enthusiasm was replaced with ambivalence and then condemnation (Bilgrei, 2016). The social location of the drug changes. Spice moves to become a 'dirty' drug, now prevalent in prisons and among the homeless.

Supply chain configuration

The digital environment is a site of criminal innovation, moving beyond incremental fine-tuning of crime scripts and criminal resources to creating new systems and paradigms for criminal activity (Aldridge and Décary-Hétu, 2014; Gad, 2014; Horton-Eddison and Cristofaro, 2017; Kraemer-Mbula et al., 2013). The development of an open interconnected set of digital markets means disruption ends up promoting development not preventing it (Ladegaard, 2020). The digital has introduced qualities of time-space compression and product comparability. Cryptomarkets marked the creation of a new technical affordance. Criminal innovation transforms the capacity and reach of criminal activity. Cryptomarkets moved into the middle level of the drug market, connecting different dealer and customer types. Their primary transformative effect has been changing the kinds of qualities dealers and buyers need. Dealers do not necessarily need the reputation for physical toughness or the social networks that they might need when operating solely in the face-to-face market (Barratt et al., 2016). They need technical skills in addition to the organisational abilities that serve them in the offline market. It also creates new networks – people who can mediate the cryptomarkets for dealers operating offline. A key negative point in terms of market operation is that credit is so central to the offline drug market, whereas it difficult to maintain and enforce credit in a virtual dealing situation. The social economics of the market are changed by this simple technical fact (Moeller and Sandberg, 2017). This is a prime example of how the theoretical functioning of the market may undermine its social functioning. A theoretical free market assumes the basic unit of transaction is exchange. If in fact the basic unit of transaction is debt/credit then both the technical and social infrastructure look rather different and less brittle.

A significant part of cryptomarket dealings is business to business rather than business to consumer. Aldridge and Decary-Hetu (2016) inspected high priced listings on the Silk Road marketplace. Estimating wholesale being over US$1,000 each, they calculated that 26% of Silk Road sales were for re-sale. Ecstasy generated the largest proportion, 47% being wholesale, followed by cannabis at nearly 25%. Under 20% of the revenue for psychedelics, prescription drugs, and stimulants was wholesale, and a mere 6% for opioids. There is a dynamic relationship with supply chain lengths. Chrystal meth can usually be manufactured locally, suggesting a shorter, within border supply chain. However, the supply chain length fluctuates – at times meth production has moved to localised in small lab production, while later moving to cartel controlled, trafficked supply (Shukla et al., 2012). Overall the cryptomarkets serve the 'last mile' geography of the drug ecosystem, vendors typically being located in the regions of the globe they are selling to rather than in producer countries (Dittus et al., 2017).

Gangs have started to adapt to cybercrime and the digital world very effectively to the point where street slang has developed to substitute for established cybercrime slang. Groups which combine, for example, drug importation and cybercrimes such as phishing or in-person frauds like skimming – using devices to collect victims' credit and debit card details (Leukfeldt and Roks, 2020). The fabric of urban space is digital – social life is digitally mediated – identity and expression matter to instrumental activity. This multi-form criminal activity shows a willingness to take up multiple illegal opportunities as they arise and depending on risk and profitability (see also Kelly's chapter in this volume).

Labour structure is being redefined by the digital, for example, money mules are becoming more important and fulfil a role linking different criminal networks while also being a high-risk/low-reward role (Leukfeldt and Kleemans, 2019). Social contacts are vital in online and offline dealing. The division of labour reconfigures risk for different participants. Money mules are more traceable and more likely to be caught by police. They also burn quickly, as their accounts are shut down when misuse is traced to them.

Innovation as a source of novelty and harm

Transformative criminal innovations are those which allow crime to be committed at lower cost, with lower skill, lower social capital, or which create novel categories of crime. On the other hand, the law often overreaches in its attempts to get ahead of criminal innovation. I examine two sources of innovation: internal and external. Internal development can be seen in the changes in cryptomarkets since Silk Road was closed down. Markets move from centralised market-controlled escrow to decentralised multisig – a decentralised signing system that is governed by the blockchain (Horton-Eddison, 2017) as a result of scams and law enforcement (Horton-Eddison and Cristoforo, 2017). The later Silk Road 2.0 scam where the administrators used the site to steal from dealers and customers, and the FBI takedown of Silk Road alerted users to the fact that market controlled, centralised escrow was no guarantee that their bitcoins were safe. Indeed, escrow represents a significant vulnerability and a tempting target. Horton-Eddison and Cristofaro's (2017) corpus analysis showed changes in community attitudes towards escrow as a result of these events. This has gone from centralised escrow to multi-signature escrow to nothing at all in the case of some markets. One psychedelic market I studied rejects all systems that are not user controlled.

Harm is generated and distributed in society and part of that is through criminal activity (Hall, 2019). So, harm can be spread without actors being necessarily maliciously motivated. They may act out normative identities (individualist, entrepreneurial) while doing that (Ancrum and Treadwell, 2017). Online dealers may be motivated by rational concerns but like the platforms themselves, rational acts can spread and increase harm from drug use, as well as allow users to evaluate risks and make considered choices about the drugs they buy. As in other spheres, dealing practice is mostly 'mundane and consensual', if not public (Zaitch, 2005). However, dealing is increasingly supply-chain led, particularly in the area of synthetic opioids such as fentanyl and carfentanil and benzodiazepines, which are the areas where the greatest increases in drug harms are being recorded (National Records of Scotland, 2019; Pardo et al., 2019). What this means is that increasingly harmful drugs are being introduced into the supply chain as a result of dealer/producers' needs and interests rather than consumer demand.

Changes in attitudes and the technology are likely to be a process of co-development and diffusion where technology has to be proven workable before being promoted. Cryptomarket technology places demands on its users. They must be competent and able to take advantage of it to increase security. Not everybody is, and the effect of the last mile distribution being disrupted by the pandemic has meant new users have moved onto the darknet who may not have the cultural capital required to navigate it well. The second barrier to its use is the same with any escrow. Vendors have more power in a seller's market and can simply refuse to use escrow at all and insist on immediate finalisation (Moeller et al., 2017). Trust matters but experience has made users sceptical of the worth of trust-centralising systems like market encryption and escrow.

Innovation is not an unalloyed good and can drive increased harm. The spread of synthetic opioids has involved steep change in the intensity and potency of drugs along with the institutionalisation of embodied harm in structurally damaged communities, emptied of resilient, lateral structures (Pardo et al., 2019). Micro-production is possible at a sophisticated technical level. Rather than the crude and prone to explosion meth lab, facilities can be sophisticated in small form. Micro-production and the growth of the Chinese chemical industry mean law enforcement cannot constrain supply very easily. Here the internet is acting as a way of spreading knowledge about production methods, and distributed production systems, rather than being a mode of distribution itself. Make this bigger – so we have to go beyond 'the digital' to understand how digital technologies are embedded in wider shifts in political economy, which illicit developments ride on.

The digital dealing sphere is often presented as freeing, but it draws users into a sphere increasingly governed by state and private institutions to a depth that would be difficult to achieve with the face-to-face market. Suppliers are increasingly dictating what is being sold. The move to fentanyl was pushed by the needs of suppliers, not in response to demand (Pardo et al., 2019). A critical driver for the expansion of fentanyl is the wider distribution of production, pushed by supply rather than demand. Supplier power has grown, and this is affirmed by the cryptomarkets where supply dominance is assisted by the market mechanisms that are employed. Recent developments illustrate that the 'consumer is king' model does not apply in practice, outside of specific contexts. Consumers are free in a narrow sense, to choose between similar offerings. Market power is concentrated in the hands of suppliers. This may be significant in terms of new harms produced by the switch to synthetic opioids. Users are having to adapt to production decisions taken to serve the interests of suppliers. Producer interests lie in cost control, reducing supply chain risk and disruption.

We may have a dual track market, with a demand-led, privileged user set and a producer-led, less powerful user set. Both are transformed in different ways with the digital. The lowest rung of the drug trade is not profitable and the lowest level mules and dealers will bear most of the costs to little gain. Dependence and extreme deprivation can harm trust and the networks needed to survive (Bourgois, 1998). The trade can be flat and networked at some points, hierarchal and ruthless at others. Within community predation is often the biggest threat to drug users and dealers, much more so than law enforcement. A drug dealer might engage in thousands of trades without attracting the attention of the police, while being exposed much more frequently to robbery, aggression and betrayal from peers. That makes the ability to navigate the social space of dealing, employing the right social capital and stance, very important to their continued survival. There are also infrastructural harms and hidden costs, such as the significant environmental cost of running the bitcoin network. Changes in the variety, combination and demand have followed shifts in supply chain capacity and in sourcing of some aspects of drug production. Increasing potency has been used as a sales tactic as with Xanax dealers.

Conclusion

With technology there is always an expectation that it will somehow abstract transactional relationships from human life (Dodd, 2018). It never does and cannot. In many ways it is non-mainstream communities that have been fastest to adopt digital technology – to create new forms of communication and trust, and also at risk from the enclosure of the digital commons through data mining, fingerprinting, surveillance, automated censorship. Digital platforms have influenced dealing in both the shape of demand and the role and power of the supply chain. Initial supply chain disruption has been rapidly reconfigured into a firmly supplier-led market focused on synthetic opioids, and a more choosy but still supplier-concentrated digital market focused on recreational and smart drugs. There are noticeable differences between communities that are very online and those that are not, and people who restrict online interaction to tight range of topics and platforms. For example, the informational elite are quite narrow in their internet use, with a tight relationship between small sets of integrated, self-reinforcing users.

The rapid introduction of new drugs, and new ways of using existing drugs in new combinations, new uses for illicit drugs and new configurations of drug user communities, challenges both existing frameworks for understanding risk and harm, and the ability of researchers and service providers to interpret trends and link them to changes in society and policy. The future is a new era of micro-production, using distributed industrial technology to evade regulation. As with other areas of the capitalist economy, apparently democratic distribution of the means of production and open dissemination of information can go along with concentration of ownership and power through sophisticated lab to letterbox platforms. What digital dealing has shown is the importance of affordances, rather than platforms. Platforms – whether social media or cryptomarkets – come and go. Dealers learn to navigate and innovate affordances and these should be the focus of research and policing to come.

Acknowledgements

The author would like to thank Ben Collier for his help with the literature for this chapter.

References

Afilipoaie A and Shortis P (2018) *Crypto-Market Enforcement–New Strategy and Tactics.* Swansea: Global Drug Policy Observatory.

Afroz S, Garg V, McCoy D, et al. (2013) Honor among thieves: A common's analysis of cybercrime economies. *2013 Ecrime Researchers Summit (Ecrs).* Available at: https://ieeexplore.ieee.org/document/6805778

Aldridge J and Décary-Hétu D (2014) *Not an "e-Bay for Drugs": The Cryptomarket "Silk Road" as a Paradigm Shifting Criminal Innovation.* Rochester, NY: Social Science Research Network.

Aldridge J and Décary-Hétu D (2016) Hidden wholesale: The drug diffusing capacity of online drug cryptomarkets. *International Journal of Drug Policy* 35: 7–15. DOI: 10.1016/j.drugpo.2016.04.020

Ancrum C and Treadwell J (2017) Beyond ghosts, gangs and good sorts: Commercial cannabis cultivation and illicit enterprise in England's disadvantaged inner cities. *Crime, Media, Culture* 13(1): 69–84. DOI: 10.1177/1741659016646414

Bakken SA and Demant JJ (2019) Sellers' risk perceptions in public and private social media drug markets. *International Journal of Drug Policy*: S0955395919300659. DOI: 10.1016/j.drugpo.2019.03.009

Bancroft A and Scott Reid P (2016) Concepts of illicit drug quality among darknet market users: Purity, embodied experience, craft and chemical knowledge. *International Journal of Drug Policy* 35: 42–49. DOI: 10.1016/j.drugpo.2015.11.008

Bancroft A, Squirrell T, Zaunseder, A, et al. (2019) Producing trust among illicit actors: A techno-social approach to an online illicit market. *Sociological Research Online.*

Barratt MJ, Ferris JA and Winstock AR (2016) Safer scoring? Cryptomarkets, social supply and drug market violence. *International Journal of Drug Policy* 35: 24–31. DOI: 10.1016/j.drugpo.2016.04.019

Barratt MJ, Coney L, Aldridge J, et al. (2017) Who initiates drug use through cryptomarkets? In: *The 11th International Society for the Study of Drug Policy*, 1 January 2017. Available at: https://espace.library.uq.edu.au/view/UQ:690040 (accessed 16 November 2017).

Bilgrei OR (2016) From "herbal highs" to the "heroin of cannabis": Exploring the evolving discourse on synthetic cannabinoid use in a Norwegian Internet drug forum. *International Journal of Drug Policy* 29: 1–8. DOI: 10.1016/j.drugpo.2016.01.011

Bourgois P (1998) The moral economies of homeless heroin addicts: Confronting ethnography, HIV risk, and everyday violence in San Francisco Shooting Encampments. *Substance Use & Misuse* 33(11): 2323–2351. DOI: 10.3109/10826089809056260

Bratspies RM (2018) *Cryptocurrency and the Myth of the Trustless Transaction*. ID 3141605, SSRN Scholarly Paper, 10 March. Rochester, NY: Social Science Research Network. Available at: https://papers.ssrn.com/abstract=3141605 (accessed 16 May 2018).

Bright DA and Sutherland R (2017) "Just doing a favor for a friend": the social supply of ecstasy through friendship networks. *Journal of Drug Issues* 47(3): 492–504. DOI: 10.1177/0022042617704004

Broséus J, Rhumorbarbe D, Mireault C, et al. (2016) Studying illicit drug trafficking on darknet markets: Structure and organisation from a Canadian perspective. *Forensic Science International* 264: 7–14. DOI: 10.1016/j.forsciint.2016.02.045

Childs A, Coomber R, Bull M, et al. (2020) Evolving and diversifying selling practices on drug cryptomarkets: An exploration of off-platform "direct dealing." *Journal of Drug Issues*: 0022042619897425. DOI: 10.1177/0022042619897425

Cunliffe J, Martin J, Décary-Hétu D, et al. (2017) An island apart? Risks and prices in the Australian cryptomarket drug trade. *International Journal of Drug Policy* 50(Supplement C): 64–73. DOI: 10.1016/j.drugpo.2017.09.005

Décary-Hétu D and Dupont B (2013) Reputation in a dark network of online criminals. *Global Crime* 14: 175–196. DOI: 10.1080/17440572.2013.801015

Demant J, Munksgaard R, Décary-Hétu D, et al. (2017) Going local on a global platform. A critical analysis of the transformative potential of cryptomarkets for organized illicit drug crime. In: *International Society for the Study of Drug Policy*, Aarhus, 2017.

Dittus M, Wright J and Graham M (2017) Platform criminalism: The "last-mile" geography of the darknet market supply chain. *arXiv:1712.10068 [cs]*. Available at: http://arxiv.org/abs/1712.10068

Dodd N (2018) The social life of bitcoin. *Theory, Culture & Society* 35(3): 35–56. DOI: 10.1177/0263276417746464

Dupont B, Côté A-M, Savine C, et al. (2016) The ecology of trust among hackers. *Global Crime* 17(2): 129–151. DOI: 10.1080/17440572.2016.1157480

Ellis A (2019) A De-Civilizing Reversal or System Normal? Rising Lethal Violence in Post-Recession Austerity United Kingdom. *The British Journal of Criminology* 59(4): 862–878. DOI: 10.1093/bjc/azz001

Europol (2017) *Crime in the Age of Technology–Europol's Serious and Organised Crime Threat Assessment 2017*. The Hague. Available at: www.europol.europa.eu/newsroom/news/crime-in-age-of-technology-%E2%80%93-europol%E2%80%99s-serious-and-organised-crime-threat-assessment-2017 (accessed 17 March 2020).

Foley S, Karlsen J and Putniņš TJ (2018) Sex, drugs, and bitcoin: How much illegal activity is financed through cryptocurrencies? Available at: https://papers.ssrn.com/abstract=3102645 (accessed 23 January 2018).

Gad M (2014) Crimeware marketplaces and their facilitating technologies. *Technology Innovation Management Review* 4(11): 28–33.

Hall A (2019) Lifestyle drugs and late capitalism: A topography of Harm. In: Raymen T and Smith O (eds.), *Deviant Leisure: Criminological Perspectives on Leisure and Harm*. Palgrave Macmillan. Available at: www.palgrave.com/gp/book/9783030177355 (accessed 8 August 2019).

Hall A and Antonopoulos GA (2015) License to pill: Illegal entrepreneurs' tactics in the online trade of medicines. *Economic and Organized Cross-Border Crime in Times of Crisis*. Nijmegen: Wolf Legal Publishers.

Hall A and Antonopoulos GA (2016) *Fake Meds Online: The Internet and the Transnational Market in Illicit Pharmaceuticals*. London: Palgrave Macmillan.

Horton-Eddison M and Cristofaro MD (2017) *Hard Interventions and Innovation in Crypto-Drug Markets: The Escrow Example*. Swansea: Global Drug Policy Observatory.

Janetos N and Tilly J (2017) Reputation dynamics in a market for illicit drugs. *arXiv:1703.01937 [stat]*. Available at: http://arxiv.org/abs/1703.01937 (accessed 10 September 2019).

Jawaheri HA, Sabah MA, Boshmaf Y, et al. (2018) When a small leak sinks a great ship: Deanonymizing Tor hidden service users through bitcoin transactions analysis. *arXiv:1801.07501 [cs]*. Available at: http://arxiv.org/abs/1801.07501 (accessed 30 January 2018).

King P (2019) Islamic State group's experiments with the decentralised web. In: *European Counter Terrorism Centre (ECTC) Advisory Network, 9–10 April 2019, at Europol Headquarters, The Hague*, 2019, p. 9.

Kraemer-Mbula E, Tang P and Rush H (2013) The cybercrime ecosystem: Online innovation in the shadows? *Technological Forecasting and Social Change* 80(3): 541–555. DOI: 10.1016/j.techfore.2012.07.002

Ladegaard I (2017) "I pray that we will find a way to carry on this dream": How a law enforcement crackdown united an online community. *Critical Sociology*: 089692051773567. DOI: 10.1177/0896920517735670

Ladegaard I (2018) We know where you are, what you are doing and we will catch you: Testing deterrence theory in digital drug markets. *The British Journal of Criminology* 58(2): 414–433. DOI: 10.1093/bjc/azx021

Ladegaard I (2020) Open secrecy: How police crackdowns and creative problem-solving brought illegal markets out of the shadows. *Social Forces*: soz140. DOI: 10.1093/sf/soz140

Lane J (2018) *The Digital Street*. Oxford University Press. Available at: www-oxfordscholarship-com.ezproxy.is.ed.ac.uk/view/10.1093/oso/9780199381265.001.0001/oso-9780199381265 (accessed 27 May 2020).

Leukfeldt ER (Rutger) and Kleemans ER (Edward) (2019) Cybercrime, money mules and situational crime prevention: Recruitment, motives and involvement mechanisms. In: Hufnagel S and Moiseienko A (eds.), *Criminal Networks and Law Enforcement Global Perspectives on Illegal Enterprise*. 1st ed. Routledge. DOI: 10.4324/9781351176194

Leukfeldt ER (Rutger) and Roks RA (Robert) (2020) Cybercrimes on the streets of the Netherlands? An exploration of the intersection of cybercrimes and street crimes. *Deviant Behavior* 0(0). Routledge: 1–12. DOI: 10.1080/01639625.2020.1755587

Lusthaus J and Varese F (2018) Offline and local: The hidden face of cybercrime. *Policing: A Journal of Policy and Practice*. DOI: 10.1093/police/pax042

Maddox A, Barratt MJ, Allen M, et al. (2016) Constructive activism in the dark web: Cryptomarkets and illicit drugs in the digital 'demimonde.' *Information, Communication & Society* 19(1): 111–126. DOI: 10.1080/1369118X.2015.1093531.

Martin J (2014) Lost on the Silk Road: Online drug distribution and the 'cryptomarket.' *Criminology and Criminal Justice* 14(3): 351–367.

Martin J (2017) Cryptomarkets, systemic violence and the 'gentrification hypothesis.' *Addiction* 113: 797–804.

Masson K and Bancroft A (2018) 'Nice people doing shady things': Drugs and the morality of exchange in the darknet cryptomarkets. *International Journal of Drug Policy* 58: 78–84. DOI: 10.1016/j.drugpo.2018.05.008

Matthews B, Collier B, McVie S, et al. (2019) Administrative data as a novel source of information on postal drug delivery in Scotland: A spatial analysis of illegal consignment seizure data. *International Journal of Population Data Science* 4(3). 3. DOI: 10.23889/ijpds.v4i3.1182

May T and Hough M (2004) Drug markets and distribution systems. *Addiction Research & Theory* 12(6): 549–563. DOI: 10.1080/1606635041233l323119

Moeller K and Sandberg S (2017) Debts and threats: managing inability to repay credits in illicit drug distribution. *Justice Quarterly* 34(2): 272–296. DOI: 10.1080/07418825.2016.1162321

Moeller K, Munksgaard R and Demant J (2017) Flow my FE the vendor said: Exploring violent and fraudulent resource exchanges on cryptomarkets for illicit drugs. *American Behavioral Scientist* early online(v). DOI: 10.1177/0002764217734269

Mohamed AR (2012) *Dorm Room Dealers: Drugs and the Privileges of Race and Class.* Boulder, CO: Lynne Rienner Publishers.

Moore T and Christin N (2013) Beware the middleman: Empirical analysis of bitcoin-exchange risk. In: *Financial Cryptography and Data Security.* Springer, pp. 25–33. Available at: http://link.springer.com/chapter/10.1007/978-3-642-39884-1_3 (accessed 11 November 2014).

Moyle L, Childs A, Coomber R, et al. (2019) #Drugsforsale: An exploration of the use of social media and encrypted messaging apps to supply and access drugs. *International Journal of Drug Policy* 63: 101–110. DOI: 10.1016/j.drugpo.2018.08.005

Munksgaard R and Demant J (2016) Mixing politics and crime–the prevalence and decline of political discourse on the cryptomarket. *International Journal of Drug Policy* 35: 77–83. DOI: http://dx.doi.org/10.1016/j.drugpo.2016.04.021

National Records of Scotland, (2019) *Drug-Related Deaths in Scotland, 2018.*

Nicholas R (2008) *The Impact of Social Networks and Not-For-Profit Illicit Drug Dealing on Illicit Drug Markets in Australia.* Hobart: National Drug Law Enforcement Research Fund.

Pardo B, Taylor J, Caulkins J, et al. (2019) *The Future of Fentanyl and Other Synthetic Opioids.* RAND Corporation. DOI: 10.7249/RR3117

Pasquale F (2015) *The Black Box Society the Secret Algorithms That Control Money and Information /c Frank Pasquale.* Cambridge: Harvard University Press.

Sandberg S and Pedersen W (2009) *Street Capital: Black Cannabis Dealers in a White Welfare State.* Policy Press.

Shukla RK, Crump JL and Chrisco ES (2012) An evolving problem: Methamphetamine production and trafficking in the United States. *International Journal of Drug Policy* 23(6). Special Focus Issue: Drug Production and Drug Markets: 426–435. DOI: 10.1016/j.drugpo.2012.07.004

Smith GJD, Bennett Moses L and Chan J (2017) The challenges of doing criminology in the big data era: Towards a digital and data-driven approach. *The British Journal of Criminology* 57(2): 259–274. DOI: 10.1093/bjc/azw096

Spicer J (2019) 'That's their brand, their business': How police officers are interpreting county lines. *Policing and Society* 29(8): 873–886.

Srnicek N (2016) *Platform Capitalism*. Oxford, UK: Polity Press. Available at: http://ebookcentral.proquest.com/lib/ed/detail.action?docID=4773843 (accessed 29 April 2020).

Storrod ML and Densley JA (2017) 'Going viral' and 'Going country': The expressive and instrumental activities of street gangs on social media. *Journal of Youth Studies* 20(6). Routledge: 677–696. DOI: 10.1080/13676261.2016.1260694

Urbanik M-M and Haggerty KD (2018) '#IT'S dangerous': The online world of drug dealers, rappers and the street code. *The British Journal of Criminology* 58(6): 1343–1360. DOI: 10.1093/bjc/azx083

Valeriano B, Jensen BM and Maness RC (2018) *Cyber Strategy: The Evolving Character of Power and Coercion*. Oxford University Press. Available at: www-oxfordscholarship-com.ezproxy.is.ed.ac.uk/view/10.1093/oso/9780190618094.001.0001/oso-9780190618094

Van Hout MC and Bingham T (2014) Responsible vendors, intelligent consumers: Silk Road, the online revolution in drug trading. *International Journal of Drug Policy* 25(2): 183–189. DOI: 10.1016/j.drugpo.2013.10.009

Vuolo M and Matias J (2020) Sources of drug acquisition among females and males in the European Web Survey on Drugs. *International Journal of Drug Policy* 81: 102777. DOI: 10.1016/j.drugpo.2020.102777

Williams ML, Burnap P and Sloan L (2017) Crime sensing with big data: The affordances and limitations of using open-source communications to estimate crime patterns. *The British Journal of Criminology* 57(2): 320–340. DOI: 10.1093/bjc/azw031

Wortley R (2012) Affordance and situational crime prevention: Implications for counter terrorism. In: *Terrorism and Affordance*. A&C Black, p. 17.

Zaitch D (2005) The ambiguity of violence, secrecy, and trust among Colombian drug entrepreneurs. *Journal of Drug Issues* 35(1): 201–228. DOI: 10.1177/002204260503500110

Zuboff S (2015) Big other: surveillance capitalism and the prospects of an information civilization. *Journal of Information Technology* 30(1): 75–89. DOI: 10.1057/jit.2015.5

16

CRYPTOMARKETS AND ORGANISED CRIME

An ethnographic life history

Craig Kelly

As Treadwell (2012) states, criminology as a discipline has been slow to conceptualise the way in which cyber-related criminality converges within and impacts the traditional criminal landscape. This combined with the notion of the dark figure of crime (Coleman and Moynihan, 1996) raises various questions around the validity of the National Crime Agencies' proposal in 2019 that there are 4,542 organised crime groups active in the United Kingdom. This hints that the figure is perhaps vastly underestimated and some aspects of drug distribution within the contemporary context are becoming increasingly hidden crimes (Reiner, 1996; Barret et al., 2016). This chapter seeks to elaborate on the nature of advances in drug distribution, aided via the 'dark web'.

Utilising an ethnographic life history approach (Goodey, 2000) this chapter seeks to contextualise how the convergence of advanced technology with global organised crime has interacted with local markets (Hobbs, 1998). The data was obtained throughout a year-long ethnographic project and a series of in-depth life history interviews. The participant in this study has an extensive history of involvement within British organised crime, specifically the supply of numerous illicit drugs such as cannabis, cocaine and, on occasion, crack cocaine. After serving a custodial sentence in relation to the supply of three kilos of cannabis and half an ounce of cocaine, the modus operandi of his offending behaviour was adapted in order to avoid detection from both existing organised crime groups and law enforcement agencies. This was achieved through the utilisation of online drug markets, which from this point will be referred to as cryptomarkets. Utilising the ethnographic life history approach therefore offers the opportunity of a 'looking glass' into the transformative nature of illicit drug supply at a grass roots level in the United Kingdom. Cryptomarkets have been receiving increasing attention within academia (Martin, 2014, 2019; see also Bancroft's

DOI: 10.4324/9781351010245-19

chapter in this volume). However, the studies from academia are often overtly cyber-centric and have failed to question how such changes to transnational drug trafficking were affecting 'glocal' (Hobbs, 1998:416) supply chains.

Drug supply through the ether

The utilisation of the internet for aspects of criminality and criminal supply change is not new (Wall, 2001, 2007). Whilst much attention within academic circles has concentrated upon offences such as fraud (Glenny, 2012), hacking services (Décary-Hétu and Giommoni, 2017; Sterling, 1998; Coleman, 2015) and the distribution of child pornography (Bartlett, 2016; Casanova et al., 2000), scant attention has been paid to illicit substances, although this is a growing area (Barratt, 2016). Despite popular perception, supplying drugs on the internet is not a new trend. The first ever transaction on the internet was conducted by students from the University of Stanford using ARPANET – an early incarnation of the internet designed by the United States Military – to sell a small amount of cannabis (Markoff, 2006; Bartlett, 2016). Since this initial transaction, and arguably the first ever cybercrime, rudimentary drug markets have frequently emerged on the web. The vast majority of these however were relatively crude, a prime example being the Farmers Market.[1] Such websites were located on what is known as the surface web and were atypically easily detectable, usually run by a collective of liberal drug users supplying hallucinogens (Bartlett, 2016; Goodman, 2015).

In 2011 however, notice boards and chat rooms across the surface web began discussing a sophisticated e-commerce website, designed to look and function as licit websites such as Amazon and e-bay (Martin, 2014). The website was located not on the surface web as previous drug market websites had been, but on the deep web, only accessible through the encrypted Tor browser (Haraty and Zantout, 2014). Quickly, the online hacking community coined the term 'cryptomarkets' (Aldridge and Décary-Hétu, 2014) to describe this style of cyber-drug market – the most infamous of which being Silk Road.

Developed well beyond the previous rudimentary websites such as the Farmers Market, Silk Road included searchable listings of products, rating systems and even complaint buttons (Aldridge and Décary-Hétu, 2014). The website was revolutionary in the development of drug trafficking, operating on an escrow system to protect the investment of both users and vendors. The rating system also ensured that the quality of the products sold was of a high standard, diminishing the two most detrimental aspects of the previous attempts of internet supply chains (Martin, 2014). In short, online drug retail had been commercialised through the integration of multiple technologies which anonymised all parties (Haraty and Zantout, 2014) and effectively circumnavigated traditional drug supply chains. A person could now order high-quality Afghan heroin from their living room, which would be delivered by their local courier service a few days later. Crucially, this enabled customers to purchase substances from their countries of production, negating the reductions of purity typically found within traditional drug market supply chains (Bancroft and Reid, 2015).

The popularity and reach of the primary website – Silk Road – expanded rapidly, with around 1,200 retail requests being sent through the service in every two-hour period whilst it was active (Biryukov et al., 2013). The Federal Bureau of Investigation (FBI), upon apprehending the alleged founder Ross Ulbricht, estimated an income from the website between 1.2 and 2 billion dollars in a three-year period (Bartlett, 2016). The investigation and eventual apprehension of Ulbricht took three years and thrust the underground website into the public fore (Bartlett, 2016). Despite this effectively being one of the largest drug distributions ever uncovered, relatively little attention was paid within academic circles to the rapidly developing involvement of serious organised crime.

Disorganised crime and entrepreneurial culture

Of the research available on cryptomarkets, much is of a quantitative nature which focuses largely upon the cyber transactions and networks (Décary-Hétu and Giommoni, 2017; Aldridge and Décary-Hétu, 2014, 2016; Christin, 2013; Dolliver and Kenney, 2016; Barratt et al., 2014; Barratt et al., 2016). Aldridge and Décary-Hétu (2016) utilised a quantitative approach to gain an insight into the use of cryptomarkets by drug dealers, rather than the typical customers who purchased substances from the websites for personal use. The research evidenced that drug suppliers were indeed utilising the websites to source substance for retail. Due to the quantitative cyber-centric approach however, little attention to the development of traditional drug markets and how this could potentially influence or be mirrored by the emerging markets was considered.

In the United Kingdom it is long recognised that organised crime is in fact disorganised. As Hignett (2012:288) states, 'what we are often witnessing as the underworld evolves is largely the formation of opportunistic, mutually profitable linkages between independent criminal organisations'. This has historically been seen internationally with the work of Thrasher (1967) first highlighting the 'fluidity' of the criminal community in America and confounded by Haller (1990). The lack of monopolisation within criminal markets across Europe was highlighted by Dorn et al., (1992) who noted the absence of a 'Mr Big' controlling the supply of illicit substance within the United Kingdom.

The work of Hobbs (1995, 1997, 1998 and 2001) and Winlow (2001) is perhaps most influential on the understanding of organised crime and drugs within the context of the United Kingdom. Their work highlights the ways in which economic factors have influenced the degradation of traditional organised criminal culture, introducing the transformation of marginalised working-class individuals who are denied traditional class-based opportunities. Such cultural changes which removed the opportunity of young British males to confirm their masculinity through traditional employment, largely due to globalisation, produced new opportunities to 'attain and maintain relevant status goals and experience the illicit stimulation that deviancy so often provides' (Winlow, 2001:162). The opportunities referenced relate to the transformation from traditional conflict-oriented criminal culture to the rise of entrepreneurial criminal culture. As Hignett (2012) details, contemporary organised crime is inextricably linked to the global economy and has served to redefine criminal activity by creating decentred and unpredictable trading economies (Hobbs, 1997).

As Hobbs (1995) demonstrates, the criminal milieu mirrors the legitimate market. Technological advancement has evidently shaped the activities of serious organised crime offenders. This can be seen in various instances, such as the case study of Dick Pooley's safe cracking skills becoming inextricably redundant (ibid.). More contemporary examples of note include the increasing use of mobile phones to aid the drug supply networks within British custodial establishments (Treadwell et al., 2019) and various social media applications and websites utilised for the distribution of counterfeit goods (Antonopoulos et al., 2018).

As legitimate markets have become increasingly dependent upon technology and virtual market places, so too have illicit markets. As Hobbs (1997) contended, the global trends in criminal supply chains are inextricably linked to the local. British drug markets are composed of a multitude of brokers and acquaintances who sell or facilitate drugs for little to no financial gain to friends which is 'minimally commercial' yet still profit driven. This highlights that, whilst the cyber-centric and quantitative explorations of the cryptomarkets are valuable for understanding the overall trend, an understanding of how such changes are affecting British drug supply networks is important. Advances in technology and global markets (both licit and illicit) are evidently interconnected to the British criminal milieu. The cryptomarkets are clearly being used to procure illicit substances in weights more substantially than we would typically associate with personal use (Aldridge and Décary-Hétu, 2016). To fully contextualise this view, it is pertinent to introduce and detail the life history of the participant – 'Paul' to enable a complete understanding.

Paul – From pre-school to post-sentencing

Born into a military family in late 1981, the research participant, referred to under the pseudonym Paul grew up on a small council estate in Yorkshire. His father had recently left the military, resulting in a rather turbulent period within the family due to a lack of basic income. His father began engaging in various temporary forms of employment and low-level criminality. The change eventually took its toll on his parents' relationship, resulting in the marriage breaking down when he was around five years old and his father moving to London. It was not until his mid-twenties, during a prison visit with his then estranged father that Paul learnt the move to London was prompted by a local organised crime group pursuing his father over a £4,000 debt, which Paul eloquently summarises as follows:

> He had to fuck off, they was [sic] going to put one in him, And through a million to one chance I end up working for his son. Couldn't make it up!"

Following the collapse of the marriage his mother met a new partner who soon moved into the family home with his own children. Paul regarded this as a turning point which clearly still affects him. He recounted on numerous occasions in a harrowing manner, a string of abuse and neglect he was subjected to from this point onwards in his life. Relative deprivation clearly played a key role within his formative years as persistent bullying led to his early abandonment of the education system. On numerous occasions Paul drew upon the internalised sense of alienation he felt within this period. When discussing the reason he is estranged from his mother, he explained that whilst the house was '*one of the nicest on the estate, but my clothes were always shite'*. This was compounded by the all-boys school he attended which was '*half full of posh lads and half full of estate lads*', with Paul citing he was neither. He states that he

> Wasn't posh enough for the rich kids but wasn't poor enough to fit in with the estate lads. I was always kind of an outsider like that. I mean I could of chilled with the estate lads but I didn't fit in there because I wouldn't kick the shit out of someone for no reason! I ain't a fighter, I'm a lover [laughs].

Paul recounts he was spending much of his time at the home of friends whose parents were extremely liberal by his early teens. He recalls most evenings being spent in front of the family games console smoking cannabis resin. By the age of fourteen he had begun using amphetamines most days, binging on MDMA and LSD (Ecstasy and acid) at the weekend. To complement his usage he would occasionally sell small quantities of cannabis to his friends' parents, as he details:

> Basically, how it first started, thirteen, fourteen. Paper round and a five-pound draw. Everyone else got pocket money, I don't get that, got to hustle it really. So, when I am like sixteen, seventeen I can't afford to smoke with how much I am working…Yano, when I said I was fourteen at my mates' house … I got shown by older people that were respectable, I mean they were dodgy, yeah they were dodgy, but they showed you how life should be.

By the age of seventeen, Paul left the family home and struggled to lay the foundations of stability he deeply desired. Until aged twenty-three he transitioned through various jobs within the service sector. Constraints to his ability to work as quickly as his colleagues as he is partially blind in one eye hindered his job security. Job insecurity combined with his drug usage resulted in him living in numerous hostels and shared houses in this period. Within this time period Paul also discloses moving into a hostel with a high prevalence of crack cocaine users. A short period of crack cocaine use followed. He moved into a squat with '*a can of beer and a pot noodle'*, not leaving for three weeks whilst he got himself clean. He also details a short spell supplying ecstasy in the local clubbing scene but stopped upon his brothers' arrest and incarceration for a near identical venture. Throughout this time he continued to distribute cannabis to provide a semblance of security, averaging sales of around two ounces a week.

Aged twenty three, Paul met a girl in the local pub and they quickly developed a relationship. Now reliant on cannabis distribution as his sole source of income, Paul found it increasingly difficult to source good-quality cannabis in the local market from his usual contacts. His partner suggested he speak to her brother-in-law (Swan) who he had met at various family gatherings in the past. Paul saw Swan a few days later and they agreed that he could 'tick' a few ounces of cannabis and return the money at a later date. Once the business arrangement was agreed Swan produced a gym bag from under the dining room table and Paul states it then dawned upon him his new business associate was not his *'usual type of criminal'*. Once he opened the bag, he found half a kilo of cannabis and agreed that he would return with £1,600 shortly after.

A brief encounter with a past associate the next day resulted in Paul offloading the half kilo in one sale and earning a small profit of £400. He explains that he decided to sell it cheap as ensuring it was sold was the best course of action in the situation. The next day he returned to his new Swan to clear his debt, at which point another bag was given to him containing a full kilo. Paul explains that he continued to sell the cannabis in half kilos to various contacts whilst still selling his own small quantities of cocaine. When asked what motivated him to escalate his illicit conduct so drastically, he explains:

> I wanted to keep the girl I was with in the comfort, but I was thrown into a world I knew nothing about. I knew gangsters, I had come across them. But I didn't know that world. But I thought fuck it.

Swan was a major distributor of cannabis across the UK, importing cannabis and heroin from Dutch and Spanish associates. The overall business was funded between Swan, in his mid-twenties, and an older individual well known within the local criminal community. Below Swan were about ten to fifteen young men, including Paul. Within a year of their first encounter Paul explains he had around seven individuals around the country who sourced their cannabis from himself exclusively. These individuals were based in various towns and cities from Yorkshire to Wales. Each of these people then resold the kilos of cannabis bought from Paul to street-level dealers and local gangs, leading Paul to estimate he had at least one to two hundred street dealers selling his cannabis. This setup was generic across the six other individuals buying cannabis from Swan.

Paul discusses briefly the protection afforded to him from the organisation, citing that if he and another dealer associated with the organisation had an issue it was resolved by Swan. On the protection afforded he details:

> There was one guy that was trying to have me over for a few grand and there was a phone call telling him not to bother. I had another bunch of lads from the pub who were trying to do me over, it basically kicked off and they were told if they went near me, spoke to me or even looked at me they were going to have their pub burnt down. I didn't know that though, I didn't find out until a few years later. So, I was protected to a degree but I didn't realise how protected I was, I think it was designed that way so you don't go around thinking you're untouchable. What they are saying is your own problems are your own problems and they only step in if it will affect the money. But they want you to make a mistake and trap you like you get a good batch then a batch that is shit and tell you to go fuck yourself. Like I know full well people were told to deal with me who wouldn't usually deal with me. They never mentioned that though, I found out later. They didn't want me going around using their name and thinking I'm untouchable.

The majority of the individuals to whom Paul sold cannabis were friends from his teenage years who had relocated around the country or their associates. By the age of twenty-five, a conservative estimate of the drugs he was selling is given – amounting to a minimum of four kilos of cannabis a week and three ounces of cocaine. The cocaine was sourced from a separate supplier, a fact Swan was aware of as he regularly bought the cocaine he used himself from Paul.

Paul discloses that his own drug use grew exponentially alongside his illicit career. By mid-2006 he was consuming around half an ounce of cocaine a week alongside his habitual cannabis use. The majority of the profit garnered was spent on parties and designer goods for his partner. In 2007 with his business still expanding, at this time selling around eight kilos of cannabis a week, Paul made a delivery to the midlands. It was unusual for him to make deliveries, usually he paid a small entrusted circle of associates to take such risks. However, for a reason he cannot remember, on the return leg of the delivery he made he was stopped by the police. He claims that this was not an unfortunate coincidence, stating the person that was supposed to be making the trip had informed the police. He was arrested and charged for the possession of half a kilo of cannabis. When the case reached court, Paul was given a suspended sentence due to it being his first arrest.

Six months later, whilst lying in bed, groggy from the previous night of hedonism, the police raided his flat. Within his home the police search uncovered three kilos of cannabis, half an ounce of cocaine, a stun gun and £25,000 in cash. Paul laughs as he recites the events of that morning. He explains he still considers himself lucky the police had not arrived the previous morning when they would have stumbled across an extra six kilos of cannabis. Overall in his time working with Swan's organisation, Paul estimates he earned a profit of around £2,000,000. A fact missed by the police as his legal defence was that of a dependent drug user intimidated into using his flat as a warehouse for drug dealers. He explained that he feared for his life therefore could not identify those responsible. However, despite what Paul terms as luck, due to the police raid he was in debt to Swan for £25,000 and sentenced to custody. Paul was ordered to serve forty-two months alongside the activation of the two months suspended sentence he had incurred during his earlier arrest. Over the next few years Paul served his custodial sentence across various areas of the prison estate. It was during the final stage of his sentence when Paul first heard of cryptomarkets (the original Silk Road website) from a fellow inmate who was utilising it to source drugs he would then distribute within the prison.

Paul – Bail hostels to cryptomarkets

For the two years following his release from custody Paul says he paid his way through life in the only way he felt he could, selling small quantities of cocaine and '*ticking the boxes*' the probation services requested. Within two years he had paid £10,000 of his debt off. He was still regularly receiving threats from Swan. After a particularly unnerving demand for more money Paul goaded his ex-associates to come to his address and '*beat him to death*'. Throughout the night the gang rang him and told him they were driving to his home, on each occasion he told them to be quick and get on with it. He recalls that he was:

> Absolutely shitting it, but they wouldn't leave me be and they were threatening my family. I just thought fuck it, I'll get a good punch in and accept my fate!

Neither Swan nor his associates arrived at his home or requested the last £10,000 he owed them. During this period, he came across an individual called James, an aloof fellow who he could not gauge and avoided when possible. James lived in one of the various probation-approved hostels Paul called home. By 2015 Paul ceased selling cocaine as his supplier had disappeared. It is unclear from the interviews where. For the next few years Paul continued selling small amounts of cannabis to fund his own habit whilst looking for legitimate employment, a task he found increasingly difficult.

Since his time within the open prison, and increasingly whilst in various hostels, Paul had heard talk of websites from which you could order drugs and have them delivered to your door. Upon a chance meeting with James in a local pub the idea to use such websites grabbed Paul's attention. Paul describes that throughout the evening James told him of these websites. He declared that if you ignore the burgeoning cocaine freebase habit of James's, he is '*an incredibly intelligent man who spends most of his days on his computer*'. The pair discussed at length the prospect of using the websites and eventually, in June 2016, Paul invested £300 in the venture and they placed their first order. Paul explains that ordering from the dark net is not as simple as it appears. Although the cryptomarkets are extremely easy to find once Tor software is installed, cryptocurrency offers practical issues:

> It takes us six weeks to set up, he takes that £300 and puts it into bitcoin. So we have set up the account but we can't buy the bitcoin. You need your passports and that to get your account set up. Then to verify the bank account we need to do a small transaction, but then we find out there is a cash point in (name of city redacted) that you can go and pair your phone up with and put the bitcoin into your phone and send it anywhere in the world. It is like money gram. So, the bitcoin passes through loads of computers, say twenty. Each one is like a digital receipt of the transaction and takes a miniscule amount of the bitcoin for the transaction. So now we don't need a central bank, it takes like points of a penny off. Then because these computers basically replace the central bank you can send me, like from me to you, and no one ever knows it was done! There is no trace apart from the computers it gets sent through. So, we get the bit coin, order the stuff, some ten grams of MDMA for seventy pounds was the first order if I remember right; and it turned up. That was the beginning of it, a chance conversation. I had the money and he was smart enough to do it so I said let's do it.

Once the pair had sourced a means to deposit bitcoin, they could then purchase their order. Paul explains that, in order to limit their chance of being caught and held accountable by the authorities they have devised a system which, to date, has proved successful. Within this system, a third member is required, Paul recruited Steven.

Steven and Paul each put forth 50% of the money to purchase the illicit substance. James orders the drug of choice from the cryptomarkets, under the name of a previous tenant at Steven's home. Steven receives the package a few days later, addressed to the previous tenant. On the package, Steven writes return to sender, therefore if the police do conduct a raid there is no evidence that he knew what was held inside. A few days later Paul will collect the package and sell the contents. Each package only contains a relatively small quantity of drugs, usually around ten grams which affords a way to minimise evidence of intent to supply if they are apprehended. The drugs bought from the cryptomarkets by the trio are eclectic. The following passage recounts in some detail the business setup and the product choice:

> I've bought acid, MDMA, ketamine, coke, solids, base. Base[2] is kind of a niche market, but a lot of people take it. It is a bread and butter drug, a council estate drug. There are a lot of people who take it every day so I know I can sell it, it's a guaranteed sale. I got the ketamine and the acid because I don't want to deal with coke, I end up sniffing it. So, I want to get drugs I will only dabble in myself or don't really take. I will only buy weed on personal level; can get it half price off the net but it stinks and you're not going to make that much money off it. For the risk you take, even if you ten shot it off it's not worth the risk. Like when I sell weed,

> I will sell anything, any weight, if I've got the right price I will sell it to you. I'm probably only selling a couple of ounces. If I sell it in tens, I'm making £150, in ounces I'm making £40. I normally sell in quarters though so I make £80 off two ounces but I smoke that a week. On the other drugs, once everything has gone out, I probably make like £300 every three weeks, hundred quid a week. I take the lion's share. I get my pal 15% on the total order, I give the lad half of the wholesale price, so if I get ten grams MD delivered to his house, I am telling him I am getting it at, selling it in eighths at like fucking, £60 an eighth. So call that three, £180. So I will give him half of that and keep the rest. So I just don't tell him I am selling it in grams and take a bigger profit. So right now there is the lad who does the internet and gets a cut of the order, there is the lad who puts the money up and gets it delivered to his house, he gets the half and I get the rest, but I raise my profit by not telling him I am doing it by the gram. I couldn't do it on my own, I don't have the know-how. At first, I was giving him twenty five percent of my profit but then he decided that was too steep and went to fifteen percent of the order rather than the profit. So, we kind of hashed it out so it's economically viable for us both.

Paul states he does not risk ordering cannabis due to the potent smell, although during a discussion I was privy to in the course of the research, it is apparent that another drug dealer in the city is ordering large quantities of cannabis directly to his home from the same cryptomarkets. This risk analysis, such as the decision to not source cannabis from the markets, is displayed throughout the time the research was conducted. When asked why Paul chose to utilise the cryptomarkets as opposed to conventional drug suppliers and what problems he has come against with both markets comparatively, he detailed the following:

> It works kind of like pirate bay. If I download something off your site and I leave a review on your site that is good, your credit rating goes up. It's all on you send something to me, I put a review on like amazon. Your rating goes up and so does mine. If there are bad reviews then you lose customers. You tend to find… we have had some problems on it. You get from level one to level eight. Once they get to eight, they might pull an exit scam, they run for a month without sending anything out and bounce with the money which is what happened to us. The first guy we used, we used him like six times, on like the seventh or eighth time he bounces and takes the money. He did it to all the customers. So we don't use level one, two or three. We tend to use between four and six, they are still building and at like level eight they might pull an exit scam.
>
> It is a lot of effort to go to, but once it is set up I don't have to ring around saying 'Have you got? Have you got?'. It is there, on the screen, they have got it, I know I've got it. I don't have to deal with anybody I just order it and it comes whereas with somebody on the street you have

> to phone around, haggle, you turn up and it might not be… If you say to someone on the web it is not what they said it was they ain't going to punch you in the face. Basically, if you ring a dealer up and say that was short, look at the beef I had with Mo over two grams. On the net if you get bounced it is cheap and it's not personal. Monetary wise yes but it's not your mate who just ripped you off. You can leave feedback on the site and there is not a repercussion. If you sell me something and I go around and tell everyone your gear is shit there is a come back on it whereas if I say on the net everyone can see its shit, I can tell everyone it is shit and there is no comeback. It is a shop, it's exactly like shopping in a proper shop. And normally on the page it will have terms and conditions like, if you haven't ordered three things in the past, we ain't going to give you a re-ship but you're more likely to get like at least a fifty percent re-ship if you have. Or they might give you a refund or a hundred percent re-ship. On the street, you might get ripped off and there is a beef. On the net it is just business. I mean on the street I have heard of people being dead, not breathing over beef. On the net I won't put more than three or four hundred on it. You can order kilos on there, but if I was to order a kilo it would be a face to face thing with somebody. It's a calculated risk init, it's not worth than putting a thousand pound down.
>
> Plus, the quality is much higher on the net, the price is much lower and so is the risk. The only risk is at customs. If I was to buy a gram of MDMA on the street it is £35 to £40, I can buy ten grams at £4 a gram, so even if I lose the ten grams, so what? I've made that on the next deal! There's risks, I had some K off there the other week it wasn't brilliant. Just won't use him again.
>
> So over a year I make like £5,200 and my drugs are free. It isn't for making money it's for making my money free. Not because I want to be a drug dealer because I don't. But I don't want to be going out on the street.

Towards the end of the research study, the trio found an alternative method of transferring currency into bitcoin, opening a bank account in Germany which they now utilise. This change of tact was cited as a response to Brexit, which they state served to damage profit margins due to the fluctuating exchange rates. The total profit garnered over the time the group was active was dubious although Paul estimates they have made around £10,000. He stated that more money could be made but he was erring on the side of caution, seeing his illicit business as a way to ensure he always had his own cannabis and money to furnish his new family home.

McDonaldization of drug distribution

Pauls' rationalisation for utilising the cryptomarkets demonstrates the application of Ritzer's (2015) theory of McDonaldization, which can be utilised as a means of understanding the rise of the cryptomarkets and their subsequent transition into the British organised crime milieu. McDonaldization was first developed by Ritzer in the early 1990s as a means to analyse the increasing homogenisation of culture within the globalised political economy, driven by the underpinning principles of the fast food industry as a means to demonstrate. Such homogenisation has been recognised as implicating upon substance use and how it has shaped the contemporary service economy (Hayward and Turner, 2018). Throughout the transcript evidence is put forth which can be applied to each of the four tenants of the theory as detailed below:

- *Efficiency* – Paul details his rationalisation for exploiting the cryptomarkets as a source for his illegal commodities through the efficiency of the service in comparison to the conventional drug market avenues. The ability to see exactly what the organisation is going to order and reports of the quality ensure an efficient source of supply in comparison to the traditional means of sourcing drugs. The ability to locate the supplier from the computer, negating the traditional means of contacting various suppliers to locate his source, also ensures that further efficiency is afforded to the business model.
- *Calculability* – The organised crime group distributes a much smaller amount of illicit substances in comparison to the previous group Paul was affiliated with. The cryptomarkets negate a large portion of actors whose involvement within the trafficking substantially increase the retail price of such substances. Using the prices of MDMA from the cryptomarkets to demonstrate this, Paul can source ten grams of the substances for the average price of one gram at a street level. The ability to increase the profit margin so considerably therefore allows the organisation to distribute smaller amounts of illicit substances whilst still netting a substantial profit. Coupling this with the decreased size of the overall organisation and the niche substances they can guarantee access to ensures an increased calculability for the overall business model.
- *Predictability* – The review system utilised on the cryptomarkets combined with the propensity for vendors to reissue substances that do not arrive or are intercepted by customs and exiles ensures a predictability within the business model. This, alongside the regularity of deliveries from the time of order to the time of delivery, ensures that the group can predict the availability of the stock and when they can distribute it at a street level, thus ensuring an enhanced service for their customers. As Paul states, much of the time spent within the traditional drug markets by figures such as himself is spent attempting to source substances to sell, the cryptomarkets add an unparalleled level of predictability.
- *Control* – The risk minimisation referenced in relation to both the decreased possibility of disputes with other street dealers and the reliance on the customer reviews for the vendors to ensure the availability of their market ensures an incomparable level of control when utilising the cryptomarkets.

> As Ritzer (2015) highlights, the minimisation of human interaction is key to the control of an organisation which is exactly what the cryptomarkets offer organised crime groups such as the one discussed in this chapter.

Overall, the introduction of cryptomarkets has offered some semblance of bureaucratic structure to illicit markets. Such developments in the formalisation of the markets offer an unprecedented possibility of 'taming' what is typically viewed as a volatile shadow economy, demonstrated by the harm reduction advice often embedded within the online markets (Bancroft and Reid, 2015). Though it must be recognised that such views are vastly overestimated within the media and in popular culture, further work is essential in investigating the viability of applying the work of Ritzer (2015) to cryptomarkets and the knock of effects in a robust manner. Though, within the context of this study, it is put forth that McDonaldization could be intrinsically linked to the phenomenon, with emerging organised crime groups viewing the utilisation of cryptomarkets as a rational choice (Aldridge and Askew, 2017).

Cryptomarkets and disorganised crime

As shown within the discussion of the application of McDonaldization, the cryptomarkets offer a mirror to the legitimate commodities markets which proposes a form of 'civilising process' to the distribution of illicit substances. For individuals such as Paul who view violence as an unpalatable predisposition within their line of work, the cryptomarkets offer an alluring alternative which maximises their entrepreneurial interests (Winlow, 2001) whilst negating much of the risk (Goldstein, 1985; Reuter, 2009; Volkan et al., 2002; Johnson, 2015; Treadwell et al., 2020). This was crucial to Paul, who perceived his illicit activity as a means to avoid the worst excesses of the service economy (Lloyd, 2018) which was his only alternative income stream (see Salinas' chapter on doubling up in this volume). As Hobbs (1998:408) observes, 'the organisation of criminal labour mirrors trends in the organisation of legitimate labour'. Therefore, the introduction of cryptomarkets, which closely mirror traditional e-commerce websites (Aldridge and Décary-Hétu, 2014) and wider consumer culture, could be perceived as a hyperbolic transformation of the drugs trade, demonstrating Hobbs' perspective.

The study of Paul and his latest venture into organised crime substantiates the qualitative data put forth by Aldridge and Décary-Hétu (2014). The utilisation of the cryptomarkets demonstrates Hignett's (2012) observation of the propensity of organised crime groups to evolve alongside technological advancement. This transformation further substantiates the evolution of opportunistic, mutually profitable organised crime groups (Hignett, 2012). This indicates that the influence of technology will increasingly perpetuate the opportunistic alliances, sole traders and leaderless networks traders identified by Pearson and Hobbs (2001:6–7). This transition potentially exacerbates the redundancy of traditional archaic organised crime groups (Hobbs, 1995). Evidenced is that the organised crime groups utilising the markets include individuals that would not traditionally be associated with the drugs trade (Paul partners), therefore alluding the changing nature of organised crime which increasingly accommodates the opportunity to profit for those who lack traditional street capital. The cryptomarkets allow the utilisation of criminal opportunities to facilitate a wider section of economically marginalised members of society to be able to confirm their masculinity through involvement deviancy (Winlow, 2001). Individuals such as those Paul operates alongside, whose traditional propensity to utilise deviancy could have been hampered by the level of conflict-orientated criminal culture within traditional drug markets, are now offered an alternative route. The anonymity of cryptomarkets has furthered the criminal entrepreneurialism and offered further normalisation of the criminal environment. As Hobbs (2001) explains, professional crime evolves alongside the legitimate economic order and contemporary professional criminals are businessmen who merely trade commodities in line with market principles. The cryptomarkets facilitate and fundamentally exacerbate this notion, but also minimise the risks.

Addressing risk as a mitigating factor

A recurring theme within the data included in this chapter is that of risk. Most prominent was the risk posed to Paul by other members of the criminal milieu (Ellis, 2016 and Treadwell et al., 2020). As is apparent when reviewing the life course of Paul, his transition into early criminality was spurned via his vulnerability as an adolescent. A key factor within this was his inability to utilise consumer symbolism (Hall et al., 2008) nor violence (Ellis, 2016) to forge his identity throughout the early stages of his life course. As can be seen within this period, his retreat into drug usage and low-level distribution served to counteract such deficits, especially through the entrepreneurial (Hobbs, 2001) approach to challenges such as homelessness. As he states he is a *"lover not a fighter"*, a part of his identity that caused him much turmoil and lasting trauma in his adolescence. Once he had become involved within the professional criminal market at a level akin to a warehouse manager (Pearson and Hobbs, 2001), in a business strategy resembling an early incarnation of contemporary county lines operations (Densley et al., 2018), such aversion to violence as a risk became a mitigating factor in his approach. Partially shielded, though unaware of the protection offered via the organisation, Paul was still targeted on one occasion for inter-criminal victimisation in the form of taxing (Treadwell et al., 2020). As stated upon the second arrest which led to his incarceration, he was in possession of a stun gun. He details that he was given this weapon to protect himself and more importantly the money and drugs he was storing after his front door was kicked off and a group of men attempted to tax him (Treadwell et al., 2020). Again this highlights the underlying and arguably most prominent risk to those involved in professional criminality, such as drug distribution. Following his incarceration the continual threat of violent reprisal was vocalised via the group he was now estranged from – furthering the likelihood of interpersonal violence. Historically, such threats of violence had already underpinned much of his early trauma (Ellis, 2016) once the context of his father fleeing to London as he owed money to Swan's father over two decades previously is taken into account.

It became apparent throughout the project that the calculation of risk underpinned much of the justification for Paul transitioning into the utilisation of cryptomarkets to source his illicit product. Such calculation is best viewed as a rational choice (Akers, 1990; Fader, 2016). Not only did he utilise individuals not usually involved within the criminal milieu (in the context of drug distribution) but the choice of substances he chose to market was rather niche, therefore lessening the possibility of other groups identifying his distribution activities. Using marketing strategies to identify drug markets, which would allow a steady flow of custom whilst not rivalling more embedded and traditional criminal networks, was key to his approach.

Secondly, the utilisation of cryptomarkets to avoid detection displays a level of maturity within the approach to risk in the discussion of police detection. On numerous occasions whilst working under Swan, Pauls' actions overtly disregarded known risks in the pursuit of profit in an attempt to maximise financial benefits. Little attention in this period was given to protecting his accumulation of wealth through money laundering or minimising the risk of being caught in possession of illicit substances. With the fledgling organised crime group he formulated utilising cryptomarkets it is clear that attention was paid to minimise the chance of detection through the very nature of his changing drug importation. Alongside this greater attention was paid to develop robust strategies which would disguise the movement of illicit money accrued from the venture.

The work of Beck (1992) can be drawn upon to make sense of the changes in approach utilised by Paul as business strategies. The concept of risk society highlights how modernity and globalisation have created manufactured risk – risks brought forth by human agency. It is long acknowledged that illicit trade mirrors licit trade, effectively emulating each other within the continuum brought forth by capitalism. As Hobbs (1995) observes, the criminal milieu often develops to utilise technology in tandem with technological advancement. Within this case study it is observable that Paul's risk aversion has allowed him to develop an illicit business model, utilising advances in technology which have sought to address the manufactured risk of both inter-criminal violence and criminal justice detection. Furthermore, the niche drugs he opted to distribute are in his own words 'bread and butter drugs' ensuring a continual, accessible but risk-adverse business plan. It is highlighted by Beck (1992) that a class distinction is evident within the risk society. He proposed that risk is stratified, much in the same manner as wealth, thus amplified within the lower social strata. This chapter proposes that an ever-clearer distinction is available within developments in the criminal milieu and professional crime. Paul's street capital (Sandberg and Pederson, 2009) was evidently fragile – thus within the criminal milieu he straddled the lower strata. He recognised throughout the case study the protection afforded to him whilst aligned with Swan's organisation and his overall aversion to violence. For Paul the use of cryptomarkets and the choice of substances he opted to market were calculated to minimise both inter-criminal and criminal justice responses.

Conclusion

This chapter has sought to give a contextual overview of how the development and proliferation of cryptomarkets have influenced the traditional drug crime nexus within the United Kingdom. As previously stated, the vast majority of work within the area has focussed upon the markets themselves or substance users, failing to regard the work of Wall (2007) who brought attention to the fact that cybercrime is not an entirely separate entity of criminal activity that fails to interact with the offline world (with the exception of Martin, 2014). Just as academia has failed to fully engage with the wider context of the technological shift (Treadwell, 2012), the vast majority of police responses have been focussed upon the upper tier of cryptomarkets distribution, most notably with the targeting of Silk Road but more recently against the Alphabay, Hansa, Dream, Valhalla and Wall Street marketplaces.

This study exposes the gap within current literature identifying how the National Crime Agencies' inference of 4,542 organised crime groups active within the United Kingdom is likely to be unrepresentative within the reality of a criminal landscape that is rapidly changing due to technological advancements (Treadwell et al., 2019; Hall and Antonopoulos, 2016; Hall and Antonopoulos' chapter in this volume). It is important to note that such changes effectively expand the breadth of actors who can engage with serious criminality yet remain wholly undetected and recognised within current approaches. As highlighted throughout, organised criminality in the United Kingdom has always mirrored the legitimate economy. Just as globalisation pushed forth a new age of efficiency within business models which account for risks, the emergence and convergence on advanced technology (Décary-Hétu and Giommoni, 2017) has allowed the scope for a diverse range of criminal actors to utilise their entrepreneurial skills within criminal markets they would previously have been manipulated within. It is unlikely that we will observe a large proportion of traditional drug distribution networks dissipate in the near future being replaced by cryptomarket activity. As can be seen within the case study of Paul though, it is likely that some criminal actors will utilise the cryptomarkets as their main acquisition point. This will facilitate an increasingly diverse plethora of substances and criminal actors in some sections of the British drug trade due to the minimised risk of harms.

Notes

1 The Farmers Market (often referred to as Adamflowers) was an illicit drugs market that appeared on the surface web in 2006. By 2010 the market had moved onto the dark web and could only be accessed using the TOR service. The website was shut down by the DEA in operation Adam Bomb in 2012. Prior to being compromised, the website was estimated to have grossed around $2,500,000, selling various substances including cannabis, mescaline, LSD and DMT.

2 Cocaine freebase (base) is similar to crack cocaine in that it is typically smoked though it can be injected. The effects are also similar to crack cocaine, producing a similar euphoric effect that lasts around three minutes. Unlike powdered cocaine, freebase is not produced using acid – instead the production process effectively purges the substance of the hydrochloride. Ether is used and dissolved in water alongside powdered cocaine and benzene to produce cocaine sulphate. This process results in a substance that is close to 100% pure. Cocaine freebase is similar to crack cocaine; however, freebase is flammable at lower temperatures and residual ether is often present within the final product. The process of producing cocaine freebase comes with greater risks due to the flammability of ether. As the substance is too volatile (often resulting in the user being burnt by the residual ether whilst inhaling the product), crack cocaine has become much more popular over the last three decades.

References

Akers, R. (1990). Rational choice, Deterrence, and social learning theory in criminology: The path not taken. *The Journal of Criminal Law and Criminology*, 81(3), 653–676. [Online] Available at: http://dx.doi.org/10.2307/1143850 [Accessed 22 June 2019].

Aldridge, J. and Askew, R. (2017). Delivery dilemmas: How drug cryptomarket users identify and seek to reduce their risk of detection by law enforcement. *International Journal of Drug Policy*, 41, 101–109. [Online] Available at: http://dx.doi.org/10.1016/j.drugpo.2016.10.010 [Accessed 22 June 2017].

Aldridge, J. and Décary-Hétu, D. (2014). Not an 'Ebay for drugs': The cryptomarket 'Silk Road' as a paradigm shifting criminal innovation. *SSRN Electronic Journal.* [Online] Available at: http://dx.doi.org/10.2139/ssrn.2436643 [Accessed 22 June 2019].

Aldridge, J. and Décary-Hétu, D. (2016). Hidden wholesale: The drug diffusing capacity of online drug cryptomarkets. *International Journal of Drug Policy*, 35, 7–15. [Online] Available at: http://dx.doi.org/10.1016/j.drugpo.2016.04.020 [Accessed 22 June 2017].

Antonopoulos, G., Hall, A., Large, J., Shen, A., Crang, M., and Andrews, M. (2018). *Fake goods, real money: The counterfeiting business and its financial management.* Bristol: Policy Press.

Bancroft, A., and Reid, S. (2015). Concepts of illicit drug quality among darknet market users: Purity, embodied experience, craft and chemical knowledge. *International Journal of Drug Policy*, 35, 42–49. [Online] Available at: https://doi.org/10.1016/j.drugpo.2015.11.008 [Accessed 17 January 2020].

Barratt, M., Ferris, J. and Winstock, A. (2014). Use of Silk Road, the online drug marketplace, in the United Kingdom, Australia and the United States. *Addiction*, 109(5), 774–810. [Online] Available at: http://dx.doi.org/10.1111/add.12470 [Accessed 22 June 2017].

Barratt, M. (2016). Everything you always wanted to know about drug cryptomarkets* (*but were afraid to ask). *International Journal of Drug Policy,* 25, 1–6. Available at: www.sciencedirect.com/science/article/abs/pii/S0955395916302274?via%3Dihub [Accessed 17 January 2020].

Barratt, M., Ferris, J., and Winstock, A. (2016). Safer scoring? Cryptomarkets, social supply and drug market violence. *International Journal of Drug Policy,* 35, 22–31. Available at: http://dx.doi.org/10.1016/j.drugpo.2016.04.019 [Accessed 17 May 2019].

Bartlett, J. (2016). *The Dark Net.* New York: Melville House Publishing.

Beck, U. (1992). *Risk Society: Towards a New Modernity.* London: Sage.

Biryukov, A., Pustogarov, I., Thill, F., and Weinmann, R. (2013). Content and popularity analysis of TOR hidden services. *Distributed Computing Systems Workshops*, pp. 188–193.

Casanova, M., Solursh, D., Solursh, L., Roy, E., and Thigpen, L. (2000). The history of child pornography on the internet. *Journal of Sex Education and Therapy*, 4, 245–251.

Christin, N. (2013). Travelling the Silk Road: A measurement analysis of a large anonymous online marketplace. In: *22nd International Conference on World Wide Web.*

Coleman, C., and Moynihan, J. (1996). *Understanding Crime Data: Haunted by the Dark Figure.* Buckinghamshire: Open University Press.

Coleman, E. (2015). *Hacker, Hoaxer, Whistle-Blower, Spy: The Many Faces of Anonymous.* London: Verso.

Décary-Hétu, D., and Giommoni, L. (2017). Do police crackdowns disrupt drug cryptomarkets? A longitudinal analysis of the effects of Operation Onymous. *Crime, Law and Social Change*, 67(1),55–75. [Online] Available at: http://dx.doi.org/10.1007/s10611-0169644-4 [Accessed 22 June 2019].

Densley, J., McLean, R., Deuchar, R., and Harding, S. (2018). An altered state? Emergent changes to illicit drug markets and distribution networks in Scotland. *International Journal of Drug Policy*, 58, 113–120.

Dolliver, D., and Kenney, J. (2016). Characteristics of drug vendors on the TOR network: A cryptomarket comparison. *Victims & Offenders*, 11(4), 600–620. [Online] Available at: http://dx.doi.org/10.1080/15564886.2016.1173158 [Accessed 23 June 2019].

Dorn, N., Levi, M., and King, L. (1992). *Traffickers: Drug Markets and Law Enforcement.* London: Routledge.

Ellis, A. (2016). *Men, Masculinities and Violence: An Ethnographic Study.* Abingdon: Routledge.

Fader, J. (2016). Selling smarter, not harder: Life course effects on drug sellers risk perceptions and management. *International Journal of Drug Policy*, 36, 120–129. [Online] Available at: http://dx.doi.org/10.1016/j.drugpo.2016.04.011 [Accessed 22 June 2019].

Glenny, M. (2012). *Dark Market.* London: Vintage.

Goodey, J. (2000). Biographical lessons for criminology'. *Theoretical Criminology,* 4(4), 473–498.

Goodman, M. (2015). *Future crimes: Inside the Digital Underground and the Battle for Our Connected World.* London: Corgi Books.

Goldstein, P. (1985). The drugs/violence nexus: A tripartite conceptual framework. *Journal of Drug Issues*, 15(4), 493–506. [Online] Available at: http://dx.doi.org/10.1177/002204268501500406 [Accessed 22 June 2017].

Haraty, R., and Zanout, B. (2014). The TOR data communication system. *Journal of Communications and Networks,* 16(4), 415–420. [Online] Available at: http://dx.doi.org/10.1109/jcn.2014.000071 [Accessed 22 June 2019].

Hall, A., and Antonopoulos, G. (2016). *Fake Meds Online.* London: Palgrave Macmillan UK.

Hall, S., Winlow, S., and Ancrum, C. (2008). *Criminal Identities and Consumer Culture: Crime, Exclusion and the New Culture of Narcissism.* Oxford: Taylor & Francis.

Haller, M. (1990). Illegal enterprise: A theoretical and historical interpretation. *Criminology*, 28(2), 207–236. [Online]Available at: http://dx.doi.org/10.1111/j.17459125.1990.tb01324.x [Accessed 22 June 2017].

Hayward, K., and Turner, T. (2018). Be more VIP': Deviant leisure and hedonistic excess in Ibiza's 'Disneyized' party spaces. In T. Raymen and O. Smith (Eds.), *Deviant Leisure: Criminological Perspectives on Leisure and Harm*. Switzerland: Palgrave Macmillan.

Hignett, K. (2012). Transnational organised crime and the global village. In F. Allum and S. Gilmore (Eds.), *Routledge Handbook of Transnational Organised Crime*. Oxford: Taylor & Francis, pp. 282–289.

Hobbs, D. (1995). *Bad Business: Professional Crime in Modern Britain*. Oxford University Press.

Hobbs, D. (1997). Professional crime and the myth of the underworld. *Sociology*, 31(1), 57–72.

Hobbs, D. (1998). Going down the glocal: The local context of organised crime. *The Howard Journal of Criminal Justice*, 37(4), 407–422.

Hobbs, D. (2001). The firm: Organised crime on a shifting terrain. *British Journal of Criminology*, 41, 549–560.

Johnson, L. (2015). Drug markets, travel distance, and violence: Testing a typology. *Crime & Delinquency*, 62(11), 1465–1487.

Lloyd, A. (2018). *The harms of work: An ultra-realist account of the service economy*. Bristol: Bristol University Press.

Martin, J. (2014). *Drugs on the dark net: How cryptomarkets are transforming the global trade in illicit drugs*. Basingstoke: Palgrave Macmillan.

Martin, J., Munksgaard, R., Coomber, R., Demant, J., and Barratt, M. (2019). Selling drugs on darkweb cryptomarkets: Differentiated pathways, risks and rewards. *British Journal of Criminology*. [Online] Available at: https://doi.org/10.1093/bjc/azz075

Markoff, J. (2006). *What the Dormouse Said: How the Sixties Counterculture Shaped the Personal Computer Industry*. London: Penguin Books.

National Crime Agency. (2019). *National Strategic Assessment of Serious and Organised Crime*. National Crime Agency.

Pearson, G. and Hobbs, D. (2001). *Middle Market Drug Distribution*. Home Office Research Study 227. London: Home Office.

Reiner, R. (1996). The case of the missing crimes. In R. Levitas and W. Guy (Eds.), *Interpreting Official Statistics*. London: Routledge.

Reuter, P. (2009). Systemic violence in drug markets. *Crime, Law and Social Change*, 52(3), 275–284. [Online] Available at: http://dx.doi.org/10.1007/s10611-009-9197 [Accessed 22 June 2017].

Ritzer, G. (2015). *The Mcdonaldization of Society*, 8th edn. London: Sage.

Sandberg, S., and Pederson, W. (2009). *Street Capital: Black Cannabis Dealers in a White Welfare State*. Bristol: Policy Press.

Shaw, C. (1968). *The Jack-Roller: A Delinquent Boy's Own Story*. London: The University of Chicago Press.

Sterling, B. (1998). *Hacker Crackdown, Law and Disorder on the Electronic Frontier*. New York: Bantam Publishing.

Thrasher, F. (1967). *The Gang: A Study of 1,313 Gangs in Chicago*. Chicago, IL: University of Chicago Press.

Treadwell, J. (2012). From the car boot to booting it up? eBay, online counterfeit crime and the transformation of the criminal marketplace. *Criminology & Criminal Justice*, 12(2), 175–191.

Treadwell, J., Ancrum, C., and Kelly, C. (2020). Taxing times: Inter-criminal victimization and drug robbery amongst the English professional criminal milieu. *Deviant Behavior,* 1, 57–69. DOI: 10.1080/01639625.2018.1519136

Treadwell, J., Gooch, K., and Barkham Perry, G. (2019). *Crime in Prison: Where Now and Where Next?* Office for the Police and Crime Commissionaires, Midlands Region.

Volkan, T., Wright, R., and Fornango, R. (2002). Drug dealers, robbery and retaliation. Vulnerability, deterrence and the contagion of violence. *British Journal of Criminology,* 42(2), 337–351.

Wall, D. (2001). *Crime and the Internet.* London: Routledge.

Wall, D. (2007). *Cybercrime: The Transformation of Crime in the Information Age.* London: Polity.

Winlow, S. (2001). *Badfellas: Crime, Tradition and New Masculinities.* Oxford: Berg.

17

IMAGE AND PERFORMANCE-ENHANCING DRUG (IPED) SUPPLIERS AND THEIR MOTIVES

Following the evidence

Katinka van de Ven, Kyle J.D. Mulrooney and Honor Townshend

Introduction

In a recent commentary, Mulrooney et al. (2019) discussed how certain 'narratives of harm' have tended to dominate discourses around the use of image and performance-enhancing drugs (IPEDs), particularly focussing on anabolic-androgenic steroids (henceforth, steroids). These views, exacerbated by a sensationalist media, tend to pathologise people who use IPEDs, exaggerate health and social risks, and ignore the role of 'pleasure' in consuming these substances. Subsequently, the authors argue, the dominance of the narrative of harm and ignorance of the reality of individual and social harms caused by these drugs more specifically has meant the prioritisation of repressive policy approaches to dealing with steroid use in society (see also van de Ven, Dunn, & Mulrooney, 2018). Indeed, without nuance, the public and policymakers are presented with a distorted reality from which to respond to the recreational use of steroids and other IPEDs.

Similarly, when it comes to the suppliers of IPEDs, a very narrow stereotype exists regarding the 'organised', violent, profiteering IPED dealer (van de Ven, 2016), which oversimplifies the everyday realities of people who produce, sell, buy and use these substances. Sport authorities, and especially the World Anti-Doping Agency (WADA), have long sought to add some 'legal' muscle to their fight against doping by involving law enforcement in anti-doping initiatives (Fincoeur, Ven, & Mulrooney, 2015; Mulrooney & van de Ven, 2015; van de Ven & Mulrooney, 2014; Van de Ven & Mulrooney, 2017a). To this end, WADA has consistently widened the anti-doping nets by advocating for stricter regulations and harsher punishments of doping supply chains, emphasising supply reduction in their efforts to curb demand. Importantly, on a number of occasions, WADA has taken the stance that doping (i.e. IPEDs) supply chains are controlled

DOI: 10.4324/9781351010245-20

in large part by 'mafia-type' organised crime (Hoberman, 2011; van de Ven & Mulrooney, 2014). In addition, sport and law enforcement officials often suggest that the individuals and groups involved in dealing IPEDs are purely interested in making profit and do not care about the health and well-being of people who use these substances (Fincoeur et al., 2015). Yet, scant evidence exists to support these claims and, perhaps more important, research shows that many IPED suppliers solely supply to friends and have little interest in making a profit (e.g. Kraska, Bussard, & Brent, 2010; van de Ven & Mulrooney, 2017b).

Ross Coomber (2006) in his book *Pusher Myths* debunks several myths regarding what is commonly understood about who a drug dealer is and how they operate. He argues that an overly simplistic characterisation of drug dealers as 'dealing in death', 'preying on the young and innocent' and 'spreading addiction with little care or regard for those they entangle' is unhelpful in trying to understand the drug problem and, ultimately, how this can be resolved. Following this line, in this chapter we argue that the view of organised crime controlling the market for IPEDs, in which dealers are solely driven by profit, is not only inaccurate but also unhelpful in responding to this illicit market. Conversely, we illustrate that a wide range of people are involved in this market and they supply IPEDs for a variety of reasons. This chapter is not an apologia for IPED suppliers but as Coomber (2006: iv) notes in his book, '[a]knowledging complexity and misinformed perspectives should never be confused with a failure to stand tall, the opposite is in fact true and paying lip service to simplistic images that are politically palatable is, of course, the easy option'. To this end, the aim of this chapter is to empirically review what we currently known about the production and supply of IPEDs by examining the current available literature on this topic. In this regard, the key questions that guide this chapter were as follows:

1. Who is involved in the illicit production and/or supply of IPEDs?
2. What are the motives to illicitly produce and/or supply IPEDs?

Methodology

We reviewed studies that explicitly examined the production and supply of IPEDs, with steroids being the primary drug being supplied. We specifically focussed on steroids as they generally are the main type of enhancement drug being studied and because it is the primary IPED being targeted by law enforcement (e.g. see van de Ven et al., 2018). In addition, steroids are also the oldest type of IPEDs, having been consumed since the late 1940s, and in the greatest amount (Evans-Brown et al., 2012). In this chapter, we will, however, use the term IPEDs as users often take a mix of enhancement drugs in their pursuit of bodily perfection (Salinas, Floodgate, & Ralphs, 2019). Due to the expertise of both van de Ven and Mulrooney in the field on the production and supply of IPEDs, it was expected that the literature in this field would be sparse. Due to the anticipated limited number of studies in this field, as well as the use of a variety of different qualitative methodologies and lack of outcome measures (making statistical analysis not possible), a systematic review or meta-analysis would not have been suitable. While we conducted a systematic search, we analysed the findings of the studies narratively in that we qualitatively summarised evidence on this topic using systematic methods to collect and interpret studies. This review therefore focussed on comprehensively and critically analysing the 17 studies to gain a better understanding of the production and supply of IPEDs.

Eligibility criteria

There were no date restrictions placed on the search due to the limited literature on the production and supply of IPEDs. Inclusion criteria comprised English and Dutch language peer-reviewed studies and research reports commissioned by the government and other bodies (e.g. WADA) that examined the production and supply of IPEDs, particularly steroids. Studies were excluded if their primary focus was on the use of IPEDs and not its supply, or if steroids were not the primary drug being produced and/or supplied. Monographs, single chapters, edited collections and PhD dissertations were excluded as well.

Search strategy

Papers that focussed on the production and/or supply of IPEDs were identified by carrying out searches on the major bibliographic databases that index international journals commonly used in the drug/doping field, and more generally within public health and criminology, including PubMed, PsycInfo, Science Direct, Cochrane, Sports Discus, Web of Science and Wiley Online, and Google Scholar. Reference lists of published works were also checked. Search terms included the type of substance (e.g. steroids) in combination with terms related to the type of offence (e.g. supply) (see Table 17.1).

Analysis

Two authors (HT and KV) conducted the database searches and screened the titles and abstracts of all publications obtained by the search strategy. The database searching, checking of reference lists and consulting with experts resulted

TABLE 17.1 Search terms

Type of substance (all fields)	*Type of offence (all fields)*
steroids OR doping OR testosterone OR 'performance and image enhancing drugs' OR 'image and performance enhancing drugs' OR IPED OR PIED	traffic* OR production OR supply* OR share OR sell*

in a total of 17 articles which met the inclusion criteria. Data extraction was done manually in Word Processor by one author (HT), using a coding schedule which identified the primary offence (production and/or supply), the production/supply source, the 'type' of supplier, and the motives for producing and/or supplying IPEDs (see Table 17.2). Grounded in the dealer typology of Sandberg (2012, pp. 1137–1138), the following distinction is made between types of IPED suppliers: (1) producers: people who manufacture their own steroids and other IPEDs, (2) exporters: people who gather the goods from producers and sell them across national borders, (3) smugglers: people who move IPEDs over the border, (4) importers: people who receive the consignment in the recipient country, (5) distributors: people who sell large quantities and make substantial amounts of money, (6) dealers: people who regularly sell medium and small quantities to users, and make some money, (7) helpers: people who sell small quantities to friends; they do not usually regard themselves as dealers, but as 'helpers', and they do not make much money; (8) online suppliers: people who sell IPEDs online via (fake) overseas or local pharmacies, illegal IPED-selling websites, social media platforms, forums and/or the deep web. Notably, these types may overlap, for example, if the producer is also a supplier and supplies via the internet. The coding instrument was piloted on a sub-sample of the articles (10%) (HT and KV). This was followed by a rigorous discussion by all three authors to refine the categories and to compare the results. The final full-text examination was then conducted by one author (HT).

Findings

In total 17 studies examined the production and/or supply of IPEDs. The countries where this phenomenon has been explored include the USA (Kraska et al., 2010), UK (Antonopoulos & Hall, 2016; Coomber et al., 2014; Hall, Koenraadt, & Antonopoulos, 2017; Salinas et al., 2019), Belgium (Fincoeur et al., 2015; van de Ven & Koenraadt, 2017; van de Ven & Mulrooney, 2017b), France (Fincoeur et al., 2015), the Netherlands (Fincoeur et al., 2015; Hall et al., 2017; Koert & Van Kleij, 1998; Oldersma, Snippe, & Bieleman, 2002; van de Ven & Koenraadt, 2017; van de Ven & Mulrooney, 2017b), Australia (Maycock & Howat, 2007; van de Ven et al., 2018) and Italy (Cordaro, Lombardo, & Cosentino, 2011; Paoli & Donati, 2015) (some studies took place in multiple countries). All studies used qualitative research methods, particularly ethnographic field research, semi-structured interviews, surveys and/or analysed online resources, policy documents and court cases.

IPED sources and their suppliers

IPEDs differ from most drug markets as many of these substances are also medicine and can be legally obtained via a prescription. As Paoli and Donati (2015: 37) point out, the legal status of IPEDs

TABLE 17.2 An overview of the included studies (N=16)

Author(s)/year and summary	*Country and year(s) of study*	*Design, participants, setting and analysis*	*Production/supply source*	*Motives*	*Supplier type(s)*
1. Kraska et al., 2010. This qualitative study reports findings on the production and (online) supply of IPEDs in the United States within fitness and bodybuilding communities.	US, 2005–2006	1. Mixed methods including 15 months of ethnographic field research (N=1 central informant; 12 sub-informants). Setting: gyms and bodybuilding competitions. Thematic analysis. 2. Quantitative content analysis of IPED-selling websites (N=186). Setting: online. Descriptive statistics.	IPEDs obtained via: – People selling via overseas (online) pharmacies; – People selling via IPED-selling websites (non-pharmacy); – Through contacts in the gym (e.g. gym members); – Healthcare professionals (doctors, pharmacists, etc.); and/or – Producing own steroids (i.e. 'Home-brewing').	– Produce/supply to make profit; – Helping out training buddy/friends; – Supply to off-set costs of own use; – Supply to off-set costs of pursuit of bodybuilding career; – Produce steroids to be able to control quality; and/or – Produce own IPEDs as it is cost-effective.	Helpers, distributors, dealers, importers, producer and/or online suppliers
2. Antonopoulos and Hall, 2016. This study provides an account of the social organisation of the steroid trafficking business in the UK.	UK, 2013–2015	1. Virtual ethnography. Setting: forums, online pharmacies and social networking sites. Jun 2013–Mar 2014. 2. Traditional ethnography. Setting: gym in England. Jan 2014–Feb 2015. Interviews during fieldwork including users (N=13), former users (N= 6), dealers (N=7), semi-professional MMA fighters	IPEDs obtained via: – Offline sellers (e.g. individuals who own or regularly frequent gyms, or are somehow connected to a gym owner); – Online sellers (via IPED-selling websites (non-pharmacy) such as social media, forums, classified sections and the dark web;	– Produce/supply to make profit; – Devotion to sport; – Social status; and/or – Brokers of 'masculinity' (Noted as: 'addiction' to inter-men admiration, informal competition with friends and the contribution of a collective 'gym identity').	Producers, distributors, importers, dealers and online suppliers

(*continued*)

TABLE 17.2 Cont.

Author(s)/year and summary	*Country and year(s) of study*	*Design, participants, setting and analysis*	*Production/supply source*	*Motives*	*Supplier type(s)*
		(N=4), amateur sportsmen (N=6), gym employees (N=3) and NHS psychologists (N=3). Thematic analysis. 3. Semi-structured interviews. Setting: MHRA, the National Crime Agency and Interpol (N=6). Thematic analysis. 4. Media analysis. Types: Newspapers, open-access online resources (from health organisations and drug agencies), bodybuilder magazines (sample size unknown). Content analysis.	– Through friends; and – Employee-sellers (gym managers and/or personal trainers who do not use steroids).		
3. Brennan et al., 2018. Qualitative study exploring online communal activity around the practice of home-brewing steroids amongst individuals who inject steroids.	Online, 2016	– Online data collection. Setting: steroid-specific forums. Method: Systematic internet searches (Google). N=6 forums. N=25 top threads. Inclusion/exclusion criteria applied. Final N=14. Content analysis of threads.	IPEDs obtained via: – People selling via overseas (online) pharmacies; – People selling via IPED-selling websites (non-pharmacy); – Through contacts in the gym (e.g. gym members); – Healthcare professionals (doctors, pharmacists, etc.);	– High risks associated with online purchase (i.e. low quality and risk of scam/fraud) – Produce of steroids to ensure quality.	Producers, dealers, distributors, helpers and online suppliers

			– Producing own steroids (i.e. 'Home-brewing'); and/or – Through friends.		
4. Coomber et al., 2014. This study aims to show what the IPED market looked like in a UK town in 2013: how it operated; how different users sought out and purchased their IPED; the beliefs they held about the IPED they sourced; and the methods they employed to feel confident in the authenticity of their purchases.	UK, 2013	– Semi-structured interviews (N=32) with 25 IPED users (8 were also 'social supplier's), 4 local gym owners/managers and 3 local IPED dealers. Setting: Service Delivery Agency and multiple gyms in Plymouth, England. Rapid appraisal.	IPEDs obtained via: – People selling via IPED-selling websites (non-pharmacy); and/or – Through contacts in the gym (e.g. gym members).	– Produce/supply to make profit; and/or –Production of steroids to ensure quality. –Helping out training buddy/friends	Distributors, online suppliers, importers and dealers
5. Fincoeur et al., 2015. This study aims to assess contemporary anti-doping policy and question how these may impact upon illicit IPED networks.	Belgium, France and the Netherlands, 2014	Empirical data from two research projects. The first project relies on (Belgium and France): – Semi-structured in-depth interviews (N=81) with: policy-makers, law enforcement officers, active	IPEDs obtained via: – Organised crime groups; – People selling via IPED-selling websites (non-pharmacy); – Through contacts in the gym (e.g. gym members); – Through friends; and/or	– Helping out training buddy/friends; – Cultural prestige amongst peers; and/or – Produce/supply to make profit;	Dealers, importers, helpers, producers and online suppliers

(continued)

TABLE 17.2 Cont.

Author(s)/year and summary	*Country and year(s) of study*	*Design, participants, setting and analysis*	*Production/supply source*	*Motives*	*Supplier type(s)*
		and retired elite cyclists, and other stakeholders (team doctors, sports physicians, team managers). Thematic analysis; The second project relies on (Belgium and the Netherlands): – trafficking cases (N=65) initiated by the criminal justice agencies – Ethnographic fieldwork conducted at bodybuilding sites for a time period of 2 years. Content analysis; – Semi-structured interviews (N=30) with law enforcement officers, (non)competitive bodybuilders and recreational weight-trainers. Thematic analysis; and – Content analysis of Belgian and Dutch news articles concerning IPED use and supply.	– Healthcare professionals (doctors, pharmacists, etc.)		

6. Hall et al., 2017. This study outlines the nature and dynamics of the trade of illicit pharmaceuticals (including IPEDs) including the roles played by each national context as nodes in the global supply chain.	UK and the Netherlands. Study (1) 2013–2014, Study (2) 2014–2015	Empirical data from two research projects. The first project relies on (UK): – Virtual ethnography. Setting: Online communities (e.g. online sellers). (Jun 2013–Mar 2014). – Traditional ethnography. Setting: A gym in North East England known for IPED use. – Semi-structured interviews (N=45) with consumers, suppliers and professionals (outside of the gym environment). (Jan 2014–Feb 2015). Thematic analysis. – Secondary data: Legal casework from the UK Medicines and Healthcare products Regulatory Agency (N=6). Content analysis. The second project relies on (Netherlands): – Legal casework from cases regarding the sale or distribution of illicit medicines (N=69) – Semi-structured interviews (Total N=78) with suppliers (N=30), consumers (N=9)	IPEDs obtained via: – Organised crime groups (not in traditional sense but often 'small and often ephemeral enterprises'); – People selling via IPED-selling websites (non-pharmacy); – Through contacts in the gym (e.g. gym members); – Other online platforms (e.g. forums); and/or – Other criminal activity (e.g. fraudulent – Healthcare professionals (doctors, pharmacists, etc.)	– To support cost of own use; – Devotion to sport; and/or – Produce/supply to make profit.	Helpers, dealers and online suppliers

(continued)

TABLE 17.2 Cont.

Author(s)/year and summary	*Country and year(s) of study*	*Design, participants, setting and analysis*	*Production/supply source*	*Motives*	*Supplier type(s)*
		and various officials (N=38). Setting: Work environments of individuals, public places (e.g. restaurants) and via phone. Thematic analysis. – of discussion platforms and websites (N=17) that were used to sell and trade illicit weight loss drugs and sexual enhancers. Content analysis. – Prevalence study amongst (N=50,860) Dutch respondent, with in-depth analysis of consumers of illicit medicine (N=985). Analysis methods: unknown.			
7. Maycock and Howat, 2015. This study aims to demonstrate the influence of social capital on transition into IPED use, illegal IPED use experiences and risks of detection.	Australia, 2006	– Participant observation of male steroid-using subgroups such as security workers, bodybuilders, sportspeople, personal trainers and dealers (N=147). 434 hours spent in the field. Setting: 8 different gyms, workplaces, nightclubs, homes and cafes.	IPEDs obtained via: – Through contacts in the gym (e.g. gym members); and/or – Through friends.	– Helping out training buddy/friends; – Supply to off-set costs of own use; – Social reciprocity (e.g. acceptance and reverence from peers within the community) – Produce/supply to make profit.	Helpers and dealers

		– Semi-structured interviews with select group of people encountered during the fieldwork (N=42) including users, dealers and other relevant stakeholders (e.g. Police Service managers of security companies and health workers). Ten of the interviewed subjects were tracked >3 years and interviewed on a regular basis. Data was given a validity rating regarding its reliability and managed by NUD. IST. Data was then divided into categories and analysed (as per symbolic interaction grounding) for evidence of social capital.			
8. Oldersma et al., 2002. This study aims to provide insight into the extent and nature of illegal trafficking of IPEDs in the Netherlands.	The Netherlands, 2001–2002	– Interviews (N=61) with key informants and specialists of various agencies such as users, dealers, law enforcement personnel and lawyers. Thematic analysis.	IPEDs obtained via: – Organised crime groups; – People selling via IPED-selling websites (non-pharmacy) – Through contacts in the gym (e.g. gym members); and/or – Through professional sport contacts.	N/A	Helpers, distributors, dealers and online suppliers

(continued)

TABLE 17.2 Cont.

Author(s)/year and summary	*Country and year(s) of study*	*Design, participants, setting and analysis*	*Production/supply source*	*Motives*	*Supplier type(s)*
9. Koert and van Kleij, 1998. This report examines the supply of IPEDs in the Netherlands.	Netherlands, unknown	– Analysis of trafficking cases in the Netherlands (sample size unknown but <10) and of (inter)national bodybuilding magazines and books (sample size unknown). – Interviews with people from the fitness/bodybuilding scene including users, dealers and other key people (e.g. sport physicians and fitness trainers) (N=62), with law enforcement personnel (e.g. the police) (N=11) and other key people such as GPs, chemists and researchers (N=14). Thematic analysis. – Analysis of IPED-selling websites (sample size unknown). Content analysis.	IPEDs obtained via: – Organised crime groups; and/or – People selling via overseas pharmacies; and/or – Healthcare professionals (e.g. doctors and pharmacists). – Through contacts in the gym (e.g. gym members and managers) and supplement companies. – Producing own steroids (i.e. 'Home-brewing').	– Produce/supply to make profit; – Helping out training buddy/friends; and/or – Supply to off-set costs of own use.	Distributors, helpers, dealers and importers
10. van de Ven et al., 2018. This paper explores the empirical reality of the influence of organised crime groups on the production and supply of IPEDs in Australia.	Australia, 2010–2016	– An analysis of Australian IPED production and supply cases and media reports (N=144) obtained through Factiva database and public online court records (e.g. via media reports). Content analysis.	IPEDs obtained via: – Through contacts in the gym (e.g. gym members); – Organised crime groups. – Through friends; – Through professional sport contacts;	N/A	Distributors, helpers, dealers, importers and online suppliers

			– Through the security sector; and/or – Healthcare professionals (e.g. doctors and pharmacists). – Producing own steroids (i.e. 'Home-brewing').		
11. van de Ven and Koenraad, 2017. This article explores the relationship between online suppliers of IPEDs and their customers.	Netherlands and Belgium. Study (1) 2012–2014; Study (2) 2014–2015	Empirical data from two research projects. The first project relies on (Netherlands/ Belgium): – Analysis of IPED-related cases (N=64). Obtained through the police, the health care inspectorate, the public Prosecution Service and the Fiscal Information and Investigation Service in the Netherlands (N=33) and from the Hormonencel in Belgium (N=31). Purposive sampling to select online specific cases (N=17). Content analysis. – Semi-structured interviews with Belgian/Dutch authorities (N=32) and (online) dealers (N=15). Thematic analysis.	IPEDs obtained via: – People selling via overseas (online) pharmacies; – Healthcare professionals (e.g. doctors and pharmacists); – People selling via IPED-selling websites (non-pharmacy); – Through contacts in the gym (e.g. gym members); and/or – Through friends.	– Produce steroids to be able to control quality; – Produce/supply to make profit.	Distributors, dealers and online suppliers

(continued)

TABLE 17.2 Cont.

Author(s)/year and summary	*Country and year(s) of study*	*Design, participants, setting and analysis*	*Production/supply source*	*Motives*	*Supplier type(s)*
		– Analysis of steroid-selling websites (N=10). Content analysis. The second project relies on (Netherlands) (Jan 2014–Aug 2015): – Semi-structured interviews with officials (N=39), suppliers (N=32) and consumers (N=10). Thematic analysis. Analysis method: – Analysis of court case files regarding the illicit supply of lifestyle drugs (N=69) that could be found at three archives: the Dutch Health Care Inspectorate (N=49), the Public Prosecution Service (N=14) and the Fiscal Information and Investigation Service (N=6). Content analysis. – Analysis of discussion platforms and websites (N=17) that were used to sell and trade illicit weight loss drugs and sexual enhancers. Content analysis.			

12. Van de Ven and Mulrooney, 2017. This article seeks to account the individual reasons for the sale and distribution of IPEDs within bodybuilding subcultures.	Netherlands and Belgium, 2010–2011 and 2012–2014	– Analysis of IPED-related cases (N=64). Obtained through the Police, the Health Care Inspectorate, the Public Prosecution Service and the Fiscal Information and Investigation Service in the Netherlands (N=33) and from the Hormonencel in Belgium (N=31). Content analysis. – Ethnographic field research. Setting: Supplement shops, gyms, bodybuilding competitions and a posing workshop. – Interviews with law enforcement personnel and other stakeholders (e.g. physicians and anti-doping officials) (N=32) and (online) IPED dealers (N=15). Thematic analysis. – Analysis of IPED-selling websites (N=10). Content analysis.	IPEDs obtained via: – People selling via IPED-selling websites (non-pharmacy); – Producing own steroids (i.e. 'Home-brewing'). – 'Generalist dealers' (e.g. hairdressers, bus drivers). – Through contacts in the gym (e.g. gym members); and/or – Through friends.	– Social reciprocity (e.g. acceptance and reverence from peers within the community) – Produce/supply to make profit; – Devotion to sport; – Helping out training buddy/friends; – Supply to off-set costs of own use; and/or – Produce steroids to be able to control quality.	Distributors, helpers, dealers, importers and/or online suppliers

(continued)

TABLE 17.2 Cont.

Author(s)/year and summary	*Country and year(s) of study*	*Design, participants, setting and analysis*	*Production/supply source*	*Motives*	*Supplier type(s)*
13. Salinas et al., 2019. This paper presents the findings of a qualitative study looking at the use and supply of IPEDs in a 'hardcore' bodybuilding gym in Northern England.	UK, 2019	– Overt systematic observation ethnography consisting of: recording conversations and observations via field notes and digital photography. (N=64 hours). Setting: Bodybuilding gym in England. Thematic analysis. – In-depth semi-structured interviews (N=20) with gym owner and managers (both of whom were IPED users and 'commercial' suppliers), a female personal trainer/IPED user, and with 17 of the gym members who were recruited and interviewed directly on site (16 of whom were IPED users). Thematic analysis.	IPEDs obtained via: – People selling via IPED-selling websites (non-pharmacy); – Through contacts in the gym (e.g. gym members); and/or – Through friends.	– Produce/supply to make profit – Social reciprocity (e.g. acceptance and reverence from peers within the community) – Devotion to sport; and/or – Helping out training buddy/friends.	Distributors, helpers, dealers and/or online suppliers
14. Cordaro et al., 2011. This study aims to identify a representative sample of steroid-selling websites and to evaluate their characteristics,	Italy, 2009	– Analysis of steroid-selling websites (N=30). Content analysis.	IPEDs obtained via: – People selling via IPED-selling websites (non-pharmacy); and/or – People selling via overseas online pharmacies	N/A	Online suppliers

available products and additional information available.					
15. Paoli and Donati, 2015. This study examines the production and distribution of IPEDs in Italy.	Italy, 2013	– Content analysis of major anti-doping investigations conducted by Nuclei Anti-Sofisticazione (N=80). Thematic analysis. – Media analysis from three major Italian news outlets: Ansa, Agi and Adnkronos. Thematic analysis. – Analysis of IPED-related criminal investigations (N=46). Content analysis. – Semi-structured interviews (N=35) with NAS officers, criminal prosecutors, policymakers and other experts. Thematic analysis. – Obtained data on the use of steroids amongst Italy's adults (15–64-year-old) from the Dipartimento Politiche Antidroga (Drug Control Department).	IPEDs obtained via: – Through contacts in the gym (e.g. gym members); – Healthcare professionals (e.g. doctors and pharmacists) – Through professional sport contacts; – Organised crime groups; – Through friends; – 'Generalist dealers' (e.g. hairdressers, bus drivers). – People selling via IPED-selling websites (non-pharmacy) – Through the security sector; and/or – Animal/livestock sector (e.g. veterinary physicians and breeders).	– Produce/supply to make profit – Devotion to sport career, prestige and sport success; – Group solidarity; – Supply to off-set costs of own use; and/or – Improvement to physique	Distributors, dealers, helpers, producers, online suppliers

(*continued*)

TABLE 17.2 Cont.

Author(s)/year and summary	*Country and year(s) of study*	*Design, participants, setting and analysis*	*Production/supply source*	*Motives*	*Supplier type(s)*
		– Requested and obtained statistical data on the number of police reports to the Judicial Authority and court verdicts for doping and other related offenses during 2001–2010, which the Italian Statistical Office (Istat) calculated explicitly for this study.			
16. Athey and Bouchard, 2013. This study discusses the Bay Area Laboratory Conservative (BALCO) scandal involving the production and distribution of steroids to professional athletes from late 1990s until 2003.	USA, 2013	Secondary media analyses to develop a social network analysis perspective including: – Transcripts of court proceedings including legal documents (N=3) and court cases (N=9). – Online and print media (e.g. Wada) and newspaper/ magazine articles (N=25) dated between 2003 and 2009. – Archival interview data (e.g. ABC News interview with BALCO founder) and – Grand jury testimonials. All source types were given a reliability scoring and data was triangulated and weighted in accordance with these scores in order to determine the coding	IPEDs obtained via: – Supplement companies; – People selling via IPED-selling websites (non-pharmacy); – People selling via overseas (online) pharmacies; Through contacts in the gym (e.g. gym members); – Healthcare professionals (e.g. doctors and pharmacists); and/or – Through professional sport contacts.	N/A	Producers, online suppliers and distributors

		of actors to be validated against the socio-matrix.			
17. Turnock, 2020. This study is an ethnographic narrative case study of a single steroid 'brewing' and supply operation in South-West England; exploring how 'drift' into IPED supply occurs in the local market, how steroid powders are accessed online, the process by which these powders are 'manufactured' into injectable steroids and the business and customer-oriented practices of local market suppliers who distribute the finished product.	England, 2015	Ethnographic narrative case study Extended (~60 min) loosely-structured interview Grounded in author's previous research which consisted of a broader ethnography of several gyms which featured interviews and fieldwork (N=1)	IPEDs obtained via: – People selling via IPED-selling websites (non-pharmacy) – Through contacts in the gym (e.g. gym members) – Through friends – Producing own steroids (i.e. 'Home-brewing').	– Supply to off-set costs of own use – Helping out training buddy/friends – Social reciprocity (e.g. acceptance and reverence from peers within the community) – Produce/supply to make profit	Producers, importers, distributors, dealers, Helpers, exporters and/or online suppliers

> suffer[s] the burden and ambiguity of contextual specificity; that is, in some contexts, the products, including their supply, are "legal" and in others they are not. In that way they are more like typical diverted pharmaceutical products, and less like traditional illicit substances, such as cocaine, heroin, and cannabis.

Indeed, most countries prohibit the production, supply and possession of traditional drugs while IPEDs are also legitimate, well-established pharmaceutical products (e.g. used to treat testosterone deficiency in men). As a result, there are many sources through which people may obtain IPEDs – from gym buddies to online IPED-selling websites (see Coomber-Moore and colleague's chapter in this volume). An overview can be found in Table 17.2.

There is the legal market where IPEDs are manufactured, distributed and sold through the regulated supply chain, for instance, via online pharmacies and general practitioners. To obtain steroids and other enhancement drugs via this route a prescription is needed; however, as many people use these substances for non-medical reasons (Mulrooney et al., 2019), they are generally illegally obtained, for example, via illicit IPED-selling websites, the dark web, friends and personal trainers. The findings illustrate that the individuals and groups involved in this illicit market can be divided into people active in the gym scene (e.g. training buddy and fitness manager), supplement industry (e.g. supplement store owners), security industry (e.g. bouncers), healthcare industry (e.g. pharmacists and general practitioners), members of the organised sport world (e.g. sport physicians and coaches), people working in the animal/livestock sector (e.g. veterinary physicians and breeders), people with no distinctive profession or occupation (e.g. hairdressers and bus drivers) and/or people who produce their own steroids (also known as 'home-brewing and 'underground steroid labs') (see Table 17.2). The gym and healthcare industry seem to make up a large chunk through which IPEDs are illegally diverted and illicitly supplied (Oldersma et al., 2002; Paoli & Donati, 2015; van de Ven et al., 2018).

In addition, online sources seem to have become a growing source to purchase and sell IPEDs (e.g. see Cordaro et al., 2011; Hall & Antonopoulos, 2015; van de Ven & Koenraadt, 2017), and are mentioned in 15 of the 17 articles. There are various sources via which online suppliers can advertise and/or offer their products – ranging from online pharmacies to 'IPED-selling websites'. Online pharmacies are pharmacies that operate over the Internet and can be both legitimate and illegitimate. Legitimate online pharmacies usually set up online sites to simplify the ordering process and compete with larger companies. However, there are a large numbers of illegitimate online pharmacies in operation which offer 'prescription only medicines' without a prescription (Hall et al., 2017). These websites attempt to mimic legitimate online pharmacies by providing, for example, scientific information on medicine and having photographs of health professionals.

There are however many illegitimate websites that do not try to portray themselves as online pharmacies and it is clear that these 'IPED-selling websites' are owned by illegal sellers and do not attempt to deceive their customers (van de Ven & Koenraadt, 2017). The online IPED sellers of these websites often produce their own steroids illegally and generally have a unique brand name (as opposed to mimicking an existing pharmaceutical brand) or sell brands from other illegal producers. This means that pharmaceutical companies have never manufactured the brands produced by these underground steroid labs and they only exist in the underground economy. There are also online sellers who make use of e-commerce markets, second-hand vending websites (e.g. Alibaba and Amazon) or the deep web, and tend to not only sell enhancement drugs, but also equipment to produce IPEDs, such as pill presses and other production materials (e.g. vials and capsules) (Hall & Antonopoulos, 2015 and Hall and Antonopoulos' chapter in this volume). Finally, there are several online sources that play an indirect role and appear to be primarily used to advertise, communicate about and find information on IPEDs such as social media (e.g. Twitter), forums (e.g. bodybuilding forums) and online communication tools (e.g. Skype).

The six articles that report on the involvement of organised crime groups illustrate that these groups seem to play a limited role in the production and supply of IPEDs. Indeed, following the literature which has explored the question of organised crime groups and IPED dealing specifically, it is suggested that they form just one small section of a broader market. There is an extremely broad supply base due to the ease at which these drugs can be obtained and there is a wide user base. The ready availability of IPEDs seems to reduce opportunities for organised crime groups to control or have significant influence in this market (e.g. see Paoli & Donati, 2015; van de Ven et al., 2018). In addition, when specifically looking at professional sports, the evidence suggests that the athlete's entourage (e.g. sport physicians and coaches) play an important role in supplying these substances to athletes (Athey & Bouchard, 2013; Fincoeur et al., 2015; Paoli & Donati, 2015).

Finally, illegal 'underground steroids labs' or 'home-brewing' are a prominent point of consideration within contemporary literature and discussions regarding IPEDs, and specifically steroids. While home-brewing is only mentioned in six of the articles assessed in this chapter, it is an imperative consideration with regard to the contemporary supply of IPEDs due to its seemingly increasing prevalence (Brennan et al., 2018; Kraska et al., 2010; Van de Ven, 2017). Despite the increased legal implications of home-brewing in many countries, both users and suppliers are turning to this technique in large part due to the general lack of priority regulating this underground market has amongst police forces and the ease with which steroids can be produced (Antonopoulos & Hall, 2016; Van de Ven, 2017). Indeed, the ease with which these raw materials can be imported from China or other Asian countries, combined with the relative simplicity of converting these cheap precursor chemicals into steroids, makes this an interesting route to obtain steroids.

Motivations to produce and/or supply IPEDs

In four articles the motives to produce and/or supply IPEDs were not discussed; these were excluded from the analysis for this section. In 12 of the 13 articles profit was mentioned as a driver for IPED suppliers. Profit levels varied between IPED suppliers; with some earning just enough to cover their own consumption or to support their bodybuilding career, while others reported that they made enough for luxury consumption and enhanced lifestyles (e.g. see Hall et al., 2017; Koert & Van Kleij, 1998; Paoli & Donati, 2015; Salinas et al., 2019; van de Ven & Koenraadt, 2017; van de Ven & Mulrooney, 2017b). Profit for some dealers was clearly an important driver for them to be involved in this illicit market, either from the very beginning or later on in their dealing career as their illegal business expanded.

Nevertheless, while profit is an important driver, this does not mean that IPED suppliers always try to scam their customers. The data shows that many of the IPED suppliers actually invest in their customers and strive to deliver IPEDs of a 'high standard' (Kraska et al., 2010; Maycock & Howat, 2007; van de Ven & Koenraadt, 2017), regardless of whether they were driven by profit or not. These (online) suppliers not only strive to create customer value but also seek to sustain a large customer base over time. This makes sense from a business perspective as having a reliable customer base generates long-term revenue. For example, in research undertaken by van de Ven and Koenraadt (2017) on online IPED suppliers, 'responsible vending' was an important theme. Online suppliers would incorporate several strategies to attract, satisfy and retain customers, such as offering information regarding steroids (e.g. post-cycle advice, how to inject) and advice on training (e.g. training schedule and type of exercises), providing product information and guidance by phone or email, and/or offering products free of charge when customers are not satisfied. Although suppliers have no assurance of the quality of the IPEDs (i.e. 'being of high standard') they sell – as the quality generally is quite poor (Coomber et al., 2014) – suppliers employ various tactics in an attempt to minimise the risks of selling poor-quality IPEDs such as sourcing from reputable suppliers, personal research and testing, and 'freebie' testing by customers. The fact that suppliers try to minimise the risk of selling poor-quality IPEDs is not unique to this illicit market. Looking at other drug markets we see that suppliers in general do not cut drugs with problematic diluents or retail in ways that cause health problems to their customers – not only for financial reasons but also because of personal ethics and values (e.g. see Coomber, 2006).

Importantly, the identification of factors additional to monetary gain is a recurrent theme throughout the assessed literature, with all 13 articles discussing non-profit-related motivations such as helping out a training buddy/friends, supplying IPEDs to off-set costs of own use and/or their pursuit of a body-building career, producing steroids to be able to 'control' for quality and/or producing steroids as it is cost-effective. The findings show that people who supply IPEDs often do not consider themselves as dealers, despite the fact that some make substantial profits, and many appear to be predominately involved to cover the costs of their own use or to provide a 'community service' (e.g. see Kraska et al., 2010; van de Ven & Mulrooney, 2017b). For example, van de Ven and Mulrooney's (2017b) research suggests that these IPED dealing groups and individuals are often driven by motivations derived from their social and cultural embeddedness in the bodybuilding subculture wherein they are 'over-socialised' into the structure and culture of bodybuilding, and follow the cultural scripts that come with their group affiliation and organisation. As a result of the cultural context in which these transactions occur, IPED dealers in these bodybuilding subcultures are often not far removed from an individual's IPED use (e.g. being part of their everyday life) and IPED dealing networks amongst bodybuilders are more likely to consist of friends or 'friends of friends', tied together by threads of collective meaning. Ultimately, the rationale for these people to be active in these illegal activities seems to come from participating in certain subcultures rather than pursuing profitable economic opportunities. Indeed, the involvement of 'social suppliers' seems to be quite common in the bodybuilding scene (Coomber et al., 2014), where the mentors, personal trainers or co-trainers of people new(er) to bodybuilding share or facilitate the purchase of steroids for little or no profit.

In relation to professionals sports, Paoli and Donati (2015) suggest in their research on IPED trafficking in Italy that the more closely connected suppliers were to professionals sports, the more non-financial reasons (e.g. sport success) played a role for being active in this market. Take, for example, sport physicians who distribute IPEDs to elite athletes. Like athletes, these suppliers often 'over-conformed' (Coakley & Pike, 2009) to the norms and values of organised sport due to their close personal involvement. These suppliers are less interested in making profit and more loyal to the sets of beliefs, norms and rules, of which the sport culture is comprised. This is not to argue that financial aspects do not play a role at all, or that the supply of drugs is irrational, but that there are other motivating factors in determining the market behaviour of these types of dealers beyond pure 'utility maximisation' (Seddon, 2005).

Limited research exists on the production of IPEDs (home-brewing), including the motivations of producers, but the primary reasons for people to produce their own steroids mentioned in the articles often relate to trying to produce steroids to control for the quality and avoiding online scams. These producers purchase raw steroid ingredients (often from Asian countries) and the subsequent production and use (followed in some instances by social supply) is considered a safer alternative both within the milieu of health and financially. As noted by Brennan, Wells and Van Hout (2018: 5), 'the social meanings attached to manufacturing AAS [steroids] in the home dictate that homebrewing is a safer method of injecting AAS than buying from an unknown source online'.

Discussion

When it comes to the question of who supplies IPEDs and what their motives are, data suggests that there are multiples types of suppliers in this market and that they are driven by multiple and often overlapping reasons. Yet, we can come to a number of more specific conclusions based upon the analysis of the data. First, there are numerous sources (e.g. online pharmacies, health professionals, contacts in the gym and organised crime groups) through which IPEDs are supplied, particularly given their legal status and the fact that regulatory enforcement varies dramatically. Second, and closely connected to this, there are a variety of types of suppliers in the IPED market, from those in the gym and security industry to healthcare professionals and organised crime groups. Yet, the gym and healthcare industry seem to play a key role through which IPEDs are diverted and illicitly supplied (Paoli & Donati, 2015; van de Ven et al., 2018). Third, for some dealers profit was an important driver, yet this varied in terms of being the primary motivation to begin dealing or as an added benefit as the illegal business expanded. Additionally, profit levels tended to differ, with some studies indicating participants were leading luxury or enhanced lifestyles on account of their dealing while others made just enough to cover their own supply or to share with friends.

Fourth, and following this line, the notion of 'social supply' or 'minimal commercialism' (Coomber et al., 2018) appears to be a strong and recurrent theme in the extant literature. For instance, while often times monetary considerations were absent as motivations to sell these drugs, socio-cultural rationales were emphasised including helping out training partners or sustaining one's own consumption, itself often connected to participation in certain subcultures such as bodybuilding. Indeed, even where profits are made, many of those who supply IPEDs did not consider themselves as 'dealers' but rather as providing a wider service to their communities. Notably, these notions of social supply did not appear to be impacted by more informal mediums of supply as, for example, van de Ven and Koenraadt (2017) note that online dealers strove to provide a quality service to consumers for a variety of reasons, market-based and otherwise, while home-brewing or underground labs may also be utilised in the name of 'quality control'. Fifth, in contrast to many legal and regulatory authorities, according to the available evidence organised criminal groups do not appear to play a primary role in the market for IPEDs. Rather, the wide user base coupled with an extremely broad supply base means that these drugs are readily available, reducing opportunities for organised crime groups to control or have significant influence in this market (ACC, 2011; Paoli & Donati, 2015; van de Ven et al., 2018).

The myriad of sources of supply and the types of suppliers and their motivations stem in large part from the policy context in which many of these studies were undertaken. Indeed, there are many legal grey areas when it comes to the production, use and supply of these substances and, even where clearly illegal,

legal enforcement is a relatively low priority (in most countries). Subsequently, legal risks are low, and opportunities are high (social, economic or otherwise) inviting a multitude of suppliers and sources. This, however, is not to suggest that a law and order approach would curb the supply of these drugs. Rather, as evidenced by other recreational drugs markets, where there is demand there is supply. Subsequently, increased risk often merely means the presence of suppliers who are willing, or have the structural and economic capacity, to take higher risks and reap greater rewards (e.g. increased drug prices, monopolisation of market, etc.). Indeed, as noted by van de Ven (2016), where legal risks became too severe, social and minimal commercialist suppliers withdrew from the market, leaving greater opportunity for those whose primary occupation is that of drug supply (e.g. organised crime groups).

Limitations

The primary limitation of this review stems from the fact that the bulk of research into the production and supply of IPEDs focuses on gym or bodybuilding subcultures. Consequently, it is perhaps not surprising that many dealers report benevolent motivations of supplying drugs to those within their subculture. Moreover, as most studies are focussed on the end of the distribution chain and on bodybuilding/fitness settings, it could be that the involvement of organised crime groups has been underestimated. The research that has sought to examine the role of 'organised crime' groups specifically supports the notion that, on the whole, they play a limited role, yet such studies are very few in number. On the other hand, we do know that organised crime groups tend to filter their specific target markets to find the most profitable sectors within these, which in this context is bodybuilding/fitness industry (Fincoeur et al., 2015; Paoli & Donati, 2015). With this in mind, it is reasonable to hypothesise that if there were evidence of a high involvement of organised crime groups, it would be found within this potentially highly profitable sub-sector, appealing to the financial motivations of said groups.

Furthermore, there are more general limitations of the review methodology employed here that must be considered. While reviews can be very useful for summarising the literature and providing guidance to policymakers, the absence of a more systematic approach to selecting and analysing the articles can lead to the inclusion of studies with poor methodological design as well as the potential for author bias. We sought to overcome these issues by clearly stipulating our selection criteria and creating a coding schedule, with the analysis and interpretation of the data being done by all three authors. Additionally, this was also remedied by the fact that the pool of literature from which we had to pull was rather small and therefore author bias was diminished given our ability to have rather broad and encompassing inclusion criteria. Yet, while we may have achieved data saturation and avoided instances of author bias in sample selection, the absence of literature on the topic at hand may limit the generalisability of the findings outlined here.

Conclusion

Authorities must remember that dealers are not 'equally destructive' (Caulkins & Reuter, 2009). Rather, as Van Hout and Bingham (2014) note, 'the adaptable nature of drug markets, online or otherwise, and displacement 'pushdown/pop up' creates opportunity [e.g. law enforcement] for reshaping such markets to make the most harmful sub-market of drug vending unattractive for vendors'. Thus, given the evidence on sources of supply and the types of those who supply them, those with a stake in addressing the issues of IPED production, supply and use must not use a one-size-fits-all approach. Rather, as this chapter has shown, policymakers and other relevant parties should consider a plurality of factors (e.g. social, economic and cultural) when designing, evaluating and implementing IPED-related supply reduction interventions such as law enforcement efforts, and not rely on over-simplistic, yet politically palatable, calls to crack down on drug dealers and organised crime.

References

ACC. (2011). Organised Crime in Australia. Retrieved from www.acic.gov.au/publications/unclassified-intelligence-reports/organised-crime-australia-2017.

Antonopoulos, G.A., & Hall, A. (2016). 'Gain with no pain': Anabolic-androgenic steroids trafficking in the UK. *European Journal of Criminology, 13*(6), 696–713. doi:10.1177/1477370816633261

Athey, N.C., & Bouchard, M. (2013). The BALCO scandal: The social structure of a steroid distribution network. *Global Crime, 14*(2–3), 216–237. doi:10.1080/17440572.2013.790312

Brennan, R., Wells, J.S.G., & Van Hout, M.C. (2018). "Raw juicing"–an online study of the home manufacture of anabolic androgenic steroids (AAS) for injection in contemporary performance and image enhancement (PIED) culture. *Performance Enhancement & Health, 6*(1), 21–27. https://doi.org/10.1016/j.peh.2017.11.001

Caulkins, J.P., & Reuter, P. (2009). Towards a harm-reduction approach to enforcement. *Safer Communities, 8*(1), 9–23.

Coakley, J.J., & Pike, E. (2009). *Sports in Society: Issues and Controversies.* London: McGraw-Hill Education.

Coomber, R. (2006). *Pusher Myths: Re-situating the Drug Dealer.* London, UK: Free Association Books.

Coomber, R., Moyle, L., Belackova, V., Decorte, T., Hakkarainen, P., Hathaway, A., Laidler, K.J., Lenton, S., Murphy, S., Scott, J., Stefunkova, M., van de Ven, K., Vlaemynck, M., & Werse, B. (2018). The burgeoning recognition and accommodation of the social supply of drugs in international criminal justice systems: An eleven-nation comparative overview. *International Journal of Drug Policy, 58*, 93–103. https://doi.org/10.1016/j.drugpo.2018.05.010

Coomber, R., Pavlidis, A., Santos, G.H., Wilde, M., Schmidt, W., & Redshaw, C. (2014). The supply of steroids and other performance and image enhancing drugs (PIEDs) in one English city: fakes, counterfeits, supplier trust, common beliefs and access. *Performance Enhancement & Health, 3.* doi:10.1016/j.peh.2015.10.004

Cordaro, F.G., Lombardo, S., & Cosentino, M. (2011). Selling androgenic anabolic steroids by the pound: Identification and analysis of popular websites on the

Internet. *Scandinavian Journal of Medicine and Science in Sports, 21*(6), e247–e259. doi:10.1111/j.1600-0838.2010.01263.x

Evans-Brown, M.J., McVeigh, J., Perkins, C., & Bellis, M.A. (2012). *Human Enhancement Drugs. The Emerging Challenges to Public Health.* Liverpool: Liverpool John Moores University.

Fincoeur, B., Ven, K., & Mulrooney, K.J. (2015). The symbiotic evolution of anti-doping and supply chains of doping substances: How criminal networks may benefit from anti-doping policy. *Trends in Organized Crime, 18.* doi:10.1007/s12117-014-9235-7

Hall, A., & Antonopoulos, G.A. (2015). License to pill: Illegal entrepreneurs' tactics in the online trade of medicines. In van Duyne, P.C., Maljevic, A., Antonopoulos, G.A., Harvey, J., and von Lampe, K. (Eds.), *The Relativity of Wrongdoing: Corruption, Organised Crime, Fraud and Money Laundering in Perspective.* Nijmegen: Wolf Legal Publishers.

Hall, A., Koenraadt, R., & Antonopoulos, G.A. (2017). Illicit pharmaceutical networks in Europe: Organising the illicit medicine market in the United Kingdom and the Netherlands. *Trends in Organized Crime, 20*(3), 296–315. doi:10.1007/s12117-017-9304-9

Hoberman, J. (2011). 'Athletes in handcuffs?': The criminalization of doping. In McNamee, M. & Møller, V. (Eds.), *Doping and Anti-Doping Policy in Sport: Ethical, Legal and Social Perspectives* (pp. 99–110). London: Routledge.

Koert, A.W.A., & Van Kleij, R. (1998). *Handel in Doping; een verkennend onderzoek naar de handel in dopinggeduide middelen in Nederland.* Nieuwegein: Arko Uitgeverij.

Kraska, P.B., Bussard, C.R., & Brent, J.J. (2010). Trafficking in bodily perfection: Examining the late modern steroid marketplace and its criminalization. *Justice Quarterly, 27.* doi:10.1080/07418820902814013

Maycock, B., & Howat, P. (2007). Social capital: Implications from an investigation of illegal anabolic steroid networks. *Health Education Research, 22.* doi:10.1093/her/cym022

Mulrooney, K., van de Ven, K., McVeigh, J., & Collins, R. (2019). Steroid madness–Has the dark-side of AAS been over-stated? In Van de Ven, K., Mulrooney, K. & McVeigh, J. (Eds.), *Human Enhancement Drugs* (pp. 1–6). UK: Routledge.

Mulrooney, K.J.D., & van de Ven, K. (2015). *Why organised crime should not be used to shape anti-doping policy.* Retrieved from UK: https://theconversation.com/why-organised-crime-should-not-be-used-to-shape-anti-doping-policy-42385

Oldersma, F., Snippe, J., & Bieleman, B. (2002). *Doping en handel; onderzoek naar de aard en omvang van dopinghandel en ontwikkeling van indicatoren.* Retrieved from https://repository.wodc.nl/handle/20.500.12832/2610

Paoli, L., & Donati, A. (2015). *The Sports Doping Market.* New York: Springer.

Salinas, M., Floodgate, W., & Ralphs, R. (2019). Polydrug use and polydrug markets amongst image and performance enhancing drug users: Implications for harm reduction interventions and drug policy. *International Journal of Drug Policy, 67*, 43–51. https://doi.org/10.1016/j.drugpo.2019.01.019

Sandberg, S. (2012). The importance of culture for cannabis markets: Towards an economic sociology of illegal drug markets. *The British Journal of Criminology, 52*(6), 1133–1151. doi:10.1093/bjc/azs031

Seddon, T. (2005). Drugs, crime and social exclusion: Social context and social theory in British drugs–crime research. *The British Journal of Criminology, 46*(4), 680–703. doi:10.1093/bjc/azi079

Soni, A., & Nasrulla, F. (2018). Be careful of these instant muscle builders. *The Tribune.* Retrieved from www.tribuneindia.com/news/trends/be-careful-of-these-instant-muscle-builders/631509.html

Turnock, L. A. (2020). Inside a steroid 'brewing' and supply operation in South-West England: An 'ethnographic narrative case study. *Performance Enhancement & Health, 7*(3–4), 100152, ISSN 2211-2669.

van de Ven, K. (2016). 'Blurred lines': Anti-doping, national policies, and the performance and image enhancing drug (PIED) market in Belgium and the Netherlands. *Performance Enhancement & Health, 4*(3), 94–102. https://doi.org/10.1016/j.peh.2016.03.003

Van de Ven, K. (2017). Illicit performance and image enhancing drug markets. In Siegel, D. & Nelen, H. (Eds.), *Contemporary Organized Crime: Developments, Challenges and Responses* (pp. 25–45). New York: Springer.

van de Ven, K., Dunn, M., & Mulrooney, K. (2018). Performance and image enhancing drug (PIED) producers and suppliers: A retrospective content analysis of PIED-provider cases in Australia from 2010–2016. *Trends in Organized Crime*, 1–11. https://doi.org/10.1007/s12117-018-9348-5

van de Ven, K., & Koenraadt, R. (2017). Exploring the relationship between online buyers and sellers of image and performance enhancing drugs (IPEDs): Quality issues, trust and self-regulation. *International Journal of Drug Policy, 50*, 48–55. doi:10.1016/j.drugpo.2017.09.004

van de Ven, K., & Mulrooney, K.J.D. (2014). Anti-doping 'on steroids': Bigger, stronger, and faster. Retrieved from http://ph.au.dk/en/research/research-areas/humanistic-sport-research/research-unit-for-sports-and-physical-culture/international-network-of-doping-research/newsletters/december-2014/inhdr-commentary-van-de-ven-mulrooney/

Van de Ven, K., & Mulrooney, K.J.D. (2017a). *Drug Testing High School Athletes and Fitness.* US: ABC-CLIO.

van de Ven, K., & Mulrooney, K.J.D. (2017b). Social suppliers: Exploring the cultural contours of the performance and image enhancing drug (PIED) market among bodybuilders in the Netherlands and Belgium. *International Journal of Drug Policy, 40*, 6–15. doi:10.1016/j.drugpo.2016.07.009

Van Hout, M.C., & Bingham, T. (2014). Responsible vendors, intelligent consumers: Silk road, the online revolution in drug trading. *International Journal of Drug Policy, 25*(2), 183–189.

18

ILLICIT PHARMACEUTICAL SUPPLY

Moving beyond common assumptions about drugs and drug dealing

Alexandra Hall and Georgios A. Antonopoulos

Introduction

A good deal of literature in criminology on drugs and drug dealing focuses on the most established and widely prohibited recreational drug markets in cocaine, heroin, cannabis and synthetics. In recent years there has been a move to better understand 'new drugs', particularly since the introduction and prohibition of novel psychoactive substances. Less time, however, has been spent researching the actors and structures involved in the illicit pharmaceutical supply chain. Yet arguably the trade is the largest global market for criminal entrepreneurs (Finlay, 2011; IRACM, 2013). Our research in recent years has attempted to fill a hole in that gap, by offering the first in-depth and empirically grounded criminological analysis of the illicit pharmaceutical trade (Hall and Antonopoulos, 2015; Hall and Antonopoulos, 2016; Antonopoulos and Hall, 2016; Hall et al., 2017; Hall and Antonopoulos, 2019; Hall, 2019; Kotze and Antonopoulos, 2019).

We have been researching the market in pharmaceuticals since 2012, conducting extensive fieldwork in online and offline contexts to collect rich empirical data on the supply and demand dimensions of the illicit trade. In 2016 we published *Fake Meds Online* (Hall and Antonopoulos, 2016), which exposed a booming global market in illicit medicines that is increasingly, but not solely, facilitated by the Internet. The trade in illicit medicines offers a prescient example of late-modern shifts in the way drugs are bought and sold, challenging many of the common assumptions currently held about drugs and drug dealing—about the 'usual suspects' involved in drug supply, their preferred business models, the types of products for sale and the embeddedness of the shadow economy and practices in legal processes and systems. We have written elsewhere about the role of technology in the trade (Hall and Antonopoulos, 2015; 2016), the complexities of consumer demand (Hall and Antonopoulos, 2016; Hall, 2019; Kotze

DOI: 10.4324/9781351010245-21

and Antonopoulos, 2019), and we are currently developing further work on the rise of what we term the *digital drug prosumer.* However, in this chapter we will shift the focus to offer a synopsis of our findings as they relate to the themes of the present collection—drug markets and drug dealing—with an emphasis on the global political economy of supply.

The chapter begins with a short historical overview of the illicit medicine trade. We then discuss some of the key political and economic processes, structures and spaces through which a huge growth in illicit medicine supply has been facilitated in recent decades. This will include a discussion of trade routes, parallel trading practices and the use of special economic zones. A discussion of the physical flows of illicit medicines follows, which explores crucial zones of production, transit and distribution. Finally, building on this, the trade's social organisation is briefly reviewed in order to outline some of the actors (both licit and illicit) involved in each stage of the global supply chain. Throughout the study we draw on primary and secondary data collected from an integrated research methodology that comprised of online and offline ethnographies—which included interviews and observations with active suppliers and consumers of illicit medicines, private stakeholders and enforcement officers—analysis of the UK health regulatory agency's investigative case files, analysis of data from the in-house counterfeiting team of a global pharmaceutical company, and various secondary media and academic sources (see Hall and Antonopoulos, 2016).

Pharmaceutical falsification: a brief outline

A vast range of products that encompass diverse 'shades' of legality constitute the global illicit market in pharmaceuticals, which can leave the market prone to definitional confusion among non-experts. Overall, the market is made up of a range of counterfeit, falsified, unlicensed and substandard medicines and medical devices. The term 'counterfeit' medicines relates to products that infringe intellectual property rights; 'falsified' medicines encompass all pharmaceuticals falsely claiming to be an authentic product; 'substandard' medicines are genuine products that do not meet national regulatory standards; and 'unlicensed' pharmaceuticals can be generic or branded products legally produced abroad yet sold in a country with different licensing agreements in order to by-pass existing intellectual property laws and patents (see Hall and Antonopoulos, 2016). Grey and black markets in almost all classes of medicine can be identified, from 'lifesaving' medicines used to treat cancer and HIV through to 'lifestyle' medicines used to enhance performance and image. We use the term *illicit medicines* to incorporate all the above, including adulterated and counterfeit medicines as well as medicines that were legally produced but sold without a license.

Pharmaceutical falsification has a long history. According to Bate (2008), as intensive research and development products, counterfeit medicines have threatened our healthcare since the nineteenth century, when technology advanced and entrepreneurs involved in counterfeiting realised the opportunity for high profit with low risk of detection and prosecution. By the late nineteenth century there were deep concerns in Britain about the adulteration of medicines which led to the passing of the Food, Drink and Drugs Acts of 1872 and 1875 and the Poisons and Pharmacy Act of 1908. One well-known historical example of pharmaceutical tampering occurred in 1982 when Johnson & Johnson found out that bottles of its extra-strength Tylenol capsules were laced with cyanide (JDSU, 2010). Since the late twentieth century, however, the international trade in both legitimate and illegitimate economies has expanded at an unprecedented rate, the result of which is that a vast amount of illicit goods—including pharmaceuticals—now permeate the global market. This has been particularly apparent since the late 1970s, when specific political and economic events precipitated an ideological shift towards a neoliberal paradigm of competitiveness and openness in the global market economy (see Harvey, 2005). Wholesale deregulation and the opening up of national economies to processes of globalisation and marketisation freed up the movement of capital and accelerated the financialisation of the global economy. These processes had concrete effects on criminality and a facilitating impact on the supply and demand of illicit goods; just as legitimate private industries profited from these changes, so too did the illegitimate industries that ran alongside them.

These macroeconomic processes had a formative effect on the growth of the illicit medicine market. According to official figures from the World Health Organization, by 2010 global counterfeit drug sales alone reached $75 billion. A 'conservative estimate' is that ten per cent of total pharmaceutical drug sales are counterfeit (Wertheimer and Wang, 2012: 5; see also WHO, 2012). Further statistics estimate that across the world up to one million people die each year after consuming counterfeit medicinal drugs (Southwick, 2013), most of whom reside in the Global South. In Europe, a 2012 study with 5,000 European citizens across five nation states found five per cent of consumers suspected that they had received a counterfeit prescription drug while one per cent were sure they had. This suggests that up to 12.8 million consumers were exposed to counterfeit medicines in those countries (Jackson et al., 2012). Bearing in mind the broader focus here on illicit medicines, not counterfeits alone, and of the inherent dark nature of this illicit market, we can suspect that a much larger market is in operation, the true size and scope of which is currently opaque to statistical representations. However, it is also important to question the extent of the risks posed by illicit medicines, and the vested interests some have in protecting the market in patented drugs (Braithwaite, 1984). Overall, statistics and official accounts are problematic and demand further methodological rigour within a qualitative framework to expose the nature and complex dynamics of this far-reaching trade—one in which patterns of crime and harm are evident in each stage of the global supply chain (Hall, 2019).

Throughout our research we found that a number of specific late-capitalist international trade relations and practices, accompanied by the liberalisation of markets globally, had been principal determining factors that helped expand the illicit medicine trade. Indeed, some of the most significant findings from our research related to the global supply chain, where a political economy perspective helped us expose the use of historically established trade routes, legal trade policies, the extraterritorial spaces of special economic zones and a range of associated production and distribution hubs.

Historically established trade routes

The emergence of globalisation and the market economy in Central and Eastern Europe after the collapse of the Soviet Union increased the number of illicit economies. Business people in the region began investing in illegal activities and the Balkans became a busy transit zone for illicit goods and services shipped from manufacturers situated in South and East Asia and the Middle East—usually headed to 'richer' consumer economies in Western Europe and the USA (see Portes et al., 1991). We found evidence of this in cases relating to illicit medicines. Our evidence also suggests that Russia has become one of the largest producers of illicit medicines and West Africa a central geographic area for the distribution of illicit goods, a position achieved by developing illicit drug routes through Latin America and taking advantage of the increased availability of illicit medicines produced in China.

As Ellis (2009) argues, the neoliberal structural adjustment period in the 1980s, along with widespread corruption among heads of state implicated in the trafficking of drugs, destabilised legitimate economies in some West African states. Various smuggling routes that had emerged in the trade of cocaine and heroin in the 1950s facilitated intensified activity. Working from bases in countries such as Liberia, with its ideal transport facilities by sea and air and use of the dollar, West African traffickers became integral to the global transit and trafficking of illicit goods, establishing themselves as a vital node in the arterial distribution process. West African diasporic communities also situated themselves in useful locations around the globe, clearly positioned to continue business relations with drug producers. For example, traffickers operating in the large Nigerian community in Mumbai took advantage of India's position as a global leader in pharmaceutical production, and similar operations were set up in various parts of South Africa. Another crucial causal factor has been the nature and dynamics of Nigerian and other West African 'organised crime' syndicates. The social composition of their business model is notably flexible, or what is now often labelled an 'adhocracy', far more suited to the modern-day business environment than the traditional hierarchical structure (see Ellis 2009: 185). For these reasons we can identify an important West African connection in both the illicit pharmaceutical and narcotics trades. The illicit medicine trade offers a profitable low-risk opportunity (see IRACM, 2013), which is why many formerly involved in relatively high-risk narco-trafficking have recently moved into the trade (see also Bate, 2008). The African connection in the illicit pharmaceutical trade is confirmed by data we collected from law enforcement agencies, the in-house anti-counterfeiting team of a large pharmaceutical company, and in discussions with African pharmaceutical company workers based in the UK, who specifically identified a South African connection in relation to production processes (see also Angop, 2013).

The developing connection between Africa and China is also an important factor. As Ellis notes, 'with the recent emergence of China as a major diplomatic and business operator in Africa', alongside the history of Chinese criminals situated on the continent, collaborative developments in 'new illicit markets in China' have emerged (Ellis, 2009: 196). One of the primary examples is the illicit pharmaceutical trade. The Chinese–Angolan connection is a particularly interesting point to consider. Data on seizures that we collected from a pharmaceutical company suggest that a direct trade route in illicit medicines from China through Angola to Europe and beyond is now in full operation. This new illicit trade route is the product of a relationship originally forged via legitimate political and economic arrangements that began to take shape when resource-rich Angola, struggling to pay debts built up during the war for independence, was offered an oil-backed loan by China at a better rate than the International Monetary Fund (Ford, 2013). Now trade relations between the nations have intensified and a Chinese diaspora in various Southern, Eastern and West African countries is well positioned to nurture business relations in both legal and illegal markets. As Haugen notes,

> [t]he pace of growth in the commercial relations between China and African countries in the past decade has been remarkably high. Trade between China and Africa grew by an average of 28 per cent per annum between 1999 and 2009 in terms of monetary value adjusted for inflation.
>
> *Haugen, 2011: 160*

Latin America's relationship with West Africa, forged in the trade of cocaine to Europe, has also been effective in presenting opportunities for the illicit medicine trade. One example is that of Guinea-Bissau's involvement in the illicit cocaine trade from Latin America to Europe (see UNODC, 2007). Latin America is second only to Asia as a region where a large number of 'incidents' of counterfeit medicines have been reported (IRACM, 2013: 17). Our data from a pharmaceutical company verify that claim. One notable example is a set of trade routes to Africa that have developed out of Colombia, where manufacturers producing large quantities of illicit medicines and packaging have exploited the routes already established via the traditional cocaine trade to distribute their products.

The use of special economic zones

Another crucial politico-economic process facilitating the illicit medicine trade is the establishment of the so-called special economic zones (SEZs), which include free ports, free trade zones and export processing zones. From the manufacturing of huge swathes of commodities in an export development zone, such as that situated in Chittagong in Bangladesh, to the transiting of products through free ports and free zones located in China, Nigeria, the United Arab Emirates (UAE) and Indonesia, these designated geographical zones are regularly used to transit illicit medicines. As deregulated conduits, free zones offer the unrestricted movement of commodities in spaces with the least resistance in terms of tax, policing, and health and safety. As designated extraterritorial areas with reduced or removed tariffs and duties and relatively lax customs controls, they are ideal locations for counterfeit products to be placed in transit before being distributed around the globe. With the arrival of the final stage of globalisation in the late twentieth century, containerisation became a popular means of transiting goods but also a particularly popular way of concealing and smuggling illicit products. This highlights the essential and ubiquitous links between legal and illegal in global capitalism as a system of accumulation (see Nordstrom, 2007; Hudson, 2015).

SEZs are the perfect illustration of the logic of late capitalism, inasmuch as they are designed to offer loosened economic laws, sitting 'outside' the standard regulatory structure and therefore exempt from the nation state's laws that govern their physical geographical location. For example, they guarantee business-friendly economic environmental factors such as the free flow of capital, lower taxes on imports and exports, and working conditions with no minimum wage or working hours, all of which support profit maximisation, attract inward foreign investment and guarantee less risk in terms of policing. The rise of the newly developing industrial economies as the production hubs of the world (EFPIA, 2012), historically established criminal distribution channels and networks, and the formation of global SEZs combine to play an important role in the supply of illicit medicines and can be analysed as part of a general process of global capitalist zoning (Neveling, 2015).

Parallel trade

The politically enforced economic application of deregulation, free international trade agreements and the opening up of markets has facilitated and encouraged the global trade in illicit medicines. In the European Union (EU) internal market, with its lack of restrictions, this process is supported by the flow of products created by the legal practice of parallel trade. There is no space to fully explore the history of parallel trade, which, as part of the move to an EU single market, includes issues of intellectual property (IP), competition and regulatory law. Nor is there space here to consider the possible impact of Brexit. However, it is important to include a brief examination in our analysis of illicit medicine supply.

In short, parallel trade is based on the free movement of trade in the EU internal market and is permitted under Articles 28 and 81 of the European

Commission Treaty for the Free Movement of Goods and Service within the Internal Market of the EU countries. Parallel trade can be said to be in operation when a product is purchased by a trader in a country where the price is cheaper and re-exported, without the authorisation of the owner of intellectual property rights, to another country where the product secures a higher price (see Maskus, 2002). The trade is 'legal by virtue of the rule of regional exhaustion of trademark rights applied in the EU and the EEA' (EAEPC, 2013). However, while free trade occurs with the voluntary participation of all parties, parallel trade 'opposes the interests and wishes of the affected manufacturers' (Graham cited in Wagner, no date: 5).

The UK is one of the largest and most lucrative EU markets 'targeted' by parallel pharmaceutical traders, who *legitimately* exploit price differentials between states to profit from countries where higher prices result in higher profit margins. Drawing on data from the British Association of European Pharmaceutical Distributors, the professional body that represents British parallel traders, Morgan (2008) estimates that the parallel pharmaceutical trade in the UK 'is worth 13 per cent of total UK drug sales of £9–10 billion', although the estimate across the EU is much smaller—between two and three per cent. The European Association of Euro-Pharmaceutical Companies (EAEPC), which represents European parallel traders, states that the parallel pharmaceutical trade in Europe is an 'integral part of the European pharmaceutical market that adds value to society by introducing price competition and a supplementary layer of product safety'. This statement seems to contradict the slogan on their website from a pharmaceutical executive, 'the paramount aim is to go for the best price in every country' (EAEPC, 2013). Profit maximisation is legitimated because it is seen as crucial to the functioning of free trade practices in the internal market. Yet in practice parallel traders are pitted against wholesalers and large pharmaceutical companies. As Satchwell notes, '[i]n the UK, hospitals and Primary Care Trusts are encouraged by the government, as the monopoly tax-funded payer for services, to buy drugs from the cheapest possible source' and turn to parallel traders in order to do so (2004: 11). The EU commission states that in theory this should reduce prices for the consumer and promote healthy competition. However, the EU's permission given to parallel trade in pharmaceuticals has had an enabling impact on the trade in illicit medicines in a number of ways.

Parallel trade incentivises the illegal trade in medicines because the principle of free movement on which the trade is based lifts barriers and opens up competition in prices between states. In effect it also incentivises the counterfeiting of medicines and makes detection more difficult. The process of importing, re-importing, repackaging and reselling provides many opportunities for illicit medicines to enter the legitimate supply chain, offering higher profit margins because the original product will have been bought at a cheaper price. The repackaging process also means 'pristine packaging is available to be used for counterfeit products, although the redundant packaging is *supposed* to be destroyed' (Satchwell, 2004: 12, emphasis added). Moreover, trademark owners are prohibited from preventing repackaging of their products if it is deemed to have no adverse effect on the original manufactured goods (see Laing 2005). Therefore, by default the regulatory system condones the passing of medicines through numerous countries and sellers before they reach the final distributor who supplies direct to the consumer. Occasionally legitimate drugs can be replaced with falsified or substandard medicines, or products that have been through a process of 'salting'—whereby legitimate products are bulked out with counterfeit products—while *en route* to another market. Overall, the principle we can draw from this is that the longer the drug distribution channels the more vulnerable the legitimate supply chain becomes, and the more opportunities are presented for the supply of illicit medicines.

Actors involved in the illicit medicine trade have recognised the opportunities presented by parallel trade in the EU and practice illegal parallel trade. Morgan (2008) reported that the Medicines and Healthcare products Regulatory Agency (MHRA) had recalled nine cases of illicit medicines in the UK over a three-year period and 'a further five cases caught at wholesaler level before they reached the market' (Morgan, 2008, np.). One infamous case in the summer of 2007 involved a number of items entering the supply chain as a direct result of parallel trading, including products used to treat psychosis, blood clots and cancer: 'Some 40,000 packs of tablets were seized by the MHRA and up to a further 10,000 were recalled' (ibid.). Peter Gillespie—whose defence was that he believed he was involved in a legal parallel trade from France—was convicted as the ringleader of a network involved in one of the most serious breaches of the laws that govern the UK pharmaceutical supply chain. In 2011 he was sentenced to eight years in prison and was fined £5.6 million (Gregory, 2013). The illicit medicines he sold were packaged in French but had been produced in China and shipped to Singapore. They were then 'bought by a wholesaler in Luxembourg who sold them on to a Belgian wholesaler and another based in Liverpool, who in turn sold them to UK parallel importers' (Morgan, 2008). This is one of the *known* cases of illegal parallel trade, highlighting the problems associated with a long and complex distribution chain with little regulation opening up the EU to counterfeiters. This type of business practice, operating largely outside of the new EU legislation on falsified medicines, must be regulated with more vigour if it is to continue without posing serious risks to the health of European citizens.

Our evidence suggests that parallel trade can offer opportunities for criminals involved in illicit medicine distribution, as well as increasing prices by enforcing competition between states in legitimate import–export transactions. These anomalies emphasise the downside and the limits to the free movement of trade, where the so-called competition leaves patients open to consuming fakes, and patients in some countries where specific pharmaceutical products sell at a lower price are unable to access the products they require as parallel trade creates shortages in supply. For instance, it has been reported that patients in Greece find it more difficult to acquire certain medicines used to treat epilepsy and bipolar disorder because once these products reach the country they are usually re-exported to the UK or Germany for a higher end-price (see Morgan, 2008; see also Cassidy, 2012). This also presents opportunities for counterfeiters to capture the gap in the market created in Greece, by supplying illicit products in place of the products that are unobtainable through legitimate avenues. In these situations, the boundaries between legitimate and illegitimate pharmaceutical supply become indistinct.

Moreover, the online market has also been expedited by parallel trade, wherein the complexities and weaknesses in the drug distribution chain are exploited by illegal parallel traders largely involved in selling products over the Internet. Our research indicates that the Internet plays a pivotal role in this illegal trade in the UK and free market principles such as parallel trade increase the commercial opportunities and lower the legal risks associated with it (Hall and Antonopoulos, 2016). Therefore, to suggest simply that the trade in illicit medicines exists outside of legitimate political and economic structures and the pharmaceutical industry is misleading. The trade cannot be regarded as 'outside' of the processes of the legitimate political economy, because within the neo-liberal variant of the legitimate political economy enabling structures have been introduced that allow, and in some ways tacitly encourage, the illegitimate trade in pharmaceuticals to flourish. Both parallel trade within the EU internal market and the shipment of illicit goods entering the UK via historically established trade routes and distribution circuits including SEZs—from Asia and Latin America, through central Europe, the UAE or West Africa—are crucial features of the overall trade in illicit medicines.

The channels and networks of production and distribution

A variety of channels and networks—both virtual and physical—through which the illicit medicine trade is put into practice have recently established themselves. In terms of the physical flows, it is generally understood that the trade in illicit medicines follows a common pattern from production and distribution through to consumption. The trade is widely dispersed in geographical space, and the products are manufactured and packaged, often in stages, before being transited and distributed through a variety of trade routes in a complex supply chain, frequently taking advantage of the SEZs situated around the globe. Production centres are to be found mainly in South Asia (India, Pakistan and Bangladesh), China, Russia and Latin America, and distribution tends to be at its most active state in large networks in parts of the Middle East, Africa and Central Europe. Drawing on data from the OECD, Pryswa points out that '75% of counterfeit medicines in the world come from China and India and half of these products transit through Dubai to conceal their origin' (IRACM, 2013: 18). From the regulatory holes in Chinese manufacturing to the movement of goods through free trade zones in the UAE, we have found a variety of geographical zones involved in the trade. Therefore, we propose a zonal model to help determine and understand the operation of the routes through which the physical flows of illicit medicines take place.

Zones of production

There has been a general shift in the pharmaceutical market, which is re-contextualising and affecting both the legitimate and illegitimate industries. The burgeoning trade in generics is the key priority for large pharmaceutical companies to tackle, while counterfeits in comparison pose a lower risk to their dominant market share (KPMG 2012). Similarly, suggesting a tangible crossover between legitimate and illegitimate markets, the most significant production hubs involved in the trade of illicit medicines are located in India, Pakistan, China and Hong Kong, where numerous chemical and equipment companies are manufacturing the active pharmaceutical ingredients (APIs) and devices needed to produce illicit medicines. It has been suggested that India is the largest supplier of counterfeit drugs (see Wertheimer and Wang, 2012: 6). India is also the world's largest producer of generic drugs, closely followed by China and an increasing contribution from Russia and some Latin American states. We found evidence to suggest that other major players involved in this stage of the process are Russia, Nigeria and the Philippines. Nevertheless, clandestine factories have also been found in Ukraine, Indonesia, Thailand, Colombia, Bolivia, Paraguay, Turkey and Iraq.

The rise of newly economically advanced countries, sometimes referred to as BRIC (Brazil, Russia, India and China) countries, offers distinct economic advantages in terms of the production of medicines. In China and India manufacturing costs are as much as 40 per cent cheaper than competitors in other states because of the relative affordability of labour and resource price differentials. These countries are major commercial platforms where counterfeit products have been historically produced. The large existing legitimate pharmaceutical industries producing generic and branded products in these countries also offer opportunities for counterfeit operations, which are sometimes illicit operations running alongside legitimate production and distribution processes.

There are various organisational scales of production (see Yar, 2008). They range from small-scale operations running from an individual's home, through medium-scale operations including legitimate factories functioning counterfeit operations at night, to large-scale industrial illicit operations or clandestine factories. There are also various and distinct stages in production: the chemical production of APIs, pill pressing, packaging, repackaging and so on. These may be based in one place or in a variety of places. Usually, raw materials/APIs are produced in China and India, but sometimes these materials are then 'smuggled' through porous borders into countries in Africa, Latin America and Eastern Europe for secondary production, which includes pressing pills and packaging. Packaging is of utmost importance, especially for products targeting developed countries such as the UK. Processes of packaging and repackaging are located in various geographic locations, sometimes free trade zones that lie *en route* as the products are in transit.

Zones of transit and distribution

As Wertheimer and Wang point out, the trade in pharmaceuticals includes 'several intermediaries', which 'increases the opportunities for counterfeiters' (2012: 41). The use of shell companies and the Internet and e-commerce in the distribution process is significant (see IRACM, 2013; Yar, 2008). However, in terms of physical flows between the chemical manufacturer, the pharmaceutical producer and the importer country we can find several points of transit and distribution, which, with parallel trade in the EU internal market, also means that various avenues are opened up for trade in illicit medicines once products reach the EU. Our evidence suggests that the following regions are zones of transit and distribution significantly implicated in the illicit medicine trade (this is by no means an exhaustive list):

- The Middle East—the UAE, Jordan and Iraq.
- Central and Eastern Europe—Russia, Kazakhstan and Ukraine.
- West, East and South Africa—Nigeria, Angola, Benin and Cameroon.

We have already noted that a large number of free zones in Nigeria and the UAE have been implicated in the illicit medicine trade. In the Middle East, the UAE—and Dubai in particular—as Bogadich points out,

> offers way stations for goods moving around the globe. Since most of the shipments do not officially enter the country, there are fewer bureaucratic entanglements. In the emirates' zones, the usual requirement for local ownership of companies is waived, and there are no import and export fees or income tax.
>
> *Bogadich, 2007*

Therefore, free trade zones offer the opportunity 'to hide–or sanitize–a drug's provenance, or to make, market or re-label adulterated products' (ibid.). The products are then passed through a multitude of distribution channels before reaching their destinations. The supply chain of a batch of illicit medicines may start in China and be transited in Dubai before heading through Caribbean island states to the USA, to Europe and back again before landing in the UK. These distribution channels vary and take advantage of porous borders and container-based shipping. Counterfeiters are aware that the longer the distribution chain, the harder the products are to detect. Alongside the shipping industry, a retired customs officer we interviewed revealed that rail routes into Europe from China are regularly used to transport containers of illicit medicines, which in the context of the new rail route connecting China, Kazakhstan, Azerbaijan,

Georgia and Turkey, could significantly increase in the near future (see Port Technology, 2015).

The social organisation

The trade in illicit medicines can involve a number of online sites and services to market products and maintain financial flows, and we have explored in detail elsewhere how the Internet has changed the market in illicit medicines (Hall and Antonopoulos, 2015; 2016.). This chapter has outlined some of the facilitating politico-economic processes and structures. In many instances we have found legitimate and illegitimate companies in both online and offline contexts becoming associates—whether knowingly or not—in the illicit medicine trade. From here, having shifted the focus onto the global supply chain, we can outline some of the actors involved and their organisation. This highlights the breadth and complexity of the global pharmaceutical supply chain, which exists on a continuum connecting online and offline spheres, global and local spaces, and licit and illicit practices (Hall et al., 2017).

A number of actors and various operational structures are involved in the processes of manufacturing, formulating, distributing and selling illicit pharmaceuticals. Functional roles range from obtaining raw materials, primary manufacture of APIs, formulation of APIs (drug synthesis) including pressing and coating, and packaging and repackaging, to marketing, advertising, online selling and transportation of the final products. In order to manufacture illicit medicines actors must produce or obtain both the APIs and the packaging that is comparable to popular branded products (Wertheimer and Wang, 2012: 2). For large-scale operations this requires a skilled workforce and plants/factories with necessary equipment for the various stages of the production process, and a team of people involved in the distribution of the products both online and offline. Overall, the actors involved in the illicit medicine trade, excluding the legal pharmaceutical companies whose merchandise is produced legally but traded illegally, include the following:

1. ***Producers:*** These individuals and associated organisations are involved in producing (and selling) illicit medicines to wholesalers or criminal entrepreneurs/crime groups, or less often, in the small-scale selling of their own products over the Internet. Their skills range from amateur to professional:
   a. *Amateurs*—individuals with no formal training possibly buying wholesale online and pressing pills at home to sell to UK consumers.
   b. *Semi-professionals*—these individuals are not pharmaceutical professionals but have built up the skills to produce a fairly accurate product.
   c. *Professionals*—actual professionals who have become involved in the counterfeit business.

2. ***Chemical engineers:*** These individuals, usually working on behalf of an API service, are involved in chemical processing and produce and supply the controlled substances. They produce the APIs, but also the substances used as filters or binders to bulk out the medicines. Enteric coating also needs to be produced (some reports show it tends to be the indigestibility of the coating, not the adulterated APIs, which causes more harm to the consumer). Thousands of chemical compounds are used in pharmaceutical production in a variety of forms of drug synthesis. These manufacturing personnel can range from skilled chemists with experience in the industry to those with no skills and experience following recipes/directions, and these services may be clandestine or legitimate. Sometimes the raw materials are shipped to other countries for pressing/production, then to another for packaging/repackaging.
3. ***Equipment producers and installers:*** Any operation needs specific equipment designed to make the required pharmaceuticals, from basic laboratory equipment to powder blenders and testers, tablet presses and capsule printers. This requires the equipment to be produced and installed by those with the technical knowledge and skills. The equipment and installation in clandestine operations may be carried out by legitimate companies who may know or not know of the illegitimacy of the operation.
4. ***Non-specialised workers:*** As in most production and distribution businesses, a range of workers are needed for menial tasks at all levels of the operation(s). These might include lifting and moving stock, packing shelves and so on.
5. ***Packaging producers:*** Including those involved in printing trademarks and barcodes.
6. ***Workers in health-related establishments:*** Those who are responsible for obtaining merchandise or other materials (e.g. cleaners collecting empty bottles), who may become implicated in supplying packaging materials to counterfeiters.
7. ***Transportation intermediaries:*** At different stages of the operation, from pre-packaging, post-production and final distribution channels via air, land and sea. For example, freight trucking companies and lorry drivers and pilots (see Kennedy and Wilson, 2015 for more on the role of legitimate intermediaries in the transportation of counterfeit goods).
8. ***Warehouse/storage providers:*** A variety of premises are used to store illicit medicines at their various stages of production and distribution, ranging from warehouses to shipment containers. The providers of these services are implicated in the trade.
9. ***Importers:*** The procurers and importers funding operations, who buy illicit medicines in bulk, buy numerous domain names acquired from website owners and advertise for web designers and drop shippers. Products can be imported either as bulk active ingredients or in dosage form. One well-documented case in the UK is that of Simon Martin Hickman, who ran a

multi-million-pound website selling fake pills used to treat sexual dysfunction, along with a variety of other sexual aids. The MHRA seized more than £14 million in assets from this Manchester-based criminal entrepreneur in 2012.

10. ***Organised crime groups:*** A criminal entrepreneur may be part of a larger organisation that bulk-buys medicines and domain names and use similar online pharmacy templates. There are larger organisations known to law enforcement, some with links to the Russian mafia and Chinese triads and so on (see Bate, 2008; Hall and Antonopoulos, 2015). In some cases, traditional organised crime groups are hired by legitimate wholesalers and rival pharmaceutical companies in China in order to settle competition between companies (see UNODC, 2010).
11. ***Intermediaries/brokers:*** The middlemen putting relevant people in contact with one another and developing trade and transportation routes. This category can include members of diasporic groups well situated to continue business relations and make new contacts. They may oversee the smooth operation of the business or may simply put relevant people in contact with one another. Here there can be a crossover with the role of counterfeiters and criminal entrepreneurs. Overall, this group consists of those who are able to see 'social holes' and connect others involved in supply (see IRACM 2013).
12. ***Retail sellers:*** As opposed to the importers, most of the sellers are, what Dorn et al. (1992) call, 'opportunistic irregulars', who have a small opportunity to profit from the business. They include user-sellers (Antonopoulos and Hall, 2016; see also Moyle and Coomber, 2015; Koenraadt and van de Ven, 2017).
13. ***Shell companies/covers/trading companies:*** Commercial organisations that often do not specialise in the medicine trade but act as the cover for illicit medicine supply. For instance, travel companies and fashion accessory companies have been found to be supplying illicit medicines. Some are simply diversifying, and medicinal drugs are part of a larger racket involving the selling of a variety of illicit goods.
14. ***Drop shippers:*** A UK-based individual can become involved in the trade as a drop shipper by searching affiliate websites and answering adverts, some simply asking 'do you want to earn money?'. Individuals expressing interest are then sent a template for a website attached to one of a group of domain names bought in bulk by a large criminal operation from a legitimate web-hosting company, along with shipments of illicit medicines, which they then sell in smaller quantities to online customers via their OP or a range of other online sites. The individual drop shipper then begins trading in illicit medicines supplied to their home address by the criminal organisation. They are paid per shipment they make, which heightens their desire to sell more. These drop shippers are also involved in re-routing goods in the supply chain (see also Palmer 2013 on the role of drop shippers).

15. ***Travellers/smugglers***: Carrying relatively small quantities over borders to be supplied to customers who have bought online.
16. ***Illegal parallel traders***: Those illegally involved in buying illicit medicines in one market to sell at a higher price in another.
17. ***Corrupt officials:*** This can include corrupt customs officers and border police situated at transit points globally involved in distribution. In free trade zones staff members have been known to 'turn a blind eye'.
18. ***Postal delivery services:*** It guarantees that the merchandise traded online reaches customers in the 'real' world. This is one aspect of the infrastructure that largely involves legitimate companies (the large courier firm FedEx was recently indicted in the USA on charges of conspiracy to deliver illicit pharmaceuticals; see Walker, 2014).
19. ***Postal workers:*** Such as postal delivery workers involved in the transport of wholesale quantities over borders and small-scale amounts sent through national postal routes. The MHRA arrested two postal delivery workers in 2013 involved in distributing unlicensed Indian erectile dysfunction (ED) drugs in the UK (Waldron, 2013).
20. ***Affiliates and sub-affiliate networks:*** Commercial entities that act as intermediaries to market the products of larger businesses online and are then paid for each referral their marketing succeeds in capturing.
21. ***Domain name registrars/web-hosting companies***: There are several web-hosting companies specifically implicated in the trade. It is from these companies that illegal OPs are made available via the web, and where domain names are bought and registered.
22. ***Rogue website designers:*** They design the templates to be used by criminal organisations and drop shippers as online pharmacies.
23. ***E-commerce merchant traders/Internet merchant account suppliers:*** In order to collect payments from customers a payment gateway will be required on the site used for supply, which is a link to a merchant account. These are supplied by merchant service providers which include those available from large commercial banks.
24. ***Other financial services:*** Services such as Western Union or high street banks can be used to collect payment or 'clean up' revenue.
25. ***Internet intermediaries, e-commerce sites and social networking sites***: Google, Facebook, Ebay, Twitter and Instagram are used as sites for supply and have become implicated in the trade.
26. ***Payment gateways and payment processors***: Which are required for credit card transactions and to move money between customer's and merchant's acquiring banks.

We acknowledge that these roles may shift and may be undertaken by the same actor or organisation—for example, the counterfeiters may run operations where the chemical engineers and packaging producers are in the same organisation. It may be that an operation is producing and packaging on the same site, or there may be some degree of outsourcing. It could be that a logistics company involved is responsible for a range of tasks during the distribution process, from storage to transport. Finally, we need to be aware that these are commercial enterprises with networks of actors involved during various stages and with varying degrees of transparency. Some of those involved may be unaware of their involvement in an illicit market. What the above simply does is begin to outline the broad range of actors that can be involved in a complex drugs supply chain, such as the illicit pharmaceutical trade. A broader focus on the 'social life' of drugs as they move through each region of the global capitalist economy can offer a more comprehensive picture of a trade's social organisation.

Conclusion

This chapter has focused on a criminological analysis of the global supply chain in pharmaceutical drugs to examine some of the complex dynamics shaping the physical flows of illicit medicines around the world. First, we explored the political economy of supply, which exposed the use of historically established trade routes, SEZs and parallel trading practices in the illicit pharmaceutical supply chain. Second, we proposed a zonal model that outlined the most regularly utilised channels and routes through which illicit medicines are produced and distributed. Third, the chapter briefly explored the social organisation of the illicit medicine trade, listing the range of actors involved in the complex supply chain. Throughout this research we have examined the trade's material flows as they are entrenched in the structures of the global political economy and global supply chains.

In the current neoliberal era, unregulated wholesale systems, misguided trade barriers, variations in intellectual property laws and the differential characteristics of producer and consumer economies encourage the supply of illicit medicines (see Passas, 1999). The trade is contingent on porous borders and trade routes, and it has become more widespread and intense as a direct result of the deregulation of international trade and liberalisation of financial markets from the 1980s. Indeed, the financial centres of the world compete for the capital return of criminal enterprise. Ever since the abolition of many capital exchange controls, the offshore banking industry has been able to 'clean up' and store accumulated assets (Shaxson, 2011; Hudson, 2015). This is just one of the entry points through which 'legitimate' businesses and economic institutions can become implicated in this 'illegitimate' trade.

Throughout this research we unearthed numerous ways in which the trade is entrenched in the extralegal (Nordstrom, 2007; see also Hall, 2012). At every point in the supply chain we have found some sort of formative role played by the legal industry. The nature and dynamics of the legal pharmaceutical industry in the context of global capitalism has bolstered the illegal industry that has emerged in its shadow, in many respects calling into question our ability to draw a clear distinction between each. To fully understand the trade we have therefore positioned our analysis in a critical discussion of late-modern capitalist dynamics. After all, the trade in illicit medicines does not exist in a vacuum but in many ways depends upon overarching processes of neoliberal globalisation, which include the current forms of pharmacy service found throughout the globe, wider national and local healthcare provisions and the general cultural, economic and technological environments that constitute and reproduce the overall neoliberal context.

Overall, the supply of illicit medicines is embedded in inseparable and interrelated political forces, economic processes and technological advancements that blur the boundaries of legality but it is also socially and culturally rooted, requiring the formation of networks of actors situated on a range of sites. The complex nature and dynamics of the trade in illicit pharmaceuticals demands researchers to employ a range of new methods, concepts and theories in drugs research that blur the distinctions between once detached categories of analysis. It is only then that we can begin to fully understand the changing landscape of drug dealing and illicit drug markets in the twenty-first century.

References

Angop. (2013) 'Over 100 Tonnes of Illicit Medicines Seized in Southern Africa'. *Agencia Angola Press*. Retrieved 8/4/16, from www.portalangop.co.ao/angola/en_us/noticias/africa/2013/9/41/Over-100-tonnes-illicitmedicines-seized-Southern-Africa,dd68cbd6-7b7a-48fb-b129-3ccc44961ea8.html

Antonopoulos, G.A. and Hall. A. (2016) 'Gain With No Pain': Anabolic-Androgenic Steroids Trafficking in the UK'. *European Journal of Criminology,* 13(6), 696–713.

Bate, R. (2008) *Making a Killing: The Deadly Implications of the Counterfeit Drug Trade.* Washington: AEI Press.

Bogadich, W. (2007) 'Counterfeit Drugs' Path Eased by Free Trade Zones'. *New York Times.* Retrieved 2/2/18, from www.nytimes.com/2007/12/17/world/middleeast/17freezone.html?pagewanted=1&_r=1

Braithwaite, J. (1984) *Corporate Crime in the Pharmaceutical Industry.* London: Keegan Paul.

Cassidy, N. (2012) 'Patients Struggle to Buy Drugs in Cash-Strapped Greece'. *BBC News Online.* Retrieved 7/6/14, from www.bbc.co.uk/news/business-18423966

Dorn, N., Murji, K. and South, N. (1992) *Traffickers.* London: Routledge.

EAEPC. (2013) *How Does It Work?*. Retrieved 6/11/13, from http://eaepc.chiemgau-net.de/en/how-does-it-work/

EFPIA. (2012) *The Pharmaceutical Industry in Figures.* Brussels: EFPIA.

Ellis, S. (2009) 'West Africa's International Drug Trade'. *African Affairs*, 108(431), 171–196.

Finlay, B.D. (2011) *Counterfeit Drugs and National Security.* Washington, D.C.: The Stimson Centre.

Ford, N. (2013) 'Locals Want Bigger Share of $40bn Industry'. *African Business,* 397(May), 16–29.

Gregory, J. (2013) *Counterfeits Peddler Fined £5.6m after UK's 'Most Serious' Supply Chain Breach.* Retrieved 26/11/13, from www.chemistanddruggist.co.uk/news-content/-/article_display_list/15947486/counterfeitspeddler-fined-5-6m-after-uk-s-most-serious-supply-chain-breach

Hall, A. (2019) 'Lifestyle Drugs and Late Capitalism: A Topography of Harm'. In Raymen, T. and Smith, O. (eds.), *Deviant Leisure: Criminological Perspectives on Leisure and Harm* (pp. 161–186). London: Palgrave Macmillan.

Hall, A. and Antonopoulos, G.A. (2015) 'License to Pill: Illegal Entrepreneurs' Tactics in the Online Trade of Medicines'. In van Duyne, P.C., Maljevic, A., Antonopoulos, G.A., Harvey, J. and von Lampe, K. (eds.), *The Relativity of Wrongdoing: Corruption, Organised Crime, Fraud and Money Laundering in Perspective* (pp. 229–252). Nijmegen: Wolf Legal Publisher.

Hall, A. and Antonopoulos, G.A. (2019) *Fake Meds Online: The Internet and the Transnational Market in Illicit Pharmaceuticals.* Basingstoke: Palgrave Macmillan.

Hall, A., Koenraadt, R. and Antonopoulos, G.A. (2017) 'Illicit Pharmaceutical Networks in Europe: Organising the Illicit Medicine Market in the United Kingdom and the Netherlands'. *Trends in Organized Crime.* Online First, doi: 10.1007/s12117-017-9304-9

Hall, S. (2012) *Theorizing Crime and Deviance: A New Perspective.* London: Sage.

Harvey, D. (2005) *A Brief History of Neoliberalism.* Oxford: Oxford University Press.

Haugen, H.Ø. (2011) 'Chinese Exports to Africa: Competition, Complementarity and Cooperation between Micro-Level Actors'. *Forum for Development Studies*, 38(2), 157–176.

Hudson, M. (2015) *Killing the Host: How Financial Parasites and Debt Destroy the Global Economy.* New York: Avalon.

IRACM. (2013) *Counterfeit Medicines and Criminal Organisations.* Paris: IRACM.

Jackson, G., Patel, S. and Khan, S. (2012) 'Assessing the Problem of Counterfeit Medications in the United Kingdom'. *International Journal of Clinical Practice*, 66(3), 241–250.

JDSU. (2010) *Pharmaceutical Counterfeiting, Tampering, and Diversion: Solutions for Addressing a Growing Threat.* Los Angeles, CA: JDSU.

Kennedy, J.P. and Wilson, J.M. (2015) Charting the Course: The Roles and Responsibilities of Ocean-Going Transportation Intermediaries in the Distribution of Counterfeit Goods. Center for Anti-Counterfeiting and Product Protection Paper Series. Retrieved 8/4/16, from http://a-capp.msu.edu/sites/default/files/Intermediary%20Liability__FINAL.pdf

Koenraadt, R. & Van de Ven, K. (2017) 'Exploring the Relationship between Online Buyers and Sellers of Image and Performance Enhancing Drugs (IPEDs): Quality Issues, Trust and Self-Regulation'. *International Journal of Drug Policy*, 50, 48–55.

Kotze, J. and Antonopoulos, G.A. (2019) 'Boosting Bodily Capital: Maintaining Masculinity, Aesthetic Pleasure and Instrumental Utility through the Consumption of Steroids'. *Journal of Consumer Culture.* Online First. https://doi.org/10.1177/1469540519846196

KPMG. (2012) *An Overview of Risk and Disclosure in the Global Pharmaceutical and Life Sciences Industry.* Retrieved 2/1/14, from www.kpmg.com/global/en/issuesandinsights/articlespublications/pages/risk-and-disclosure-in-the-global-pharmaceutical-industry.aspx

Laing, B.A. (2005) 'Parallel Trade in Pharmaceuticals: Injecting the Counterfeit Element into the Public Health'. *NC Journal of International Law and Commercial Regulation,* 31(4), 847–900.

Maskus, K.E. (2002) *Parallel Imports in Pharmaceuticals: Implications for Competition and Prices in Developing Counties.* Final report to the World Intellectual Property Organisation.

Morgan, O. (2008) 'Parallel Trade in Drugs Puts EU Patients at Risk'. *The Guardian Online.* Retrieved 13/9/13, from www.theguardian.com/business/2008/jun/29/pharmaceuticals

Moyle, L. and Coomber, R. (2015) 'Earning a Score: An Exploration of the Nature and Roles of Heroin and Crack Cocaine "User-Dealers"'. *The British Journal of Criminology,* 55(3), 534–555.

Neveling, P. (2015) 'Free Trade Zones, Export Processing Zones, Special Economic Zones and Global Imperial Formations 200 BCE to 2015 CE'. In Ness, I. and Cope, Z. (eds.), *The Palgrave Encyclopedia of Imperialism and Anti-Imperialism* (pp. 1007–1016). Basingstoke: Palgrave Macmillan.

Nordstrom, C. (2007) *Global Outlaws: Crime, Money, and Power in the Contemporary World.* Los Angeles, CA: University of California Press.

Palmer, E. (2013) 'China Cooperating with Big Pharma to Fight Counterfeiting'. *Fierce Pharma Manufacturing,* January 22, p. 1.

Passas, N. (1999) 'Globalisation, Criminogenic Asymmetries, and Economic Crime'. *European Journal of Law Reform,* 1, 399–423.

Port Technology. (2015) *China-Kazakhstan's Massive Cargo Connection.* Retrieved 6/4/16, from www.porttechnology.org/news/china_kazakhstans_massive_cargo_connection

Portes, A., Castells, M. and Benton, L.A. (eds.). (1991) *The Informal Economy: Studies in Advanced and Less Developed Countries.* Baltimore, MD: John Hopkins University Press.

Satchwell, G. (2004) *A Sick Business: Counterfeit Medicines and Organised Crime.* The Stockholm Network.

Shaxson, N. (2011) *Treasure Islands: Uncovering the Damage of Offshore Banking and Tax Havens.* New York: St. Martin's Press.

Southwick, N. (2013) *Counterfeit Drugs Kill 1 Million People Annually: Interpol.* 26/11/13, from www.insightcrime.org/news-briefs/counterfeit-drugskill-1-million-annually-interpol

UNODC. (2007) *Cocaine Trafficking in West Africa: The Threat to Stability and Development.* Retrieved 3/11/13, from www.unodc.org/documents/data-and-analysis/west_africa_cocaine_report_2007-12_en.pdf

UNODC. (2010) *The Globalisation of Crime: A Transnational Organised Crime Threat Assessment.* Vienna: UNODC.

Wagner, W.J. (no date) *Cross-Border Trade in Pharmaceuticals: Free Trade or Illegal Trade.* Ottawa, ON: Gowlings.

Waldron, J. (2013) *Seven Arrested Over Illicit Medicines Postal Smuggling Scheme.* Retrieved 30/11/13, from www.chemistanddruggist.co.uk/news-content/-/article_display_list/16053734/seven-arrested-over-illicit-medicinespostal-smuggling-scheme

Walker, T. (2014) 'FedEx Facing Drug-Trafficking Charges over Illicit Pharmaceuticals'. *The Independent,* July 20. Retrieved 30/11/13, from www.independent.co.uk/news/business/news/fedex-facing-drugtrafficking-charges-over-illicit-pharmaceuticals-9616936.html

Wertheimer, A.I. and Wang, P.G. (eds.). (2012) *Counterfeit Medicines Volume I: Policy, Economics and Countermeasures.* Hertfordshire: ILM.

WHO. (2012) *Substandard/Spurious/Falsely Labelled/Falsified/Counterfeit Medical Products: Report of the Working Group of Member States.* Geneva: WHO.

Yar, M. (2008) 'The *Other* Global Drugs Crisis: Assessing the Scope, Impacts and Drivers of the Global Trade in Dangerous Counterfeit Pharmaceuticals'. *International Journal of Social Inquiry,* 1(1), 151–166.

19

DRUG MARKETS AND DRUG DEALING

Time to move on

Tammy C. Ayres and Stuart Taylor

Introduction

> The greatest trick the devil ever pulled was convincing the world he didn't exist.
>
> *Verbal Kent in The Usual Suspects, Singer, 1995*

While the previous chapters of this book provide nuanced insights into drug markets, their focus is on the illicit risks aligning with dominant socio-legal constructions of drugs – ensuring that the most harmful drug markets remain invisible. In this chapter, we therefore seek to expand these boundaries to provide a more encompassing consideration of these often-neglected markets. We do this in two ways. Firstly, we illustrate how normative constructions of drug markets lead to a narrow focus on illegal drugs and the relative omission of legal markets. This is a process, which strengthens the arbitrary drug apartheid, a system of legal privilege rooted in capitalist interest and ideology. Secondly, we highlight how critical drug scholars unintentionally reinforce prevailing understandings of drug markets through a fetishism with the 'new' and a desire to protect the vulnerable. Resultantly, we argue that a reconceptualisation of our criminological imagination is required in order to expose the drug apartheid and reveal the full spectrum of drug market actors and harms.

Underpinning this chapter is the contention that the arbitrary frameworks governing the legality of different substances construct a drug apartheid (Buchanan, 2015) – a hierarchical system of segregation that privileges certain drug markets while criminalising others. Resultantly, contemporary drug policies, justified by their purported ability to mitigate drug-related harms, contradictorily serve to enhance their scope and severity (Taylor, Buchanan and Ayres,

DOI: 10.4324/9781351010245-22

2016). The laws governing the supply of 'drugs', their criminalisation and subsequent punishment are not premised on a science of harmfulness, instead history, not harm dictates their erroneous demarcation. Yet the legitimacy of the drug apartheid is maintained through a reductionist drugs discourse, which obfuscates nuanced knowledge and presents fallacy as fact (Taylor, 2016). Adherence to dominant constructions of drug use and supply by government, the media, the public and (importantly for this chapter) the research community, serves to conceal the full spectrum of drug market harms – particularly the harm of non-drugs such as sugar, medicines, alcohol and tobacco. Instead the dominant status quo serves to disavow the illegitimacy and harmfulness of the current system of drug prohibition and its resultant apartheid. Simultaneously, this discourse abdicates responsibility for drug-related harms onto minorities of problematic substance users and illicit drug dealers while disavowing the influence of consumer capitalism, structural social inequalities and, indeed, drug policy itself in shaping these damaging outcomes and its subsequent harms. Ultimately, this process ensures that the reality underpinning the legitimacy of the current system of drug prohibition – that it is premised on the exigencies of Capitalism rather than the harmfulness of the so-called drugs (Ayres, 2017, 2020a, 2020b; Paley, 2014) – remains hidden. Consequently, those with vested economic and moral interests in the drug apartheid continue to flourish while its casualties continue to amass – casualties that disproportionately fall along the lines of race, gender and class, and which tend to be concentrated in the Global South (Ayres, 2020b; Paley, 2014).

Criminologists, keen to expose the inherent contradictions of drug prohibition, its opaque reasoning and its damaging outcomes, have developed an ever-evolving critique of its processes (Brownstein, 2013; Pryce, 2012). Resultantly, they help us move beyond the stereotypes, myth, and supposition that predominate assumed knowledge (Taylor et al., 2016). The preceding chapters of this book provide examples of this, identifying as they do, new and emerging trends, providing invaluable, nuanced insights into drug dealing, encouraging us to move beyond normative assumptions by recognising the diversity of actors engaged in contemporary drug markets. They therefore reveal a spectrum of hereupon unseen drug market-related issues and harms, moving the critical debate forward. Or do they? This book on 'drug dealing' focuses on those illegal/illicit drug markets that routinely populate the reductionist drugs discourse. In doing so, it ignores the most prevalent and powerful drug dealers within society – those pharmaceutical companies who supply prescription medications; those corporations which monopolise the supply of caffeine; those conglomerates who dominate the global supply of alcohol and tobacco; and those food manufacturers who supply daily doses of sugar to us all. As such, this book stands accused of feeding into the normative parameters of the drug apartheid, constructing global understandings of drug use, drug dealing and drug markets through a narrow, conventional lens.

Resultantly, this chapter argues that there is a need to reconceptualise our understanding of drugs, drug dealing and drug markets in order to contest the drug apartheid, by showing that the supply of legal drugs by large corporations is as if not more harmful than the supply of illicit drugs by the evil and amoral drug dealers. Key to this contestation is a reworking of our criminological imagination. There is a need to reposition attention onto the wider sphere of substance use to recognise the full spectrum of drug markets and actors and to highlight the harmful practices of legitimate substance suppliers as opposed to simply illegal entrepreneurs. In doing so we refocus our attention onto the drug market-related harms experienced by the majority rather than those encountered by the minority. For while the harmful implications of the status quo are experienced most acutely by socially marginalised populations, the processes of the drug apartheid permeate the entire social strata, making us all susceptible to its damaging outcomes, throwing dubious light on drug prohibitions' purported ability to protect society from drug-related harm.

The drug apartheid: how did we end up here?

Speaking to their seven-year-old niece recently, one of the authors learnt that a 'drugs' education event had taken place at her school. She explained that the pupils had been informed of what drugs were – illegal substances – and told in no uncertain terms that these were bad, should never be taken, and that drug dealers were dangerous. In response, I took her to a café and asked what she wanted and why – a hot chocolate, I like the taste and how it makes you feel. I explained that hot chocolate contained drugs, that those drugs tasted good and gave her energy, and if used in moderation were relatively safe but that used excessively could be very harmful. I explained that the same applies to illegal drugs but that the system of prohibition enhanced the risks associated with them. We then (after I declined her request for a second hot chocolate) took a walk around town, with me pointing out all the outlets that offered medicines, tobacco, alcohol, sugar and caffeine. I explained that these businesses all sold substances that were as equally beneficial/harmful as those sold by illegal drug dealers. She looked confused. I was reminded of the entrenched nature of societal constructions of drug markets.

Our response (in a social, legal and political sense) to substance use is governed more by the profile of who manufactures or uses a drug than the inherent toxicity or risks associated with it. So, while pharmaceutical companies, the alcohol and tobacco industry, purveyors of caffeine, and food and drink manufacturers who laden their products with sugar cause the greatest proportion of drug-related harms, they simultaneously enjoy a position of legal privilege (Taylor et al., 2016). But how did we end up here?

Drugs and what we constitute/define as drugs are historically tied to the exigencies of capitalism and its establishment across the globe (Ayres, 2020a, 2020b; Courtwright, 2001; Paley, 2014). Despite the popular portrayal of 'drugs' subverting capitalism and corrupting society, this is a myth created to disavow the realities underpinning a system of governance that is not only unscientific, but also potentially more harmful than the substances it purports to protect us from (MacCoun and Reuter, 2001). Instead, the demarcation of privileged legal drugs from unprivileged illegal drugs is interwoven with colonialism, trade, empire, slavery, exploitation, the advancement of global consumer capitalism and the contemporary political economy (Farrell, 1997). As Fisher (2009: 8) notes, 'capitalism subsumes and consumes all of previous history', so while drug prohibition is contemptuously framed as grounded in notions of harm, addiction and the protection of society from dangerous substances, this constitutes an '(unconscious) fantasy structuring our social reality' (Žižek, 1989: 33). Instead, the prohibition of some drugs but not others is historically tied to ruthless trading companies, ethnic cleansing, slavery and indentured labour to open up markets and create trade networks spanning the globe – networks, which were integral to the current system of free trade, its well-established trade routes and contemporary global capitalism (Buxton, 2006; Courtwright, 2001). History distinguished (erroneously) between legitimate trade/supply in these substances and illegitimate criminal supply, despite large monopolies/corporations like the East India Trading Company partaking in the same merciless undertaking[1] as that employed by criminal entrepreneurs (Hall, 2012) – a process that has been refined but is equally apparent today (see Ayres and Treadwell's chapter and Salinas' chapter in this volume).

When discussing drug supply and trafficking, large companies and multinational corporations are largely omitted from the discussion – as evidenced by their absence within the content of this book (barring Linnemann and Medley's chapter proceeding this one). Although some texts concerned with drug dealing offer tentative understandings of the opium trade (and indeed, the British government's role within this – see Barton, 2011; Coomber, 2006), the majority of this literature focuses on the usual suspects: the criminal entrepreneur, social suppliers, terrorist and organised crime groups. This means that the actions of those corporations and conglomerates which legitimately manufacture and sell drugs at extortionate prices, withhold lifesaving medications from people who need them, poison people, inflict deformities[2] and cause more deaths than all illicit drugs and illicit drug dealers combined, are sidelined. So, despite provoking widespread harm, such organisations fail to arouse the same level of attention as the stereotypical 'death dealers' of illegal substances. Consequently, these companies are neither held to account nor criminally prosecuted for their role in the supply of drugs. This is despite the fact that adverse drug reactions from legitimate pharmaceutical drugs are one of the leading causes of morbidity and mortality in health care – it is the sixth leading cause of death worldwide – despite being preventable (Hacker, 2009; Singer and Baer, 2009), and two of the most popular drugs, tobacco and alcohol, kill millions globally, and have been deemed the biggest threat and by far the worst drugs for human health (Peacock, Leung, Larney et al. 2018), and yet they are legal. Instead, organisations such as pharmaceutical companies are seen as legitimate producers and suppliers of safe drugs that we all need to keep us healthy and cure disease. Simultaneously, we ignore their underhand and unscrupulous business practices that are not only unethical but also harmful (Hagopian, 2015; Singer and Baer, 2009) – with big pharma providing the gold standard here through its stifling of generic competition, twisting of health policy in their favour, and payment of doctors and medical experts to not only promote and endorse their product, but also prescribe it to their patients[3] (Feldman and Frondorf, 2017; Singer and Baer, 2009).

Thus, despite being premised on notions of harm, addiction and danger, the historical control and regulation of some drugs (e.g. cocaine and heroin) but not others (e.g. alcohol and tobacco[4]) can be linked to big business and its multinational corporations that are premised on the exigencies of capitalism and its pursuit of profit (Ayres, 2020a, 2020b; Farrell, 1997; Paley, 2014). Yet this is hidden and renounced along with the harms embedded in these capitalist markets of consumption. Instead, fantasy conceals the systemic violence inherent in capitalism and its circuits of consumption (Smith and Raymen, 2018; Winlow and Hall, 2016; Žižek, 2008). Hence, drugs, particularly illegal, unprivileged drugs, are blamed for societal ills, seen as both polluting and dangerous (Douglas, 1969), held responsible for causing crime, addiction, disease and death, destroying communities, families, individuals and town centres (Ayres and Taylor, 2020). They therefore function as a fetish, giving body to inconsistency (Žižek, 1989), serving to negate the systemic causes underpinning these ills, as 'capital can never openly admit that it is a system based on inhuman rapacity' (Fisher, 2014: 36). Rather than acknowledge the systemic violence underpinning society, we admonish some drugs but not others, seeking to eradicate their flawed consumption, flawed consumers, and flawed amoral and evil sellers. We therefore centre attention on dangerous drugs, dangerous groups, excessive and dangerous consumption, and selling practices, while diverting attention away from the systemic violence that masks the paradoxical nature of capitalism (Žižek, 2006) and its harmful circuits of production, supply and consumption.

The drug apartheid: the current situation

While the historic control and regulation of drugs was bound to Capitalist economic interest, this simultaneously acted as a civilising process, premised on notions of morality, religion, race and class – with some drugs moralised and seen as a vice, while others were not (Buxton, 2006; Courtwright, 2001; Withington, 2014). Hence, the use of certain substances by certain people was construed as socially acceptable, even attracting respect and gravitas, while the use of other substances by other people was construed as morally indignant and indicative of the danger posed by their race, ethnicity, gender and class. This process was tied to capital and power, which manifested as inequality that amounts to a form of objective violence, which pervades society (Žižek, 2008).

The continuation of this process into the contemporary has been stark with illegal drug markets disproportionately associated with certain types of people, with the drug apartheid celebrating certain substance use as culturally relevant and socially embedded, and other substance use as culturally offensive and socially repugnant. Despite those users who use the latter substances representing a minority of all drug users, they have been framed as *the* drug users, with representations, understandings and responses to the drugs problem rooted in a focus on this minority. This acts to reinforce the legitimacy of the drug apartheid as good people use acceptable non-drugs, and bad people use unacceptable drugs.

Table 19.1 illustrates the numerical foundations of the drug apartheid and the inverse funnel through which substance use is constructed. For while 2.97 million people in England and Wales report illegal drugs use during the previous year (with an estimated 300,783 opiate and crack cocaine users, 550,000 ecstasy users, 875,000 cocaine users and 2.4 million cannabis users), these numbers are dwarfed by those who use legal substances. For example, the 2 million individuals in England who illicitly use prescription painkillers, the 6.1 million who identify as smokers, the 25.9 million who drink alcohol and the estimated 31.9 million caffeine users.

So, while 90% of the population use the non-drug caffeine, just 9% use illegal drugs, with only a fraction of these identified as users of those drugs (heroin and crack cocaine) deemed the most problematic (Taylor, 2008). The drug apartheid, however, takes attention away from the prevalent legal markets while the reductionist drugs discourse simultaneously deflects attention away from the wider body of individuals engaged with illegal drug markets (Taylor, 2011). Instead, it centres upon a minority group of heroin/crack (and increasingly spice/synthetic cannabinoids) users who represent a comparatively small segment of drug markets. In doing so, the status quo is maintained with the momentum of the drug apartheid camouflaging the most destructive drug market-related harms within society – obesity, tooth decay, loss of sleep, liver disease, cancer and the prescription practices of the medical profession.

Hence, while our gaze is drawn to those drug markets deemed to be the most dangerous and therefore outlawed via the 1961 UN Single Convention of Narcotic Drugs, we invisiblise the corporate promotion of sugary foods, alcohol, caffeine, tobacco and pharmaceuticals. Despite an increasing recognition of the harms associated with these licit substances, their social, legal and political construction as non-drugs endures – a process that this very book, for the most part, stands accused of reinforcing. For while this text provides an invaluable insight into the contemporary drug dealing landscape, it continues the linear trend of exploring illegal drug and/or illicit and 'grey' markets, and the contemporary developments associated with them.

This process of demarcating legal drug markets from illegal ones – to the extent that they are not even seen as *drug* markets – is bolstered by a neoliberal self-responsibilisation agenda, which ascribes the problematic use of legal substances to an irresponsible minority (who eat too much sugar, binge drink, etc.). A minority that can usually be found in the lower socio-economic classes where their 'relentless monstering' (Fisher, 2009: 77) reinforces the need for governance structures which civilise those transcending acceptable behavioural

TABLE 19.1 Estimated trends within the last year among adult population of England (and Wales)

Population	*Number*	*Region*	*Source*
Opiate and/or crack cocaine users	300,783	England	Hay, dos Santos and Swithenbank, 2018
Ecstasy users	550,000	England and Wales	Home Office, 2018
Dependent alcohol users	595,131	England	Pryce, Buykx, Gray et al., 2017
Cocaine users	875,000	England and Wales	Home Office, 2018
Non-prescribed painkiller users	2.0 m	England	Rhodes, 2018
Cannabis users	2.4 m	England and Wales	Home Office, 2018
Any illegal substance users	2.97 m	England and Wales	Home Office, 2018
Tobacco users	6.1 m	England	ONS, 2018a
Alcohol users	25.6 m	England	ONS, 2018b
Individuals prescribed medication	25.9 m	England	NHS Digital, 2018
Caffeine users	31.9 m	England	Estimate for 2018[14]

boundaries. This consequently provides a smokescreen for the harmful practices of legitimate drug market enterprises (Babor, Robaina, Brown et al., 2018; McCambridge, Kypri, Miller et al., 2014).

A good illustration of this is the supply/use of alcohol in UK airports. Alcohol is freely available in airports, no matter what the time of day, as they sit outside the usual UK licensing conditions. Here the substance regarded by some as the most harmful societal intoxicant (Nutt, King and Phillips, 2010) enjoys a position of legal privilege while other less harmful substances are prohibited (with low level drug mules who carry such substances arrested for trafficking). The unrestricted availability of alcohol has encouraged an informal tradition of people having 'the first drink of the holiday' at times that would otherwise be frowned upon – within the liminal airport departure lounge; however, this represents an accepted consumption practice of alco tourism (Bell, 2008). Yet recent media attention has seen a flurry of interest around airport alcohol consumption due to those irresponsible consumers who drink too much and negatively impact the leisure consumption of others, via delayed or redirected flights (Cox and Slater, 2018; Tahir, 2018; Allen and Cardy, 2017; Godfrey, 2017). Resultantly, a recently launched aviation industry campaign cautions 'one too many: fly responsibly or you could pay the price', threatening consumers that disorderly behaviour will lead to hefty fines/prison (One Too Many, 2019). Here a differentiation is established between appropriate and inappropriate drug market engagement, justifying the development of a system of punitive control to respond to such irresponsible behaviour. Meanwhile, airport businesses such as Burger King encourage customers to 'replace your adult meal drink with a beer'; while executive airport lounges offer unlimited alcoholic drinks packages; and airline companies serve an array of alcoholic beverages on board which are essential to their profitability. So, while the purveyors of alcohol enjoy drug market liberalisation, the responsibility for any ensuing problems is directed upon the flawed consumers themselves, particularly those that do not adhere to contemporary hedonism that combines pleasure with control and restraint; to prosper one must engage in risk, but not too much risk (Žižek, 2008).

Furthermore, this process ensures the self-perpetuation of the capitalist status quo (and de facto the drug apartheid) through the increasing encouragement for society to consume in more responsible ways, with products that are less likely to cause harm (to them and others), supposedly. Resultantly, contradictory governance structures, formulated around fallacious conceptualisations of harm, are able to operate in plain sight. For example, despite the growing realisation that drugs such as alcohol and tobacco are, in relation to other legal and illegal substances, comparatively harmful, this has not led to their prohibition. Instead, Capitalism has harnessed this harmfulness to justify some of the highest sin taxes in the world[5] on their supply and sale. These taxes, increasingly disguised as health taxes (e.g. on sugar), aim to control harmful patterns of consumption, while also promoting health, as health has become commodified, individualised and deadly (Hall and Antonopoulos, 2019; Singer and Baer, 2009; Winlow and

Hall, 2016). As Fisher (2009: 77) notes, 'there's no doubt that late capitalism certainly articulates many of its injunctions via an appeal to (a certain version of) health'. Yet this too is an illusion. Instead, these new healthier and less harmful substances act as a corrosive form of symbolism aimed at advancing capitalism and the interests of the plutocratic elite (Hall, Winlow and Ancrum 2008; Ayres, 2020a). The version of health promoted is not based on scientific evidence or genuine well-being, particularly in relation to mental health. Instead 'a reductive, hedonic model of health which is all about feeling and looking good' (Fisher, 2009: 73) is prioritised as survival and competitive success becomes a 'matter of appearance and surface impressions' (Ewen and Ewen, 1982: 265) in a society where representation has overtaken reality (Baudrillard, 1994). We currently live in a 'derealization ... of everyday reality' (Satre as cited in Jameson, 1991: 19). Rather, these new drugs are Žižek's (2005: 151) chocolate laxative, 'a product containing the agent of its own containment' and an array of new drugs and substances purporting to be miracle cures have flooded the market (see Ayres, 2020a). Drugs that will not only supposedly improve our health and well-being as well as denoting a desirable and healthy lifestyle, but superior products that are also ethical, sustainable and ecologically sound as capitalist profiteering is acceptable if countered by charity (Žižek, 2005).

Capitalism's drive for profit also shapes innovation and product development, as new drugs are created, marketed and sold as innovative and safer alternatives, despite the reality, since some of these medicines, foods and drugs contain toxic poisons (e.g. Botox, lead, mercury, aluminium) that actually cause harm (Romanowski and Schueller, 2013; Singer and Baer, 2009; Tucker, Fischer, Upjohn et al. 2018). New substances like heroin, made by pharmaceutical giant Bayer, were proffered as 'a safe non-addictive' antidote to the adverse consequences of morphine addiction but created a new and worse problem of heroin addiction[6] (Buxton, 2006; Farell, 1997), illustrating Derrida's (1995: 235) point about *pharmakon* '*both* as poison *and* as antidote'. This can also be seen in the contemporary e-cigarette and vaping industry that offers a supposedly 'healthier' alternative to smoking, despite inconclusive evidence (Arnold, 2014; Pisinger, 2015). Ironically, those same manufacturers whose products prompted such concerns in the first instance are now promoting those that are refining our consumption practices (the food industry and no added sugar products; the tobacco industry and vaping; the alcohol industry and low-strength drinks). In today's contemporary marketplace 'we find a whole series of products deprived of their malignant property' providing us with a '*reality itself* deprived of its substance' (Žižek, 2002: xxvi) – a false reality that has become more real than reality itself. Instead, consumers believe that they are buying and consuming drugs devoid of their dangerousness or at least safer than their illegal counterparts as they are sold by legitimate companies. Although, the fight against these dangers is also one of the 'main investments of today's biopolitics'; 'no wonder marijuana is so popular among liberals who want to legalize it–it already IS a kind of opium without opium' (Žižek, 2003: 167). This may also help to explain why despite substances like ecstasy, LSD and psilocybin mushrooms being less harmful than cannabis (Nutt et al., 2010), cannabis is the drug that has been deemed safest to legalise first; a populist-driven decision, rather than one rooted in science (see Taylor et al., 2016).

While such a direction of travel may appear to result in a welcome reduction in (non)drug-related harms, it simultaneously reinforces the legitimacy of legal drug markets – framing flawed consumption on a minority who fail (or are unable) to engage with these products in a civilised and sensible manner (pregnant women who smoke cigarettes; street drinkers who consume high-strength white cider; obese people who eat too much sugar). Consequently, the irrational practices of consumers, rather than the nature of the consumer market and its sellers, attract denunciation (Winlow and Hall, 2016). For example, media representations of the purchase and smoking of cigarettes by those who are pregnant or dependent on welfare prompt public disapproval as this represents an irresponsible choice (Hookway, Elmer and Frandsen, 2017; van der Bom, Paterson, Peplow et al., 2018), while the health risks associated with their unhealthy habit also threaten the health of us all (Matthews-King, 2018). Restrictions on smoking in public and private places, the addition of gruesome warning pictures to packs of cigarettes and a substantial increase in tobacco taxation on the surface indicate a turn against neoliberal notions of market freedom. Yet in essence, such moves legitimise the freedom of the tobacco market by turning attention towards a minority of irresponsible smokers, pushing them to switch to vaping and e-cigarettes, which is not only deemed safer, but also touted as a quick-fix solution to smoking cessation. By restricting the available choices (and therefore limiting the freedoms) of this group of irresponsible smokers, the remainder can continue to engage with tobacco use at their liberty, albeit for a price in the exclusive members clubs/venues for cigar aficionados which attract contradictory media headlines emphasising their 'glamourous' and 'luxury' nature (Foulkes, 2017; Prynn, 2018).

This process serves to sideline calls to prohibit the highly profitable[7] tobacco industry, while encouraging exclusivity, in addition to the self-perpetuation of the tobacco market through less risky, hence more responsible branded products (e.g. e-cigarettes, Nicorette and vaping) which can be consumed in public and private spaces. Alternatives the media portray as healthy substitutes (Jennings, 2018), which drive a billion-dollar industry that is set to grow exponentially to $43 billion by 2023 (RM, 2018). Meanwhile, the emergence of new civilised consumer markets which further extend the scope of (non)drug-related harm, such as lifestyle and performance enhancing products (Hall and Antonopoulos, 2019; Koenraadt and van de Ven, 2018, see also chapters in this book by Hall and Antonopoulos, and van de Ven, Mulrooney and Townshend) or beauty products and dietary supplements (Ayres, 2017, 2020a), belie any overall reduction in capitalism's damaging drug-related practices.

The processes mapped out here reinforce common sense assumptions of drug markets and drug dealing. While on the one hand this book challenges such dominant narratives by deconstructing the homogeneous drug dealer label, it simultaneously (albeit unintentionally) bolsters the existing drug apartheid by underlining the drug/non-drug divide. This removes notions of 'drug dealing' away from the legitimate supply of legal substances and instead focuses attention on those producers, traffickers and suppliers of illegal substances. Hence, we must scrutinise our acquiescence to toxic consumption, as well as the role that drug scholars play in this process; is the continued academic fetishism with 'new' emerging illegal drug phenomena, coupled with the persistent desire to identify and help those most affected by drug markets, further entrenching the drug apartheid?

Bolstering apartheid? Academic fetishism and laudability in the neoliberal university

Taylor (2016: 111) argues that 'contemporary drugs research has developed a recognisable pattern' which 'reaffirms the themes of the reductionist discourse' and 'suppresses the development and dissemination of alternative knowledge'. This critique is based on those referred to as 'political compliant' academics who undertake governmentally funded projects which focus on a narrow array of issues and outcomes drawing on unrepresentative samples. In fact, the field of drugs is rife with research premised on unrepresentative samples and unrepresentative populations, like those in treatment and/or the criminal justice system, that perpetuate the dominant status quo confirming that drug use causes crime, addiction, immorality, disease and death, destroying communities, families and the individual. The reality is very different, as the majority of drug users are not addicted let alone in treatment or caught up in the criminal justice system. This is also true of drug dealers since the research in this area is sparse, particularly when you ascend to the higher levels of drug trafficking, and what there is, illustrates the same racial, gender and socio-economic disparities found in the possession offences since they come from the lower end of the supply chain (Beckett, Nyrop and Pfingst, 2006; Bewley-Taylor, Hallam and Allen, 2009; Stuntz, 1998). Resultantly, the understanding/knowledge base underpinning 'drug supply' and 'drug use' is not only one-sided, but also biased and stereotypical as the reality goes unnoticed. Instead of acknowledging the reality of drugs, their supply and their consumption, the destructive nature of illegal drugs is clearly depicted in the medicalised discourse of disease and contagion, where drugs are seen as a scourge on society, being pushed on to innocent consumers by evil drug dealers that infect the masses and destroy civilisation, while the real 'root' causes are disavowed.

Yet this bolstering of the normative is perhaps equally applicable to critical scholars, who, through a desire to either debunk or further understand the place, role and inferences of drug markets, inadvertently feed into this process. This is prompted by an academic fetishism to perpetually focus on the 'new'. Yet within the field of drug markets, we must question: whether any contemporary developments should be construed as 'new'; whether such developments warrant attention; and whether by focussing on such issues, we are advancing knowledge or restricting our ability to contend the status quo. To elaborate, Potter and Chatwin (2018) critique how novel psychoactive substances (NPS) have been framed as a distinct and new category of drugs and, in doing so, question the enhanced focus on this emergent issue by scholars. Simultaneously, however, they note that 'of course, academics should respond to the issues of the day–particularly those working in the field of policy, or those seeking to understand contemporary social issues' (Potter and Chatwin, 2018: 330). Yet the assumption that we should 'respond to the issues of the day' is indicative of such fetishism. As academics, we may equally assume a questioning of whether contemporary drug market developments warrant attention. Yes, different types of drug markets emerge (e.g. GBH, NPS), as do different modes of manufacturing (e.g. meth labs, hydroponics) and dealing mediums (e.g. mobile phones and apps, the dark net, drones, county lines). Yet these do not represent anything 'new'. They represent the evolution and modernisation of historical processes, which politically compliant and critical scholars alike have poured time, money and careful thought into for over a century. Similarly, the issues and harms related to these markets are established problems given a fresh twist, that is, their use by certain populations, who they place at risk, their supply by otherwise law-abiding/criminal elements, their availability in prisons and the health issues they cause.

We therefore have to question whether our fetishist desire to debunk and explore the 'new' simply serves to revamp what we already know. This is highlighted throughout this book, from Wilson's chapter on amphetamine supply in the 1950s and 1960s by pharmaceutical giant Smith, Klein and French through to Kelly and Bancroft's chapters on cryptomarkets and cryptocurrencies that characterise a segment of online contemporary drug supply. Furthermore, does this research seek change and if so how, as the greatest utility of research into drug markets and users seems to be to those authorities that seek to implement and enforce prohibitionist strategies (and increasingly those private industries whose technologies supposedly ameliorate associated problems – see Taylor, Ayres and Jones, 2020). Instead of proffering the rediscovery and reapplication of ideas and theories from yesteryear, criminology needs to offer 'a theoretical and empirical account of the now' (Winlow, 2012: 9). Such thinking may be dismissed (particularly by the preceding chapter authors) through an insistence that research into contemporary drug markets is crucial as this builds a more critical empirical evidence base through which we may assess drug policy and contest the drug apartheid. Yet through continually focussing on emerging illegal drug phenomena, we bolster the notion that drug market harms are novel instead of recognising that they are grounded in historic, hegemonic drug policy ideology and what constitutes 'business as usual'. An ideology that relies on 'a crucial paradox' (Žižek, 2008:15) – a paradox that has been normalised and is reflected in the use, production and supply of substances.

Simultaneously, this thinking may sit uncomfortably with those dedicated to the advancement of frontline drug services who strive to support vulnerable populations via 'new' knowledge informing the evolution of harm reduction services. Yet harm reduction services in the UK have been reduced 'to the point of almost elimination' (Fisher and Measham, 2018: 19) and outside a small number of projects, the impact of such research is minimal. However, there are no treatment programmes or services that drug dealers can access, unless they are also a drug user, and their vilification and condemnation are represented/embodied in some of the harshest punishments available across the globe, which include death (see Sander, Girelli and Fernández, 2020). Concurrently, by focussing on the 'new' we continue our linear trend of concentrating on minority populations – as such emerging phenomena by their nature centre on marginal drug market actors. Yet this further risks strengthening the drug apartheid through re-emphasising the current segregation between the legal and illegal, which protects the majority. Critical drugs scholars (the authors included) have spent considerable time and energy scrutinising the (often harmful) inferences of drug markets on those marginalised and powerless groups. Inadvertently, however, when we unveil how the drug apartheid harms the minority (of illegal drug actors), we unintentionally bolster its underpinning raison d'être – that the majority are being protected by it.

This belies that every member of society is impacted, in some form, at some time in their life, by obesity, tooth decay, loss of sleep, liver disease, cancer or the prescription practices of the medical profession, as the causes of these harms are culturally accommodated, embedded and promoted. There is a need, therefore, to redirect our attention from the harms of the minority towards the harms of the majority. As by doing so we illustrate that we are all vulnerable – therefore avoiding the moral side-step of current policy whereby viewing certain subpopulations as more vulnerable than others limits the need to proactively address their needs – as being vulnerable is another way of indicating a peripheral (and less worthwhile) social status (Stevens, 2018). While a dedication to minority groups may therefore be laudable (and on occasion, lessen the harms they are exposed to), it aligns with the inverse funnel through which the drug apartheid is formulated and legitimised. There is, therefore, a need to question the value of such research, as despite evidencing the often-harmful implications of drug markets, its utility in moving the debate forwards is dubious.

This malaise is indicative of the realist rock and radical hard place drug researchers often find themselves torn between. For as far as we may wish to move beyond academic fetishism in order to develop a more encompassing structural contestation and reconceptualisation of drug markets, the realist in us wants to learn more about these, to mitigate the harms they invoke and to effect change in the here and now. Furthermore, such research sits comfortably within the neoliberal university, allowing scholars to attain funding for 'innovative' projects, publish 'new' knowledge, have potential impact on future drugs policy, and deliver research-informed teaching. As long as they avoid being too radical, too political and do not undermine the dominant status quo. Instead they simultaneously risk complicity with dominant drug narratives, which restrict the emergence of a macro/meso level critique of drugs policy that encompasses all drug markets, including those run by legitimate organisations and transnational corporations. A call to look at these drug markets replicates historical calls from critical criminologists to look at crimes of the powerful and a move away from state-defined notions of crime to one of social harm (Hillyard and Tombs, 2007). While this movement has recently gathered momentum once again (Hall and Winlow, 2015; Smith and Raymen, 2018), the context of the neoliberalism and marketisation of higher education has stilted any disciplinary progress.

As Winlow (2012) contends, the pressure and parameters instilled by the neoliberal university have stifled and stalled criminology's disciplinary dialectic. Consequently, academic freedom has been eroded and we now occupy an era of academic repression, where conformity is championed and 'not rocking the boat' is proffered as a guaranteed route towards career advancement (Juergensmeyer, Nocella and Seis, 2020). Although once politicised and critical institutions, universities have been reconstituted as non-political, non-critical and non-controversial corporations as they all compete for their market share of students and competition is increasingly premised on measurability and metrics (Juergensmeyer et al. 2020; Spence, 2019). However, metrics and league tables merely represent the university's ability to play the 'corporate game' and take 'intellectual short cuts in order to improve statistics' (Spence, 2019: 762). Concurrently, this has deleterious consequences for both the production and dissemination of knowledge as research of 'questionable social value' is produced that permits the university to posture itself as a world leading institution but is actually mediocre and has no real-world use (Spence, 2019). Instead of being critical spaces and 'sites of contention … where people can reflect on, as well as challenge, the orthodoxy of academic knowledge, the structure and rules of the broader society, or the actions of those at the highest level of power' (Castro as cited in Juergensmeyer et al., 2020: 6), universities have become another neoliberal institution where conformity is exerted, expected and rewarded by internal and external forces (Juergensmeyer et al., 2020; Spence, 2019). 'Where everyone is entitled to an opinion, but no firm conclusions are to be reached' as academics position themselves 'as calculating, dispassionate *subjects of rationality*' (Winlow, 2012: 8–9). Instead academia has become like the Internet, 'interpassive networks of like-minds who confirm, rather than challenge, each other's assumptions and prejudices' (Fisher, 2009: 75). It is these neoliberal risk-averse institutions that censure and advise against research into drug trafficking, particularly the higher tiers of drug supply chains, particularly those that operate in other, often more unstable (e.g. Afghanistan and Mexico) countries, as the ethics committee is there to mitigate against risky research and control the production of knowledge (Winlow and Hall, 2012).

Perhaps as much as there is a need to expose the drug apartheid, there is a need to expose our inadequate investigation of such issues and the restrictions placed on contemporary academics. Perhaps as much as there is a need to reconceptualise what we understand to be 'drug markets', there is an equally pressing need to reconceptualise our criminological exploration of such issues (Winlow, 2017) – particularly when the latter is serving to bolster the former. While reconceptualising our role as drug researchers requires careful, collective deliberation and action, it represents a crucial facet to imagining the most effective way of contesting the drug apartheid.

Conclusion: contesting apartheid

As Seddon (2016: 415) observes, 'it will only be when the 'false self-evidence' of the drug concept is shaken hard enough that it falls apart, that we will finally see the arbitrary boundaries between intoxicants drawn a century ago disappear like markings 'drawn in sand at the edge of the sea'. There is a need therefore for 'systems of drug control to be completely re-imagined and re-conceptualized to reduce the harm they cause' as 'the problems of drug markets cannot be solved with recourse to the ideologies of governance that support and maintain their very existence' (Wakeman, 2014: 236). Hence, we must 'move beyond the conceptual frame to which the status quo is tethered' (Seddon, 2016: 396) to illustrate how drug prohibition and domestic drug polices serve as 'resources, tools, instruments, designed and then used to criminalize, demoralize, incapacitate, fracture and sometimes eliminate those problem populations' (Box, 1983: 7). Simultaneously recognising that drug laws serve as a 'trick to deflect our attention away from other, even more serious crimes and victimizing behaviours, which objectively cause the vast bulk of avoidable death, injury and deprivation' ensuring they 'exclude many similar, and in important respects, identical acts' which are likely to be committed more frequently by powerful individuals' (Box 1983: 9). Instead Western liberals focus on acts of violence that cause them outrage, while they fetishistically disavow the real constituent of the global situation and its inherent harm, as ideology subjectively invisibilises our reality and we are blinded to the objective violence of the world (Žižek, 2008).

The key message emanating from this chapter is that the drug apartheid and its tools of drug prohibition and the reductionist discourse need dismantling as current approaches to (non)drug markets are prompting more harm than they prevent. There is a need, therefore, to reconstruct drug markets on a social, legal, economic and political level and to redress the harms consequentially caused. While such a task represents a daunting proposition due to the imposing structures of the capitalist status quo, drugs scholars can help build a momentum for change but only if they reconsider their current role. Hence, there is a need for them to move away from the 'new', to refocus on the established and to transfer attention away from the minority onto the majority. It is up to contemporary drug scholars to widen the criminological imagination and extend the concept of drugs and drug supply to look at the production and supply of non-drugs – non-drugs which cause more harm than all illicit drugs combined.

The production and supply of these legal non-drugs is big business[8] and they are often more harmful than many illicit drugs sold by drug dealers. However, these harms are disavowed. Both drugs and non-drugs cause environmental, social and health harms, not to mention sustaining global economic inequalities, which are further exacerbated by illicit drugs being prohibited (see Ayres, 2020b; Taylor et al. 2016). This is, however, denied as illicit drugs provide a convenient scapegoat for many of society's ills, while non-drugs, which occupy a privileged position, have their harms routinely disavowed and obscured. Instead focus and condemnation are reserved for illicit drugs, despite there being little science corroborating the demarcation underpinning this drug apartheid, which is actually an ideological fantasy dressed up as reality (Žižek, 1989). Even ethical non-drugs like fair trade coffee (caffeine) are not what they seem, as ideology serves to conceal the paradoxical nature of consumer capitalism and its 'unbalanced, uncanny structure' (Žižek, 1989: 82). Instead Fairtrade coffee is a gimmick that does not benefit farmers or have the purported positive impact consumers believe it to have, with evidence suggesting it is corrupt and can actually be quite harmful, particularly to other farmers, as much of the money disappears into 'a great grey hole' (Griffiths, 2012; Ruben and Fort, 2012). Instead 'the Fairtrade industry makes false claims and suppresses significant information, which constitutes unfair trading' (Griffiths, 2012: 372). These gimmicky marketing strategies that incorporate social responsibility and warrant a higher price tag are routinely attached to everyday non-drugs and their supply, but they can also be found in the production and supply of illicit drugs, particularly those sold online, which are also marketed as 'Fairtrade' and 'organic' (Martin, 2014) to ease the conscience (and guilt[9]) of the consumer. Unfortunately, this is often an illusion, a marketing ploy widely known as 'bluewashing' or 'greenwashing' (for a review, see Brisman and South, 2016), as everyone is duped into consuming the right products/drugs and obtaining them from the right sources or supply/origin as everyone is told to consume, but to do so ethically. However, the reality remains, there is no such thing as ethical consumption despite capitalism's attempts to convince consumers otherwise as consumerism is now routinely accompanied by charity (Žižek, 2005).

Other suppliers of non-drugs like pharmaceutical companies rip of/exploit States and their citizens via price gouging despite no improvement in quality,[10] tax dodging, huge profit margins notwithstanding the development of these drugs are largely funded by the taxpayer and other public bodies. Big pharma manipulate the market, and have also been accused of political corruption and lobbying.[11] Pharmaceutical companies cause global harm and cause thousands of deaths each year, via unsafe adulterated drugs, adverse drug reactions, overcharging, pollution[12] and their impact on the environment, which have devastating and irreversible effects on wildlife, water supplies, pollution and global warming (Jorge and Clemente, 2019; Meller and Ahmed, 2019). Yet it is the producers and suppliers of illicit drugs that are vilified, blamed and criminalised for production and trafficking offences that attract the harshest sentences available in the world that include death, as morality is used to demarcate between acceptable and unacceptable drugs, as well as acceptable and unacceptable means of producing, supplying and procuring these drugs. There are no producers and suppliers of non-drugs who have been imprisoned for life or sentenced to death regardless of the harms inflicted by their products – an inconsistency that supports the drug apartheid and the ideological obstacles which hinder the effective evidence base policy.

The drug apartheid was and continues to be built on moral purpose. While this moral purpose is publicised as the protection of the majority of society from drug-related harm, this represents a distraction from the fundamental moral driver of drug prohibition – the perpetuation of the capitalist status quo and the social and economic purposes this serves. Resultantly, we erroneously associate drug market problems only with illicit drugs, with specific minority groups, disproportionately clustered along the lines of race, ethnicity, gender and class and disparately associated with the Global South. There is a need, therefore, to expose prohibition's inability to achieve its touted aim – that it fails to protect the majority of society, as its harms are omnipresent and permeate us all. Instead we ignore the objective violence metered out around the globe and are complicit in its functioning despite pretending not to know (Žižek, 2008). Instead corporate interests are prioritised, while the chocolate laxative and opium without opium mindset mean that no one is willing to confront the true cause or the reality as ideology naturalises inconsistencies so that they are no longer recognised as inconsistencies. Real problems and their cause are routinely desublimated into entertainment and popular culture, which disguises the truth by deflecting attention away from the destructive practices of legitimate business and anything that undermines the dominate status quo (Žižek, 1991). Practices that also apply to drugs and drug supply (Ayres and Taylor, 2020; Boyd, 2002; Taylor, 2008), as drug policy and drug prohibition are framed as essentialism (Taylor, 2016) and stereotypical caricatures are created and maintained around drugs and their supply (Boyd, 2002). Despite being no more or less harmful than some non-drugs, illicit drugs are scapegoated as an evil scourge on society – a scourge that destroys everything it touches. This morally informed shock and outrage at illicit drugs and the evil death dealers that supply them are focused on, while the horrors, violence and injustices that sustain them (banks, governments, oligarchs and conglomerates[13]) preclude a realistic understanding of the issues and finding effective subsequent solutions. The result is ineffective, erroneous and harmful explanations and answers that are masqueraded as the truth, as 'individualistic psychologically based solutions to drug issues' are emphasised, 'rather than examining social, political, and legal factors that shape drug use' and supply (Boyd, 2002: 398). It ignores the evidence base – science – and props up the illegitimate drug apartheid that has nothing to do with harm/harmfulness and protecting the public, and everything to do with contemporary ideology and the exigencies of consumer capitalism.

Instead critical drug scholars need to move this debate forward and not only expand what we mean by drugs, so it includes legal and illegal substances, but also the harms arising from these drugs that includes their production, supply and consumption. Legal non-drugs do not necessarily mean safe and illegal drugs do not necessarily mean dangerous. Consideration needs to be given to all drugs in society that includes how their benefits might be exploited, their harms mitigated and the destructive outcomes arising from the structures of governance that surround them alleviated/eliminated. First, however, the contemporary hurdles of consumer capitalism and its subsequent capital realism (Fisher, 2009) need to be overcome, alongside changes to the contemporary university, if we are to ever consider bringing about real change. In fact, many drug epidemics throughout history have been caused by doctors' over-prescribing practices and the underhand practices of pharmaceutical companies – whether we are talking about amphetamines in the UK (see Wilson's chapter in this volume) or the recent opioid crisis in the USA (see Linnemann and Medley's chapter in this volume) where Johnson & Johnson has been described as 'drug kingpin' and part of the pharmaceutical industry cartel. This highlights that the drug apartheid is as entrenched and omnipresent as it ever has been, which emphasises the continued need to go above and beyond this. It is time to move on!

Notes

1 According to Hall (2012:253), 'Capitalist "undertaking", in the pure sense of "getting things done" to serve the interests of the self, whilst risking harm to others'.

2 There are many examples where drugs have caused irreversible damage to its users. From Thalidomide in the 1950s which led to children born with congenital malformations, through to the contemporary high strength natural herbal antioxidants like green tea, which have been shown to cause liver and kidney damage (EFSA Panel, 2018; Singer and Baer, 2009).

3 In Canada, big pharma paid $151m to doctors and hospitals in 2017–2018 (Russell and Lieberman, 2019), while NHS doctors were receiving up to £100,000 a year from pharmaceutical companies in consultation fees (Malnick, 2016).

4 Tobacco financed the American Revolution, sugar sustained transnational slavery (Courtwright, 2001).

5 With 82–90% of the recommended retail price (RRP) for tobacco being tax and between 55–79% of the RRP for alcohol being tax, generating a total of £27.6 billion in taxes each year (Eads, 2017; TMA, 2017).

6 Heroin was ten times stronger than morphine (Buxton, 2006) and two to three times stronger than opium.

7 In 2017, the oral tobacco and nicotine market was worth an estimated US$12.5 billion (BAT, 2018).

8 The global opiate painkiller market in 2018 was worth $25.5billion (GVR, 2019), in 2017 the antidepressant market was worth $14.11billion (AMR, 2018a), the global alcoholic drinks market was valued at $1,439 billion in 2017 (AMR, 2018b), the global vaping and e-cigarette market was worth $12.41billion in 2019 (GVR, 2020) and the global sugar market was worth $75.617 billion in 2018 (RM, 2019).

9 Guilt arises from obeying the superego command to enjoy and from not being happy and fulfilled as enjoyment has become mandatory and we are forever thinking we are not enjoying properly or enough (Zizek, 1989). According to Zizek (1989), there is no subject without guilt.
10 Some of the most popular medications have tripled in price and this market has grown eight times faster than general inflation rates (Jorge and Clement, 2019).
11 In the 2016 congressional elections the pharma industry spent more than $62 million on political campaigns and in 2018 spent more than $283 million on lobbying (Meller and Ahmed, 2019).
12 The contamination of water sources with antimicrobial drugs by pharmaceutical companies (combined with mass misuse of antibiotics and poor sanitation) has had grave consequences in India, where an estimated 58,319 new-borns die from multidrug-resistant infections every year (see Laximnarayen et al. 2013).
13 The two largest privately held companies in the US – Koch Industries and Cargill – are in the top 100 air polluters (PERI, 2019).
14 In the absence of any UK data relating to caffeine use, this figure represents an estimate using the only available study into caffeine use amongst a country's population – that of the USA (see Frary, Johnson and Wang, 2005). This study identified 90% of the adult population as caffeine users. The total presented here therefore is admittedly a crass estimate for the UK, identifying 90% of the total number of those of working age in England (35,543,544).

References

Allen, P. and Cardy, P. (2017) Drunken Brits Brawl on Ryanair Flight to Ibiza–Then Fight with Police after Diverted Plane Lands. *The Mirror,* 26 August.

AMR (Allied Market Research). (2018a) *Antidepressant Drugs Market.* Canada: AMR.

AMR (Allied Market Research). (2018b) *Alcoholic Beverages Market.* Canada: AMR.

Arnold, C. (2014) Vaping and Health: What Do We Know about E-Cigarettes? *Environmental Health Perspective,* 122(9): A244–A249.

Ayres, T.C. (2020a) Substances: The Luxurious, the Sublime and the Harmful. In S. Hall, T. Kuldova and M. Horsley (Eds.), *Crime, Harm and Consumerism* (pp. 108–122). London: Routledge.

Ayres, T.C. (2020b) The War on Drugs and Its Invisible Collateral Damage: Environmental Harm and Climate Change. In A. Brisman and N. South (Eds.), *Routledge International Handbook of Green Criminology* (pp. 239–259). London: Routledge.

Ayres, T.C. (2017) Drugs, Leisure, Consumption and Harm. *BSC Newsletter* (winter): 20–26.

Ayres, T.C. and Taylor, S. (2020) The Media and Intoxication. In F. Hutton (Ed.), *Cultures of Intoxication* (pp. 239–261). Basingstoke: Palgrave MacMillan.

Babor, T., Robaina, K., Brown, K., Noel, J., Cremonte, M., Pantani, D., Peltzer, R. and Pinsky, I. (2018) Is the Alcohol Industry Doing Well by 'Doing Good'? Findings from a Content Analysis of the Alcohol Industry's Actions to Reduce Harmful Drinking. *BMJ Open.* doi: 10.1136/bmjopen-2018-024325

Barton, A. (2011) *Illicit Drug Use and Control* (2nd edition). Oxon: Routledge.

BAT (British American Tobacco). (2018) The Global Market Trends Affecting Our Industry. Available at: www.bat.com/group/sites/UK__9D9KCY.nsf/vwPagesWebLive/DO9DCKFM (accessed 12 December 2019)

Baudrillard, J. (1994) *Simulcra and Simulation.* Michigan: University of Michigan Press.

Beckett. K., Nyrop, K. and Pfingst, L. (2006) Race, Drugs and Policing: Understanding Disparities in Drug Delivery Arrests. *Criminology* 44(1): 105–137.

Bell, D. (2008) Destination Drinking: Toward a Research Agenda on Alcotourism. *Drugs: Education, Prevention and Policy* 15(3): 291–304.

Bewley-Taylor, D., Hallam, C. and Allen, R. (2009) *The Incarceration of Drug Offenders: An Overview.* London: Beckley Foundation.

Box, S. (1983) *Power, Crime and Mystification.* Tavistock: London.

Boyd, S. (2002) Media Constructions of Illegal Drugs, Users, and Sellers: A Closer Look at *Traffic. International Journal of Drug Policy,* 13(5): 397–407. doi.org/10.1016/S0955-3959(02)00079-8

Brisman, A. and South, N. (2016) Consumer Technologies, Crime and Environmental Implications. In M.R. McGuire and T.J. Holt (Eds.), *The Routledge Handbook of Technology, Crime and Justice* (pp. 310–324). London: Routledge.

Brownstein, H. (2013) *Contemporary Drug Policy.* Abingdon: Routledge.

Buchanan, J. (2015) Ending Prohibition with a Hangover. *British Journal of Community Justice,* 13: 55–74.

Buxton, J. (2006). *The Political Economy of Narcotics: Production, Consumption and Global Markets.* London: Zed Books.

Coomber, R. (2006) *Pusher Myths: Re-Situating the Drug Dealer.* London: Free Association Books.

Courtwright, D. (2001) *Forces of Habit: Drugs and the Making of the Modern World.* Cambridge, MA: Harvard University Press.

Couzens, G. (2018) 'A dios!' Passengers Cheer as 'Drunk and Aggressive' Irish Couple Are Escorted off Ryanair Flight after They Forced It Divert to Northern Spain. *Daily Mail,* 11 January.

Cox, C. and Slater, C. (2018) Ryanair Flight from Manchester to Ibiza Turned Back over 'Disruptive' Passenger. *Manchester Evening News,* 18 September.

Derrida, J. (1995) *Points: Interviews, 1974–1994.* California: Stanford University Press.

Douglas, M. (1969) *Purity and Danger.* London: Routledge.

Eads, L. (2017) UK Alcohol Duty Rates to Rise with Inflation. *The Drinks Business,* 8th March.

EFSA (European Food Safety Authority) Panel (2018) Scientific Opinion on the Safety of Green Tea Catechins. *EFSA Journal,* 16(4): 1–89.

Ewen, S. and Ewen, E. (1982) *Channels of Desire.* London: McGraw-Hill.

Farrell, A. (1997) Addicted to Profit: Capitalism and Drugs. *International Socialism,* 77.

Feldman, R. and Frondorf, E. (2017) *Drug Wars.* Cambridge: Cambridge University Press.

Fisher, M. (2014) *Ghosts of My Life: Writings on Depression, Hauntology and Lost Futures.* Ropley: Zero-Books.

Fisher, M. (2009) *Capitalist Realism.* Ropley: Zero-Books.

Fisher, H. and Measham, F. (2018) Night Lives: Reducing Drug-Related Harm in the Night Time Economy. Available at: http://volteface.me/publications/night-lives/ (accessed 12 January 2019).

Foulkes, N. (2017) London's Most Glamorous Venues for Cigar Lovers. *Financial Times,* 17 November.

Frary, C., Johnson, R. and Wang, M. (2005) Food Sources and Intakes of Caffeine in the Diets of Persons in the United States. *Journal of the American Dietetic Association,* 105(1): 110–113.

Godfrey, K. (2017) Drunken Passengers Are CHEERED at after They're Removed from a Diverted Flight. *The Express,* 22 June.

Griffiths, P. (2012) Ethical Objections to Fairtrade. *Journal of Business Ethics*, 105(3): 357–373.

GVR (Grand View Research). (2019) *Opioids Market Size, Share and Trends Analysis Report by Product, by Application, by Region, and Segment Forecasts, 2019–2026*. San Francisco: GVR.

GVR (Grand View Research). (2020) *E-cigarette and Vape Market Size, Share & Trends Analysis Report by Product, by Component, by Distribution Channel, and Segment Forecasts, 2020–2027*. San Francisco: GVR.

Hacker, M. (2009) Adverse Drug Reactions. In M. Hacker, W.S. Messer II and K.A. Bachmann (Eds.), *Pharmacology: Principles and Practice* (pp. 327–352). New York: Elsevier.

Hall, A. and Antonopoulos, G. (2019) The (Online) Supply of Illicit Lifestyle Medicines: A Criminological Study. In K. Van de Ven, K. Mulrooney and J. McVeigh (Eds.) *Human Enhancement Drugs* (pp. 173–187). London: Routledge.

Hall, S. (2012) *Theorizing Crime and Deviance*. London: Sage.

Hall, S. and Winlow, S. (2015) *Revitalizing Criminological Theory*. London: Routledge.

Hall, S., Winlow, S. and Ancrum, C. (2008) *Criminal Identities and Consumer Culture: Crime, Exclusion and the New Culture of Narcissism*. Cullompton: Willan.

Hagopian, J. (2015) *The Evils of Big Pharma Exposed*. Global Research. Available: www.globalresearch.ca/the-evils-of-big-pharma-exposed/5425382 (accessed 12 January 2020)

Hari, J. (2015) *Chasing the Scream: The First and Last Days of the War on Drugs*. London: Bloomsbury.

Hay, G., dos Santos, A.R. and Swithenbank, Z. (2018) *Estimates of the Prevalence of Opiate Use and/or Crack Cocaine Use, 2014/15: Sweep 11 Report*. Liverpool: Public Health Institute, Liverpool John Moores University.

Hillyard, P. and Tombs, S. (2007) From Crime to Social Harm. *Crime, Law and Social Change*, 48(1–2): 9–25.

Home Office. (2018) *Drug Misuse Declared: Findings from the 2017/18 Crime Survey England and Wales*. London: Home Office.

Hookway, N., Elmer, S. and Frandsen, M. (2017) Risk, Morality and Emotion: Social Media Responses to Pregnant Women Who Smoke. *Health, Risk & Society*, 19(5–6): 246–259.

Jameson, F. (1991) *Postmodernism, or, the Cultural Logic of Late Capitalism*. Durham: Duke University Press.

Jennings, K. (2018) British MPs Push E-Cigarettes as Health Benefit. *Politico*, 17th August.

Jorge, M. and Clemmer, F. (2019) High Prescription Costs Are Just One Way Big Pharma Drug Companies Rip Us Off. *USA Today*, 16th December.

Juergensmeyer, E., Nocella, A.J. and Seis, M. (2020) *Neoliberalism and Academic Repression: The Fall of Academic Freedom in the Era of Trump*. Boston: Brill.

Koenraadt, R. and van de Ven, K. (2018) The Internet and Lifestyle Drugs: An Analysis of Demographic Characteristics, Methods, and Motives of Online Purchasers of Illicit Lifestyle Drugs in the Netherlands. *Drugs: Education, Prevention and Policy* 25(4): 345–355.

Laxminarayan, R., Duse, A., Wattal, C., Zaidi, A., Wertheim, H., Sumpradit, N., Vlieghe, E., Hara, G., Gould, I., Goossens, H., Greko, C., So, A., Bigdeli, M., Tomson, G., Woodhouse, W., Ombaka, E., Peralta, A., Qamar, F., Mir, F., Kariuki, S., Bhutta, Z., Coates, A., Bergstrom, R., Wright, G., Brown, E. and Cars, O. (2013) Antibiotic Resistance–The Need for Global Solutions. *The Lancet: Infectious Diseases*, 13(12): 1057–1098.

McCambridge, J., Kypri, K., Miller, P., Hawkins, B. and Hastings, G. (2014) Be aware of Drinkaware. *Addiction*. 109(4): 519–524.

MacCoun, R.J. and Reuter, P. (2001) *Drug War Heresies*. Cambridge: Cambridge University Press.

Malnick, E. (2016) Individual NHS Doctors Receiving £100,000 per Year from Drugs Firms. *The Telegraph*, 30th June. Available at: www.telegraph.co.uk/news/2016/06/30/individual-nhs-doctors-receiving-100000-per-year-from-drugs-firm/ (accessed 25 November 2019).

Martin, J. (2014) *Drugs on the Dark Net How Cryptomarkets are Transforming the Global Trade in Illicit Drug*. Basingstoke: Palgrave.

Matthews-King, A (2018) 'Thirdhand smoke' in carpets and furniture could pose health risk, scientists warn. *The Independent,* 9th May.

Meller, A. and Ahmed, H. (2019) How Big Pharma Reaps Profits While Hurting Everyday Americans. *Centre for American Progress*, 30th August.

NHS Digital. (2018) *Prescriptions Dispensed in the Community–England*. Available at: https://digital.nhs.uk/data-and-information/areas-of-interest/prescribing (accessed 7 February 2019).

Nutt, D., King, L.A. and Phillips, L.D. (2010) Drug Harms in the UK: A Multicriteria Decision Analysis. *Lancet,* 376(9752): 1558–1565.

One Too Many. (2019) Fly Responsibly or You Could Pay the Price. Available at: www.onetoomany.co.uk/ (accessed 1 February 2019).

ONS (Office for National Statistics). (2018a) *Adult Smoking Habits in Great Britain: 2017. ONS Statistical Bulletin*. London: Office for National Statistics.

ONS (Office for National Statistics). (2018b) *Adult Drinking Habits in Great Britain: 2017. ONS Statistical Bulletin*. London: Office for National Statistics.

Paley, D. (2014) *Drug War Capitalism*. Edinburgh: AK Press.

Peacock, A., Leung, J., Larney, S., College, S., Hickman, M., Rehm, J., Giovino, G.A., West, R., Hall, W., Grifiths, P., Ali, R., Gowing, L., Marsden, J., Ferrari, A.J., Grebley, J., Farrell, M. and Degenhardt, L. (2018) Global Statistics on Alcohol, Tobacco and Illicit Drug Use: 2017 Status Report. *Addiction*, 113(10): 1905–1926.

PERI (Political Economy Research Institute). (2019) *Toxic 100 Air Polluters Index* (2019 Report, Based on 2017 Data). Massachusetts: PERI.

Pisinger, C. (2015) *A Systematic Review of Health Effects of Electronic Cigarettes*. Denmark: CPH.

Potter, G. and Chatwin, C. (2018) Not Particularly Special: Critiquing 'NPS' as a Category of Drugs. *Drugs: Education, Prevention and Policy* 25(4): 329–336.

Pryce, R., Buykx, P., Gray, L., Stone, T., Drummond, C. and Brennan, A. (2017) *Estimates of Alcohol Dependence in England based on APMS 2014, Including Estimates of Children Living in a Household with an Adult with Alcohol Dependence*. Available at: www.sheffield.ac.uk/polopoly_fs/1.693546!/file/Estimates_of_Alcohol_Dependence_in_England_based_on_APMS_2014.pdf (accessed 7 February 2018).

Pryce, S. (2012) *Fixing Drugs: The Politics of Drug Prohibition*. Basingstoke: Palgrave MacMillan.

Prynn, J. (2018) A Luxury Smoking Lounge and Cigar Shop Has Opened at the Ritz. *Evening Standard,* 24 May.

Rhodes, D. (2018) NHS Accused of Fuelling Rise in Opioid Addiction. *BBC,* 15 March. Available at: www.bbc.co.uk/news/uk-england-43304375 (accessed February 5 2019).

RM (Research *and Markets)*. (2019) *Global Sugar Market–Forecasts from 2019 to 2024*. Ireland: RM.

RM (Research *and Markets).* (2018) *Vapor Products Market–Global Outlook and Forecast 2018–2023.* Ireland: RM.

Romanowski, P. and Schueller, R. (2013) *It's OK to Have Lead in Your Lipstick.* Chicago: Brains Publishing.

Ruben, R. and Fort, R. (2012) The Impact of Fair Trade Certification for Coffee Farmers in Peru. *World Development*, 40(3): 570–582.

Russell, A. and Lieberman, C. (2019) Big Pharma Paid $151M to Doctors, Hospitals in 2017–18, but We Don't Know Who Got Paid or Why. *Global News*, 19th August. Available at: https://globalnews.ca/news/5769443/big-pharma-paying-doctors-hospitals/ (accessed November 26 2019).

Sander, G., Girelli, G. and Fernández, A. (2020) *The Death Penalty for Drug Offences 2019.* London: Harm Reduction International.

Seddon, T. (2016) Inventing Drugs: A Genealogy of a Regulatory Concept. *Journal of Law and Society,* 43(3): 393–415.

Singer, M. and Baer, H. (2009) *Killer Commodities: Public Health and the Corporate Production of Harm.* Lanham: AltaMira Press.

Springer, B. (1995) *The Usual Suspects.* Polygram.

Sander, G., Girelli, G. and Fernández, A. (2020) *The Death Penalty for Drug Offences: Global Overview 2019.* London: Harm Reduction International.

Smith, O. and Raymen, T. (2018) *Deviant Leisure: A Criminological Perspective. Theoretical Criminology,* 22(1): 63–82.

Spence, C. (2019) Judgement' versus 'Metrics' in Higher Education Management. *Higher Education*, 77: 761–775.

Stevens, A. (2018) 'Being Human' and the 'Moral Sidestep' in Drug Policy: Explaining Government Inaction on Opioid-Related Deaths in the UK. *Addictive Behaviors.* DOI: 10.1016/j.addbeh.2018.08.036

Stuntz, W.J. (1998) Race, Class and Drugs. *Columbia Law Review,* 98(7): 1795–1842.

Tahir, T. (2018) 'Deplorable' Passenger Forces Jet2 Flight to Ibiza to land in France Following 'Disgraceful' Behaviour with Blow-Up Doll in front of Children. *Daily Mail,* 11 June.

Taylor, S. (2016) Moving beyond the Other. *Tijdschrift over Cultuur and Criminaliteit* 6: 100–118.

Taylor, S. (2011) New Strategy, Usual Suspects: A Critique of Reducing Demand, Restricting Supply, Building Recovery. *Criminal Justice Matters,* 84(1): 24–26.

Taylor, S. (2008) Outside the Outsiders: Drugs, Drug Use and the Media. *Probation Journal* 55(4): 369–388.

Taylor, S., Ayres, T.C. and Jones, E. (2020) Enlightened Hedonism? Independent Drug Checking amongst a Group of Ecstasy Users. *International Journal of Drug Policy,* Online First. doi.org/10.1016/j.drugpo.2020.102869

Taylor, S., Buchanan, J. and Ayres, T.C. (2016) Prohibition, Privilege and the Drug Apartheid: The Failure of Drug Policy Reform to Address the Underlying Fallacies of Drug Prohibition. *Criminology and Criminal Justice* 16(4): 452–469.

TMA (Tobacco Manufacturers' Authority). (2017) *Tobacco Taxation in the UK.* London: TMA.

Tucker, J., Fischer, T., Upjohn, L., Mazzera, D. and Kumar, M. (2018) Unapproved Pharmaceutical Ingredients Included in Dietary Supplements Associated with US Food and Drug Administration Warnings. *JAMA Open Network* 1 (6): 1–11.

van der Bom, I., Paterson, L., Peplow, D. and Grainger, K. (2018) 'It's not the Fact They Claim Benefits but Their Useless, Lazy, Drug Taking Lifestyles We Despise': Analysing

Audience Responses to Benefits Street Using Live Tweets. *Discourse, Context and Media,* 21: 36–45.
Wakeman, S. (2014) 'No one wins. One Side Just Loses More Slowly': The Wire and Drug Policy. *Theoretical Criminology* 18(2): 224–240.
Withington, P. (2014) Introduction: Cultures of Intoxication. *Past and Present* 222(9): 9–33.
Winlow, S. (2017) What Lies Beneath? Some Notes on Ultra-Realism, and the Intellectual Foundations of the 'Deviant Leisure' Perspective. Available at: www.academia.edu/36915549/What_lies_beneath_Some_notes_on_ultra-realism_and_the_intellectual_foundations_of_the_deviant_leisure_perspective (accessed 22 November 2018).
Winlow, S. (2012) IS IT OK to Talk about Capitalism Now? Or, Why Criminology Must Take a Leap of Faith. In S. Winlow and R. Atkinson (Eds.), *New Directions in Crime and Deviancy* (pp. 21–39). Abingdon: Routledge.
Winlow, S. and Hall, S. (2016) Criminology and Consumerism. In P. Carlen (Ed.), *Criminologias Alternativas* (pp. 1–34). Buernos Aries: IEA.
Winlow, S. and Hall, S. (2012) What Is an 'Ethics Committee'? Academic Governance in an Epoch of Belief and Incredulity. *The British Journal of Criminology* 52(2): 400–416.
Žižek, S. (2008) *Violence.* New York: Picador.
Žižek, S. (2006) *The Parallax View.* Cambridge: MIT Press.
Žižek, S. (2005) *The Metastases of Enjoyment.* London: Verso.
Žižek, S. (2003) Homo Sacer as the Object of the Discourse of the University. *Cités,* 16, 25–41.
Žižek, S. (2002) *For They Know Not What They Do.* London: Verso.
Žižek, S. (1991) *Looking Awry.* Cambridge: MIT Press.
Žižek, S. (1989) *Sublime Object of Ideology.* London: Verso.

20

SIDE *AFFECTS* MAY VARY

Palliative capitalism, punitive capitalism and US consumer culture

Travis Linnemann and Corina Medley

In late August 2015, a hitherto unknown hedge fund manager and pharmaceuticals executive named Martin Shkreli emerged from the flow of the 24-hours news cycle, as the loathsome face of predatory capitalism. Soon known by the pejorative moniker "Pharma Bro", Shkreli earned his proverbial fifteen minutes of disrepute for helping engineer an overnight increase—from $13.50 to $750 per pill—in the cost of the AIDS drug, Daraprim. Defending the move, Shkreli insisted not only of its legality, but its shrewd rationality arguing, "if there was a company that was selling an Aston Martin at the price of a bicycle, and we buy that company and we ask to charge Toyota prices, I don't think that that should be a crime" (Ramsey, 2015). On this point Shkreli was technically correct, as the hike was not illegal, a fact punctuated by Daraprim's patent holder, Turing Pharmaceuticals' refusal to re-price the drug in the face of full-throated public outrage. Indeed, it seems that Shkreli's sin was not transgressing law, some obscure code of ethics or even ruthless profiteering, but rather, playing by the rules of his particular industry and simply being honest about it. Called among other things, a "morally bankrupt sociopath", "scumbag", "garbage monster" and "everything wrong with capitalism", one of the few insults not lobbed at Pharma Bro, was *drug dealer*, an epithet apparently reserved for those who profit from selling other kinds of drugs, in other kinds of markets.

For more than a century, the so-called drug dealers have haunted the American imagination, figuring almost Jungian archetypes of xenophobic anxiety and racial animus. From surplus Chinese laborers who were targets of the nation's first drug laws, Mexican immigrants blamed for "reefer madness", the so-called "Negro Cocaine Fiends" of the Jim Crow South, Colombian traffickers, Bloods and Crips, "white trash meth cooks", to the ambiguous threats of "drugs and gangs" used by Donald Trump to declare a national emergency and "build the wall", drugs and drug dealers have offered a formidable, malleable, perhaps universal

DOI: 10.4324/9781351010245-23

adversary with which to stir populist angst and mobilize a far-reaching politics of security (Neocleous, 2016).[1] While this long parade of racist caricatures might reveal and diagnose distinct currents of cultural sentiment, in the century-long history of the US drug war, characters like Shkreli have rarely, if ever, risen to the level of pop-cultural folk devil.[2] Characterizing immutable concerns for "street" rather than "suite" crimes, pharmaceutical companies and their representatives have mostly escaped the scrutiny of criminalization and the dishonor of the drug dealer label by aggressively lobbying lawmakers and marketing their products, no matter how closely they resemble "street drugs", under the sheltering rationality of science (Greene and Herzberg, 2010). Today, critical observers watch this process unfold in real time, as off-the-books operators are pushed out of now legal cannabis markets by corporate interests and their celebrity partners (Martha Stewart, Snoop Dog, Rob Gronkowski, etc.) (Mull, 2019). With this obvious, however troublesome observation in mind, we begin by approaching the appearance and disappearance of drugs and drug dealers from the US political economic landscape and socio-political imaginary through the prism of Mark Fisher's (2009) capitalist realism.

Bubbling to the surface

Famously captured by Margret Thatcher's smug insistence "there is no alternative" capitalist realism signals the demise of the collective ability to organize or even imagine a world outside capitalism's confines (Fisher, 2009:2). This stifling atmosphere of resignation not only regulates work, education and leisure, but sets the parameters of cultural production, acting as an invisible barrier constraining thought and action (Fisher, 2009:16). Bolstering this barrier is a business ontology which convinces subjects to imagine themselves as just that, solitary agents wholly responsible for success or failure within their given market arenas. Under such a system, writes Annie McClanahan, a whole range human endeavors such as education cease to be a means to "know thyself" and a social good worthy of collective commitment and instead become a crude instrument of self-investment, deployed to maximize and advertise "human capital" (McClanahan, 2019:112). The self-interest and self-blame demanded by such a system are a particularly effective strategy of class rule. Individuated, responsibilitized subjects will, as such, blame themselves for perceived failures, rather than seeking to challenge social structures, which they have been convinced do not actually exist. In the aggregate then, capitalist realism entails a sort of affective pacification, described by Fisher as collective depression, in which the many have abandoned solidarity and the hope of collective action to the grim belief that their circumstances can and in fact will get worse (Fisher, 2018:749, see also Fleming, 2019).[3]

By cultivating ruthless self-interest alongside self-blame, capitalist realism not only constrains the political imagination, but also drives a process that permits and disowns its own morbid symptoms. This is what Fisher means when he insists that capitalist realism "has nothing to do with the Real. On the contrary, the Real is what realism has continually to suppress" (Fisher 2018: 433). In *The Plague of Fantasies*, Slavoj Žižek relatedly describes how the subject's inner fantasy life is rarely contained at "unfathomable depths" and invariably bubbles to the surface, exposing its secret contradictions and conflicts (Žižek, 1997:4). This becomes evident when a previously respected, or at least benign person acts out violently. Of course, friends and associates will insist that "he seemed to be such a nice guy", but if we look closely warning signs are also typically there. Žižek's point is that for the subject, internal contradictions and antagonisms materialize externally. At the level of ideology, the case of Shkreli, Turing Pharmaceuticals and Daraprim can be read in precisely this way. The outrage at Shkreli's ruthless profiteering diagnoses the antagonisms which the overriding ideology of capitalist realism, to continue, must disavow. Rather than placing his actions in context and then using them to launch a sustained attack on price rigging, for-profit health care or a critique of the broader social system which feeds upon its own symptoms, ambiguity and disinterested irony instead ruled the day, individuating Shkreli's behaviors, transforming him into "Pharma Bro", a man with an eminently "punchable face".[4] Meanwhile, his adept operation within the confines of neoliberal capitalism was in fact revered by keepers of that order, evidenced by the universities, including Harvard, which invited him to campus to speak.

Under the tread of capitalist realism, subjects not only internalize the system's contradictions, but embody and reproduce them as well. There is, as Fisher put it, "an isomorphic relationship between the social and individual disorders of capitalism" (Fisher, 2009:436). Rather than being the only system that works, the "mental health plague" of many capitalist societies "*suggests that it is inherently dysfunctional, and that the cost of it appearing to work is very high* (emphasis ours) (Fisher, 2009:19). Mimicking the volatility and fragility of the market, conditions such as bipolar disorder can be read as symptoms of the inner workings of capitalism—its pathological contradictions and conditions bubbling to the surface of social life. He writes,

> With its ceaseless boom and bust cycles, capitalism is itself fundamentally and irreducibly bi-polar, periodically lurching between hyped-up mania (the irrational exuberance of 'bubble thinking') and depressive come-down. (The term 'economic depression' is not accident, of course). *To a degree unprecedented in any other social system, capitalism both feeds on and reproduces the moods of the populations. Without delirium and confidence, capital could not function* (our emphasis).
>
> *Fisher 2009: 35*

Recognizing and attempting to make sense of the isomorphic relationship between the social and individual disorders of what he similarly calls affective capitalism, in his book *Life in Pain*, John Fitzgerald (2020) drawing on Brian Massumi's ontopower, describes processes where capital creates or enables the conditions necessary for the expansion of certain markets. He writes, "Ontopower creates the conditions for the successful deployment of biopower onto segments of the population" effectively "giving life" to productive parts of the population, while simultaneously finding ways to weed out those populations deemed unproductive (Fitzgerald, 2020:55). In his account of the contradictory policy responses to illicit drug users, Jesse Proudfoot makes a similar observation, seeing both punitive and supportive programs emerging from the same libidinal economy. He suggests that in a state of ambiguity the related but contradictory desires to care for and punish drug users—as with the tensions between love and hate—are worked out in a dialectical relationship that produces a number of results, including social policy (Proudfoot, 2019:220-1). Both supportive "harm reduction" efforts such as methadone maintenance treatment for opioids users and draconian practices which foreground police and prisons are therefore driven by the twin desires for and to control illicit enjoyment.

Following these insights, in what follows, we map two distinct, but overlapping dimensions that both enlist and reproduce the ideology of capitalist realism by depoliticizing and profiting from its ailments, while also finding new ways to enlist the fearsome specter of the drug dealer and drugs themselves in pacification projects underpinning the broader class war. In the first instance, we describe what we call *palliative capitalism*, a set of social relations in which legal pharmaceutical drugs and their producers, marketers and distributors profit from treating or attempting to treat the conditions that capitalism creates. As with bi-polar disorder, consider the apparent "epidemic" of attention deficit hyperactivity disorder (ADHD) and its variants. At a time when social media feeds, streaming video, text messaging and the like deliver a self-curated deluge of frenetic stimulation and when email, video conferencing and virtual offices tether us perpetually to work and school, how can we not reject the individuating notion that this "disease" results solely from biology? If, as Fisher observes, ADHD is a pathology, "it is a pathology of late capitalism—a consequence of being wired into the entertainment-control circuits of hypermediated consumer culture" (Fisher 2009: 25). Just as the data generated by our online activities and lives have been commodified and sold back to us (Wark, 2019), drugs meant to aid our ability to succeed as individuals in our increasingly bureaucratized and managed world—to provide "impulse control", to help us "stay on task" and concentrate on tedium—are a boon for capital. Already hugely profitable, in 2006 ADHD medications brought in some $4.7 billion dollars for their manufacturers, a number which, by 2015, had nearly tripled to $12.7 and is now expected to top 17 billion in 2020 (Keshavan, 2016).[5] It cannot be understated that these made-legal pharmaceutical drugs are the primary excepted method to help the individual cope with and adapt to an invariably corrosive system. On a competitive treadmill, where falling behind means social and economic death, the mantra *there is no alternative* normalizes a system of over-prescription and overreliance on pharmaceutical products. As such, we might best understand the pharmaceutical industry not only as actual drug-dealers, but the pushers and peddlers of capitalist realism itself.

Moving on from corporate drug dealers who peddle remedies to capitalism's ills, in the chapter's latter half we return to the common understanding of drugs, drugs users and drug dealers as social harms. Mapping the relations of what we call *punitive capitalism*, we identify a politics and their adjoining innovations and practices that seek not to ameliorate, but to control and punish. Under conditions of punitive capitalism, the illicit drug market provides potent enemy figures for the state and its police to align against. Meanwhile, made-legal drug markets administered by the Shkrelies of the world dissolve into a background of conventionality and their products find new uses in the pacification (Hatch, 2019) and in some instances, extermination of superfluous and threatening populations (Smith, 2018).

Here the overriding, but disavowed assumption is that drug control efforts are driven not by the desire for public safety. As Suzanna Reiss succinctly puts it, drugs and by extension drug dealers have never been targets, but rather *tools* deployed for and by political power (Reiss, 2014:1). Rather than an arena of crime control, the drug war is understood as a low-intensity conflict which brings pacification—elimination of superfluous populations, fabrication of individual and market relations—into the domestic frame through the articulation of an "emergency situation" a "clear and present danger" which threatens to undo social order itself (Neocleous, 2011:202). As Dawn Paley (2014) has shown, the specter of warring cartels and potentials for "narcoterrorists" to sneak or "spill" across the southern US board, helped win public support and funding for drug war initiatives that were actually designed to clear the way for Western business interests in Colombia, Mexico and other states across the Global South. Even more acutely, within the US interior, pharmaceutical drugs are increasingly used to manage prisoners and court-ordered "patients"—many of whom, ironically, ran afoul with the law for drug violations—in the broad system of confinement that Anthony Ryan Hatch calls *captive America* (Hatch, 2019). The plan to govern and control the swelling population of those living as captives, he speculates, "is to move them from their institutional cells to new locations *inside their own brain cells*, into mental prisons that perform the same work as the old physical barracks or hospital rooms" via proliferating psychopharmaceutical technologies of pacification (emphasis original, Hatch, 2019:9). For Hatch and for us, the US "correctional" population is quite plainly a captive market, made for and delivered by the state to its corporate partners.

While we document a grim and bloodied history, the tortured affects and actors upon which capital feeds also offer opportunity to build a radical politics with which to reveal and challenge capitalist realism. Toward this aim, we read both the palliative care available under capitalist realism and the system built to pacify, punish and exterminate its lumpen detritus as symptoms of a broader ideology which insists that your problems are your own and if you fail to succeed and fall between the cracks, only you are to blame.

Ask your doctor if palliative capitalism is right for you

Each year, heart disease, cancer, stroke, diabetes and Alzheimer's disease are among the leading causes of death in the US, claiming over 1.5 million lives annually.[6] While rates of deaths from these diseases have remained relatively stable over the last decade, during the same period deaths by suicide, alcoholism and drug overdose have increased dramatically. According to the US Centers for Disease Control, suicide is now the second leading cause of death among the young (aged 15–34 years),[7] while the 70,980 lives lost to drug overdose in 2019 outpaced both murder and automobile accidents combined.[8] Described by some as "diseases or deaths of despair", researchers have linked the rising morbidity in the US to concurrent declines in measures of psychosocial well-being (Case and Deaton, 2015; Columbia University Mailman School of Public Health, 2018). As these data suggest, there seems to be a verifiable link, observed by Fisher (2009) and others (see, for instance, James, 2007) between rising rates of mental illness and the conditions of life under the forms of neoliberal capitalism practiced in US, UK and Australia (i.e. increased bureaucratic surveillance and punitive discipline, lack of affordable housing and health care, volatile economy and labor market). Underlying or perhaps driving collective depression, Fisher locates what he calls *reflexive impotence,* a recursive affect emerging from the recognition that things are bad and exacerbated by the perceived inability to do anything about it (Fisher 2009: 21). The lack of individual and collective agency marked by collective depression and reflexive impotence reinforces the widely held understanding of mental health problems as wholly individual and pathological conditions, best managed anesthetically and importantly, not cured by pharmaceutical drugs (Buck-Morss, 1992; de Sutter, 2018). Under such a system, the best one can hope for is to tolerate and not succumb—by way of alcoholism, drug overdose or suicide—to their life circumstances. Sadly, as we know, increasing numbers of people do in fact succumb to the most pernicious effects and *affects* of neoliberal capitalist.

Though the picture is incomplete, recent estimates indicate that nearly 17% of the adult US population is taking at least one psychotropic drug (Moore and Mattison, 2017). Of course, this measure leaves us wanting, as it only captures the lucky, yet increasingly few who have access to adequate health care. Nevertheless, if there is one thing that this statistic reveals about the inner psychic life of the contemporary US, it is that the problems *of* capitalism are not problems *for* capitalism. Indeed, what could be more in keeping with the noxious conditions of capitalist realism than to profit from managing—*actively not-eliminating*—the conditions it creates? Among the starkest examples of this toxic symbiosis are pharmaceutical products engineered, prescribed and distributed to help users cope with the dysfunctions built into the system.

Take, for instance, the psychotropic drug Abilify (aripiprazole) which has, in recent years, been one of the most often prescribed, hence profitable drugs of the US pharmaceutical market, generating approximately $7 billion dollars in sales in 2013 alone.[9] An antipsychotic designed to treat schizophrenia and bipolar disorder, the drug became a boon for its manufacturers Bristol-Myers Squibb, when physicians began to prescribe it off-label for depression and a host of other ailments like anxiety and insomnia.[10] Already profitable on its own, Abilify is useful for our argument, as it was rebranded as a panacea for those already suffering from depression and for those whose existing medications were not working. Abilify therefore became one of the most profitable drugs in the US by capitalizing on an established market, with the promise of making ineffective medications more effective. In other words, while it was already an economically viable, though not necessarily efficient treatment, under the guise of palliative capitalism Abilify generated even more money for its patent holders and investors, by failing just slightly better.[11] Like so many other medications, Abilify's manufacturers also warn that it may cause a number of adverse reactions, including the compulsion to "gamble, binge eat, shop, and have sex".[12] Not only are these side effects the consummate hedonic behaviors of capitalist realism, they of course might also necessitate further psycho-pharmaceutical care. What Abilify makes clear then is that the goal of palliative care under capitalist realism is to manage—*actively not cure* a particular difficulty. And because conditions such as depression and bipolar disorder, which Abilify is intended to treat, are always individualized and pathologized, their root causes in social relations and the broader social order remain unacknowledged and unremedied. Always a half-measure, the fix is meant for the subject not the system.

Even more benign pharmaceutical drugs such as those intended to treat high-cholesterol—another widely prescribed and profitable category of medications—result directly from late-capitalist consumption practices.[13] In a society in which medical and food systems are governed by powerful corporations, alternatives to pharmaceutical care, such as adjusting one's diet and reducing consumption of animal products, are somehow deemed irrational. In other words, rather than making a substantive change that might benefit individuals, animals, the environment and society as a whole, the insidious ethic of palliative capitalism transforms suffering into profit, seeking not to ameliorate individual conditions, but to manage them indefinitely.

While drugs such as these diagnose many of the contradictions of palliative care under capitalist realism, we, of course, find an even more potent distillation, the present "opioid crisis".[14] The recent rise in overdose deaths from opioids, while unprecedented, is in no way an accident of demographics or product of some collective lapse in moral judgment. As Emily Witt succinctly put it, the causes of the opioid crisis are manifold:

> They include, but are not limited to: the country's dysfunctional privatised healthcare system, which makes it possible for addicts to accumulate doctors willing to prescribe painkillers in a way they can't in the UK; a corrupt regulatory agency beholden to the industry it was tasked with regulating; a punitive legal paradigm that criminalises drug users instead of helping

> them; an abstinence-only approach to treating drug addiction that impedes evidence-based medication-assisted treatment; corporate greed; a political class that takes marching orders from the lobbyists of said corporations; entrenched poverty, joblessness and hopelessness; and a general epistemological failure when it comes to ideas about what 'drugs' are, which psychoactive chemicals are safe and which are dangerous, *and what a drug dealer is supposed to look like* (emphasis ours).
>
> *Witt, 2019*

As Witt adeptly notes and as the US public is still learning, the manufacturers and *dealers* of OxyContin (Oxycodone), Purdue Pharma and the Sackler family, its key stakeholders, lie at the center of a decade-long marketing and sales strategy which has made the deaths of hundreds of thousands of people a grim reality. Now in what researchers call its third wave, the opioid crisis began with institutionalization of the OxyContin market, before regulation, scarcity and an uptick in global production broadened the demand for heroin and then later fentanyl.[15] As one of the many lawsuits filed against Purdue and the Sacklers in recent years alleges plainly, "Eight people in a single family made the choices that caused much of the opioid epidemic (Zezima and Bernstein, 2019)".

Prior to Purdue's monumental intervention into the opioids market, it was much more difficult for patients to access opioids legally. Historian Keith Wailoo (2014), for instance, documents how in the 1970s and 1980s the US government erected significant roadblocks making it difficult for those on disability to receive medical treatment for pain. In keeping with the mantra of the rising neoliberal order, the logic seemingly was that the underserving poor were either exaggerating their needs, or simply not a good use of scarce resources (Fitzgerald, 2020). This all changed with a multifaceted campaign led primarily by Purdue, to normalize the use of high quantities of opioids to manage pain. The first step of the campaign was to downplay the addictive potentials of opioids and to attack and discredit the notion that the drugs themselves actually gave users pleasure. The argument that the drugs were not addictive was fortified by a single one-hundred-word commentary published in the *New England Journal of Medicine* in 1980 (Porter and Jick, 1980). Unscientific and anecdotal, the now notorious letter was passed off as peer-reviewed science and used in promotional materials and by drug reps to calm doctors anxious about over-prescribing opioids (Van Zee, 2009). Decoupling opioids from pleasure or as Proudfoot (2019) specifies "illicit enjoyment", the wellspring of ameliorative and punitive social responses to drug users was also accomplished with the aid of the academic community. Citing studies documenting a condition called "pseudoaddiction", Purdue argued that users' symptoms negated any pleasure they might derive from the drug. As Fitzgerald explains, "the argument was that chronic pain (cancer) patients weren't really addicted because the pain negated any euphoria from the drug. Without euphoria, there was no pleasure, and as such, there could be no real addiction" (Fitzgerald, 2020:48).

At a party celebrating the launch of OxyContin in 1996, Dr. Richard Sackler predicted the drug would "be followed by a blizzard of prescriptions that will bury the competition" (Armstrong, 2019). That year, the American Pain Association (which has now declared bankruptcy in anticipation of rulings against the organization for its role in the opioids crisis) in conjunction with Purdue endorsed a plan to recognize pain as the fifth vital sign. Four years and significant political work later, the campaign succeeded, with pain codified as the fifth vital sign in a law passed by the Clinton administration—blowing the made-legal market for opioids wide open (Coleman, 2019).

While accurate, Sackler's blizzard was a localized forecast, targeting regions of the US most beset by collective depression and reflexive impotence. As Beth Macy (2018) describes in her book *Dopesick,* the rural US, particularly New England and central Appalachia "already full of shuttered factories, Dollar General stores, along with burgeoning disability claims", was a natural proving ground for Purdue's wares (Macy, 2018:32). With the help of data-mining firms, Purdue targeted doctors in the Northeast who served oft-injured laborers in the logging and fishing industries and Appalachian doctors who likewise cared for miners. Backed by Washington lobbyists who among other things succeeded in gutting of Food and Drug Administration (FDA) restrictions on television advertising of narcotic drugs, the marketing program which included direct "education" of prescribing doctors and "front groups" to advocate for opioid-based pain management helped make OxyContin the top selling opioid worldwide, reaping an estimated 35 billion dollars for Purdue since its introduction (Fitzgerald, 2020). But as the money and bodies piled up, so did scrutiny.

No less than five years after forecasting an OxyContin blizzard, Sackler had pivoted, devising another plan to protect his company and family's interests as questions concerning Purdue's role in the opioid crisis began to mount. "We have to hammer on the abusers in every way possible", he wrote in an email, "They are the culprits and the problem. They are reckless criminals (Armstrong, 2019)". Again, a battalion of think tanks, public relations firms, media consultants and expert spokespersons stood at the ready to defend the family and their profits. For instance, Dezenhall Resources, the same public relations firm that defended Exxon Mobile and the convicted Enron fraudster Jeffrey Skilling, cultivated an "anti-story" which wrote off overdose victims as irresponsible junkies. Sally Satel, an Ivy League psychiatrist turned corporate shill, was out front early, writing essays, giving (TEDx) talks and appearing in the news media to fight negative publicity. Satel who is also a "resident scholar" at the right-wing American Enterprise Institute—to which Purdue had donated heavily—helped advance the narrative that misguided "opiophobia" was keeping legitimate "pain patients" from necessary care. With a sort of perverse "guns don't kill people, people kill people" logic, Satel absolved Purdue, insisting "the very people who seek drugs are often the ones least psychologically equipped to handle them. This is a tragic reality of addiction, but it is not fundamentally the fault of the drug" (Satel, 2011). That the burgeoning overdose crisis was laid at the feet of the "least psychologically equipped" (i.e. morally defective, emotionally weak), rather than the manufacturers, dealers, politicians and the broader social structures that had authorized it, is very much in keeping with palliative care under capitalist realism. Again, the suggestion is that your problems are your own, so just go ahead and take the drugs, but be sure to follow the instructions.

With the help of friendly lawmakers who facilitated doctor shopping and pill mills, the sophisticated "anti-story" did for a time allow Purdue to continue to reap their ill-gotten gains (Chappell, 2017). The windfall, however, seems to have come to an end. In 2007, Purdue Pharma paid 635 million, at the time the largest settlement in US history, to 26 US states for misleading doctors and patients and failing to properly administer and regulate OxyContin (Van Zee, 2009) and in late 2019, it filed for bankruptcy protection in US federal court (Spector, 2019). While Purdue may ultimately go under, this does not mean that any of its personnel or the Sacklers will suffer criminal penalties.

Like other family dynasties, the drug trade, legal or otherwise, made the Sacklers one of the wealthiest families in the world (Keefe, 2017). As James Bradley (2009) suggests in his book *The Imperial Cruise*, several elite US families including the Cabots, Lowells and Kirklands made their fortune from the opium trade, while it is also long rumored that Joseph Kennedy made his family's fortune bootlegging during prohibition (Maier, 2014). Like Cabot, Lowell, Kirkland and Kennedy the name Sackler appears on buildings throughout the US, a morbid symptom—not unlike a rash or boil—of the material externality of palliative capitalism and the grim consequences of capitalist realism. More critically then, the museums, galleries, libraries and other spaces meant to be monuments to the beneficence of great men reveal and remind of the treachery of a system that allows some to profit greatly from the despair and misery of others. As the former chair of the psychiatry program at the Duke University School of Medicine described,

> I don't know how many rooms in different parts of the world I've given talks in that were named after the Sacklers ... Their name has been pushed forward as the epitome of good works and of the fruits of the capitalist system. But, when it comes down to it, they've earned this fortune at the expense of millions of people who are addicted. It's shocking how they have gotten away with it.
>
> *Keefe, 2017*

While the Sacklers and their ilk no doubt intend for their charitable donations to win them good will (and sizeable tax deductions) from an uncritical public while pushing their predatory relations deep inside neoliberalism's interior, there are some who recognize them for what they are, demonic sigils of the most ruthless sort of accumulation. Indeed, activist groups PAIN Sackler, ACTUP and others exist solely to reveal in Max Haiven's words, the vanity of the super-rich, "who use their violently extracted wealth to transmute the world's cultural reassures into branded monuments to the destruction of world civilisation in the name of profit" (Haiven, 2019:664).

To pacify, punish and eliminate

While palliative capitalism feeds on the system's dysfunctions, punitive capitalism is a set of political and economic relations mobilized to profit from the pacification, punishment and at times disposal of capitalism's misfits and cast-offs. In the broadest sense, punitive capitalism operates through a drug war, which has long been used by the US to extend police power beyond its sovereign boundaries and provide ideological cover for its geopolitical goals. From controlling commodities and markets prior to, during and after World War II (Frydl, 2013; Reiss, 2014) to disguising counterinsurgency war as "drug control" (Kuzmarov, 2008) the US drug war has always been, first and foremost, a project of accumulation. As Horace Bartilow (2019) writes, drug control is a "corporatist regime predicated on protecting free market capitalism and for leveraging corporate penetration into foreign markets (Bartilow, 2019:2)". Calling the drug war a "long term fix for capitalisms woes" Paley has shown how US aid to Colombia in the late 1990s and Mexico in the mid-2000s opened and secured markets for Western business interests by displacing and dispossessing indigenous communities and small-scale agricultural producers and by locating and eliminating grassroots resistance (Paley, 2014). Both aid plans were followed by massive increases in lethal violence, with some 200,000 deaths in Mexico since 2006, as counterinsurgency war unfolded (Paley, 2014). Particularly when combined with counter-terror work under the sign of "narcoterror" the drug war brings the low-intensity conflict of counterinsurgency to the US interior, providing an ideological catch-all for violent and invasive policing regimes.

Beginning with undercover by and bust programs, no-knock raids and asset forfeiture and ending with vast disciplinary archipelago of community-based "treatments", drug courts, jails and prisons the US drug war is shot through with opportunities for accumulation (Tiger, 2013; Kaye, 2019). Not unlike Hatch's critique of *captive America*, a growing body of ethnographers show how profits made from the battle against drug addiction sustain a system that traps subjects in a circuit of faltering and punitive treatments (McKim, 2017; Flores and Barahona-López, 2019). In her study of opioid-dependent homeless women in Boston, Kimberly Sue (2019) documents the capital generated from those unfortunate souls suspended in liminal cycles between prison, jail, residential treatment and the streets. Not lost on those caught up in drug war's gears, Serenity, a homeless opioid user, explains how people like her are "money in the pocket" of the corrections industry.

> Because you're job security for them. That's money in their pocket. They really don't give two shits, especially for someone like me who is a frequent flyer. They just give up. Oh well. She's coming back; she's not going to go

> [to a program] … I'm a lost cause … the prisons industries keep making more and more money off people like me, because that's what we do.
>
> *Sue, 2019:19*

Like palliative care under capitalist realism, the pharmaceutical "technocorrections" industry, as Hatch (2019) calls it, clearly profits from managing not curing its ailments. Setting it apart from palliative care under capitalist realism are drug war practices designed not only to pacify but also to vindictively punish and eliminate the visible symptoms of its internal contradictions—drug users and dealers.

Like his articulated policies and general human sensibilities, Donald Trump's approach to drugs and drug dealers unsurprisingly provides a stark distillation of capitalist realism's most punitive dimensions. Openly dismissing the viability of harm reduction, the resilient but facile politics of "just say no" and "really big, really great advertising" (fear appeals) aimed at the young have charted the course of Trump's drug policy. While it opened new funding sources, neither his theatrical declaration of the opioids crisis as a national emergency nor the symbolic donation of a portion of his Presidential salary has had any real impact on opioid consumption or resulting deaths. Conversely, Trump's tax policies have made it more difficult for drug users to access treatment through Medicaid programs. All the while, the same companies that profited greatly from the sale of opioids continue to profit from treating its resulting symptoms.[16] As with the manipulation of the Daraprim market, increased demand, engineered shortages and price hikes have driven the aggregate sales of the anti-overdose drug Naloxone from 20 million in 2011 to 280 million in 2016, with profits now expected to exceed 900 million by 2026 (Denvir, 2017; Watson, 2019).

Still, at a time when corporate drug dealers are raking in massive profits both from supplying the opioid market and from providing products to deal with its disastrous effects, there are some who choose to punish by withholding lifesaving treatments. Dan Picard, an administrator of a small Ohio community, made national news when he proposed a grotesque "three strikes" policy to address the financial strain of responding to drug overdoses. For those served by city emergency services, Picard suggested that local courts order first-time patients to complete community service work equal to the costs of their care. On a second case, Picard suggested the amounts be doubled and on a third he suggested that the city withhold medical services imposing a *de facto* death sentence (Szalavitz, 2017).[17] Defending the cruel proposal, Picard reaffirmed the ruthless logic of capitalist realism "you are on your own" and of punitive capitalism, seeking to send the "message to the world that you don't want to come to Middletown to overdose because someone might not come with Narcan and save your life. We need to put a fear about overdosing in Middletown" (Richter, 2017). While on the one hand seemingly endorsing a form of brutal deterrence, on the other hand, Picard admits his was principally a monetary concern. "It's not a proposal to solve the drug problem", he explained, the proposal "is in regard to the financial survivability of our city. If we're spending $2 million this year and $4 million next year and $6 million after that, we're in trouble. We're going to have to start laying off. We're going to have to raise taxes (Wootson, 2017)". Offering his support to Picard, the local Sheriff vowed that those in his employ would neither carry nor administer Naloxone, quipping that any deaths were not his fault, but the fault of users "when they stick that needle in their arm (Wootson, 2017)". As we have written elsewhere, the ruthless neglect that would allow people to die of an easily treatable condition requires an understanding of the problem that not only places blame squarely at the feet of the dead, but marks them for death (Linnemann and Medley, 2019).

Even more in keeping with the vindictive politics of targeting drug users for lethal neglect, anonymous administration insiders describe how Trump routinely compares drug dealers to serial killers and openly longs for their executions. "He often jokes about killing drug dealers" one informant alleged, "He'll say, 'You know the Chinese and Filipinos don't have a drug problem. *They just kill them* (Swan, 2018)". While human rights groups and his own State Department have denounced the wholesale murder authorized by Rodrigo Duterte's drug war, Trump has no such reservations. In a phone call to Duterte just after he took office, Trump gushed,

> I just wanted to congratulate you because I am hearing of the unbelievable job on the drug problem … Many countries have the problem, we have a problem, but what a great job you are doing and I just wanted to call and tell you that.
>
> *Sanger and Haberman, 2017*

In a speech a short time later, Trump boldly declared "We can have all the blue-ribbon committees we want, but if we don't get tough on drug dealers we're wasting our time. And that toughness includes the death penalty" (Trump, 2018). The next day in fact, Trump's then Attorney General, Jeff Sessions, transformed rhetoric to practice, issuing a memo strongly encouraging federal prosecutors to seek the death penalty in drug trafficking cases. Invoking the specter of "drug traffickers, transnational criminal organizations and violent street gangs" Sessions urged prosecutors to "consider every lawful tool at their disposal" including the "pursuit of capital punishment". Citing a handful of never-before-used statutes passed by Congress during the early 1990s "crack panic",[18] Sessions made the case for the death penalty to "aid in our continuing fight against drug trafficking and the destruction it causes in our nation" (Sessions, 2018). Of course, the Sacklers and the myriad others at Purdue, McKesson, Cardinal Health, Amerisource Bergen and so on would never be targets of Trump and Session's campaign.[19] Not only does this very public move continue the century-long drug war campaign against the racialized poor, it hides the misdeeds of those who operate in the made-legal market in plain sight.

Bringing the vile ethics of punitive capitalism to their logical conclusion, Fentanyl Citrate, the drug that has contributed to thousands of overdose deaths in the third wave of the opioids crisis, has recently been used in conjunction with other pharmaceutical drugs to administer the death penalty in at least one US state. In August 2018, the State of Nebraska executed a 60-year-old double murderer using a combination of Fentanyl Citrate, the widely prescribed sedative Diazepam (Valium), the muscle relaxer Cisatracurium (Nimbex) and Potassium Chloride.[20] With the death of this particular prisoner and those to follow, we find an odd cocktail of pharmaceutical drugs characterizing a mix of lethal ideologies under capitalist realism. On one end of the market built to profit from neoliberal capitalism's failures is a system that offers only an ineffectual pharmaceutical band aid, while on the other end is the fearsome retribution of the state, its police, prisons and execution chambers. To us, it is clear, capitalist realism offers neither hope for the vulnerable nor mercy for the condemned.

Good for something

Fisher, who struggled his whole life with and eventually succumbed to depression, knew all too well that the corrosive affects that haunted his mind were social in origin. The problem to which he returned again and again was how to translate the academic understanding of collective depression and reflexive impotence into a political program for social change. Getting at this question, Fisher concludes his essay *Good for Nothing,* rather hopefully, writing,

> The rebuilding of class consciousness is a formidable task indeed, one that cannot be achieved by calling upon ready-made solutions–but, in spite of what our collective depression tells us, it can be done. Inventing new forms of political involvement, reviving institutions that have become decadent, converting privatised disaffection into politicised anger: all of this can happen, and when it does, who knows what is possible?
>
> *Fisher, 2018:749*

"Who knows?", *indeed*. Had he lived to see the still unfolding developments of 2020, Fisher would no doubt have been horrified by governmental incompetence and mounting death, but we suspect, heartened by movements rising against the violence of capital and police, those who enforce the categories legal and illegal and make real the distinctions between Shkreli, Sackler and the alterity of "drug dealers". Displacing, for now, the sneering inner voice of institutionalized self-doubt and self-interest, are multitudes—from Black Lives Matter marches in Tokyo, to "dads with leaf blowers" in Portland—standing up for one another and, importantly, between the vulnerable and police, "*the violence of the commodity made flesh* (Clover, 2016:126)". While far from perfect and far from finished, the burgeoning movement against state violence signals the anger and just maybe the repoliticization of those backed into a corner by a system that has thus far offered no alternative.

Notes

1 Dugan Meyer (2020) calls the various forms taken by the gang member or in our case the drug dealer, the "whatever object" of security politics.
2 Here we follow Kathleen Frydl (2013) and Suzzanne Reiss (2014) who show how the drug war as a method of economic warfare precedes Nixon's declaration by decades.
3 Fisher speculates that Post-Fordism and neoliberalism have only exacerbated these conditions making them more visible, with "invisible plague" of psychiatric and affective disorders that has spread, silently and stealthily, since around 1750 (i.e. the very onset of industrial capitalism) (Fisher 2009: 35).
4 According to several commentators, hatred of Shkreli may also reflect the "punchability" of his face. https://thinkprogress.org/we-asked-scientists-just-how-punchable-is-martin-shkrelis-face-b460e544d3ee/
5 "To be bored simply means to be removed from the communicative sensation-stimulus matrix of texting, YouTube and fast food; to be denied, for a moment, the constant flow of sugary gratification on demand (Fisher 2009: 24)." "The consequence of being hooked into the entertainment matrix is twitchy, agitated interpassivity, an inability to concentrate or focus (Fisher 2009: 24)."
6 www.cdc.gov/nchs/fastats/leading-causes-of-death.htm
7 www.washingtonpost.com/news/to-your-health/wp/2018/06/07/u-s-suicide-rates-rise-sharply-across-the-country-new-report-shows/?utm_term=.68450aa3ac7d.
8 www.drugabuse.gov/related-topics/trends-statistics/overdose-death-rates
9 See sales data here: www.drugs.com/stats/abilify
10 Bristol-Myers was subsequently fined for its off-label marketing campaign: See: www.biopharmadive.com/news/bristol-myers-hit-with-marketing-fine-for-abilify/432130/
11 As one of the Top 10 advertised drugs we cannot discount the influence of advertising and sales in Abilify's rise. Physicians are undoubtedly integral to the process of becoming a top-selling drug. Without doctors willing to prescribe the drug, whether that is for its original purposes or for the range of non-psychotic disorders it eventually encompassed, the drug would not be successful. They are, in effect, the dealers for the drug companies. And the advertisers are the pushers.
12 www.fda.gov/Drugs/DrugSafety/ucm498662.htm. FDA Drug Safety Communication: FDA warns about new impulse-control problems associated with mental health drug aripiprazole (Abilify, Abilify Maintena, Aristada) (look up format for government reports/warnings; pdf available online) U.S. Food and Drug Administration. 05-03-2016
13 In addition to high cholesterol, many other common ailments (obesity, acid-reflux) are at least in part food related.
14 While we in no way seek to diminish the suffering or lives lost to these drugs, we remain skeptical of the language of epidemic, crisis and emergency as they often signal the state's deployment of police power towards its aim of pacification. (See Neocleous, 2011.)
15 Fitzgerald (2020) marks the waves of the opioids crisis as such: OxyContin 1996, Heroin 2010, Fentanyl 2013.

16 Not to be outdone, Richard Sackler is in the approval process for a new treatment for opioid addiction: www.npr.org/2018/09/11/646657455/family-with-oxycontin-patent-has-another-to-wean-patients-off-oxycontin

17 "We'll have that list and when we get a call, the dispatcher will ask who is the person who has overdosed. And if it's someone who has already been provided services twice, we'll advise them that we're not going to provide further services, and we will not send out an ambulance" (Wootson, 2017).

18 (18 U.S.C. § 1959); (18 U.S.C. § 924(j)); (21 U.S.C. § 848(e)); (18 U.S.C. § 3591(b)(1)).

19 As of the time of this writing, the following companies have been held liable in state and/or federal US courts for their role in the opioid crisis: Southwood Pharm, Cardinal Health, Amerisouce Bergen, McKession, Masters Pharm, Sunrise Wholsale, Harvard Medical Group, Key Source Medical, Omnicare, CVS, Walgreens, UPS, FedEx, CVS Health, Mallinckrodt (Fitzgerald, 2020).

20 Suspecting it was the source of the drugs the Nebraska Department of Corrections intended use on Moore, the German manufacturer Fresenius Kabi managed to temporarily delay the execution on grounds that the state had obtained the drugs through improper or illegal means (Berman, 2018).

References

Armstrong, D. (2019). Inside Purdue Pharma's Media Playbook: How It Planted the Opioid "Anti-Story" Propublica.org. Retrieved: www.propublica.org/article/inside-purdue-pharma-media-playbook-how-it-planted-the-opioid-anti-story?utm_source=pardot&utm_medium=email&utm_campaign=majorinvestigations

Bartilow, H. A. (2019). *Drug War Pathologies: Embedded Corporatism and US Drug Enforcement in the Americas.* UNC Press Books.

Berman, M. (2018). Nebraska becomes the first state to use fentanyl in an execution. *Washington Post.* Retrieved: www.washingtonpost.com/news/post-nation/wp/2018/08/14/nebraska-prepares-for-first-u-s-execution-using-fentanyl/

Buck-Morss, S. (1992). Aesthetics and anesthetics: Walter Benjamin's artwork essay reconsidered. October, *62*, 3–41.

Bradley, J. (2009). *The Imperial Cruise: A Secret History of Empire and War.* Hachette, UK.

Case, A. and Deaton, A. (2015). Rising morbidity and mortality in midlife among white non-Hispanic Americans in the 21st century. *Proceedings of the National Academy of Sciences*, *112*(49), 15078–15083.

Chappell, B. (2017). Tom Marino, Trump's Pick as Drug Czar, withdraws after Damaging Opioid Report. (National Public Radio). Retrieved: www.npr.org/sections/thetwoway/2017/10/17/558276546/tom-marino-trumps-pick-as-drug-czar-withdraws-after-damagingopioid-report

Coleman, J. J. (2019). Whatever happened to the decade of pain control and research? In J. F. Peppin, J. J. Coleman, K. K. Dineen, & A. J. Ruggles (Eds.), *Prescription Drug Diversion and Pain: History, Policy and Treatment.* Chapter 4 (pp. 78–109). New York: Oxford University Press.

Columbia University's Mailman School of Public Health. (2018, September 27). Deaths of despair: The opioid epidemic is just part of the problem: Rising medical costs may be the biggest contributor to declines in life-expectancy. *ScienceDaily.* Retrieved February 17, 2019 from www.sciencedaily.com/releases/2018/09/180927164235.htm

Denvir, D. (2017). These pharmaceutical companies are making a killing off the opioid crisis. *The Nation.* Retrieved: www.thenation.com/article/these-pharmaceuticalcompanies-are-making-a-killing-off-the-opioid-crisis/

De Sutter, L. (2018). *Narcocapitalism: Life in the Age of Anesthesia*. London: Wiley.

Fitzgerald, J. (2020). *Life in Pain: Affective Economy and the Demand for Pain Relief*. New York: Springer.

Fisher, M. (2009). *Capitalist Realism: Is There No Alternative?*. Portland: John Hunt Publishing.

Fisher, M. (2018). *K-Punk: The Collected and Unpublished Writings of Mark Fisher*, edited by Darren Ambrose. London: Repeater Books.

Fleming, P. (2019). *The Worst Is Yet to Come: A Post-Capitalist Survival Guide*. London: Watkins Media.

Flores, J., & Barahona-López, K. (2019). "It's like everyone's trying to put pills in you": Pharmaceutical violence and harmful mental health services inside a California Juvenile Detention Center. *Critical Criminology*, *27*, 643–662.

Frydl, K.J. (2013). *The Drug Wars in America, 1940–1973*. Cambridge: Cambridge University Press.

Greene, J. A., & Herzberg, D. (2010). Hidden in plain sight marketing prescription drugs to consumers in the twentieth century. *American Journal of Public Health*, *100*(5), 793–803.

Haiven, M. (2019). our opium wars: The ghosts of empire in the prescription opioid nightmare. *Third Text*, *32*(5–6), 662–669.

Hatch, A.R. (2019). *Silent Cells: The Secret Drugging of Captive America*. Ann Arbor: University of Minnesota Press.

James, O. (2007). Selfish capitalism and mental illness. *The Psychologist*, *20*(7), 426–428.

Kaye, K. (2019). *Enforcing Freedom: Drug Courts, Therapeutic Communities, and the Intimacies of the State*. Columbia: Columbia University Press.

Keefe, PR. (2017, October 30). The family that built an empire of pain. *The New Yorker*. Retrieved: www.newyorker.com/magazine/2017/10/30/the-family-that-built-an-empire-of-pain

Keshavan, M. (2016, May 23) Tasty and easy to take, a new ADHD drug alarms some psychiatrists. Retrieved: www.statnews.com/2016/05/23/adhd-drug-concerns/

Kuzmarov, J. (2008). From counter-insurgency to narco-insurgency: Vietnam and the international war on drugs. *Journal of Policy History*, *20*(3), 344–378.

Linnemann, T. and Medley, C. (2019). Down and out in Middletown and Jackson: Drugs, dependency, and decline in JD Vance's capitalist realism. In. A. Harkins, & M. McCarroll (Eds.), *Appalachian Reckoning: A Region Responds to Hillbilly Elegy*. West Virginia University Press.

Macy, B. (2018). *Dopesick: Dealers, Doctors and the Drug Company that Addicted America*. Bloomsbury: Apollo Books.

Maier, T. (2014). The secret boozy deals of a Kennedy, a Churchill, and a Roosevelt. *Time*. Retrieved: https://time.com/3529756/kennedy-churchill-roosevelt-investment-deal/

McClanahan, A. (2019). Serious crises: Rethinking the neoliberal subject. *Boundary 2: An International Journal of Literature and Culture*, *46*(1), 103–132.

McKim, A. (2017). *Addicted to Rehab: Race, Gender, and Drugs in the Era of Mass Incarceration*. New Brunswick: Rutgers University Press.

Meyer, D. (2020). Security symptoms. *Cultural Geographies*, 28(2). https://doi.org/10.1177/1474474020933892

Moore, T.J., & Mattison, D.R. (2017). Adult utilization of psychiatric drugs and differences by sex, age, and race. *JAMA Internal Medicine*, 177(2), 274–275.

Mull, A (2019). America's best drug dealers are A-list celebrities. *The Atlantic.* Retrieved: www.theatlantic.com/health/archive/2019/11/celebrities-legal-weed/602233/?utm_campaign=the-atlantic&utm_medium=social&utm_source=facebook&fbclid=IwAR0uK5yO_trFxO_kik_fI4R7NrDD-_A_nF-GqOouL11AG5zucSVxd9aQ8zE

Neocleous, M. (2011). 'A brighter and nicer new life': Security as pacification. *Social & Legal Studies, 20*(2), 191–208.

Neocleous, M. (2016). *The Universal Adversary: Security, Capital and 'The Enemies of All Mankind'.* London: Routledge.

Paley, D. (2014). *Drug War Capitalism.* Baltimore: AK Press.

Porter, J. and Jick, H. (1980). Addiction rare in patients treated with narcotics. *New England Journal of Medicine, 302,* 123.

Proudfoot, J. (2019). The libidinal economy of revanchism: Illicit drugs, harm reduction, and the problem of enjoyment. *Progress in Human Geography, 43*(2), 214–234.

Ramsey, L. (September 22, 2015). A pharma CEO tried to defend his decision to jack up the price of a critical drug by 5,000%–and it backfired. *Business Insider.* Retrieved: www.businessinsider.com/martin-shkreli-defends-daraprim-price-2015-9

Reiss, S. (2014). *We Sell Drugs: The Alchemy of US Empire.* Berkley: University of California Press.

Richter, E. (2017). Middletown Councilman Has 'No Regrets' about Overdose Comments. *Journal-News.* Retrieved: www.journal-news.com/news/middletown-councilman-has-regretsabout-overdose-comments/iRyfMw7KvWABWfUUw8qV6H/

Sanger, D. and Haberman, M. (2017). Trump praises Duterte for Philippine drug crackdown in call transcript. *The New York Times.* Retrieved: www.nytimes.com/2017/05/23/us/politics/trump-duterte-phone-transcript-philippine-drug-crackdown.html

Satel, S. (2011). Keeping OxyContin out of the wrong hands. *Boston Globe.* Retrieved: https://sallysatelmd.com/articles/2001/keeping-oxycontin-out-of-the-wrong-hands/

Sessions, J. (2018). Memorandum from Jefferson Sessions, U.S. Attorney Gen. to U.S. Attorneys, guidance regarding use of capital punishment in drug-related prosecutions. Retrieved: www.justice.gov/opa/press-release/file/1045036/download

Smith, M. (2018). Fentanyl used to execute Nebraska inmate, in a first for U.S. *New York Times.* www.nytimes.com/2018/08/14/us/carey-dean-moore-nebraska-execution-fentanyl.html

Spector, M. (2019). OxyContin maker Purdue Pharma files for bankruptcy protection. Reuters.com. Retrieved: www.reuters.com/article/us-purdue-pharma-bankruptcy-idUSKBN1W1058

Swan, J. (2018). Exclusive: Trump privately talks up executing all big drug dealers. Axios.com. Retrieved: www.axios.com/exclusive-trump-privately-talks-up-executing-all-big-drug-dealers-1519595170-402cc386-8729-4684-a7ef-a5bf31876afa.html

Szalavitz, M. (2017). Ohio lawmaker suggests letting people die if they've overdosed twice before. *Vice.com.* Retrieved: https://tonic.vice.com/en_us/article/zmejd9/ohio-lawmaker-danpicard-three-strikes-let-people-die-if-theyve-overdosed-twice-before

Tiger, R. (2013). *Judging Addicts: Drug Courts and Coercion in the Justice System* (Vol. 6). New York: NYU Press.

Trump, D. (2018). Remarks by President Trump on combatting the opioid crisis. *The White House.* Retrieved: www.whitehouse. gov/briefings-statements/remarks-president-trump-combatting-opioid-crisis/ [Accessed on 7 May 2018].

Van Zee, A. (2009). The promotion and marketing of OxyContin: Commercial triumph, public health tragedy. *American Journal of Public Health, 99*(2), 221–227.

Wailoo, K. (2014). *Pain: A Political History*. Maryland: John Hopkins University Press.

Wark, M. (2019). *Capital Is Dead*. London; New York: Verso.

Watson, J. (2019). Naloxone spray market to reach USD 928.1 million By 2026. Reports and Data. Retrieved: www.globenewswire.com/news-release/2019/05/01/1813611/0/en/Naloxone-Spray-Market-To-Reach-USD-928-1-Million-By-2026-Reports-And-Data.html

Witt, E. (2019). Dopesick by Beth Macy; American Overdose: The opioid tragedy in Three Acts by Chris McGreal: Dreamland: The true tale of America's opiate epidemic by Sam Quinones. *London Review of Books, 41*(7), 23.

Wootson Jr. C.R. (2017). One politician's solution to the overdose problem: Let addicts die. *Washington Post*. Retrieved: www.washingtonpost.com/news/to-yourhealth/wp/2017/06/28/a-council-members-solution-to-his-ohio-townsoverdose-problem-let-addicts-die/

Zezima, K. and Bernstein, L. (2019, February 1). Lawsuit claims Sackler family disregarded safety, opioid addiction in Purdue push to profit from OxyContin. *Washington Post*. Retrieved: www.washingtonpost.com/national/lawsuit-claims-sackler-family-disregarded-safety-opioid-addiction-in-purdue-push-to-profit-from-oxycontin/2019/02/01/5d29e072-2660-11e9-90cd-dedb0c92dc17_story.html?noredirect=on&utm_term=.751a37fd8033

Žižek, S. (1997). *The Plague of Fantasies*. London: Verso.

CONCLUSION

> The average drug trafficking organization, meaning from Medellin to the streets of New York, could afford to lose 90 percent of its profit and still be profitable. Now think of the analogy. GM builds a million Chevrolets a year. Doesn't sell 900,000 of them and still comes out profitable. That is a hell of a business, man. That is the dope business.
>
> *Robert Stutman, a former DEA agent*

The final chapter of this edited collection attempts to draw the preceding chapters together, before going on to offer some final thoughts on the issues that have arisen relating to drug dealing in the twenty-first century. The chapters of this book illustrate the cutting-edge research being undertaken by internationally renowned scholars into the manufacture and supply of drugs across the globe. One of the main themes evident across these contributions is the profits to be made from drug dealing and supply to make it an attractive and lucrative business to increasingly diverse sections of the populace. While not all drug dealers make huge profits – and some do it merely to obtain free drugs and/or to pay for their own drug use – the above example outlines the profits to be made and the economic potential of the drug trade, which illustrates why, despite its best efforts, prohibition, criminalisation and punishment have had little impact on drug production and supply, either locally or globally. In fact, the literature illustrates the adverse failure of prohibition to restrict the supply of drugs, even during the most recent coronavirus disease 2019 (Covid-19) pandemic, which saw entire countries locked down (see UNODC, 2021). Despite the additional Covid-19 restrictions, most of the drugs trade continued unabated, further illustrating the inefficacy of prohibition.

DOI: 10.4324/9781351010245-24

Prohibition: outdated, failing and harmful

The failure of prohibition to effectively curb the production and supply of drugs, however, is unsurprising and is largely attributable to the demand for drugs, which culminates in the balloon/conveyor-belt effect[1] (see Rolles et al., 2016) that arises from the logistics of the market. This was seen during the Covid-19 pandemic, which saw methods of drug supply shift with an increase in the delivery of drugs by mail, sea and private aircraft (UNODC, 2021). Illustrating that despite interdiction efforts and the 50-year war on drugs, while there is demand there will always be supply (even during a global pandemic), which means 'overall drug supply (as evidenced by various indicators of increasing production, declining prices and increasing potency) has been largely unimpeded by the multibillion-dollar investments' that enforce prohibition (GCDP, 2012: 12–13). Instead, prohibition and interdiction efforts disproportionately fall on and harm producer countries and/or those in the Global South (Ayres, 2020a; McSweeney, 2015). Despite five decades of waging a war on drugs, drug trafficking and production has increased, with some drug markets expanding in recent years (see NCA, 2021; UNODC, 2021). In fact, the only noticeable effect prohibition has had in that time is to cause harm on a global scale (e.g. corruption, environmental degradation, ill-health, political instability, violence) to users and dealers alike (see Rolles et al., 2016 for more information), which is something that it continues to do, despite the lack of evidence underpinning it (Pearson and Hobbs, 2001; Taylor et al. 2016).

Despite the dearth of evidence underpinning the current system of prohibition, and its discriminatory and harmful effects, the focus on supply reduction[2] and its accompanying rhetoric legitimises some of the harshest punishments for drug dealers that exist around the world, which includes the death penalty (HRI, 2021). However, such draconian punishments are reserved for the usual suspects rather than the powerful unusual suspects who seem to operate with impunity[3] despite causing significant harm. Instead of focusing on harm, prohibition is premised on the political and scientific idiosyncrasies that seem to determine the legality of certain substances and thus the criminality of their users and/or suppliers, which is not only discriminatory but is more harmful than some of the drugs it purports to protect us from (MacCoun and Reuter, 2001; Rolles et al., 2016; Taylor et al., 2016). Instead, the war on drugs epitomises the neoliberal ethos and its hegemonic ideology about some (unprivileged) substances and some (unprivileged) users. In true neoliberal ethos drug prohibition distinguishes between the deserving and undeserving citizen to produce excluded populations that warrant social control and punishment (Bauman, 2001; Wacquant, 2009). While the free trade agreements, foreign policies and neoliberal restructuring define today's drug markets and have actually facilitated 'financial capital' and resource exploitation by the Global North and its transnational corporations to gain power over other lands, particularly resource-rich producer/transit countries often located in the Global South, this is often concealed under the guise of reducing supply (see Paley, 2014).

Reducing the supply of drugs is believed to help control the drug problem and is but one concern that drives public commitment to enforcing drug laws that prohibit illicit drugs globally. Supply reduction initiatives aim to stop drugs at their source by destroying crops and disrupting networks in order to reduce the quantity of illicit drugs entering the country, thus driving up the price and subsequently discouraging use. However, while there is demand there will always be supply, and as the United Nations Office on Drugs and Crime (UNODC) has identified, 'the collision of rising demand with a prohibitionist global drugs control system has created a criminal market of staggering proportions that is undermining governance, stability and the rule of law across the world' (Rolles et al., 2016: 11). However, the illicit drug market is not only dominated by criminal drug trafficking organisations – also known as transnational Organised Crime Groups (OCGs) – but also involves legitimate businesses (e.g. banks, solicitors firms, delivery companies and even Royal Mail). Like legitimate businesses OCGs have diversified their operations and became involved in new lucrative entrepreneurial (business) opportunities (e.g. arms/weapons trafficking, extortion, kidnapping, human smuggling/trafficking and modern slavery) in order to maximise profit, minimise loss and protect themselves from the competition (Paley, 2014) as most OCGs/drug traffickers are engaged in a 'plurality of business activities[4]' (Paoli, 2003: 174). While one would expect other forms of criminality in illicit supply chains, evidence also suggests that some of these criminal endeavours – extortion, corruption and modern-day slavery – are also present in the supply chains of legal (privileged) drugs and the legitimate businesses involved in the production and supply.

Whether it is corrupt practices of British American Tobacco (see BBC, 2021) or the pollution, environmental degradation and modern-day slavery that exist in the supply chains of legal substances like tobacco, coffee, tea or medicines from Big Pharma, or the companies' repeated convictions for fraud, price fixing and the production and marketing of harmful – often fatal – drugs (Braithwaite, 1984; LeBaron, 2021; Singer and Baer, 2009; Upright, 2017), these practices are largely overlooked and rarely prosecuted despite causing global harm. Instead, these harms are disavowed perpetuating the illusion that only illegitimate drugs, their manufacturers and suppliers are harmful – after all, they are unregulated – thus rationalising their control and prohibition (Taylor et al., 2016) as they are seen as a threat to the dominant status quo.

Drug trafficking and its links to serious and organised crime, terrorism and violence are seen as undermining capitalism and as a significant threat to national security both here in the UK and abroad, which is indoctrinated in a range of national and international policies and strategies, despite their derisory evidence base. Instead of acknowledging the finer nuances of these clandestine markets and how they are inextricably tied to the legitimate global political economy and capital, this is ignored. Instead, the West's concealed coercion is disavowed as is its role in the global drug trade as prohibition serves Western hegemonic interests and the foreign policy of those in the Global North by refusing to acknowledge the logic of the market and the fact that Western demand drives supply, and until this is eliminated, any supply reduction measures remain futile (see Ayres, 2020a). Despite the expenditure spent on supply reduction there is very little evidence to support the efficacy of these initiatives, particularly when it comes to those targeting the upper tiers of illicit supply chains, including how crime networks link up and are financed (Pearson and Hobbs, 2001). Instead, knowledge gaps exist that limit our understanding of drug supply as well as the evidence base underpinning policy and practice, which is largely missing.

Research, knowledge and the academy

Research on drug supply and trafficking is limited. It relies on official statistics as well as research conducted with incarcerated populations and law enforcement agencies, which further skews the knowledge base in this area. Although the global drugs trade is estimated to be worth billions – more than most transnational corporations, and in some instances, more than the gross domestic products (GDPs) of some States/Countries – estimates vary considerably, as the true extent of the illicit drug trade is unknown and largely based on guestimates. This is because obtaining reliable data on illicit drug production and its supply is problematic and difficult to monitor due to its clandestine nature. In fact, the data that is available often describes low-level and/or unsuccessful drug dealers, which provides a distorted picture of the drug trade and those operating within it. As Coomber highlights at the start of the book, research predominately focuses on the most visible (e.g. what is assumed or 'known' from prior research) and, as such, continues 'to over simplify and over homogenise what, and who, a drug dealer *is* and what a drug market looks like'. Therefore, by adopting narrow methodological and stereotyped lenses only the 'surface aspects of drug supply and exchange' are focused up, which creates a 'one-dimensional perspective' that results in 'unhelpful interventions levied on many of those prosecuted for supply offences'. It must also be acknowledged, however, that research is also limited by the academy itself and its marketisation as research has become more restricted.

In the neoliberal university, the Research Excellence Framework (REF) and its metrics alongside ethics approval systems are being used to prevent certain research topics being studied (see Kaufmann, 2021). Instead, 'applying for ethical clearance is increasingly viewed as a hollow and burdensome process, which requires the applicant to say the right things and tick the right boxes' (Winlow and Hall, 2012: 12), particularly in the field of crime and criminality, which is often deemed to be beyond minimum risk and thus problematic to the increasingly non-political, risk-averse research-intensive university. While ethics committees supposedly seek to protect individuals (participants and researchers) from harm/danger – and the institution from costly lawsuits – the reality is quite different. Ethics committees are increasingly seen as part of the bureaucracy pervading the contemporary neoliberal university and its marketisation, which prioritises certain academics, certain subjects/disciplines and certain methodologies over others that ultimately control the production of knowledge (Kauffman, 2021; Spence, 2019). This alongside the emphasis on metrics means research is produced of questionable social meaning and value as academics play the system, misrepresent the numbers and adopt formulaic approaches to their outputs to ensure they are not too radical, controversial or political but that they advance their careers enough by making only incremental contributions to existing knowledge (Alvesson et al., 2017; Spence, 2019; Winlow and Hall, 2012; Winlow, 2021). Consequently, as Spence (2019: 762) highlights:

> a marketised environment is encouraging institutions to take all sorts of intellectual short cuts in order to improve statistics on student satisfaction and employability. Overall, the pursuit of excellence, as currently conceived by UK HEIs, engenders mediocrity. HEIs would be much better advised to stick to Humboldtian ideals of cultivating critical minds rather than the instrumentalism of student satisfaction scores or nurturing a culture of 'big hits' in 'top journals' for academics.

In fact, the prioritisation of metrics and customer (student) satisfaction stifles true academic enquiry, innovation and debate, as frenetic competition is promoted and 'drab uniformity' is encouraged to ensure consistency so that 'no student consumer is disadvantaged' (Winlow, 2021: 8).

Rather than being a critical voice producing knowledge in their respective areas, the main aim of a university is to climb league-tables, avoid complaints – and thus reputational damage that may discourage fee-paying customers – and to ensure that the research undertaken is uncontroversial, as universities seek to distance themselves from academics who engage with provocative, and often political, topics (Kauffman, 2021). Academics that do not conform are seen as delinquent troublemakers who often find themselves in scope for redundancy and/or facing disciplinary action. This approach is also failing their students by 'producing graduates who lack the critical thinking skills that are actually required to enter the graduate labour market and make informed life choices' (Spence, 2019: 768). In fact, the new pursuit of excellence pervading UK higher education institutions – through the Research and Teaching Excellence Frameworks (REF/TEF) – instead engenders mediocrity and has deleterious consequences for both staff and students as well as 'knowledge production and knowledge transfer' (Spence, 2019: 761). These neoliberal, customer-focused, risk-averse institutions censure and advise against research into controversial and risky topics like drug trafficking and organised crime as ethics committees inadvertently end up limiting, prioritising and controlling research and thus the production of knowledge as they have become inextricably tied to the logistics of the market and the wider political economy (Kauffman, 2021; Spence, 2019; Winlow and Hall, 2012).

While ethics committees are there to eliminate unethical research practices, the reality, particularly in criminology, is quite different. Rather than minimise harm, the ethics committee – often comprised predominately of 'white, secular, middle-class, middle-aged and liberal' academics (Winlow and Hall, 2012: 410) – embodies and perpetuates harm as well as many of the dominant myths surrounding drugs, their users and their suppliers. In the many ethics applications the authors have completed, they have grown tired of responding to comments/queries that have no bearing on the reality of doing research in this area and actually indoctrinate and perpetuate some of the myths surrounding drugs, their users and their suppliers (e.g. how can drug users give informed consent?). In fact, as scholars working in this area have highlighted, many of the ethical practices governing research and indoctrinated and enforced by university ethics committees actually have the opposite effect and not only have the potential to cause our participants harm but may also result in a long prison sentence at Her Majesty's pleasure.

Individuals committing illegal acts should not be asked to sign a consent form as it opens them up to the potential of a criminal investigation and subsequent prosecution, while the researchers involved – despite having a professional responsibility to protect their research participants – may be summoned to give evidence – including information about those who participated in the research[5] – which means they could therefore end up being complicit in the prosecution of their research subjects (Coomber, 2002a, 2002b; Sandberg and Copes, 2012). Such practices also invariably – and often negatively – impact the ability to gather participants as well as the quality of the data gathered (e.g. non-compliance of interviewees) since most ethics committees expect researchers to add a caveat to their application to ensure the data collected falls within the limitations of the law – a condition which consequently obligates a researcher to report serious crime/harm to the authorities, even if it is the focus of their research. Therefore, ethics committees are increasingly limiting cutting-edge research in this area, as well as potentially increasing the harm arising from such projects. Consequently, ethics committees are increasingly being seen by academics as part of the administrative and managerialist culture currently pervading the neoliberal university, which like most things in post-modernity prioritises representation over reality, in the Baudrillardian (1998) sense.

The university – like most things in society – is deprived of its substance, it is not neutral but has been co-opted into the libidinal economy of capitalism where it reinforces the capitalist reproduction of symbolic reality while 'obfuscating the unfreedom on which it relies' (Žižek, 2003: 3). Even when researchers are granted ethical approval to undertake research with criminal drug dealing populations – which is unlikely, particularly in relation to the higher echelons of drug trafficking that is perceived as violent and dangerous[6] – the fragmented nature of the drug market (and other illicit markets) also makes research in this area difficult to undertake as the lower-level dealers rarely know much about the market structures and supply chains above them (Pearson and Hobbs, 2001). In fact, trying to gauge the size/extent as well as the nature of drug markets and their actors – like most drug statistics – is like trying to do a jigsaw with half of the pieces missing or 'a jigsaw in which each piece comes from a different set' (Pearson and Hobbs, 2001: 58).

Therefore, there is also a need to collect more incisive data on the production, price and purity of each substance at each of the different stages of these global supply chains (Pearson and Hobbs, 2001). Although a more accurate picture of the 'world drug situation' is provided by the UNODC World Drug Reports, even these have their limitations (e.g. not all countries respond, the statistics are often bias and influenced by local governments and is based on regional and national guestimates of cultivation and production) (see Mansfield, 2011). Instead, drug production and cultivation statistics are often 'guestimates' based on a range of indicators that are not always corroborative or able to facilitate meaningful comparisons, whether that is between countries and regions or over time. Instead, aggregate data is used to assess the efficacy of supply side efforts, which can hide important differences (e.g. between groups/sub-groups) as well as lead to a high chance of identifying false positives and negatives in the data (Mansfield, 2011). This is exacerbated further by the inconsistencies and corruption that pervades illicit (and legal) drug markets, which also impacts the official statistics as politicians, prosecutors, judges, banks and the police are also active in the drug business:

> Government deal-making with segments of drug traffickers illustrates how the drug war is also used to attack a segment of traffickers and the political class, while others are given a free hand in ensuring their product makes it to market.
>
> *Paley, 2014: 121*

In fact, around the globe governments and states take a cut of the illicit earnings in return for turning a blind eye to illicit activity. However, this is omitted from the official discourse and its statistics alongside the actions of legitimate corporations (e.g. pharmaceutical companies) and actors (e.g. doctors) manufacturing and supplying licit (and illicit) substances. Instead, this is disavowed and hidden. Thus, ascertaining the true extent of drug supply is like trying to do a jigsaw puzzle with most of the pieces missing, which is unlikely to change while drugs remain prohibited and their markets illicit. However, it is not just the drug trade that is profitable, but also the war on drugs, which has been a source of profit for corporations, governments and states for many years (Meehan 2011; Paley 2014). In other words, while the war on drugs has done little, if anything, to curb the illegal drug trade, it has been a tremendous source of profit for state-corporate entities as the distinction between licit and illicit, businessperson and criminal-entrepreneur has become culturally, politically and economically blurred.

The blurring of licit with illicit: there is no business like the dope business

It is not just the legality of the actors and organisations that have become obscured. The legality of drug markets also varies by geographic location and substance, illustrating another layer of complexity that further blurs the divide/distinction between licit and illicit since what is illegal in one country is not necessarily illegal in another country, further complicating the manufacture and supply chains of an increasingly diverse array of substances (e.g. medicines, illicit drugs, performance and image enhancing drugs/human enhancement drugs [PIEDS/HED], dietary supplements). In fact, the preceding chapters outline the dynamic and ever-evolving nature of drug markets and the diverse actors and organisations that operate within them, as drug dealing has become increasingly differentiated (Coomber, 2010). Therefore, this final chapter attempts to bring these diverse and varying accounts together. Although this book has tried to present a pertinent and contemporary overview of the drugs trade, it has to a certain extent focused on the stereotypical, traditional notion of the drug dealer, and one which aligns with the dominant socio-legal construction of drugs that reflects and perpetuates the drug apartheid[7] (Taylor et al., 2016).

While it is clear that illegal drugs and illicit markets dominate the literature on drug supply and trafficking – as reflected in the first half of this edited collection – the second half of the book starts to examine quasi-legal and legal markets and suppliers in an attempt to broaden the debate and move the focus of drug manufacturing and supply forward, away from the powerless to incorporate the powerful, which includes legitimate actors and organisations that are often excluded from the official discourse on drugs and their supply. This omission is despite the fact that the supply and/or the manufacture of drugs by legitimate actors (e.g. doctors) and companies has often fuelled illicit drug use and supply (e.g. by over prescribing, see Wilson's chapter in this volume). This along with the corrupt and criminal practices of producers and suppliers of legal drugs – many of which replicate those found in illicit markets – is seen and treated very differently from the illicit drug dealer who is still subject to some of the harshest and most draconian punishments meted out around the world. Instead, the criminal practices in the supply chains of legal drugs by legal actors are dealt with very differently, if at all. Such practices are routinely hidden and legitimised by those in power or seen as unintentional even unavoidable, rather than attribute to corruption and criminality. Rarely is anyone held to account let alone punished, and instead the company is merely fined illustrating the unequal application of the criminal law, as those in power – the powerful – actually enjoy much protection from the criminal law as their misdemeanours/crimes are dealt with via fines and regulation. Therefore, any criminal punishment – as with other areas of criminality – disproportionately effects certain groups – the powerless – particularly those that are already disadvantaged and marginalised as drug policy and legislation disproportionately discriminates along the lines of class, race/ethnicity and gender – something that is captured in the aforementioned chapters. Despite the widespread acknowledgement, that prohibition and its accompanying laws are discriminatory; most government expenditure (domestically as well as globally) is spent on supply reduction and law enforcement, despite the lack of evidence base underpinning their efficacy. The missing evidence base may explain their failure to effectively reduce the supply of drugs or to deter people from becoming embroiled in drug markets and their illegal supply chains, which are constantly evolving and mutating. In fact, it must be recognised that drug prohibition and its laws have had little impact on drug use and/or drug production and supply despite estimates that enforcing global prohibition costs USD$100 billion a year. However, this seems unsurprising when compared to the drug trade itself, which is estimated at USD$330 billion a year (Rolles et al., 2016: 22). While there is limited evidence that law enforcement initiatives may have some short-lived localised impact on supply chains (see UKDPC, 2008), the money to be made from the illicit drug trade – as well as some of the other substances mentioned (e.g. PIEDS/HEDS, fake medications, the pharmaceutical industry) – means that there will always be someone willing to take the risk due to the profit margins to be made.[8] Although these are mostly accrued by the wealthier consumer countries and those higher up the supply chains (e.g. businesses, organised crime groups, states/governments, banks, terrorist organisations and insurgent groups), the financial incentives are huge and remain a key driving factor (Eastwood, Fox and Rosmarin, 2016; Rolles et al., 2016) across substances, markets, countries and socio-economic contexts. Along these trade routes however – in the name of prohibition – the legitimate economy, states/countries and governments are undermined; producer and transit countries are negatively harmed; environmental degradation and climate change are inflicted (argued elsewhere by Ayres 2020a as constituting a form of state-induced ecocide); businesses and agriculture are monopolised; vulnerable people and countries are exploited; income inequality is exacerbated and economic growth rates stilted; as well as destroying indigenous homelands and cultures (see Rolles et al., 2016).

Despite the increase in revenue spent on supply reduction, production has increased, drugs have become cheaper and, in some instances, purer (NCA, 2021; UNODC, 2021). Instead, the key beneficiaries of supply reduction initiatives are the state via the criminal justice system, their organisations and agents (Rolles et al., 2016). In fact, the 'relationship between the supply of illicit drugs, the demand for them and enforcement activities remain somewhat poorly conceptualised, under-researched and little understood' (May and Hough, 2004: 558) and not much has changed. Some of this is attributed to research limitations in this area, which perpetuate the stereotypical conception of the evil and amoral drug dealer, despite the truth. In fact, rather than stopping the flow of drugs, the money spent fighting the war on drugs has actually 'bolstered a war strategy that ensures transnational corporations access to resources through dispossession and terror' (Paley, 2014: 15) as anti-drug policies sustain and prioritise the expansion of capitalism and its exploitative practices as the production and supply of drugs is, and always has, prioritised the exigencies of capitalism (Ayres, 2020a, 2020b; Courtwright, 2001; Paley, 2014). However, this is disavowed, and instead illicit drugs and their dealers are blamed for subverting capitalism and undermining the dominant status quo as they have historically been associated with others/otherness.

Drugs, particularly the unprivileged illicit ones, have always been seen as coming from outsiders as only people different from us manufacture and supply them (see Becker, 1963; Coomber, 2006). The reality, however, as the chapters of this book have shown, is very different from the imaginary, which may explain why the unusual suspects are often overlooked and ignored, not only in research, but also in policy and practice. Instead, drug policy is premised on the stereotypical minority. Illicit drug dealers are seen as problematic, amoral and dangerous people/groups that corrupt society – whether it is the gypsies in Spain or the Jamaican Yardies in London – as a reductionist discourse around some drugs, their users and suppliers dominates (see Taylor et al., 2016).

The demonic drug dealer and their motivation to deal in death

In fact, the historical demonisation of drug dealers focuses on the usual suspects, which sees drug dealers as a threat to the dominant – often Western – status quo, capitalism and society's – largely Western – sociocultural norms, despite the reality. Instead, drug dealers are mostly rational economic actors. They see themselves as service providers selling commodities that meet the demands of the customer. In fact, drug supply – like many other forms of contemporary employment, including the new 'gig economy' (see the chapter by Salinas in this volume) – has come to represent a precarious form of work with flexible hours and a lack of employee benefits (e.g. sick pay and holiday pay) as the individual entrepreneur is held accountable for their own fate and fortune 'as freedom and enduring satisfaction are available to all those who desire success badly enough to make the required sacrifices' (Hall et al., 2008: 38). However, not all drug supply is about profit and not everyone deals drugs to make money, although most suppliers deal drugs to obtain some form of advantage, which may (or may not) include free drugs.

In Wilson's chapter on the *Northern Soul* scene, even those that burgled the chemist shops to obtain pharmaceutical grade amphetamines were part of the scene and not driven by the profit motive. In fact, 'the chemist burglars seldom sold to individual users unless cajoled by a friend or associate' illustrating what Wakeman (2016) and others refer to as the 'moral economy' of drug use (see Moyle's chapter also in this volume). This notion of the supportive network of drug users is argued to be a social cultural reaction or resistance to the imperatives of post-industrial consumer capitalism. This notion however can be challenged and some (see Ancrum and Treadwell, 2016) contend that the overarching aim of social supply is less about caring for the needs of fellow drug users and more about ensuring their own individualistic needs, as most dealers get something out of these transactions – usually free drugs (see Moyle's chapter) – illustrating the neoliberal promotion of narcissistic individualism, entrepreneurship and innovation. Although drug dealers, for the most part, are rational economic actors, there is little evidence to suggest that they plan or aspire to become involved in the drugs trade as Heal's and other chapters in this edited collection have shown. Instead, people find themselves in situations where they have few alternatives and where they have no option but to take advantage of their 'good fortune' (see Morgan's chapter in this volume) and any other entrepreneurial opportunities that come their way.

Drug dealing for some was emancipatory, in that it provided individuals with economic freedom – economic freedom they would be unlikely to achieve via legitimate avenues – that involved the conspicuous consumption of the trinkets and status symbols that demarcate success and show others that you have made it in contemporary society (Hall et al., 2008; Treadwell and Ayres, 2014). Like other forms of crime, drug dealing was an 'instrument for achieving fantasised positions of social distinction and respect in consumer culture' (Hall et al., 2008: 13). Thus, the distribution of drugs for many included in this book was a form of work or at least a means of supplementing their insecure and often inadequate incomes. As Reuter and colleagues (1990: ix) found, 'drug dealing is an underground version of moonlighting', which is something clearly evidenced in this edited collection.

Therefore, the preceding chapters offer an insight into the heterogeneous nature of drug dealing, which is highly differentiated as are the substances being bought and sold within these markets. The substance market not only includes traditional illicit drugs but also legitimate medications that are siphoned off and sold illicitly on the black market, for example, IPEDS/HEDS, fake medications, precursor chemicals[9] (many of which are diverted from legal markets) as well as legal substances like alcohol, tobacco and dietary supplements. This plethora of substances are for many an integral part of surviving and excelling in contemporary society as the increasingly diverse array of pills and potions promise to satisfy our every want and desire, as we all strive for perfection (see Ayres, 2019, 2020b; Hall, 2019). They fulfil an increasingly diverse array of functions for increasingly diverse sections of the populace (Ayres, 2019, 2020b; Boys et al., 2001) as the entrepreneurial consumer is the role model of social subjectivity and individuals become entrepreneurs of themselves and their own lives (Bauman, 2001; Bröckling, 2007). In fact, what this edited collection shows is that drugs/substances are 'a fact of everyday life' (South, 1999: 4) whether that is their use and/or their manufacture and supply. Substances are not used and supplied by deviant others – the outsiders (Becker, 1963) – but are instead used and supplied to varying degrees by normal everyday (entrepreneurial) people that at times see drug dealing as a meaningful form of employment, particularly when it is compared to their other options.

In fact, the plurality of factors (social, economic and cultural) underpinning people's involvement in the drug trade have been evidenced in the chapters of this book, and must be taken into consideration when implementing policy and legislation, which tends to focus – disproportionately and discriminatorily – on the usual suspects and the drug dealing of the powerless – the low-level street dealers. As highlighted by Wacquant (2011: 438):

> like crime fighting, drug prohibition and supply reduction initiatives have 'been elevated to the rank of government priority and 'insecurity'–understood narrowly in strict reference to lower-class street offending, despite the mounting wave of corporate criminality–[which] has been turned into a driver of election campaigns and raw materials for re-asserting state sovereignty.

Therefore, for many, drug dealing is a rationale response to the situations people find themselves in, which are in some instances beyond their control, or at least imposed on them externally (e.g. immigration policy and initiatives to reduce drug supply) but hinder their ability to find employment in the legitimate economy. No one in this book aspired to be a drug dealer, but instead saw it as a way to survive and prosper – achieve a better life – in contemporary neoliberal society, where individuals are responsible for their own chances and choices, as well as the risks arising from those choices as people only have themselves to blame for their own (mis)fortune (Bauman, 2001; Hall et al., 2008).

The dominant perception is that drug dealers make the wrong choices, which subsequently attracts condemnation and punishment, while society's sociocultural norms that sublimate the systemic violence of consumer capitalism are ignored (Ayres, 2019, 2020b; Raymen and Smith, 2016; Žižek, 2008). Instead, the wider political economy and its innate violence are disavowed despite the fact that many of the issues and harms associated with drug supply are actually attributed to the wider political economy, government policy and legislation. As South (1995, cited in Ruggiero and South, 1995: 193) has pointed out previously, 'the escalation in organised forms of crime can be interpreted as the inevitable outcome of the parallel escalation of the war against drugs'. While there is no denying the levels of violence in drug markets is exacerbated by prohibition, its subsequent policing initiatives and free market competition between different groups, it also shows that drug dealing (and its markets) cannot be divorced from the wider political economy, as drugs are just another commodity to be bought, sold and consumed (Ruggiero and South, 1995).

As with most commodities around the world, the drug trade has developed and been reorganised as technology has advanced. Substances have also diversified alongside the sellers as the boundaries between licit and illicit have become increasingly blurred. However, rarely is the supply of legal – privileged – substances considered in the drug dealing/trafficking literature despite their use and supply being equally if not more harmful than many of their illicit counterparts. Instead, adherence to dominant constructions of drugs and their supply serves to conceal the full spectrum of drug market harms, particularly the harms arising from legal non-drugs, their manufacture and supply chains. Like other markets, global drug markets have evolved and developed alongside technology. Whether we are referring to the shift to closed markets facilitated by pagers and mobile phones or the more recent use of social media and smart-phone applications that offer encrypted and secure platforms, new technology has constantly changed the way drugs are dealt, however, they also create new challenges for both law enforcement and public health. Although drug markets and dealing has evolved, the themes and similarities between this book and Eurodrugs – written nearly thirty-years ago – are very similar. However, like other areas of criminology, drug markets have undergone changes that demand a re-appraisal of the 'conventional theory' (subcultures and anomie) 'usually employed for their interpretation' (Ruggiero and South, 1995: 11) and require the use of different methodologies by researchers.

The preceding chapters of this book provide examples of new and emerging trends, providing invaluable and nuanced insights into drug dealing, encouraging us to move beyond normative assumptions by recognising the diversity of actors engaged in contemporary drug markets. Drug dealers range from organised crime groups to old-age pensioners,[10] however by focusing on the new and the most visible – as this book does – the linear trend of concentrating on minority populations and marginal drug market actors continues, which may actually inhibit the advancement of knowledge, fail to challenge the dominant status quo and create homogenised and overly simplistic understandings of drug markets and drug dealers all of which perpetuate the drug apartheid.

The drug apartheid

The drug apartheid is an arbitrary division of substances 'that has privileged the use of certain substances and outlawed the use of other substances, a corrupt system that has much to do with who uses the drugs and little to do with the risks posed by the drugs' (Taylor et al. 2016: 459). Thus, the supply of legal drugs and their market prospers within neoliberalism, while the illicit drug trade is framed as corrupting society causing many of its ills, while the substances themselves are deemed so harmful that they warrant criminalisation and punishment, despite the fact there is much cross-over (pharmacologically) between privileged/legal and unprivileged/illegal substances and their markets. Instead, the harms arising from legal substances and their supply are disavowed, while the focus on illegal drugs serves to legitimise the current system of drug prohibition and its resultant apartheid as the most severe and draconian punishments are saved for the evil and amoral drug dealer. Focusing on illicit drug markets and their violence detracts from the objective violence in the current system of consumer capitalism (Žižek, 2008) as harm is located within the social structures of contemporary society (Hall et al., 2008; Pemberton, 2015; Raymen and Smith, 2016). It is in this context that drug supply (and use) must be understood.

The current drug apartheid conceals the full spectrum of drug market harms and instead focuses on the usual suspects – illicit drugs and their suppliers – while the manufacture and supply of licit, privileged drugs, is largely omitted and disavowed. Instead, the advertising and promotion by pharmaceutical companies and doctors is not subject to the same scrutiny and criticism as those involved in the illicit drug trade, who are blamed for ruining people's lives, communities and businesses, as well as causing global corruption, violence and economic instability. However, this over-simplification is complicit with the wider reductionist discourse espoused by politicians, commercial enterprise, researchers and the public alike. As the editors of this book have argued elsewhere, drug dealers see themselves as entrepreneurial service providers who are merely meeting the demands of the customer. They do not see themselves as deviant criminals that push drugs onto innocent victims. Instead, drug dealing is a form of work, and a preferable form of work at that, particularly when compared to the other opportunities proffered to them by the legitimate and illegitimate economy. In fact, what is evidenced from the chapters of this book is that the drug market is decentralised, highly fragmented and diverse. It is a constantly mutating network of diverse actors and organisations that are transient and reactive so as to avoid detection, enforcement and prosecution, which is all largely driven by market forces.

The production and supply of drugs/substances is a market-driven process that provides huge revenues for both legitimate (corporations, governments, states) and illegitimate (insurgent groups and organised criminals) actors and organisations. While there is demand for illicit drugs in consumer countries,[11] there will always be *someone* willing to grow drug crops to meet that demand and generate a profit – which is why drugs have been impossible to eradicate and why prohibition, by itself, does not work.[12] Instead, we must observe that market forces are a major factor in the global trade in drugs (and its inherent fluctuations) and the intricacies of supply and demand. However, global drug policies have ignored such forces prioritising supply reduction over demand reduction initiatives despite the dearth of evidence underpinning them both. The evidence base underpinning supply reduction is missing as very little is actually known about successful drug dealers or those that occupy the higher echelons of the drug trafficking chains (Pearson and Hobbs, 2001). Whether we will ever obtain an accurate picture of the drug trade is questionable, particularly while it remains an illicit activity. Therefore, drugs – their production, supply and use – must be understood in the political economy of neoliberal consumer capitalism, which promotes the entrepreneurial values of competitiveness, self-interest, individual empowerment and decentralisation creating self-interested actors that embody the neoliberal ideal of market-orientated entrepreneurship as evidenced among the diverse actors that deal drugs.

Drug dealers see themselves as entrepreneurs, heeding the neoliberal call to be a competitive and enterprising individual striving for success while also being responsible for their own fate. In contemporary neoliberalism, we are all expected to exploit unexploited opportunities and become burgeoning 'entrepreneurs', which 'produces a model for people to understand what they are and what they ought to be' – a form of subjectification – as 'acting entrepreneurially is the very condition of participation in social life' (Bröckling, 2007: iii). Therefore, drug dealers – on both a local and a global scale – exploit the entrepreneurial opportunities they have for illicit gains, using skill sets that are often no longer valued in the legitimate economy in order to 'stand out and fit in' as people seek individual recognition and distinction via consumption (Hall et al., 2008: 203) as everyone consumes themselves into being (Bauman, 2001). However, drug dealers are still seen as something we should not be as the demonisation and scapegoating of drug dealers never gets old.

Some final thoughts

Subsequently this book shows that drug markets are highly differentiated, heterogeneous and diverse phenomena that are constantly mutating. While they include diverse sections of the populace, what is clear from the chapters of this book is that drug dealers are for the most part ordinary people who look to improve their lives and that of their families, which they are unable to achieve via the legitimate economy and its supposed meritocracy. Whether it was low wages, variable hours, poor housing, schooling, social, immigration or employment policies, the push and pull factors outlined in this book varied considerably; however, all were inextricably tied to the legitimate political economy and surviving in contemporary society. For those involved in the research that adorns the pages of this book, the monetary rewards outweighed the risks of arrest and punishment, and yet drug policy and its legislation continue to focus on criminal sanctions that are imposed on the usual suspects, the unprivileged drugs and the unprivileged populations that manufacture and supply them, while the 'boys and girls next-door' remain 'comfortably shielded from criminal justice scrutiny by race and class-based privileges' (see Mohamed and Fritsvold's chapter in this volume). Like legislation and policy, this book, like the majority of research on drug dealing, tends to focus on the usual suspects, the lower-level dealers from poor, marginalised communities and countries, although it does contain the odd exception.

While academia has continually tried to create typologies of drug dealers, human beings do not fit neatly into categories. While these categories have been replicated to a certain extent in policy and legislation to try and differentiate between dealers,[13] legislation still criminalise the most vulnerable and marginalised drug dealers. The diversity and heterogeneity of drug supply markets means that policy, practice and legislation cannot adopt a homogeneous one-size-fits-all approach to drug trafficking, particularly when the current system of regulation and prohibition is full of contradictions – contradictions that emulate the wider contradictions and inequalities characteristic of neoliberal consumer capitalism and its inherently ambiguous, exclusionary and harmful policies (Ayres, 2019, 2020a, 2020b). Therefore, focusing on the control of risky and dangerous substances, and risky and dangerous individuals/groups who manufacture and supply them, detracts from the contradictions and systemic violence of neoliberal consumer capitalism and its inherent paradoxes, which feed into the fantasy that to fix these contradictions we must exclude the problematic drug dealer (Ayres, 2020b; Žižek, 1993), while ignoring the embeddedness of drugs and the illicit economy in legitimate processes, systems and organisations. Although legitimate substances and their supply chains are seen as less harmful, the reality is quite different; however, this is disavowed. Instead, a reductionist discourse around drugs and their supply is maintained and perpetuated which fuels the belief that has seen an extension of prohibitive drug laws and the implementation of ever more punitive responses to drug supply as those in power strive towards a drug-free world (see UNDCP, 1998), whatever that means. While it was always unclear how prohibition and the war on drugs were supposed to defeat and eliminate drugs, it is obvious that this is an unrealistic target when drugs are inextricably tied to the very system that seeks to prohibit them. Rather than subvert capitalism, drugs – their use and supply – are very much part of the system and its perpetuation (Ayres, 2019, 2020a, 2020b; Courtwright, 2001; Paley, 2014).

However, one of the main issues remains that of prohibition, which ignores scientific evidence and instead criminalises the supply of certain substances by certain people in certain countries – but not others – which personifies the drug apartheid (see Taylor et al., 2016). While it is clear that prohibition has been ineffective, which may be attributed to the lack of evidence base underpinning it, it has caused untold harm around the world (see Rolles et al., 2016) and as McCoun and Reuter (2001: 62) highlight, 'a policy that costs society more than the harms it mitigates is difficult to justify', particularly when these harms disproportionately effect the Global South (Ayres, 2020a) and the most vulnerable (Taylor et al., 2016; Wacquant, 2009). In fact, the dominance of the Global North is evidenced not only in this book – an omission on our part, although we did ask some scholars from the Global South[14] – but also in the research, policies and legislation that govern the manufacture, supply and use of drugs across the globe. These promote a predominately Westernised view of drugs, their use and how they should be controlled; Westernised initiatives that place the onus on producer and transit countries located in the Global South and ignore market logistics that are driven by demand, demand that tends to be concentrated in the Global North (see Ayres, 2020a). Instead of focusing on reducing demand in the Global North and dealing with wider socio-economic and cultural inequalities it is easier to blame the evil drug dealer and the unprivileged drugs that they supposedly push onto innocent people, especially children.

In contemporary society, drug dealers are individuals that fail to make the 'right' choices (Bauman, 2001). They are individually pathologised and demonised as evil and amoral people that deal in death, despite the reality. Instead, representation and a simulacrum of the drug dealer dominate (Baudrillard, 1998). Illicit drug dealers are instead scapegoated, portrayed as the demons and monsters responsible for all of society's ills, which maintains the social and racial hierarchy's integral to the ideological machinery that also detracts from the objective violence of consumer capitalism (Žižek, 2008). The prohibition of some substances but not others and the policies and legislation that enforce it are contradictory, discriminatory, harmful and prioritise the expansion of capitalism and the interests of those in power (Ayres, 2020b; Paley, 2014). Therefore, prohibition and the war on drugs with all its ambiguities is an 'ideological state apparatus' (Žižek, 2002: 16) that wages on despite its deleterious global effects (Rolles et al. 2016).

Despite the inefficacy of prohibition and a growing acknowledgement that the war on drugs has been a global failure that causes more harm than many of the drugs it prohibits, this is fetishistically disavowed, which allows everyone to carry on regardless; 'they know very well how things really are, but still they are doing it as if they did not know' (Žižek, 1989: 30). This also means that having a reasoned debate about drugs is impossible as anyone that questions the dominant status quo – like Professor Nutt – is ridiculed, undermined and disbelieved despite the wealth of scientific evidence supporting their claims. Consequently, as Taylor and colleagues (2016) argue,

> unless a mature, scientific and evidence-based approach is adopted to drug policy reform is adopted that clearly starts to expose, challenge and dismantle the very foundations of the drug apartheid any new regulatory framework or so-called reform is arguably little more than repackaged prohibition.

As such, there are four final considerations arising from this book that seek to address some of the shortcomings identified in the preceding chapters:

(1) There is a need to reconceptualise our understanding of drugs, drug dealing and drug markets in order to contest the drug apartheid (see Taylor et al., 2016). We need to incorporate the manufacture and supply of quasi-legal and legal substances by large corporations and by legitimate actors to provide a more nuanced and realistic picture of drug supply harms that include the powerful and the privileged, rather than just focusing on the powerless and unprivileged people and substances – the usual suspects.

(2) Research in this area should be expanded to incorporate the unusual suspects that supply legal drugs under a façade of legitimacy. More research also needs to be conducted on the higher echelons of the drug trade, how it's financed and the role of legitimate actors/businesses involved, however, it must also be acknowledged that this type of research produces 'dirty knowledge' (Ferrell, 1997: 7) that can put both the researcher and their participants at risk. This risk is currently exacerbated by the contemporary neoliberal university and its ethics committees, which insist on signed consent forms and research that ensures the data collected falls within the limitations of the law. While

the dangers associated with this type of research must be acknowledged (see Bloor et al. 2008) and mitigated against, it should not stifle academic enquiry and research, which leads us onto the next point.

(3) More support needs to be provided by the academy and its ethics committees to facilitate risky research into crime and criminals, which includes drug dealing. As the chapters of this book already show, some people are already undertaking stellar research in this area but they may also be risking life and livelihoods as academics jump through the necessary ethical hoops just to get their research authorised.

(4) Leading on from the first two points, if there is to be a reappraisal of drug dealing, then there needs to be a reconsideration of theory and the theories used to explain drug trafficking in contemporary society, which has changed substantially, thus rendering many traditional theories redundant. In line with growing demands for a shift to looking at social harm rather than the law and legal prohibition would also benefit this area as it would allow scholars to focus on the embedded and normalised harms arising from those in power, its organisations agents and legislation alongside those arising from the everyday functioning of capitalism (Hall and Winlow, 2015; Pemberton, 2015; Raymen and Smith, 2016). The use of different methodologies by researchers may also be necessary as technological advancements are constantly changing the way drugs are manufactured and supplied. Further consideration should also be given to not only how researchers protect themselves but also their participants.

(5) Lastly, and this is nothing new, but there needs to be a reform of the current drug laws. Everyone knows the war on drug has failed, is harmful, discriminatory and unjust, and yet it continues to impact most on the most vulnerable, while the privileged – countries, substances and people – are ignored. Although drug law reform seems to be gathering momentum, as Taylor and colleagues (2016: 4) argue, it needs to be rooted in science rather than being a 'populist driven decision' as we have seen in relation to cannabis. It must also be acknowledged that the state, governments and their political, economic and law enforcement machines remain part of the problem as they target the usual suspects while ignoring those in powerful and privileged positions, which includes drugs/substances and the people that use and supply them.

What is clear is that drug dealers are normal everyday people just trying to survive in contemporary society, and drugs are just another commodity to be bought and sold in consumer capitalism. As Nigel South (1999: 4) said, drugs – licit and illicit – are 'a fact of everyday life', and this is never truer than in contemporary neoliberal society.

Overall, the chapters of this edited collection emphasise the underlying and deep-seated social and economic inequalities that characterise capitalism as a key factor in the supply of drugs as well as crime more generally. The drugs trade is an attractive option for a diverse array of legal and illegal organisations, businesses and actors, including normal everyday people, particularly as the inequality gap gets wider and the rich get richer. It is in this context that drug supply must be viewed, as people increasingly seek to eke out a living and take advantage of every opportunity available to them not only to survive but also to thrive. Although everyone is subject to the same social pressures of neoliberal consumer capitalism, not everyone is equally placed to achieve them. This however is fetishistically disavowed, as the harmful capitalist dynamic behind drug supply remains hidden, which serves to conceal the full spectrum of drug market harms, particularly the harms arising from privileged legal non-drugs, their manufacture and supply chains (Ayres, 2020b; Žižek, 1989), which are excluded. Like other areas of criminology, surely it is time to refocus the lens of drug manufacture and supply to include the powerful and more unusual suspects rather than continuing to scapegoat and demonise the most vulnerable and powerless. It is hoped that this collection will go some way in bringing about that change in focus and provoke a new emphasis on the realities of contemporary global drugs markets.

Notes

1 The balloon effect is where 'tighter controls in one place produces a swelling (namely, an increase) in another place' (Rolles et al. 2016: 21); therefore, as law enforcement cracks down on one supply route, another will become more popular as drug producers mobilise to meet demand.

2 Supply reduction initiatives reduce the production, supply and availability of illicit drugs, which may involve destroying crops and/or disrupting the trafficking.

3 See the recent ruling on the bankruptcy plan for the maker of OxyContin, Purdue Pharma, who will pay USD$4.5bn (£3.3bn) to settle lawsuits related to the crisis, and although the Sackler family will relinquish control of Purdue Pharma, they will have immunity from future lawsuits relating to the opioid crisis.

4 According to the EMCDDA (2019a: 13), illicit drugs represent the most valuable market to Organised Crime Groups in the EU, with 'more than one third of the 5,000 OCGs identified in the EU's Serious and Organised Crime Threat Assessment (SOCTA) 2017 were directly involved in the drug market' and around 'two-thirds of those engaged in the drug trade were also involved in other criminal activities'.

5 Not just by authorities here in the UK but also by third party states (e.g. USA) using reciprocal international treaties, which is likely to burgeon alongside the increasing use of the Internet and World Wide Web (Coomber, 2002a).

6 There are inherent risks in undertaking criminological research with criminal populations, particularly when it comes to the higher echelons of OCGs, which must be taken into consideration by university ethics committees as there have been incidents – albeit rare – where researchers have been raped, kidnapped, tortured and killed while undertaking research in the field. In the area of drugs, Ken Pryce who was a Jamaican criminologist died in Jamaica whilst investigating international drug networks in the Caribbean (see Bloor, Fincham and Sampson, 2008; Mahmood, 2008).

7 The drug apartheid is a hierarchical system of segregation that privileges certain drug markets whilst criminalising others (see Taylor et al., 2016).

8 The overall mark-up from farm gate to the consumer is 16,800% for heroin and 15,800% for cocaine (see Wilson and Stevens, 2008).
9 A topic omitted from this book despite evidence illustrating the trade in precursor chemicals and cutting agents (the bash industry) had become a desirable alternative to some drug dealers due to the huge profits and reduced risk involved in this trade (e.g. some are legal to buy and sell, can be used legitimately) (EMCDDA, 2019b).
10 For example, Roger and Sue Clarke aged 72 and 71 were caught trafficking cocaine into Europe on a luxury Caribbean cruise (Keeley, 2019).
11 The demarcation between 'user' and 'producer' countries is becoming increasingly blurred due to an increase in drug use in both 'producer' and 'transit' countries.
12 If prohibition is to be maintained, instead of prioritising supply reduction, supply and demand reduction initiatives need to be integrated (Kramer et al., 2014) and an evidence base used to inform both strands of drug policy.
13 The Sentencing Council Guidelines (2012) examines the role of the dealer in the transaction in an attempt to differentiate between social supply and drug dealing proper, where they make a profit.
14 If any Global South scholars are interested in contributing to an edited collection on drug dealing in the Global South, then please contact either Tammy or Craig.

References

Alvesson, M., Gabriel, Y., and Paulsen, R. (2017) *Return to Meaning: A Social Science with Something to Say*. Oxford: Oxford University Press.

Ancrum, C. and Treadwell, J. (2016) Beyond ghosts, gangs and good sorts: Commercial cannabis cultivation and illicit enterprise in England's disadvantaged inner cities. *Crime, Media, Culture,* 13(1), 69–84.

Ayres, T.C. (2020a) The war on drugs and its invisible collateral damage: Environmental harm and climate change. In A. Brisman and N. South (Eds.), *Routledge International Handbook of Green Criminology* (pp. 239–259). London: Routledge.

Ayres, T.C. (2020b) Substances: The luxurious, the sublime and the harmful. In S. Hall, T. Kuldova and M. Horsley (Eds.), *Crime, Harm and Consumerism* (pp. 108–122). London: Routledge.

Ayres, T.C. (2019). Substance Use in the Night-Time Economy: Deviant Leisure? In T. Raymen and O. Smith (Eds.), *Deviant Leisure: A Criminological Perspectives on Leisure and Harm* (pp. 135–160). Basingstoke: Palgrave Macmillan.

Baudrillard, J. (1998) *Consumer Society: Myths and Structures*. London: Sage.

Bauman Z. (2001) Consuming life. *Journal of Consumer Culture*, 1(1), 9–29.

BBC (2021) British American Tobacco negotiated bribe for Mugabe, new evidence suggests. 13 September, 1.

Becker, H. (1963) *Outsiders*. Glencoe: Free Press of Glencoe.

Bloor, M., Fincham, B., and Sampson, H. (2008) *Qualiti (NCRM) Commissioned Inquiry into the Risk to Well-being of Researchers in Qualitative Research*. Cardiff: Cardiff University.

Boys, A., Marsden, J., and Strang, J. (2001) Understanding reasons for drug use amongst young people: A functional perspective. *Health Education Research: Theory and Practice,* 16 (4), 457–469.

Braithwaite, J. (1984) *Corporate Crime in the Pharmaceutical Industry*. London: Routledge.

Bröckling, U. (2007) *The Entrepreneurial Self*. London: Sage.

Coomber, R. (2010) Reconceptualising drug markets and drug dealers—the need for change. *Drugs and Alcohol Today*, 10(1), 10–13.

Coomber, R. (2006) *Pusher Myths: Re-Situating the Drug Dealer.* London: Free Association Books.

Coomber, R. (2002a) Editorial: Protecting our research subjects, our data and ourselves from respective prosecution, seizure and summons/subpoena. *Addiction Research & Theory*, 10(1), 1–5.

Coomber, R. (2002b) Signing your life away?: Why research ethics committees (REC) shouldn't always require written confirmation that participants in research have been informed of the aims of a study and their rights–the case of criminal populations. *Sociological Research Online*, 7(1), 218–221.

Courtwright, D. (2001) *Forces of Habit: Drugs and the Making of the Modern World.* Cambridge, MA: Harvard University Press .

Eastwood, N., Fox, E. , and Rosmarin, A. (2016) *A Quiet Revolution.* London: Release.

European Monitoring Centre for Drugs and Drug Addiction (EMCDDA) (2019a) EU Drug Markets Report 2019. Lisbon: EMCDDA.

European Monitoring Centre for Drugs and Drug Addiction (EMCDDA) (2019b) Drug precursor developments in the European Union. Luxembourg: EMCDDA.

Ferrell, J. (1997) Criminological Verstehen: Inside the immediacy of crime. *Justice Quarterly*, 14, 3–23.

Global Commission on Drug Policy (GCDP) (2012) *The War on Drugs and HIV/AIDS How the Criminalization of Drug Use Fuels the Global Pandemic.* GCDP: Geneva.

Hall, A. (2019) Lifestyle drugs and late capitalism: A topography of harm. In O. Smith and T. Raymen (Eds.), *Deviant Leisure and Social Harm* (pp. 161–186). London: Policy Press.

Hall, S. and Winlow, S. (2015) *Revitalizing Criminological Theory.* London: Routledge.

Hall, S., Winlow, S. and Ancrum, C. (2008) *Criminal Identities and Consumer Culture: Crime, Exclusion and the New Culture of Narcissism.* Cullompton: Willan.

Harm Reduction International (HRI) (2021) *Death Penalty For Drug Offences: Global Overview 2020.* London: HRI.

Kaufmann, E. (2021) *Academic Freedom in Crisis: Punishment, Political Discrimination, and Self-Censorship.* London: CSPI.

Keeley, G. (2019) Cocaine cruise pensioners jailed for eight years. *The Times*, Friday 27th September.

Kramer, T., Jensema, E., Jelsma, M., and Blickman, T. (2014) *Bouncing Back: Relapse in the Golden Triangle.* Amsterdam: Transnational Institute.

LeBaron, G. (2021) The role of supply chains in the global business of forced labour. *Journal of Supply Chain Management,* 57(2), 29–42.

MacCoun, R.J. and Reuter, P. (2001) *Drug War Heresies: Learning from Other Vices, Times, and Places.* Cambridge: Cambridge University Press.

Mahmood, C.K. (2008) Anthropology from the Bones: A memoir of fieldwork, survival, and commitment. *Anthropology and Humanism*, 33(1–2), 1–11.

Mansfield, D. (2011) *Assessing Supply-Side Policy and Practice: Eradication and Alternative Development.* Geneva: GCDP.

May, T. and Hough, M. (2004) Drug markets and distribution systems. *Addiction Research & Theory*, 12(6), 549–563.

McSweeney, K. (2015) *The Impact of Drug Policy on the Environment.* New York: Open Society Foundations.

Meehan, P. (2011) Drugs, insurgency and state-building in Burma: Why the drugs trade is central to Burma's changing political order. *Journal of Southeast Asian Studies*, 42(3), 376–404.

NCA (2021) *National Strategic Assessment of Serious Organised Crime.* London: NCA

Paoli, L. (2003) *Mafia Brotherhoods.* New York: Oxford University Press.

Paley, D. (2014) *Drug War Capitalism*. Edinburgh: AK Press.

Pearson, G. and Hobbs, D. (2001) Middle market drug distribution. Home Office Research Study 227. London: Home Office.

Pemberton, S. (2015) *Harmful Societies*. Bristol: Polity.

Raymen, T. and Smith, O. (2016) What's deviance got to do with it? Black Friday sales, violence, and hyper-conformity. *British Journal of Criminology,* 56(2), 389–405.

Rolles. S., Murkin, G., Powell, M., Kushlik, D., Saunter, N. and Slater, J. (2016*) The Alternative World Drug Report* (2nd edition). Bristol: TDPF.

Ruggiero, V. and South, N. (1995) *Eurodrugs: Drug Use, Markets and Trafficking in Europe*. London: UCL Press.

Sandberg, S. and Copes, H. (2012) Speaking with ethnographers: The challenges of researching drug dealers and offenders. *Journal of Drug Issues,* 43(2), 176–197.

Sentencing Guidelines for Drug Offences (2012) *Drug Offences: Definitive Guidelines*. London: Sentencing Council.

Singer, M. and Baer, H. (2009) *Killer Commodities: Public Health and the Corporate Production of Harm*. Lanham: AltaMira Press.

South, N. (1999) *Drugs: Cultures, Controls and Everyday Life*. London: Sage.

Spence, C. (2019) Judgement' versus 'metrics' in higher education management. *Higher Education,* 77, 761–775.

Taylor, S., Buchanan, J., and Ayres, T.C. (2016) Prohibition, privilege and the drug apartheid: The failure of drug policy reform to address the underlying fallacies of drug prohibition. *Criminology and Criminal Justice* 16(4), 452–469.

Treadwell, J. and Ayres, T.C. (2014) Talking prada and powder: Cocaine use and supply among the football Hooligan Firm. In J. Treadwell and M. Hopkins (Eds.), *Football Hooliganism, Crime and Crowd Control: Contemporary Themes in Relation to Research and Theory* (pp. 49–70). Basingstoke: Palgrave Macmillan.

UKDPC (2008) *Tackling Drug Markets and Distribution Networks in the UK*. London: UKDPC

UNDCP (1998) *A Drug-Free World: We Can Do It*. New York: UNDCP.

UNODC (2021) *COVID-19 and Drugs: Impact Outlook*. Vienna: UNODC.

Upright, E. (2017) From tea to tobacco: which everyday products are most at risk of modern slavery links? *Thomson Reuters Foundation*, 16 June.

Wacquant, L. (2011) From public criminology to the reflexive sociology of criminological production and consumption. *British Journal of Criminology*, 51, 438–448.

Wacquant, L. (2009) *Punishing the Poor: The Neoliberal Government of Social Insecurity*. London: Duke University Press.

Wakeman, S. (2016) The moral economy ofheroin in austerity Britain. *Critical Criminology*, 24, 363–377.

Wilson, L. and Stevens, A. (2008) *Understanding Drug Markets and How to Influence Them. Report 14*. Oxford: The Beckley Foundation.

Winlow, S. and Hall, S. (2012) What is an 'ethics committee'? Academic governance in an epoch of belief and incredulity. *The British Journal of Criminology* 52(2): 400–416.

Winlow, S. (2021) Beyond measure: On the marketization of British universities, and the domestication of academic criminology. *Critical Criminology*, Online First.

Žižek, S. (2008) *Violence*. New York: Picador.

Žižek, S. (2003) Homo Sacer as the object of the discourse of the university. *Cités* 16, 25–41.

Žižek, S. (2002) *Welcome to the Desert of the Real*. New York: Verso.

Žižek, S. (1993) *Tarrying with the Negative*. Durham: Duke Press.

Žižek, S. (1989) *Sublime Object of Ideology*. London: Verso.

INDEX

Note: Page numbers in *italics* indicate figures and in **bold** indicate tables on the corresponding pages.

Printed in the United States
by Baker & Taylor Publisher Services